Critical Guide to
Catholic Reference Books

RESEARCH STUDIES IN LIBRARY SCIENCE
Bohdan S. Wynar, Editor

No. 1. *Middle Class Attitudes and Public Library Use.* By Charles Evans, with an Introduction by Lawrence Allen.

No. 2. *Critical Guide to Catholic Reference Books.* 2nd ed. By James Patrick McCabe, with an Introduction by Russell E. Bidlack.

No. 3. *An Analysis of Vocabulary Control in Library of Congress Classification and Subject Headings.* By John Phillip Immroth, with an Introduction by Jay E. Daily.

No. 4. *Research Methods in Library Science. A Bibliographic Guide.* By Bohdan S. Wynar.

No. 5. *Library Management: Behavior-Based Personnel Systems. A Framework for Analysis.* By Robert E. Kemper.

No. 6. *Computerizing the Card Catalog in the University Library: A Survey of User Requirements.* By Richard P. Palmer, with an Introduction by Kenneth R. Shaffer.

No. 7. *Toward a Philosophy of Educational Librarianship.* By John M. Christ.

No. 8. *Freedom Versus Suppression and Censorship.* By Charles H. Busha, with an Introduction by Peter Hiatt, and a Preface by Allan Pratt.

No. 9. *The Role of the State Library in Adult Education: A Critical Analysis of Nine Southeastern State Library Agencies.* By Donald D. Foos, with an Introduction by Harold Goldstein.

No. 10. *The Concept of Main Entry as Represented in the Anglo-American Cataloging Rules. A Critical Appraisal with Some Suggestions: Author Main Entry vs. Title Main Entry.* By M. Nabil Hamdy, with an Introduction by Jay E. Daily.

No. 11. *Publishing in Switzerland: The Press and the Book Trade.* By Linda S. Kropf.

No. 12. *Library Science Dissertations, 1925-1972: An Annotated Bibliography.* By Gail A. Schlachter and Dennis Thomison.

No. 13. *Milestones in Cataloging: Famous Catalogers and Their Writings; 1835-1969.* By Donald J. Lehnus, with an Introduction by Phyllis A. Richmond.

No. 14. *Weeding Library Collections.* By Stanley J. Slote.

No. 15. *Library of Congress Subject Headings: Principles and Application.* By Lois Mai Chan.

No. 16. *Theory and Practice in Library Education: The Teaching-Learning Process.* By Joe Morehead.

No. 17. *AACR 2 Headings: A Five-Year Projection of Their Impact on Catalogs.* By Arlene Taylor Dowell.

No. 18. *Library Science Dissertations, 1973-1981: An Annotated Bibliography.* By Gail A. Schlachter and Dennis Thomison.

No. 19. *Library of Congress Subject Headings: Principles and Application.* 2d ed. By Lois Mai Chan.

No. 20. *Critical Guide to Catholic Reference Books.* 3d ed. By James Patrick McCabe.

Critical Guide to Catholic Reference Books

Third Edition

James Patrick McCabe

With an Introduction by
Russell E. Bidlack
Dean Emeritus of the School of Library Science
University of Michigan

Libraries Unlimited, Inc.•Englewood, Colorado•1989

LIBRARIES UNLIMITED, INC.
P.O. Box 3988
Englewood, Colorado 80155-3988

Library of Congress Cataloging-in-Publication Data

McCabe, James Patrick.
 Critical guide to Catholic reference books / James Patrick McCabe; with an introduction by Russell E. Bidlack. -- 3rd ed.
 xiv, 323 p. 17x25 cm. -- (Research studies in library science ; no. 20)
 Bibliography: p. 263
 Includes indexes.
 ISBN 0-87287-621-7
 1. Catholic Church--Bibliography. 2. Reference books--Catholic Church. I. Title. II. Series.
 Z674.R4 no. 20
 [Z7837]
 [BX1751.2]   JUL   9 1996
 020 s--dc19
 [016.282]   89-2835
                                              CIP

CONTENTS

Preface xi

Introduction xiii

CHAPTER I – GENERAL WORKS 1
Bibliography 1
    Bibliographies of Bibliography 2
    General Bibliographies 2
    Manuscripts 3
    Rare Books 4
    Selection Aids 5
    National Bibliographies 11
Libraries 16
    General Works 16
    Library Science 17
General Dictionaries and Encyclopedias 20
    American and British 22
    Dutch 29
    French 29
    German 31
    Italian 32
    Japanese 34
    Mexican 34
    Polish 34
    Spanish 35
Periodicals 35
    History and Bibliography 35
    Union Lists 38
    Indexes 38
Societies 39
    Directories 40
Biography 41
    Indexes 41
    General Biography 42
    American 44
    British 47
    Canadian 48
    German 48
    Mexican 48

CHAPTER I – GENERAL WORKS – *Continued*

Lives of the Saints 49
    Sources 49
    Dictionaries and Collections 51

Genealogy 56
    Heraldry 56
    Names 56

CHAPTER II – THEOLOGY 57

Religions 57
    Denominations 57
    History of Religions 60

General Theological Works 61
    Bibliography 61
    Sources 65
    Dictionaries and Encyclopedias 92
    Handbooks and Manuals 95
    History 98
    Bio-Bibliography 98

Theological Disciplines 99
    Apologetics 99
    Dogmatic Theology 100
    Moral Theology 107
    Pastoral Theology 112
    Ascetical and Mystical Theology 116
    Ecumenism 120

Liturgy 121
    General Works 121
    Liturgical Books 123
    Dictionaries and Encyclopedias 130
    Handbooks and Manuals 132
    History 135
    The Mass 136
    The Divine Office 136
    Prayers 137
    Eastern Rites 138

CHAPTER III – THE HUMANITIES 139

Philosophy and Psychology 139
    Philosphy 139
    Psychology 152

Literature 153
   General Works 153
   Individual Authors 157
   Quotations 160
   Genres 161
   Britain 163
   France 164
   Germany 165
   Latin Literature 165

Music and Hymnology 166
   Bibliography 166
   Collections 167
   Indexes 168
   Dictionaries and Encyclopedias 168
   Handbooks 169
   History 170

Fine and Applied Arts 171
   Handbooks 171
   Symbolism 171
   Architecture 176
   Vestments and Ecclesiastical Dress 176

CHAPTER IV — SOCIAL SCIENCES 178
  General Works 178
   Bibliography 178
   Sources 178
   Dictionaries and Encyclopedias 179
   Handbooks 180

  Education 181
   Bibliography 181
   Sources 182
   Dictionaries and Encyclopedias 182
   Handbooks 182
   Directories 182
   Higher Education 183
   History 185

  Sociology 186
   General Works 186
   Social Work 187
   Etiquette and Customs 189

  Statistics 190
   General Yearbooks and Directories 190
   National Yearbooks and Directories 192

CHAPTER IV – SOCIAL SCIENCES – *Continued*

Economics...201
    Bibliography..201
    Sources 202

Political Science..202
    Bibliography..202
    Sources 202
    Dictionaries and Encyclopedias...............................203

Canon Law..203
    Bibliography..203
    Texts and Sources.......................................204
    Indexes...206
    Dictionaries and Encyclopedias...............................207
    Handbooks and Commentaries................................208
    History...209
    Eastern Canon Law......................................209
    Treaties 209

Geography..210
    Guidebooks..210
    Atlases 210

CHAPTER V – HISTORY.................................212

General Church History..................................212
    Bibliography..212
    Sources 212
    Dictionaries and Encyclopedias...............................213
    Handbooks...214
    Biography 216
    Archeology 217

History by Periods......................................217
    Ancient 217
    Medieval 219
    Modern 223

American Church History.................................225
    Guides 225
    Bibliography..226
    Sources 227
    Dictionaries and Encyclopedias...............................229
    Handbooks...230

The Papacy...230
    Bibliography..230
    Sources 231
    Dictionaries and Encyclopedias...............................236
    History...236

CHAPTER V — HISTORY — *Continued*

Councils..238
    Sources 238
    Council of Trent (1545-63)...................................239
    Vatican Council I (1869-70)..................................240
    Vatican Council II (1962-65).................................240
    Dictionaries..242
    Handbooks 243

Religious Orders..243
    General Works...243
    Sources 244
    Indexes...244
    Individual Orders...250

Appendix 1 — Diocesan Reference Publications.................261

Appendix 2 — Bibliographies Consulted.......................263

Author/Title/Subject Index..................................267

PREFACE

Preparing this third edition has been rewarding and informative. Of the 243 new entries included, over 160 of them were published after 1978. The rest are older works discovered in my research or pointed out to me by readers. Some thirty-eight titles listed in the second edition have been revised and are listed in their new editions. New publications of Catholic reference works are most numerous, naturally, in the theological disciplines (Chapter II). The appearance of the new Code of Canon Law in 1983 generated thirteen new entries in Chapter IV. Other new titles are distributed fairly evenly throughout the other subject areas.

This work was originally written in another form as a Ph.D. dissertation for the School of Library Science of the University of Michigan, and it owes its existence to the members of the doctoral committee who originally decided to accept the topic and to the members of the dissertation committee: Dr. Russell Bidlack, Chairman, Drs. Kenneth Vance, John Reidy, and Edmond Low, and Sister Mary Claudia Carlen, all of whom were most kind in offering advice and sound criticism despite very busy schedules. Another member of the Michigan faculty whom I consulted was Dr. Raymond Kilgour who served on the committee until his retirement in April 1968.

Sister Mary Claudia, whose name appears frequently in this bibliography, supplied perhaps the most aid and encouragement as a result of her expertise in the field of Catholic bibliography, and much of the research was done at her library at Marygrove College, Detroit, Michigan.

Other libraries where I received welcome and aid were at the University of Michigan, the Catholic University of America, Villanova University, the University of Pennsylvania, Allentown College, and the Library of Congress.

Mrs. Phyllis Vogel typed the manuscript with great patience and skill; and Mrs. Kathryn Stephanoff corrected the proof sheets.

INTRODUCTION

In 1971, when the first edition of this work appeared, *Wilson Library Bulletin* said of it: "The *Critical Guide to Catholic Reference Books* is distinguished for the quality of its annotations, the informed selection of its titles and the fullness of its bibliographic data, reflecting the scholarly judgement of its author" (XLVI [September 1971], p. 84). Similar accolades greeted the second edition in 1980. Reviewers have praised the work for its comprehensive scope, logical organization, frequency of cross references in the annotations, and its excellent index. Indeed, the unanimously positive reception of this work and its popularity with libraries of all types have prompted the publisher and author to attempt this third edition, which has been enlarged by more than twenty percent in the number of titles included and thoroughly revised where necessary in the material carried over from the second edition.

A number of bibliographical studies of Catholic literature have been done in recent years, but these works have been primarily concerned either with guiding the reader to the "best books" on a particular subject or with listing all books by and/or about Catholics and Catholicism published in a given period or place. In the present work, James McCabe has compiled a much more comprehensive guide in the area of Catholic bibliography than has been attempted previously. He has provided a critical introduction to over fifteen hundred of the most important reference books in English and foreign languages whose contents or point of view relate in some way to Catholicism.

In formulating a definition of a reference work, McCabe has gone beyond the conventional definition and, like Constance M. Winchell in her *Guide to Reference Books*, has included books "which, while intended primarily to be read through for either information or pleasure, are so comprehensive and accurate in their treatment and so well provided with indexes that they serve also as reference books" (8th edition, Chicago, American Library Association, 1967, p. xiv). The books listed fall into two classes: 1) those dealing with topics peculiar to the Church, such as liturgy and other theological disciplines; and 2) those dealing with the social sciences, literature, the arts, and similar subjects to which Catholics have traditionally contributed a unique perspective.

In selecting titles from this body of literature for inclusion here, McCabe introduced a number of limitations which have added to the practicality of his list. Only published works currently available to the researcher in the United States are included. Rare or very old books have been omitted unless they are unusually important or unique. While the main emphasis is on works in English, foreign-language titles have been freely included if they are widely known, comprehensive in scope, and scholarly; if there is no English-language equivalent; or if they are more up to date than similar English-language works or translations.

Also included are many works written or sponsored by non-Catholics where those works dealt exclusively or in large part with the Church. In general, however, books by non-Catholics on topics such as patrology and scripture, which are of common interest to all Christians, have been excluded in favor of a more thorough listing of works from Catholic sources. While scholars in these fields may justly feel that this results in an unbalanced list, it is a fact that there are several general bibliographies that include those titles deliberately excluded by McCabe.

Catholic authorship alone, however, has not been enough to justify the inclusion of a reference work. The contents or point of view must relate in some way to Catholicism. Hence, a science dictionary written by a Catholic has not been included, nor has any work whose Catholic authorship in no way makes it distinguishable from other books on the same topic. Periodicals have not been included except those of a bibliographic nature or that publish annual bibliographies.

The critical opinions cited here are largely from Catholic sources, a fact that detracts somewhat from the objectivity of the work; however, non-Catholic and secular media have not as a rule covered the more obscure Catholic reference works, and opinions from these sources were simply not available for the majority of books included in this bibliography.

The subject arrangement resulted largely from the nature of the books themselves and follows the general Dewey Decimal outline used in other guides to reference works. The theology classification is based upon the traditional divisions in Catholic theology.

McCabe has made a significant contribution to bibliography. While limited strictly to Catholic materials, his guide provides a valuable addition to ecumenical studies and will be used by researchers for many years to come in their study of the structure, history, and teachings of the Catholic Church.

Ann Arbor, Michigan   Russell E. Bidlack

I
GENERAL WORKS

BIBLIOGRAPHY

The works included in this chapter are those listing books not exclusively on one subject, but covering the Catholic Church or Catholic writers in general. Six types of bibliographies are listed:

Bibliographies of Bibliography. The best surveys of Catholic bibliography are to be found in works listed elsewhere in this chapter. One of the most recent of these is an essay by Sister Mary Claudia Carlin, I.H.M., which appears in the *Catholic Bookman's Guide* (A19, pp. 35-74). Older studies may also be found in William T. O'Rourke's *Library Handbook for Catholic Readers* (A74, pp. 207-259), and Stephen Brown's *Introduction to Catholic Booklore* (A16), from which the chapter of "Catholic Bibliography" was revised and reprinted in Brother David Martin's *Catholic Library Practice* (A78, v. 1, pp. 97-199).

General Bibliographies. Since the beginning of the history of printing there have been several attempts to compile a universal bibliography as well as a universal Catholic bibliography, but in neither category has there been any notable success. For lists of the Catholic attempts, most of which are too rare or inaccurate for this study, see the works of Barrow (A1) and Sister Claudia (A19) mentioned above. Pérennè's *Dictionnaire* (A4) is one of the last attempts—and a limited one at that.
Library catalogs such as the *Acton Collection* (A2) and the *NUC Bibliography of the Catholic Church* (A3) are also grouped in this category although they have not been compiled for that purpose.

Manuscripts. There are no comprehensive catalogs of specifically Catholic manuscripts, but Kristeller's *Latin Manuscript Books* (A7) covers a large portion of the field. Catalogs of manuscripts dealing with specific topics and countries will be found listed in the appropriate sections of this book.

Rare Books. In addition to the works listed here, the bibliographies of Merrill (A50), Finotti (A49), and Parsons (A51) should also be consulted for American Catholic incunabula.
In British Catholic bibliography, the term "recusant" is used to refer to the Catholic population after the break with Rome in 1558. Because of the fugitive nature of their publishing activities, recusant works are among the rarest Catholic books in English.

Selection Aids. Because of the Church's traditional position on reading and the safe-guarding of faith and morals, book selection aids based on these principles were numerous. Many of these works used a code system indicating moral evaluations and suitability for different age groups. Not all works listed here are so oriented: *The Catholic Bookman's Guide* (A19) and the *Guide to Catholic Reading* (A15) concern themselves with listing the best books for the Catholic reader. The inclusion of the *Index* (A45) is merely for historical purposes.

National Bibliography. Of all the countries represented on this list, the United States is the leader in bibliographic control of Catholic literature. The Catholic Library Association, through the *Catholic Periodical and Literature Index* (A160) has provided a systematic and comprehensive listing of Catholic material since 1959 when it assumed responsibility for the *Guide to Catholic Literature* (A56) which was later merged with the *Catholic Periodical Index*. Happily this work also lists many foreign Catholic publications which helps compensate for the lack of a methodical approach to Catholic bibliographic control in almost every other country in the world.

BIBLIOGRAPHIES OF BIBLIOGRAPHY

A1   Barrow, John Graves. **A Bibliography of Bibliographies in Religion**: Based upon [a] Ph.D. Dissertation, Yale University, 1930. Ann Arbor, Edwards Bros., 1955. 489p. LC 55-8299.

"Attempts to bring together all separately published bibliographies in the field of religion" (Preface). Arranged chronologically under subject headings. Some critical observations in the annotations, but most are very brief and simply descriptive. Chapter eight deals with the Catholic Church (pp. 207-259) and Catholic material is included in other subject divisions. Author and title index.

GENERAL BIBLIOGRAPHIES

A2   **Acton Collection: Classes 1, 2, 3, 6, 7: Papacy, Canon Law, Religious Orders, Counter-Reformation.** Cambridge, 1910. 504p. (Cambridge University Library Bulletin, Extra Series). LC 9-18441.

"This bulletin contains the titles of those books in the Acton Collection on the subjects listed which were not previously in the University Library" (Preface). Titles are arranged by the Cambridge Library classification system with an author index. Lord Acton, an outstanding Catholic scholar in history, planned and edited the first edition of the *Cambridge Modern History* and collected almost 60,000 books on the Church for which no complete catalog has been compiled.

A3   **A Bibliography of the Catholic Church: Representing Holdings of American Libraries Reported to the National Union Catalog in the Library of Congress.** London, Mansell, 1970. 527p. ISBN 7201-0134-4.

This excerpt from the *National Union Catalog, Pre-1956 Imprints* includes more than 16,000 entries beginning "Catholic Church." These include all papal and Roman documents, all liturgical books, the Roman Catechism, all the codes of canon law, many local Church documents coming under the heading "Catholic Church in . . . ," and all treaties made between the Vatican

State and other countries. Locations are given in the usual NUC style. Those familiar with the type of material entered under "Catholic Church" will be aware of the limitations of this list, and users should realize that the cross references to other volumes of the NUC are given, but are useless unless one can consult the complete Catalog.

A4   Pérennès, François Marie. **Dictionnaire de bibliographie catholique: présentant l'indication et titres complèts de tous les ouvrages qui ont été publiès dan les trois langues: grecque, latine et française, depuis la naissance du christianisme en tous pays, mais principalement en France, pour et sur le catholicisme, avec le divers renseignements bibliographiques qui peuvent en donner l'idée la plus complète ... Suivi d'un Dictionnaire de bibliologie par M. Brunet.** Paris, Migne, 1858-66. 6v. LC 2-572.

"Severely criticized for its arrangement but does have a *Table des auteurs*. From the point of view of scientific bibliography, the work is not wholly satisfactory. There is no attempt at annotation, nor at discrimination between what is valuable and what almost worthless. ... Since the publication of Pérennès' Dictionary nothing on so large a scale, and at the same time, with so wide a scope would seem to have been attempted." (Stephen J. M. Brown, "Catholic Bibliography," in *Catholic Library Practice*, ed. by Bro. David Martin [Portland, OR, University of Oregon Press, 1947-50], v. 1, p. 107). Incorporates and supersedes previous works of this kind. An exhaustive bibliography of previous bibliographical works will be found in vol. I, p. xxix of Migne's *Encyclopédie théologique* (A122) of which this work is a part.
vol. I-IV: Pérennè's Dictionnaire; vol. V: Brunet's Dictionnaire de bibliologie catholique; vol. VI: Supplément. Classified arrangement with author index.

A5   Vatican. Biblioteca vaticana. **The Books Published by the Vatican Library, 1885-1947: An Illustrated Analytic Catalogue.** Trans. by Mary E. Stanley. Vatican City, Apostolic Library, 1947. liv, 183p. LC 48-6039.

Lists 250 works in three classes: 1) "Catalogues of Manuscripts," 2) "Studies and Texts," 3) "Illustrated Editions." Forthcoming works in the same fields are listed in a special section. The detailed annotations by Dr. Nello Vian are in two parts: historical and descriptive, and contents notes. Finely printed with illustrations of title pages, mss., etc. Index.

MANUSCRIPTS

A6   Jolliffe, P. S. **A Check-List of Middle English Prose Writings of Spiritual Guidance.** Toronto, Pontifical Institute of Medieval Studies, 1974. 253p. LC 75-302818. ISBN 0-88844-351-X. (Subsidia mediaevalia, 2).

Items are listed in 15 groups according to the type of contents. Indexes of incipits, authors and titles, and acephalous items are included. Identification and location of manuscripts are given as are references to printed versions when they exist. Bibliography: pp. 237-253.

A7   Kristeller, Paul Oskar. **Latin Manuscript Books before 1600: A List of the Printed Catalogues and Unpublished Inventories of Extant Collections.** 3rd ed. New York, Fordham University Press, 1960-65. 284p. LC 66-3585.

(First published in *Traditio*, 6:227-317, 1948 and 9:393-418, 1953.)

Composed of three sections: A. Bibliography and statistics of libraries and their mss. collections; B. Works describing mss. in more than one city; C. Printed catalogs and handwritten inventories of individual libraries arranged by city. The 1965 issue contains a supplement of additions and corrections. Analyzes lists covering more than one collection, gives complete bibliographical information, locations, and number of mss. indexed in each list. Mss. not examined by the author are indicated as are the sources of his information. A valuable tool. No index.

A8   Revell, Peter, comp. **Fifteenth Century English Prayers and Meditations: A Descriptive List of Manuscripts in the British Library.** New York, Garland, 1975. 137p. LC 75-6579. ISBN 0-8240-1098-1.

Arranged broadly by subject with indexes for authors, initia and manuscript number. The entries are bibliographically complete.

RARE BOOKS

AMERICAN

A9   Greenly, Albert H. **A Bibliography of Father Richard's Press in Detroit.** Ann Arbor, Clements Library, 1955. 48p. LC A56-299.

Lists 52 items printed by Father Richard between 1809-1816, many of which are religious in nature, e.g., prayer books, catechisms, etc. A carefully done rare book catalog.

A10   **The Sutro Library Catalogue of Works on the Catholic Church by Spanish, Portuguese, and Spanish-American Writers before 1800.** Comp. under the direction of Charles D. O'Malley, by the personnel of the W.P.A. Sacramento, CA, State Library, 1941. (Its Occasonal Papers, Bibliographical Series, No. 3, Pt. 1.) LC 41-52656.

A catalog of books, pamphlets, broadsides and manuscripts, dealing with the history, theology and liturgy of the Catholic Church. Annotations are supplied for most items as are full transcriptions of title pages for all works printed before 1600. The arrangement is alphabetical by author. No indexes.

BRITISH

A11   Allison, Anthony Francis and David Rogers. **A Catalogue of Catholic Books in English Printed Abroad or Secretly in England, 1558-1640.** Bogner Regis, Eng., Arundel Press, 1956. 2 v. (Biographical Studies, v. 3, no. 3-4.) LC A57-2353.

Designed as a supplement to Pollard and Redgrave's *Short Title Catalogue* (London, Bibliographical Society, 1926), this work lists 930 items giving S.T.C. numbers for works already listed there and indicating those not.

Arranged alphabetically by author, supplying title page transcriptions, additional bibliographical information and locations in libraries. See *also* Clancy, *English Catholic Books, 1641-1700* (A13).

Guernsey Books of Great Britain has recently undertaken a reprinting project called "English Recusant Literature, 1558-1640" consisting of 633 titles selected from this catalog.

A12 Byrns, Lois. **Recusant Books in America, 1559-1640.** New York, P. Kavanagh Hand-Press, 1959- . v. LC 59-35772.

Brief title entries for fugitive Catholic books preserved in American libraries. May be used in conjunction with Allison and Roger's *Catalogue* (A11).

A13 Clancy, Thomas H. **English Catholic Books, 1641-1700: A Bibliography.** Chicago, Loyola University Press, 1974. 157p. LC 74-704. ISBN 0-8294-0231-4.

This "provisional list" continues Allison's *Catalogue* (A11). 1139 items are cited in the main body of the work plus 381 borderline items in an appendix. The arrangement is by main entry with generous cross references, an index of publishers, a chronological index and an index of translators, editors and compilers. Locations, shelf numbers and some additional descriptive information are supplied.

A14 **Recusant Books at St. Mary's Oscott.** New Oscott, St. Mary's Seminary, 1964-1966. 3 pts. in 1 v. LC 72-222552.

Lists 3,365 items with descriptive annotations. "Short title indexes." Projected in four parts; to date lists 3,365 items with descriptive annotations. "Short title indexes."

SELECTION AIDS

GUIDES

A15 Bernard, Jack F. **A Guide to Catholic Reading: A Practical Handbook for the General Reader on Every Aspect of Catholic Literature with Descriptions of More than 750 Books of Catholic Interest.** By Jack F. Bernard and John J. Delaney. Garden City, NY, Doubleday, 1966; Image, 1966. vi, 392p. LC 66-20941.

An annotated guide, arranged by subject including mostly in-print books. Excludes highly technical, juvenile and liturgical works. Each subject section is preceded by an introductory essay. The annotations supply all pertinent bibliographical information plus a description of the contents. Emphasis is on modern works easily read by the general public, but it is not limited by the restriction to in-print works. List of publishers. Title and author index.

A16 Brown, Stephen James Meredith. **An Introduction to Catholic Booklore.** London, Burns, Oates and Washbourne, 1933. vii, 105p. (Catholic Bibliographical Series, No. 4) LC 34-5782.

The first part of this work has been revised and published in *Catholic Library Practice* (A78), pp. 97-119. Covers Catholic bibliographies, book selection, reference books and Catholic publishing. *The Catholic Bookman's Guide* (A19) updates this work somewhat although the two do not have exactly the same scope and purpose. Fr. Stephen Brown was an outspoken and opinionated Irish Jesuit with all the wit and knowledge peculiar to that class. These traits are as evident in his treatment of "Catholic booklore" and his many other bibliographical works as if he were writing the history of Catholicism under British Protestant rule, which, in a way, is what he does. Now largely out of date, this work was widely quoted and is still useful for its coverage of older foreign works. Index. Bibliographies.

A17 Catholic Library Service. **Catalog and Basic List of Essential First-Purchase Books.** New York, Paulist Press, 1962. 152p. LC 61-66571.

An annotated author list of about 1,600 books recommended for Catholic elementary school libraries. Indexes by title, grade and Dewey Decimal classification number.

A18 Freudenberger, Elsie. **Reference Works in The Field of Religion, 1977-1985: A Selective Bibliography.** Haverford, PA, Catholic Library Association, 1986. 65p. LC 87-101762. ISBN O-8750-7037-X.

Lists 155 works by type with fine descriptive annotations. Not limited to Catholic works or authors.

A19 Regis, Sister Mary, ed. **The Catholic Bookman's Guide: A Critical Evaluation of Catholic Literature.** New York, Hawthorn Books, 1962. 638p. LC 62-12956.

A selective, annotated bibliography of books by Catholics or of Catholic interest, emphasizing books in-print and in English—although important foreign and out-of-print books are included. Arranged by subject each section was compiled by an expert and is preceded by an introductory essay with annotations for most titles. The purpose of the work is to provide something like a *Reader's Advisor* for Catholic books. The quality of the selection and criticism varies from chapter to chapter.

"The essays, which are concise but comprehensive should interest all scholars and be required reading for reference librarians; and the bibliographies which have been compiled by subject experts can be confidently used by all libraries as check lists for acquiring basic materials or appraising present holdings" (*Catholic Educational Review*, LXII [May, 1964], p. 355).

GENERAL BOOKS

A20 **Best Sellers: The Semi-Monthly Book Review.** Scranton, PA, University of Scranton, 1941-1987. 46 v. Semi-monthly. LC A42-2236.

Reviewers for this journal were mostly Catholics and members of the faculty at the University of Scranton. When applicable, ethical and moral questions were raised. Children's Books were systematically rated for objectionable contents.

A21 **Bibliographie catholique, revue critique des ouvrages de religion, de philoso-phie, d'histoire, de littéraire, d'éducation.** Paris, Bureau de la Bibliographie catholique, 1841-89. 80 v. Monthly. LC 7-6619.

Reviewed about 300 books per year of interest "to clerics, mothers and fathers, heads of institutions, persons of both sexes, parish libraries, Christian reading groups." Only works in French were covered. Indexes for each volume and cumulated indexes for volumes 1-15 (1841-1856) and 16-30 (1856-1863).

A22 **Bollettino bibliografico internazionale.** Roma, Pia Società de San Paolo, 1947- . v. Monthly. LC 63-27665. (Title varies.)

Annotated, classified and selective bibliography of Italian books on all sub-jects, especially religion (theology and philosophy). Moral evaluations are given. Indexes in each issue.

A23 **Books by Catholic Authors in the Cleveland Public Library: A Classified List.** Comp. and ann. by Emilie Louise Haley. Cleveland, Cleveland Public Library, 1911. 4+232p.

This work serves as a fine example of several catalogs of this type compiled early in the century by both librarians and clergymen. Although designed for patrons of a specific library, some, like the Cleveland list, were so exten-sive that they could be used as selection tools or author checklists. Other American libraries that issued similar lists were Baltimore, Grand Rapids, Kansas City, Louisville, Milwaukee, Pittsburgh and Utica, New York. (Cf. *Library of Congress Author Catalog*)

A24 Carey, Mother Marie Aimee. **A Bibliography for Christian Formation in the Family.** Glen Rock, NJ, Paulist Press, 1964. 175p. LC 64-15491.

"Contents: Christian Marriage, Christian Atmosphere in the Home, Liturgy, Prayer, Bible Lives of the Saints, Sex Education, Catechetical Instruction, Apostolic Formation, Christian Culture, Children's Books, Religious Voca-tions, Pamphlets." An annotated bibliography with an author index.

A25 Catholic Library Association. **C.L.A. Booklist.** Haverford, PA, Catholic Library Association, 1942-70. 28v. Annual. LC 45-10454. (Title varies.)

A fine selection tool with a surprisingly broad scope. Lists the "best books published within the year by Catholic authors or of special Catholic concern" (Preface, 1963). Subject lists are selected and annotated by such specialists as Sister Melania Grace, Dom Bernard Theall, and Edmund Burke. No longer published.

A26 Dalglish, William A., ed. **Media for Christian Formation: A Guide to Audio-Visual Resources.** Dayton, OH, Pflaum/Standard, 1969-73. 3 v. il.
v 1. Media for Christian Formation. 1969. LC 78-79711. ISBN 0-8278-0400-8. v.2. Media Two. 1970. LC 70-120399. ISBN 0-8278-0402-4. v 3. Media Three. 1973. LC 70-120399. ISBN 0-8278-0414-8.

A useful tool listing and evaluating over 1,000 films, filmstrips, posters, records, and tapes from Catholic, Protestant and non-religious sources. Evaluative anno-tations indicate age levels and denominational limitations, if any. Alphabetical arrangement by title with a detailed subject index, list of sources, and a directory of film, filmstrip and tape libraries.

A27   **Enciclopedia de orientación bibliográfica.** Director: Tomás Zamarriego. Barcelona, J. Flors, 1964-65. 4 v. LC 65-53526.

Lists about 100,000 items in Spanish, French, English, Italian, German, Portuguese, and Latin. Attempts to include the basic books and articles for every field of knowledge, especially theology, religion, and the humanities. Over 600 specialists chose the titles and wrote the critical and descriptive annotations. "Very useful for graduate students, teachers, and librarians" (*Theological Studies* XXVI [Sept., 1965], p. 530), but the work's vast scope limits its depth such that only some of the most well known works in each language are listed for each subject. Author and subject indexes.

A28   Instituto Nacional del Libro Español. Feria nacional del libro católico. **Selección de libros católicos españoles, 1939-1952.** Barcelona, 1952. 351p.

A29   Instituto Nacional de Libro Español. **Libros de religión. El Libro Español,** Supplementos, **no.2.** Madrid, Instituto Nacional del Libro Español, 1959.

Over 6,000 Spanish titles published 1939-1959; the ideal Catholic collection covering the Bible, patristics, theology, the spiritual life, the Church, the apostolate, literature, religious art and periodicals. Author index.

A30   **Lectuur-repertorium: auterslijst bevattende Bibliografische nota's en 300 portretten van auteurs behorende tot de Nederlandse en de algemene literatuur, met waarde en vakaanduiding van 90,000 literaire en vulgariserende werken,** sanengesteld door net A.S.K.B. Onder Redactie van Jovis Baers. Antwerpen, Vlaamsche Boekcentrale, 1952-54. 3 v. LC 53-15682.

A reader's guide to general and popular literature in Dutch giving moral evaluations.

A31   Tavagnutti, Mario Sigismondo. **Katholisch-theologische bücherkunde der letzten funfzig Jahre.** Wien and Leipzig, Verlag Austria, Drescher und comp, 1891. 4 v.
    v. 1 Hagiographia (LC 6-28301); v. 2 Christologische bibliographie (LC 34-41023); v. 3 Mariologische bibliographie (LC 6-25026); v. 4 Biblioteca catholica Societatis Jesu. (LC 6-25025).

A series of bibliographies of German and Latin works published from 1840 to 1890. "An important work" (Stephen J. M. Brown, "Catholic Bibliography," in *Catholic Library Practice*, ed. by Bro. David Martin [Portland, OR, Portland University Press, 1947-50], v. 1, p. 108).

CHILDREN'S BOOKS

A32   **Children's Catalog: Catholic Supplement.** Selected by a Committee of the Catholic Library Association, Sister M. Fidelis, Chairman. New York, Wilson, 1949. 25p.

Arranged in the same manner as the *Children's Catalog*. No more issues published.

A33 Fullam, Raymond B. **Spiritual Books for Catholic Youth: An Annotated and Graded List of Spiritual Books for Catholic Youth from 13 to 19 Years Old.** With an introduction by Harold C. Gardiner. St. Louis, Queens Work, 1952. 51p. LC 52-1170.

This is an example of many similar lists (*see* Regis [no. A19]) designed for readers in the "lower and upper teens." Arranged in broad subject categories covering the lives of the saints, Christ, scripture, prayer, Church history, doctrine, Mary. Author and title indexes.

A34 Kelley, Marjorie E. **In Pursuit of Values: A Bibliography of Children's Books.** New York, Paulist Press, 1973. 44p. il. LC 73-87029. ISBN 0-8091-1803-3.

"Books which can help children grow in values by developing moral reasoning" (Preface). Items are annotated and arranged by grade level.

A35 Noonan, Eileen F. **Books for Catholic Elementary Schools.** Haverford, PA, Catholic Library Association, 1982. 14p. LC 843-137683.

An annotated bibliography of 100 books suitable for elementary school libraries. Covers a variety of subject areas, excluding religion, for which see A36.

A36 Noonan, Eileen. **Books for Religious Education in Catholic Secondary Schools.** Rev. ed. Haverford, PA, Catholic Library Association, 1986. ii, 18p. LC 86-208006. ISBN O-8750-7039-6.

An annotated subject list with a list of publishers.

A37 Kircher, Clara J., comp. **Behavior Patterns in Children's Books: A Bibliography.** Washington, DC, Catholic University of America Press, 1966.v 132p. LC 66-18693.

Replaces the author's earlier work *Character Formation through Books* (3rd ed. Washington, DC, Catholic University of America Press, 1952). Lists books by grade level (1-12) giving for each book a brief annotation and a list of the character traits or virtues stressed in the book. Index of character traits, author and title indexes.

A38 **Senior High School Library Catalog with the Catholic Supplement.** 10th ed. New York, Wilson, 1972. 1373p. LC 72-3819. ISBN 0-8242-0475-1.

The Catholic Supplement lists over 900 books and is arranged exactly like the general section. Titles are selected for their "relevance for Catholic schools because of their subject, authorship or special relationship to the curriculum of Catholic High Schools" (Preface. 8th ed.) by a committee of the Catholic Library Association. Because of the limited scope of this list it tends to be more useful than the main catalog. The 11th ed., 1977 does not contain a Catholic Supplement, nor do subsequent editions.

A39 Sztore, Mary Virginia. **Student's Values in Drugs and Drug Abuse.** Haverford, PA, Catholic Library Association, 1976. 32p.

Contains annotated listings of books and A-V materials as well as definitions of drugs.

COLLEGE READING

A40   **Focus: An Annotated Bibliography of Catholic Reading.** By Donald Smyth
and others. Washington, DC, National Newman Club Federation, 1962.
134p. LC 63-738.

Prepared by the Jesuits of Woodstock College primarily for Catholic college
students at secular universities but also helpful for the Catholic college library
selector because of its curriculum oriented arrangement. First published in
1951, it has been revised twice, 1956 and 1962. The annotations are descriptive and evaluative and the selection is not limited to books by Catholic
authors. List of publishers. No index.

A41   Grace, Sister Melania, and Gilbert C. Peterson. **Books for Catholic Colleges:
A Supplement to Shaw's List of Books for College Libraries.** Comp. under
the auspices of the Catholic Library Association. Chicago, A.L.A., 1948.
134p. LC 48-11124.

A42   Grace, Sister Melania, and Gilbert C. Peterson. **Books for Catholic Colleges:
A Supplement to Shaw's List of Books for College Libraries. Supplements,**
1948-49; 1950-52; 1953-55.

Originally intended as a supplement to the standard college library list
(Charles Bunsen Shaw, *A List of Books for College Libraries* [Chicago,
A.L.A., 1931]). Titles were selected by vote by Catholic College Librarians.
The work was undertaken because the needs of a Catholic college curricu-
lum obviously require an expanded list in the fields of philosophy and
religion. History, literature and Romance languages are also well represented.
The arrangement of titles is by broad subject group with form subdivisions.
No annotations. Author, title, subject index.

For a time this work was updated by supplemental lists appearing in
*C.U.L.S.: The Quarterly Newsletter of the College and University Section
of the Catholic Library Association*, but this seems to have been discontinued.

INDEX LIBRORUM PROHIBITORUM

A43   Bujanda, Jésus Martinez de. **Index des livres interdits.** Sherbrooke, Québec,
Centre d'Études de la Renaissance, 1984- . v. LC 86-206056. ISBN 2-76220-029-6.

A work projected in ten volumes, which contains an annotated list of the
contents of the Indexes published by various authorities throughout the centuries.
The publication history and library locations are given for each item. Historical
essays, the original texts of the Indexes and numerous tables and indexes are also
supplied.

A44   Burke, Redmond Ambrose. **What Is the Index?** Milwaukee, Bruce, 1952.
x, 129p.

Although the Index is no longer binding in ecclesiastical law (*Acta Apostolicae Sedis*, LXIII, June 1966, P. 445), this work is still useful as a clear, if
sometimes inaccurate, explanation of perhaps the most famous censorship
device in history. "Tables of books contained in the Index." Index.

A45 **Index librorum prohibitorum, SS. mi D. N. Pii PP. XII iussu editus, anno MDCCCCXLVIII.** In Civitate Vaticana, Typis Polyglottis Vaticanis, 1948; Westminster, MD, Newman, 1948. xxiv, 508p.

Formerly updated by periodic lists in *Acta Apostolicae Sedis* (E120). No more titles will be added in the future, however; nor will new editions of the *Index* be published by Rome.

A46 Pernicone, Joseph Marie. **The Ecclesiastical Prohibition of Books.** Washington, DC, Catholic University of America Press, 1932. 267p. (C.U.A. Studies in Canon Law, no. 72).

A scholarly history of the *Index* and an explanation of the Church's position on censorship.

REFERENCE BOOKS

A47 Catholic Library Association. **C.L.A. Basic Reference Books for Catholic High School Libraries.** Comp. by a committee of the C.L.A. 2nd ed. Haverford, PA, C.L.A., 1963. 47p.

The first edition, compiled by Sister Mary Naomi, appeared in 1959. A basic list, well selected and annotated, covering all subject areas, not just religion. Arranged by Dewey classification.

Annual, annotated lists of reference books may be found in the *Catholic Library World*, December issues.

SISTERS' BOOKS

A48 Harmer, Sister Mary Fabian. **Books for Religious Sisters: A General Bibliography.** Washington, DC, Catholic University of America Press, 1963. 184p. LC 63-11580.

A reading list for nuns in which "The religious, cultural, and recreational requirements of the sisters were considered. Professional materials, medical and nursing books, educational methods, texts, as well as highly specialized works on particular subjects were omitted as was science" (Preface). Brief descriptive annotations are given, and important works are starred for first purchase. Arrangement is classified including sections on bibliography and reference. Index of authors.

NATIONAL BIBLIOGRAPHIES

AMERICAN–EARLY

A49 Finotti, Joseph Maria. **Bibliographia catholica americana: A List of Works Written by Catholic Authors and Published in the United States. Part I. from 1784 to 1820 Inclusive.** New York, The Catholic Publication House, 1872. 318p. LC 1-657. Reprinted: New York, B. Franklin, 1971. LC 74-149232. ISBN 0-8337-1128-8. (No more parts published) (Includes a catalogue of Mathew Carey's works, p. 268-291, 296-299.)

The first attempt at American Catholic bibliography and a well done, if not complete, one. The list is especially weak in foreign language works printed in the U.S. Finotti himself admitted (Preface) to omitting most German titles, and a separate list of French additions was compiled in 1952 (A46). Arranged in alphabetical order by author. Complete bibliographical information is given along with much historical and biographical information. The list is based primarily on Finotti's personal library. Originally he intended to cover the years 1784 to 1875. Sales of the first volume were so poor, however, that he abandoned the project. At his death in 1879 his library was sold. 1,492 items were listed in the catalog. (*Catalogue of the Library of the Late Rev. Joseph M. Finotti . . . To be sold at auction . . .* [New York, C. C. Shelley, 1879], iv, 142p. LC 13-5161).

Wilfrid Parsons, whose *Early Catholic Americana* (A51) supersedes this work, said of it:

> Those who have read this book will appreciate both the delightfully whimsical style and the genuinely bibliographical passion which made it something unique in its field . . . It was a gallant attempt to do, at great odds, the same work for early Catholic Americana that Joseph Sabin was doing at the same time for general Americana. (*Early Catholic Americana* [New York, Macmillan, 1939], p. v)

A50 Merrill, William Stetson. **Catholic Authorship in the American Colonies Before 1784.** Washington, DC, Catholic University of America Press, 1917. 18p. LC 18-1698.

Reprinted from *Catholic Historical Review*, v. III (1917), pp. 308-325. A brief, historical essay precedes the detailed listing of the forty-seven books by Catholic authors printed before 1784. For works printed in America after this date *see* Finotti (A49) and Parsons (A51).

A51 Parsons, Wilfrid. **Early Catholic Americana: A List of Books and Other Works by Catholic Authors in the United States, 1729-1830.** New York, Macmillan, 1939. xxv, 282p. Reprinted: Kennebunkport, ME, Milford House, 1973. LC 73-4826. ISBN 0-87821-137-3.

A52 Parsons, Wilfrid. **List of Additions and Corrections to Early Catholic Americana: Contribution of French Translations (1724-1820) by Forrest Bowe.** New York, Franco-Americana, 1952. x, 101p. LC 39-6755.

A bibliography of 1187 numbered items covering 300 more titles than Finotti but not giving the same wealth of bibliographical and historical information found in that work—there are almost no notes or annotations; but Parsons does provide a fine introductory essay on the history of American Catholic publishing. The same standard of inclusion is used here as in Finotti—any book written by a Catholic. Complete bibliographical information is given as well as locations in thirty different libraries. Special tables list the works published by Mathew Carey.

The supplement by Bowe lists 282 items most of which are translations from the French. Annotations explain why the work did not appear in Parsons. Alphabetical arrangement by author. Chronological index and title index.

71 additional items located at Catholic University Library are listed by T. Schmidt in "Early Catholic Americana: Some additions to Parsons" (*American Catholic Historical Society of Philadelphia. Records*, LXXXVI [March-December, 1975], pp. 24-32).

AMERICAN–CURRENT

A53 Benziger Brothers. **Catalogue of All Catholic Books in English.** New York, Benziger Brothers, 1912. 39, 183p. LC 12-29448.

"This Catalog contains practically all Catholic books published to-day in all English-speaking countries, with the exception of pamphlets, prayer books, and school books" (Title page). Contains portraits of many Catholic authors of the day. 5,521 items are listed in brief entries. The arrangement is by broad subject category. Author and subject indexes.

A54 **The Catholic Bookman: International Survey of Catholic Literature.** Grosse Pointe, MI, W. Rimig and Co., 1937-44. 7 v. Monthly, 1937-38; bimonthly, 1939-44. LC 41-3127.

Each issue contained articles on Catholic books and authors; the "Catholic Book Index" (an author-title-subject index with annotations); and "The Catholic Magazine Index" (a subject and author index to about 20 periodicals, which served to update the *Catholic Periodical Index*). After 1939 this section became the "Catholic Survey of all Current Literature," indexing Catholic periodicals for book reviews.

Easily the best journal of its kind; currently the *Religious Book Review* (A58) serves roughly the same purpose.

A55 Catholic University of America. **Theses and Dissertations: A Bibliographical Listing, Keyword Index and Author Index. Cumulation, 1961-1967.** Washington, DC, Catholic University of America Press, 1970. LC 70-113459.

"Indexes 5,458 masters', licentiate and doctoral theses accepted at Catholic University" (Introduction). A computerized listing giving full bibliographic information.

A56 **Guide to Catholic Literature, 1888-1967: An Annotated, Author, Title Subject, Bibliography of Books by and about Catholics, With a Selection of Catholic Interest Books by Non-Catholic Authors.** Comp. by Catherine M. Pilley. Haverford, PA, Catholic Library Association, 1940-68. 8 v. Annual, cumulated quadrennially. LC 41-8156.

(Imprint varies. Formerly published by Walter Romig, Grosse Pointe, MI. Now combined with the *Catholic Periodical Index* to form the *Catholic Periodical and Literature Index* [A160].)

Although by no means complete, especially in its coverage of European publications, this work filled a gap in Catholic bibliography admirably. It covered books and pamphlets including juvenile literature, and it supplied biographical notes for each author. Annotations were descriptive and critical with references to book reviews appearing in periodicals.

In 1959, when the Catholic Library Association took over publication, juvenile literature was dropped as were references to reviews since these were available in the *Catholic Periodical Index*.

The merger with *C.P.I.* has resulted in a much more useful bibliography and a technically more acceptable tool, since the older volumes of the *Guide* were often difficult to follow typographically.

Brown described it as "a very important work, fully supplying the desiderata of Catholic bibliographers. A great work bound to be of immense service to writers and readers whether Catholic or not" (*Catholic Library Practice* [A78], p. 114).

"A valuable possession for Public and University Libraries" (*Wilson Library Bulletin*, XXVI [November, 1951], p. 278).

A57 Maddrell, Jane G. **Bibliography of Catholic Books Published during 1948- Listed According to Subject**. Kansas City, KS, Bibliographic Pub. Co., 1949- . v. Annual.

Apparently only one issue of this subject list appeared.

A58 **Religious Book Review**. Williston Park, NY, 1970- . v. Quarterly. LC 76-14546. (Title varies: *Religious Book Guide*, 1970-71.)

(Preceded by *Catholic Book Merchandiser*, 1958-67; *Catholic Bookseller and Librarian*, 1967-69.)

Contains articles on the religious book trade, libraries, authors, advance news of books and paperbacks. The "Subject Guide to New Religious Books" is a bimonthly, annotated list with author and title indexes.

More ecumenical in coverage than its predecessors, but the emphasis is on Catholic publications.

A59 **Religious Reading 1-** . Washington, DC, Consortium Press, 1975- . v. Annual. LC 77-641847. ISBN 0147-8109.

Descriptive annotations are provided for each of the 1,500 to 2,000 titles listed annually. The listing is alphabetical by title under seven broad subject categories with subsections. Author and title indexes are supplied as well as a directory of publishers. Coverage is limited to English language books published in the United States. Catholic, Protestant and Jewish titles are included.

A60 Willging, Eugene Paul. **Catalog of Catholic Paperback Books**. New York, Catholic Book Merchandiser, 1961-66(?). 5 v. Annual. LC 63-25734.

Published as the April-May issue of the *Catholic Book Merchandiser*, one of the predecessors of the *Religious Book Review* (A58). Listed Catholic interest books, as well as books by Catholic authors, by author with descriptive annotations. Title and subject indexes.

A61   Willging, Eugene Paul. **The Index to Catholic Pamphlets in the English Language.** Washington, DC, Catholic University of America Press, 1937-53. 6 v. Irregular. LC 37-7135. (Title and imprint vary.) v. 1. 1937; Supp. 1939; v. 2. 1937-1942; v. 3. 1942-1946; v. 4. 1946-1948; v. 5. 1948-1950; v. 6. 1950-1952.

An annotated, classified list with classified and alphabetical indexes. The pamphlet is still a popular form of religious literature and such a thorough and easy to use bibliography would be useful today.

CZECHOSLOVAKIA

A62   Tumpach, Josef. **Bibliografie české katolické literatury náboženské od roku 1828 až do konce roku 1913.** Výdano v pamět osmdesátiletého jubilea "Časopisu katolického duchovenstva" a padesatiletého jubilea "Dědictví sv. Prokopa". Sest. Jos. Tumpach a Ant. Podlaha. V Praze, Nákl, Dědictví sv. Prokopa, 1912-23. 5 v. (2319p.). LC 63-56674.

Books and periodical articles in a classified listing with an index in volume five.

FRANCE

A63   **Catalogue collectif des livres religieux.** Paris, Union des Éditeurs Exporteurs Français d'Ouvrages de Religion, 1952- . v. LC 53-17407.

Each volume listed approximately 4,000 books in classified order with author and subject indexes.

A64   **Catalogue collectif des livres de culture religieuse en langue française: 1965, 1966, 1967.** Paris, UDEFOR, Union des éditeurs française d'ouvrages de religion, 1968. iv. 188p. LC 77-359901.

A classified, annotated bibliography with indexes of authors and titles.

GERMANY

A65   Rennhofer, Friedrich. **Bücherkunde des katholischen Lebens: Bibliographisches Lexikon der religiösen Literatur der Gegenwart.** Wien, Brüder Hollinek, 1961. xii, 360p. LC 61-40952.

A subject listing of over 12,000 titles published between 1940-1960 in Germany, Austria and Switzerland. No annotations. Author index and list of German Catholic publishers.

ITALY

A66   **Catalogo generale del libro cattolico in Italia.** Roma, Unione Editori Cattolici Italiani, 1950(?)- . v. Annual. LC 54-39498.

Arranged by subject, subarranged by publisher then author. Gives complete bibliographical information and prices. No annotations. Author and subject indexes.

POLAND

A67   Bar, Joachim Roman. **Polska bibliografia teologiczna za lata 1940-1948.** Warsaw, Akademia Teologii Katolickiej, 1969. 210p. LC 75-9762.

A68   Bar, Joachim Roman. **Polska bibliografia teologii i prawa kanonicznego za lata, 1949-1968.** Warsaw, Adademia Teologii Katolickiej, 1972. 445p. LC 74-209156.

Classified bibliographies with author indexes.

A69   **The Catholic Book in Poland, 1945-1965: Classified Catalogue.** Prepared by Maria Pszczólkowska. Translated by Danuta Karcz and Jolanta Ronikier. Warszawa, Ars Christiana, 1966. 544p. LC 68-5057.

Contains descriptive annotations in English.

SOUTH AMERICA

A70   **Bibliografía teologica comentada del area Iberoamericana.** Buenos Aires, Instituto Superior Evangélico de Estudios Teológicos, 1974- . v. Annual. LC 85-10333.

An ecumenical bibliography of religion covering books and articles in classified order with author and subject indexes.

LIBRARIES

General Works. The books listed in this section, while they may be of interest primarily to librarians, are also valuable to the general researcher; the Catholic Library Association's *Directory* (A71) is a guide to Catholic collections throughout the country; and the classification schedules (A82 and A83) could serve as guides to the organizing of religious knowledge although they are both in need of revision.

The Catholic Library Association, founded in 1921, is an organization of about 4,000 members involved with Catholic libraries and is open to any person or institution interested in its purposes. (For a complete history see "History of the Catholic Library Association" by Sister Consolata Maria, published serially in the *Catholic Library World*, beginning with XXXVI [April, 1965], p. 526.) The Association publishes the monthly *Catholic Library World*, *The Catholic Periodical and Literature Index* and many other reference works on this list.

GENERAL WORKS

DIRECTORIES

A71   Catholic Library Association. **Handbook and Membership Directory.** Haverford, PA, 1940- . v. Annual. LC 52-26054.

Contains the Constitutions and Bylaws of the Association, a list of individual members with a geographical index, and a complete description of all committees, councils, local units, sections, and roundtables.

A72   Moberg, David O. **International Directory of Religious Information Systems.** Milwaukee, WI, Marquette University, 1971. 88p. LC 75-156952.

A list of 66 data bases, indexing and abstracting services, libraries and information centers, giving name, personnel, history, description of services, accessibility and source of financial support. Indexes.

A73   Ruoss, G.M. **A World Directory of Theological Libraries.** Metuchen, NJ, Scarecrow Press, 1968. 220p. LC 68-12632.

A geographical listing of over 1,700 theological libraries giving the name, address, denomination, and year of founding. Institution Index. Religious Group Index.

HANDBOOKS

A74   O'Rourke, William Thomas. **Library Handbook for Catholic Readers.** New York, Bruce Pub. Co., 1937. xiv, 184p. LC 37-13544.

(First edition, 1935, entitled *Library Handbook for Catholic Students.*)

A general guide to libraries and literature for Catholic college-level students and the intelligent general reader. Some topics covered include "The Card Catalog," "Classification," "General Reference Works," "Periodical Indexes," "Pamphlets and Clippings," and "Bibliographies." The chapters are made up of text and annotated bibliographies. Foreign language material is covered throughout the book as well as in an appended bibliography of "Foreign Catholic Reference Works," also annotated. Other appended bibliographies: philosophy, sociology, classical Greek and Latin literature and antiquities. Worthy of being revised.

LIBRARY SCIENCE

ADMINISTRATION HANDBOOKS

A75   **Catholic Library Association. Paris Library Manual.** Villanova, PA, Catholic Library Association, 1959. 72p. LC 59-15681.

Contains "how to" information about organizing a library plus lists of books and periodicals for first purchase.

A76   Catholic Library Association. **Parish Library Manual: Suggested Books for First Purchase: Supplement 1964.** Haverford, PA, Catholic Library Association, 1965. 20p.

Lists about 100 new titles in subject order.

A77   Corrigan, John T. **Guide for the Organization and Operation of a Religious Resource Center.** Haverford, PA, Catholic Library Association, 1977. 78p. il. LC 77-670038.

A useful manual for establishing and operating a small parish library. Contains helpful information about administration, facilities, supplies, acquisition, processing and organizing materials and services. Appendixes include a D.D.C. scheme outline, a subject heading list, and a directory of publishers. Replaces *The Parish and Catholic Lending Library Manual* edited by Vincent Schneider (Haverford, PA, CLA, 1965).

A78   Martin, Brother David. **Catholic Library Practice.** Portland, OR, 1947-52. 2 v. il. LC 44-6329.

A series of studies by authorities in the field, covering the place of the library in various Catholic institutions, Catholic bibliography, library education, publishing, etc. Most of the essays are well written, of substantial length, and include a bibliography. The chapter on "Catholic Bibliography" was written by Fr. Stephen Brown and is a revision of his *Introduction to Catholic Booklore* (A16).

An excellent work, the only one of its kind, but now seriously out of date. Index.

A79   Schneider, Vincent P., ed. **The Parish and Catholic Lending Library Manual.** 2nd. ed. Haverford, PA Catholic Library Association, 1965. 64p. LC 65-4102.

A "how to" manual covering organization, acquisitions, cataloging, and other technical services.

CATALOGING CODES

A80   Biblioteca vaticana. **Rules for the Catalog of Printed Books.** Trans. from the 2nd. Italian ed. by Thomas J. Shanahan, Victor A. Schaefer, and Constantin T. Vesselowski; ed. by Wyllis E. Wright. Chicago, American Library Association, 1948. xii, 426p. LC 48-7079.

A fine example of a cataloging code covering author entry, descriptive cataloging, subject headings and filing in one volume incorporating the best in the "Anglo-American" tradition; in fact, as the preface points out, "the circumstances and personnel under which the rules were prepared produced the unexpected result that for many years the most complete statement of American cataloging practice was available only in the Italian language."

Although it should be useful in any large library, it is especially valuable in the Catholic library because of the nature of the materials for which it was devised, i.e., Bible entries based on the Vulgate version. Saints' names are given in Latin, but the section on subject headings has been adapted for English usage.

A81   Kapsner, Oliver Leonard. **A Manual of Cataloging Practice for Catholic Author and Title Entries: Being Supplementary Aids to the A.L.A. and Vatican Library Cataloging Rules.** Washington, DC, Catholic University of American Press, 1953. ix, 107p. (Catholic University of America Studies in Library Science, 2.) LC A53-7313.

One of the smallest of Kapsner's many library reference works but certainly not the least useful. It was designed to supplement the Vatican and 1949 A.L.A. codes and could be used by any library cataloging Catholic material, especially liturgical books (both Latin and Eastern), religious orders, and names in religion. Its treatment of the Bible is probably of interest only in Catholic libraries. Other types of entries covered include popes, saints, documents, monastic rules and the use of the heading "Catholic Church" in Catholic collections. Many examples are furnished for each rule, and reference is consistently made to related rules in the A.L.A. and Vatican codes. Should be updated to conform to recent AACR2 practices.

CLASSIFICATION SCHEDULES

A82   Lynn, Jeannette Murphy. **An Alternative Classification for Catholic Books: Ecclesiastical Literature, Theology, Canon Law, Church History, for Use with the Dewey Decimal, Classification décimale, Library of Congress Classifications.** 2nd. ed. rev. by Gilbert C. Peterson. Supplement (1965) by Thomas G. Pater. Washington, DC, Catholic University of America Press, 1965. 514p. LC 66-1593.

Essentially based on the Library of Congress system, modifying it by changing locations and adding a third letter. Valuable for its plentiful and detailed tables of liturgical books, papal documents, religious orders, and local Church government. The introductory essay on classifying Catholic Church materials is also of value.

A83   Walsh, Richard J. **A Modification and Expansion of the Dewey Decimal Classification in the 200 class.** Haverford, PA, Catholic Library Association, 1963. iv, 123p.

Originally devised in 1941 and reprinted in 1963. A workable scheme for Catholic libraries, but now considerably out of date, especially in the light of post-conciliar developments.

Later revisions of Dewey are probably more adaptable to heavily Catholic collections than the original scheme—and are certainly more frequently revised.

SUBJECT HEADINGS

A84   Kapsner, Oliver Leonard. **Catholic Subject Headings.** General editors: Catherine M. Pilley, Mathew R. Wilt. Haverford, PA, Catholic Library Association, 1981. ii, 240p. LC 81-140344. ISBN 0-87507-009-4.

A long awaited revision of the fifth edition, 1963. "Updated with current usage reflecting the changes in terminology since Vatican II and supplemented by the *Catholic Periodical Index* and the ninth edition of the *Library of Congress Subject Headings.*"

GENERAL DICTIONARIES AND ENCYCLOPEDIAS

Catholic dictionaries and encyclopedias generally fall into two major categories: those primarily concerned with theological topics, and those treating a wide variety of topics (usually in the humanities) from a Catholic point of view. This chapter lists only the latter. (See Chapter II for the former.) Within the second category there is a subdivision represented by the difference, for example, between the *New Catholic Encyclopedia* (A105) and *Der Grosse Herder* (A123). The first is primarily a religious work in which the editors have omitted any topic they considered irrelevant; the second deliberately covers all topics, but with a religious viewpoint where applicable. Small, one-volume dictionaries not limited to strictly theological terms are also included here.

Two works dominate the English-language list of encyclopedias—*The Catholic Encyclopedia* (A89) and the *New Catholic Encyclopedia* (A105), which does not completely replace the older work.

According to *The Catholic Encyclopedia and its Makers* (A179, p. liv. ff.), the actual work on the *Encyclopedia* was begun in 1905 when the editors held their first meeting in New York and organized the Robert Appleton Company (later the Encyclopedia Press), which remained an entirely independent company formed for the special purpose of publishing and distributing the *Encyclopedia*. After 1922 when the last volume had appeared and it had published a biographical directory of its contributors (*The Catholic Encyclopedia and its Makers*) and two supplements (A91 and (A92), the Company was dissolved.

The next two attempts to compile a similar work (in 1927-29 and 1936) were by different companies although some of the same persons were involved in editing and contributing to them. The first of these, *Universal Knowledge* (A114), was modeled after *Der Grosse Herder*; only two volumes ever saw print. In 1936 the Gilmary Society of New York issued one promising volume of an expanded and revised edition (A93), but finally had to be content with issuing a loose-leaf *Supplement* (A92) to the original *Encyclopedia*.

Finally, in 1958, Cardinal Stritch suggested the undertaking of a new Catholic encyclopedia to the Board of Trustees of the Catholic University of America ("Background information on the *New Catholic Encyclopedia*" *Catholic Library World*, XXXIX [January, 1968], p. 358), which approved a plan for editing it under the auspices of the University. They purchased the right to use the name and the remaining sets of the old *Catholic Encyclopedia* from the Gilmary Society, and an arrangement was reached with the McGraw-Hill Book Company to publish the work while leaving full editorial control of the contents to the University. The rector of the University, Bishop William J. McDonald, was appointed editor in chief, and the work was begun. But by 1962, it became apparent from the backlog of editorial work that a change was in order; a greatly expanded, full-time staff of editors was organized under the Rev. John P. Whalen, and the editing was finally completed in 1966, only one year behind the projections made in 1959. In the late spring of 1967, the sturdily bound and handsomely printed, fifteen-volume set went on sale. In 1974 a supplementary volume appeared (A106), and another (A107) in 1979.

Of the more popular one-volume dictionaries and encyclopedias, probably the most widely known and useful are Attwater's *Catholic Dictionary* (A86), Addis' *A Catholic Dictionary* (A85) and the *Catholic Encyclopedia Dictionary* (A94). Unfortunately, these are out of date, and none of the more recent works are as well done. Hardon's *Modern Catholic Dictionary* (A102) falls short of filling this gap because of serious omissions and a theologically conservative stance.

Foreign Language Works. Unhappily for those readers whose knowledge of languages is limited to English, the best and most comprehensive reference works on the Church are still available only in other languages. This bibliography contains all the large, important works and many of the smaller or popular ones that are widely used, unique, or more up-to-date than similar works in English. These criteria have been applied to foreign works in the individual subject lists in subsequent chapters also.

Ranking very high, if not the highest, on the list of foreign countries producing the greatest number and the most scholarly Catholic reference works is France, where two of the largest series of Catholic encyclopedias in existence have been published. The first of these appeared in the nineteenth century under the direction of the prolific editor and controversial priest, Jacques Paul Migne (see Henri Leclercq "Migne," *Dictionnaire d'archéologie chrétienne*, t. 11, pt. 1, p. 942-57). After a disagreement with his bishop in 1825 over his pamphlet on "Liberté", he moved to Paris where he edited and wrote extensively for two periodicals and founded a printing establishment for the inexpensive production of theological works to encourage the scientific study of the sacred sciences by the clergy. Among the huge sets he edited and printed were a 28-volume commentary on the scriptures, 28 volumes on theology, 102 volumes on preaching and the 378-volume Greek and Latin patrologies (B169-B173). His *Encyclopédie théologique* (A122) was published in three different series from 1844-1873 and totals 170 volumes.

A series of disasters and controversies ended Migne's ambitious plans for raising the intellectual level of the French clergy. In 1868 a fire broke out in his printing plant destroying millions of francs' worth of plates; and in 1870 the Franco-Prussian War took its toll. Migne's career ended under suspension from his priestly duties by the Archbishop of Paris who was opposed to the more commercial aspects of the business which eventually grew to include the production and sale of religious articles; and under the displeasure of Rome, which condemned his practice of selling books for Mass stipends. In spite of all this he did manage to produce a "universal library for the Clergy" (J. P. Kirsch, "Migne," *New Catholic Encyclopedia*, IX, p. 827) of over 2,000 volumes, many of which are still the standard editions in their fields. His *Imprimerie Catholique* employed over 300 persons and developed many time- and money-saving typographical techniques.

The second of the monumental French works, known collectively as the *Encyclopédie des sciences religieuses* (A120), has been appearing regularly since 1907 under the direction of the Letouzey Firm of Paris, which also publishes a series of more popular Catholic reference works. Individual parts of the series are listed in various chapters of this work according to subject.

Germany has also produced a number of impressive general Catholic works along with its well known, but more strictly theological works, such as the *Lexikon für Theologie and Kirche* (B192), not listed in this part of the bibliography. The chief producer of these works has been the House of Herder in Freiburg im Bresgau, founded in 1801 by Bartholomaus Herder (Franz Meister, "Herder," *Catholic Encyclopedia*, VII, p. 251-53). His son Karl Raphael Herder was responsible for beginning the two standard German Catholic reference works: the *Kirchenlexikon* (A127) and the *Konversations Lexikon* now called *Der Grosse Herder* (A123).

Moroni's *Dizionario* (A135) and the *Enciclopedia cattolica* (A131) are the chief Italian contributions to this field; the first is significant for its comprehensiveness and detail and the second for its scholarship and relative currentness.

The first volume of a large, important Polish Catholic encyclopedia (A139) appeared in 1973 and was well received by scholars. In 1982, volume 1 of the *Enciclopedia de la Iglesia Católica en Mexico* (A138) appeared. This handsomely produced work, projected in twelve volumes, has the distinction of being the most up-to-date, general Catholic encyclopedia.

AMERICAN AND BRITISH

A85   Addis, William Edward and Thomas A. Arnold. **A Catholic Dictionary: Containing Some Account of the Doctrine, Discipline, Rites, Ceremonies, Councils and Religious Orders of the Catholic Church.** Rev. by T. B. Scannell; further rev., with additions by P. E. Hallet. 17th ed. London, Routledge and Kegan Paul, 1960. viii, 860p. (First published, 1886.)

A fine dictionary, more scholarly than most, with many long articles. There are no bibliographies as such, but sources of information are indicated, and a list of reference works used appears in the front of the volume. No biography.

A86   Attwater, Donald. **A Catholic Dictionary.** New York, Macmillan, 1961. xvi, 552p. (First published in 1931 as the *Catholic Encyclopaedic Dictionary.*)

Among the most popular one-volume Catholic dictionaries in English. Has gone through 3 editions and many printings in England and the U.S. It is a "general work of quick reference to the signification of words, terms, names and phrases in common use in the philosophy, dogmatic and moral theology, canon law, liturgy, institutions and organization of the Catholic Church" (Preface). Biographies are included but limited mostly to saints.

A87   Broderick, Robert Carlton. **Catholic Concise Dictionary.** Rev. by Placid Hermann and Marion A. Habig. Chicago, Franciscan Herald Press, 1966. xi, 330p. LC 66-14726. (First published, 1944, under the title *Concise Catholic Dictionary.*)

A dictionary of terms with short, easy-to-read definitions; no biography or bibliography. "Some definitions do not seem adequate . . . [but] one of the most commendable features of the book is the large number of terms pertaining to Oriental rites" (*Social Justice Review*, LXI [December, 1968], p. 282).

A88   Broderick, Robert Carlton. **The Catholic Encyclopedia.** Nashville, Thomas Nelson, 1976. 612p. il. LC 76-10976. ISBN 0-8407-5096-X.

A recent addition to the popular, one-volume Catholic dictionary field. This work is most valuable for its coverage of new terms and practices. It contains 4,000 entries and is, therefore, not as comprehensive as Nevins' *Maryknoll Catholic Dictionary* (A104) which contains 10,000 entries. Covers Catholic beliefs and practices, some abbreviations and names of religious orders, but is not strong in biography. The illustrations are well done but of little practical value. Both the *Critic* (XXXV [Spring, 1977], p. 74) and *Theological Studies* (XXXVIII [Spring 1977], p. 602) describe it as theologically conservative in tone.

A89   The Catholic Encyclopedia: An International Work of Reference on the
       Constitution, Doctrine, Discipline, and History of the Catholic Church.
       New York, The Encyclopedia Press, 1905-22. 16 v.

A90   The Catholic Encyclopedia: An International Work of Reference on the
       Constitution, Doctrine, Discipline, and History of the Catholic Church.
       Supplementary Volume, Containing Revisions of the Articles on Canon
       Law According to the Code of Canon Law . . . 1917.

A91   The Catholic Encyclopedia: An International Work of Reference on the
       Constitution, Doctrine, Discipline, and History of the Catholic Church.
       Supplement I, 1922 (v. 17). LC 30-23167.

A92   The Catholic Encyclopedia: An International Work of Reference on the
       Constitution, Doctrine, Discipline, and History of the Catholic Church.
       Supplement II, New York, The Gilmary Society, 1950-58.

       For over fifty years this work was the chief source of information on the
       Catholic Church in English-speaking countries. Its longevity is the result,
       no doubt, of the stability of the Church, at least up until 1962, but it must
       also be attributed to the competency of its contributors and editors and
       the comprehensiveness of its scope. As stated in the preface, "it is not
       exclusively a church encyclopedia, nor is it limited to the ecclesiastical
       sciences and the doings of Churchmen. It records all that Catholics have
       done, not only in behalf of charity or morals but also for the intellectual
       and artistic development of mankind."

       The work is frequently criticized for its polemical approach to Protestants,
       e.g. the articles on Luther, Calvin, and similar figures, but more often it
       is lavishly praised for its illustrations, bibliography, biography, historical
       articles, general scope, and quality of scholarship. Collison, for example,
       says, "it is rich in philosophical, literary, historical, and fine arts material;
       with so wide a scope that librarians often use it as a supplementary source
       in their search for materials" (Robert Collison, *Encyclopedias: Their History
       through the Ages*, 2nd. ed. [New York, Hafner, 1966], p. 218). Winchell,
       although she points out that it is not so comprehensive as the great French
       Catholic works, remarks on its usefulness in "medieval literature, history,
       philosophy, art, etc." (Constance M. Winchell, *Guide to Reference Books*
       [Chicago, A.L.A., 1967], p. 219.)

       Volume 16 contains supplementary articles, a very thorough index, and a
       reading guide to the contents.

A93   The Catholic Encyclopedia: A General Work of Reference for Art, Bio-
       graphy, Education, History, Law, Literature, Philosophy, the Sciences,
       Religion, and the Church. Rev. and enl. ed. New York, the Gilmary Society,
       1936- . v. LC 36-10935.
          V. 1. *A-* . (No more volumes published.)

A94   **The Catholic Encyclopedia Dictionary, Containing 8500 Articles on the Beliefs, Devotions, Rites, Symbolism, Tradition and History of the Church; Her Laws, Organizations, Dioceses, Missions, Institutions, Religious Orders, Saints; Her Part in Promoting Art, Science, Education and Social Welfare.** Comp. and ed. under the Direction of the editors of *The Catholic Encyclopedia*. New York, The Gilmary Society, 1941. iii, 1095p. LC 41-5257. (Published in 1929 under the title *The New Catholic Dictionary*)

Now largely out of date; many of its articles were abridged from *The Catholic Encyclopedia*. All are signed or documented. Contains biographies. No bibliographies. Classified index. Still regarded as "the most useful dictionary" (*Catholic Library World*, XXXVI [May-June, 1965], p. 617).

A95   **The Catholic Encyclopedia for School and Home.** New York, McGraw-Hill, 1965. 12 v. il. LC 65-20114.

A96   **The Catholic Encyclopedia for School and Home. Supplementary Volume.** New York, McGraw-Hill, 1968. 211+40p. il.

A97   **The Catholic Encyclopedia for School and Home. The Contemporary Church: Supplement.** New York, Grolier, 1974. viii, 264p. il.

A popular work, intended for the general reader and for use in schools, which has been published recently enough to incorporate many of the changes inaugurated by the Second Vatican Council. The scope of the work has been defined in the preface as "one which would support and enrich the high school curriculum, which was the inflexible norm to determine the inclusion or exclusion of subjects and the amount of space to be allotted to each."

Over 1,200 contributors wrote for the work and are listed with their qualifications in Volume 12. The bibliography—there are no individual bibliographies after each article—is also in Volume 12. This classified "Reading List," as it is called, was designed "to take the reader one step beyond what he has read in any given article" (Preface to "Reading List"). Most of the books were chosen because they were either in-print or otherwise available. Many fine works are included, but the lack of indexes or at least of a more detailed classification scheme makes them difficult to locate quickly.

This is "a well written, well edited, and well illustrated source of mid-century Catholic thought on both religious and secular subjects," according to *Subscription Books Bulletin*. "Though not strong on music, science and technology, it augments general encyclopedias in its biographies of religious figures and its attention to subjects directly related to the religions of the world." (*Booklist and Subscription Books Bulletin*, LXIII [July, 1967], p. 1113.)

A98   **Catholic Reference Encyclopedia.** n.p. Catholic Educational Guild, 1968. 6 v. il. LC 68-1321.

A popular, short article encyclopedia that could well have been printed in one or two volumes.

A99   **Corpus Dictionary of Western Churches.** Ed. by T. C. O'Brien. Washington, DC, Corpus Publications, 1970. xviii, 820p. LC 78-99501.

Almost 100 authorities from all faiths have contributed to this ecumenical dictionary. There are articles for each of the Churches listed in the *Yearbook of American Churches*, biographical and topical articles. Most of them contain brief bibliographies. The majority of the contributors are Catholic, but "Happily, there is little if any trace of pre-conciliar triumphalism" (*America*, CXXII [February 21, 1970], p. 199.) Cross references are indicated throughout.

A100   **The Encyclopedia of Religion.** Editor in chief, Mircea Eliade; editors, Charles J. Adams et al. New York, Macmillan, 1987-88. 16 v. LC 86-5432. ISBN 0-02-909480-1.

The first attempt in over forty years to update the **Encyclopedia of Religion and Ethics** (Edinburgh, Clark, 1908-1926). Covers all religions and religious topics including the religious history of all races. "Not conceived as a dictionary, with entries covering the entire vocabulary in every field of religious studies. Rather, it was conceived as a system of articles on important ideas, beliefs, rituals, myths, symbols, and persons that have played a role in the universal history of religions from Paleolithic times to the present day" (Preface). Contains many articles of Catholic interest and many contributors are Catholic scholars. Index, vol. 16.

A101   **Encyclopedic Dictionary of Religion.** Ed. by Paul Kevin Meagher, Thomas C. O'Brien, Consuelo Maria Aherne. Philadelphia, Sisters of St. Joseph; Washington, DC, Corpus Publications; Distributed by Catholic University Press, 1979. 3 v. LC 78-62029. ISBN 0-9602572-3-3.

A comprehensive dictionary of religion written mostly by Catholic authors. Most articles are short but only the briefest do not contain cross references and some bibliography. "The articles are written objectively and from an ecumenical point of view, although those on controversial topics clearly reflect Roman Catholic positions" (*Wilson Library Bulletin,* LIV [January, 1980], p. 332).

A102   Hardon, John A. **Modern Catholic Dictionary**. Garden City, NY, Doubleday, 1980. xiii, 635p. LC 77-82945. ISBN 01385-12162-8.

Defines over 5,000 items "dealing with Catholic faith, worship, morals, history, canon law, and spirituality" (Introduction). Biographies are not covered. An Appendix contains the Creed, a list of popes, ecclesiastical calendars for the Roman and Byzantine rites and a list of U.S. and Canadian religious orders. "A distorted and unattractive picture of the modern Catholic Church. The modern Catholic dictionary still waits to be written" (*America* CXLII [April 26, 1980], p. 365).

A103   Hardon, John A. **Pocket Catholic Dictionary**. Garden City, NY, Image Books, 1985. xv, 510 p. LC 85-5790. ISBN 0-3852-3238-1.

Abridged edition of A102. 2,000 entries.

A104   Nevins, Albert J. **The Maryknoll Catholic Dictionary.** Wilkes-Barre, PA, Dimension Books; New York, Grosset and Dunlap, 1965. wvii, 710p. LC 65-15436.

A comprehensive one-volume dictionary; it is "intended to meet the needs of users in the U. S. and Canada and incorporates the many changes in the Church's liturgy and discipline coming about as a result of the Council" (Preface). Includes terms, doctrines, feasts, practices, religious orders; with appendixes of abbreviations, forms of address, patron saints, Catholic organizations, popes, biographies of American and Canadian Catholics and saint's names. It appears to be reasonably up-to-date and useful but has been criticized for superficiality and omissions (*Catholic Library World*, XXXVI [May-June, 1965], Pp. 617-618).

A105   **New Catholic Encyclopedia: An International Work of Reference on the Teachings, History, Organization, and Activities of the Catholic Church and on All Institutions, Religions, Philosophies, and Scientific and Cultural Developments Affecting the Catholic Church from Its Beginning to the Present.** Prepared by an editorial staff at the Catholic University of America. New York, McGraw-Hill, 1967. 15 v. il. LC 66-22292.

This work acknowledges its lineage to *The Catholic Encyclopedia* (Preface), but it is an entirely new work. It contains some 17,000 signed articles, each with a bibliography. In the tradition of the older work the *N.C.E.* covers not just Catholic topics but many general subjects from a Catholic point of view. Over 4,800 scholars contributed to the work and their names and qualifications are listed in the last volume; many of them are non-Catholics. "There are, however, some startling omissions," as one reviewer points out, "Congar, Rahner, Weigel, Diekmann, Schillebeeckx, J. C. Murray, Gilson, Maritain" (*Choice*, IV [June, 1967], p. 390). Over 300 maps and 7,500 illustrations are included. Biography is a strong point although no living persons are included. The last volume contains an extensive bibliography of the reference and other works most frequently cited (pp. 207-26), and the computerized index compiled by Sister Claudia Carlen, I.H.M.

A comparison of the older work with the new will reveal a tendency to shorten historical articles and articles dealing with older topics. This, of course, is what one hopes for in a new work so that current issues may be treated at greater length, but it should serve to warn librarians not to discard the older work too hastily.

For extensive appraisal of the *Encyclopedia*'s theological aspects *see* the *American Ecclesiastical Review* (CLVIII [September, 1968], pp. 161-71) and the *Catholic Biblical Quarterly* (XXIX [October, 1967], pp. 661-5) for the scriptural contents.

Library Journal described the articles as "uniformly excellent, both in scholarship and readability. There are fine articles on art, music and architecture and an especially complete coverage of Scholastic philosophy. The many Biblical articles, . . . 140 pages, make up a complete Biblical encyclopedia. . . . A credit to American Catholic scholarship" (*Library Journal*, XCII [April 15, 1967], p. 1618). Daniel Callahan, on the other hand, criticized the work for the "consistently overlooked . . . discrepancy between ideal and reality in Catholic life and institutions" and for its inclusion of "a vast amount of straight 'secular' material" such as anthropology and the nature of nuclear energy (*New York Times Book Review*, September 10, 1967, p. 8).

The ecumenical tone of the work was strongly praised by the *Times Literary Supplement* (September 28, 1967, p. 899).

A106   New Catholic Encyclopedia: An International Work of Reference on the Teachings, History, Organization, and Activities of the Catholic Church and on All Institutions, Religions, Philosophies, and Scientific and Cultural Developments Affecting the Catholic Church from Its Beginning to the Present. Volume XVI, Supplement, 1967-1974. Ed. by David Eggenberger. Washington, DC, Publisher's Guild, in association with McGraw-Hill, 1974. 520p. il.

Contains new articles on such contemporary issues as Underground Church, Theology of Dissent, Women as Priests, Exclaustration, Laicization, etc. Of the 440 articles, 127 are biographies of notable Catholics recently deceased. Most of these articles are accompanied by a portrait and a bibliography. Unfortunately only two of the biographees are women. Articles on unrelated, purely secular topics such as Space Exploration continue to be inserted. The quality of the illustrations is somewhat below that of the original set. The *Supplement* is nevertheless a valuable addition to the *Encyclopedia*.

A107   **New Catholic Encyclopedia: An International Work of Reference on the Teachings, History, Organization, and Activities of the Catholic Church and All Institutions, Religions, Philosophies, and Scientific and Cultural Developments Affecting the Catholic Church from Its Beginning to the Present. Volume XVII, Supplement, Change in the Church.** Prepared by an editorial staff at the Catholic University of America. Washington, DC, Publishers Guild in association with McGraw-Hill, 1979. xv, 812p. LC 66-22292. ISBN 0-07-0102-35-X.

Nearly 800 articles based on the theme "Change in the Church." " '*The Supplement*' is self-contained but is also designed to bring out the impact of postconciliar thought and life on earlier entries in the *Encyclopedia*" (Preface). Bibliographies. Index.

A108   **The New Catholic Peoples' Encyclopedia.** Ed. by Edward G. Finnegan. New and revised edition. Chicago, Catholic Press, 1973. 3 v. il. LC 73-10485. ISBN 0-8326-2001-7. (Published in 1965 as *Virtue's Catholic Encyclopedia*.)

Good for basic information for school and home use. Brief articles without bibliography.

A109   **The New Library of Catholic Knowledge.** Advisory editors, Illtud Evans, et. al. New York, Hawthorn Books, 1963-64. 12 v. il. LC 63-11044.

The volumes cover such topics as the Old and New Testaments, Church history, the lives of the saints, Church government, liturgy and Church art and architecture. Volume twelve is a dictionary and index. Directed to the school and family library, some of the contributors are, nevertheless, experts in their fields. "Delightfully readable, clear and straightforward" (*New Blackfriars*, XLVI [May, 1965], p. 488). Very brief bibliographies are supplied at the end of each volume.

A110   Pegis, Jessie Corrigan. **A Practical Catholic Dictionary**. Garden City, NY, Hanover House, 1957; New York, All Saints, 1961 (paper). 258p. LC 57-6297.

A popular work designed for general readers and students. Brief entries. Not an improvement over earlier works in this list (*Worship*, XXXI [November, 1957], pp. 619-20).

A111   Pfeiffer, Harold A. **The Catholic Picture Dictionary**. Illus. by R. and K. Wood. New York, Duell, Sloan and Pearce, 1948. 156p. LC 48-5835.

Illustrations of Church furnishings, vestments, ceremonies, etc., and identifications of some major works of art.

A112   **The Twentieth Century Encyclopedia of Catholicism**. Ed. by Henri Daniel-Rops. New York, Hawthorn Books, 1958-68. 150 v.

Originally published in French under the title *Je sais, je crois*, edited by Henri Daniel-Rops, the renowned French lay theologian. This "encyclopedia" is actually a series of separately bound monographs, each indexed and containing a "Select Bibliography." The set is divided into sixteen parts made up of from five to fifteen volumes, each dealing with some aspect of a broad subject such as knowledge and faith, the truths of the faith, scripture, man, Church history, Church organization, the Church and the modern world, literature, art, science, Christian religions, and non-Christian religions.

The index (vol. 150) by Joseph Sprug covers subjects only. The *Critic* said of the work:

> It is not intended for the specialist in theology, but aimed rather at the layman, seeking to give him an intelligent grasp of all the major aspects of Catholicism. French bibliographies have been completely redone for the English-speaking reader and contain only works in English; however, they are not as complete as could be desired. Since the work is written on the popular level, it tends to blur the distinction between propositions that belong to the deposit of faith and those that are merely theological opinion. But by and large it is a welcome addition to Catholic literature in English (*Critic*, XVIII [January, 1959], p. 23).

Most of the volumes were reviewed favorably as they appeared.

A113   **Twentieth Century Catholicism. A Periodic Supplement to the Twentieth Century Encyclopedia of Catholicism**. New York, Hawthorn Books, 1965- . v. LC 65-3716. (No more volumes published)

(Editor 1965, Lancelot Capel Sheppard)

Intended to be a supplement to the main set by "revising, strengthening, and improving" the material that is directly related to the different volumes in the series.

A114   **Universal Knowledge: A Dictionary and Encyclopedia of Arts and Sciences, History and Biography, Law, Literature, Religions, Nations, Races, Customs and Institutions**. Ed. by Edward A. Pace, Conde B. Pallen, Thomas J. Shahan, D. D., James J. Walsh, John J. Wynne; assisted by numerous collaborators. New York, The Universal Knowledge Foundation, Inc., 1927-29. v. 1-2; A-Byzantium. LC 27-8564.

Planned as a twelve-volume encyclopedia by some of the editors of the *Catholic Encyclopedia*, covering general knowledge, not just religious topics, but written from a Catholic point of view in the manner of *Der Grosse Herder* (A123). Most of the articles in the first two volumes were rather short, and only major articles were signed and had bibliographies which were not very extensive.

DUTCH

A115   **Encyclopaedie van het Katholicisme.** Onder redactie van E. Hendrikx, J. C. Doensen en W. Bocxe. Antwerpen, 't Groeit, 1955-56. 3 v. LC 57-24409.

A much smaller work than *De Katholieke encyclopaedie* (A116), but limited more to religious topics; also contains biographies and bibliography.

A116   **De Katholieke encyclopaedie.** 2. druk, onder redactie van P. van der Meer, F. Baur en L. Engelbregt. Amsterdam, Uitg. Mij. Joost van den Vondel, 1949-55. 25 v. LC 50-15191.

One of the largest general Catholic encyclopedias published in the twentieth century although the articles themselves are extremely brief. Includes theology, history, biography, geography, religions, science and natural history somewhat in the manner of *Der Grosse Herder* (A123). Bibliographies are supplied but are brief and cover mostly Dutch works. The index is not analytical.

FRENCH

A117   **Catholicisme: hier, aujourd'hui, demain. Encyclopédie en sept volumes.** Dirigée par G. Jacquement. Paris, Letouzey et Ané, 1947- . v. LC A51-863.

Published by the same firm that produces the *Encyclopédie des sciences religieuses* (A120), this work is intended to cover a general range of subjects from a Catholic point of view but more briefly than in their monumental series. Seven volumes are projected. Most of the articles have bibliographies appended or contained in the texts; all are signed and some run to lengths of several pages.

The Catholic Library World declared that:
> The articles are written authoritatively and scientifically including the most up-to-date information on each topic. There is a large number of contributors qualified in various subject fields, most of them belonging to the faculties of seminaries, religious scholasticates and Catholic institutions of higher education. Emphasis is on French subjects. (*Catholic Library World*, XXIX [March, 1948], pp. 203-4).

A118   **Dictionnaire practique des connaissances religieuses.** pub. sous la direction de Joseph Bricourt. Paris, Letouzey et Ané, 1925-29. 6 v. and supplement. LC 25-20237.

A general religious encyclopedia covering doctrines, sects, history, biography, archeology, Church government, etc., all from a Catholic point of view.

Good for biographies, especially of French Catholics. The emphasis is on French topics and viewpoints. Alphabetical and classified indexes.

A119   **Dictionnaire du foyer catholique: Apporte, sous le classement alphabétique, les responses à toutes les questions que peut se poser un catholique de XXe siècle.** Paris, Librairie des Champs-Elysées, 1956. xv, 892p. LC 57-31390.

A popular dictionary covering terms, concepts, biography, history, etc. Also published in a Spanish edition: *Diccionario del hogar católico* (A140).

A120   **Encyclopédie des sciences religieuses, redigée par les savants catholiques. les plus éminents de France et l'étranger.** Paris, Letouzey et Ané, 1907- . v. Part 1. Dictionnaire de la Bible, by F. G. Vigoroux and L. Pirot. 1907-12. 5 v. Supplément, 1928- . v. *See* (B85); Part 2. Dictionnaire de théologie catholique, by A. Vacant and others. 1909-50. 15 v. Tables générales. 1951- . v. *See* (B139). Part 3. Dictionnaire d'archéologie chrétienne et de liturgie by F. Cabrol and H. Leclerq. 1928-53. 15 v. in 30. *See* (B294). Part 4. Dictionnaire d'histoire et de géographie ecclésiastiques, by A. Baudrillart. 1929- . v. *See* (E7). Part 5. Dictionnaire de droit canonique, by A. Villien and E. Magnin. 1935- . v. *See* (D146).

Each of these works is listed and evaluated separately in this bibliography. In general, one can say of them that no more complete treatment of their subject fields can be found in reference form, or perhaps in any other form. Each article is of monograph length, is signed, and contains an extensive bibliography both in the text and in a separate list.

The series is listed in every standard bibliography of reference works and is given the highest praise. Both Winchell and Walford call them works of the highest quality of scholarship and bibliography. Dutcher says of them, "Each of these works, in its own field, approximates the scale of the series as a whole" (George M. Dutcher, *A Guide to Historical Literature* [New York, Macmillan, 1936], p. 119); and Paetow predicted that "this set will be the largest work of reference on religion in any language" (Louis J. Paetow, *Guide to the Study of Medieval History* [New York, Crofts, 1931], p. 16).

The only general criticism one can level against the work is one common to many French publications, namely, the delayed schedule of publication of the individual dictionaries, which is so serious that the early volumes are usually out-of-date before the set is half complete. Attempts at updating through supplements usually tend to make the work more difficult to use and are themselves on a delayed schedule.

A121   Follain, Jean. **Petit glossaire de l'argot écclésiastique.** Paris, J.J. Pauvert, 1966. 50p. LC 67-50944.

An interesting if small collection of French ecclesiastical slang.

A122   Migne, Jacques Paul. **Encyclopédie théologique, ou Série de dictionnaires sur toutes les parties de la science religieuse** . . . publiée par m. l'abbé. Migne . . . Paris, Chez l'éditeur, 1845-73. 168 v. in 170. LC 46-45278.

Although now quite out of date, this set contains some sections that have never been replaced by later works. It is actually a series of over 100 multi-volume dictionaries or encyclopedias on separate subjects, not all of which are theological. Some of these will be found listed individually in this bibliography.

Among the better known parts are the *Dictionnaire de la Bible*; *de la liturgie catholique*; *des héresies*; *de toutes les religions du monde*; *de géographie*; *de la biographie*; *d'anthropologie*; *des sciences politiques et sociales*; *universel de mythologie*; *des sciences physiques et naturelles*; *de technologie*; and *universel de philologie sacrée*. These dictionaries are made up of articles or brief treatises on various aspects of the main subject, arranged in alphabetical order. Many are of unequal value, are poorly printed, and contain typographical errors. Nevertheless, it is not likely that a work of such a comprehensive scope will ever be attempted again with the same success, if indeed at all. Not even the extensive Letouzey series (A120) tries to match the *Encyclopédie* in this respect. See the *Library of Congress Author Catalog* for a complete list of titles in the series.

GERMAN

A123 **Der Grosse Herder; Nachschlagewerk für Wissen und Leben.** 5., neubearb. Aufl. von Herder's Konversationslexikon. Freiburg, Herder, 1952-56. 10 v.

A124 **Der Grosse Herder; Nachschlagewerk für Wissen und Leben. Erganzungsband.** 1962. 2 v.

Intended to be a general encyclopedia—not primarily religious but written from a Catholic point of view—but "by its general impartiality, scholarship, accuracy, and thoroughness has earned itself a wider audience" (Robert Collison, *Encyclopedias: Their History throughout the Ages.* 2d. ed. [New York, Hafner, 1966], p. 187).

Made up of mostly brief articles with thousands of small photographs and many larger plates. Each article has at least a very brief bibliography. Catholic subjects, biography and viewpoints are emphasized although the majority of the articles have nothing to do with religion. Volume ten, *Der Mensch in seiner Welt*, is something of a general survey of modern history, culture, philosophy, theology, etc. "A monumental compendium of the sum of human knowledge as it directly affects man's life in the universe" (*America*, XC [December 5, 1953], p. 270).

A125 **Der Neue Herder** (Verantwortliche Chefredaktion: Udo Becker und Günther Böing. Bildredaktion: Hans Quast) Neu aufl. In 6 Bänden mit einem Grossatlas. Freiburg, Herder, 1965-68. 8 v. in 7. LC 67-109030.
v. 7-8. Der neue Herder Handatlas.

An abridged version of *Der Grosse Herder* with briefer articles and more limited scope. Some updating on information in the larger work. Many cross references; thousands of illustrations. Coverage of Catholic terms, biography, etc. is strong.

A126 Rathberger, Alphonse Maria. **Wissen Sie Bescheid? Ein Lexikon religiöser und weltanschaulicher Fragen.** Neubearb. von Rudolf Fischer-Wollpert. 16 überarb. und erw. Aufl. Augsburg, Winfried-Werk, 1970. 772p. LC 71-542141.

A standard Austrian Catholic dictionary. The articles are of moderate length and contain references to Vatican II documents and other sources. Subject index.

A127   Wetzer, Heinrich Joseph. **Wetzer und Welt's Kirchenlexikon: oder, Encyklopädie der Katholischen Theologie und iher Hülfswissen schaften.** 2. aufl., von dr. Franz Kaulen . . . Freiburg, Herder, 1882-1901. 12 v. LC 39-4413.

A128   Wetzer, Heinrich Joseph. **Wetzer und Welt's Kirchenlexikon: oder, Encyklopädie der Katholischen Theologie und iher Hülfswissen schaften. Namen und Sachregister.** 1903. xxxviii+604p. (First published 1847-1856.)

Although this work was intended primarily as a theological, not a general encyclopedia, the scope is almost as inclusive as the *Catholic Encyclopedia*, which describes the work as:

the first comprehensive attempt to treat everything that had any connection with theology encyclopedically in one work and also the first attempt to unite all the Catholic savants of Germany, who had hitherto pursued each his own path, in the production of one great work . . . It had great influence on the subsequent intellectual activity of Catholicism (Franz Meister, "Herder," *Catholic Encyclopedia*, VIII, p. 256).

In its day, it was recognized as the most important Roman Catholic encyclopedia (George M. Dutcher, *A Guide to Historical Literature* [New York, Macmillan, 1936] , p. 238), but has now been replaced by later works from the same firm.

ITALIAN

A129   Ceccaroni, Agostino. **Piccola enciclopedia ecclesiastica: Agiografia, biografie, missione cattoliche, ordini religiosi, liturgia, inni sacri, eretici e scismatici, religioni acattoliche, sistemi filosofici, diocesi d'Italia, santuari di Maria, fasti eucaristici, feste e calendari, arti sacre, citazioni bibliografiche, curiosità, aneddoti.** Appendice aggiornata a tutto il 1952 dal don Angelo Ciceri Milano, A vallardi, 1953. 1294+301p. LC A54-656. (First published in 1898 as *Dizionario ecclesiastico illustrato*.)

Contains brief, unsigned articles with no bibliographies. The text is that of the 1898 edition with a supplement.

A130   **Dizionario ecclesiastico.** Sotto la direzione dei rev. mi mons. Angelo Mercati e mons. Augusto Pelzer, con la collaborazione di numerosi e noti specialisti. Redattore capo Antonio M. Bozzone. Torino, Unione Tipografico—Editrice, 1953-58. 3 v. il. LC A54-340.

Does not cover art, history, music, etc. as much as the larger works, but contains many biographies especially of minor Italian church figures. Many illustrations. Short, signed articles with bibliographies.

A131   **Enciclopedia cattolica.** Città del Vaticano, Ente per l'Enciclopedia cattolica e per il Libro cattolico, 1949-54. 12 v. il. LC A50-1313.

A work in the grand style of the *Enciclopedia italiana*, written by the best Italian scholars with excellent bibliographies and illustrations. Biographies of popes, saints, rulers and other notables are accompanied by representations of them from works of art; articles on artists are supplemented by illustrations of their works; and there are numerous pictures of cathedrals, shrines, and monasteries. Collison praises it especially for these illustrations (Robert Collison, *Encyclopedias: Their History Throughout the Ages* 2d. ed. [New York, Hafner, 1966] , p. 219), and *Theological Studies* called it a "Summa humanistica, which is written from an entirely Catholic point of view, and at the same time, modern, expert and beautifully reproduced. Librarians and theological students will especially appreciate the work because of the abundance of information about authors, journals, societies, documents, legal phrases, hymns, and famous books and series. The treatment of science is adequate, but the sciences are subordinated to the more humane forms of human endeavor" (*Theological Studies*, XVI [March, 1955] , p. 109).

The scope of the work is not limited to Italy, or even to Europe, but articles on the United States and American Church history are exceedingly brief, almost to the point of being worthless. The two American encyclopedias must be used to complement this set.

A132   **Enciclopedia del cattolico.** Milano, A. Mondadori, 1953. 3 v. il. LC 54-25069.

Volume one covers scripture, the history of Christianity, Catholicism, liturgy and the apostolate in a series of popular essays with an index. Volumes two and three comprise a short-article encyclopedia of Catholicism.

A133   **Enciclopedia del cristianismo,** diretta da Silvio Romani. Segretario di redazione: Rodolfo Sommaruga. Roma, Casa Editrice Taraffi, 1947. lxiii, 1356p. LC 49-20177.

A short-article dictionary, covering Church doctrines, biography and terms.

A134   **Enciclopedia ecclesiastica,** pubblicata sotto la direzione dell' eccellenza mons. Adriano Bernareggi . . . Segretario di direzione sac. prof. Angelo Meli . . . Milano, F. Vallardi; Torino, Pontificia Marietti, 1942-55. v. 106. il. LC 45-15153.

A well illustrated and handsomely printed, general Catholic encyclopedia which was abandoned in progress, no doubt as a result of the appearance of the *Enciclopedia cattolica* (A131).

A135   Moroni, Gaetano. **Dizionario di erudizione storico-ecclesiastica da S. Pietro sino ai nostri giorni** . . . Venezia, Tipografia Emiliana, 1840-61. 108 v. in 53. LC 1-19053. (Title varies slightly.)

Moroni was the private secretary to Popes Gregory XVI and Pius IX and wrote the *Dizionario* singlehandedly from his own knowledge and experience and from printed sources. The *Catholic Encyclopedia* said of it that while it is "a mine of interesting data and authoritative in matters concerning the Pontifical Court, the organization of the Curia, and the administration of the Papal states; in matters of history, it depends upon the writers whom the author consulted. It is, however, not a well-ordered or homogenous work; but these defects may be readily forgiven in view of the fact that the author did his work alone, without real collaboration, and wrote at times sixteen hours a day" (U. Benigni, "Moroni," *Catholic Encyclopedia*, X, p. 576). No bibliographies are given in the work, but it is rich in biographies of obscure Church figures.

JAPANESE

A136   Jōchi Daigaku. **Katorikku Daijiten (Encyclopedia of Catholicism)**. Fuzanbo, 1940-60. 5 v.

Published by the Jesuits of the Sophia University in cooperation with Herder of Germany. The work is printed entirely in Japanese characters except for the bibliographies. According to the *Tablet*, "many of the articles are translations from *Der Grosse Herder* [A103], but others have been written by Japanese authorities—notably, Chief Justice Kotaro Tonaka, Japan's leading Catholic layman, who wrote on international law" (*Tablet*. CC [December 27, 1952], p. 538).

The scope includes the "history, doctrines, dogmas, organization, literature, etc. of Catholicism, including that in Japan" (Nihon no Sanko Toshe Henshu Linkai, *Guide to Japanese Reference Books* [Chicago, A.L.A., 1966], p. 30). Bibliographical references after the articles and in a supplement in volume five.

A137   Satō, Seitarō. **Ecclesiastical Japanese**. By F. X. Satō. Tokyo, Hara Shobo, 1959-60. 2 v. LC 60-4901.

For each word covered, the use of the term in a sentence or paragraph is given along with a translation into phonetic Japanese and Japanese characters. Index of terms.

MEXICAN

A138   **Enciclopedia de la Iglesia Católica en México**. Director, José Rogelio Alvarez. Ciudad de México, Enciclopedia de México, 1982- . v. LC 84-147776. ISBN 9-6871-6701-7. Volume 1. A-Benedicto.

Projected in twelve volumes. A comprehensive, general Catholic encyclopedia. Articles range from one paragraph to several pages in length. Beautifully illustrated in color and black and white. Longer articles contain bibliographies.

POLISH

A139   **Encyklopedia katolika**. Komitet redakcyjny Wincenty Granat. Pod red. Feliksa Gryglewicza, Romualda Lukaszyka, Zygmunta Sulowskiego. Lublin, Tow Naukowe Katolickiego Uniwersytetu Lubelskiego, 1973- . v. LC 75-56208.
  Vol. 1, Aiw-Baptýsci

An important, original work of Polish Catholic scholarship, produced by the Catholic University of Lublin. The articles tend to be long, are signed, and contain bibliographies. "One must not look for revolutionary points of view in such a work; one can only demand solid and objective information, which is what this encyclopedia provides" (*Journal of Ecumenical Studies*, XII [Summer, 1975], p. 415).

SPANISH

A140 **Diccionario del hogar católico.** Barcelona, Editorial Juventud, 1962. 1179p.

A revision of the French *Dictionnaire du foyer catholique* (A119).

A141 **Enciclopedia de la religión cathólica.** Barcelona, Dalmau y Jover, 1950-56. 7 v. LC A52-7374.

Although the *Enciclopedia universal ilustrada europeo-americana* (Barcelona, Espasa, 1905-33. 8 v. in 81) may be credited with a Catholic viewpoint (William T. O'Rourke, *Library Handbook for Catholic Readers* [Milwaukee, Bruce Publ. Co., 1937], p. 30), this is the only available, deliberately Catholic, Spanish encyclopedia. The first volume brought on itself such a storm of protest over its poor binding and typography and high price (*Catholic Library World*, XXIII [April, 1952], p. 228) that the work was redesigned. Even so, the quality of the printing and illustrations leaves much to be desired. Articles are unsigned and are no more than four or five lines long, for the most part, and there is no bibliography. Except for its specifically Spanish articles and biographies, there is little to recommend in this work.

PERIODICALS

The early history of American Catholic periodicals has been admirably written by Eugene Willging and Herta Hatzfeld (A155), both of the Catholic University of America. Unfortunately, the manner of its publication has not been equally admirable. The first series, dealing with states having very brief publishing histories, was printed as a series of articles in the *Records of the American Catholic Historical Society* beginning in September, 1954. The second series has been printed by Catholic University in a series of mimeographed parts, all of which are out of print.

Users of Catholic periodicals have been greatly aided since 1930 by *The Catholic Periodical Index*, now *The Catholic Periodical and Literature Index* (A160), published by the Catholic Library Association. If the Association did nothing else—and it has many other worthwhile projects—this work alone would be justification enough for its existence.

HISTORY AND BIBLIOGRAPHY

A142 **Catalogue sélectif de publications religieuses françaises et d'inspiration.** Paris, Union Nationale des Editeurs-Exporteurs de Publications Françaises, 1971. 96p. LC 74-186294.

A listing of religious newspapers and magazines published in France. Catholic, Protestant, Orthodox and Jewish publications are included. Classified arrangement with a title index.

A143 **Catholic Press Directory**, 1023-. New York, Catholic Press Association, 1923-. v. Annual. LC 23-11774. (Title and imprint vary.)

The best source of accurate and up-to-date information on Catholic newspapers, magazines, and other serial publications, supplying names, addresses, personnel, advertising information, circulation, and special features or editions. U. S. and Canadian, English and foreign language publications are included. Geographical arrangement with title index.

A144 **Catholic Press in India: Directory**. Bombay, Institute of Communication Arts, St. Xaviers College, 1976. 174p. LC 77-902971.

In alphabetical order by title, the language, frequency, circulation, purpose, staff, and address are given for each newspaper or magazine.

A145 **The Catholic Writer Yearbook . . . A Comprehensive Directory of Catholic Publications and their Manuscript Needs**. Ed. by Edoardo Marolla. Pence, WI, Marolla Press, 1942- . Annual. LC 45-53356.

(No more volumes published?)

Indicates magazines that accepted and paid for manuscripts and what type of material was accepted. Full information given for all periodicals.

A146 Corrigan, John T., ed. **Periodicals for Religious Education Resource Centers and Parish Libraries: A Guide to Magazines, Newspapers and Newsletters**. Haverford, PA, Catholic Library Association, 1976. 39p.

An annotated list of religious periodicals suitable for high school and parish libraries. The arrangement is alphabetical by title. Full bibliographic information is supplied.

A147 Culkin, Harry M. **Guide to Current Catholic Diocesan Newspapers in Microform**. Brooklyn, NY, Culkin, 1979. 231. LC 80-112287.

A list of the microform editions of 141 U.S. Catholic diocesan newspapers. Locations given. Indexes.

A148 Eilers, Franz-Josef, ed. **Christian Communication Directory Africa**. Published by Catholic Media Council (Aachen); World Association for Christian Communication (London); Lutheran World Federation (Geneva); Paderborn, Schöningh, 1980. 544p. LC 81-472045. ISBN 3-506-722113-1.

Arranged by country. A joint Catholic and Protestant effort at media documentation. Gives the name, director, address, objectives, and activities for religious publishers and media producers.

A149 Eilers, Franz-Josef, ed. **Christian Communication Directory Asia**. Published by Catholic Media Council (Aachen); World Association for Christian Communication (London); Lutheran World Federation (Geneva). Paderborn, Schöningh, 1982. 1036p. ISBN 3-506-72214-X.

The aim of this volume is "to collect all relevant information on Christian media institutions in Asia ... news and information services, publishing houses, printing presses, periodicals, radio/tv stations, radio/tv production studios, A-V film centers, research and training institutions" (Introduction). The arrangement is alphabetical by country. The names of the institutions, addresses, personnel, objectives, founding dates and publications are listed for each entry. An index lists the names of the institutions and titles of periodicals in one alphabet.

A150 Gaines, Stanley J. **Publisher's Guide: Catholic Journals, Academic and Professional**. River Forest, Commission on Journals, Academic and Professional, 1961. ix, 85p.

Lists of journals arranged by subject fields.

A151 Istituto per le Scienze Religiose di Bologna. Biblioteca. **Catalogo delle publicazioni periodiche**. Bologna, Istituto per le Scienze Religiose di Bologna, 1971. LC 73-345991.

A listing of the periodicals received by the Library in alphabetical order by title.

A152 Lucey, William Leo. **An Introduction to American Catholic Magazines**. Philadelphia, n.p., 1953. 95p. LC 56-26831.

Covers the history of American Catholic magazines from 1865 to 1900. Index of Periodicals. Index of Names.

A153 Poulat, Emile. **Les "Semaines religieuses": approche socio-historique et bibliographique des bulletins diocésains français**. 2d. éd. Lyon, Université de Lyon II, Centre d'Histoire du Catholicisme, 1973. 100p. LC 75-11880.

A list, with an introductory essay, of 19th century diocesan weekly bulletins held by the *Bibliotheque Nationale*. Each entry gives a description of the contents and a brief history of the publication. Arranged by diocese.

A154 St. Mary's College, St. Mary, KS, St. Peter Canisius' Writers' Guild. **The Catholic Writer's Magazine Market**. Milwaukee, Bruce Pub. Co., 1943. 96p. LC 43-17649.

Gives names, addresses, editorial requirements, and rates for 150 U. S. Catholic periodicals.

A155 Willging, Eugene Paul, and Herta Hatzfeld. **Catholic Serials of the Nineteenth Century in the United States: A Descriptive Bibliography and Union List. Second Series**. Washington, DC, Catholic University of America Press, 1959- . pts. LC 59-4623.

The First Series appeared in the *Records of the American Catholic Historical Society*. (See "Introduction" to part 10 for a complete list.)

The Second Series covers states with longer publishing histories; each section is made up of an historical introduction, an annotated list of serials arranged by cities and towns, an extensive bibliography of sources, and various appended charts and tables. There is also a general bibliography for the entire work reprinted in each section. Annotations are mainly historical and descriptive but contain some critical commentary. Foreign language publications printed in the U. S. are also covered.

UNION LISTS

A156   Chicago Area Theological Library Association. **Union List of Serials.** 1st. ed. Chicago, 1974. iv, 673p. LC 74-176319.

Lists religious and theological periodical holdings for 22 member libraries of which 5 are Catholic institutions. Annuals and monograph series are not included. The arrangement is alphabetical by title. Publisher's names are also included along with the holdings of each library.

A157   Fitzgerald, Catherine Anita. **A Union List of Catholic Periodicals in Catholic Institutions on the Pacific Coast.** Ann Arbor, MI, Edwards Bros., 1957. 94p. LC 57-59033.

The holdings of the cooperating libraries are indicated along with the name, dates and place of publication of the periodicals. Many serial publications not usually thought of as periodicals are included. Lists 450 items plus a list of periodicals not held by the libraries.

A158   Vatican. Biblioteca vaticana. **Catalogo delle pubblicazioni periodiche esistenti in varie biblioteche di Roma e Firenze.** Città del Vaticano, 1955. xiii, 495p. LC A56-2502.

The 9,000 periodicals listed here are limited to those devoted to "the moral disciplines, history, philology, and art" (Preface). Apparently the "moral disciplines" include philosophy, theology and religion in general. While not limited to Catholic libraries, the list contains mostly Catholic titles, and gives complete bibliographical information.

INDEXES

A159   **Catholic Magazine Index.** Detroit, Romig, 1937-38. 3 v. in 1. LC A40-165.

A cumulated author-subject index to 20 Catholic periodicals which appeared originally in the *Catholic Bookman* (A54).

A160   **The Catholic Periodical and Literature Index. A Cumulative Author-Subject Index to a Selective List of Catholic Periodicals and An Author-Title-Subject Bibliography of Adult Books by Catholics with a Selection of Catholic-Interest Books by Other Authors.** Haverford, PA, Catholic Library Association, 1930- . v. Bimonthly. Cumulated biennially. LC 70-649588.

Formerly called the *Catholic Periodical Index* (1930-66). Has undergone continual improvement and expansion with every volume. *Catholic Library World* described it in 1967 as:

> a complete author and subject index to 126 periodicals with selective indexing to an additional 100 titles. Periodicals from the United States, Belgium, Canada, England, France, Germany, Ireland, Italy, Spain, and Vatican City are included. Only a few of the 226 titles are covered by other periodical indexes. The Index is particularly strong in the fields of theology, Church history, Bible studies, and religion. Seventy percent of its entries deal with other subjects such as agriculture, anthropology, art, education, history, journalism, library science, literature, medicine, music, nursing, philosophy, political science and sociology. (*Catholic Library World*, XXXIX [September, 1967], p. 91)

Currently 153 periodicals are indexed in full with no partial indexing, and, as the new title indicates, books are also listed since 1968 when the *Guide to Catholic Literature* (A56) was merged with this work.

In recent years the *Index* has been put on a more prompt publishing schedule, and the typography and printing methods have been improved, resulting in greater legibility and clarity of arrangement. Not the least of its values is the indexing of practically all Catholic book reviews most of which are not covered by the standard book review indexes—*Book Review Digest*, *Index to Book Reviews in the Humanities*, or *Book Review Index*. Many foreign titles are covered by these reviews. Motion picture and play reviews are also indexed.

Another excellent feature of this work is the complete indexing of the texts in all languages of papal, conciliar, diocesan, and other official Church documents, most of which appear in periodicals and newspapers. Commentaries and excerpts are also listed.

The Catholic Periodical and Literature Index is truly an indispensable work for any library that collects Catholic periodicals because of its wide and unique coverage both in titles and subject matter.

A161   **Abridged Catholic Periodical and Literature Index.** Haverford, PA, Catholic Library Association, 1983- . v. Bimonthly, no cumulations. LC 83-587. ISSN 0737-3457.

Indexes about 30 titles. No cumulated editions published. Suitable for the small high school or parish library.

SOCIETIES

There is no single, comprehensive international directory of Catholic organizations. The *Catholic Almanac* (D90) contains a list of international and U. S. societies, and the *Directory of Religious Organizations in the United States* (A163), published in 1982 is a welcome ecumenical tool which provides quite thorough coverage of Catholic societies. Additional information on Catholic societies will be found in the various local and national directories and almanacs in Chapter IV. Religious orders are treated separately in Chapter V.

DIRECTORIES

A162 Alfaro, Carlos. **Guiá apostolicá latinoamericana.** Barcelona, Editorial Herder, 1965. xv, 591p. LC 65-6741.

A directory of Latin American, Catholic organizations dedicated to apostolic activities, including organizations made up of the hierarchy, the laity, and religious. Both national and international organizations are listed giving names, addresses, officers, history, purpose and publications. Index of names, organizations and subjects.

A163 **Directory of Religious Organizations in the United States.** 2nd ed. Falls Church, VA, McGrath, 1982. 518p. LC 84-223812. ISBN 0-8434-0757-3.

An alphabetical list of 1,628 religious organizations of all sects. Lists affiliations, officers, address and telephone numbers, publications, and meetings, and provides a brief history and description. Religious orders were included in the first edition (Washington, DC, Consortium, 1977) but are excluded from this edition. No indexes. A subject index would be useful.

A164 **Ecumenism Around the World: A Directory of Ecumenical Institutes, Centers and Organizations.** 2nd. ed. Roma, Friars of the Atonement, 1974. ix, 163p.

Ecumenical organizations are listed and described in both English and French. Brief histories, affiliation, purpose, libraries, publications and staff members are provided. Index.

A165 Preuss, Arthur. **A Dictionary of Secret and Other Societies.** St. Louis, MO, B. Herder Book Co., 1924. xi, 543p. LC 24-9579. Reprinted: Detroit, Gale, 1966. LC 66-21186. ISBN 0-8103-3083-0.

All information is documented. Written for Catholics with emphasis on anti-Catholic groups, although many non-secret and purely benevolent or patriotic organizations are included. Alphabetical arrangement with an index of names, subjects and organizations.

A166 Sugranyes de Franch, Ramon. **Les organisations internationales catholiques.** Paris, Fayard, 1972. 89p. LC 74-331167. (Le Christ dans le monde, 12.)

A study of modern Catholic international organizations including an "annexe" of 30 organizations giving their addresses and a brief description.

A167 Whalen, William Joseph. **Handbook of Secret Organizations.** Milwaukee, Bruce Pub. Co., 1966. viii, 169p. LC 69-26658.

Compiled, as was Preuss' work, "to be of use to those concerned with dual membership in the Church and a secret society" (Preface). Based on questionnaires and presenting a fairly balanced account of traditionally anti-Catholic groups. Select bibliography, p. 163-64. Index.

A168   Willging, Eugene Paul and Dorothy E. Lynn. **A Handbook of American Catholic Societies**. Scranton, PA, Catholic Library Association, 1940. 24p. LC 41-4710.

Covers national societies only. Gives address, purpose, history and publications. Alphabetical arrangement by name with subject index.

BIOGRAPHY

Reference sources for Catholic biography comprise a large number of works, some very old and famous. The works listed in this section, however, represent less than one-third of the biographical materials in the entire work since there is a separate section for the lives of the saints (A205-A244) and for religious orders (E170-E264). General encyclopedias should not be overlooked as a source of biography (A85-A141), nor should the literature section of Chapter III which contains a list of biographies of authors (C88-C118).

Indexes. There are no current continuing indexes of Catholic biography of the nature of *Wilson's Biography Index* (New York, H. W. Wilson Co., 1947-); however, this tool serves rather well for Catholic material and may be supplemented by the *Catholic Periodical and Literature Index* (A160).

General Biography. In addition to the works listed here, many fine sources of biography for the early writers of the Church may be found in the Patrology section of Chapter II.

National Biographies. Gillow's *Literary and Biographical History* (A198) is the only complete dictionary of national biography in this list in that it covers clergy and laity. For other countries, the works included below must be used in conjunction with the various general national biographies such as the *Dictionnaire de biographie francaise*. (See Sheehy's *Guide to Reference Books* [Chicago, A.L.A., 1986], pp. 279-313, for a complete list of titles).

The *American Catholic Who's Who* (A196) is the only continuing, contemporary biographical dictionary still publishing. Delaney's *Dictionary of American Catholic Biography* (A188) is an up-to-date source for U.S. Catholics.

INDEXES

A169   Brown, Stephen James Meredith. **International Index of Catholic Biographies**. 2nd. ed. rev. and greatly enl. London, Burns, Oates and Washbourne, 1935. xix, 287p. (Catholic Bibliographical Series, no. 3.) LC 37-1357.

An index to nearly 10,000 individual biographies in book form published during the nineteenth century or later (up to 1935), and including books in foreign languages. Biographies are confined, as one might expect, to saints and beati, other Catholics notable for their holiness, and famous Catholics in good standing with the Church; there are no James Joyces on this list. Some Catholic biographical series are listed in an appendix.

A170   Chevalier, Cyr Ulysse Joseph. **Répertoire des sources historiques du moyen age, . . . Bio-bibliographie.** Nouv. éd. refondue, cor. et considérablement augm. . . . Paris, A. Picard et Fils, 1905-7. 2 v. in 4. LC 5-9616. Reprinted: New York, Kraus, 1959. LC 75-77037. ISBN 0-527-1670-2, v.1. 0-527-16710-X, v. 2.

The *Bio-bibliographie* is an alphabetical list of medieval names giving a very brief biographical description and a complete bibliography of the person's life, influence, and criticism of his works—but not a list of his works. Generally regarded as the most complete work of its kind for the Middle Ages, it is, nevertheless, difficult to use because of the huge number of cryptic references crammed into tightly packed columns of print. For example, St. Augustine's name is followed by five double-columned pages of references. The books are arranged in alphabetical order by main entry, but "no attempt has been made to weed out worthless material; good, bad, old and new accounts are jumbled together in long alphabetical lists" (Louis J. Paetow, *Guide to the Study of Medieval History*, [New York, Crofts, 1931], p. 7). The scope of the work, however, makes it a valuable tool; it covers the period from early Christianity to A.D. 1500, including no end of obscure names. Brown refers to it as "a monument of erudition" (Stephen J. M. Brown, "Catholic Bibliography" *Catholic Library Practice*, ed. Bro. David Martin [Portland, OR, University of Oregon Press, 1947-50], v. 1, p. 109).

GENERAL BIOGRAPHY

A171   Ceillier, Remi. **Histoire générale des auteurs sacrés et ecclésiastiques.** Paris, L. Vivès, 1858-63. 14 v. in 15. LC 1-17812.

Contains the lives and commentaries on the works of writers from Old Testament times to the end of the thirteenth century. The articles are quite long and thoroughly documented. Long extracts from the works of the authors are given along with contemporary criticism. The arrangement is chronological, but there are indexes in each volume, as well as a two-volume general index.

A172   Delaney, John J., and James Edward Tobin. **Dictionary of Catholic Biography.** Garden City, NY, Doubleday, 1961. xi, 124p. LC 62-7620.

A biographical dictionary of "outstanding Catholics from the time of the Apostles to the present day (1961)" (Preface). Contains over 16,000 brief entries much like those found in *Webster's Biographical Dictionary* (Springfield, MA, Merriam, 1962) with just a little more detail. Many entries have bibliographies citing one or two sources, usually in English; chief written works are listed also. There are appendixes of patron saints, iconography, popes and similar topics. The *Catholic Historical Review* called it a very useful reference work but criticized its scanty bibliography and several inaccuracies and omissions which could be corrected easily enough in later editions (*Catholic Historical Review*, XLIX [April, 1963], p. 135).

A173   Eubel, Conrad. **Hierarchia catholica medii et recentioris aevi: sive Sum-
morum pontificum S.R.E. cardinalium, ecclesiarum antistitum series e
documentis tabularii praesertim Vaticani collecta, digesta, edita.** Editio altera.
Monasterii, Sumptibus et Typis Librariae Regensbergianae, 1913-23. v. 1-6.
Reprinted with vol. 7. Patavii, "Il Messaggero di S. Antonio," 1960-68. 7 v.
LC 3-19932.

(Volumes 1-3 entitled *Hierarchia catholica medii aevi*.)

Gives considerably more detail than Gams (A174)—histories of each diocese,
boundaries, a list of bishops and auxiliaries with the names of their conse-
crators, the dates and sources of information. Brief lives of the popes and
cardinals are also given. The work was originally intended to cover only the
period from 1198 to 1431, but in 1901 work was begun on new volumes to
bring it up to the present day. Currently it covers up to the year 1846. Index
of names and places.

A174   Gams, Pius Bonifacius. **Series episcoporum Ecclesiae catholicae, quotquot
innotuerunt a beato Petro apostolo.** 2., univeränderte aufl. Leipzig, K. W.
Hiersemann, 1931. xxiv, 963p. LC 34-32814.

A175   Gams, Pius Bonifacius. **Series episcoporum Ecclesiae catholicae, qua series,
quae apparuit 1873 completur et continuatur ab anno ca. 1870 ad 20 febr.
1885.** iv, 148p. (First edition, 1873-86.)

A list of all the bishops of each diocese in the Church beginning with Peter
to the year 1875 giving the dates of their installation and death. The names
and dates of local councils are also given. Arranged geographically with
indexes.

A176   **I Grandi del Cattolicesimo: Enciclopedia Biografica,** a cura di P. Gini G.
Roschini e A. Santelli, con la collaborazione di oltre 130 insigni studiosi
divetta da C. Carbone. Roma, Ente Librario Italiano, 1955-58. 2 v. il.

An international biographical dictionary with major emphasis on Italian
Catholics. Illustrations are drawn from works of art where possible. The
bibliographic citations vary from encyclopedia articles to primary sources.

A177   Smith, Sir William. **A Dictionary of Christian Biography, Literature, Sects,
and Doctrines.** Ed. by William Smith and Henry Wace. London, J. Murray,
1877-87. 4 v. LC 12-3122.

A companion to the author's *Dictionary of Christian Antiquities* (London,
Murray, 1876-80). The emphasis is on the Fathers, but many other persons
are listed, including some non-Christians who influenced the Church. Bibliographies—mostly Protestant works—are supplied. Covers up to the time of
Charlemagne. Revised in 1911 by Wace and Piercy (A178).

A178   Wace, Henry, and William C. Piercy, eds. **A Dictionary of Christian Biography
and Literature to the End of the Sixth Century A.D., with an Account of
the Principal Sects and Heresies.** London, J. Murray, 1911. xi, 1028p.
LC 12-1409.

A revised and abridged version of Smith's *Dictionary* (A177). The articles are shorter, but bibliographies are still included.

GENERAL BIOGRAPHY—CONTEMPORARY

A179 **The Catholic Encyclopedia and Its Makers.** New York, The Encyclopedia Press, Inc., 1917. viii, 192p. il. LC 17-24119.

Contains brief biographies and portraits of the 1,452 contributors to the *Catholic Encyclopedia*, many of whom were foreign, but most of whom were living American Catholics at the time. Lists of written works are given as well as the titles of the articles they wrote for the *Encyclopedia*.

A180 MacEoin, Gary.and the Committee for the Responsible Election of the Pope. **The Inner Elite: Dossiers of Papal Candidates.** Kansas City, KS, Sheed, Andrews and McMeel, 1978. xxx, 300p. il. LC 78-17845. ISBN 0-8362-3105-8.

Published shortly before the death of Pope Paul VI, this collection of biographies of members of the College of Cardianls was intended to familiarize the world with the choice of candidates. Unfortunately the biographies are undocumented, informally written, and replete with unsubstantiated quotations and anecdotes. The biographies are arranged by geographic areas with an index of names and an introduction explaining the history of papal elections. Names of members of the Committee for the Responsible Election of the Pope, and the "100 contributors" are not supplied.

A181 **Who's Who in the Catholic World.** Ed. by S. S. Taylor and L. Melsheimer. Düsseldorf, L. Schwann Verlag, 1967- . v.
v. 1. Europe: A Biographical Dictionary Containing about 5,500 Biographies of Prominent Personalities in the Catholic World.

Gives typical information including publications. Appended lists of the hierarchy, religious orders, institutions, organizations and Vatican officials, including diplomats. Apparently ceased publication.

AMERICAN

A182 Campbell, Thomas Joseph. **Pioneer Laymen of North America.** New York, The America Press, 1915. 2 v. il. LC 15-10062.

The lives of about fifteen North American explorers, traders, politicians, and soldiers are given along with portraits and a general bibliography. The sketches are written on a popular level but are rather long and detailed.

A183 Campbell, Thomas Joseph. **Pioneer Priests of North America, 1642-1710.** New York, Fordham University Press, 1980-19. 3 v. LC 8-22530.

Brief lives of the early Jesuits and other priests who worked among the Iroquois, Hurons, and early colonists in the U. S. and Canada. No bibliography.

A184   **Catholic Builders of the Nation: A Symposium of the Catholic Contribution to the Civilization of the United States.** Prepared under the Editorship of Constantine E. McGuire with the Collaboration of Rev. James Gillis, Admiral W. S. Benson, J. J. Walsh, and others. New York, Catholic Book Company, 1935. 5 v. il. LC 35-3511.

A comprehensive work, certainly out of date, but useful for the period it covers. The work is actually a series of essays divided into five sections: Catholicism and the Building of the Nation; . . . and the Nation's Social Development; Catholics in Science, Industry and Service; . . . in the Liberal Professions; and the Catholic Contribution to Education. Most of the studies are followed by bibliographies. The use of this work as a collected biography is greatly aided by a general index in volume five.

A185   Clarke, Richard Henry. **Lives of the Deceased Bishops of the Catholic Church in the United States: With an Appendix and an Analytical Index.** New York, R. H. Clarke, 1888. 3 v. LC 33-24578.

The first important collected biography of the American hierarchy. (*See* Code's *Dictionary* [A187], pp. vii-xiv, for a complete list of these works). The biographical sketches, arranged in chronological order, average thirty pages in length for over 100 bishops. There is, however, no bibliography or index.

A186   Code, Joseph Bernard. **American Bishops, 1964-1970.** St. Louis, MO, Wexford Press, 1070. 25p. LC 79-289632.

Brief biographies of the more than 100 bishops named since the publication of A187. "Miscellanea" includes thirteen tables dealing with the American hierarchy.

A187   Code, Joseph Bernard. **Dictionary of the American Hierarchy, 1789-1964.** New York, J. F. Wagner, 1964. 452p.

The most complete and up-to-date work available covering more than 850 prelates. The entries are brief and factual and contain only basic information. Unfortunately only principal written works are listed and sources given only for "contested facts." At the end of the book there are thirty-three very useful appendixes having to do with chronology, succession, geographical origins, residential and titular sees, necrology and related topics. A fine work as far as it goes, but it could include more by way of biographical data. The introduction (pp. vii-xiv) describes earlier works on the same topic.

A188   Delaney, John J. **Dictionary of American Catholic Biography.** Garden City, NY, Doubleday, 1984. 621p. LC 83-25524. ISBN 0-385-178786.

A collection of some 1,500 well-written if brief biographies of deceased American Catholics. For authors, major works are listed, but no other bibliography is supplied. "The work is surprisingly thorough" (*Theology Today*, XLII [April, 1985], p. 149).

A189   Finn, Brendan A. **Twenty-four American Cardinals: Biographical Sketches of those Princes of the Catholic Church Who Either Were Born in America**

or Served There at Some Time. Boston, B. Humphries, 1948. 475p. ports. LC 48-6031.

Informal biographies with portraits. No bibliography.

A190   Liederbach, Clarence A. **America's Thousand Bishops: From 1513 to 1974 . . . From Abromowicz to Zuroweste.** Cleveland, Dillon/Leiderbach, Inc., 1974. 67p. LC 73-94081. ISBN 0-9132-2809-5.

Supplies names, sees and dates of birth and death. A brief introductory essay surveys the highlights of the history of America's bishops.

A191   Lonsway, Jesse William. **The Episcopal Lineage of the Hierarchy in the United States, Revised 1790-1963** by Jesse W. Lonsway and Aaron Pembleton. 2nd. ed. Cincinnati, Episcopal Lineage, 1965. 46p. il. LC 67-1887.

(Includes table "Catholic Hierarchy in the United States.")

Traces the apostolic succession in the American hierarchy in a series of some twenty tables and diagrams and several explanatory essays.

A192   O'Donnell, John Hugh. **The Catholic Hierarchy of the United States, 1790-1922.** New York, AMS Press, 1974. xiv, 223p. LC 73-3558.

Originally written as a thesis for the Catholic University of America, this manual provides brief biographies and bibliographies for each prelate. The arrangement is chronological under the name of each diocese.

A193   **Photo Directory of the United States Catholic Hierarchy.** Huntington, IN, Our Sunday Visitor, 1985. 134p.

Contains the name, diocese, date of ordination and photograph of each member of the American hierarchy.

A194   Reuss, Francis Xavier. **Biographical Cyclopedia of the Catholic Hierarchy of the United States, 1789-1898.** Milwaukee, Wiltzius, 1898. 129p.

Code (A187) describes this work as "more serviceable than any work that came before or after it" (p. vii). Its biographies are shorter than Clarke's (A185) but are more concise and scholarly.

A195   Thornton, Francis Beauchesne. **Our American Princes: The Story of the Seventeen American Cardinals.** New York, Putnam, 1963. 319p. Ports. LC 63-9674.

Brief, informal biographies of the first 17 Americans to be made cardinals. Each sketch is from 30 to 40 pages long. Bibliography, pp. 313-14. Index.

AMERICAN BIOGRAPHY—CONTEMPORARY

A196   **The American Catholic Who's Who,** 1934/35- . Detroit, W. Romig, 1935-71. Washington, DC, N. C. News Service, 1972- . v. Biennial. LC 11-1094.

An earlier attempt at a continuing biographical dictionary was made in 1911 (Georgina Pell Curtis, *American Catholic Who's Who* [St. Louis, Herder, 1911]); however, no more editions appeared from this source. Romig's work has been appearing regularly since 1934. In each entry he gives the typical "who's who" type of information—profession, parentage, education, positions held, titles and dates of written works. The information is gathered by questionnaire and revision is done by biographees for each edition. Qualifications for inclusion are not indicated in a preface or introduction to the work; and while clergymen seem to outnumber laymen, one would be hard pressed to find the name of even a locally known Catholic not included in the work.

BRITISH

A197 **Biographical Studies, 1534-1829, Materials toward a Biographical Dictionary of Catholic History in the British Isles from the Breach with Rome to Catholic Emancipation.** Bogner Regis, Arundel Press, 1951-53. 3 v. (1953- . Title changed to *Recusant History*)

For the first three years of its existence this serial was devoted exclusively to printing bio-bibliographical articles in the manner of Gillow (A198) as a supplement to that work. After 1953 the articles were of a less restricted nature.

A198 Gillow, Joseph. **A Literary and Biographical History, or Bibliograpical Dictionary of the English Catholics from the Breach with Rome in 1534 to the Present Time** . . . . London, Burns and Oates; New York, Catholic Pub. Soc. 1885-92. 5 v. LC 1-771. Reprinted: New York, B. Franklin, 1968. LC 74-6323.

(2,000 biographies)

Easily the best national Catholic biographical dictionary; an excellent supplement to the *Dictionary of National Biography* (London, Smith, Elder, 1908-09. 22 v.). It is an expansion and continuation of the biographies by Hugh Tootell in Dodd's *Church History of England* (Wolverhampton, 1737-42, 3 v.). Authors, martyrs, confessors, clergymen, artists, and members of the professions are included with bibliographical references for each entry and full, annotated lists of works for authors. The length of the entries varies from a single paragraph to several pages. Father Brown described the work as "a Catholic bibliographical work of outstanding value and importance. . . . In its five bulky volumes every scrap of writing by an English Catholic since the Reformation is recorded with painstaking exactitude. It ought not to be ignored by any serious historian of modern England." (Stephen J. M. Brown, "Catholic Bibliography," in *Catholic Library Practice*, ed. Brother David Martin [Portland, OR, University of Portland Press, 1947-50], v. 1, p. 114).

A199 Kirk, John. **Biographies of English Catholics in the Eighteenth Century: Being part of His Projected Continuation of Dodd's Church History.** Ed. by John Hungerford Pollen, S. J., and Edwin Burton. London, Burns and Oates, 1909. xvi, 293p. LC 9-14581.

This work should also be used as a supplement to Gillow (A198) for the period it covers. According to the introduction, more than half the names listed are not to be found in that work.

BRITISH BIOGRAPHY–CONTEMPORARY

A200   **Catholic Who's Who.** London, Burns and Oates, 1908- . v. Annual.

The thirty-fifth and apparently last edition of this series (1952) included notable living prelates, clergy, and laymen of Great Britain and the Commonwealth but not Ireland. From 1908 to 1935 it was titled the *Catholic Who's Who and Yearbook.*

CANADIAN

A201   Liederbach, Clarende A. **Canada's Bishops: From 1120-1975 . . . From Allen to Yelle.** Cleveland, Dillon/Liederbach, Inc., 1975. 64p. LC 73-94082. ISBN 0-9132-2810-9.

Contains a 50 page introductory essay on Canada's hierarchy as well as a list of the names, sees and dates of each bishop.

GERMAN

A202   Korff, Heinrich. **Biographica catholica: Verzeichnes ein Werken über Jesus Christus, sowie über Heilige, selige Ordensleute, Ehrewurdige und fromme Personen, Konvertiten Meister der christlichen Kunst, hervorragende und verdiente katholische Männer und Frauen 1870-1926.** Freiburg, Herder, 1927. vii, 280p.

An index or bibliography of more than 7,000 individual and collected biographies published in German from 1870 to 1926. The books listed include lives of Christ, the saints, clergy and laity. Individual biographies are arranged by the name of the subject and collections by the name of the author.

A203   Kosch, Wilhelm. **Das Katholische Deutschland, biographisch—bibliographisches Lexikon.** Augsburg, Hass und Grabherr, 1933-40. v. 1-5 + fasc. 3. LC 34-2159.

Unfortunately never completed. The last fascicle brought the biographies up to the letter *S* in the alphabet. The entries are rather short, but full lists of written works are given, as well as photographs and portraits in many cases. The period covered seems to be mostly from the seventeenth century on, but there are some entries from earlier periods.

MEXICAN

A204   Valverde Téllez, Emeterio. **Bio-bibliografía eclesiástica mexicana, 1821-1943.** Dirección y prólogo de José Bravo Ugarte. México, Editorial Jus, 1949. 3 v. (Collección de estudios históricos.) LC 49-6422.
        V. 1-2. Obispos A-Z; V. 3. Sacerdotes.

Each entry consists of a biographical sketch of reasonable length and a full bibliography of written works. The treatment of bishops is considerably more extensive than that of priests.

LIVES OF THE SAINTS

Hagiography is a science of no little importance to the student of literature, fine arts, and history, as well as to the religious scholar. For an excellent introduction to this field, Hippolyte Delehaye's *Legends of the Saints* (Notre Dame, IN, University of Notre Dame Press, 1966) should be consulted.

Father Delehaye was a member of the Society of Bollandists, a group of Belgian Jesuits organized in 1651 by Jean Bolland to gather, study, and publish source material on the lives of the saints in order to identify in them the purely legendary elements patently derived from local and ethnic mythologies. (*See* Delehaye's *Work of the Bollandists through Three Centuries* [A214]). After several false starts, the *Acta sanctorum* (A205), containing the texts of all the known lives of the saints whose feast days fall in January, was published along with critical commentary, variants, etc. The work won immediate scholarly acceptance and has continued, with many interruptions, until the present day.

Dictionaries and Collections. Popular collections of the lives of the saints are more than plentiful, even from non-Catholic sources. In this bibliography only the most comprehensive, recent, and widely used works are listed. Works with essentially the same contents but designed for use in the study of iconography are to be found in the fine arts section of Chapter III (pp. 000-000).

SOURCES

A205   **Acta sanctorum quotquot toto orbe coluntur, vel a catholicis scriptoribus celebrantur quae ex latinis et graecis, aliarumque gentium antiquis monumentis collegit, digessit, notis illustravit Joannes Bollandus . . . servata primigenia scriptorum phrasei.** Operam et studium contulit Godefridus Henschenius . . . Edito novissima, curante Joanne Carnandet . . . Parisiis, V. Palme, 1863-1931 (Jan.-Nov. v. 1-85 in 67) il.

A206   **Acta sanctorum quotquot toto orbe coluntur, vel a catholicis scriptoribus celebrantur quae ex latinis et graecis, aliarumque gentium antiquis monumentis collegit, digessit, notis illustravit Joannes Bollandus . . . servata primigenia scriptorum phrasei. Ad Acta sanctorum . . . supplementum.** Volumen complectens auctaria Octobris et Tabulas generales. Scilicet Ephemerides et Indicem alphabeticum decem priorum mensium . . . cura et opere L. M. Rigollot. 1875. 2 v. LC 25-11972.

A207   **Acta sanctorum quotquot toto orbe coluntur, vel a catholicis scriptoribus celebrantur quae ex latinis et graecis, aliarumque gentium antiquis monumentis collegit, digessit, notis illustravit Joannes Bollandus . . . servata primigenia scriptorum phrasei. Supplément aux Acta sanctorum pour des vies de saints de l'époque mérovingienne** par M. l'abbé C. Narbey. Paris, Le Soudier, 1899-19. 2 v. LC F-1945.

The volumes of the main set contain the acts or lives of the saints reprinted from the original sources gathered from the libraries of Europe, with annotations and commentaries on the various copies of manuscripts, lists of variants in the texts of different editions, and commentary "which solved, or at least tried to solve, every problem to which the texts of the Acts could give rise, in the matter of chronology, geography, history, philological interpretation, . . . with an erudition and a method which could be called absolutely unknown, hitherto" (Charles de Smedt, "Bollandists," *Catholic Encyclopedia*, II, p. 632).

The lives of the saints are arranged in this work, as in many others, in the order of the occurrence of their feasts in the calendar year. There have been three different editions of the *Acta*: the original Antwerp edition, the first volume of which appeared in 1643; the Venetian edition, published from 1764-1770, covering up to the sixth volume for September, "the whole printing of which teems with typographical blunders" (de Smedt, p. 639); and finally, the Paris edition, 1863-1869, covering up to the tenth volume for October. "This edition reproduces exactly, volume by volume, the original one except for the months of January and June," which have been arranged differently (de Smedt, p. 639).

A208   **Analecta Bollandiana.** Bruxelles, Société des Bollandistes; Paris, Picard, 1882- . v. Quarterly.

A209   **Analecta Bollandiana. Indices in tomos XXI-XL (1902-1922); XLI-LX (1923-42).** 3 v. LC 32-22256.

A periodical supplement to the main set which reprints newly discovered materials, additional commentaries and bibliographies, and reviews hagiographic literature.

A210   **Bibliotheca hagiographica graeca.** 3 éd., mise a jour et considérablement augmentée par François Halkin. Bruxelles, Société des Bollandistes, 1957. 3 v. (Subsidia hagiogrpahica, no. 8a.) V. 3., Supplément, appendices et tables.

A211   **Bibliotheca hagiographica latina antiquae et mediae aetatis.** Ediderunt Socii Bollandiani . . . Bruxellis 1898-1901. 2 v. (Subsidia hagiographica, no. 6, 12.) LC 4-21796.

A212   **Bibliotheca hagiographica latina antiquae et mediae aetatis. Supplementi editio altera auctor.** 1911. 355p.

A213   **Bibliotheca hagiographica orientalis.** Ediderunt Socii Bollandiana, Bruxellis, apud editores Beyrouth Syrie Imprimerie catholique, 1910. xxiii, 287p. (Subsidia hagiographica, 10.) LC 11-1338.

This and the three preceding works are bibliographies of the saints arranged alphabetically by the names of the saints listing all the literature relating to their lives and works written in Greek, Latin, and Oriental languages before the sixteenth century, with references to printed versions.

A214   Delehaye, Hippolyte. **The Work of the Bollandists through Three Centuries, 1615-1915.** Princeton, Princeton University Press, 1922. 209p. LC 22-8148.

A history of the Bollandists and their work with a special chapter on the "Bibliography" (pp. 235-269) of the Society's major publications.

A215   Jocobus de Voragine. **The Golden Legend; or Lives of the Saints as Englished by William Caxton.** London, J. M. Dent and Co., 1900. 7 v.

Voragine was the archbishop of Geneva, renowned for his holiness and love for the poor, who wrote perhaps the most famous book of the Middle Ages, the *Legenda aurea*, or as he entitled it, the *Legenda sanctorum*. It is a collection of the lives of the saints based on legends and folklore of the people of his times. It is an excellent example of the type of literature the Bollandists were trying to identify and discredit as legend. The full Latin text was last printed in Leipzig (Graesse) in 1850.

A216 Musurillo, Herbert Anthony, comp. **The Acts of the Christian Martyrs.** Introduction, texts and translations by Herbert Musurillo. Oxford, Clarendon Press, 1972. lxxiii, 379p. LC 72-177389. ISBN 0-1982-6806-8.

A selection of 28 very early acts are presented in the original Greek or Latin as well as in English translation in an attempt to illustrate primative Christian belief and late Roman Empire politics. A long, scholarly introduction with notes is indexed, as are the texts and their notes.

DICTIONARIES AND COLLECTIONS

A217 Attwater, Donald. **A Dictionary of Saints: Based on Butler's Lives of the Saints,** complete ed. New York, P. J. Kenedy, 1958. vii, 280p. LC 58-12556.

"With each entry . . . an index reference is given to the fuller treatment in 'Butler'" (1956 ed. [A227]).

A218 Attwater, Donald. **Martyrs, from St. Stephen to John Tung.** London, Sheed and Ward, 1958. xviii, 286p. LC 65-8330.

Over 60 martyrs or groups of martyrs are listed with narratives of their lives and a "Bibliography of Sources" for each saint (pp. 226-36).

A219 Attwater, Donald. **The Penguin Dictionary of Saints.** 2nd ed. REv. and updated by Catherine Rachel John. Harmondsworth, Eng. and New York, Penguin, 1983. 352p. GB 84-17488. ISBN 0-14-051-123-7.

Brief entries for about 750 saints indicating symbols of the saint in paintings and sculpture. Glossary.

A220 Baring-Gould, Sabine. **The Lives of the Saints.** New and rev. ed. Edinburgh, J. Grant, 1914. 16 v. il. LC A16-1094.

This is a non-Catholic work but includes many post-Reformation saints. For each day there is a list of saints with biographies, many illustrations, source of the cult (i.e. martyrologies, etc.), and a history of the cult. Attempts to distinguish between fact and legend, but now much out of date. Volume sixteen: "Additional lives of English martyrs, Cornish, Scottish and Welsh saints and a full index to the entire work."

A221 Bentley, James. **A Calendar of Saints: the Lives of Principal Saints of the Christian Year.** New York, Facts on File, 1986. 256p. LC 86-10626. ISBN 0-8160-1682-8.

Brief inspirational biographies of the saints, one for each day of the year. Illustrations from paintings or sculptures are provided for each saint, Index.

A222   **Bibliotheca sanctorum.** Roma Istituto Giovanni XXIII nella Pontificia
Universita lateranense, 1961-69. 12 v. LC 66-37318.

A large collection, on a markedly more scholarly level than Butler (A225);
containing long, signed articles with large bibliographies and many illustrations
taken from works of art. The articles for major saints are divided into sections
for biography, analysis of their influence, their thought and writing, and iconography. While this work is not on the level of the *Acta sanctorum* in size or
thoroughness, it may well be the next best thing. The illustrations, all black
and white, are well-chosen and reproduced.

A223   **The Book of Saints: A Dictionary of Persons Canonized or Beatified by the
Catholic Church.** Comp. by the Benedictine Monks of St. Augustine's Abbey,
Ramsgate. 5th ed. entirely revised and re-set. New York, Crowell, 1966.
xii, 740p. LC 66-22140.

Probably the most useful one-volume work in the field in that it covers about
2,200 saints with a rare degree of accuracy and integrity, accountable, no
doubt, to the fact that it has gone through five revisions. Sources of information are documented.

A224   Butler, Alban. **Butler's Lives of the Saints.** Edited by Michael Walsh. Concise ed.
San Francisco, Harper and Row, 1985. xiv, 466p. LC 84-48781. ISBN
0-060-69251-0.

Arranged by feastday, the number of saints included has been reduced to one per
day. Anglo-Saxon and American saints have been favored. The index is that of
the complete edition (A225) with boldface type for the names of those saints
included in this work.

A225   Butler, Alban. **The Lives of the Saints.** Originally compiled by Alban Butler;
now ed., rev, and supplemented by Herbert Thurston. London, Burns, Oates,
and Washbourne, 1926-38. 12v. LC 26-15085. (First published, 1756-59.)

A226   Butler, Alban. **The Lives of the Saints. Supplementary Volume** by Donald
Attwater, 1949.

Certainly one of the oldest and most popular works in English in this field.
The arrangement is the same as in the *Acta sanctorum*, from which, of
course, most of the material was drawn. There is one volume for each
month in this unabridged version, for which one may use Attwater's
Dictionary of Saints (A217) as an alphabetical index. Butler's work was
not intended to be scholarly although it does contain some critical commentary and bibliographical references; its main object "is to present a
short but readable and trustworthy account of the principal saints who are
either venerated liturgically (with a mass and office) in the Western Church
or whose names are familiar to English-speaking Catholics" (Preface). The
1926-28 revision by Thurston, Leeson, and Attwater makes an even greater
attempt at pointing up the legendary matter in the traditional lives and to
indicate what facts can be verified through history or legitimate tradition.
Homilies of a devotional nature are included. In English-speaking countries
this has long been the standard work; *America* referred to it as a "classic
for 200 years" (XCV [June 16, 1956], p. 288); and in the preface to his
abridged version (A217), Attwater commented:

This is a Herculean and scholarly work. Butler was not, as many were inclined to think, a credulous and uncritical writer, an epitome of those hagiographers whose object is apparently at all costs to be edifying. He is as critical a hagiographer as the state of knowledge and available materials of his age would allow.

A227   Butler, Alban. **Lives of the Saints**, complete ed. Ed., rev., and supplemented by Herbert Thurston and Donald Attwater. New York, Kennedy, 1956. 4 v. LC 56-5383. Reprinted: Westminster, MD, Christian Classics, 1981. 4 v. ISBN 0-8706-1046-5.

In number of entries this work is an expansion of Butler's work—from 1,486 to 2,565 lives. But it is also an abridgement in that Butler's eighteenth century verbosity and homilies have been cut. Based on the Thurston revision of Butler (1926 [A225]). The indexing of this set is complete, with individual indexes in each volume and a general index in volume four.

A228   Delaney, John J. **Dictionary of Saints**. Garden City, NY, Doubleday, 1980. 647p. LC 79-7783. ISBN 0-385-13594-7.

"An up-to-date, easy-to-use compendium of factual information about some five thousand saints" (Introduction). Very brief entries. No bibliography. Indexes of patrons and symbols. Tables of popes and world rulers. Byzantine and Roman calendars.

A229   **The Encyclopedia of Catholic Saints**. Philadelphia, Chilton Books, 1966. 12 v. LC 66-28561.

Based on the French work *Les saints de tous les Jours* by Robert Morel (Paris, Le Club du Livre Chrétien). The arrangement is by calendar—one volume per month with an index in volume twelve. Biographies are given for only the major saint of the day, but others are listed. Could easily have been bound in one volume.

A230   Englebert, Omer. **The Lives of the Saints**. Trans. by Christopher and Anne Fremantle. New York, D. McKay Co., 1951. xi, 532p. LC 51-11328.

Short articles on major saints in the calendar arrangement with index. Minor saints are also mentioned with dates and places of birth and death. ". . . a one-volume work that strives to add flesh and bones to a skeleton sketch and that attempts to place a saint before us as a living reality" (*American Ecclesiastical Review*, CXXV [August, 1951], p. 155).

A231   Farmer, David Hugh. **The Oxford Dictionary of Saints**. New York, Oxford University Press, 1982. xxiv, 439p. LC 82-237064. ISBN 0-19-283036-8.

Covers all English saints; important saints of Ireland, Scotland and Wales; and a selection of other well-known saints. Articles are brief but contain bibliographies of primary and secondary sources. Good for some obscure names.

A232   Holweck, Frederick George. **A Biographical Dictionary of the Saints, with a General Introduction on Hagiology**. St. Louis, MO, B. Herder Book Co., 1924. xxix, 1053p. LC 24-20782. Reprinted: Detroit, Gale, 1969. LC 68-30625. ISBN 0-8103-3158-6.

More comprehensive than most Catholic works because of its inclusion of "personages who have attained veneration only among heretics and schismatics" (Preface). Although old, this is a carefully done work, listing sources of information and definitive biographies.

A233   **The Saints: A Concise Biographical Dictionary.** Ed. by John Coulson. New York, Hawthorn Books, 1958. 496p. il. LC 58-5626.

Brief entries with illustrations drawn from works of art: a useful one-volume work furnishing "succinct and authentic information . . . on some 2,230 saints" (*Critic*, XVI [June-July, 1958], p. 14). Sources of information are noted.

A234   **Saints and Feast Days: Lives of the Saints: With a Calendar and Ways to Celebrate.** Chicago, Loyola University Press, 1985. 180p. ISBN 0-8294-0505-4.

Designed for use in schools, this work gives lives of saints or descriptions of feast days with suggestions for class activities to commemorate the day. Brief "Bibliography for Saints and Feast Days". No index.

A235   **Vies des saints et des bienheureux, selon l'order de calendrier, avec l'historique des fêtes par les Bénédictins de Paris.** Paris, Letouzey, 1935-56. 12 v.

A236   **Vies des saints et des bienheureux, selon l'order de calendrier, avec l'historique des fêtes par les Bénédictins de Paris. Supplément et tables générales.** v. 13. 1959.

Long biographical sketches of the saints taken from the *Acta sanctorum* and other sources (listed after each article); comparable to Butler (**A225**).

WOMEN

A237   Dunbar, Agnes Baillie Cuninghame. **A Dictionary of Saintly Women.** London, G. Bell and Sons, 1904-05. 2 v.

Based largely on the *Acta sanctorum* from which the author seems to have chosen only the most remarkable and even absurd incidents. The articles are short and contain, in addition to biographical information, facts about the cult and symbolism. Sources of information are indicated. Index of last names.

CANDIDATES

A238   Congregatio pro Causis Sanctorum. **Index ac status causarum beatificationis servorum Dei et canonizationis beatorum.** Città del Vaticano, Typis Polyglottis Vaticanis, 1975. vii, 402p.

Since 1969 the Congregation for Causes of the Saints has been charged with the processes of beatification and canonization. This work is a list of those whose cause for canonization has been introduced, giving their present status—"Servant of God," "Venerable," or "Blessed"—and biographical information. Officials working on their causes are also listed as are references to any printed documents that exist.

EASTERN SAINTS

A239   Attwater, Donald. **Saints of the East.** New York, P. J. Kenedy, 1963.
190p. LC 63-11328.

A series of twenty-four biographies of saints who lived in the East before
the schism. "Unfortunately this book does not measure up to (Attwater's)
previous standards; . . . nevertheless (it) is extremely important because there
is so little available in the English language on Eastern hagiography" (*Best
Sellers*, XXIII [September 16, 1953], p. 205).

AMERICA

A240   Habig, M. A. **Saints of the Americas.** Huntington, IN, Our Sunday Visitor,
1974. 384p. il. LC 74-15269. ISBN 0-8797-3880-4.

The biographies of 45 saints and *beati* are given in this popularly written
work. Documentation is supplied, but the material is handled uncritically.

BRITAIN

A241   Baring-Gould, Sabine, and John Fisher. **The Lives of the British Saints: The
Saints of Wales and Cornwall and Such Irish Saints as Have Dedications in
Britain.** London, Society of Cymmrodorion, 1907-13. 4 v. il. LC 8-11526.

The approach is scholarly, based on original manuscripts in prose and verse.
Some articles are very short, each is thoroughly documented and there are
numerous illustrations of saints, symbols, and some maps. Genealogies and
many original texts are supplied. No attempt is made at a critical selection
of materials in the light of legend vs. history. Index and appendix.

A242   Doble, Gilbert Hunter. **Lives of the Welsh Saints.** Cardiff, University of Wales
Press, 1971. x, 248p. LC 76-596679. ISBN 0-900768-68.

The lives of five early Welsh saints with bibliography and original sources.
Edited for publication by D. Simon Evans. "Tackles with a degree of real
success almost intractably difficult material" (*Tablet*, CCXXV[October 16,
1971], p. 1002).

A243   Doble, Gilbert Hunter. **The Saints of Cornwall.** Chatham, Parrett and Neves,
1960-70. 5 v. LC 61-37764.

A reprinting of the author's *Cornish Saints Series*, a collection of pamphlets
published 1923-1944. This version is edited by Donald Attwater. Arranged
geographically by volume, providing biography, bibliography and excerpts
from original source material.

IRELAND

A244   O'Hanlon, John. **Lives of the Irish Saints, with Special Festivals and the
Commemoration of Holy Persons, Compiled from Calendars, Martyrologies
and Various Sources relating to the Ancient Church History of Ireland.**

Dublin, Duffy; London, Burns; New York, Benziger, 1875-1903. 9 v. and
7 pts. of v. 10 (Jan. 1 to Oct. 21).

(No more volumes published.)

A monumental work never completed. Its nine volumes go only through October in the traditional arrangement, but the set is valuable as far as it goes for its lengthy biographies. No index has been provided, but other sources could be used to find the feast day.

GENEALOGY

The three works in this section dealing with names were inspired by the Christian custom of naming children after saints. Latin forms of the name are given because these were formerly used in the baptism and confirmation ceremonies.

HERALDRY

See also Galbreath's **Papal Heraldry** (E137).

A245   Brassard, Gérard. **Armorial des évêques du Canada; album historico-héraldique contenant les protraits et les armoires des évêques du Canada depuis mgr. de Montmorency de Laval jusqu'à date, avec notice biographique pour chacun.** Montréal, P. Q., Mercury Pub. Co., 1940. 403p. il. LC 41-24694.

A246   Brassard, Gérard. **Armorial of the American Hierarchy: The Roman Catholic Church in the United States of America.** Worcester, MA, Stobbs Press, 1956- . v. LC 56-1847.
   (V. 2 has title Biographical and Heraldic Dictionary of the Catholic Bishops in America: The South Atlantic States.)

Brief biographies of each member of the hierarchy, portraits, and color reproductions of arms with documented explanations, are given along with the arms of Dioceses and States.

NAMES

A247   Attwater, Donald. **Names and Name Days.** London, Burns, Oates and Washbourne, 1939. xi, 124p. LC 40-11692. Reprinted: Detroit, Gale, 1968. LC 68-30595. ISBN 0-8103-3108-X.

A dictionary of Christian names selected by the compiler giving the meaning, language of origin, the Latin form and a note on the principal saint of that name. Appendixes of patrons, etc.

A248   Egger, Carl. **Lexicon nominorum virorum et mulierum.** Romae, Studium, 1957. ix, 197p. LC A57-5785.

Gives the Latin, French, Spanish, English, and German equivalents under the Italian form of the name with cross references from each form.

A249   Smith, Edward Francis. **Baptismal and Confirmation Names Containing in Alphabetical Order the Names of Saints with Latin and Modern Language Equivalents, Nicknames, Brief Biography, Representation in Art and Pronunciation, with a Daily Calendar of Feasts and Lists of Patron Saints.** New York, Benziger Bros., 1935. iii, 280p. LC 35-7834.

Cross references to other forms of names are supplied.

II

THEOLOGY

RELIGIONS

Works devoted to the study of religions and the history and origin of religion are included in this section. The most recent, comprehensive survey of religious beliefs may be found in the *Enciclopedia delle religione* (1970-76 [B19]). Gründler's *Lexikon der Christlichen Kirchen und Sekten* (B2), Hardon's *Religions of the World* (B4), and *Protestant Churches of America* (B3) are still useful, but are in need of some updating. Perhaps when it is completed Piepkorn's *Profiles in Belief* (B207) will become the standard work.

When speaking of the Christian churches of the East, the term "uniate" is often applied to those in union with Rome although members of these Churches have traditionally preferred to be called Eastern Catholics. The oriental series by Fortescue (B10, 11, 12) is part of a projected four-volume work left incomplete by the author. The third volume, *The Uniate Eastern Churches*, was finished by George D. Smith. Although older than Attwater's work (B8), this series is much more detailed.

Few of the works on the history of religion are useful as guides to current thought, but they have not yet been replaced by similar works of equal scholarship and reference value.

DENOMINATIONS

HANDBOOKS

B1   Algermissen, Konrad. **Christian Denominations.** Translated by Joseph W. Grundner. St. Louis, MO, Herder Book Co., 1945. v, 105p. LC 45-5798. (Translation of *Christliche Sekten und Kirchen Christi*)

"The author's ecclesiology and Church history are undistinquished. However, there is a great deal of worthwhile information about the smaller Protestant religious societies and a fair account of the most important movements for the reunion of Christendom" (*American Ecclesiastical Review*, CXVI [April, 1946], p. 314).

This has long been a standard work—emphasizing the relationship of the Catholic Church to other religions. Arrangement: "Separated Churches of the East," "Protestantism"—i.e. denominations by groups, and "Christian Reunification." Index.

B2   Gründler, Johannes. **Lexikon der Christlichen Kirchen und Sekten unter Berücksichtigung der Missionsgesellschaften und zwischenkirchlichen Organisationen.** Wien, Herder, 1961. 2 v. LC 62-39512.
> Section I. Die katholische Kirche; Section II. Die nichtkatholischen Kirchen, Sekten, Missiongesellschaften und zwischenkirchlichen Organisationen; Section III. Statistik; Section IV. Übersichten; Section V. Personen-Orts-und-Sachregister.

> One of the most comprehensive and up-to-date handbooks of Christian denominations. The treatment of the Catholic Church is general in nature with separate articles for each rite. The name, headquarters, history and description of missionary activities are given for each sect. The statistical section covers membership and clergy; sources of information are indicated. Bibliography, v. 2., pp. 140-46. "Recommended as a very convenient reference" (*Catholic Historical Review*, XLVIII [January, 1962], p. 294).

B3   Hardon, John A. **Protestant Churches of America.** Rev. edition. Westminster, MD, Newman Press, 1966. xxiii, 373p.

> Part I, "Major Protestant Denominations" treats fourteen religious groups giving their history, doctrines, ritual and worship, organization and government, statistics and references. Part II, "Minor Protestant Sects," treats these in related groups; and Part III, "Statistics on Religious Bodies in the United States," contains a series of tables on membership, finances, etc., furnished by the churches themselves. "Objective" and "readable" (*American Ecclesiastical Review*, CXXXVI [April, 1957], p. 284). Index.

B4   Hardon, John A. **Religions of the World.** Westminster, MD, Newman Press, 1963. x, 539p. LC 63-12236.

> A comprehensive survey designed for the general reader covering primitive religion, ten Oriental religions and seven major religious families "of Judaic origin." The extensive bibliography (pp. 487-505) was criticized for being confined to English language titles only (*Theological Studies*, XXVI, [March, 1965], p. 102), but "all in all Hardon has written a very useful book, which can be warmly recommended to the readers for which it is primarily intended." Index.

B5   Hardon, John A. **The Spirit and Origins of American Protestantism: A Source Book on its Creeds.** Dayton, OH, Pflaum Press, 1968. xvi, 516p. LC 68-21241.

> (Includes "Confessional Index of the Protestant Churches of America.")

> A collection of the statements of belief of the major Protestant denominations to serve the "growing need in the ecumenical movement" (Introduction). Divided into two parts: "European Reformation Movements" and the "Free Church Tradition." The documents reprinted include creeds, cathechisms, articles, etc. Reflecting on the fragmentation of Christianity represented here, one reviewer states, "Altogether it is probably better to have such a book than not" (*Jubilee*, XVI [June, 1968], p. 46). Analytic index.

B6 **Whalen, William Joseph. Minority Religions in America.** Rev. ed. New York, Alba House, 1981. vi, 226p. LC 81-3664. ISBN 0-8189-0413-5.

"A concise summary of the history, beliefs and practices of thirty minority religions in the U.S. ..., combining accurate factual data with general principles and expressing it in lucid, up-to-date language" (*America*, CX [January 18, 1964], p. 111). Classified bibliography, pp. 189-194. Index.

B7 Whalen, William Joseph. **Separated Brethren: A Survey of Protestant, Anglican, Eastern Orthodox, and Other Denominations in the United States.** 3rd rev. ed. Huntington, IN, Our Sunday Visitor, 1979. 252 p. LC 79-83874.

A survey for American Catholics of Protestant, Eastern Orthodox, Old Catholic and Polish National churches in the United States. The first two chapters offer a general overview of the differences between Catholic and non-Catholic Christians. Each major denomination is given a separate treatment with emphasis on similarities to and differences from the Catholic Church. The work is not apologetic in tone or purpose. Index.

EASTERN CHURCHES

B8 Attwater, Donald. **The Christian Churches of the East.** Rev. edition. Milwaukee, Bruce Pub. Co., 1961. 2 v. (First published in 1935 under the title, *The Catholic Eastern Churches*)

Volume one devotes a chapter to each of the five uniate rites except the Byzantine, which receives more detailed treatment. For each of these rites there is given a short bibliography, a history, a summary of its present state, and a description of its liturgy and customs. There is also a chapter on Eastern monasticism. Volume two does much the same thing for the Orthodox Church as well as for the Nestorians and Monophysites. Both volumes contain bibliographies, glossaries and indexes. "Long established as the standard work on the subject in English" (*Eastern Churches Quarterly*, XIV [Winter, 1961], p. 262).

B9 Attwater, Donald. **A List of Books About the Eastern Churches.** Newport, RI, St. Leo Shop, 1960. xvii, 221p. LC 60-40006.

Lists 200 titles, with an introductory bibliographical essay. Pamphlets and papal documents are also included.

B10 Fortescue, Adrian. **The Lesser Eastern Churches.** London, Catholic Truth Society, 1913. 468p. il.

Covers the Nestorians, Copts, Abyssinians, Jacobites, Malabars, Armenians, giving their history, social and political backgrounds, liturgical books and rites, with references to sources. Contains some minor inaccuracies (*America*, X [March 28, 1914], p. 595).

B11 Fortescue, Adrian. **The Orthodox Eastern Church.** London, Catholic Truth Society, 1916. xxxiii, 451p. LC 17-14537. Reprinted: Freeport, NY, Books for Libraries Press, 1971. LC 70-179520. ISBN 0-8369-6649-X.

The history, theology, liturgy and structure of the Orthodox Church are covered in a popular style " of no less conspicuous merit than more scholarly works" (*Catholic World*, LXXXVI [March, 1908], p. 832). Bibliography, pp. xxi-xxxiii.

B12   Fortescue, Adrian. **The Uniate Eastern Churches: The Byzantine Rite in Italy, Sicily, Syria and Egypt.** Ed. by George D. Smith. London, Burns, Oates, and Washbourne, 1923. xxiii, 244p. LC 24-11215.

A thorough treatment by geographical areas with many bibliographical references, but now seriously out of date. "An admirable introduction to the subject of Oriental rites" (*Catholic World*, CXIX [April, 1924], p. 138).

HISTORY OF RELIGIONS

B13   Anwander, Anton. **Die Religionen der Menscheit; Einfürung in Wesen und Geschichte der Ausserchristi. Gottesvorstellungen mit einen Religionsgeschichte.** 2 aufl. Freiburg, Herder, 1949. xxi, 400p.

Compiled by an expert in the field. Malclès criticized the work for its lack of scholarly apparatus (Louis Noëlle Malclès, *Les sources du travail bibliographique* [Geneve, E. Droz, 1950-58], v. 2, p. 347); it does, however, have a bibliography (pp. 379-387).

B14   Bricout, J. **Où en est l'histoire des religions?** Paris, Letouzey et Ané, 1911-12. 2 v. LC 12-15889.

Arranged by religious or racial groups, with a bibliography for each section. General index in volume II.

B15   Mitros, Joseph F. **Religions: A Select, Classified Bibliography.** Louvain, Editions Nauwelaerts; New York, Learned Publications, 1973. xix, 435p. LC 77-184042. ISBN 912116-08-0. (Philosophical Questions Series, 8).

The first part (of seven) of this work deals with research and writing in the disciplines of religion. The remaining six parts are bibliographies, mostly annotated, of reference books: non-Christian religions, Catholicism, Protestantism, the Fathers, Scripture and periodicals. The listings are alphabetical under subject headings with an author index at the end of the work. Most of the works listed are in English.

B16   Pinard de la Boullaye, Henri. **L'étude comparée des religions: essai critique.** 3ᵉ éd. rev. et augm. Paris, G. Beauchesne, 1929-31. 2 v.

A guide to, and a history of the science of the history of religions, "expounding adequately all theories of comparative religion," to be prized for its "genuine erudition and judicious estimates" (*American Ecclesiastical Review*, LXXIII [July, 1925], p. 106). Although there is no index, the reference value of this work, as the *Guide to Historical Literature* points out, lies in its ample bibliographies and full discussions of major works (American Historical Association, *Guide to Historical Literature* [New York, Macmillan, 1963], p. 45).

B17   Rousselot, Pierre. **Christus: manuel d'histoire des religions.** 8e éd. rev.
       Paris, Beauchesne, 1948. 1367p.

"The work of some of the best Catholic specialists in the world today"
(*Catholic World,* XC [November, 1912] , p. 243). In a number of brief,
clear essays, the contributors attempt to disprove a completely evolutionary
theory of religion. The reference value of this work lies in its comprehensive
scope, clarity of arrangement and many bibliographies.

DICTIONARIES AND ENCYCLOPEDIAS

B18   Anwander, Anton. **Wörterbuch der Religion.** 2. neubearb. Aufl. Würzburg,
       Echter-Verlag, 1962. 636p. LC 66-96243.

A useful dictionary of the history of religions which covers concepts and
theories of this science as well as information concerning the present status
of religions in various countries and other miscellaneous information.
Theological Studies had high praise for the uniform and masterly approach
of this one-man work to current problems (X [March, 1949] , p. 142).

B19   **Enciclopedia delle religione.** Firenze, Vallecchi, 1970-76. 6 v. il. LC 73-
       540666.

A large, scholarly work by numerous Italian theologians and other scholars.
The articles deal with religions and religious topics; those articles dealing
with major religions are of monographic length. Articles are signed and
contain cross references and long bibliographies of sources in many languages.

B20   König, Franz Cardinal. **Religionswissenschaftliches Wörterbuch die Grund-**
       begriffe. Freiburg, Herder, 1956. Col. 954. LC 57-37135.

Pre-classic, classical, Eastern and present-day religions are covered in moderately brief articles with bibliographies—mostly of German works. "A
creditable piece of scholarship . . . almost indispensable for chaplains of
Newman Clubs and students of non-Catholic and Catholic universities"
(*Theological Studies*, XVIII [June, 1957] , p. 272).

GENERAL THEOLOGICAL WORKS

BIBLIOGRAPHY

The works listed in Chapter I under general bibliography pp. 1-17, 35-38
should also be consulted for theology, especially the *Catholic Periodical and Literature
Index* (A160), the bulk of which is, in fact, devoted to theology of one sort or another.
The works listed in this section are those covering theological literature exclusively.

The most important, comprehensive, continuing theological bibliography
is the *Elenchus bibliographicus* (B28) published by the University of Louvain as an
annual issue of its *Ephemerides theologicae.* Another excellent source of continuing
bibliography is the quarterly annotated list contained in *Theology Digest*, a journal
published by the School of Divinity of St. Louis University. The selection of titles
and descriptive annotations are done by Father Charles Heiser, S.J.

B21   Alhadef, John Joseph, comp. **National Bibliography of Theological Titles in Catholic Libraries.** Los Gatos, CA, Alma College, 1965-70. 3 v. LC 76-16969.

An author catalog based on the theological collection of Alma College and, later (vols. 2 and 3), other Jesuit College and seminary libraries. Catholic University and St. John's College, Minnesota, also participated. Location symbols are supplied.

B22   Bleistein, Roman and Elmar Klinger, eds. **Bibliographie Karl Rahner: 1924-1969.** Freiburg im Breisgau, Herder, 1969. 111p. LC 77-425999.

B23   Bleistein, Roman, ed. **Bibliographie Karl Rahner: 1969-1974.** Freiburg im Breisgau, Herder, 1974. 47p. LC 75-556201. ISBN 3-4511-7039-6.

These two bibliographies list a total of 2,859 works in chronological order. The first collection has a subject index.

B24   **Bulletin de théologie ancienne et médiéval.** Louvain, Abbaye du Mont César, 1929- . v. Quarterly. LC A41-4816.

Issued as a bibliographical supplement to *Researches de théologie ancienne et médiéval*, this work supplies quarterly, annotated lists of books and articles dealing with patristic and medieval theology. The annotations are critical and detailed. Subject and name indexes.

B25   Center for Reformation Research. **Early Sixteenth Century Roman Catholic Theologians and the German Reformation: A Finding List of CRR Holdings.** Saint Louis, Center for Reformation Research, 1975. LC 75-315894.

The CRR collects source material on the history of the Reformation and has published several lists such as this. Twenty-one theologians are covered. Biographies as well as bibliographies are provided. CRR holdings are in microform.

B26   Doohan, Leonard. **The Laity: A Bibliography.** Wilmington, DE, Michael Glazier, 1987. 159p. LC 87-45006. ISBN 0-89453-617-6.

A bibliography of books and articles arranged in classified order based on broad subject categories and source, e.g. Papal documents, Church documents, episcopal documents. Index of names.

B27   Dreesen, G. ed. **Bibliographia academica: Faculteit der Godgeleerheid, Faculty of Theology.** Louvain, Universitaire Pers, 1972. 348p. (Anna nuntia lovaniensa, 18.) LC 74-316628.

A bibliography of the 1972 faculty members of the Theology school at Louvain. The arrangement is by rank—i.e. professors, lecturers, etc. Index of authors.

B28   **Ephemerides theologicae lovaniensis. "Elenchus bibliographicus."** Louvain, Université catholique, 1924- . v. Annual.

"One of the most excellent and serviceable of the various 'elenchi.' . . . A very thorough instrument covering both book and periodical sources. It is organized around traditional theological subjects and encompasses these in detail. . . . There is a fine index of authors that leads one to the item immediately" (Charles Harvey Arnold, "Philosophy and Religion," *Library Trends*, XV [January, 1967] , p. 471). International in coverage. List of periodicals analyzed.

B29   Gagné, Armand. **Répertoire des thèses des facultés ecclésiastiques de l'Université Laval, 1935-1960.** Quebéc, Université Laval, 1960. iii, 191. (Etudes et recherches bibliographiques, no. 2.) LC 75-225426.

A listing of 129 dissertations by subject with indexes.

B30   Gla, Dietrich. **Systematisch geordnetes Repertorium der katholisch-theologischen Litteratur, welche in Deutschland, Österreich und der Schweiz seit 1700 bis zur Gegenwart (1900) erschienen ist.** Mit zahlreichen litterarhistorischen und kritischen Bemerkungen und einem Personen und Sachregister. Bearbeitet und hersaugegeben von dr. theol. Dietrich Gla. Paderhorn, F. Schöningh, 1895-1904. 2 v. LC 5-35452.

Arranged under 142 subject headings, this annotated bibliography covers books and articles. Father Brown considered it a "valuable work" of Catholic bibliography ("Catholic Bibliography," *Catholic Library Practice* [A78] , v. 1., p. 109).

B31   Glorieux, Palémon. **Répertoire de maitres en théologie de Paris au XIIIe siècle.** Paris, Librarie Philosophique J. Vrin, 1933-34. 2 v. LC AC33-3713.

Bio-bibliographies of 425 theologians arranged by religious orders. Manuscript locations are supplied as are the titles of works about each author.

B32   Loidl, Franz. **Die Dissertationen der Katholische-Theologischen Fakultät der Universität Wien, 1831-1965.** Vienna, Herder, 1969. 106p. (Wiener Beiträge zur Theologie, Bd. 25.) LC 79-422365.

An alphabetical listing by author giving the title, format (typed or handwritten), and library location.

B33   Marcos Rodríguez, Florencio. **Los Manuscritos pretridentinos hispaños de ciencias sagradas en la Biblioteca Universitaria de Salamanca.** Salamanca, Universidad Pontificia de Salamanca, 1971. 262-501p. LC 73-328070.

Descriptions of some 800 manuscripts with indexes for authors and first lines.

B34   O'Brien, Elmer. **Theology in Transition: A Bibliographical Evaluation of the Decisive Decade, 1954-1964.** New York, Herder and Herder, 1965. 282p. (Contemporary Theology.) LC 65-13486.

Contains six bibliographic surveys covering Theological Trends, Old Testament, New Testament, Patristics, Liturgy, Theology in Transition. Each essay is followed by an extensive bibliography. "A great service to teachers and students of theology" (*Theological Studies*, XXVII [May, 1966] , p. 460). Subject and author indexes.

B35   Principe, Walter Henry and Ronald E. Diener. **Bibliographies and Bulletins in Theology.** Toronto, Pontifical Institute of Medieval Studies, 1967. 44l. LC 67-82397.

An annotated bibliography of bibliographies in theology. The arrangement is classified. No indexes.

B36   **Rassegna di letteratura tomistica.** Napoli, Edizione Domenicane Italiane, 1966- . v. ISSN 0557-6857.

See (C6) for complete description. Covers many theological works as well as philosophical ones.

B37   **Répertoire général de sciences religieuses: bibliographie hors commerce.** Publiée avec le concours de la Direction des relations culturelles au Ministère des affaires étrangères pour le Service bibliographique du Centre d'études Saint-Louis-de-France. Rome, L'Airone; Paris, Alsatia Colmar, 1950- . Année. LC A54-5915.

Very broad scope—among the more strictly Catholic-interest sections are Théologie Catholique, Droit canonique et ecclésiastique, Missions catholique, and many others dealing with scripture, Church history, religious education and art. Lists books and articles from over 1,000 periodicals. International in coverage.

B38   Snyderwine, L. Thomas. **Researching the Development of Lay Leadership in the Catholic Church Since Vatican II: Bibliographical Abstracts.** Lewiston, NY, E. Mellen Press, 1987. 192p. LC 87-12224. ISBN 0-88946-241-0.

Lists and abstracts books and articles published from 1965 to 1985. Author, title, and subject indexes.

B39   Stegmüller, Friedrich. **Repertorium commentariorum in Sententias** Petri Lombardi. Wurzburg, F. Schöningh, 1947. 2 v. LC 48-25394.

A comprehensive list of medieval doctoral theses, all of which took this form. Gives descriptive annotations and locations. Volume two contains indexes of first words, authors, scribes and professors.

B40   Steiner, Urban J. **Contemporary Theology: A Reading Guide.** Collegeville, MN, Liturgical Press, 1965. vi, 111p.

A selected, annotated bibliography of current theological books covering scripture, liturgy, ecumenics, moral and pastoral theology, psychology, sociology, Church history and Christian art. The annotations, many of which are critical, are careful and detailed. Author index.

B41   Willaert, Leopold. **Bibliotheca Janseniana Belgica. Répertoire des imprimés concernant les controverses théologiques en relation avec le jansénisme dans les Pays-Bas catholiques et le pays de Liège aux XVIIe et XVIIIe siècles.** Namur, 1949-51. 3 v. (Bibliothèque de la Faculte de Philosophie et Lettres de Namur, facs. 4, 5, 12.) LC A51-1584.

Contains over 1,400 books and articles on the Jansenist heresy along with the names of libraries with extensive holdings in this literature. Limited to works by Belgian authors, printed in Belgium, or dealing with Belgium.

SOURCES

The Scriptures, the teachings of the Fathers of the Church and the documents of the popes and councils are the major sources of Catholic theology. The major collections of papal and conciliar documents, however, are listed in Chapter V (E98-E169) with the history of the popes and councils.

B42   Palmer, Paul F. **Sources of Christian Theology.** Westminster, MD, Newman Press, 1955- . v. LC 55-1503.

V. 1. Sacraments and Worship: Liturgy and Doctrinal Development of Baptism, Confirmation and the Eucharist. 1955; V. 2. Sacraments and Forgiveness: History and Doctrinal Development of Penance, Extreme Unction and Indulgences. 1960; V. 3. Christ and His Mission: Christology and Soteriology. 1966. (No more volumes published.)

These are the first volumes in a series "designed to present in English translation and in topical arrangement the basic texts and documents which have shaped Catholic theological teaching" (General Foreword). Future volumes were to cover the priesthood, celibacy, marriage, God, sin and grace, the Church, Mary. The documents are selected from early liturgies, the Fathers, the councils and official pronouncements of the Holy See. Also included are selctions from the writings of Protestant Reformers which illustrate their views on the topics covered when they differ from the Catholic teaching. Indexes in each volume.

B43   **Textus et Documenta in usam exercitationum et praelectionum academarum.** Roma, Pontificia Universita Gregoriana, 1932- . v.

Series philosophica.
Series theologica.

A continuing series of source material with commentaries, notes and bibliography. The texts are those of theologians, philosphers, and the Fathers as well as official Church documents.

SCRIPTURE

Texts

Since the Council of Trent, the official version of the Bible for Catholics has been St. Jerome's Latin translation or Vulgate written in the fifth century and revised many times. Trent also called for a revision, one of the results of which became known at the Clementine version after Pope Clement VIII by whom it was issued in 1592. It was not until 1907, however, that a modern scientific attempt was made to reconstruct the original text of St. Jerome; the first volume of this version—*Biblia Sacra* (B44)— was not published until 1926, and the work is still in progress.

For over three and one-half centuries the standard English version of the Bible for Catholics was the Douay-Rheims, a translation of the Vulgate made by Gregory Martin, an English Catholic who took refuge in the Catholic College at Douay (1578) and later at Rheims (1593). Many minor revisions of this text have been made throughout the centuries, the most widely known of which was that by Bishop Richard Challoner of London (1741 and 1777) who modernized some word forms and expressions and completely rewrote the notes. The edition listed here (B47) contains the original Douay-Rheims text but with the Challoner notes.

In 1941 the American Episcopal Committee of the Confraternity of Christian Doctrine authorized a new translation to be done by the Catholic Biblical Society of America. As the work progressed, and sections appeared in print, it became known as the Confraternity Edition (B48). In 1970, however, with the completion of the Old Testament and the revised New Testament, the entire work was reissued as *The New American Bible* (B51). This version was to become the official text for use in liturgical books; however, some books have been approved using other texts such as the *Jerusalem Bible* (B39). Nevertheless, this version has the distinction of being the only modern English language version of the Bible translated completely and anew from the original languages. A promising development in recent years has been the appearance of several editions of "common versions" for Christians of all faiths, e.g., *The Catholic R.S.V.* (B45) and the *Oxford Annotated Bible* (B53).

B44   **Biblia Sacra iuxta latinam vulgatam versionem ad codicum fidem, iussu Pii pp. XI, cura et studio monachorum Sancti Benedicti Commissionis pontificiae a Pio pp. X institutae sodalium praeside Aidano Gasquet, S.R.E. cardinale edita.** Romae, Typis Polyglottis Vaticanis, 1926- . v. LC 29-179.

This scholarly edition contains extensive notes comparing almost every word with other versions in Latin and other languages including the original Greek and Hebrew. For each book, introductory, historical, and bibliographical material is provided "the result of which is a text considerably different from the Clementine version" (Fitzmyer [B63], p. 28).

B45   **The Holy Bible, Containing the Old and New Testaments. Revised Standard Version. Catholic Edition.** Prepared by the Catholic Biblical Association of Great Britain. Toronto, Camden, T. Nelson, 1966. xvi, 1005+250p. LC 66-2323. Translated from the original tongues, being the version set forth A.D. 1611; Old and New Testaments revised A.D. 1881-1885 and A.D. 1901, Apocrypha revised A.D. 1894; Compared with the most ancient authorities and revised A.D. 1952, Apocrypha revised A.D. 1957.

No textual changes were made in the Old Testament, but the books are in the Catholic canonical order. In the New Testament, Appendix II contains a list of changes made in the text. Interpretative notes and the selection of variant readings have been done in accordance with Catholic teachings. In some respects the arrangement is considered superior to other R.S.V. editions (*New Blackfriars*, XLVII [August, 1967], p. 609).

B46   **The Holy Bible: A Translation from the Latin Vulgate in the Light of the Hebrew and Greek Originals. Authorized by the Hierarchy of England and Wales and the Hierarchy of Scotland.** Trans. by Monsignor Knox. New York, Sheed and Ward, 1956. vii, 913+285p. LC 57-459.

A one-man translation by Msgr. Ronald Knox, the late, brilliant English writer. As a literary work, this translation is a pleasure to read, but it is not highly respected by Biblical scholars (*American Ecclesiastical Review*, CXXIII [December, 1950], p. 479).

B47   **The Holy Bible, Douay Version. Translated from the Latin Vulgate.**
       (Douay, A.D. 1609: Rheims, A.D. 1582) with a preface by H. E., the
       Cardinal Archbishop of Westminster. London, Catholic Truth Society,
       1963. 128+351p.

       The text is the original Douay-Rheims version without the Challoner
       modifications. His notes, however, are included.

B48   **The Holy Bible: Translated from the Original Languages with Critical Use
       of All the Ancient Sources by Members of the Catholic Biblical Association
       of America.** Paterson, NJ, St. Anthony Guild Press, 1952-61. LC 52-13526.

       This edition usually referred to as the "Confraternity Edition" was actually
       begun in 1941 when the American Episcopal Committee of the Confraterni⸱
       of Christian Doctrine issued a translation of the New Testament based on
       the Latin Vulgate (Paterson, NJ, St. Anthony Guild Press, 1941). In 1943
       Pope Pius XII, in his encyclical *Divino Afflante Spiritu*, urged Biblical
       scholars to return to the original languages for new translations of the
       Scripture. The Catholic Biblical Association thus began translating the Old
       Testament from Hebrew, Aramaic or Greek texts. The fifth volume, the
       revised New Testament was never issued in this series. Instead it became
       part of the *New American Bible* (B51).

B49   **The Jerusalem Bible.** Gen. ed., Alexander Jones. Garden City, NY, Double-
       day, 1966. xvi, 1547+498p. LC 66-24278.

       Produced by the Dominican Bible School in Jerusalem and first published
       in French in 1948, this edition contains an entirely new English translation
       based on the French and "a fresh look at the Hebrew and Greek" (Preface),
       which had been generally acclaimed as the best modern English translation
       until the appearance of *The New American Bible* (B40). The scholarly
       apparatus—notes, commentary and appendixes—has been revised to reflect
       the latest scriptural thinking. In his guide (B63), Fitzmyer calls this "the
       best of modern scholarship" (p. 24); elsewhere it has been described as "the
       finest Catholic annotated English version of the Bible with excellent refer-
       ence features, cross references and an index of Biblical themes" (*Worship*,
       XL [December, 1963], p. 663). See B52.

B50   Merk Augustinus, ed. **Novum testamentum graece et latine: Apparatu critico
       instructum.** 10th ed. Rome, Pontifical Biblical Institute, 1984. 47, 873p. (Scripta
       Pontificii Instituti Biblici, v. 65.)

       The Greek and Latin texts are printed side by side with notes for each.

B51   **The New American Bible; Translated from the Original Languages, with
       Critical Use of All the Ancient Sources by Members of the Catholic Bibli-
       cal Association of America, With Textual Notes on Old Testament Readings.**
       Paterson, NJ, St. Anthony Guild Press, 1970. 21+1103+426p. LC 71-141768.

       The Old Testament sections of this version began appearing in 1952 (*See*
       [B48] in four volumes as the "Confraternity Edition." When the New
       Testament was completed, however, the entire work was re-revised and
       issued as the *New American Bible*. It is the text that is most frequently
       printed in liturgical books for use at Mass and other ceremonies. Scholars

agree that it is the best translation in the American idiom and that it is remarkably faithful to the most ancient texts and original languages. In this edition there are 127 pages of notes explaining every deviation from the original languages. These have not been reprinted in many of the subsequent editions. For an extensive review by a Lutheran scholar see *Catholic Biblical Quarterly*, XXXIII (June, 1971), pp. 405-9.

B52   **New Jerusalem Bible.** Garden City, NY, Doubleday, 1985. xvi, 2108p. LC 85-16070. ISBN 0-385-14264-1.

Introductions and notes are based on the 1973 French revised version. The English translation, however, was made directly from the Hebrew, Greek and Aramaic. Where these texts admit of more than one interpretation, the lead of the *Bible de Jéresalem* has been followed. "Supplements" or appendices include a chronological table, genealogies, a calendar, tables of measures and money, alphabetical table of the major footnotes, index of persons, maps, and an index of maps.

B53   **The New Oxford Annotated Bible with the Apocrypha: Revised Standard Version, containing the 2nd. ed. of the New Testament.** Ed. by Herbert G. May and Bruce M. Metzger. New York, Oxford University Press, 1973. xxviii, 1564p, xxii+298p. il. LC 72-96564.

First published in 1965. This edition includes the 1971 translation of the New Testament and three new supplementary articles. Annotations and articles explain differing viewpoints between Catholics and Protestants. Thus "we have the first really common English version of the Bible and an annotated one at that" (*Theological Studies*, XXVII [March, 1967], p. 173).

B54   **Nova Vulgata Biblorum Sacrorum editio: Sacros. Oecum. Concilii Vaticani II ratio habita.** Iussu Pauli PP. VI recognita; auctoritate Ioannis Paulis PP. II promulgata. Vatican City, Libreria Editrice Vaticana, 1979. xiii, 2154p. LC 84-152401.

The new revised Latin Vulgate edition of the Bible with notes.

B55   Rhymer, Joseph, ed. **The Bible in Order.** Garden City, NY, Doubleday, 1976. xxxii, 1917p. LC 75-11363. ISBN 0-385-11062-6.

An arrangement of the text of the *Jerusalem Bible* in the order in which the books were written. Also contains a "Chronological Table" comparing world history with Biblical events.

B56   **Westminster Version of the Sacred Scriptures.** Gen. editors, the Rev. Cuthbert Lattey and the Rev. Joseph Keating. London, Longmans, 1913- . v.

The British equivalent of our Confraternity edition, this version is also based on scholarly study of the original texts and has been in progress since 1913. In 1933 the New Testament was completed. This version is frequently printed in combination with the Douay Old Testament.

Gospel Harmonies

These versions of the New Testament attempt, in a four column arrangement, to present a complete chronological account of the life of Christ and to point up the differences and similarities of the four Gospel narratives.

B57 Hartdegen, Stephen J. **A Chronological Harmony of the Gospels Using the Revised Text of the Challoner-Rheims Version of the New Testament.** Paterson, NJ, St. Anthony Guild Press, 1942. xxv, 22op. LC 42-21021.

A four column arrangement that makes for easy visual reference; an outline of the chronology and several indexes are supplied.

B58 Johnston, Leonard. **A Harmony of the Gospels in the Knox Translation.** Ed. by Leonard Johnston and Aidan Pickering. New York, Sheed and Ward, 1963. xii, 252p. LC 63-17147.

Arranged by major events in the life of Christ. Index.

B59 Steinmueller, John E. **A Gospel Harmony Using the Confraternity Edition of the New Testament.** New York, W. H. Sadlier, Inc., 1942. xl, 166p. LC 42-3775.

Bibliography

The most comprehensive and complete bibliographic tool for Scriptural studies is the *Elenchus bibliographicus* (B60). Other works listed here, such as Fitzmyer (B63) and Marrow (B69) are brief but useful introductions to the bibliography of the field.

B60 **Biblica: "Elenchus bibliographicus "** Romae, Pontificio Instituto Biblico, 1920- . v. Annual. LC 32-12677.

An international classified bibliography of books and articles on scriptural topics without any annotations but with references to book reviews. Presently lists nearly 7,000 items. The most comprehensive bibliography in its field and "an indispensable tool for biblical research" (Fitzmyer [B63], p. 127).

B61 **Bibliographie biblique.** Montréal, Facultés de théologie et de philosophie de la Compagnie de Jésus, 1958. xix, 398p.

Covers over 9,000 Catholic Biblical writings in French, Latin, and English published from 1920-1957. Classified arrangement with no author or title indexes, but useful for grouping all the literature of the period under subject headings.

B62 Chambers, Bettye Thomas. **Bibliography of French Bibles: Fifteenth- and Sixteenth-Century French-Language Editions of the Scriptures.** Genève, Droz, 1983. 548p. LC 83-219034.

A descriptive bibliography of 554 items with a list of library locations. No indexes.

B63   Fitzmyer, Joseph A. **An Introductory Bibliography for the Study of Scripture.** Rev. ed. Rome, Biblical Institute Press, 1981. xi, 154p.

An annotated bibliography of 550 books dealing with the Bible. Annotations are long and descriptive. References to critical reviews of most of the titles are supplied. Arranged by type of work. Author index.

B64   Fitzmyer, Joseph A. **The Dead Sea Scrolls: Major Publications and Tools for Study.** With an addendum (January, 1977). Missoula, MT Scholars Press for the Society of Biblical Literature, 1977. 171p. ISBN 0-88414-053-9.

A classified list of published editions of the scrolls and works about the scrolls, their discovery, and the Qumram community. Explains how the scrolls are identified and provides outlines of the contents of some of them. Index of Modern Authors, Index of Biblical Passages.

B65   Hester, Goldia. **Guide to Bibles in Print.** Austin, TX, R. Gordon and Associates, 1966- . v. LC 66-22742. ISSN 0072-8241.

Covers English and foreign language Bibles with separate lists for each version, Catholic and non-Catholic.

B66   Humphrey, Hugh. **A Bibliography for the Gospel of Mark, 1954-1980.** New York, E. Mellon Press, 1981. xviii, 163p. LC 81-18717. ISBN 0-88946-916-4.

Based on the entries for "Mark" in the *Elenchus bibliographicus Biblicus* (B60), 1954 to 1978. 1,599 items are listed. Index of Authors.

B67   Langevin, Paul-Emile. **Bibliographie Biblique. Biblical Bibliography. Biblische Bibliographie. Bibliografia Biblica. 1930-1983.** Quebec, Presses de l'Universite Laval, 1972-1985. 3v. LC 72-225363. ISBN 2-7637-7060-6.

Lists articles and books in French, English, German, Italian, and Spanish in a classified arrangement with a broad subject index for each language and an author index. Tens of thousands of items are listed. "A mammoth task. The utility researchers will find in it will amply repay the efforts the editor has invested" (*Catholic Biblical Quarterly*, XXXV [October, 1973], p. 540).

B68   Malatesta, Edward. **St. John's Gospel, 1920-1965: A Cumulative and Classified Bibliography of Books and Periodical Literature on the Fourth Gospel.** Rome, Pontifical Biblical Institute, 1967. xxviii, 205p. (Analecta Biblica, v. 32.) LC 70-386588.

A classified bibliography of John's Gospel derived from *Elenchus Bibliographicus* (B60). Author Index. Reviewer Index.

B69   Marrow, Stanley B. **Basic Tools of Biblical Exegesis: A Student's Manual.** Rome, Biblical Institute Press, 1978. 91, (8)p.

215 titles are included in this annotated list designed for scripture students in seminaries. "Selective, but Marrow has adroitly selected" (*Theological Studies*, XXXVIII [March, 1977], p. 196). The 1978 edition is a reprint of the 1976 edition with additions and corrections printed at the end of the volume.

B70   Nickels, Peter. **Targum and New Testament: A Bibliography Together with a New Testament Index.** Rome, Pontifical Biblical Institute, 1967. xi, 88p. (Scripta Pontificii Instituti Biblici, v. 117.) LC 73-505376.

Targums are Aramaic versions of the Old Testament. "The purpose of this bibliography is to acquaint exegetes with Targum—New Testament relationships." Arrangement is by books of the N.T. Books and articles included.

B71 O'Callaghan, Edmund Bailey. **A List of Editions of the Holy Scriptures, and Parts Thereof Printed in America previous to 1860.** Albany, Munsell and Rowland, 1861. liv, 415p. il. LC Z247. Reprinted: Detroit, Gale Research, 1966. LC 66-25690.

Lists and describes in detail all editions of the Bible, Catholic and Protestant, English and foreign language, published in America. Arranged chronologically with indexes for titles, translators, editors, publishers, etc.

B72 Pope, Hugh. **English Versions of the Bible.** Rev. and amplified by Sebastian Bullough. St. Louis, Herder, 1952. ix, 787p. LC 52-10359. Reprinted: Westport, CT, Greenwood Press, 1972. LC 73-152600. ISBN 0-8371-6035-9.

A narrative history of English versions of the Bible beginning with "Saxon versions and glosses." Thoroughly documented and clearly written. Fr. Pope was a British Dominican scripture scholar. He does not claim to be complete as to all texts and editions, but the work did fill a need for unified treatment of Protestant and Catholic versions. For more recent treatment see F. F. Bruce's *The English Bible* (New York, Oxford, 1961).

B73 Pullen, G.F., ed. **Catalogue of the Bible Collections in the Old Library at St. Mary's Oscott, c. 1472-1850.** Sutton Coldfield, St. Mary's Seminary, 1971. xxii, 208p. LC 74-167164.

An alphabetical listing of over 1,500 texts and commentaries. "Short Title Index".

B74 St. John's University, Collegeville, MN. **Library Index to Biblical Journals.** 5th ed. Ed. by Thomas Peter Wahl. Collegeville, St. John's Univ. Pr., 1971. 1 v. (unpaged). LC 73-27544.

An index to 22 biblical journals arranged by a complex subject-numerical system. Indexes.

B75 Shea, John Dawson Gilmary. **A Bibliographical Account of Catholic Bibles, Testaments and Other Portions of the Scripture Translated from the Latin Vulgate and Printed in the United States.** New York, Carmoisy Press, 1859. 48p. LC 1-17017. Reprinted: New York, Gordon Press, 1980.

Describes about sixty American Catholic editions of the Bible and provides a brief history of Catholic versions in English.

B76 Stegmüller, Friedrich. **Repertorium Biblicum Medii Aevi.** Matriti, Consejo Superior de Investigaciones Científicas. Instituto Francisco Suáres, 1950-61. 7 v. LC 53-17384.

An exhaustive listing of apocryphal texts, Biblical prologues, and patristic and medieval commentaries on the Bible giving opening and closing words, contents notes and references to printed texts. No indexes are included, but the work is still quite an achievement and "a necessary addition to any library or institute where biblical studies are encouraged" (*Downside Review*, LXX [Spring, 1952], p. 229-30).

B77 Steinmueller, John E. **A Companion to Scripture Studies.** Rev. and enl. ed. New York, J. F. Wagner, 1962-69. 3 v. Reprinted: Houston, TX, Lumen Christi, 1972.

Covers the major reference works and provides introductory essays on the latest advances and methods in the field. Such topics as texts and versions, inspiration, the canon, interpretation, exegesis, archaeology and geography are covered and extensive bibliography provided. Volumes two and three are devoted to the Old and New Testaments respectively, while volume one covers general topics. *America* praised this edition for its up-to-dateness both in text and bibliography (CVII [October 6, 1962], p. 859). Indexes in each volume.

Abstract Journals

B78 **Internationale Zeitschriftenschau für Bibelwissenschaft und Grenzgebiete. International Review of Bible Studies. Revue internationale des études bibliques.** Stuttgart, Verlag Katholisches Bibelwerk, 1951/52- . v. Semi-annual. LC 54-22523.

"One of the most valuable bibliographical surveys of Scripture studies" (Sister Mary Claudia Carlen, "Bibliography of Catholic Bibliographies," unpublished bibliography in the Archives of the Marygrove College Library, Detroit, MI). Books and articles are abstracted and references given to reviews in a classified arrangement with author indexes. The abstracts are in French, German or English, but books in other languages are covered.

B79 **New Testament Abstracts.** Weston, MA, Weston College of the Holy Spirit, 1956- . v. LC 60-40637.

Published by the Jesuits of Weston College three times per year, this is an "extremely useful tool for both New Testament specialists and theologians" (Fitzmyer [B63], p. 127). Periodical articles only are abstracted, but coverage includes Protestant and Jewish literature as well as Catholic.

B80 **Old Testament Abstracts.** Washington, DC, Catholic Biblical Assoc. of Amer., 1978- . v. (3 nos. per year.) LC 78-643261. ISSN 0364-85f91.

Indexes over 350 journals, Catholic, Protestant, Jewish and Orthodox. Abstracts average 350 words in length. Each issue lists and abstracts about 50 monographs also. There are annual Author, Citation and "Words in Hebrew and other Ancient Languages" indexes. "Indispensable for scholars in the Old Testament field" (*Homiletic and Pastoral Review*, LXXIX [January, 1979], p. 76).

Concordances and Indexes

The making of concordances has been much simplified through the use of computers. Fischer's concordance to the *Vulgate* (B84) is a good example of how thoroughly and completely they can be done using this method. *A Complete Concordance to the New American Bible* (B88) is available thanks to computers.

B81 Bechis, Michael. **Repertorium biblicum, seu Totius Sacrae Scripturae concordantiae iuxta vulgate editionis exemplar Sisti V. pontif. maximi**

iussu recognitum et Clementis VIII. Auctoritate editum praeter alphabeti-cum ordinem in grammaticalem redactae a sac. Michaele Bechis et Leoni papae XIII dictae. Taurini, B. Canonica et Fil., 1887-88. 2 v. LC 22-24318.

Gives only the single word with references; the context is not indicated.

B82   **The Combined Biblical Dictionary and Concordance for the New American Bible.** Charlotte, NC, C.D. Stampley Enterprises, 1971. 252p. LC 77-27265

A dictionary of biblical names and a concordance to very few common words – all in one alphabet. Not a very useful work. See (B88).

B83   Dutripon, François Pascal. **Concordantiae Bibliorum sacrorum vulgatae editionis, ad recognitionem iussu Sixti V. pontif. max., Bibliis adhibitam recensitae atque emendatae ac plusquam viginti quinque millibus versiculis auctae insuper et notis historicis, geographicis, chronicis locupletatae.** Parisiis, Belin-Mander, 1838. xxiii, 1484p. LC 10-717.

A thorough concordance to the Vulgate, supplying personal and place names with brief identifications, and all other words with their contexts. Brief summaries of each book of the Bible are given as well as a glossary of the Latin forms of Hebrew names. Now replaced by (B84).

B84   Fischer, Bonifatius. **Novae concordantiae bibliorum sacrorum iuxta Vulgatam versionem critice editam.** Stuttgart-Bad Canstatt, Fromman-Holzboog, 1977. 5 v. (svii, 5699 columns.) LC 78-358497. ISBN 37728-0638-4.

A completely new concordance produced by computer directly from the text. 22 frequently used words are omitted. Inflected forms of a word are grouped under the first form. The entries include the sentence or phrase in which the word is used and the citation to the text. This is the most exhaustive concordance to the Vulgate ever produced and replaces the three works listed above for those who can afford it or who have need for indexing at such a level.

B85   Kiefer, William J. **Biblical Subject Index.** Westminster, MD, Newman Press, 1958. 197p. LC 58-8757.

Not a concordance, but a subject index listing references to the text under headings devised by the author. Suitable for preachers and religion teachers and those not interested in the exhaustive references supplied by concordances.

B86   Martinez, Ernest R. **Hebrew- Ugaritic Index with an Eblaite Index to the Writings of Mitchell J. Dahood: A Bibliography with Indices of Scriptural Passages, Hebrew, Ugaritic, and Eblaite Words and Grammatical Observations, Critical Reviews, Doctrinal Dissertations and Related Writings.** Rome, Biblical Institute Press, 1967-81. 2 v. (Scripta Pontificii Instituti Biblici, 116.)

An alphabetical listing of words with references to the writings of Father Dahood in which the word has been defined or explained. Bibliography. Scriptural Indexes.

B87   **Modern Concordance to the New Testament.** Ed. and rev. following all current English translations of the New Testament by Michael Darton. Garden City, NY, Doubleday, 1977. xviii, 786p. LC 77-365063. ISBN 0-385-07901-X.

Based on the French *Concordance de la Bible, Nouveau Testament* (Paris, Ed. du Cerf, 1970). This concordance is "thematic and verbal. The presentation is by subject matter: 341 themes subdivided under their Greek roots according to sense" (Introduction). The texts of the citations are from the *Jerusalem Bible*. English Index, Greek Index, Index to Proper Names, List of Greek roots. "This English concordance at last makes it possible for the non-Hellenist to do comparatively serious and first-hand work on the New Testament. For such a student the concordance could be said to be the most important tool published since Cruden" (*Tablet*, CCXXX [November 27, 1976], p. 1147).

B88   Nelson's Complete Concordance to the New American Bible. Stephen J. Hartdegen, gen. ed. Nashville, Thomas Nelson, 1977. 1274p. LC 77-22170. ISBN 0-8407-4900-7.

A verbal concordance of 18,000 key words found in the *New American Bible* (B51). The context of the word is given along with the chapter and verse. A list of 150 prepositions and other very common words not indexed is given in the Preface.

B89   Peultier, E. Concordantiarum universae sacrae Scripturae thesaurus. Paris, Lethielleux, 1939. 1238, xvp.

Divided into two parts: *Tabulae Syntopticae*—tables of genealogies, catalogues, laws, descriptions of buildings, rites, etc., and *Concordantiae verbales*.

B90   Seubert, Aloysius H. The Index to the New Testament, and The Topical Analysis to the New Testament. Lemon Grove, CA, Universal Publications, 1955. vii, 122+142p. LC 58-26854.

A combination subject index and verbal concordance. The "Topical Analysis" is an extended table of contents of the New Testament. The index section is alphabetical in arrangement.

B91   Thompson, Newton Wayland. Complete Concordance to the Bible (Douay Version). By Rev. Newton Thompson, S.T.D., and Raymond Stock. St. Louis, MO, Herder Book Co., 1945. 1914p. LC 45-8426. (First edition called: *Concordance to the Bible* [Douay Version], 1942)

An exhaustive index of words and proper names giving the context of the word and exact references to its use. Numbers are listed in a separate section in numerical order.

B92   Thompson, Newton Wayland. Verbal Concordance to the New Testament (Rheims Version). Baltimore, John Murphy, 1928. 294p. LC 30-13898.

Words are given in context.

B93   Williams, Thomas David. A Concordance of the Proper Names in the Holy Scriptures. St. Louis, MO, Herder Book Co., 1923. 1056p. LC 23-11894.

A biographical and geographical dictionary providing brief identifications along with references to the text. The complete quotation in which the name is found is also given.

Dictionaries and Encyclopedias

Dictionaries of Biblical terms, characters and place names are plentiful, and many excellent ones not published by Catholics are also available and useful for their treatment of more specialized topics. Of the works listed here, Vigouroux's *Dictionnaire de la Bible* (B113) is the most comprehensive and scholarly. Bauer's *Encyclopedia of Biblical Theology* (B94) and Léon Dufour's *Dictionary of Biblical Theology* (B78) are fine, up-to-date English language works on a lesser scale.

B94   Bauer, Johannes Baptist, ed. **Encyclopedia of Biblical Theology**. London, Sheed and Ward, 1970. Reprinted: New York, Crossroad Press, 1981. 3 v. LC 81-626. ISBN 0-8245-0042-3.

First edition titled *Sacramentum Verbi* (New York, Herder, 1970). A translation of the 3rd edition of *Bibel theologisches Wörterbuch;* issued in England as *Bauer Encyclopedia of Biblical Theology* (Sheed and Ward, 1970). This is an important, scholarly work by well known European experts. The articles are moderately long and contain bibliographies. "One can not agree with all the positions taken . . . but readers can find here solid biblical interpretation presented within a framework of Catholic tradition" (*Catholic Biblical Quarterly*, XXXIII [April, 1971] , p. 237). A "Supplementary Bibliography" of works published since the 3rd German edition is supplied along with an "Analytical Index of Biblical References," an "Index of Biblical References" and an "Index of Hebrew and Greek words."

B95   **Catholic Biblical Encyclopedia: Old and New Testaments**. By John E. Steinmueller and Kathryn Sullivan. New York, J. F. Wagner, 1956. 2 v. in 1. il.

A general encyclopedia of the Bible covering biography, history, archeology and geography on a level suitable for the general reader. Although it is considered "a worthwhile volume" (*Worship*, XXXI [January, 1957] , p. 93), it is handicapped by its arrangement—the mere binding together of two separate dictionaries on the Old and New Testaments with an index of cross references from one section to the other. There is, however, much good, brief reference information in the more than 4,100 articles.

B96   Dheilly, Joseph. **Dictionnaire biblique**. Tournai, Desclée. 1964. 1260p.

A 2,500 article encyclopedia covering the usual range of topics for the general reader in a "brief, handy, complete, and up-to-date manner" (*Etudes*, CCCXXI [July-August, 1964] , p. 139). No bibliography. Classified subject index.

B97   **Encyclopedia of the Bible**. General ed.: P. A. Marijnen, gen. ed. Trans. from the Dutch by D. R. Welsh with emendations by Claire Jones. Englewood Cliffs, NJ, Prentice-Hall, 1965. vi, 248p. il. LC 64-23557.

(Trans. of *Elseviers encyclopedie van de Bijbel*.)

A small, brief-entry dictionary by Protestant and Catholic scholars.

B98   **Encyclopedic Dictionary of the Bible**. Trans. and adapt. by Louis F. Hartman. New York, McGraw-Hill, 1963. 2634 col. LC 63-9699. (Trans. of A. van der Born's *Bijbels Woordenboek*.)

The usefulness of this work is proven by its translation and adaptation into several foreign languages—the German *Bibel-lexikon* (Haag 1957); the Italian *Dizionario biblico* (Gennero, 1960); the French *Dictionnaire encyclopédique de la bible* (Mont Césare, 1960); and the Spanish *Diccionario de la biblia* (Barcelona, 1963) (*Theological Studies*, XXV [March, 1964], p. 75).

The work is general in coverage and includes articles on biography, philosophy, theology, history, geography and archeology, ranging in length from a short paragraph to several columns. Many articles have bibliographies, and there are frequent references to the text (Hebrew and Greek). This is a translation and adaptation of the second revised Dutch edition of 1954-57.

B99   **Exegetisches Wörterbuch zum Neuen Testament.** Hrsg. von Horst Balz und Gerhard Schneider. Stuttgart, Kohlhammer, 1980-83. 3 v. LC 79-382065. ISBN 3-17-004774-4.

Alphabetical arrangement by Greek word. Each entry contains a bibliography and an article on the word in question. Cross references.

B100   Grabner-Haider, Anton. **Praktisches Bibellexikon.** Unter Mitarbeit katholischer und evangelischer Theologen. Freiburg, Herder, 1969. xiviii, 127p. col. LC 77-558777.

An ecumenical Bible dictionary by more than 50 contributors containing brief entries on a wide variety of Biblical topics.

B101   Haag, Herbert. **Breve diccionario de la Biblia.** 3a. ed. Barcelona, Herder, 1985. viii, 658col. ISBN 8-425-40623-4.

Spanish translation of the German edition of *Bibel-Lexikon* (Einsiedeln, Benziger, 1968). The original work was based partially on Van den Born's *Bijbels Woordenboek* (B98), but also contains much new and original material by more than 100 of the leading biblical scholars of Europe. Each article is signed and contains a bibliography. "Best work of its kind on the market" (*Catholic Biblical Quarterly*, XXXV [January, 1969], p. 95).

B102   Léon-Dufour, Xavier, ed. **Dictionary of Biblical Theology.** 2nd. ed., rev. and enl. Trans. under the direction of P. Joseph Cahill. Revisions and new articles trans. by E. M. Stewart. New York, Seabury, 1973. xxxii, 712p. LC 73-6437. ISBN 0-8164-1146-8.

Written from a theological point of view. Such topics as grace, death and election are explained in the light of the Old and New Testaments in moderately long articles which have been subdivided by subject. Respected by scholars of all denominations, this work was hailed as coming from "the best of French-speaking exegetes both in France and other countries," and as "a truly admirable work deserving translation into other languages" (*Catholic Biblical Quarterly*, XXIV [October, 1962], p. 443). The second edition is based on the 1968 French edition. Each article has been thoroughly revised and forty new articles have been added. "An excellent tool for synthesizing Biblical thought" (Ibid., XXXVI [July, 1974], p. 415).

B103 Léon-Dufour, Xavier. **Dictionary of the New Testament.** Trans. from the 2nd. rev. French ed. by Terence Pendergast. New York, Harper and Row, 1980. 458p. LC 79-3004. ISBN 0-06-062100-1-X.

Defines over 1,000 words, terms, names and concepts found in the New Testament "which require an explanation, historical-geographic, archeological, literary, or theological" (Preface). The explanations are brief and are accompanied by references to the text. A 51-page introduction gives an overview of the New Testament world. Index of Greek Words. "The text manages to balance thoroughness of detail with readability" (*Catholic Biblican Quarterly*, XLIV [January, 1982], p. 151).

B104 McKenzie, John Lawrence. **Dictionary of the Bible.** Milwaukee, Bruce Pub. Co., 1965. xviii, 954p. il. LC 65-26691.

Like Léon-Dufour (B102) this work is theological rather than factual in emphasis. It has been recommended especially for the theological content of its articles and the individual coverage of each book of the Bible "despite its high price and some minor printing errors" (*Catholic Biblical Quarterly*, XXVIII [April, 1966], p. 153). It is the work of one man, but eight experts in the field checked his work. In addition to giving his own opinions in most articles, McKenzie also cites those of other authorities or indicates the trend of modern scholarship. No bibliographies are supplied for individual topics.

B105 Nolli, Gianfranco. **Lessico biblico.** Roma, Studium, 1970. 1161p. LC 71-487793.

A Biblical dictionary based on the Vulgate text. Covers persons, places and topics. Frequent references to and quotes from the text.

B106 Odelain, O. and R. Séguineau. **Dictionary of Proper Names and Places in the Bible.** Garden City, NY, Doubleday, 1981. xl, 479p. LC 79-8030. ISBN 0-385-14924-7.

Lists, defines, and gives biblical references to 3,500 proper names found in the *Jerusalem Bible.* Appendices contain numerous lists and chronologies.

B107 **Podręczna encyklopedia biblijna: dzielo zbiorowe pod red.** Eugeniusza Dąbrowskiego. Poznań, Ksieg. św. Wojciecha, 1959. 2 v. LC 62-29955.

According to the *Catholic Biblical Quarterly* this is "the first work of its kind in Polish literature; . . . with extensive bibliographies and some minor errors; . . . but which must be considered monumental in that it was composed entirely by Polish scholarship" (XXIV [March, 1964], p. 193). Treats such topics as inspiration, history, textual criticism, individual books, biblical theology and archeology. Classified arrangement with an Index of Articles, but no analytical index.

B108 Richards, Hubert J. **ABC of the Bible.** Milwaukee, Bruce Pub. Co., 1967. 216p. LC 67-30413.

An attempt to "put the findings of modern biblical scholarship at the disposal of those who might be discouraged by an overabundance of technical detail" (Foreword). The material was drawn largely from *Virtue's Catholic Encyclopedia* (see A108) and covers biblical "history, geography, literary forms, and theological terms pertinent to the Bible without all the paraphernalia of scholarship. . . . A most helpful dictionary" (*America*, CXIX [December 7, 1968], p. 600). No bibliography.

B109   Rolla, Armando, ed. **Enciclopedia della Bibbia**. Torino, Elle Di Ci, 1969-1971. 6 v.

An Italian revision and translation of the Spanish *Enciclopedia de la Biblia* (Barcelona, Garriga, 1963). Contains moderately long signed articles including proper names, with bibliographies. Handsomely bound and illustrated. (*Estudios Biblicos*, XXXIII [1964], pp. 335-38).

B110   Rouet, Albert. **A Short Dictionary of the New Testament**. New York, Paulist Press, 1982. 177p. LC 81-82435. ISBN 0-8091-2400-9.

The thirty-three articles in this brief work "help the reader of the New Testament rediscover the environment which shaped the lives of the people of that time" (Introduction). No bibliographies. An index would be useful.

B111   Spadafora, Francesco. **Dizionario biblico**. 3. ed. Riv. ed ampliata. Roma, Editrice Studium, 1963. xviii, 658p. LC 67-117932.

Contains brief signed articles with bibliographies by 27 Italian biblical scholars.

B112   Staudacher, Joseph M. **Lector's Guide to Biblical Pronunciations**. Huntington, IN, Our Sunday Visitor, 1975. 72p. LC 75-14609. ISBN 0-8797-3773-5.

A guide to the pronunciation of some 800 difficult place names that appear in the readings used at Mass. Pronunciations are indicated by a simple system of respelling explained in the introduction.

B113   Vigouroux, Fulcran Grégoire. **Dictionnaire de la Bible, contenant tous les noms de personnes, de lieux, de plantes, d'animaux mentionnés dans les Saintes Écritures, les questions théologiques, archéologiques.** Publié par F. Vigoroux avec le concours d'un grand nombre de collaborateurs. Paris, Letouzey et Ané, 1907-12. 5 v. il. LC 10-20843.

B114   Vigouroux, Fulcran Grégoire. **Dictionnaire de la Bible, contenant tous les noms de personnes, de lieux, de plantes, d'animaux mentionnés dan les Saintes Écritures, les questions théologiques, archéologiques. Supplément.** Publiés sous la direction de Louis Pirot avec le concours de nombreux collaborateurs. 1926- . v.

The largest, most comprehensive and scholarly Catholic biblical encyclopedia; now largely out of favor with scholars, this work was begun in 1907 under the editorship of Vigouroux, a professor of Scripture at Saint Sulpice and the *Institute Catholique* at Paris, the "bulk of whose work was apologetical, largely concerned with defending the Bible's historicity." Yet, according to Chirico, "conservative as he was in temperament, he was open to new currents in biblical studies" (Peter F. Chirico, "Vigouroux," *New Catholic Encyclopedia*, XIV, p. 668).

In addition to the standard topics found in biblical encyclopedias—names of persons, places, plants and animals, and theological, historical and archeological topics—this monumental work includes biographical and critical articles on biblical scholars, bibliographies of their works and criticism of them.

The work had become so outdated as early as 1928, when Pirot became editor, that he abandoned plans for a revision and began issuing a *Supplément*, still in progress, of the same proportion as the original work. Upon the death of Pirot, André Robert became editor, and he in turn was replaced by H. Cazelles in 1956. Methods and emphasis in scriptural scholarship have been changing so rapidly in the last few decades that most of the *Supplément* is now in need of a revision, but it must still be considered a work "indispensable to the biblical scholar" (Fitzmyer [B63], p. 73).

B115   Vincent, Albert Léopold. **Lexique biblique. Horssérie de la collection "Bible et vie chrétienne."** Tournai, Casterman, 1961. xii. 472p. LC 63-45648.

Very brief entries for names and topics with references to the text.

Commentaries

Biblical commentaries differ from the encyclopedias and dictionaries not so much in content as in arrangement. Usually they are arranged in the order of the books of the Bible and in some cases (*The Anchor Bible* [B116] and the *Old* and *New Testament Reading Guides* [B124, B125]) they follow the text line by line. *The Jerome Biblical Commentary* (B121) and *A New Catholic Commentary on Holy Scripture* (B121) are both excellent, up-to-date, one-volume commentaries.

B116   **The Anchor Bible.** Intro., translation, and notes. Garden City, NY, Double-day, 1964- . v. LC 64-55388.

An interfaith venture on the part of a group of Catholics, Protestants and Jews. Thirty-eight volumes containing a new translation and extensive commentary are projected. Some bibliography is supplied. The opinions expressed are considered "up-to-date, yet marked by scholarly restraint" (*Cross Currents*, XV [Summer, 1965], p. 306).

B117   Brown, Raymond Edward. **The Jerome Biblical Commentary.** Ed. by Raymond Brown, Joseph A. Fitzmyer, and Ronald E. Murphy. Englewood Cliffs, NJ, Prentice Hall, 1968. 2 v. in 1. LC 68-9140.

The first section or "volume" deals with each of the books of the Old Testament giving history, outlines and a very detailed commentary teeming with bibliographical references. The second section does the same for the New Testament and contains fifteen additional studies on general biblical topics. *Catholic Biblical Quarterly* termed this a "magnificent, monumental . . . commentary on the Bible . . . a successful blending of the contributions of fifty scholars into a moderate, modern, intelligently critical, comprehensively balanced companion to the Bible" (XXXI [July, 1969], p. 405). The reviewer goes on, however, to criticize some sections for bland consensus scholarship and one-sidedness (pp. 407-08). Index of subjects and persons, but not of the bibliographies.

B118   Knox, Ronald Arbuthnott. **A New Testament Commentary for English Readers.** London, Burns, Oates and Washbourne, 1953-56. 3 v. LC 54-34236.

Volume 1 covers the Gospels; 2, the Acts and St. Paul; 3, the other epistles and the Apocalypse. The commentary is meant to be used in conjunction with Knox's translation of the New Testament (B46). It is aimed at the layman, not the biblical scholar. "A clear and succinct explanation of the text . . . that makes it easy and pleasant reading" (*Catholic Biblical Quarterly*, XVII [July, 1955], p. 521). Running titles help to locate specific topics or incidents. Each volume has an index.

B119   McEleney, Neil J., ed. **Pamphlet Bible Series: A Commentary and Complete Text of the Old and New Testaments**. New York, Paulist Press, 1960-71. 46 v. LC 60-9284.

The text used is the Confraternity Edition. Commentary is printed in the front of each pamphlet followed by the text. There are also quizzes on the commentary and on the text in each volume. "Reviewers have commented on the bizarre illustrations, wide margins and paucity of commentary compared with the price ... but as for the quality of the commentaries, the list of eminent contributors vouches for their excellence" (*Catholic Biblical Quarterly* XXIV [April, 1962], p. 237).

B120   McKenzie, John Lawrence, ed. **New Testament for Spiritual Reading**. New York, Herder and Herder, 1969-71. 25 v.

The titles in this series were translated from the German *Geistliche Schrift-lesung* originally edited by Wolfgang Trilling. "The books are not commentaries in the learned sense of the word, nor introductions, nor critical works and were not written for the specialist, though they will have much to say to him" (*Clergy Review*, LV [May, 1970], p. 414). Contains text and commentary.

B121   **A New Catholic Commentary on Holy Scripture**. Reginald C. Fuller, gen. ed.; Leonard Johnston, Old Testament ed.; Conleth Kearns, New Testament ed.; with a Foreword by the Cardinal Archbishop of Westminster. London, Nashville, Nelson, 1969. xix, 1377p. il. LC 79-108360. ISBN 0-17-122010-2.

A thorough revision of *A Catholic Commentary on Holy Scripture* (New York, Nelson, 1953). There is a commentary for each book of the Bible as well as 30 other articles on specific topics. Each article and commentary contains bibliographical notes. This work is largely the product of British Catholic scholars (although there are some American contributors), whereas the *Jerome Biblical Commentary* (B117) is primarily an American work. "The varying treatment of topics or of the interpretation of individual books found in these two great achievements will enrich our common Catholic understanding of the Bible" (*America*, CXXIII [November 21, 1970], p. 437). A very detailed index adds to the reference value of this work.

B122   **New Testament Message: A Biblical-Theological Commentary**. Wilfred Harrington, O.P. and Donald Senior, C.P., editors. Wilmington, DE, M. Glazier, 1979-81. 22 v. ISBN 0-89453-124-7.

In the first volume of this series, *Interpreting the New Testament*, the editor explains various forms of literary and biblical criticism. The subsequent volumes, each by a Catholic author, deal with an individual book or part of a book of the New Testament. The complete text of the N.T. is not supplied. William Heidt severely criticized this series for its lack of Catholic sources in the bibliographies and other lapses from orthodoxy. (*Homiletic and Pastoral Review*, LXXXI [April, 1981], pp. 75-79).

B123   **Old Testament Message: A Biblical-Theological Commentary.** Carroll
        Stuhlmueller, C.P. and Martin McNamara, M.S.C., editors. Wilmington, DE, M.
        Glazier, 1981-84. 23 v. ISBN 0-89453-235-9.

        The first volume of this series is titled *Interpreting the Old Testament: A
        Practical Guide* in which principles of literary, biblical and other types of
        criticism are explained. Each subsequent volume deals with a book or group of
        books of the Old Testament in a popular style with bibliographies for each book.
        The complete text is not given. "While to be commended for popular instruction,
        it can occasionally result in a too-simple approach. However, the occasions,
        happily, are few" (*Clergy Review*, LXVIII [June, 1983], p. 222).

B124   **New Testament Reading Guide.** Collegeville, MN, Liturgical Press, 1960.
        14 v.

B125   **Old Testament Reading Guide.** Collegeville, MN, Liturgical Press, 1965- . v.
        il. LC 65-2824.

        A series of pamphlets, each devoted to a book or group of books of the
        Bible; considered "the finest available in English for laymen" (Fitzmyer, [B63], p.
        53). Where available, the Confraternity text is used, accompanied by an
        introduction and extensive commentary in the form of notes. No bibliography or
        index is provided, but the "Review Aids" and "Discussion Topics" are helpful
        features.

B126   Robert, André. **Guide to the Bible: An Introduction to the Study of Holy
        Scripture.** Pub. under the direction of A. Robert and A. Tricot. 2nd. ed.
        rev. and enl. Trans. by Edward P. Arbez and Martin R. P. McGuire. Paris,
        New York, Desclée Co., 1960- . v. LC 60-50336. (Trans. of *Initiation
        biblique*.)

        To be completed in two volumes. "A very useful manual for the student"
        (Fitzmyer [B63], p. 53). Attempts to describe the chief problems and
        the present state of the science of exegesis and to point out the direction
        of current research. Rich in bibliography. Index.

B127   Robert, André. **Introduction to the New Testament.** Ed. by A. Robert
        and A. Feuillet. Trans. from the French by Patrick W. Skehan and others.
        New York, Desclée, 1965. xviii, 912p. il. LC 65-15631.

B128   Robert, André. **Introduction to the Old Testament.** 1968. xxv, 650p.
        LC 68-25351. (First published as *Introduction à la Bible*, 1954-62.)

        The contributors are well known French Biblical scholars, each of whom
        has written an essay and bibliography on some aspect of Biblical studies—
        political, religious, and literary backgrounds or commentaries on parts of
        the Bible. "Though not intended for a strictly scholarly audience, this
        is the best informed and most modern Catholic introduction to the O.T.
        and N.Y." (Fitzmyer [B63], p. 53). The bibliographies have been undated
        and adapted for the English speaking reader. Index of authors and subjects.

B129   Wikenhauser, Alfred. **New Testament Introduction.** Trans. by Joseph Cun-
        ningham. New York, Herder and Herder, 1958. 579p. LC 58-5870. (German
        title: *Einleitung in das Neue Testament*.)

Covers each of the books of the New Testament as well as such topics as textual origins, canonicity, history and sources of study; each section is preceded by a bibliography. *Theological Studies* had some criticism of the indexes of persons and subjects but recommended the work highly for teachers and priests (XX [March, 1959], pp. 114-16).

B130   Woods, Ralph Louis, ed. **The Catholic Companion to the Bible.** Philadelphia, Lippincott, 1956. 313p. LC 56-6416.

Contains brief excerpts from the writings of well over 100 saints, theologians and scholars grouped under three broad categories: "The Nature, Value and Authority of the Bible," "The Old Testament," and "The New Testament." "An erudite and easy to read volume" (*Catholic Biblical Quarterly*, XVIII [October, 1956], p. 468). An author index gives references to the complete works from which the excerpts were taken.

Atlases

B131   Grollenberg, Luc H. **Atlas of the Bible.** Trans. and ed. by Joyce M. H. Reid and H. H. Rowley. London, Nelson, 1957. 165p. LC 58-31964. (First published in Dutch as *Atlas van de Bijbel*.)

Contains thirty-five colored maps and countless photographs, but "the text is not as highly esteemed as that of the Westminster Atlas" (Fitzmyer [B63], p. 94). Valuable for its recentness, geographical index and treatment of the Dead Sea Scrolls.

B132   Grollenberg, Luc H. **Shorter Atlas of the Bible.** Trans. by Mary F. Hedlund. Edinburgh. T. Nelson, 1959. 196p. LC 60-1540.

Contains a revised text but fewer maps and photographs.

B133   Lemaire, Paulin and Donato Baldi. **Atlas biblique: Histoire et Géographie de la Bible.** Louvain, Éditions du Mont César, 1960. 343p.

Covers twenty periods of Bible history with maps, illustrations, charts and text. Geographical, Greek, Latin, subject and other indexes. "Grollenberg's *Atlas* (B131) makes its maps and history serve the Bible, whereas this atlas has a strong tendency to make Bible serve its maps and history" (*Études*, CCCXIII [April, 1962], p. 123).

B134   Seraphin, Eugene William, and Jerome A. Kelly. **Maps of the Land of Christ, the Holy Places of Scripture.** Correlated with the Life of Christ by Isidore O'Brien. Rev. ed. Paterson, NJ, St. Anthony Guild Press, 1947. vi, 58p. il. LC 48-10107.

Twenty maps illustrating the life of Christ and "Points of Special Interest" are contained in this small work. The plates are fair but not exceptional by today's standards. Numerous charts and tables are provided covering parables, miracles and geographical information.

PATROLOGY

All Christian writers, orthodox and heretical, up to Gregory the Great (d. 604), or Isidore of Seville (d. 636) in the West and to John Damascene (d. 749) in the East are considered Fathers of the Church according to Quasten (*Patrology* [B143], v. 1., p. 1). Actually the dates vary with almost each authority, but authors after the ninth centruy are usually not termed Fathers. Patristical writings are important sources of Christian theology and philosophy for both Catholics and Protestants.

The most important patristical reference works are the texts themselves. These have been published in several monumental collections, the most complete but unsatisfactory of which is that by Abbé Jacques Migne (B169-B173). Numbering nearly 400 volumes, this series contains the same kinds of typographical errors found in his *Encyclopédie théologique* (A122).

In 1953, however, the first volume of a projected replacement for Migne appeared: *Corpus Christianorum: Series Latina* (B158-B162); and in 1977 the first volume of the *Series Graeca* (B158) was published. Edited by the Benedictine monks of St. Peter's Abbey, Belgium, these series promise to be the most accurate and complete of the many collections attempted throughout the history of the Church.

There are many fine guides to the literature of the Fathers among which Quasten's (B143) and Altaner's (B135) stand out for their reference value and recency.

Guides

B135   Altaner, Berthold. **Patrology**. Trans. by Hilda C. Graef. New York, Herder and Herder, 1960. xxiv, 659p. LC 58-5869.

A guide to patristic literature, containing bio-bibliographies of patristic writers, history and bibliography of anonymous works, notes on editions of famous works, and historical background of the age. Translated into French, Spanish and Italian as well as English. "By all odds the most complete and adequate coverage of the patristic field within the capacity of one tidy volume" (*American Ecclesiastical Review*, CXXIV [April, 1951], p. 315). A ninth German edition was published in 1980; (*Patrologie: Leben, Schriften und Lehre der Kirchenväter*. Freiburg, Basel, Herder, 1980. xxii, 672p).

B136   Bardenhewer, Otto. **Geschichte der altkirchlichen Literatur**. Freiburg, Herder, 1913-32. 5 v. LC 31-29064.

Includes Eastern and Western literature up to the end of the fifth century; this is a "work of exceptional critical value illustrating a wide range of patristical erudition and cautious application of the best principles of modern criticism. . . . It is a court of final reference in its special province" (*Catholic World*, LXXVII [April, 1903], p. 117-18). Each chapter is followed by an extensive bibliography. Index in each volume; no general index.

B137   Bardenhewer, Otto. **Patrology: the Lives and Works of the Fathers of the Church**. Trans. from the 2nd. ed. by Thomas J. Shahan. St. Louis, Herder, 1908. xvii, 680p. LC 12-35566.

Now quite out of date in its bibliographies but still an important work for its concise and critical biographies and the detailed information given on spurious and apocryphal works. In its day it was praised by "eminent patristic scholars, both for its accurate treatment of its subject and for the fullness of its bibliographies" (*America*, II [November 27, 1904], p. 182).

B138   Cayre, Fulbert. **Patrologie et histoire de la théologie.** 4. éd. Paris, Société de S. Jean L'Evangeliste, 1944-47. 3 v.

A work valuable for its comprehensiveness in respect both to the number of authors and the length of the period covered—down to St. Francis de Sales (d. 1622). Designed for use by seminarians, it covers the history of dogma and positive theology and the history and principles of spirituality in addition to patristics. The arrangement is bio-bibliographical covering each author in chronological order.

B139   Labriolle, Pierre Champagna de. **Histoire de la littérature latine chrétienne.** 3. éd. rev. et augm. par Gustav Bardy. Paris, Belles Lettres, 1947. 2 v. (Collection d'Études anciennes).

See annotation (B140).

B140   Labriolle, Pierre Champagna de. **History and Literature of Christianity from Tertullian to Boethius.** Trans. from the French by Herbert Wilson; with an introductory foreword by His Eminence Cardinal Gasquet. New York, A. A. Knopf, 1924. xxiii, 555p. LC 25-4946.

A scholarly work covering the history of Christian literature down to the end of the sixth century. Each chapter is preceded by a critical bibliographical essay. The studies of authors go into great detail on the influences shaping their work, their influence on others, their lives and an analysis of their works. The work is generally respected, but *America* faulted this translation for "many serious errors" (XXXIII [August 22, 1925], p. 452). Index and tables.

B141   Ortiz de Urbina, Ignacio. **Patrologia syriaca.** Romae, Pont. Institutum Orientalium Studiorum, 1958. 250p.

Covers heretical, orthodox, anonymous and some post-patristic writers giving detailed bio-bibliographies for each.

B142   Puech, Aimé. **Histoire de la littérature grecque chrétienne depuis les origines jusqu'à la fin du ive siècle.** Paris, Société d'édition "Les Belles Lettres," 1928-30. 3 v. (Collection d'études anciennes.) LC 30-29051.

Planned as a companion volume to Labriolle's history of Latin literature (B139, B140) and executed in the same style.

B143   Quasten, Johannes and Angelo di Berardino. **Patrology**. Westminster, MD, Christian Classics, Inc., 1983-86. 4 v. LC 83-72018.
V.1.   The beginnings of Patristic Literature, by Johannes Quasten. ISBN 0-8706-1084-8.
V.2.   The Ante-Nicene Literature after Irenaeus, by Johannes Quasten. ISBN 0-8706-1085-6.
V.3.   The Golden Age of Greek Patristic Literature from the Council of Nicaea to the Council of Chalcedon, by Johannes Quasten. ISBN 0-8706-1086-4.
V.4.   The Golden Age of Latin Patristic Literature from the Council of Nicea [*sic*] to the Council of Chalcedon, by Angelo de Berardino. ISBN 0-8706-1126-7.

Originally published in English, this work has appeared in German, Italian and French translations. In the English version, much emphasis is put on indicating the best modern translations of the authors in question. The work consists of bio-bibliographical essays on each of the Fathers, including anonymous writers, a general bibliographical introduction and essays on the history and background of the period. With the appearance of the first volume in 1950, the *Catholic Library World* remarked: "This is a monumental work of detailed scholarship giving new dimensions to the two series currently being published in this country: *The Fathers of the Church* (B155) and *Ancient Christian Writers* (B153). Invaluable for bibliographical data and indispensable for libraries with patristic holdings"(XXII [November, 1951], p. 60).

Bibliography

B144   **Bibliographia patristica: Internationale patristische Bibliographie.** Hrsg. von W. Scheemelcher. Berlin, De Gruyter, 1956- . v. Annual. LC 61-31447.

A classified listing of books and articles with references to book reviews compiled by scholars of all faiths. Over 1,000 items per year are covered. Volume one began with literature published from 1956. Author indexes. No annotations.

B145   **Bibliographia patristica: Internationale patristische Bibliographie. Supplementum 1- .** Berlin, W. de Gruyter, 1980- . Irregular. Dupp. 1. Voces: Eine Bibliographie zu Wörten and Begriffen aus der Patristik (1918-1978).

A bibliography of studies of Greek and Latin words found in the Fathers. Indexes.

B146   **Bulletin d' ancienne littérature chrétienne latine.** Maredsous, Belgium, Abbaye de Maredsous, 1921-38. 2 v. LC 38-25988.

Books and articles are listed in two sections: biblical, and non-biblical literature. Section Two covers authors up to the 12th century in chronological order. Indexes.

B147   Crouzel, Henri. **Bibliographie critique d'Origène**. Publié avec le concours du Centre national de la recherche scientifique de France. Le Haye, Nijhoff, 1971. 685p. (Instrumenta Patristica, 8A.) LC 72-322809.

B148   Crouzel, Henri. **Bibliographie critique d'Origeñe. Supplément.** Steenbrugis, in Abbatia Sancti Petri; Hagae Comitis Martinus Nijhoff, 1982- . v. (Instrumenta Patristica, 8A.)

Works about Origen are listed chronologically with author and subject indexes.

Indexes

B149   Dekkers, Eligius. **Clavis patrum latinorum, qua in novum Corpus christianorum edendum optimas quasque scriptorum recensiones a Tertulliano ad Bedam commode recludit Eilgius Dekkers, opera usus qua rem praeparavit et iuvit Aemilius Garr.** Editio altera, aucta et emendata. Steenbrugis, In Abbatia Sancti Petri, 1961. xxvii, 640p. (Sacris erudiri, 3.2).

        A key to the confusing array of patristic editions both in the large collections listed below and in other sources. Four approaches are given: the chronological, in the main body of the work; by names of authors and works; by subjects; and by opening words. Brief biographies are given for important authors with bibliographies arranged by subject. This work is a companion to the *Corpus Christianorum: Series Latina* (B159) for which it serves as a catalog or prospectus.

B150   Geerard, Maurice. **Clavis patrum graecorum.** Turnhout, Brepols, 1974- . v. LC 79-11461.

        A guide to the Greek patristic literature from the ante-Nicene fathers to John of Damascene including synodal and conciliar literature. Bibliographical information and references to commentaries are provided for each item. This work, like Dekkers (B149), is a companion or prospectus for the *Corpus Christianorum* (B158), but for the Greek series. Projected in four volumes; volume four will be a series of indexes and tables.

B151   Kraft, H. **Clavis patrum apostolicorum; catalogum vocum in libris patrum qui dicuntur apostolici non raro occurrentium** adiuvante Ursula Früchtel congressit, contulit conscriptsit Henricus Kraft. Munich, Kösel Verlag, 1963. viii, 501p. LC 66-48039.

        A concordance to the writings of the Greek and Latin Fathers. Each writer is listed alphabetically and followed by a list of words for which definitions are given in Latin for Greek terms and German for Latin terms. Citations to sources are given. There is a list of sources on p. viii.

B152   **Biblia patristica: index des citations et allusions bibliques dans la littérature patristique.** Centre d'analyse et de documentation patristiques, équipe de recherche associée au Centre national de la recherche scientifique, J. Allenbach ... et al. Paris, Éditions du Centre national de la recherche scientifique, 1975-1980, 3 v. LC 75-405618. ISBN 2-222-01802-1.
        Vol. 1. Des origines à Clément d'Alexandrie et Tertullien.
        Vol. 2. Le troisième siècle, Origène excepté.
        Vol. 3. Origène.

        An exhaustive verse by verse index of citations to the use of each text in the works of the Fathers.

Collections

English Language

B153   **Ancient Christian Writers: The Works of the Fathers in Translation.** Ramsey, NJ, Paulist Press, 1946- . v. LC 48-22835. ISSN 0066-1597.

A bit more scholarly in its approach than *The Fathers of the Church* (B155) both in its introductions and copious notes. According to *Theological Studies,* the series "measures up in a high degree to the aims stated in the general introduction—philological precision and theological understanding" (LXXXI [March, 1947], p. 150-51). Bibliographies of other modern translations in a number of languages are also provided.

B154   **The Ante-Nicene Fathers: Translations of the Writings of the Fathers down to A.D. 325.** The Rev. Alexander Roberts and James Donaldson, editors. New York, C. Scribner's, 1899-1900. 10 v. LC 38-33157.

Contains writings of the Fathers who lived before the Council of Nice, 325. Many explanatory notes and scriptural references. Subject index in each volume. "Indispensable in the library of every scholarly Catholic" (*Catholic World*, CXXIII July, [1926], pp. 562-63). General index in vol. 9.

B155   **The Fathers of the Church: A New Translation.** Washington, DC, Catholic University of America Press, 1947- . v. LC 48-14069

Projected in 100 volumes. While it does provide some bibliography it is "non technical . . . and footnotes are few" (*America*, LXXVIII [November 1, 1947], p. 134). There is an introduction to each volume, a general index and a scriptural index. This series and *Ancient Christian Writers* (B153) are the only 20th century attempts of a comprehensive nature to render the writings of the Fathers into contemporary English and are therefore, important not only to Catholic scholars, but to English speaking Christians of all denominations. Originally this work was published by the Catholic University of America, but in 1978 editorial responsibility was assumed by Consortium Books.

B156   **A Select Library of Nicene and Post-Nicene Fathers of the Christian Church.** Ed. by Philip Schaff in connection with a number of patristic scholars of Europe and America. New York, The Christian Literature Company, 1887-94. 14 v. LC 35-25976.

B157   **A Select Library of Nicene and Post-Nicene Fathers of the Christian Church. Second Series.** Trans. into English with prolegomena and explanatory notes under the editorial supervision of Philip Schaff . . . and Henry Wace. 1890-1900. 14 v. LC 1-17019.

Covers from St. Augustine to Gregory the Great, including the canons and decrees of the "seven ecumenical councils of the undivided Church." Each work is indexed.

Original and Other Languages

B158   **Corpus christianorum: Series graeca.** Turnhout, Brepols, 1977- . v.

B159   **Corpus christianorum: Series latina.** Turnhout, Brepols, 1953- . v.

B160   **Corpus christianorum: Continuatio mediaevalis.** Turnhout, Brepols, 1966- . v.

B161   **Corpus christianorum: Series apocryphorum.** Turnhout, Brepols, 1983- . v.

B162   **Corpus christianorum: Instrumenta lexicologica latina.** Turnhout, Brepols, 1982- . v.

"Designed to supplant Migne's *Patrologia* (B169-173) with new critical texts of the best of those currently extant; the series follows the critical catalogue or prospectus of E. Dekker's *Clavis patrum latinorum* (B149)" (Library of Congress).

Almost thirty years ago, the Benedictine monks of St. Peter's Abbey, Steenbrugge, Belgium, in collaboration with the Brepols publishing firm, announced definite plans for "the issue . . . of a new collection of all early Christian texts, according to the best existing editions, more or less on the lines laid down by Dom Pitra and the Abbé Migne. " This New Migne, stretching to the front edge of the Carolingian Renaissance and promising the best possible critical edition of every early Christian text (not only works specifically patristic, but also conciliar, hagiographical, and liturgical texts, burial inscriptions, diplomas, etc.) as well as pertinent non-Christian authors, was an audacious undertaking. But it was stimulated by an unsatisfactory situation, frustrating to student and scholar: some texts were out of print, others simply out of reach; even if obtainable, Migne (PL and PG), for all its value, was a century old; *Sources chrétiennes* was in its infancy, and its first volumes could not supply a Greek text; earlier volumes of both the Vienna corpus (B164) and the Berlin (B168) were beyond acquiring, and even these admirable series are far from complete and are not in every instance satisfactory.

A division into three series—Latin, Greek, and Oriental—was considered imperative. The Latin series would be the first to see the light of day, beginning in 1951 (such was the hope; the first volume appeared in 1953), with ten years thought sufficient for the publication of the contemplated 120 volumes from Tertullian to Bede (the estimate of volumes was later revised to 160, then to 175, again to 180). The projected rate of publication has not been maintained. In the twenty-four years between 1953 and the end of 1976, 85 volumes have appeared (an average of 3.5 a year) and the enumeration of the volumes (e.g., 162, 162A, 162B) indicates that the total number of Latin volumes will exceed 200.

Happily, the general editors of CC have decided to launch the Greek series without awaiting the termination of the Latin. Once again it is a question of bringing together critical editions now scattered far and wide and of filling the lacunae of unedited and inadequately edited texts. A preliminary task was indispensable: to establish a *Clavis patrum Graecorum*, a kind of master plan corresponding to the *Clavis patrum Latinorum* (B149), the remarkable 640-page inventory of Latin ecclesiastical writers from Tertullian to Bede put together by Dom E. Dekkers. CPG's content and structure would stem from the same principles that commanded CPL: (1) list the patristic writings that have come down to us, including fragments; (2) mention for each text the most useful editions, with a special place for PG; (3) offer bibliographies on the tradition and establishment of the text; (4) list ancient translations, not only Latin but Syriac, Armenian, Georgian, Coptic, and Arabic; (5) indicate questionable authenticity. At least three content-volumes are envisaged. Only the second has appeared, by Maurice Geerard, *Scriptores saeculi IV* (B150), a 708-page volume on the writers from Alexander of Alexandria to John Chrysostom; the third (fifth to eighth centuries) is in the press, the first (ante-Nicene) is in progress. A fourth volume may well be needed, to handle the Byzantine literature from the ninth to the fifteenth centuries. An indices-initia-tabulae volume is expected to conclude the Clavis. (Walter J. Burghardt, [*Theological Studies* XXXVIII (December, 1977), pp. 765-67].

B163   **Corpus scriptorum christianorum orientalium**, curantibus I. B. Chabot, I. Guidi, H. Hyvernat, B. Carra de Vaux, I. Forget, et A. Vaschalde. Louvain, Secretariat du Corpus S. C. O., 1903- . v. LC 37-14334.

A monumental collection expected to number hundreds of volumes, this series covers Syriac, Coptic, Ethiopic, Arabian and Armenian texts, printed in their original languages and a Latin or modern language translation. Introduction, notes and bibliographies accompany each text. When it is completed, this series will be a "monument to Catholic scholarship" (*America*, X [March 7, 1914], p. 525).

B164   **Corpus scriptorum ecclesiasticorum latinorum.** Editum consilio et impensis Academiae litterarum caesareae vindobonensis. Vindobonae, C. Geroldi, 1866- . v. LC 7-26284.

The "Vienna Corpus," which when completed will cover up to the end of the seventh century. Each text is accompanied by lengthy introductions, bibliographical notes and indexes of names, places and subjects.

B165   Glorieux, Palémon. **Pour revaloriser Migne: tables rectificatives.** Lille, Facultés Catholiques, 1952. 82p. (Cahier Supplémentaire aux melanges de science religieuse, 9.) LC 60-32633.

Supplies corrections as to the authorship of some of the works reprinted in Migne (B169) *Series Latina.*

B166   Graffin, René. **Patrologia orientalis.** Paris, Firmin-Didot, 1907-49. 26 v.

An older collection covering the same languages as the C.S.C.O. but on a much more selective basis. French translations are given along with the original versions. Both Catholic and Protestant scholars contributed to this collection. Each item is indexed. Intended to complement Migne.

B167   Graffin, René. **Patrologia syriaca complectens opera omnia SS. patrum, doctorum scriptorumque catholicorum quibus accedunt aliorum acatholicorum auctorum scripta quae ad res ecclesiasticas pertinent quotquot syriace supersunt, secundum codices praesertium londinenses, parisienses, vaticanos.** Parisiis, Firmin-Didot, 1894-1926. 3 v. LC 38-33826.

Includes writers up to the year A.D. 320. The texts are in Syriac and Latin, and a Lexicon (concordance) is printed in volume three. Index. Also designed to complement Migne.

B168   **Die grieschischen christlichen Schriftsteller der ersten drei Jahrhunderte.** Berlin, Akademie Verlag, 1897- . v.

Covers writers after the third century as well. Introductions and indexes are in German and texts in Greek. Regarding this series and the C.S.E.L. (B164) Quasten observed: "To the Academies of Vienna and Berlin falls the honor of having started two series of patristic writings that endeavor to combine philological accuracy and completeness" (*Patrology* [B143], v. 1, p. 14).

B169   Migne, Jacques Paul. **Patrologiae cursus completus, seu bibliotheca universalis omnium SS. patrum, doctorum, scriptorumque ecclesiasticorum. Series latina,** a tertulliano ad Innocentum III. Parisiis, Migne, 1844-80. 221 v.

B170   Migne, Jacques Paul. **Patrologiae cursus completus, seu bibliotheca universalis omnium SS. patrum, doctorum, scriptorumque ecclesiasticorum. Supplementum,** accurante Adalberto Hamman. Paris, Garnier, 1958- . v.

B171   Migne, Jacques Paul. **Patrologiae cursus completus, seu bibliotheca universalis omnium SS. patrum, doctorum, scriptorumque ecclesiasticorum. Series Graeca,** a S. Barnaba ad Photium. Parisiis, Migne, 1857-66. 161 v. in 166.

B172   Migne, Jacques Paul. **Patrologiae cursus completus, seu bibliotheca universalis omnium SS. patrum, doctorum, scriptorumque ecclesiasticorum. Series Graeca. Indices digessit Fernandus Cavallera.** Parisiis, Garnier, 1912. LC 18-10316.

B173   Migne, Jacques Paul. **Patrologiae cursus completus, seu bibliotheca universalis omnium SS. patrum, doctorum, scriptorumque ecclesiasticorum. Series Graeca. Index locupletissimus.** Theodorus Hopfner. Paris, Geuthner, 1928-39. 2 v.

Still the most comprehensive collection of patristic texts. Greek texts are accompanied by Latin translations. This work contains typographical errors similar to those described in the *Encyclopédie théologique* (A122) and was sometimes based on uncritical editions of the originals. So bad are the misprints that Quasten recommends using the older editions Migne reprinted (*Patrology* [B143], v.1, p.1).

B174   Pitra, Jean Baptiste, Cardinal. **Spicilegium solesmense complectens sanctorum patrum scriptorumque ecclesiasticorum anecdota hactenus opera, selecta e graecis orientalibusque et latinis codicibus.** Graz, Akademische Druck-U. Verlagsanstalt, 1962-63. 4 v.

Contains the texts of some Greek and Latin writings not found in the above works. Hymns, the writings of some pagan philosophers and works on Greek canon law are included along with the usual fare. Each volume is indexed for subjects, names and definitions of terms.

B175   Pitra, Jean Baptiste, Cardinal. **Analecta sacra spicilegio solesmensi parata.** Farnborough, Gregg, 1966. 4 v. LC 67-101479.

        A continuation of (B132) containing Greek hymns, writings of Ante-Nicene Fathers, etc. Indexes in each volume.

B176   **Sources chrétienne.** Directeurs-fondateurs: H. DeLubac, S. J. et J. Danielou, S. J. Paris, Les Editions du Cerf, 1942- . v.

        A series of individual texts, some of which have not appeared elsewhere. Original versions are given along with French translations. Introductions, notes, and indexes are provided.

Dictionaries

B177   Blaise, Albert. **Dictionnaire latin français des auteurs chrétiens.** Revu spécialment pour le vocabulaire théologie par Henri Chirat. Strasbourg, Le Latin Chrétien, 1954. 865p. LC 55-23762.

        Covers non-classical words and meanings used from the first to the seventh centuries and is especially concerned with theological terms. Quotations with exact references are given to illustrate the definitions.

B178   Blaise, Albert. **Lexicon latinitatitis medii aevi: Praesertim ad res ecclesiasticas investigandas pertinens. Dictionnaire latin-francais des auteurs du Moyen-Âge.** Turnholti, Typographi Brepols, 1975. lxviii, 970p. LC 75-541872.

        A dictionary of terms used especially by Christian authors covering the "sciences ecclésiastiques" and scholastic philosophy. Citations from literature are given for important words.

B179   **Dizionario patristico e de antichità cristiane.** Diretto da Angelo Di Berardino. Casale Monferrato, Marietti, 1983- . v. LC 83-213006. ISBN 88-211-6706-2. Volume 1. A-Ful.

        Made up of many brief articles and some longer (4-5pp.). All articles contain bibliography. Covers both names and topics.

B180   **A Patristic Greek Lexicon.** Ed. by G. W. H. Lampe. Oxford, New York, Clarendon, 1976. xlviii, 1568p. LC 77-372171. ISBN 0-1986-4213-X.

        Provides meanings and history of theologically important words as used by the Fathers from the first to the ninth centuries, and includes words not so important but which have been inadequately treated in other Greek lexicons. Although criticized for not being a complete patristic dictionary in itself, the work is recognized as "A landmark in patristic scholarship" (*Theological Studies*, XXIV [September, 1963], p. 462).

B181   Souter, Alexander, comp. **A Glossary of Later Latin to 600 A.D.** Oxford, Clarendon Press, 1949. 454p. LC a50-7994.

        Contains definitions of Latin words and phrases that appeared from 180 to 600 A.D. which includes the writings of many Church Fathers. References to authors and works are provided.

DICTIONARIES AND ENCYCLOPEDIAS

While the *Lexikon für Theologie und Kirche* (B192) and the *Dictionnaire de théologie catholique* (B185) are not likely to be replaced either in scholarship or size, there are some newer theological dictionaries more adapted to current trends and, therefore, perhaps more useful. Chief among these are Rahner's *Sacramentum mundi*: An Encyclopedia of Theology (B197) and his *Dictionary of Theology* (B195) which, in addition to being up-to-date, are as scholarly as one could expect works of their size to be. *The New Dictionary of Theology* (B194) is a fine, new one-volume work.

B182   Bouyer, Louis. **Dictionary of Theology**. Trans. by Charles Underhill Quinn. New York, Desclée Co., 1965. xi, 470p. LC 66-13370.

Aims to "give precise definitions of theological terms and at the same time to provide a concise synthesis of Catholic doctrine in terms equally understandable to layman and the specialist" (Foreword). Bibliographical references are limited to Church documents, biblical texts, the *Summa* and one or two commentaries. *Commonweal* blamed it for deficiencies in cross references but compared it favorably to Rahner's *Dictionary of Theology* (B195) because of its objectivity (LXXXIII [February 25, 1966], p. 619).

B183   Bradley, John P., ed. **Encyclopedic Dictionary of Christian Doctrine**. Gastonia, NC, Good Will Publishers, 1970. 3 v. (The Catholic Layman's Library, v. 7-9.) LC 78-92779.

An attempt to present "the message of Christ" to the laity in the post-conciliar world. Articles are of moderate length (6 to 10pp.) with bibliographies. Very few biographical articles are included.

B184   **A Catholic Dictionary of Theology: A Work Projected with the Approval of the Catholic Hierarchy of England and Wales**. London, New York, Nelson, 1962- . v. LC 62-52257.

Still in progress and may run to four or five volumes; attempts to present "Catholic doctrines with the sources from which they are drawn in scripture and tradition; . . . not to enter into matters of Catholic discipline or canon law except where these have doctrinal importance" (Preface). Each article is signed and has an extensive bibliography in which English language works and translations predominate. The articles, ranging in length from one column to several pages, are readable but scholarly and documented. Longer articles are subdivided into numbered parts with an introductory section explaining the basis of the division. Volume one (A-Casuistry) appeared before the Second Vatican Council (1962-65), but the editors held up further publication until its close. In a review of the first volume, *America* said, "The quality of this work is so high and the need so great that one hesitates to note gaps" (CVII [January 26, 1963], p. 149), which the reviewer did, nevertheless.

B185   **Dictionnaire de théologie catholique contenant l'exposé des doctrines de la théologie catholique, leurs preuves et leur histoire**, commencé sous la direction de A. Vacant et E. Mangenot, continué sous celle de Amann avec le concours d'un grand nombre de collaborateurs. Paris, Letouzey et Ané, 1908-49. 15 v. LC A14-712.

B186   Dictionnaire de théologie catholique contenant l'exposé des doctrines de
        la théologie catholique, leurs preuves et leur histoire. Table analytique,
        t. 1-9, (A-L), 1929. 143p.

B187   Dictionnaire de théologie catholique contenant l'exposé des doctrines de la
        théologie catholique, leurs preuves et leur histoire. Tables générales, par
        Bernard Loth et Albert Michel. 1951-72. 3 v.

The largest and best known purely theological encyclopedia. Begun in 1904,
the main body of the work was completed in fifteen volumes in 1949. But
in 1951 the first fascicle of the *Tables générales* appeared, indexing and
cross referencing the information in the first fifteen volumes and containing
new articles and bibliographies. According to the Preface, "the purpose of
this work is to explain the doctrines of Catholic theology, their proofs and
their history." To do this, there are articles on all aspects of theology—
Catholic and non-Catholic; schools of theology; periods; countries; theologians; sects; and similar topics. Most of the articles are very long—some
virtually treatises done by several contributors—and contain extensive
bibliographies. Universally regarded as one of the most authoritative works
in its field, the *Dictionnaire* was reviewed almost fascicle by fascicle as it
appeared. It is listed in all standard bibliographies of reference works covering religion or history. *Theological Studies* described it as "an invaluable
reference work, proved to be so from its beginning" (XIX [December,
1958], p. 653-54).

B188   Exeler, Adolf and Georg Scherer, eds. **Glaubersinformation: Sachbuch zur
        Theologischen Erwachsenbildung.** Freiburg im Breisgau, Herder, 1971. 351p. LC
        72-312963.

Brief articles with cross references and bibliographies. No biography. Intended as
an aid in the theological education of adults. "Provides the elements of a sound
theological formation for laymen" (*Lumen Vitae*, XXVIII [March, 1973], p. 178).

B189   Fries, Heinrich. **Handbuch theologischer Grundbegriffe. Unter Mitarbeit
        zahlreicher Fachgelehrter.** München, Kösel-Verlag, 1962-63. 2 v. LC 64-
        33310.

Contains articles of several pages in length, many done by the same contributors who did the *Lexikon für Theologie und Kirche* (B192). The purpose
is to "elaborate fundamental theological concepts and describe their significance especially for Catholic theology" (Preface). Biblical origins, history,
relationships and current problems connected with these concepts are explained, and long bibliographies (mostly of German works) are supplied.
Theological Studies praised it for its conciseness, convenient size and price
compared to the *Lexikon* (XXIV [September, 1963], p. 480). Subject
index in volume two.

B190   Granat, Wincenty, ed. **Encyklopedia Katolika.** Lublin, Tow Naukowe
        Katolickiego Uniwersytetu Lubelskiego, 1973- . v. LC 75-562078.

A comprehensive theological encyclopedia including biography. Articles are of
moderate length (1 to 3p.) with extensive bibliographies. "An event in the
intellectual life of Poland ... The first time that such a work has been undertaken

in Poland (previous encyclopedias were based on translations) and by Polish
writers ... Catholic theology predominates, but the most recent thought of non-
Catholic theologians is presented" (*Journal of Ecumenical Studies*, XII [Summer,
1975], p. 415).

B191 LaBrosse, Olivier, Antonin-Marie Henry, and Phillippe Rouillard, eds.
Dictionnaire de la foi chrétienne. Paris, Éditions du Cerf, 1968. 2 v. LC
73-367698.

Volume one is an encyclopedia of very brief articles on persons and topics.
Volume two contains a series of chronological tables and lists dealing with
Church history, doctrines and documents. "Less substantial than Bouyer (B182)
and not as up-to-date, but the information in volume two makes the whole work
worthwhile" (*Études, CCC* [Janvier, 1969], p. 138).

B192 Lexikon für Theologie und Kirche: begründet von Michael Buchberger.
2., völlig neubearb. Augl., unter dem Protektorat von Michael Buchberger
und Eugen Seiterich; hrsg. von Josef Höfer und Karl Rahner. Freiburg,
Herder, 1957-67. 11 v. il. LC 58-41506.

B193 **Lexikon für Theologie und Kirche:** begründer von Michael Buchberger. 2., völlig
neubearb. Augl., unter dem Protektorat von Michael Buchberger und Eugen
Seiterich; hrsg. von Josef Höfer und Karl Rahner. **Supplement.** 1967-68. 3 v.

The best known German Catholic theological encyclopedia, recently revised
under the general editorship of Karl Rahner and Joseph Höfer. In many
short articles, and some long, this work covers theology, Church history,
non-Catholic religions and theology, canon law, liturgy, and philosophy, as
well as biographies of theologians and saints. "The contributors are all
outstanding authorities in their special fields. Bibliographies are ample and
up-to-date and are drawn from many languages" (*Downside Review*, LXXVI
[Summer, 1958], p. 299). The *American Ecclesiastical Review* credited
this edition with a "high level of excellence," praising it for its universality
of scope, clarity of presentation, and the extent of the revision done to the
1930-38 text (CLIV [January, 1966], p. 68-69). The eleventh volume contains author and subject indexes.

B194 **The New Dictionary of Theology.** Editors: Joseph A. Komnonchak, Mary
Collins, Dermot A. Lane. Wilmington, DE, Michael Glazier, 1987. vii, 1106p. LC
87-82327. ISBN 0-89453-609-5.

"Constructed around twenty-four topics which the editors believe constitute the
principal themes of the christian vision of faith. The longest and most important
articles are devoted to these themes which provide the center around which all
other articles revolve" (Preface). Only the shortest articles do not contain
bibliography. Cross references are generously supplied. The articles are well
written and explain the official position of the Church as well as other points of
view among theologians. This is an important and up-to-date English language
work with an impressive list of contributors.

B195 Rahner, Karl and Herbert Vorgrimler. **Dictionary of Theology.** 2nd. ed. New
York, Crossroad, 1981. 541p. LC 81-5492. ISBN 0-8245-0040-7.

Originally published in German as *Kleines Theologisches Wörterbuch* (10th ed. Freiburg, Herder, 1976). The first English edition was called *Concise Theological Dictionary* in Great Britain and *Theological Dictionary* in the U.S. (New York, Herder, 1965). "Intended to provide brief explanations, in alphabetical order, of the most important concepts of modern Catholic dogmatic theology for readers who are prepared to make a certain intellectual effort" (Preface). There are references to Scripture and Church documents but no bibliographies as such. Entries are restricted to terms, isms, and doctrines; no biographies are included. All articles have been revised and some substantially rewritten for this edition. "Up-to-date, modern in tone and approach as well as comprehensive in coverage" (*America*, CXIV [January 1, 1966], p. 26).

B196   Rahner, Karl. **Encyclopedia of Theology: The Concise Sacramentum Mundi.** New York, Seabury, 1975. 1841p. LC 74-33145. ISBN 0-8164-1182-4.

An abridgement of **(B197)** in which many articles have been omitted. Some new material has been added from the *Lexikon für Theologie und Kirche*, and Rahner has written several new articles for this edition.

B197   Rahner, Karl. **Sacramentum mundi: An Encyclopedia of Theology.** Ed. by Karl Rahner and others. New York, Herder and Herder, 1968-70. 6 v. LC 68-25989.

Articles are all several pages in length, signed, and have bibliographies of books in all languages. "An attempt to formulate present-day developments of the understanding of the faith, basing itself on modern investigations of the key themes of the theological disciplines" (General Preface). *Commonweal* had some critical remarks about the assignment of subject headings, the subdivision of some articles and the general difficulty of the language but gives the work substantial praise for its inclusion of topics rarely treated in the old theology, raising difficult questions and problems and for its originality of style (LXXXIX [February 28, 1969], pp. 677-78).

B198   **Westminster Dictionary of Christian Theology.** Edited by Alan Richardson and John S. Bowden. Philadelphia, Westminster Press, 1983. xvi, 614p. LC 83-14521. ISBN 0-6642-1398-7.

An ecumenical work with articles of moderate length containing bibliographies. Index of Names, but no biographies as such. "Remarkably coherent, comprehensive, and integrated" (*New Blackfriars* LXV [March , 1984], p. 140).

HANDBOOKS AND MANUALS

B199   Dyer, George J., ed. **An American Catholic Catechism.** New York, Seabury Press, 1975. xii, 308p. LC 75-7786. ISBN 0-8164-1196-4.

Arranged in the traditional question and answer format. "In most places this work handles areas of dispute with honesty and clarity . . . but also has some very serious omissions" (*Commonweal*, CII [July 18, 1975], p. 280). Index.

B200   Feiner, Johannes. **The Common Catechism: A Book of Christian Faith**.
        New York, Seabury Press, 1975. xxv,690p. LC 75-1070. ISBN 0-8164-0283-3.

        A translation of the German *Neues Glaubensbuch*, this unique work is the
        first attempt by Catholic and Protestant theologians to produce a common
        handbook of the Christian faith. The first four parts of the work deal with
        God, Jesus, Man, and Faith; the fifth part treats of "Questions in Dispute
        Between the Churches." While some theologians view this work with reser-
        vations (*Theological Studies*, XXXVI [December, 1975], p. 798), it is a
        concise statement of major similarities and differences between the faiths.
        Subject index, appendix of "Agreed Statements."

B201   Hardon, John A. **The Catholic Catechism**. Garden City, NY, Doubleday,
        1975. 623p. LC 73-81433. ISBN 0-3850-8039-5.

        A detailed statement of post-Vatican II Catholic teachings, well documented,
        whose "overriding concern is fidelity to the deposit of faith" (*Theological
        Studies*, XXXVI [December, 1975], p. 799). A detailed subject index is
        supplied.

B202   Lawler, Ronald David, ed. **The Teachings of Christ: A Catholic Catechism
        for Adults**. Huntington, IN, Our Sunday Visitor Press, 1976. 640p. LC
        75-34852. ISBN 0-8797-3899-5.

        Based on the *General Catechetical Directory* (B207), this work explains
        the teachings of the Church by means of constant reference to the Scriptures,
        the Fathers, the councils and numerous other Church documents. "Undoubt-
        edly the best manual to date for adult catechetical instruction" (*Theological
        Studies*, XXXVII [September, 1976], p. 488). Appendix of Catholic
        Prayers; Scriptural index; general index.

B203   McBrien, Richard P. **Catholicism**. Minneapolis, Winston Press, 1980. 2 v. index.
        LC 79-55963. ISBN 0-03-056907-9

        The author "intends this book as a bridge between the Church of yesterday and
        the Church of today" (Preface). In five parts and thirty chapters, McBrien
        attempts to present almost a *summa theologica* of contemporary Catholic
        theology, but always in relation to the roots of Catholicism and frequent
        references to texts and documents. Each chapter is followed by a detailed
        summary and a bibliography. Glossary. Index of Personal Names. Index of
        Subjects. "The book is monumental and should certainly be found in libraries"
        (*Theological Studies*, XLII [March, 1981], p. 140).

B204   National Conference of Catholic Bishops. **Basic Teachings for Catholic Religious
        Education**. Washington, DC, United States Catholic Conference, 1973. 36p. LC
        73-172147.

        "This text sets down the principal elements of the Christian message ... specified
        by the American Bishops ... as ... central in all religious instruction"
        (Introduction). Appendices contain the Ten Commandments, the Beatitudes, the
        Seven Precepts of the Church. Index.

B205 **A New Catechism: Catholic Faith for Adults.** Trans. from the Dutch by Kevin Smyth. New York, Herder and Herder, 1967. xviii, 510p. LC 67-29673.

The controversial Dutch attempt at a renewed catechism based on the Second Vatican Council; i.e., "The whole message, the whole of the faith remains the same, but the approach, the light in which the faith is seen, is new" (Foreword). Covers man's place in the world, various religions, Christ and the Christian religion, the sacraments and commandments, death and the resurrection. "This book is a mature study of the Catholic faith, untechnical, as its genre demands, but written by (unidentified) persons of competence, who expect work on the part of the reader; . . . which deserves better than to be put on the list of recent religious thrillers" (*America*, CXVII [February 3, 1968], p. 160).

B206 Piepkorn, Arthur Carl. **Profiles in Belief: The Religious Bodies of the United States and Canada. Vol. I. Roman Catholic, Old Catholic, Eastern Orthodox.** New York, Harper and Row, 1977. xix, 324p. LC 76-9971. ISBN 0-06-066580-7.

This is the first volume of a monumental seven volume set by the famed Lutheran scholar. The section on the Roman Catholic Church treats of its history, doctrine, nature and function and various movements within the Church. Each one of these sections is followed by documentation and bibliographies. There is a subject index for the entire volume. The treatment of the material is of a reference nature—not an in depth study. The presentation is accurate and fair. The value of the entire set, however, goes far beyond its treatment of any one denomination.

B207 Sacred Congregation for the Clergy. **General Catechetical Directory.** Washington, DC, Publications Office, United States Catholic Conference, 1971. 112p. LC 72-196137.

"The immediate purpose of the Directory is to provide assistance in the production of . . . catechisms" (Foreword). Every topic that should be contained in a catechism or catechetical course is explained. Subject index.

B208 Spirago, Franz. **The Catechism Explained.** Trans. by Richard F. Clarke. Completely new and rev. ed. by Anthony N. Fuerst. New York, Benziger Bros., 1961. 485p. LC 61-8925.

A guide to the Roman Catechism (E147) arranged in the traditional question and answer fashion but covering more than the usual doctrinal questions. *Homiletic and Pastoral Review* described this work as "a classic for half a century" (LXII [October, 1962], p. 89).

B209 **Theology Library.** By a group of theologians under the editorship of A. M. Henry. Trans. by William Storey. Chicago, Fides Pub. Assoc., 1954-58. 6 v. LC 54-10891. (Trans. of *Initiation théologique*).

Intended as a general introduction to theology for the laity. In a series of essays by more than forty collaborators, the work deals with each of the major topics or disciplines of theology and is equipped with many reference features—indexes, glossaries and bibliographies. Although valuable for its wide range of coverage, it has been criticized for lacking coherence and an accurate overview of theology (*Thought*, XXIX [March, 1954], p. 135).

B210   Vorgrimler, Herbert. **Bilan de la théologie du XXe siècle.** Paris, Casterman, 1970-71. 2 v. LC 71-524226. (Also published in German: *Bilanz der Theologie im 20. Jahrhundert.* Freiburg, Herder, 1970. 4 v.)

A survey of theological disciplines and related topics in the modern world. Articles are of moderate length, contain bibliographies, and are written by well-known authorities. Volume II contains biographical and critical studies of 12 modern theologians and an index to the entire work including the bibliographies. "Stimulating new perspectives and abundant bibliographies recommend this as a reference work of first priority" (*Lumen Vitae* [March, 1971], p. 168).

HISTORY

B211   Hocedez, Edgar. **Histoire de la théologie au XIXe siècle.** Bruxelles, Édition Universelles, 1947-52. 3 v. LC A55-1375.

The most comprehensive general history of theology, composed of large chapters divided into small subsections covering the important periods, movements and personalities in the history of theology. Extensive bibliographies follow each chapter. According to *Theological Studies*, the work "cannot be recommended highly enough" for its "concise, adequate, and concrete treatment of all movements and tendencies" (IX [March, 1948], pp. 151-53).

BIO-BIBLIOGRAPHY

B212   Farge, James K. **Biographical Register of Paris Doctors of Theology, 1500-1536.** Toronto, Pontifical Institute of Medieval Studies, 1980. xvi, 562p. LC 80-505879. ISBN 0-8884-359-5.

Presents detailed biographical and bibliographical information for 474 graduates of the Faculty of Theology of Paris. Five indexes appear at the end of the volume.

B213   Hurter, Hugo. **Nomenclator literarius theologiae catholicae theologos exhibens aetate, ratione, disciplinis distinctos.** Ed. iii emendata et aucta. Innsbruck, Wagner, 1903-13. 5 v. in 6. LC 6-21408. Reprinted: New York, Burt-Franklin, 1962. LC 72-210323.

The standard bio-bibliography of Catholic theologians; an annotated catalog of theological writers from the beginning of the Church up to 1910, giving brief biographies, full bibliographies and commentary in Latin. Approximately 40,000 items are listed with indexes for subjects in each of the six volumes. The coverage is broader than just theology: philosophy, Church history and related subjects are included. Stephen Brown described the set as "a work of truly astonishing research" ("Catholic Bibliography," *Catholic Library Practice* [A65], v. 1, p. 109).

THEOLOGICAL DISCIPLINES

The works covered in this section are grouped under six headings: 1) Apologetics, the study of the defense of the teachings of the Church especially with regard to revelation, tradition and the nature of the Church; 2) Dogmatic theology, the study of God and his activity as derived from revelation and the teachings of the Church; 3) Moral theology, the study of man and his behavior, using the same sources as in dogmatic theology; 4) Pastoral theology or practical theology, the study of the methods by which the message of the Church is brought to the world; 5) Ascetical and Mystical theology, the study of how man may attain Christian perfection; and 6) Ecumenical theology, the study of Christian reconciliation and unity, and how to attain it. Each of these fields is closely related drawing freely from one another and dealing with the same topics but with different emphases.

APOLOGETICS

BIBLIOGRAPHY

B214   Gorman, Robert. **Catholic Apologetical Literature in the United States** (1784-1858). Washington, DC, Catholic University of America Press, 1939. x, 192p. (C.U.A. Studies in Church History, v. 28.) LC 39-31558. Reprinted: New York, AMS Press, 1974. LC 73-3582. ISBN 0-404-57778-4.

A history of the books, pamphlets and tracts published in defense of the Catholic Church from 1784 to 1858. An appendix lists all the works treated.

DICTIONARIES AND ENCYCLOPEDIAS

B215   **Dictionnaire apologétique de la foi catholique, contenant les preuves de la vérité de la religion et les réponses aux objections tirées des sciences humaines.** 4 éd., entièrement refondue sous la direction de A. D'Alès avec la collaboration d'un grand nombre de savants catholiques. Paris, G. Beauchesne, 1911-22. 4 v. LC 25-20239.

The most extensive reference work in the field whose main purpose is not to explain Church teaching but to present the answers to objections raised against it. Most of the articles are long and have large bibliographies. This work has been described as:

> The most serviceable apologetic work on all matters that concern the Catholic faith and doctrine. No matter of importance that touches even remotely upon the history, teaching and discipline of the Church is neglected, and to all are given a thoroughness and completeness of treatment that brings the inquirer in touch with the best sources and surest findings (*Catholic World*, XCVIII [June, 1913], p. 410).

Unfortunately this is no longer quite so true because of the age of the work.

DOGMATIC THEOLOGY

Many of the works in this section are arranged according to the traditional subdivisions of dogmatic theology—God-one and triune, Christ, Mary, man and creation, the scriptures, the Church, the sacraments, grace, virtues and eschatology or the "last things." Among the most useful reference works in dogma are the source books (B216-224), especially Denzinger (B218), which cite the specific passages from the scriptures, the Fathers, or Church documents on which the doctrines are based. Neuner's collection (B220) is important in that it is quite recent and contains documents from Vatican II and the reign of Pope Paul VI in English.

SOURCES

B216   Cavallera, Ferdinand. **Thesaurus doctrinae catholicae, ex documentis magisterii ecclesiastici, ordine methodico disposuit Ferdinandus Cavallera.** Parisiis, G. Beauchesne, 1920. xviii, 794p. LC 22-8154.

Contains the teachings of the Church as contained in extracts from documents, papal and conciliar, arranged according to the traditional divisions of the field of theology. Chronological and subject indexes..

B217   **The Church Teaches: Documents of the Church in English Translation.** Selections trans. and prepared for publication by John F. Clarkson and others of St. Mary College, St. Mary, Kansas. St. Louis, B. Herder Book Co., 1955. xiv, 400p. LC 55-10297.

"Translations of some documents of the Church that are most frequently used and are most important for the ordinary courses of theology" (Foreword). References to Denzinger's *Enchiridion* (B218) are given, wherein one may find a citation of the complete text from which the excerpt is drawn. Not as useful a work as it was before Denzinger was translated into English. Classified and subject indexes.

B218   Denzinger, Heinrich Joseph Dominik. **Enchiridion symbolorum, definitionum, et declarationum de rebus fidei et morum.** Quod primum edidit Henricus Denzinger et quod funditus retractavit, auxit notulis, ornavit Adolfus Schönmetzer, Ed 35 emendata. Barcinone, Herder, 1973. xxxii, 954p.

The most familiar collection of this type; a handbook of the sources and texts in excerpt form on which Catholic dogmatic and moral teachings are based. The texts are arranged in chronological order and are selected from all sources except Scripture. This edition contains Vatican II Documents as well as post-Conciliar texts. Full references to complete texts are given for each quotation. Classified and alphabetical indexes.

B219   Denzinger, Heinrich Joseph Dominik. **The Sources of Catholic Dogma.** Trans. by Roy J. Deferrari from the 30th ed. of Enchiridion symbolorum. St. Louis, Herder, 1957. xxxiv, 653+67p. LC 57-5963.

Promised to be very useful but severely criticized for its theologically weak translation (see *Theological Studies*, XVIII (June, 1957), pp. 280-88). Valuable, nonetheless, for its bibliographical notes and indexes.

B220   Neuner, Josef and J. Dupuis. **The Christian Faith in the Doctrinal Documents of the Catholic Church.** 1st. U.S.A. edition, corrected. Westminster, MD, Christian Classics, 1975. xxxi, 687p. LC 75-319948.

An updating of *The Teaching of the Catholic Church as Contained in Her Documents* (New York, Alba House, 1967) containing post Vatican II documents as well as those dating from ancient Christian sources. Arranged by subject. Biblical, name and subject indexes.

B221   **Official Catholic Teachings.** Wilmington, NC, Consortium Books, 1978. 6 v. V. 1. *Christ Our Lord*, by Amanda G. Watlington. LC 78-53844. ISBN 0-8434-0714-X; V. 2. *Love and Sexuality*, by Odile M. Liebard. LC 78-53843. ISBN 0-8434-0713-1; V. 3. *Bible Interpretation*, by James J. Megivern. LC 78-53846. ISBN 0-8434-0715-8; V. 4. *Social Justice*, by Vincent P. Mainelli. LC 78-53833. ISBN 0-8434-0712-3; V. 5. *Clergy and Laity*, by Odile M. Liebard. LC 78-53848. ISBN 0-8434-0717-4; V. 6. *Worship and Liturgy*, by James J. Megivern. LC 78-53847. ISBN 0-8434-0716-6.

Over 240 documents from popes, councils and other sources are reprinted in this series in numbered paragraphs. Each volume contains a subject index referring to these numbered sections. The original documentation is reprinted with the texts and an introduction has been written for each volume by the compiler.

B222   Rouët de Journel, Marie Joseph. **Enchiridion patristicum; loci SS. patrum, doctorum scriptorum ecclesiasticorum.** Novo appendice aucta. 24. ed. Barcinone, Herder, 1969. xxvii, 817p.

A collection of 2,290 quotations from the Fathers of the Church, arranged in chronological order with a classified index and an alphabetical index of subjects, authors and titles. *See* Willis' *The Teachings of the Church Fathers* **(B224)** for an English version of the same material.

B223   Vaughan, Kenelm. **The Divine Armory of Holy Scripture.** New rev. ed., ed. by Rev. Newton Thompson. St. Louis, Herder, 1943. vi, 444p. LC 43-4795.

An arrangement of scriptural passages under the traditional theological headings with an index.

B224   Willis, John Randolph. **The Teachings of the Church Fathers.** New York, Herder and Herder, 1966. 537p. LC 66-13067.

"The aim of this book is to present a brief outline of Catholic doctrine as it appears in some of the more typical writings of the Church Fathers" (Introduction). Based on the *Enchiridion patristicum* of Rouët de Journel **(B222)** but arranged by subject rather than chronologically. References to complete texts are supplied. Index.

DICTIONARIES

B225   Parente, Pietro, Antonio Piolanti, and Salvatore Garofalo. **Dictionary of dogmatic theology.** Trans. from the 2nd Italian ed. by Emmanuel Doronzo. Milwaukee, Bruce Pub. Co., 1951. xxvi, 310p. LC 51-7704.

Brief articles with references to Aquinas and modern authors. Originally intended for the layman but also useful for the theological student. *Theological Studies* termed the articles "gems of precise, concise philosophical thought and Catholic dogma" (XIII [March, 1952], p. 164).

B226　O'Carroll, Michael. **Trinitas: A Theological Encyclopedia of the Holy Trinity.** Wilmington, DE, M. Glazier, 1987. ix, 220p. LC 86-45326. ISBN 0-8945-3595-1.

All topics, documents, councils, and persons who have written authoritatively on the Trinity are covered. Each article is supplied with a bibliography. "The reader will be in a better position to draw his/her own conclusions in faith after dipping into Fr. O'Carroll's extensive survey" (*Doctrine and Life*, XXXVII [April, 1987], p. 219).

HANDBOOKS

B227　Ott, Ludwig. **Fundamentals of Catholic Dogma.** 6th ed. Edited in English by James Canon Bastible. Trans. from the German by Patrick Lynch. St. Louis, Herder, 1964. xvi, 544p.

A basic outline of the teachings of the Church which presents essential statements of doctrine and attempts to explain the speculative, scriptural and traditional foundations of that teaching. But it has been criticized for not giving enough attention to the speculative aspects of the doctrine it presents. "It may be useful as a quick reference provided the user does not expect to receive a complete treatment on any given point" (*American Ecclesiastical Review*, CXXXIV [January, 1956], p. 69).

B228　**Sacrae theologiae summa, iuxta constitutionem apostolicam "Deus scientiarum Dominus."** Matriti, Biblioteca de Autores Cristianos, 1955-56. 4 v.

Covers all the areas of dogmatic theology, giving brief introductions and full bibliographies. Indexes in each volume with a general index in volume 4.

B229　Schmaus, Michael. **Dogma.** Westminster, MD, Christian Classics, 1984. 6 v. ISBN 0-87061-095-3.

Translation and revision of *Glaube der Kirche* (St. Ottilien, EOS-Verlag, 1979). Covers scripture, creation, Christ, the Church, sacraments, justification, and the last things. Volume one contains bibliographies for each chapter; the other volumes do not. Indexes for each volume. "An entirely fresh presentation of systematic theology that aims at incorporating all significant developments since the Second Vatican Council" (*Theological Studies*, XXX [June, 1969], p. 338).

B230　**The Teaching of the Catholic Church: A Summary of Catholic Doctrine.** Arr. and ed. by George D. Smith. 2nd. ed. London, Burns and Oates, 1963. 1334p.

A series of essays on each of the theological subject divisions, each by a different author. No bibliography, but marginal notes, concise English language treatment, and an index make this work valuable for reference. "This summary is one that no library of any serious reputation can afford to lack" (*Commonweal*, XLIX [February 1, 1949], p. 500).

B231   Tanquerey, Adolphe. **Synopsis theologiae dogmaticae ad mentem S. Thomae Aquinatis hodiernis moribus accommodata.** Parisiis Desclée. (26th ed.) 1949-50. 3 v. LC 37-13178.

B232   Tanquerey, Adolphe. **Brevior synopsis theologiae dogmaticae.** New York, Benziger, 1913.

The classic handbook for the study of dogmatic theology for generations. Both the larger set and the abridged version are rich in bibliographical references to sources and modern commentaries. Each volume has an index. Unfortunately, no revisions have been made since Vatican II.

B233   Tanquerey, Adolphe. **A Manual of Dogmatic Theology.** Trans. by John J. Byrnes. New York, Desclée, 1959. 2 v. LC 59-13235.

This is a translation of the *Brevior Synopsis* with updated text and bibliography.

CHRISTOLOGY

B234   Prat, Ferdinand. **Jesus Christ: His Life, His Teaching and His Work.** Trans. from the 16th French ed. by John N. Heenan. Milwaukee, Bruce Pub. Co., 1950. 2 v. (Science and Culture Series.) LC 50-58219.

Probably the most scholarly modern life of Christ available; it is a detailed account based on the Gospels and other ancient as well as modern authorities and contains detailed "Supplementary Notes" on social, political, geographical and other types of background information. In addition to the general index, there is a philological index which defines Greek words having more than one meaning or disputed meanings. The work is reputed to be "the best life of Christ in existence, replete with details that can be found almost nowhere else" (*America*, LXXXIV [December 16, 1950], p. 337). Tables, charts and bibliographical notes.

B235   Sabourin, Leopold. **The Names and Titles of Jesus: Themes of Biblical Theology.** Trans. by Maurice Carroll. New York, Macmillan, 1967. xviii, 334p. LC 66-22534.

Explains about 50 names or titles given to Jesus. A work "proffered not to biblical scholars . . . but presents clear summaries of the various positions that have been taken on many issues of Christology" (*Clergy Review*, LII [Sept., 1967], p. 730). Appendix of 187 additional names with scriptural references.

Sources

B236   Xiberta y Roqueta, Bartolomé María. **Enchiridion de Verbo Incarnato: fontes quos ad studia theologica collegit Bartholomaeus M. Xiberta.** Matriti, 1957. 810p. LC 58-25953.

A selection of over 2,500 passages from the Fathers and various Church documents dealing with Christ, arranged by author with a classified subject index. "A valuable service to professors and students" (*Theological Studies*, XIX [September, 1958], p. 471).

Dictionaries

B237   Bardy, Gustav. **Enciclopedia cristologica.** Alba, Ed. Paoline, 1960. xxiv, 1245p. (Multiformis Sapientia).

Covers more than the dogmatic aspects of Christology. There are articles on the influence of Christ on various religions, humanity in general, literature, and the arts. The arrangement is classified, with each section containing many long bibliographies. The work was originally published in French (1935), but the Italian translation of 1960 has been revised and updated. *Civiltà* described it as scholarly and detailed (CXI [November, 1960], p. 277).

MARIOLOGY

Bibliography

B238   Besutti, Giuseppe Maria. **Bibliografia mariana.** Roma, Marianum, 1950- . v. LC 51-27320.
        V. I. 1948-51; V. II. 1951-52; V. III. 1952-57.

A classified bibliography of books and articles on Mary with analyses of large works but no annotations. International coverage. Subject and author indexes.

B239   Marian Library, Dayton University. **Booklist of the Marian Library.** 2nd. ed. Comp. by Edmund J. Baumeister, S.M. Dayton, The Library, 1949. 200p. LC 50-16384.

A comprehensive listing of over 10,500 titles in English, French, German, Italian, Latin and Spanish. The arrangement is by author with no indexes. For a while this work was supplemented by a *Newsletter* from the same source.

Sources

B240   **Papal Documents on Mary.** Comp. and arr. by William J. Doheny and Joseph P. Kelly. Milwaukee, Bruce Pub. Co., 1955. x, 275p. LC 55-8936.

Gives texts of documents issued from 1849 to 1953 with Latin titles and brief summaries. Arranged chronologically with no index.

Dictionaries and Encyclopedias

B241   Attwater, Donald. **A Dictionary of Mary.** New York, P. J. Kenedy, 1956. viii, 312p. LC 56-10460.

"A work of quick reference to matters connected with the many aspects of the life, significance and veneration of the Blessed Virgin Mary" (Preface). A popular work in non-technical language, covering doctrines as well as organizations, shrines, devotions, legends and so forth. No bibliography.

B242   **Enciclopedia mariana "Theotócos."** Traducción del Italiano por don Francisco Aparicio. Madrid, Ediciones Studium, 1960. 902p. (Colección Mariana, 21).

A classified encyclopedia covering the full range of Marian topics, including
the history of Mariology, Marian dogmas, devotion, spirituality, Church
law and Mary, as well as her influence in literature, art and music. Bibliography is copious and indexed for authors. A subject index is also provided.

B243   **Lexikon der Marienkunde**, hrsg. von Konrad Algermissen, Ludwig Böer,
Carl Feckes, Julius Tyciak. Regensburg, F. Pustet, 1957- . v.

With the failure of the Pustet firm in 1967 the editing of this comprehensive and scholarly work was undertaken by Harrassowitz, but to date no
fascicles have appeared from this source. Actually nothing has appeared
since 1961 when the fifth fascicle was issued. What has been done is of
high quality and well printed and illustrated (*Cahiers Marials*, VII [March-
April, 1958], p. 159).

B244   O'Carroll, Michael. **Theotokos: A Theological Encyclopedia of the Blessed Virgin
Mary.** Rev. ed. with supplement. Wilmington, DE, M. Glazier, 1983. x, 390p. LC
82-82382. ISBN 0-89453-268-5.

Articles deal with all aspects of Mary's life, doctrines, and persons who are
considered authorities on the subject. Bibliographies are supplied for all articles.
"For the professional theologian it will be a *vade mecum* of recent studies (the
bibliographies have over seven thousand references)" (*Theological Studies*, XLIV
[June, 1983], p. 320).

B245   Roschini, Gabriele Maria. **Dizionario di mariologia.** Roma, Editrice Studium,
1961. xii, 517p. LC 65-45792.

Contains an article on "Bibliographia mariana" as well as the biographies
of famous Mariologists and articles with bibliographies of the same nature
as the *Enciclopedia mariana* (**B242**).

Handbooks

B246   Carol, Juniper B. **Mariology.** Milwaukee, Bruce Pub. Co., 1955-57. 3 v.
LC 55-6959.

A collection of studies in English "covering the entire theological tract
relative to Our Blessed Lady" (Introduction). Historical and other aspects
are also covered with a "high degree of scholarship" by contributors of
"international reputation" (*Theological Studies*, XIX [March, 1958], p.
109). Bibliographies are appended to each chapter and indexed by author
in volume three.

B247   Du Manoir de Juaye, Hubert. **Maria: études sur la Sainte Vierge.** Paris, B.
Beauchesne, 1949- . v. LC 51-27497.

Completed in 1964 in seven volumes with a general index volume projected.
A work of incredible detail and exceedingly rich in bibliography covering
the most minute details of Mariology.

B248   Sträter, Paul. **Katholische Marienkunde.** Paderborn, F. Schöningh, 1947-52.
3 v. LC 52-67013.

Covers sources of Marian doctrine, explanations of the doctrines, and spiritual and apostolic aspects of Mariology. Each section is done by a specialist and provided with bibliography. Index.

THE CHURCH

B249   Dulles, Avery and Patrick Granfield. **The Church: A Bibliography.** Wilmington, DE, M. Glazier, 1985. 166p.

"Our aim in compiling this bibliography is to indicate the more important ecclesiological writings" (Introduction). No periodical articles are listed. Asterisks indicate works of broad interest that serve as good introduction to the topic. No annotations. Index.

SACRAMENTS

Sources

B250   **Monumenta eucharistica et liturgica vetustissima collegit,** notis et prolegomenis instruxit Johannes Quasten. Bonnaie, P. Hanstein, 1935-37. 7 v. LC 35-37057.

A source book of patristic texts dealing with the Eucharist and other sacraments, providing brief introductions to the texts, biographies of authors, and references to the complete printed versions. Copious notes give cross references and indicate similar passages in other sources. Index in each volume.

Holy Orders

Bibliography

B251   Guitard, André and Marie-Georges Bulteau. **Bibliographie Internationale sur le Sacerdoce et le Ministère. International Bibliography on the Priesthood and the Ministry,** 1969- . Montréal, Centre de Documentation et de Recherche, Center of Documentation and Research, 1971- . v. Annual. LC 72-623148.

A continuation of the editor's *Bibliographie sur le Sacerdoce, 1966-68* published in 6 parts in 1969, this work is an exhaustive listing of books and articles dealing with Catholic, Protestant and Jewish clergy. The bulk of the material, however, seems to be Catholic literature. The arrangement is classified (29 major headings) with author and subject indexes. Almost 7,000 items are listed in the 1969 issue.

B252   Mierzwinski, Theophil T., ed. **What Do You Think of the Priest? A Bibliography on the Catholic Priesthood.** New York, Exposition Press, 1972. 95p. LC 72-86589. ISBN 9-6824-7527-0.

A selection of English language material on priests and the priesthood. Subject arrangement with author and title indexes.

B253   Morgan, John H. **The Ordination of Women: A Comprehensive Bibliography, 1960-1976.** Wichita, KS, Institute of Ministry and the Elderly, 1977. viii, 41p.

Separate lists of books and articles for and against the ordination of women. Includes Catholic and non-Catholic sources.

Sources

B254   **The Catholic Priesthood According to the Teaching of the Church.** Ed. by Pierre Veuillot. Westminster, MD, Newman Press, 1958-64. 2 v. LC 58-1447. (Trans. of *Notre sacerdoce*).

Reprints papal documents dealing with the priesthood from Pius X to Pius XII in chronological order with indexes for scripture, canon law and subjects. Each document is provided with a brief introduction.

B255   **Enchiridion clericorum: documenta ecclesiae futuris sacerdotibus formandis.** Editio 2 funditus recognita et aucta. Città del Vaticano, Typis Polyglottis Vaticanis, 1975. lxiii, 1566p. LC 77-472675.

All pertinent documents from the first century down to Pope Paul VI are reprinted in Latin or their original language. The bulk of texts, however, originated in the 20th century. Papal, conciliar and curial documents are included. Index. "It has the special virtue of all handbooks, to have accessible many documents otherwise very hard to find" (*Clergy Review*, LXII [December, 1977], p. 503).

Dictionaries

B256   **Enciclopedia del sacerdozio,** diretta dal rev. prof. Giuseppe Cacciatore C. SS. R. 2 ed. Firenze, Libreria Editrice Fiorentina, 1957. xiv, 1691+127p.

A classified encyclopedia with articles arranged under three major headings: the vocational formation of the priest, the theology of the priesthood, and the works of the priest. Each article is followed by a brief bibliography; a classified and annotated "Bibliografia generale" of over 100 pages appears at the end of the book (pp. 1531-1636). Full indexing helps to compensate for the poor reference arrangement.

MORAL THEOLOGY

The areas covered by moral theology include general principles governing human behavior, the commandments of God, the laws of the state, those of the Church, the proper use of the sacraments, and the duties and virtues to be practiced in various states of life. The most familiar reference works in this field are the guides and manuals (B271-281) such as Davis (B273) and Callan (B271), which explain moral principles and define terms with more or less brevity and clarity. Häring's *Free and Faithful in Christ* (B275) and *The Law of Christ* (B276) are unique among these works for their non-legal approach.

Contemporary bioethical problems are comprehensively treated in the new *Encyclopedia of Bioethics* (B264), an ecumenical work in four volumes edited at Georgetown University.

BIBLIOGRAPHY

B257   **Bibliography of Bioethics.** Washington, DC, Kennedy Institute of Ethics, Georgetown University, 1975- . v. Annual. LC 75-4140. ISSN 0363-0161.
Vols. 1-6 published by Gale Research Co., Detroit.
Vols. 7-9 published by Macmillan/Free Press, New York.
Vols. 10- published by The Kennedy Institute of Ethics.

Each volume lists about 2,000 books, articles and audio visual items, some with abstracts. Arranged alphabetically by subject. Author index. Title index. See B260 for monthly updates.

B258   Floyd, Mary K. **Abortion Bibliography.** Troy, NY, Whitson Pub. Co., 1970- . v. Annual. LC 72-78877. ISSN 0092-9522.

"An attempt at a comprehensive world bibliography" (Preface). Lists English and foreign language works in three sections: books (by title), articles (by title), articles (by subject). Covers literature from all sources; many Catholic items may be found in each volume. Author index; no annotations.

B259   Dollen, Charles. **Abortion in Context: A Select Bibliography.** Metuchen, NJ, Scarecrow Press, 1970. 150p. LC 75-16032. ISBN 0-8108-0337-2.

A bibliography of books and periodical articles from the years 1967-69 when the national debate was getting into full swing. No annotations. Listing is by author and title in one alphabet. Subject Index. List of sources.

B260   **New Titles in Bioethics.** Washington, DC, Georgetown University, Kennedy Institute of Ethics, Center of Bioethics Library, 1975- . v. Monthly. LC 79-3772. ISSN 0361-6347.

"A listing by subject of recent monograph additions to the National Reference Center for Bioethics Literature." Annual cumulations.

B261   Triche, Charles W. **The Euthanasia Controversy, 1812-1974: A Bibliography with Select Annotations.** Troy, NY, Whitson Pub. Co., 1975. vii, 242p. LC 75-8379. ISBN 0-87875-071-1.

1,363 items; books, parts of books and periodical articles, are listed. Not specifically Catholic literature but many Catholic sources are cited.

SOURCES

B262   **Papal Pronouncements on Marriage and the Family from Leo XIII to Pius XII (1878-1954).** By Alvin Werth and Clement S. Mihanovich. Milwaukee, Bruce Pub. Co., 1955. xiii, 189p. LC 55-12375.

Excerpts from papal encyclicals and other documents dealing with the origin and nature of marriage, its purpose and function, and the family. The editors have supplied some brief analyses of the documents and references to the complete text. General index; bibliography, pp. 172-79.

DICTIONARIES AND ENCYCLOPEDIAS

B263   **Concise Dictionary of Christian Ethics.** Ed. by Bernhard Stoeckle, with contributions by Anton Vögtle, Laurence Bright, and others. New York, Crossroad, 1979. x, 285p. LC 79-50666. ISBN 0-8245-0300-7

Contains articles of moderate length with bibliographies. Where Catholic teachings differ from Protestant, two articles appear on the same subject. "There are far too many flaws (misleading cross-references, typographical errors, omissions in the selection of articles) in this work to make it a useful reference tool" (*Theological Studies*, XLI [June, 1980], p. 453).

B264   **Encyclopedia of Bioethics.** Warren T. Reich, Editor in Chief. New York, Free Press, 1978. 4 v. LC 78-8821. ISBN 0-02-926060-4.

Initiated by the Joseph and Rose Kennedy Institute of Ethics at George-town University, this work was sponsored by various governmental and private foundations and contains articles by medical, scientific, philosophical and theological scholars of all faiths, Christian, non-Christian and Jewish. Catholics will find this a useful source of information on contemporary bioethical problems since Catholic viewpoints are consistently presented and clearly labeled. The same is true for other major religious groups. Bibliographies are long, annotated and plentiful.

B265   Hörman, Karl. **Lexikon der christlichen Moral.** 2., völlig neubearb. Aufl. Innsbruck, Tyrolia-Verlag, 1976. lxiii, 1756p. col. LC 76-488361.

Thirty-nine Austrian authorities contributed the long scholarly articles that make up this work. Bibliographies include works in all Western languages and are quite extensive. Cross references are supplied. "Can be recommended for its copious bibliographies and good and fair treatment of current questions in moral theology" (*Theological Studies*, XXXI [March, 1970], p. 210). Indexes.

B266   **Lexikon des katholischen Lebens,** hrsg. von Wendelin Rauch, unter Schrift-leitung von Jakob Hommes. Mit 16 Bildseiten und 8 schematischen über-sichten. Freiburg, Herder, 1951. xvi, 1352p. col. LC 53-17035.

Over 800 articles dealing with contemporary moral problems with bibliographies for each article and a general classified bibliography (pp. 1331-54). Classified index.

B267   Palazzini, Pietro. **Dictionarium morale et canonicum.** Romae, Officium Libri Catholici, 1962-68. 4 v. LC 63-34193.

Based on traditional Church teachings, papal instructions and the Second Vatican Council. Pietro Palazzini, "the editor and most distinguished contributor is a skilled, and well known writer on moral and canonical matters," according to the *Jurist*, which in general has high praise for the work but does point out the lack of English titles in the bibliographies, its high price, and its poor paper (XIII [April, 1963], pp. 249-52).

B268   Roberti, Francesco. **Dictionary of Moral Theology.** Comp. under the direction of Francesco Cardinal Roberti. Ed. under the direction of Pietro

Palazzini. Trans. from the 2nd Italian ed. Westminster, MD, Newman Press, 1962. xxxix, 1352p. LC 60-14828.

The only dictionary of moral theology available in English; it is made up of many brief articles covering roughly the same material found in the handbooks listed below. While it has generally received critical acclaim, there seems to be something lacking in its usefulness with regard to American customs (*Ave Maria*, XCVI [July 28, 1962] , p. 26).

B269   Rossi, Leandro and Ambrogio Valsecchi. **Dizionario enciclopedico di teologia morale.** Roma, Edizione Paoline, 1973. 1198p. LC 74-304797.

Many Italian and some foreign contributors (e.g. Bernhard Häring) have contributed to this work. Most articles are very long and arranged in sections. Each is followed by a lengthy bibliography. "Universally valid moral principles and the ancient solutions are presented in a new light inspired by the discussions pursued in this field over the past few years" (*Lumen Vitae*, XXIX [September, 1974] , p. 476).

B270   **Westminster Dictionary of Christian Ethics.** Edited by James F. Childress and John MacQuarrie. Philadelphia, Westminster Press, 1986. xvii, 678p. LC 85-22539. ISBN 0-6642-0940-8.

Most articles are of short or moderate length and contain bibliographies. Differences between Catholic and Protestant teachings are stated. Index of Names. "Entries are concise and to the point" (*Theological Studies*, XLVIII [March, 1987], p. 215).

HANDBOOKS AND MANUALS

B271   Callan, Charles Jerome. **Moral Theology: A Complete Course Based on St. Thomas Aquinas and the Best Modern Authorities.** Rev. and enl. by Edward P. Farrell, O. P. New York, Wagner, 1958. 2 v.

Does not contain any bibliography but is useful for its many definitions and thorough index. "A careful and competent revision of this 30 year old work. A complete and thoroughly modern scientific treatment of moral theology" (*Critic*, XVII [May, 1959] , p. 66).

B272   Conway, John Donald. **What They Ask about Morals.** Notre Dame, IN, Fides, 1960. x, 370p. LC 60-8445.

A popular treatment of questions concerning sin, conscience, virtues and vices, the commandments, Church regulations and other problems. The answers are notable for their clarity and frankness. An earlier work by the same author covers *What They Ask about Marriage* (Chicago, Fides, 1955. LC 55-7774). Classified Index.

B273   Davis, Henry. **Moral and Pastoral Theology.** 7th ed., rev. and enl. ed. by L. W. Geddes. New York, Sheed and Ward, 1958. 4 v. (Heythrop Series, 2.) LC A59-1591.

Covers the traditional range of topics with frequent bibliographical references, excerpts from pertinent Church documents and treatment of the pastoral aspects of moral problems. This edition has been criticized for its inadequate updating and skimpy treatment of nuclear warfare (*Clergy Review*, LX [November, 1958], pp. 694-98). Index in each volume.

B274   Grisez, Germain Gabriel. **The Way of the Lord Jesus.** Chicago, Franciscan Herald Press, 1983- . v. LC 83-1508. ISBN 0-8199-0861-4.

Volume 1. Christian Moral Principles.

"This book is constructed primarily as a textbook in fundamental moral theology for students in Catholic seminaries" (User's Guide and Preface). The answers, however, are quite extensive and written in several levels of complexity. Bold face type is used for quick, simple answers. References to Scripture, the Fathers, and other sources are provided in the text and in notes. Six indexes provide access to subjects, Scripture, Denzinger (B218), Vatican II documents, and Aquinas.

B275   Häring, Bernhard. **Free and Faithful in Christ: Moral Theology for Clergy and Laity.** New York, Crossroad, 1982. 2 v. LC 81-22155. ISBN 0-8245-0308-2.

"Twenty-five years after completing *The Law of Christ* [B276] ..., I attempt anew to offer a comprehensive presentation of Catholic moral theology" (Preface). References to sources contained in the text and in extensive notes after each chapter. Subject index for each volume. "A fresh breeze in Catholic moral theology" (*Cross Currents*, XXX [Summer, 1080], pp. 198-203).

B276   Häring, Bernhard. **The Law of Christ: Moral Theology for Priests and Laity.** Trans. by Edwin G. Kaiser. Westminster, MD, Newman Press, 1961-66. 3 v. LC 60-14826.

The most scholarly handbook of this type with much documentation and a bibliography for each section. The approach is by way of the Scriptures, the Fathers, and the liturgy rather than by merely stating dogmatic principles. "*The Law of Christ* may not be the complete answer to the call for a new approach to moral theology . . . founded upon the positive values of the Christian life, [but] it is, nevertheless, a giant stride in the right direction" (*Catholic Biblical Quarterly*, XXV [April, 1963], p. 117). Indexes in each volume.

B277   Jone, Heribert. **Moral Theology.** Trans. and Adapted by Rev. Urban Adelman. Westminster, MD, Newman Press, 1959. xxi, 610p.

Brief but clear treatment of moral questions adapted for American use with many definitions, distinctions and examples. "Recommended for its clarity, conciseness, and doctrinal accuracy" (*Revue d'Ottawa*, XXIX [April, 1959], p. 254). Index.

B278   Prümmer, Dominic M. **Handbook of Moral Theology.** Trans. by Gerald F. Shelton. Ed. for American Usage by John Gavin Nolan. New York, P. J. Kenedy, 1957. 500p.

A small handbook in much the same style as Jone (B277) but criticized by *Theological Studies* for its omission of pertinent material and inadequate adaptation for American usage (XIX [June, 1958], p. 295). Index.

B279   Prümmer, Dominic M. **Manuale theologiae moralis: secundum principia S. Thomae Aquinatis, in usum scholarum.** Editio 12 a E. M. Munch. Freiburg, Herder, 1955. 3 v.

A comprehensive work with scholarly apparatus on which the previous work was based. General index in volume three. Bibliography, v. 1, pp. XII-XXXVII.

B280   Tanquerey, Adolphe. **Synopsis theologiae moralis et pastoralis ad mentem S. Thomae et S. Alphonsi hodiernis moribus accommodata.** Paris, Desclée, 1947-48. 3 v.

B281   Tanquerey, Adolphe. **Brevior synopsis theologiae moralis et pastoralis.** Paris, Desclée, 1924. xxii, 799p. LC 25-3859.

Standard work of good reputation (cf. *Catholic World*, LXXXVI [Feb., 1903], p. 693 and *America*, VI [Dec. 30, 1911], p. 283), but now even more out-of-date than Tanquerey's dogmatic theology (B174).

PASTORAL THEOLOGY

Pastoral theology may be defined as the theological science that covers the obligation of the priest in the care of souls. Unfortunately there is no comprehensive English language reference work dealing with this topic. The *Handbuch der Pastoraltheologie* (B283) is the only work of its kind produced in the latter half of this century, but it has not been translated.

BIBLIOGRAPHY

B282   Morgan, John H. **Death and Dying: A Resource Bibliography for Clergy and Chaplains.** Wichita, KS, Institute on Ministry and the Elderly, 1977. 30p.

Covers topics related to suffering and death. About 500 books and articles are listed. No index.

HANDBOOKS

B283   **Handbuch der Pastoraltheologie. Praktische Theologie der Kirche in ihrer Gegenwart.** Hrsg. von Franz Xaver Arnold, Karl Rahner. Freiburg, Herder, 1964-72. 5 v. in 6. LC 66-66410.

A comprehensive treatise on the history of pastoral theology, influences upon it, its principles and their application to modern problems. "It is possible that the complete manual will scarcely succeed in covering all the problems set to the Church by the rapidly evolving modern world. Nevertheless, this work will render the Church a very great service in her endeavors to fulfill the *aggiornamento* sought by the Vatican Council" (*Lumen Vitae*, XXIII [March 1968], p. 189). Bibliographies of almost exclusively German works are supplied for each chapter.

B284   Zumbro Valley Medical Society. Medicine and Religion Committee. **Religious Aspects of Medical Care: A Handbook of Religious Practices of All Faiths.** St. Louis, Catholic Hospital Association, 1975. viii, 64p. LC 74-18147. ISBN 0-8712-5019-5.

Basic religious beliefs as they affect medical treatment are described for 43 different religious groups. Among the topics covered are drugs, transplants, abortion, birth control, dietary regulations, and the right to die. The statements tend to be very brief and in some cases might lead to confusion if taken too literally.

DICTIONARIES

B285   **Katechetisches Wörterbuch.** Hrsg. von Leopold Lentner in Verbindung mit Hubert Fischer, Franz Bürkli und Gerard Fischer. Wien, Herder, 1961. LC 62-68176.

Contains long, signed articles, with bibliographies, covering technical terms, biographies, organizations, the history of catechetics and the state of religious instruction in different countries. "A good, strong work edited with care; . . . excellent indexes facilitating consultation" (*Nouvelle Revue théologique*, LXXXV [March, 1963] , p. 226).

HOMILETICS

B286   Herrera Oria, Angel, Cardinal, comp. and ed. **The Preacher's Encyclopedia.** English version trans. and ed. by David Greenstock. Westminster, MD, Newman Press, 1964-65. 4 v. LC 65-2580.

Contains liturgical, exegetical and moral notes on the scriptural readings used in the Sunday mass cycle with quotations from the Fathers and other theologians and saints on the theme of the day's liturgy. Texts from the writings of the popes and literary works and a sermon outline based on the Epistle and Gospel are also given. Each volume is devoted to a particular liturgical season.

B287   Maertins, Thierry. **Bible Themes—a Source Book.** Bruges, Biblica, 1964. 2 v.

An index to scriptural texts for sermon writers. 450 subject headings of "themes" are developed in brief paragraphs, each of which is followed by a list of references to suitable quotes from Scripture. The subjects are arranged in six major categories in a classified arrangement, but an alphabetical subject index is provided along with an index for the Sundays in the liturgical year.

B288   **Recent Homiletical Thought: A Bibliography.** Nashville, Abington Press, 1967-83. 2 v. LC 67-15948. ISBN 0-8010-5613-6.

A classified annotated bibliography of books, articles and theses covering Catholic and Protestant works. Volume 1 distinguishes between the two, volume 2 does not. Coverage is from 1935 to 1979. List of periodicals indexed and author index for each volume.

B289   Rufino, Mauricio, ed. **A Vademecum of Stories.** Trans. by Richard J. Restrepo. New York, Wagner, 1967. viii, 849p.

2,276 stories are printed under 82 topics. The stories are suitable for sermons. Index.

MISSIOLOGY

Bibliography

B290   **Bibliografia missionaria, anno 1- .** Comp. dal Giovanni Rommerskirchen (et al.). Roma, Pontificia Universitaria de Propanganda Fide, 1935- . v. Annual. LC 38-36351.

Listed books and periodical articles from 1933 in a classified arrangement with subject and author indexes in each volume and cumulated every four years. Annotations were not given except for some contents notes. A supplement to **(B292).**

B291   **Ronda, James P., and James Axtell. Indian Missions: A Critical Bibliography.** Bloomington, Published for the Newberry Library by Indiana University Press, 1978. xi, 85p. LC 78-3253. ISBN 0-253-32978-7.

The first part of this work is a bibliographical essay covering the topic in general and the work of eight specific denominations, Catholics included. The second part is an alphabetical listing of the 211 works surveyed. The purpose is to select the best or most important works from a massive literature.

B292   Streit, Robert. **Bibliotheca missionum.** begonnen von P. Robert Streit, fortgeführt von P. Johannes Dindinger. Freiberg, Herder, 1916-74. 30 v. (Veröffentlichungen des Internationalen Inst. für Missionswissenschaftliche Forschung.) LC 31-2188.

The largest and most complete bibliography of Catholic mission literature; lists and annotates histories, letters, diaries, Church documents, philological works and bibliographies. The annotations are descriptive and critical and contain some biographical material. Covers the literature of America, India, Japan, the Phillippines, Korea, Indochina and Indonesia up to 1909; Africa up to 1940; China, Australia and Oceania up to 1950. Locations in European libraries are given for many works. Much of this material is primary source material for the early histories of these countries.

B293   Vriens, Livinus. **Critical Bibliography of Missiology.** With the collaboration of Anastasius Disch (mission law) and J. Wils (linguistics). English ed. Trans. from the Dutch ms. by Deodatus Tummers. Nijmegen, Bestelcentrale der V.S.K.B. Publ., 1960. (Bibliographia ad usum seminariorum, v. E2.) LC 63-36628.

Covers works on mission theory, law, methodology, history, missiography, home missions and related subjects in a classified arrangement. Introductions to each of these types of literature are provided in addition to critical annotations. Index of authors and anonymous works.

B294   Laures, John. **Kirishtan bunko: A Manual of Books and Documents on the Early Christian Mission in Japan.** 3rd. ed. Tokyo, Sophia University, 1957. xxiv, 536p. (Monumenta nipponica monographs, no. 5).

Lists books, articles, documents and manuscripts covering missionary activity "from its beginnings to the first fifty years after the reopening of Japan to foreign intercourse" (Preface). The arrangement is by publisher with a separate list for doubtful works. Author, title and subject index. Special reference to the principal libraries in Japan and more particularly to the collection at Sophia University, Tokyo. Appendix of ancient maps of the Far East, especially Japan.

Dictionaries

B295 **The Encyclopedia of Missions: Descriptive, Historical, Biographical, Statistical.** Ed. under the auspices of the Bureau of Missions by Henry Otis Dwight. 2nd. ed. Detroit, Gale Research, 1975. xii, 851p. LC 74-31438. ISBN 0-8103-4205-7. (Reprint of 1904 ed. published by Funk and Wagnalls Co., New York).

Covers some Catholic mission activity, but not very thoroughly.

B296 Neill, Stephen Charles. **Concise Dictionary of the Christian World Mission.** Nashville, Abingdon Press, 1971. xxi, 682p. LC 76-21888. ISBN 0-6870-9371-6.

More than 240 contributors, of which 20 are Catholic, have written the articles for this ecumenical work. Missionary activity of all major Christian faiths and some non-Christian groups is covered. "The editors are to be complimented for retrieving so many pieces of the puzzle of Christian mission history" (*Catholic Historical Review*, LV [October, 1973], p. 506); but for detailed information on Catholic missionary activity the reader will have to consult other sources such as the yearbooks published in missionary districts (listed in Chapter IV under "Statistics").

Directories

B297 Agenzia Internationale Fides. **Le missioni cattoliche dipendenti dalla Sacra Congregazione de Propagande Fide: storia, geografia, statistica.** Roma, Consiglio Superiore della Pontificia opera della Propagazione delle Fide, 1950. 548p.

A directory of bishops, seminaries, churches, schools and other institutions— now considerably out-of-date. Brief histories of each territory are given along with statistics. Index.

B298 United States Catholic Mission Council. **Handbook.** Washington, DC, U.S.C.M.C., 1960- . v. Biennial.

A statistical summary of the number of American missionaries sent to foreign countries by religious orders and other groups. Geographical index.

Handbooks

B299 Schmidlin, Joseph. **Catholic Mission History.** Translation ed. by Matthias Braun. Techny, IL, Mission Press, S.V.D., 1933. xiv, 862p. LC 35-604.

An outline or survey of the field from the time of Christ. Each chapter is preceded by a critical bibliography, as is the work as a whole. The extensive index also covers the bibliographies.

B300   Schmidlin, Joseph. **Catholic Mission Theory**. Trans. by Matthias Braun.
Techny, IL, Mission Press, S.V.D., 1931. xi, 544p. LC A39-485.

A guide to the literature and sources of missiology and to its aims and
methods by the former "distinguished professor of missiology at the
University of Munster" (*America*, L [March 31, 1934], p. 631); now in
need of revision in the light of the new decree on missions promulgated
at the Second Vatican Council.

Atlases

B301   Despont, J. **Nouvel atlas des missions**. Paris, L'Oeuvre de la Propagation
de la Foi, 1951. 59p. LC A51-8342.

Covers only mission territories, showing national and diocesan boundaries
and little else. History and statistics are given for each area. Index. For
more up to date coverage of mission territories *see* Emmerich's *Atlas
hierarchicus* (D 195).

ASCETICAL AND MYSTICAL THEOLOGY

The writings of the masters of the spiritual life such as St. Theresa of Avila,
John of the Cross, Francis de Sales, etc., constitute one of the greatest bodies of
literature in Christendom but have never been, and are too large to be, issued in a
single collection such as those published for the Fathers of the Church. *Classics of
Western Spirituality* (B312) is a series that publishes excerpts from selected
authors. The majority of the works listed here deal with the principles they lived and
taught. The most important work in the field is easily Viller's *Dictionnaire de
spiritualité ascétique et mystique* (B316) which covers both the history and teachings of
asceticism. A rebirth of interest in mysticism and spirituality has led to the publication
of some new and significant works such as B315, 319, and 320.

BIBLIOGRAPHY

B302   **Bibliographia internationalis spiritualitatis**. Rome, Pontificio Istituto de
Spiritualità, Edizioni dei Padri Carmelitani Scalzi, 1966- . v. Annual. ISSN
0084-7836.

Indexes books and articles under eight headings: Sources, Biblical Spirituality,
Doctrines of Spirituality, Liturgical Spirituality, The Spiritual Life, History of
Spirituality, Art and Spirituality, Allied Disciplines, Name index. Subject index.

B303   **Bibliotheca Catholica Neerlandica, impressa 1500-1727**. Hagae Comitis, M.
Nijhoff, 1954. x, 669p. LC 55-36980.

A chronological listing of devotional literature published in Holland during
the times of the Vicars Apostolic (1592-1727). Over 18,000 items are
included with only the briefest bibliographical descriptions. No annotations.
Index.

B304   Bowman, Mary Ann. **Western Mysticism: A Guide to the Basic Works**. Chicago,
American Library Association, 1978. vi, 113p. LC 78-18311. ISBN 0-8389-0266-9.

A selected bibliography of primary and secondary sources on mystics and mysticism suitable for the general reader. Arranged chronologically. Author-Title Index. Subject Index. Appendix: A Guide for Acquisition Librarians.

B305   Dagens, Jean. **Bibliographie Chronologique de la littérature de spiritualité et de ses sources 1501-1610.** Paris, Desclée, 1953. 208p. LC 54-30524.

The period covered by this bibliography is an important one in the history of Christian spirituality. The works listed here are arranged chronologically. No annotations. Author index.

B306   Dols, Jean Michel Emile. **Bibliographie der moderne devotie.** Nigmegen, Centrale Drukkerij, 1936-41. 2 v. LC 36-31896.

A selected bibliography of international devotional literature with material on the history of the literature and biographies of authors. Some periodical literature is included. No annotations.

B307   Lagorio, Valerie Marie and Ritamary Bradley. **The 14th Century English Mystics: A Comprehensive Annotated Bibliography.** New York, Garland, 1981. ix, 197p. LC 79-7922. ISBN 0-8240-9535-9.

Attempts to cover the scholarship of the past 100 years on 14th century English mysticism — especially on the five major figures of the era: Richard Rolle, the author of *The Cloud of Unknowing*, Walter Hilton, Julian of Norwich and Margery Kempe. Secondary writers and some post-Reformation and Recusant figures are also covered. 841 books and articles are listed; theses are not included. Author and subject index.

B308   Matthews, Stanley G. **Recommended Spiritual Reading Books.** Dayton, OH, Marianist Publications, 1959. 38p.

An annotated list of 308 works for spiritual reading arranged by subject with an author index. To have been supplemented and revised every five years. *See* the *Catholic Periodical and Literature Index* (A160) for many similar lists, too small or ephemeral for inclusion here.

B309   Metodio da Nembro, Carobbio Mario. **Quatrocento scrittori spirituali.** Milan, Centro Studi Cappuccini Lombardi, 1972. xvi, 465p. LC 73-316838.

A chronological study of over 600 spiritual writers from the period. Subject and author indexes.

B310   Sáenz de Tejada, José Maria. **Bibliografía de la devoción al Carazón de Jesús (ensayo).** Bilbao, Mensajero del Corazón de Jesús, 1952. 434p. LC A53-2490.

Covers books in all languages with descriptive annotations. Arranged by author with a subject index.

B311   Sawyer, Michael E. **A Bibliographical Index of Five English Mystics: Richard Rolle, Julian of Norwich, the Author of the Cloud of Unknowing, Walter Hilton, Margery Kempe.** Pittsburgh, Clifford E. Barbour Library, 1978. xiii, 126p. LC 78-110788. ISBN 0-931222-09-5.

   A listing of primary and secondary sources for each mystic. No indexes.

SOURCES

B312   **Classics of Western Spirituality: A Library of the Great Spiritual Masters.** New York, Paulist Press, 1978- . v.

   A new series, ecumenical in scope. Each volume is devoted to a single author, containing selections from his works, a preface and lengthy introduction, a selected bibliography and an index to the prefatory material as well as the texts.

B313   Jaegher, Paul de. **An Anthology of Mysticism.** Ed. with an intro. and biographical notes by Paul de Jaegher, S. J. Trans. by Donald Attwater and others. Westminster, MD, Newman Press, 1950. viii, 281p. LC A51-9826.

   A collection of brief excerpts from the writings of twenty-one Catholic mystics from St. Anselm of Foligno (1248) to Mother Marie Ste. Cecile (1929). References to complete texts in English are given.

B314   Rouët de Journel, Marie Joseph. **Enchiridion asceticum: loci SS. patrum et scriptorum ecclesiasticorum ad ascesim spectantes,** quos collegerunt M. J. Rouët de Journel et J. Dutilleul. Ed. 6. Barcinone, Herder, 1965. xxxv, 682p.

   Selected passages from the Greek and Latin Fathers of the Church. Greek works are printed in Greek and Latin. Sources are noted. Subject index.

DICTIONARIES AND ENCYCLOPEDIAS

B315   **Dictionnaire de la vie spirituelle.** Sous la direction de Stefano De Fiores et Tullo Goffi. Paris, Éditions du Cerf, 1983. xxii, 1246p. ISBN 2-204-01842-2.

   Articles deal with concepts rather than people or schools of spirituality. Most articles are from 6 to 12 pages long, are preceded by a summary and followed by a bibliography of mostly French language works. Index. "Only the high price of this volume might stand in the way of the wide circulation it so richly deserves" (*Lumen Vitae*, XXXIX [1984], p. 468).

B316   **Dictionnaire de spiritualité ascétique et mystique, doctrine et histoire,** publié sous la direction de Marcel Viller, S.J., assisté de F. Cavallera et J. de Guibert, S.J., avec le concours d'un grand nombre de collaborateurs. Paris, G. Beauchesne, 1932- . v. LC 38-24895.

   The most comprehensive reference work in this field with long, signed articles covering concepts of spiritual theology and explaining their origin and development through the centuries with frequent references to sources. The lives, written works, doctrines, mystical experiences, and influences of the masters of the spiritual life are covered, as well as many minor figures in the field. Bibliographies are given for each article with much detailed information on editions; some are subdivided by subject. Each country of the world is covered, its spiritual history by century and the individual schools of spirituality that flourished there. The "excellence characteristic of this series" has long been acknowledged by critics (*Theological Studies*, XXVI [September, 1965], p. 454).

B317 **Dizionario enciclopedico di spiritualitá.** Diretto de Ermanno Ancilli. Roma, Studium, 1975. 2 v. LC 76-522017.

A comprehensive, scholarly work covering schools of spirituality, biography and related topics. The articles are of moderate length, are signed and contain bibliographies of works in all languages.

B318 Ferguson, John. **Encyclopedia of Mysticism and the Mystery of Religions.** New York, Crossroads, 1982. 228p. LC 82-123902. ISBN 0-8245-0429-1.

Reprint of 1976 edition. Covers persons and topics from all religions, East and West. Articles range from one line to a page. Primary sources are mentioned but bibliographic citations are not supplied. A fine one-volume work on mysticism for the non-expert and a good bibliography of secondary sources" (*Theological Studies*, XXXVIII [December, 1977], p. 824).

B319 **The Westminster Dictionary of Christian Spirituality.** Edited by Gordon S. Wakefield. Philadelphia, Westminster Press, 1983. xv, 400p. LC 83-14527. ISBN 0-6642-1396-0.

An ecumenical work dealing with topics and persons from all schools of spirituality, Christian and non-Christian. All major Catholic schools of spirituality are covered. Articles are signed and include cross references and a bibliography. "The articles are models of conciseness and compression. At the same time they are accurate and up-to-date" (*Theological Studies*, XLV [December, 1984], p. 778).

HANDBOOKS

B320 **The Study of Spirituality.** Edited by Cheslyn Jones, Geoffrey Wainwright, Edward Yarnold, S.J. New York, Oxford University Press, 1986. xxix, 634p. LC 86-8380. ISBN 0-19-504169-0.

Divided into two parts: Part One is an introduction to the theology of spirituality; Part Two is a history of spirituality covering Biblical and philosophical roots, the fathers, the medieval West, the Catholic Reformation, English Roman Catholics in the 18th and 19th centuries, and current Roman Catholic spirituality. Each subsection has a bibliography. Index of Subjects. Index of Names. "A timely and relevant volume and one which will serve as a useful resource book" (*Month*, XX [January, 1987], p. 44).

B321 Tanquerey, Adolphe. **The Spiritual Life: A Treatise on Ascetical and Mystical Theology.** Trans. by Herman Branderis. 2nd. rev. ed. New York, Desclée, 1961. xlviii, 750+21p.

Covers the general principles of the spiritual life and of each of its three stages as conceived in the traditional manner—the purgative, illuminative and unitive. Each chapter has its own bibliography in addition to the general bibliography (pp. xvii-xlviii) which is arranged by period. The first edition was described as "A comprehensive epitome of the doctrines inculcated by the great spiritual teachers of the Catholic Church" (*Catholic World*, CLXV [April, 1937], p. 125).

HISTORY

B322   Bouyer, Louis. **History of Christian Spirituality**. By Louis Bouyer and others. New York, Seabury, 1963-69. 3 v. LC 63-16487.

Not primarily biographical or bibliographical in approach, but organized by school or period. There are no bibliographies as such but many bibliographical notes and frequent chapters on the literature of various topics. "The scope of the work is broad, but Father Bouyer's great knowledge and wide reading meet the challenge successfully; . . . an adequate, comprehensive manual and reference book for students and teachers alike" (*Catholic Historical Review*, L [January, 1965], p. 530). Indexes: subjects, Biblical, ancient authors, modern authors.

B323   Gautier, Jean. **Some Schools of Catholic Spirituality**. Aided by Eugene Masure and others. Trans. by Kathryn Sullivan. New York, Desclée, 1959. 384p. LC 59-12020.

A selective survey of the spirituality of the major religious orders, the *Imitation of Christ*, and contemporary French spirituality. Some bibliography is supplied, but the work has been criticized for its failure to present an adequate theological basis for the characteristics of each school (*Theological Studies*, XXI [June, 1960], p. 307). No index.

B324   Pourrat, Pierre. **Christian Spirituality**. Westminster, MD, Newman Press, 1953-55. 4 v. LC 53-5585.

A history of Christian spirituality from the early Church to the beginning of the twentieth century. Each chapter contains extensive bibliographical notes. "Meant to be a readable history, but at the same time pinpoints valuable information for handy reference" (*Catholic Library World*, XXIV [May, 1953], p. 273). Index in each volume.

ECUMENISM

BIBLIOGRAPHY

B325   **Internationale ökumenische bibliographie; International Ecumenical Bibliography; Bibliographie Oecuménique Internationale**. Mainz, Matthias-Grünewald-Verlag 1962/63- . v.

A classified annotated bibliography of books and articles covering 1) the history and present condition of churches country by country, and 2) "theological questions." A subject bibliography covers unity, God, Christ, man, Scripture, sacraments and other topics. Compiled by experts from all faiths but mostly Catholics. Index.

B326   Lescrauwaet, Josephus Franciscus. **Critical Bibliography of Ecumenical Literature**. Nigmegen, Bestel Centrale V.S.K.B., 1965. 93p. (Bibliographia ad usum seminariorum v. 7.) LC 67-124280.

An international bibliography covering 351 basic works on churches in general and by types, the Ecumenical Movement, East-West relations, the World Council of Churches, and the Roman Catholic Church and ecumenism. The annotations are detailed and critical. Selection was limited to generally available and in-print works. Author index.

B327　Puglisi, J.F. and S.J. Voicu. **A Bibliography of Interchurch and Interconfessional Theological Dialogues.** Rome, Centro pro Unione, 1984. 260p. LC 85-119787.

An extensive listing of the texts of dialogues between major faiths with lists of news reports about them and "Reflections and Reactions" to them. Arranged by the names of the churches involved in the dialogue. No indexes.

B328　Sutfin, Edward J. **A Selected Annotated Bibliography on Ecumenical and Related Matters.** Haverford, PA, Catholic Library Association, 1968. (Reprinted from *Liturgical Arts Magazine*).

Selections cover a wide variety of topics. Long and critical annotations are supplied.

DICTIONARIES AND ENCYCLOPEDIAS

B329　**Ökumene Lexikon: Kirchen, Religionen, Bewegungen.** Hrsg. in Verbindung mit Athanasios Basdekis ... (et al.) von Hanfried Krüger, Werner Löser und Walter Müller-Romheld. Frankfort am Main, Lembeck, Knecht, 1983. 1326p. LC 84-110788. ISBN 3-87476-200-9.

Brief articles dealing with ecumenical topics and names. Most articles contain bibliographies and cross references. "There are significant omissions ... The listing of world nations, giving population figures and the percentage of religious affiliations, is very helpful. Also well done is the description of each major ecumenical conference and its significance for its time" (*Journal of Ecumenical Studies*, XXI [Fall, 1978], p. 781).

LITURGY

The liturgy encompasses the public prayers and ceremonies of the Church, specifically the mass, the divine office and the administration of the sacraments. Although some general works on Eastern rites appear on this list, it is mainly devoted to the Latin rite.

GENERAL WORKS

BIBLIOGRAPHY

B330　Amiet, Robert. **Repertorium liturgicum Augustanum: Les témoins de la liturgie du Diocèse d'Aoste.** Aoste, Typo-offset, 1974. 2 v. il. LC 75-57213.

A catalogue of 291 manuscripts dealing with the liturgy of the Val d'Aosta region of Italy. An introduction to the liturgy and the liturgical books is contained in volume 1. The entries contain a complete description of the item and a bibliography. Microfilm copies are noted. Indexes.

B331   Kapsner, Oliver Leonard. **Benedictine Liturgical Books in American Benedictine Libraries: A Progress Checklist Prepared for the Library Science Section of the American Benedictine Academy.** Latrobe, PA, St. Vincent College Library, 1960. 311. LC 61-468.

A classified listing of 322 items with library locations.

B332   Rupke, Ursula Irene. **Liturgische Zeitschriften und Reihen des deutschen Sprachgebiets im 20 Jahrhundert unter Berücks. d. liturg. Bewegung u. Reform im Kath. Raum. Paderborn.** Arbeitsgemeinschaft Kath.-Theolog. Bibliotheken, 1974. xxv, 166p. LC 75-584602. (Veröffentlichungen der Arbeitsgemeinschaft Katholisch-Theologischer Bibliotheken, 2).

A survey of the German language liturgical press and liturgical reform.

B333   Vismans, Thomas A. **Critical Bibliography of Liturgical Literature** by Th. A. Vismans and Lucas Brinkhoff. Trans. from the German and ed. by Raymund W. Fitzpatrick and Clifford Howell. Nijmegen, Bestelcentrale der V.S.K.B. Publ., 1961. 72p. (Bibliographia ad usum seminariorum, v. E. 1.) LC 63-35902.

A basic, retrospective list of some 300 liturgical works with critical annotations. "Admirably complete and highly to be recommended" (*Worship*, XXXV [July, 1961], p. 466). Index.

B334   **Yearbook of Liturgical Studies.** Notre Dame, IN, Fides Pub. Assoc., 1960-67. 7 v. LC 60-15442.

Originally this work contained a series of liturgical studies and an index to liturgical articles in periodicals. Later this was expanded to include books, and annotations were added. The last volume to appear (1967) contained only an unannotated bibliography.

SOURCES

B335   **Documents on the Liturgy, 1963-1979—Conciliar, Papal, and Curial Texts.** International Commission on English in the Liturgy. Collegeville, MN, Liturgical Press, 1982. xv, 1496p. LC 82-83580. ISBN 0-8146-1281-4.

Edited and translated by Thomas C. O'Brien. A carefully edited collection of 544 documents presented in seven categories: General Principles, The Eucharist, Other Sacraments and Sacramentals, The Divine Office, The Liturgical Year, Music, Art and Furnishings. The full texts of the documents are given along with notes. Cross references to other documents are supplied. The Appendices include a chronological listing of all the documents, a classified list of document (e.g., constitutions, decrees, addresses, letters, etc.), an index of incipits (beginning words in Latin), a 53-page General Index referring back to numbered paragraphs in the texts, other indexes and lists.

B336   **Enchiridion documentorum instaurationis liturgicae.** Composuit et indice auxit Reiner Kaczynski. Torino, Marietti, 1976- . v.
        Vol. 1. 1963-1973.

Contains the texts of 180 items in numbered paragraphs with an extensive index (223 pp.). Bibliographies include references to official Latin and vernacular texts of liturgical services as well as to secondary material. "The original documents assembled in this collection can be found only by searching through dozens of other volumes" (*Jurist*, XXXVI [1976], p. 254).

B337 **Liturgiesgeschichtliche Quellen und Forschungen.** Münster, Ascherdorff, 1919- . v.

Produced at the Maria Laach Abbey, the center of the liturgical movement; a major collection of ancient and later liturgical texts as well as scholarly studies.

B338 **Notitiae: commentarii ad nuntia et studia de re liturgica.** Edita cura Sectionis pro Cultu Divino, Sacrae Congregationis por Sacrementis et Cultu Divino. Roma, Typis Polyglottis Vaticanis, 1965- . v. Monthly.

An official publication containing texts of documents bearing on the liturgy, liturgical texts themselves, and studies on liturgical topics.

B339 Seasoltz, R. Kevin. **The New Liturgy: A Documentation, 1903-1965.** New York, Herder and Herder, 1966, xivii, 707p. LC 65-13481.

A collection of papal and other Church documents dealing with the liturgical reform from the *Motu proprio* on sacred music of Pius X to the Liturgical Constitution of Vatican II. Index.

LITURGICAL BOOKS

The chief liturgical books of the Roman rite are the *Roman Missal* containing the text of the mass; the *Breviary*, containing the psalms and prayers that make up the seven parts or "Hours" of the divine office; the *Martyrology*, the official list of all the saints, not just martyrs, with brief biographies, formerly used for daily recitation at the hour of *Prime* in the office; the *Pontifical*, which contains the prayers and ceremonies of those rites ordinarily reserved to the bishop, such as the administration of holy orders and confirmation, the consecration of a church, an altar, a cemetery, the blessing of oils, and the canonical visitation of churches and religious houses; the *Ritual*, containing the prayers and cermonies used in the administration of the sacraments, funerals, processions and the formulas for blessing various objects; and the *Ceremonial of Bishops*, containing detailed directions for pontifical functions and for everything connected with the mass, directions for singing the office in cathedral churches, and for various extra-liturgical functions. *The Memorial of Rites* is also an official liturgical book but so far out-of-date that it is not included on this list.

Listed below are editions of the books both as they existed in the Tridentine era and as they now exist in the versions reformed by the Second Vatican Council. The typical editions were prepared by the Consilium for the Implementation of the Constitution on the Sacred Liturgy. For English speaking countries a vernacular version of the books was prepared by the International Commission on English in the Liturgy. American editions usually contain additional material peculiar to United States liturgical practice.

BIBLIOGRAPHY

B340   Bohatta, Hanns. **Katalog der liturgis'chen Drücke des XV und XVI Jahr-hunderts in der Herzogl. Parma'schen Bibliothek.** Wien, A. Holzhausen, 1909-10. 2 v. LC 9-18018.

      A catalog of 606 books in the liturgical collection of the library of Robert de Bourbon (Robert Bohatta).

B341   Bohatta, Hanns. **Liturgische Bibliographie des XV Jahrhunderts mit Aus-nahme der missale und livres d'heures.** Wien, Gilhofer und Ranschburg, 1911. viii, 71p. LC 12-11728.

      A supplement ot Weale's *Bibliographia liturgica* (B356), first edition, (1886) and to the author's *Bibliographie der livres d'heures* | (B364).

B342   Hoskins, Edgar. **Horae Beatae Mariae Virginis, or Sarum and York Primers, with Kindred Books and Primers of the Reformed Roman Usage together with an Introduction.** London, Longmans, Green, 1901. lvi, 577p. LC 2-9315.

      Lists 297 liturgical books printed in England from 1778-1817 with descrip-tive annotations and a directory of printers and booksellers. Indexes.

B343   Lacombe, Paul. **Livres d'heures imprimés au XV et au XVIe siècle, con-servés dan les bibliothèques publiques de Paris.** Paris, Imprimerie nationale, 1907. lxxxiv, 438p. LC 8-11532.

      598 items listed by publisher with complete transcriptions of title pages, descriptive notes and locations. Index.

B344   Pfaff, Richard W. **Medieval Latin Liturgy: A Select Bibliography.** Toronto, University of Tornoto Press, 1982. xviii, 129p. (Toronto Medieval Bibliographies; 9.) LC 82-178542. ISBN 0-8020-5564-8.

      "Aims to cover the most important sources—editions of, and literature concerning the medieval Latin liturgy" (Preface). Over 1,000 titles are listed by topic. No annotations. Author index.

HANDBOOKS

B345   Cabrol, Fernand. **The Books of the Latin Liturgy.** Trans. by the Benedic-tines of Stanbrook, St. Louis, Herder Book Co., 1932. xii, 165p. (Catholic Library of Religious Knowledge, XXIII.) LC 33-3740.

      A thorough treatment of the history and contents of the official liturgical books used in the Latin rite, with sóme coverage of various extra-liturgical books. Each chapter contains a bibliography in addition to the general bibliography. "Of deep interest to theologians, historians, and librarians" (*America*, XLVII [August 20, 1932], p. 481).

ROMAN MISSAL

      Since the post-Vatican II reforms in the mass have been implemented, the missal now commonly appears in two volumes: the *Lectionary*, containing the readings from Scripture and the *Sacramentary*, containing the prayers of the mass.

B346   **Missale romanum, ex decreto sacrosancti Concilii tridentini restitutum.**
        Summorum pontificum cura recognitum. Editio iuxta typicam. Novi
        Eboraci, Benziger, 1963. Variously paged.

        This edition contains the text of the mass essentially as it existed from
        the Council of Trent (1545-63) until the changes introduced by the Second
        Vatican Council. A good bilingual edition is the *English-Latin Roman Missal
        for the United States of America* (New York, Benziger Bros., 1966.
        1268+436+52p).

B347   **Lectionary for Mass: English Translation approved by the National Conference
        of Catholic Bishops and Confirmed by the Apostolic See.** Bible Texts from the
        Jerusalem Bible. New York, Benziger, 1970. xxvii, 976p. LC 74-23209.

B348   **Lectionary for Mass. English Translation Approved by the National Conference
        of Catholic Bishops and Confirmed by the Apostolic See.** Revised Standard
        Version, Catholic Edition. Collegeville, MN, Liturgical Press, 1970. xlii, 2078p.

B349   **Lectionary for Mass: English Translation approved by the National
        Conference of Catholic Bishops and Confirmed by the Apostolic See.**
        With the New American version of Sacred Scripture from the original
        languages made by members of the Catholic Biblical Association and
        sponsored by the Bishops' Committee of the Division of Religious Educa-
        tion (Confraternity of Christian Doctrine). New York, Catholic Book Pub.
        Co., 1970. 1122p. LC 76-23204.

        The Lectionary is a part of the newly reformed Roman Missal. It contains
        the readings (epistles and gospels) used at Mass, which have been expanded
        into a complex three-year cycle. It also contains responsorial psalms recited
        by reader and congregation after the first reading. Other prayers of the
        Mass are now found in the *Sacramentary*.

B350   **The Sacramentary: Approved for Use in the Dioceses of the United States
        of America by the National Conference of Catholic Bishops and Confirmed
        by the Apostolic See.** New York, Catholic Book Pub. Co., 1974. 84+1099p.
        il. LC 78-316089.

        "Translation by the International Commission on English in the liturgy,
        with additions and adaptations for the U.S. by the Bishops' Committee
        on the Liturgy of the *Sacramentary*." The *Sacramentary* is part of the
        new *Roman Missal* and contains the proper prayers for each day of the
        year as well as the new common parts of the mass. The scriptural readings
        used at mass are now contained in the *Lectionary*.

B351   **Le Gradual romain.** Edition critique par les moines de Solesmes. Solesmes,
        Abbaye Saint-Pierre, 1957- . v. LC A59-5351.

        The *Roman Gradual* is an outgrowth of the *Missal* and contains all the
        chants used at mass for every day of the year. The new critical edition
        will supersede the Vatican edition of 1907 and provide historical and
        bibliographical information as well.

B352   Nevins, Albert J. **General Intercessions: The Prayer of the Faithful.** Rev. and enl. ed. of *Prayers of the Faithful for Every Occasion covering the seasonal cycle, sanctoral and special feasts, pastoral masses and other occasions.* Huntington, IN, Our Sunday Visitor, 1978. 128p. LC 77-90846. ISBN 0-87973-806-5.

The "prayer of the faithful" is a part of the reformed liturgy of the mass. The prayers contained in this collection are not required texts. Each diocese or church may compose its own.

B353   Pflieger, André. **Liturgicae orationis concordantia verbalia.** Rome, Herder, 1963. xi, 740p. Prima Pars: Missale Romanum.

A concordance to the common words in the Roman Missal. Some proper names—Jesus, Mary, the apostles—are included. References to both the common and proper of the mass are given.

B354   Schuster, Ildefonso, Cardinal. **The Sacramentary: Historical and Liturgical Notes on the Roman Missal.** Trans. from the Italian by Arthur Levelis-Marke. London, Burns, Oates and Washbourne, Ltd., 1924-30. 5 v. il. LC 25-19635.

Contains general introductory material on the mass and an analysis—historical, archeological and scriptural—of every mass in the liturgical year. The arrangement is by the liturgical calendar which makes for easy reference, but there is no index or bibliography. *Catholic World* said of this work that its "high level of scholarship merits enthusiastic praise," and that the translation is "clear, fluid, and exact" (CXXIV [November, 1929], p. 508).

B355   Sloyan, Gerard Stephen. **Commentary on the New Lectionary.** New York, Paulist Press, 1975. ix, 428p. LC 75-22781. ISBN 0-8091-1895-5.

One-page commentaries on the readings for Sunday masses "intended to help the clergy and others who engage in promoting weekly divine worship—i.e. preachers, readers and music directors" (Preface).

B356   Weale, William Henry James. **Bibliographia liturgica. Catalogus missalium ritus latini ab anno MCCCCLXX IV impressorum.** Collegit W. H. Iacobus Weale, iterum edidit H. Bohatta. Londini, B. Quaritch, 1928. xxxii, 380p. LC 38-36379.

A catalog of 1,931 *Roman Missals* printed from 1474 to about 1655. Locations in libraries and complete bibliographical descriptions are given. The arrangement is by place and by religious orders, with indexes.

ROMAN BREVIARY

B357   **Brevarium romanum ex decreto sacrosancti Concilii tridentini restitutum S. Pii V. pontificis maximi iussu editum aliorumque pontificum cura recognitum, Pii papae X. auctoritate reformatum.** Editio II iuxta typicam vaticanam amplificata I. Neo Eboraci, Benziger Bros., 1943. 4 v. LC 44-23919.

This edition contains the *Vulgate* version of the psalms; for the Latin version revised by order of Pope Pius XII see any edition after 1946.

B358   **Roman Breviary in English,** Restored by the Sacred Council of Trent,
Published by Order of the Supreme Pontiff St. Pius V, and Carefully
Revised by Other Popes. Reformed by Order of Pope Pius X. According
to the Vatican Typical Edition, with new Psalter of Pope Pius XII.
Compiled from Approved Sources. With "An Incentive to Prayer" by
Francis Cardinal Spellman. Ed. by Joseph A. Nelson, New York, Benziger,
1950-51. 4 v. LC 50-2806.

Both this and **(B357)** contain the text as it existed until the recent series
of changes and omissions.

B359   **Liturgy of the Hours: Approved by the Episcopal Conferences of the
Antilles, Bangladesh, Burma, Canada, of the Pacific (CEPAC), Ghana,
India, New Zealand, Pakistan, Papua-New Guinea and the Solomons,
The Philippines, Rhodesia, South Africa, Sri Lanka, Tanzania, Uganda,
and the United States of America For Use in Their Dioceses and Confirmed
by the Apostolic See.** With Proper for the United States. New York, Catholic
Book Pub. Co., 1975-76. 4 v. LC 78-318850.

"English translation prepared by the International Commission on English
in the Liturgy." Based on the Vatican Typical Edition and published in
some editions as *The Prayer of Christians*, this version is the result of the
reforms ordered by Vatican II.

B360   **Our Lady's Daily Hours: The Little Office of the Blessed Virgin Mary,
According to the Roman Breviary, with the Latin Psalter of the Pontifical
Biblical Institute Approved by Pope Pius XII and the English Translations
of the New Testament and the Psalms Made under the Patronage of the
Episcopal Committee of the Confraternity of Christian Doctrine.** Ed. with
a complete commentary by Dominic J. Unger. Paterson, NJ, St. Anthony
Guild Press, 1954. xxv, 534p. LC 54-3109.

Used as a substitute for the *Roman Breviary* by some religious groups.

B361   Britt, Matthew. **The Hymns of the Breviary and Missal.** Rev. ed. New York,
Benziger Bros., 1936. 383p. LC 36-18952.

A collection of verse translations of 176 Latin hymns, with Latin texts,
literal translations, and notes on authorship and liturgical use. The arrangement is by place in the office with Latin and English indexes.

B362   Connelly, Joseph. **Hymns of the Roman Liturgy by Joseph Connelly.**
Westminster, MD, Newman Press, 1957. xxiii, 263p. LC 57-6438.

English prose translations of 154 hymns with annotations on authorship,
source, liturgical use and other information. Author and first line indexes.

B363   Bohatta, Hanns. **Bibliographie der breviere, 1501-1850.** Leipzig, K. W.
Hiersemann, 1937. vii, 349p. LC AC37-2642.

Lists nearly 3,000 Breviaries including Roman Breviaries, those proper
to various religious orders and to certain dioceses. Indexed by title, chronology,
publisher and place.

B364   Bohatta, Hanns. **Bibliographie der livres de' heures (horae B.M.V.) officia,
        hortuli animae, coronae B.M.V., rosaria und cursus B.M.V. des XV und
        XVI Jahrhunderts.** 2d. aufl. Wien, Gilhofer und Ranschburg, 1924.

        A catalog of 1,582 books of hours and 236 offices of the Blessed Virgin
        Mary.

B365   Britt, Matthew. **A Dictionary of the Psalter, Containing the Vocabulary
        of the Psalms, Hymns, Canticles and Miscellaneous Prayers of the Breviary
        Psalter.** New York, Benziger Bros., 1928. xxxvi, 299p. LC 29-1306.

        Defines 2,700 words used in the hymns, prayers and psalms (*Vulgate*
        version). Some Hebrew words are defined also. "A fine bit of painstaking
        and scholarly research," which also gives examples of usage (*Catholic World*,
        CXXIX [July, 1929], p. 508).

B366   Konus, William J. **Dictionary of the New Latin Psalter of Pope Pius XII.**
        Westminster, MD, Newman Press, 1959. 132p. LC 59-9407.

        Definitions of words used in the psalms with references to their use. Proper
        names are included.

B367   Batiffol, Pierre. **History of the Roman Breviary.** Trans. by Atwell M. Y.
        Baylay, M. A. From the 3rd French ed. with a new chapter on the Decree
        of Pius X. London, Longmans, Green, 1912.

        A scholarly account of the development of the Breviary from its origins to
        1911, with bibliographical notes and appendixes. Index.

ROMAN RITUAL

B368   **The Roman Ritual in Latin and English, with Rubrics and Plainchant.**
        Notation, tr. and ed. with intro. and notes by Philip T. Weller. Milwaukee,
        Bruce Pub. Co., 1946-52. 3 v. LC 47-27305.

        A complete edition of the pre-Vatican II ceremonies with indexes in each
        volume.

B369   **The Rites of the Catholic Church as Revised by Decree of the Second Vatican
        Ecumenical Council and Published by Authority of Pope Paul VI.** English
        translation prepared by the International Commission on English in the Liturgy.
        Study ed. New York, Pueblo Publishing Company, 1983. xvi, 818p. LC
        84-197201. ISBN 0-916134-15-6.

        First edition, 1978. This volume contains rites for ceremonies performed by
        priests as revised by the Second Vatican Council on English in the Liturgy. In this
        collection, the many prayers and blessings for various occasions and objects have
        been omitted and the emphasis placed on ceremonies for the administration of
        the sacraments of baptism, penance, matrimony, anointing of the sick, and
        burial. Some ceremonies for bishops are also included.

ROMAN PONTIFICAL

B370   **Pontificale romanum.** Editio typica emendata. Città del Vaticano, Typis
        Polyglottis Vaticanis, 1962-63. 3 v. il.

An edition of the pre-Vatican II version with complete texts of ceremonies and directions for their performance. Index in each volume.

B371   **Roman Pontifical Revised by Decree of the Second Vatican Ecumenical Council and Published by Authority of Pope Paul VI.** Washington, DC, International Commission on English in the Liturgy, 1978- . v.

The texts and rubrics for the administration of confirmation, holy orders and the blessings of abbots, abbesses and the reception of religious vows are contained in this version. These ceremonies are usually performed only by bishops.

B372   Puniet, Pierre de. **The Roman Pontifical: A History and Commentary.** Trans. for the Benedictines of Stanbrook by Mildred Vernon Harcourt. London, Longmans, Green, 1932- . v. LC 32-25005.

A scholarly history of the origins of the *Pontifical* with theological commentary on the ceremonies and prayers. The French version (1930-31) consists of two volumes.

CEREMONIAL OF BISHOPS

B373   **Manual of Episcopal Ceremonies Based on the Caeremoniale episcoporum, Decrees of the Sacred Congregation of Rites and Approved Authors.** By Aurelius Stehle. Rev. by Emmeran A. Rettger. 5th ed. Latrobe, PA, Archabbey Press, 1961. 2 v. LC 61-13124.

Contains detailed instructions and some texts for pre-Vatican II ceremonies. Index.

ROMAN MARTYROLOGY

B374   **Martyrologium romanum Gregorii Papae XIII editum Urbani VIII et Clementis X auctoritatae recognitum ac deindo anno MDCCXLIX Benedicti XIV opera ac studio emendatum et actum. Quarta post typicam editio iuxta primam a typica editionem anno MDCCCCXXII a Benedicto XV adprobatam.** Città del Vaticano, Typis Polyglotti Vaticanis, 1956. cxxiii, 542p.

The official version for use in the liturgy with over 200 pages of indexing by name, place, category, etc.

B375   **Martyrologium romanum: ad formam editionis typicano scholis historicis instructum.** Ediderunt Hippolytus Delehaye. Bruxelles, Sociéte des Bollandistes, 1940. xxiii, 659p. (In Acta sanctorum, t. 68. Propylaeum ad Acta sanctorum Decembris).

A critical edition based on scholarly methods devised by the Bollandists.

B376   **The Roman Martyrology: In Which Are to Be Found the Eulogies of the Saints and Blessed Approved by the Sacred Congregation of Rites up to 1961.** Ed. by J. B. O'Connell. London, Burns and Oates, 1962. xix, 412p. LC 62-21497.

An English translation of the uncritical Vatican text approved by Pope Benedict XV. Index.

B377   Russo-Alesi, Anthony Ignatius. **Martyrology Pronouncing Dictionary**. New York, E. O'Toole Co., 1939. LC 39-21766.

"Contains the Pronunciation of Over 5,000 names of Martyrs, Confessors, Virgins, Emperors, Cities and Places Occurring in the Roman Martyrology with a Daily Calendar and a List of the Patron Saints." Cites authorities for the pronunciations. Among the many appendixes is an American Martyrology arranged by state.

DICTIONARIES AND ENCYCLOPEDIAS

The most scholarly liturgical dictionary, Cabrol's *Dictionnaire d'Archéologie chrétienne et de liturgy* (B382) covers only up to the ninth century, but there are several smaller works of high quality such as Podhradsky's *New Dictionary of Liturgy* (B389) which supplies basic information on modern liturgical matters, and Davies' *Dictionary of Liturgy and Worship* (B383) which covers liturgy from an ecumenical perspective.

B378   Berger, Rupert. **Kleines Liturgisches Wörterbuch**. Freiburg im Breisgau, Herder, 1969. 404p. LC 70-459642.

Contains brief articles of a page or less in length. Cross references. No index.

B379   Braun, Joseph. **Liturgisches Handlexikon**. 2 verb. sehr verm. aufl. München, Kösel-Pustet, 1950. viii, 399p.

A small dictionary of the liturgy with no bibliography. Covers history, ceremonies, technical terms, national liturgies and so forth.

B380   Blaise, Albert. **Le vocabulaire latin des principaux thèmes liturgiques**. Ouvrage revu par Dom Antoine Dumas, O.S.B. Turnhout, Brepols, 1966. 639p. LC 67-112768.

More than a language dictionary. Limited to patristic texts on the liturgy, it serves as a liturgical index to the Fathers by giving quotations with references along with detailed definitions.

B381   Brinkhoff, Lucas. **Liturgisch woordenboek**. Samengesteld onder redactie van L. Brinkhoff, et al. Roermond, J. J. Romen, 1962- . v. (Romen's woordenboeken.) LC 65-36024.

Covers a wide variety of liturgical topics—history, doctrinal and cultural significance, and pastoral aspects of the liturgy—ignoring minor rubrical matters subject to change. "Done with the same care as other works from this publisher, perhaps surpassing them" (*Nouvelle revue théologique*, LXXXV [November, 1963], p. 992).

B382   Cabrol, Fernand. **Dictionnaire d'archéologie chrétienne et de liturgie**, publié par le r. p. dom Fernand Cabrol avec le concours d'un grand nombre de collaborateurs. Paris, Letouzey et Ané, 1907-53. 15 v. LC 3-15097.

The "most complete and scholarly work" for questions on the ancient liturgies of the Church (O'Rourke [A74], p. 119). In addition to its general coverage of pre-Carolingian social and religious life, this work covers liturgical art, architecture, music, rites, and formulas in long, signed articles with copious bibliographies. Criticism of the work has usually been in the form of unequivocal praise for its scope and scholarly detail (e.g., *Catholic Historical Review*, XV [April, 1929], p. 119, and *Month*, CI [June, 1923], p. 214).

B383   Davies, John Gordon, ed. **A Dictionary of Liturgy and Worship**. New York, Macmillan, 1972. ix, 385p. il. LC 72-90276.

A successful ecumenical dictionary with signed articles by authorities from all major Christian faiths and some non-Christian religions. In addition to technical terms, the liturgies of each sect are explained. Cross references and bibliographies are supplied. "A combination of comprehensiveness with thoroughness" (*Month*, VI [April, 1973], p. 155). See B388 for an updated version.

B384   De Angelis, Michael. **The Correct Pronunciation of Latin According to Roman Usage. With Phonetic Arrangement of the Texts of the Ordinary of the Mass, Responses at Mass Benediction Hymns and Hymns in Honor of the Blessed Virgin Mary**. Ed. by Nicholas A. Montani. Philadelphia, PA, St. Gregory Guide, 1937. 47 p. LC 37-24083. Reprinted: Chicago, GIA Publications, 1973.

Contains general rules for pronunciation along with specific texts from the mass and selected hymns.

B385   Diamond, Wilfrid Joseph. **Dictionary of Liturgical Latin**. Milwaukee, Bruce Pub. Co., 1961. 156p. LC 61-7491.

Gives English definitions for more than 1,000 words used in the liturgy. A useful work in that most of the standard Latin dictionaries are restricted to classical usage.

B386   Lercaro, Giacomo, Cardinal. **A Small Liturgical Dictionary**. Ed. by J. B. O'Connell. Trans. by J. F. Harwood-Tregear. Collegeville, MN, Liturgical Press, 1959. 248p. LC 60-4796.

Liturgical terms are briefly defined with no bibliographical references.

B387   Lesage, Robert, ed. **Dictionnaire pratique de liturgie romaine**. Paris, Bonne Presse, 1952. 1138col. LC 53-28722.

Brief, signed articles written with great clarity. Cross references; no bibliographies as such but references may be found in the text. "Throughout the work ceremonial details rather than liturgical values are stressed" (*Catholic Library World*, XXIV [May, 1953], p. 275).

B388   **New Westminster Dictionary of Liturgy and Worship**. Edited by J.G. Davies. Philadelphia, Westminster Press, 1986. xv, 544p. LC 86-9219. ISBN 0-664-21270-0.

An ecumenical work giving good coverage to Catholic topics. Some articles have bibliographies. "There is certainly much that is useful in this dictionary. However one could wish for entries on the psychology and anthropology of worship, the monastic tradition, and contemporary liturgical music" (*Worship*, LXI [March, 1987], p. 186).

B389   Podhradsky, Gerhard. **New Dictionary of the Liturgy.** English ed., by Lancelot Sheppard. Staten Island, NY, Alba House, 1967. 208p. il. LC 67-5547.

Contains longer definitions with some historical and theological background information. "An astonishing amount of historical information not easily available otherwise is compressed into a small space" (*America*, CXVII [August 19, 1967], p. 183). General bibliography, pp. 205-08.

HANDBOOKS AND MANUALS

B390   **The Church at Prayer: An Introduction to the Liturgy.** Ed. by Aimé Georges Martimort with the collaboration of R. Cabié, et al. New ed. Collegeville, MN, Liturgical Press, 1985- . v. LC 85-24174. ISBN 0-8146-1366-7.
Volume 1. Principles of the Liturgy
Volume 2. The Eucharist
Volume 3. The Sacraments
Volume 4. The Liturgy and Time

A comprehensive up-to-date treatment of the liturgy with numerous bibliographies for each section, chapter, and subdivisions of chapters. Index of names and subjects in each volume. "An extremely rich source of information about the liturgy" (*New Blackfriars*, L [November, 1969], p. 771).

B391   Eisenhofer, Ludwig, and Joseph Lechner. **The Liturgy of the Roman Rite.** Trans. by A. J. and E. F. Peeler. Ed. by H. E. Winstone. New York, Herder and Herder, 1961. 506p. LC 60-13249.

A handbook of liturgical studies, prayers, languages, actions, setting, equipment and ceremonies. "Its wealth of information and bibliography rank this book of first importance" (*New Blackfriars*, XXXIII [May, 1952], p. 299). Index.

B392   King, Archdale Arthur. **The Rites of Western Christendom.** London, Burns, Oates, 1955-59. 4 v.
V. 1. Liturgies of the Religious Orders. 1955. LC 55-4576; V. 2. Liturgy of the Roman Church. 1957; V. 3. Liturgies of the Primatial Sees. 1957. LC A59-881; V. 4. Liturgies of the Past. 1959. LC 60-4134.

Covers every important rite that has existed in the West with historical backgrounds, descriptions of ceremonies, pictures of major churches and monasteries, and excerpts from liturgical texts. Each volume is thoroughly indexed.

B393   Martimort, Aimé Georges. **L'Église en prière: introduction à la liturgie,** avec la collaboration de R. Béraudy, et al. 3. éd. rev. et corr. Paris, Desclée, 1965. xv, 950p. il.

A comprehensive survey of the liturgy, rich in bibliography, done by many
different authorities. Its four sections cover fundamentals of the liturgy,
the mass and eucharistic devotion, other sacraments and sacramentals, the
liturgical seasons and the office. "The best of its kind in any language"
(*Theological Studies*, XXIII [September, 1962], p. 484). See B390 for an updated,
English translation.

B394   Nocent, Adrian. **The Liturgical Year.** Collegeville, MN, Liturgical Press, 1977. 4
v. ISBN 0-8146-0962-7.

A detailed commentary on the liturgical seasons and each Sunday of the year
based on the readings from the Lectionary (B347-349).

B395   Parsch, Pius. **The Church's Year of Grace.** Trans. by Daniel Francis Coogan,
Jr. and Rudolf Kraus. Collegeville, MN, Liturgical Press, 1953-58. 5 v.
LC 53-3963.

A guide to the daily liturgy explaining the meaning and history of each feast
in terms of the mass and office for the day according to the pre-Vatican II
liturgical year. Meditations and biographies of saints are also included. Each
volume is arranged in two sections: the "Proper of the Seasons," i.e., Sundays
and other moveable feasts; and the "Proper of the Saints," feasts that fall
on specific dates. This was a very widely used guide to the meaning of the
liturgy by one of the authorities in the liturgical movement. Originally
written in German, the translation has been highly praised (*Books on Trial*,
XI [May, 1953], p. 287).

B396   Radó, Polikárp. **Enchiridion liturgicum: complectens theologiae sacramen-
talis et dogmata et leges.** Ed. 2. emendata et aucta. Romae, Herder, 1966.
2 v.

A "complete treatise on every possible aspect of the liturgy" (*Clergy Review*,
XL [May, 1963], p. 333) in outline form covering the liturgy in general
with special sections on the mass, office, prayers, devotions and each of the
sacraments. The text is in Latin; each section is followed by a bibliography
which is indexed in volume two. General index.

B397   Schmidt, Herman. **Introductio in liturgiam occidentalem.** Romae, Herder,
1960. xi, 849p.

A general guide to the liturgy covering its origins, documentary sources,
the liturgical revival, the sacraments and devotions, the calendar, and sacred
art and music. Despite some omissions the work has been well received for
its pastoral approach and "massive bibliography" (*Worship*, XXXV [October,
1961], p. 594-97). Index.

ORDO

The *Ordo* is a daily calendar, published in a given country or diocese, showing what feast is to be observed, what readings are to be used at mass and
what prayers are to be said in the office of the day. All ordos must conform
to the newly revised *Roman Calendar* (B399-400).

B398   **Ordo for the Celebration of the Divine Office and the Mass in the Dioceses of the United States.** Quincy, IL, Sunday Missal Service, 1977- . v.

This edition of the *Ordo* may be used in any diocese of the United States since it mentions specific commemorations observed in all dioceses. Typical information given includes name and rank of feast or observance, color of vestments to be worn, special prayers or commemorations to be used at mass and in the office, other regulations regarding types of special masses (e.g. funerals) which may be held on that day. For an example of a local *Ordo see* F1.

B399   **Liturgical Calendar and Ordo: United States of America.** Washington, DC, United States Catholic Conference, 1985- . v. Annual.

"This calendar is based on the general *Roman Calendar* (B400) promulgated by Pope Paul VI on February 14, 1969" (Introduction). Published annually, the calendar lists what feasts of the new *Roman Calendar* are to be observed on which day in the given year. Although the issues are dated for the calendar year, the arrangement is by the liturgical year which begins four Sundays before Christmas (the first Sunday of Advent). The entry for each day tells what readings are to be used at mass and what feast or saint's day, if any, is to be commemorated, the color of the vestments to be worn, and the version of the Divine Office to be recited. Individual dioceses and religious orders may issue their own versions of this calendar slightly altered for local observances.

B400   **Roman Calendar: Text and Commentary.** Washington, DC, United States Catholic Conference, 1975. ii, 135p.

A translation by the International Committee on English in the Liturgy of the *Calendarium romanum* published in 1970 by the Sacred Congregation of Rites. This revision of the liturgical year was undertaken to restore major feasts and commemorations to their proper place and to eliminate lesser known saints and those whose historical authenticity had been called into question. This document establishes what feast will occur on each day of the year and how significant the observance is to be. In two separate appendixes, the saints listed in the new calendar are named and described; and the reasons are given for dropping the saints of the old calendar. Indexes. *See also Liturgical Calendar* (399).

HANDBOOKS OF CEREMONIES

Most of the handbooks of customs and handbooks of ceremonies listed below are filled with detailed instructions on liturgical rites and furnishings and are all more or less obsolete but are included here for historical reference.

B401   Fortescue, Adrian, and J. B. O'Connell. **The Ceremonies of the Roman Rite Described.** With an appendix on "The Ceremonies of the Ritual in the U.S.A." by Frederick R. McManus. 11th ed. London, Burns, Oates and Washbourne, 1960. 428p. il. LC A60-2789.

This work, B402, and B403 are now out of date for most ceremonies but but were the standard authorities for many years and contain a wealth of information on vestments, church furniture and equipment as well as ceremonies. Index.

B402   O'Connell, Laurence John, and Walter J. Schmitz. **The Book of Ceremonies.** Rev. 1956. Milwaukee, Bruce Pub. Co., 1956. 622p. il. LC 56-3916.

Not as complete in coverage as Fortescue (B401). Index.

B403   Wuest, Joseph. **Matters Liturgical: The Collectio rerum liturgicarum.** Trans. by Thomas W. Mullaney. Re-arr. and enl. by William T. Barry. 10th rev. ed. New York, F. Pustet Co., 1959. 1171p. LC 59-3163.

Contains answers to specific problems rather than complete instructions for ceremonies. Index.

HANDBOOKS OF CUSTOMS

B404   Berger, Florence E. **Cooking for Christ, the Liturgical Year in the Kitchen.** Des Moines, National Catholic Rural Life Conference, 1949. 127p. LC 49-49579.

Arranged by liturgical seasons and feast days giving historical and liturgical information along with recipes. Index.

B405   Kaufman, William Irving. **The Catholic Cookbook: Traditional Feast and Fast Day Recipes.** New York, Citadel Press, 1965. xviii, 296p. LC 65-20541.

Francis X. Weiser and Brother Herman Zaccarelli were consultants for the liturgy and recipes respectively. Indexed for types of meals and countries of origin.

B406   Weiser, Francis Xavier. **Handbook of Christian Feasts and Customs: The Year of the Lord in Liturgy and Folklore.** New York, Harcourt, Brace, 1958. 366p. LC 58-10908.

"Written to explain the origin, history, and development of Christian feasts throughout the year of Our Lord" (Preface). Sundays, weekday practices, seasonal and special feasts are covered in well documented chapters, but there are no bibliographies as such. An index and dictionary of terms are added reference features in this work designed for the laity rather than clerics or other specialists. "A remarkable book combining scholarship and a popular readable style" (*America*, C [March 21, 1959], p. 721).

HISTORY

B407   Baumstark, Anton. **Comparative Liturgy.** Rev. by Bernard Botte. English ed. by F. L. Cross. Westminster, MD, Newman Press, 1958. 249p. LC 58-8754.

Originally issued as a series of lectures on the history of the liturgy from a comparative point of view, this work has become, through several revisions and enlargements, a handbook of the history of the literature. Well-documented in notes and an extensive bibliographical appendix (pp. 201-35) covering original texts, translations of liturgical books and the Eastern and Western rites of the Church. Criticized for being too one-sided in its presentation (*Eastern Churches Quarterly*, XII [Summer, 1958], p. 260).

B408   Oppenheim, Dom Philip. **Institutiones systematico-historicae in sacram liturgiam.** Roma, Marietti, 1937-39. 4 v.

A history of Church laws dealing with the liturgy whose main point "is to prove that the Roman Pontiff is the supreme legislator in matters liturgical," but which is "a desirable addition to reference works on the liturgy treating in detail the legal aspects of the liturgy which have received only incidental treatment in the treatises on the liturgy" (*American Ecclesiastical Review*, CII [January, 1940], p. 83). Each volume has a subject index. A general index of names is contained in volume four.

B409   Righetti, Mario. **Manuale di storia liturgica.** 3. ed. riveduta e ampliata. Milano, Editrice Ancora, 1959-66. 4 v. LC 73-30879.

Considered a standard work on the history of the liturgy (*Theological Studies*, XXVII [September, 1967], p. 640-01), this revision was begun mostly to take into account the decrees of the Second Vatican Council, but other parts of the work are also revised along with the bibliographies which abound. Index.

THE MASS

B410   Jungmann, Joseph Andreas. **The Mass of the Roman Rite: Its Origins and Development.** Trans. by Francis A. Brunner. New York, Benziger, 1950-55. 2 v. LC 51-4097. Reprinted: Westminster, MD, Christian Classics, 1986. 2 v. LC 86-71098. ISBN 0-8706-1129-1.

Covers the history of the mass from the primitive Church up to the twentieth century, the nature and forms of the mass, and the ceremonies of the mass in great detail. The entire work is a continuous source of bibliography; half of every page is taken up with notes which are indexed along with the text. "The most authoritative and complete work on the history of the growth of the liturgy of the Roman mass that has ever appeared" (*Catholic Historical Review*, XXX [February, 1956], p. 217). An important work for the student of music, fine arts and literature as well as for liturgists. Benziger issued a one-volume edition without notes in 1959.

THE DIVINE OFFICE

B411   Parsch, Pius. **The Breviary Explained.** Trans. by William Nayden and Carl Hoegerl. St. Louis, Herder, 1952. 495p. LC 52-8708.

More a guide for the proper understanding and recitation of the office than a history or commentary, although much of this type of material is included in the work. The three sections cover "Fundamental Notions," a history of the Breviary; "Constituent Parts," the elements that make up each hour; and "The Spirit of the Breviary," seasonal changes. *America* remarked that it has been written "without reference to current reforms" (LXXXVI [August 2, 1952], p. 444).

PRAYERS

B412   Bouyer, Marie Dominique. **Table Prayer.** Trans. and adap. by Anselm Jaskolka. New York, Herder and Herder, 1967. 128p. LC 67-27733.

More than 150 short prayers for various feasts and liturgical seasons.

B413   **Enchiridion indulgentiarum. Preces et pia opera in favorem omnium christifidelium vel quorumdam coetum personarum indulgentius ditata et opportune recognita.** Città del Vaticano, Typis Polyglottis Vaticanis, 1950. 679p. LC A52-1125.

Not an official liturgical book, but a source for all the prayers officially approved for use throughout the entire Church. (B414) is an English translation.

B414   **The Raccolta: or A Manual of Indulgences, Prayers and Devotions Enriched with Indulgences in Favor of all the Faithful in Church or of Certain Groups of Persons and Now Opportunely Revised, Edited and in Part Newly Translated into English from the 1950 "Enchiridion indulgentiarum-preces et pia opera" Issued by the Sacred Penitentiary Apostolic.** By Joseph P. Christopher, Charles E. Spence, and John F. Rowan, by authorization of the Holy See. New York, Benziger Bros., 1952. xvi, 626p. LC 52-8184.

Contains texts in Latin and English. Index.

B415   Rézeau, Pierre. **Répertoire d'incipit des prières françaises à la fin du Moyen Âge: addenda et corrigenda aux répertoires de Sonet et Sinclair: nouveau incipit.** Genève, Droz, 1986. 520p. (Publications romanes et francaises, 174.)

Supplements Sonet (B418) and Sinclair (B416).

B416   Sinclair, Keith V. **French Devotional Texts of the Middle Ages: A Bibliographic Manuscript Guide.** Westport, CT, Greenwood Press, 1979. xxii, 231p. LC 79-7587. ISBN 0-313-20649-X.

B417   Sinclair, Keith V. **French Devotional Texts of the Middle Ages: A Bibliographic Manuscript Guide.** First Supplement. Westport, CT, Greenwood Press, 1982. xvi, 234p. LC 82-11773. ISBN 0-313-23664-X.

Continues Sonet (B418) which lists 2,374 manuscripts; Sinclair lists 3,999 in his two volumes. The arrangement is alphabetical by incipit or opening words with indexes of owners, authors, translators, saints and other persons, and subjects. Continued by Rézeau (B415).

B418   Sonet, Jean. **Répertoire d'incipit de prières en ancien français.** Genève, E. Droz, 1956. xv, 410p. (Sociéte de publications romanes et françaises, 54.) LC 56-5898.

A listing of manuscript copies of pre-medieval prayers alphabetically by opening lines with indexes. Continued by Sinclair (B416, B417), and Rézeau (B415).

B419   **Vaterunser Bibliographie.** Hrsg. von Monica Dorneich. Jubiläumsgabe der Stiftung Oratio Dominica. Freiburg im Breisgau, herder, 1982. 240p. LC 83-118656. ISBN 3-451-19752-9.

An alphabetical listing of 20th century books and articles on the Lord's Prayer. Music and recordings since 1945 are also listed. No indexes.

EASTERN RITES

B420   Day, Peter D., comp. **Eastern Christian Liturgies: The Amenian, Coptic, Ethiopian and Syrian Rites; Eucharistic Rites with Introductory Notes and Rubrical Instructions**. Shannon, Irish University Press, 1972. 195p. LC 72-180868. ISBN 0-716-50595-9.

Presents the history of each of the rites as well as the texts of the masses. There is also a section on the externals of each rite — vestments, vessels, calendars, language, churches and hierarchy.

B421   King, Archdale Arthur. **The Rites of Eastern Christendom**. Rome, Catholic Book Agency, 1947-48. 2 v. il. LC 51-32359.

Covers in considerable detail the historical, ritual, and ceremonial information and the major liturgical texts of each of the Uniate and separated churches of the East. The *Tablet* described these two large volumes as "a notable addition to the few books we have in English about Catholic Orientals" (CXCII [April 22, 1950], p. 223-34). Both volumes have bibliographies and indexes.

B422   Raes, Alphonsus. **Introductio in liturgiam orientalem**. Roma, Pontificio Institute Orientale, 1947. 288p.

Contains more bibliography than King (B421), but also covers Uniate and separated churches with emphasis on the Byzantine. Index.

III

THE
HUMANITIES

PHILOSOPHY AND PSYCHOLOGY

PHILOSOPHY

BIBLIOGRAPHY

International bibliographic control sponsored by, or emphasizing, Catholic philosophers has been well covered in the twentieth century. The chief tool since 1934 has been the *Répertoire bibliographique de la philosophie* (C7) produced at the University of Louvain, from which also comes the *Bulletin de la philosophie médiéval* (C9).

For English language works, McLean's series: *Philosophy of the 20th Century: Catholic and Christian* (**C3 and C4**) is an important source of bibliography. Another good, general introduction to this literature is the philosophy section in Regis' *Catholic Bookman's Guide* (**A19**): "Ancient and Medieval Philosophy" (pp. 217-66); "Modern Philosophy" (pp. 267-92); and "The Philosophy of Science" (pp. 293-328).

General

C1   Brie, G. A. de. **Bibliographia philosophica, 1934-1945.** Bruxellis, Editiones Spectrum, 1950-54. 2 v. LC 51-5942.

Essentially the same as the "Répertoire bibliographique" which appeared in the *Revue philosophique de Louvain* from 1934-48. Listings are drawn from this source along with some others selected by the editor in an attempt to fill the bibliographical gaps left by the war years. Volume one is a bibliography of the history of philosophy, and volume two covers other subdivisions of philosophy. References to reviews are also given.

C2   Koren, Henry J. **Research in Philosophy: A Bibliographical Introduction to Philosophy and a Few Suggestions for Dissertations.** Pittsburgh, Duquesne University Press, 1966. 203p. LC 66-28340.

Written as a guide for graduate students in philosophy. Each chapter covers the elements of different aspects of the bibliography of philosophy: books, periodicals, reference works, bibliography. "Some of the information given is on the elementary level" (*Heythrop Journal*, IX [July, 1968], p. 346).

C3   McLean, George Francis. **An Annotated Bibliography of Philosophy in Catholic Thought, 1900-1964.** New York, F. Ungar, 1967. xiv, 371p. (Philosophy in the 20th Century: Catholic and Christian, v. 1). LC 67-24185.

"Compiled as an aid to the professor, student, and general reader" (Preface). Lists approximately 13,000 selected titles in the traditional Catholic philosophical areas "as well as works by or about Catholics of the more recent existential, personalist, or phenomenological orientations." The history of philosophy is not covered. The evaluative annotations are "remarkably objective" (*Thomist*, XXXIII [April, 1969], p. 399). Classified arrangement with index. References to reviews.

C4   McLean, George Francis. **A Bibliography of Christian Philosophy and Contemporary Issues.** New York, F. Ungar, 1967. viii, 312p. (Philosophy of the 20th Century: Catholic and Christian, v. 2.) LC 67-24186.

Wider scope than the preceding work, it also includes periodical articles. The topics covered are: Christian philosophy, contemporary philosophies, philosophy and technology, philosophy of man and God, the problem of God in a secular culture, religious knowledge and language, moral philosophy, and teaching philosophy. Over 4,000 items are listed, all of which "are significant in their fields" (*Thomist*, XXXIII [April, 1969], p. 399). No annotations are supplied. Index.

C5   Matczak, Sebastian A. **Philosophy: A Select, Classified Bibliography of Ethics, Economics, Law, Politics, Sociology.** Louvain, Éditions Nauwelaerts, 1970. xxii, 308p. (Philosophical Questions Series, 3.) LC 79-80677.

Provides brief introductions and extensive bibliographies "from the point of view of their relevance to philosophy" for the five subject fields mentioned in the title. Index of authors included.

C6   **Rassegna di letteratura tomistica.** Napoli, Edizione Domenicane Italiane, 1966- . v. ISSN 0557-6857.

Replaces *Bulletin thomiste* (Paris, Éditions du Cerf, 1924-1965).

An annual bibliographical supplement to the *Revue thomiste* covering general Catholic theology as well as philosophy. Volumes one through seven cover the years 1924-30, and volume eight, issued in four parts, covers literature from 1947 to 1953. The gaps in this set may be filled by consulting the above mentioned works and the bibliographies listed below under St. Thomas Aquinas. Coverage is international in scope, but French authors are emphasized. As the title indicates, works listed are restricted to the Thomistic or Scholastic. Classified arrangement with indexes in each volume.

C7   **Répertoire bibliographique de la philosophie.** Louvain, Institut Supérieur de philosophie, 1949- . v. Quarterly. LC 51-28726.

A general bibliography of all philosophical writings in books and periodicals covering the history of philosophy; philosophy by periods (ancient, medieval, renaissance, and contemporary); Eastern philosophy; and the various philosophical disciplines. The works listed are not just those by Catholics; on the other hand, Catholic writers are not usually overlooked. The listing is by subject with author indexes and an annual index of book reviews (November). This work is a continuation of C8.

C8   **Revue philosophique de Louvain.** "Répertoire bibliographique (1934-48)." Louvain, Société Philosophique de Louvain, 1934- . v.

The bibliography appeared as a quarterly supplement to the *Revue* (cf. Brie. *Bibliographia philosophica* [C1] for a cumulation of these lists).

Medieval

C9   Société Internationale pour l'Étude de la Philosophie Médiévale. **Bulletin.** Louvain, Secrétariat de la S.I.E.P.M., 1959- . v. Annual.

More of a guide to the year's bibliographical activity in this field than a simple listing of works. Publications are arranged by sponsoring bodies or countries of origin. Works in progress, including dissertations, are listed. The indexes make this work easy to use as a bibliography.

C10   Steenberghen, Fernand van. **Philosophie des Mittelälters.** Aus dem Französischen übers, von Ernst Schneider. Bern, A. Francke, 1950. 52p. (Bibliographische Einführungen in das Studium der Philosophie, 17).

Part of a series of unannotated, classified bibliographies compiled by philosophers from the University of Louvain. This volume covers the works on and by various philosophers and movements. Index of authors.

C11   Vasoli, Cesare. **Il pensiero medievale. Orientamenti bibliografici.** Bari, Laterza, 1971. 301p. LC 74-874226.

A bibliography of primary and secondary sources for medieval philosophers. Arranged chronologically. No indexes.

Italian

C12   **Bibliografia filosofica italiana dal 1900 al 1950.** Roma, Ed. Delfino, 1956. 4 v. LC A52-1091.

C13   **Bibliografia filosofica italiana.** Anno. 1949- . Milano, C. Mazorati, 1951- . v.

A four-volume author list of books and articles by and about Italian philosophers. Anonymous and pseudonymous works are included in volume four as is a list of Italian philosophical periodicals (cf.C14).

C14   Istituto   di studi filosofici. **Bibliografia ragionata delle reviste filosofiche italiane dal 1900 al 1955,** a cura di Enrico Zampetti. Roma, Universita, 1956. 136p. LC 57-20251.

An alphabetical list reprinted from the *Bibliografia filosofica italiana* (C12).

Spanish

C15   Martínez Gómez, Luis. **Bibliografía filosofica española e hispano-americana, 1940-1958.** Barcelona, J. Flors, 1961. xxv, 500p. (Libros "Pensamiento." Serie: Difusión, no. 1.) LC 62-39099.

    Covers books and articles previously listed in the Spanish journal *Pensamiento*. Classified arrangement with name indexes.

DICTIONARIES AND ENCYCLOPEDIAS

    The most comprehensive general dictionary of philosophy with a Catholic emphasis is in Italian. The *Enciclopedia filosofica* (C17) edited by the Centro di Studi Filosofica Christiani di Gallarate, an international association of philosophers who "accept the basic Christian affirmation but no schema allegedly deduced from it" (A. Robert Caponigri, "Gallarate Movement," *Encyclopedia of Philosophy* [New York, Macmillan, Free Press, 1967], v. 3, p. 267). Brugger's *Philosophical Dictionary* (C16) is smaller and more specifically Catholic in content. Wuellner's *Dictionary* (C20) is, of course, devoted exclusively to Scholastic philosophy.

C16   Brugger, Walter, and Kenneth Baker. **Philosophical Dictionary.** Spokane, WA, Gonzaga University Press, 1972. xxiii, 460p. LC 72-82135.

    A translation and adaptation of Brugger's *Philosophisches Wörterbuch* (13 Aufl. Freiburg, Herder, 1967). Bibliographies found in the German edition have not been included in this translation. "A remarkable work, unique because it is written from the standpoint of Thomism.. . . . American articles are not of such high order. They exclude much important Anglo-Saxon thought" (*Choice*, X [October, 1973], p. 1159).

C17   **Enciclopedia filosofica.** Venezia, Istituto per la collaborazione culturale, 1957-58. 4 v. il. LC A58-4987.

    Compiled by some 600 scholars enlisted by the founders of the Gallarate movement; contains extensive articles on basic concepts of philosophy and major philosophers, and smaller articles dealing with terms and lesser philosophers. The articles are signed and furnished with bibliographies. *Thought* said of this work that it is "a magisterial achievement some ten years in the making. . . . an indispensable tool for anyone seriously engaged in philosophical work, and no student of philosophy should fail to consult it" (XXXIV [June, 1959], p. 279).

C18   Fernandez-Garcia. Mariano. **Lexicon scholasticum philosophico-theologicum in quo termini, definitiones, distinctiones et effata seu axiomaticae propositiones philosophiam ac theologiam spectantes a B. Ioanne Duns Scoto exponontur, declarantur, opera et studio.** Ad Claras Aquas (Quaracchi), Ex Typographia Collegii S. Bonaventurae, 1910. liv, 1055p. Reprinted: Hildesheim; New York, Olms, 1974. LC 75-563297. ISBN 3-4870-5221-0.

    In three parts: (1) Grammatica speculatica, (2) Distinctiones, (3) Effata. Definitions in Latin with references to texts.

C19 Westminster. **Dictionary of Christian Ethics**. Edited by James F. Childress and John Macquarrie. Philadelphia, Westminster Press, 1986. xvii, 678p. LC 85-22539. ISBN 0-6642-0940-8.

A widely respected ecumenical work by more than 80 scholars. Catholic authorities contributed articles on specifically Catholic topics, but other articles present a Catholic viewpoint if pertinent. (See Austin Fagothey's review of this work for an interesting distinction between Catholic moral theology and Protestant Christian ethics: *Theological Studies*, XXIX [June, 1968], p. 353). Brief bibliographies and cross references follow most articles.

C20 Wuellner, Bernard. **A Dictionary of Scholastic Philosophy**. 2nd. ed. Milwaukee, Bruce Pub. Co., 1966. xviii, 339p. LC 66-24259.

Geared for the undergraduate student of Scholastic philosophy, this handy volume covers most of the technical terms used in all Scholastic disciplines, giving the part of speech, various meanings with quotations, divisions or distinctions of meanings, notes on usage, citations of principles involved in the use of the term, and references to discussions of the term in philosophical literature. A thorough introduction to the rather technical terminology of Scholasticism. "An essential item on the philosophy reference shelf" (*The New Scholasticism*, XXXI [April, 1957], p. 267).

HANDBOOKS

C21 Raeymaeker, Louis de. **Introduction à la philosophie**. 6e édition. Louvain, Publications universitaires de Louvain; Paris, B. Nauwelaerts, 1967. 320p. LC 68-104266.

Provides an introduction to the literature of philosophy, to societies, organizations and congresses, and contains a survey of the content and the history of philosophy. An English edition of this work appeared in 1948 (*Introduction to Philosophy*. New York, Joseph Wagner, 1948. 297p.).

C22 Wuellner, Bernard. **Summary of Scholastic Principles**. Chicago, Loyola University Press, 1956. 164p. LC 56-10903.

An outline presentation of all the principles of the Scholastic disciplines with reference to their appearance in St. Thomas and, in some cases, in contemporary sources. *The New Scholasticism* criticized some of Fr. Wuellner's references for being too obscure, but in general had high praise for the work (XXXII [January, 1958], p. 147). Index.

HISTORY

Both Copleston's **(C24)** and Gilson's **(C26)** histories of philosophy are significant for their recency, comprehensiveness and reference value. Copleston is especially useful for his biographical approach and clarity of style.

C23 Collins, James Daniel. **A History of Modern European Philosophy**. Milwaukee, Bruce Pub. Co., 1965. x, 584p.

(5th printing with bibliographical continuation.)

A history designed for Catholic students of philosophy covering the lives and works of eighteen modern European philosophers. The critical bibliographies of editions and studies make this a useful reference work. Index.

C24   Copleston, Frederick. **A History of Philosophy**. Westminster, MD, Newman Press, 1946-75. 9 v. LC 47-875. Reprinted: Mahwah, NJ, Paulist Press, 1986. 9 v. ISBN 0-8091-0065-7.

This comprehensive work was originally intended for Catholic seminarians. (Fr. Copleston teaches philosophy at the Gregorian University in Rome.) It is written in an easy style which Bourke describes as "good, and avoiding the jargon of Scholasticism" (Regis [A19], p. 215), but which the reviewer in *Thought* considers "at times jejune and verbose" (XXII [November, 1947], p. 404). Nevertheless, this is an important work which the same reviewer describes as "broad-minded and objective, comprehensive and scholarly, unified and well-proportioned; written from a Scholastic point of view, but not intended as a vehicle of indoctrination in Scholastic philosophy" (p. 411). Concentrating as it does on persons rather than abstract ideas, it is suitable for the interested general reader, but is also useful for reference because of its biographical arrangement and bibliographies which become more plentiful in later volumes. The first volume begins with the ancients of Greece and Rome, and the final volume ends with Sartre.

C25   Fischl, Johann. **Geschichte der Philosophie**. Graz, A. Pustet, 1948-54. 5 v. LC A51-7532.

A comprehensive and useful reference history in that it is arranged biographically with bibliographies and indexes in each volume. Father Bourke calls it an important work, but not as useful as Ueberweg's *Grundiss der Geschichte der Philosophie* (Berlin, S. Mittler und Sohn, 1928. 5 v.) (Regis [A19], p. 218).

C26   Gilson, Étienne Henry. **History of Christian Philosophy in the Middle Ages**. New York, Random House, 1955. 829p. LC 54-7802. Reprinted: Westminster, MD, Christian Classics, 1972.

An introduction, for general readers and students, to the history of Christian philosophy from Justin Martyr in the second century up to Nicholas of Cues. "By far the best general work on medieval thought" (Regis [A19], p. 244).

Arranged chronologically by philosophers, most of whom have a chapter devoted to them. The extensive bibliography (pp. 552-804) covers every name and topic mentioned in the text. An index of authors and historians is also supplied.

C27   **A History of Philosophy**. Étienne Gilson, gen. ed. New York, Random House, 1962-66. 4 v.

Although arranged in biographical order, the stress in this work is more on doctrines and theories than personal lives or influences. This is a comprehensive survey written by noted Catholic scholars with many useful reference features including a general bibliography for each period and for each philosopher, including editions of works and critical annotations of works about them, and indexes in each volume. "The series is intended both for college students and for cultivated readers who feel that perhaps Will Durant has not said the last word" (*America*, CVIII [May 25, 1963], p. 777).

C28   Maréchal, Joseph. **Précis d'histoire de la philosophie moderne: de la Renaissance à Kant.** Rev. et augm. Paris, Desclée, 1951- . v.

If completed, this work will prove a useful reference for the modern period. The first volume, originally published in 1935, covers each philosopher of the period giving his biography, teachings and a bibliography. General introductions to movements and periods are also given along with bibliographies. The reference value of the work has been acknowledged because of its detailed table of contents and exhaustive indexes, but the bibliographies have been criticized for being inadequate. (*American Ecclesiastical Review*, XC [February, 1935], p. 216).

C29   Steenberghen, Fernand van. **Histoire de la philosophie: période chrétienne.** Louvain, Publications universitaires, 1964. 196p. LC 75-215728.

Covers the period from the Fathers of the Church to the 15th century in brief articles. The life and works of major figures are given. "The Bibliography (pp. 181-06) is very short and limited in character" (*Modern Schoolman*, XLII [January, 1965], p. 226).

C30   Wulf, Maurice Marie Charles Joseph de. **History of Medieval Philosophy.** Trans. by Ernest C. Messenger. London, New York, Nelson, 1952. 3 v. LC 55-21007.

This English translation is based on the 6th French edition published in 1947 (*Histoire de la philosophie mediévale*. Louvain, Institut Supérieur de philosophie; Paris, Vrin, 1934-47. 4 v.). The arrangement is generally chronological. Each chapter is followed by a lengthy bibliography. The bibliographies in this edition have been updated to 1947. A standard work in the field.

BIOGRAPHY

Introductory bio-bibliographies for individual Catholic philosophers may be found in most of the works listed under dictionaries, histories and bibliography; nor should one ignore such fine general works as the *Encyclopedia of Philosophy* published by Macmillan in 1967.

The reference tools listed here for individual philosophers are naturally limited to those philosophers and their adherents whose writings are so voluminous that they have generated reference works to synthesize and control the literature.

C31   American Catholic Philosophical Association. **Directory of Members.** Washington, DC, 1968- . v. Annual. LC 78-5394.

Gives brief biographical information and lists publications of each member.

C32   Riedl, John Orth. **A Catalogue of Renaissance Philosophers (1350-1650).** Comp. by Robert A. Baker, Andrew J. Bakula, Thomas H. Barry and others under the direction of John O. Riedl. Milwaukee, Marquette University Press, 1940. xi, 179p. il. LC 40-9025.

A bio-bibliography of Western philosophers from Dante to Nicholas Malebranche providing a paragraph or two of biographical and critical information and a list of written works for each philosopher. A basic reference tool, praised for its usefulness and convenient arrangement, despite.the "few minor defects" which "do not affect its excellence as a whole" (*Thought*, XV [December, 1940], p. 719). Unfortunately no similar work is available for other periods in the history of philosophy.

Albert the Great

C33   Schooyans, Michel. **Bibliographie philosophique de Saint Albert le Grand (1931-1960).** São Paulo, Universidade Catòlica de São Paulo, 1961. 55p. (Separata da Revista da Universidade Catòlica de São Paulo, v. 21, fasc. 37-38.)

Lists books and articles in French, English, German, Spanish, and Italian in subject arrangement. Author index.

Anselm

C34   Evans, G.R., ed. **A Concordance to the Works of St. Anselm.** Millwood, NY, Kraus International, 1984. 4 v. LC 82-48973. ISBN 0-527-03661-7.

Based on the *Opera Omnia* (Rome, 1938-61), edited by F.S. Schmitt and *Philosophical Fragments* in the *Memorials of St. Anselm* (London, Oxford, 1969), edited by R.W. Southern. Use in context is given along with the citations. There are three indexes: "Finding List" (an index to variations in word forms); "Reverse Vocabulary Index," and "Index of Frequent Words." An exhaustive work.

Augustine

C35   Andresen, Carl. **Bibliographia Augustiniana.** 2., völlig neubearb. Aufl. Darmstadt, Wissenschaftliche Buchgesellschaft., 1973. ix, 317p. LC 74-323977. ISBN 3-534-01145-7.

Much expanded over the first edition (1962). A classified listing of monographs. No index.

C36   Bavel, Tarsicius J. van. **Répertoire bibliographique de saint Augustin, 1950-1960.** Avec la collaboration de F. van der Zande. Steenbrugis, In Abbatia Sancti Petre, 1963. Pp. 991. (Instrumenta patristica, 3.) LC 64-33473.

A classified, annotated bibliography of books and articles in all languages, published from 1950 to 1960. Thoroughly and carefully done by the monks of St. Peter's Abbey in Belgium. Index.

C37   Institut des Ëtudes Augustiniennes. **Fichier augustinien/Augustine Bibliography, Author Catalog.** Boston, G.K. Hall, 1972. 2 v. LC 72-373137. ISBN 0-8161-0947-8.

C38   Institut des Études Augustiniennes. **Fichier augustinien/Augustine Bibliography, Subject Catalog.** Boston, G.K. Hall, 1972. 2 v. LC 72-373136. ISBN 0-8161-0948-7.

The Library Catalog listing the primary and secondary sources held in this important collection.

C39   Miethe, Terry L. **Augustinian Bibliography, 1970-1980: With Essays on the Fundamentals of Augustinian Scholarship.** Westport, CT, Greenwood Press, 1982. xxii, 218p. LC 82-6173. ISBN 0-313-22629-6.

A classified listing of 4,000 books and articles with good coverage of English language works. Personal Name Index.

C40   Nebreda del Cura, Eulogio. **Bibliographia augustiniana, seu operum collectio, quae divi Augustini vitam et doctrinam quadentenus exponunt.** Rome, Cuore de Maria, 1928. 272p. LC 56-54211. Reprinted: Dubuque, IA, William C. Brown Reprint Co., 1963.

A classified bibliography of secondary sources, both books and articles.

C41   Sciacca, Michele Federico. **Augustinus.** Bern, A. Francke, 1948. 32p. (Bibliographische Einführungen in das Studium der Philosophie, 10).

An international listing of recent books and articles in subject arrangement with an author index. No annotations.

Duns Scotus

C42   Schäfer, Odulf. **Bibliographia de vita, operibus et doctrina Iohannis Duns Scoti, doctoris subtilis ac Mariani, Saec. XIX-XX.** Romae, Herder, 1955. xxiv, 223p. LC A55-7363.

Lists over 4,500 books and periodical articles in all major languages with name and subject indexes. Provides analysis of the contents of larger works.

Erasmus

C43   Haeghen, Ferdinand van der. **Bibliotheca Erasmiana. Répertoire des oeuvres d'Erasme.** Nieuwkoop, B. de Graaf, 1961. 3 v. in 1.

A bibliography of his works, his editions of other works, and books containing extracts of his works.

C44   Margolin, Jean Claude. **Quatorze années de bibliographie érasmienne, 1936-1949.** Paris, J. Vrin, 1969. 431p. LC 72-473461.

C45   Margolin, Jean Claude. **Douze années de bibliographie érasmienne, 1950-1961.** Paris, J. Vrin, 1963. 204p. LC 66-82129.

C46   Margolin, Jean Claude. **Neuf années de bibliographie érasmienne, 1962-1970.** Paris, J. Vrin; Toronto, Buffalo, University of Toronto Press, 1877. xi, 850p. LC 78-342340. ISBN 0-8020-2276-6.

Year by year listings of works by and about Erasmus including books and articles. For each item there is a lengthy abstract (in French). A full series of indexes in each volume aids in accessing the material.

Marcel

C47   Lapointe, François, and Claire Lapointe. **Gabriel Marcel and His Critics: An International Bibliography** (1928-1976). New York, Garland, 1977. 287p. LC 76-24736. ISBN 0-8240-9941-9.

Lists 1,297 works by Marcel and 1,704 critical works. The arrangement is classified, but an index of authors is included. No annotations.

Maritain

C48   Gallagher, Donald. **The Achievement of Jacques and Raïssa Maritain: A Bibliography, 1906-1961.** Garden City, NY, Doubleday, 1962. 256p. LC 62-7633.

Contains an introduction to Maritain's thought, a biography of Jacques and Raïssa and a bibliography of books, articles and parts of books written by Jacques Maritain along with books and articles about him. The bibliography of Raïssa Maritain is in a separate section. English and French language works are covered completely, other languages, insofar as the compilers could verify items. Classified arrangement with subject index.

Teilhard de Chardin

Bibliography

C49   Jarque i Jutglar, Joan E. **Bibliographie génerale des Oeuvres et articles sur Pierre Teilhard de Chardin**. Fribourg, Éditions Universitaires Fribourg, 1970. 206p. LC 75-596353.

2,228 items are listed by author. Indexes.

C50   McCarthy, Joseph M. **Pierre Teilhard de Chardin: A Comprehensive Bibliography**. New York, Garlanmd, 1981. ix, 438p. LC 78-68299. ISBN 0-8240-9783-1.

Lists 4,317 "Works About Teilhard de Chardin" and 621 editions of "Works by Teilhard de Chardin." Each section has a separate subject index. The most comprehensive bibliography on this subject.

C51   Polgár, Lásló. **Internationale Teilhard-Bibliographie, 1955-65.** Freiburg, Alber, 1965. Pp. 93. LC 66-66082.

Covers books and articles in all languages including translations. Contents notes are supplied. Classified arrangement with indexes. "This work is well organized" (*Étude*, CCCXXV [July-August, 1966], p. 132).

C52   Poulin, Daniel. **Teilhard de Chardin: essai de bibliographie, 1955-1966.** Québec, Presses de L'Université Laval, 1966. xiii, 157p. LC 67-4477.

Lists 352 books and articles by and about Teilhard along with phonograph records and books in preparation. Some descriptive annotations and contents notes are supplied. Author index.

Indexes

C53   L'Archevêque, Paul. **Teilhard de Chardin: index analytique.** Québec, Presses de l'Université Laval, 1967. vii, 175p.

A subject index to seven works in their French editions.

Dictionaries

C54   Cuénot, Claude. **Nouveau lexique Teilhard de Chardin.** Paris, Éditions du Seuil, 1968. 224p. (Études et recherches sur Teilhard de Chardin.) LC 68-142799.

Supplies definitions with examples from Chardin's writings of terms particular to his system. *Études* praises the work for not superimposing meanings from other systems, especially Scholasticism, on his concepts; "Il rendra grand service" (CCCXXX [March, 1969], p. 452).

C55   Cuypers, Hubert. ̦**Vocabulaire Teilhard de Chardin: lexique, citations, références.** Paris, Éditions Universitaires, 1963. 101p. (*Carnets Teilhard*, 5-6.)

Provides definitions of important terms and gives references to their use in the works of Chardin.

Thomas Aquinas

Bibliography

C56   Bourke, Vernon Joseph. **Thomistic Bibliography, 1920-1940. The Modern Schoolman, Supplement to Volume XXI.** St. Louis, 1945. viii, 312p. LC 45-8381.

A continuation of Mandonnet's *Bibliographie thomiste* (C58). Lists 6,667 works on St. Thomas and Thomism: his life, works and doctrines—philosophical and theological. Thoroughly indexed. No annotations. Continued by Miethe (C60).

C57   Dondaine, Hyacinthe François and H.V. Shooner. **Codices manuscript operum Thomae de Aquino.** Romae, Commissio Leonina, 1967- . v. LC 77-26801. Vol. 3, Montreal, Les Presses de l'Université de Montreal, 1985. ISBN 0-88844-559-8.

A listing by place with descriptions of autograph and non-autograph manuscripts of the works of St. Thomas.

C58   Mandonnet, Pierre Félix, and J. Destrez. **Bibliographie thomiste.** 2ᵉ éd. rev. et completée par M. D. Chenu. Paris, J. Vrin, 1960. xxii, 119p. (Bibliothéque thomiste, 1).

A retrospective classified list covering the literature up to 1920. Continued by Bour (C56) and Miethe (C60). 2,219 selected books and articles are included. Index of authors and a list of periodicals cited.

C59   **Rassegna di letteratura tomistica.** Napoli, Edizione Domenicane Italiane, 1966- . v. ISSN 0557-6857.

Replaces *Bulletin thomiste* (Paris, Éditions de Cerf, 1924-1965).

Cf. (C6). A source for current bibliography on Thomas as well as on general philosophy and theology.

C60   Miethe, Terry L., and Vernon J. Bourke. **Thomistic Bibliography, 1940-1978.** Westport, CT, Greenwood Press, 1980. xxii, 318p. LC 80-1195. ISBN 0-313-21991-5.

A classified bibliography listing 4,097 items. Author index. Continues Madonnet (C58) and Bourke (C56).

C61   Wyser, Paul. **Thomas von Aquin.** Bern, A. Francke, 1950. 78p. (Bibliographische Einführungen in das Studium der Philosophie, 13/14).

Covers editions of his works and literature dealing directly with his life and work. Author index. No annotations.

C62   Wyser, Paul. **Der Thomismus.** Bern, A. Francke, 1951. 120p. (Bibliographische Einführungen in das Studium der Philosophie, 15/16).

A classified listing of books and articles on Thomism with an author index. No annotations.

Concordances

C63   Deferrari, Roy Joseph, and Sister M. Inviolata Barry. **A Complete Index of the Summa of St. Thomas Aquinas.** Washington, DC, Catholic University of America Press, 1956. ix, 386p. LC 56-4980.

A concordance or *index verborum* supplying accompanying words or phrases to show the context of each word. Based on the Leonine edition of the *Summa* (Roma, Apud Sedum Commisionis, 1882-1948), this work lists every word in the text except such common words as *et, cum, qui,* and inflected forms. The references are to the numbered articles in the text making the work useful with any edition, even English translations.

C64   **Index Thomisticus: Sancti Thomae Aquinatis operum omnium indices et concordantiae in quibus verborum omnium et singulorum formae et lemmata cum suis frequentiis et contextibus variis modis referentur; quaeque auspice Paulo VI Summo Pontifice consociata plurium opera atque electronico IBM automato usus digessit Robertus Busa.** Stuttgard-Bad Cannstatt, Frommann-Holzboog, 1974- . v. LC 75-548922. ISBN 3-7728-0532-9.

An immense work of more than 30 large volumes consisting of a series of indexes and concordances to all of St. Thomas' works as well as doubtful works usually attributed to him. The indexes give reference to the works in coded form. The concordances, divided by parts of speech, give full quotations with references for each word and inflected form. "A monumental work of incomparable importance to Thomistic research and exegesis" (*New Scholasticism*, L [Spring, 1976], p. 237).

C65   Lohr, Charles H. **Thomas Aquinas. Scriptum super Sententiis: An Index of Authorities Cited.** Amersham, Eng., Avebury, 1980. vii, 391p. LC 80-503184. ISBN 0-86127-103-3.

A list of the authors and Scriptures quoted by Thomas in his *Writings on the Sentences of Peter Lombard.* Arranged alphabetically by author, then by work.

Dictionaries

C66   Deferrari, Roy Joseph. **A Latin-English Dictionary of St. Thomas Aquinas Based on the Summa theologica and Selected Passages of his Other Works.** Boston, St. Paul Editions, 1960. 1115p. LC 60-1846.

("Based on *A Lexicon of St. Thomas Aquinas,*" p. 4.)

Contains English definitions with no references to their use in the text.

C67   Deferrari, Roy Joseph, and Sister M. Inviolata Barry. **A Lexicon of St. Thomas Aquinas Based on the Summa theologica and Selected Passages of his Other Works.** With the technical collaboration of Ignatius McGuiness. Washington, DC, Catholic University of America Press, 1948-58. 5 v. LC A49-1297.

A dictionary of all the words used in the *Summa* and selected terms from other works giving the meaning, both in the words of St. Thomas and those of the compilers, with quotations to illustrate the meanings. Obviously the result of much toil and study, this work has been termed "a monumental achievement of American scholarship. Though it may not embody the ultimate perfection desired by some professional philosophers and theologians, it achieves its avowed purpose with remarkable accuracy and distinction" (*Catholic Library World*, XXI [May, 1950], p. 246).

C68   Schütz, Ludwig. **Thomas-lexikon: Sammlung, übersetzung und erklärung der in samtlichen werken des h. Thomas von Aquin vorkommenden kunstausdrücke und wissenschaftlichen aussprüche.** Von dr. Ludwig Schütz. 2., sehr vergrosserte aufl. Paderborn, F. Schöningh, 1895. x, 889p; Reprinted: New York, Musurgia, 1949. LC 25-20228.

A dictionary of Thomistic terms giving definitions in German and references to their appearance in major works. The first edition of this work appeared in 1895, and the 1949 version is merely a reprint of what *Franciscan Studies* describes as a standard work although compiled before later discoveries of "the true nature of some spurious works heretofore included in the canon" (IX [December, 1949], p. 457-58).

C69   Stockhammer, Morris. **Thomas Aquinas Dictionary.** New York, Philosophical Library, 1965. xii, 219p. LC 64-21468.

More of a concordance or index to the major works of St. Thomas than a dictionary. It provides quotations illustrating certain terms or concepts "that are of interest to the modern reader; items of merely medieval concern were omitted" (Preface).

Commentaries

C70   Farrell, Walter. **A Companion to the Summa**. New York, Sheed and Ward, 1938-42. e v. LC 39-1667. Reprinted: Westminster, MD, Christian Classics, 1974. 4 v. ISBN 0-8706-1117-8.

A handy reference work in that it is an explanation, or "the *Summa* reduced to popular language" (Preface), arranged in the same order and with the same numbering of articles. Indexes in each volume.

C71   Glenn, Paul Joseph. **A Tour of the Summa**. St. Louis, B. Herder Book Co., 1960. 466p. LC 60-16942.

"A condensed paraphrase of the essential teachings of the *Summa*" (Preface), retaining the original numbering. "An impressively useful compression of the *Summa* into a readable, practical workbook" (*Homiletic and Pastoral Review*, LXI [April, 1961], p. 722).

Texts

C72   Thomas Aquinas, Saint. **Summa theologica**. 1st complete American ed. trans. by the Fathers of the English Dominican Province; with synoptical charts. New York, Benziger Bros., 1947-48. 3 v. LC 47-26779..

Originally published 1912-36 in twenty-one volumes. Contains text and commentary with numerous charts and a glossary of terms. There are twenty-five indexes and guides for finding quotations and passages of the work suitable for various subject and professional fields.

C73   Thomas Aquinas, Saint. **Summa theologiae: Latin text and English Translation, Introductions, Notes, Appendices, and Glossaries**. New York, McGraw-Hill, 1964-76. 60 v. LC 63-11128.

The most recent translation, also by the Dominicans. Latin and English texts are printed side by side with introductions and copious notes. Each volume contains a number of appendixes explaining doctrinal matters not sufficiently clear in the text, a glossary of the English terms used in a philosophical sense, and an index. The appearance of the first few volumes was the occasion for much critical acclaim (e.g., *Catholic Library World*, XXXVII [May-June, 1966], p. 602).

PSYCHOLOGY

BIBLIOGRAPHY

C74   Meissner, William W. **Annotated Bibliography in Religion and Psychology**. New York, Academy of Religion and Mental Health, 1961. xi, 235p. LC A63-680.

Contains approximately 3,000 titles of books and articles dealing with the "psychological aspects of religion and the religious aspects of psychology" (Preface). The annotations are long and descriptive but not usually critical. Nevertheless, this is a useful work and should be updated.

DICTIONARIES

C75   Cirlot, Juan Eduardo. **A Dictionary of Symbols.** Trans. from the Spanish by Jack Sage. 2nd. edition. London, Routledge and K. Paul, 1971. lv, 419p. LC 72-189383. ISBN 0-7100-7177-9.

An alphabetical list of symbols and things symbolized, drawn from religion, art and literature, with long interpretive explanations. "The judgments expressed are sober and generally well measured" (*Catholic Biblical Quarterly*, XXV [April, 1963], p. 231). Bibliography, pp. 367-377. Index.

HISTORY

C76   Misiak, Henryk, and Virginia M. Staudt. **Catholics in Psychology: A Historical Survey.** New York, McGraw-Hill, 1954. 309p. (McGraw-Hill Series in Psychology.) LC 54-8803.

Intended as a supplement to the standard textbooks in the field, this work is in reality a series of bio-bibliographies of Catholic psychologists of all nations some of whom are covered in a single chapter and others grouped in one chapter. A good source for minor psychologists not covered so thoroughly in other works.

LITERATURE

GENERAL WORKS

BIBLIOGRAPHY

The bibliographical needs for students of Catholic literature will not, for the most part, be well met by the works listed here. Again, reference should be made to the general bibliographic tools listed in Chapter I, as well as to the literary bibliographies listed in Sheehey's and Walford's guides to reference works (Eugene P. Sheehey, *Guide to Reference Books* [Chicago, A.L.A., 1986] and Albert J. Walford, *Guide to Reference Materials* [London, The Library Association, 1980-87]).

C77   Menendez, Albert J. **The Road to Rome: An Annotated Bibliography.** New York, Garland, 1986. xxi, 133p. LC 85-45110. ISBN 0-8240-8687-2.

1,461 biographies, autobiographies, novels and other works dealing with conversion to Catholicism are listed by type. Author Index.

C78   **Religia a literatura.** Katolicki Uniwersytet Lubelski Zaklad Badań nad Literatur a Religijna. Lublin, Zaklad, 1972?- . v. LC 82-646524. ISSN 0208-7588. Annual.

A classified bibliography of books dealing with literature from a religious point of view. Author and subject indexes.

C79   Sagehomme, Georges. **Répertoir alphabétique de 15,500 auteurs, avec 55,000 de leurs ouvrages, romans, recits et pièces de théâtre, qualifiés quant à leur valeur morale.** 8. éd. rev. et complétée par E. Dupuis. Tournai, Casterman, 1950. xii, 732p. LC A51-2906.

The literature of all nations (with titles in French) is listed by author with arbitrary, unexplained moral evaluations given for each work.

COLLECTIONS AND ANTHOLOGIES

C80   Caponigri, Aloysius Robert. **Modern Catholic Thinkers: An Anthology.** New York, Harper and Row, 1965-66. 2 v. LC 65-9086.

Selections from contemporary Catholic writers on God, man, the Church, politics, history, culture and religion. The choice of authors is excellent, but there are no indexes. References to sources are supplied.

C81   **The Catholic Tradition.** Charles J. Dollen, James K. McGowan, James J. Megivern, editors. Wilmington, NC, McGrath Pub. Co., 1979. 14 v. LC 79-1977. ISBN 0-8434-0725-5.

Covers seven topics: The Church, The Mass and the Sacraments, Sacred Scripture, The Savior, Personal Ethics, Social Thought, Spirituality, in two volumes each. Each two-volume set contains selected writings of Catholic thinkers from the Fathers of the Church up to contemporary authors. A brief one-page introduction is provided for each author as are citations to complete works. No indexes.

C82   Chapin, John. **A Treasury of Catholic Reading.** New York, Farrar, Straus and Cudahy, 1957. 656p. LC 57-7700.

"108 selections by leading writers from St. Augustine to Bishop Sheen illustrating the diversity, variety and richness of the Catholic way of life" (Preface). Selections range from documents to literature and cover a wide variety of topics. Sources indicated. No index.

C83   Pegis, Anton Charles. **The Wisdom of Catholicism.** New York, Modern Library, 1955. 988p. LC 55-6396.

An anthology of mostly prose literature illustrating Catholic thought from St. Ignatius of Antioch to Étienne Gilson. The selections tend to be devotional and theological with some poetry and hymns. Sources are given in the bibliography, pp. 985-988.

C84   **A Primer of Medieval Latin: An Anthology of Prose and Poetry.** Compiled by Charles H. Beeson. Washington, DC, Catholic University of America Press, 1986. LC 86-8301. ISBN 0-8132-0635-9. Reprint of the 1925 edition.

Contains both religious and secular selections with helpful notes and a brief dictionary of medieval Latin words.

C85   Shuster, George Nauman, ed. **The World's Great Catholic Literature.** With an introduction by William Leon Phelps. Garden City, NY, Halcyon House, 1947. xxii, 441p. LC 48-549.

Over 200 writers are represented in this anthology of prose literature covering the entire range of Catholic history. The selections are arranged chronologically with an index of authors. "Biographical Notes" are supplied for each of the authors.

C86   Ulanov, Barry, ed. **Contemporary Catholic Thought: Faith, Hope and Love in the Modern World.** New York, Sheed & Ward, 1963. 310p. LC 62-15276.

Excerpts from the writings of nineteen leading Catholic theologians and thinkers such as Rahner, Jungmann, Marcel, Maritain and Teilhard de Chardin. The selections are grouped under the general headings Faith, Hope, and Love.

DIGESTS

C87   Magill, Frank Northern. **Masterpieces of Catholic Literature in Summary Form.** Ed. by Frank N. Magill with ass. eds. A. Robert Caponigri and Thomas P. Neill. New York, Harper and Row, 1965. xxxv, 1134p. LC 63-20740.

Contains brief digests of some 300 works of Catholic literature in the same style as the *Masterplots* series. Treatises, biographies, letters, and poetry are covered, but no fiction or drama. Would be more useful if it contained more works. Chronological arrangement with author and title index.

BIOGRAPHIES OF AUTHORS

Catholic-author books are among the most numerous and useful reference works for Catholic literature. Hoehn's *Catholic Authors* (**C91**) and Romig's *Book of Catholic Authors* (**C93**) are both done in the style of the Kunitz and Haycraft series published by the H. W. Wilson Company (1938-67); that is, they are frequently autobiographical and contain lists of works and portraits.

C88   **Catholic Authors in Modern Literature, 1880-1930.** Loretto, PA, St. Francis College, 1930. 230p. il. (*The Mariale*, v. 6).

Short biographical sketches of about 200 contemporary authors are given, with partial lists of works. Some portraits are included. Index (lists additional Catholic authors not covered in the work).

C89   FitzGerald, John Arthur. **A List of 5,000 Catholic Authors.** Ilion, NY, Continental Press, 1941. 101p. LC 41-11568.

No works are listed nor are full names given in some cases. Useful only for identification purposes.

C90   Gallery of Living Catholic Authors. **The Gallery of Living Catholic Authors Is the Catholic Literary Center of the World . . . ,** by Sister Mary Joseph. Webster Groves, MO, The Gallery, 1945. 97p. LC 45-20074.

An international list of Catholic authors supplying brief biographical information and lists of works. Covers over 400 names.

C91   Hoehn, Matthew. **Catholic Authors: Contemporary Biographical Sketches,**
       1930-1952. Newark, NJ, St. Mary's Abbey, 1948-52. 2 v. il. LC 48-2039.

       Over 1,000 biographies with photographs of living and deceased modern
       authors are contained in this useful set. The emphasis is on English speak-
       ing writers, but some Europeans whose works are translated into English
       are also included.

American

C92   Martin, David, Brother. **American Catholic Convert Authors: A Bio-**
       Bibliography. Detroit, W. Romig, 1944. xiv, 259p. LC 44-7628.

       Brief biographies and lists of works of convert authors from the eighteenth
       century to the present. References to sources of information are given. Index.

C93   Romig, Walter. **The Book of Catholic Authors: Informal, Self-Portraits of**
       Famous Modern Catholic Writers. Detroit, W. Romig, 1942-66. 6 v. LC
       42-21745.

       A fine series no longer published. Portraits are supplied along with the
       autobiographies and lists of works. Volume six contains an index to the
       entire series.

C94   Scally, Sister, Mary Anthony. **Negro Catholic Writers, 1900-1943: A Bio-**
       bibliography. Detroit, W. Romig, 1945. 152p. LC 45-3679.

       Approximately seventy-five authors are included with annotated lists of
       their writings. Index.

Italian

C95   Casati, Giovanni. **Scritorri cattolici italiani viventi, dizionario bio-bibliografico**
       ed indice analitico delle opere, con prefazione di Filippo Meda. Milano,
       R. Ghirlanda, 1928. viii, 112p. LC 29-23176.

       A carefully done work giving a few lines of biography with complete lists
       of works and editions.

German

C96   **Katholischer Literaturkalender.** Freiburg, Herder, 1891-1926. 15 v. Annual.
       LC 11-16804.

       An annual "who's who" of German Catholic writers giving names, addresses
       and titles of works.

HISTORY AND CRITICISM

C97   Alexander, Calvert. **The Catholic Literary Revival: Three Phases of Its**
       Development from 1845 to the Present. Port Washington, NY, 1968. xv,
       399p. (Essay and General Literature Index Reprint.) LC 68-16288. (First
       printed in 1935).

       Begins with Newman and Hopkins; then the Agnes Meynell group—Lionel
       Johnson, Francis Thompson, etc. and finally the post-World War I group—
       Dawson, Mackenzie, Waugh, Kaye-Smith, Hollis, and so on. Bibliographies

follow each section. "Soundly critical, contains an immense amount of information and displays a vast reading done with the utmost discernment" (*Booklist*, XXXII [February, 1936], p. 165). Index.

C98 Braybrooke, Patrick. **Some Victorian and Georgian Catholics: Their Art and Outlook.** London, Burns, Oates and Washbourne, 1932. xi, 201p. LC 33-12317. Reprinted: Freeport, NY, Books for Libraries, 1966. LC 67-22080. ISBN 8369-1325-6.

Covers Patmore, Alice Meynell, Francis Thompson, Sheehan, Conrad and Noyes. With portraits.

C99 Brown, Stephen James Meredith. **A Survey of Catholic Literature.** Pts. 1, 2 and 4 by Stephen J. Brown; pt. 3 by Thomas McDermott. Rev. ed. Milwaukee, Bruce Pub. Co., 1949. x, 281p. (Science and Culture Series.) LC 49-1416.

A unique work and, therefore, somewhat valuable if out of date. Brown did the European section and McDermott the Western Hemisphere. Limited to belles-lettres, the work includes a "General Review" from the beginnings to the end of the nineteenth century; a detailed history of the medieval period; North and South America; and contemporary literature in Europe. Each chapter is followed by a bibliography of suggested reading and a list of references. The suggested reading lists could have been more complete, but the work is still a helpful guide to a field that is more often talked about than studied in such a unified way. Index.

C100 Gardiner, Harold Charles. **The Great Books: A Christian Appraisal: A Symposium on the Program of the Great Books Foundation.** New York, Devin-Adair Co., 1949-53. 4 v. LC 49-7493.

A series of essays of Catholic scholars which attempts to evaluate the "great books" from a Christian point of view. A short, selected bibliography follows each essay. For the reader confused by the overwhelming array of philosophies and theologies contained in these works, this is a "handy, illuminating, and in a real sense, necessary *vade mecum*" (*Thought*, XXIV [June, 1949], p. 356). No indexes.

INDIVIDUAL AUTHORS

Perhaps now that computers are used so widely in the compilation of indexes, bibliographies and concordances, we may see more Catholic authors treated in the future than the few listed here.

AELFRIC THE GRAMMARIAN

C101 Reinsma, Luke Mins. **Aelfric: An Annotated Bibliography.** New York, Garland, 1987. 323p. LC 85-45125. ISBN 0-8240-8665-1.

A classified bibliography of primary and secondary sources with indexes.

DANIEL, PHILLIP, AND ELIZABETH BERRIGAN

C102   Klejment, Anne. **The Berrigans: A Bibliography of Published Works by Daniel, Phillip and Elizabeth Berrigan**. New York, Garland, 1979. xxxiii, 209p. LC 78-68214. ISBN 0-8240-9788-2.

An exhaustive listing of books, parts of books and articles with indexes. 106 selected secondary sources are also listed.

G. K. CHESTERTON

C103   Sprug, Joseph William. **An Index to G. K. Chesterton**. Washington, DC, Catholic University of America Press, 1966. xx, 427p. LC 66-30169.

An index-concordance to "all of Chesterton's writings in book form from *Greybeards at Play*, 1900, to the most recent posthumous collection, *The Spice of Life*, 1965" (Introduction). The references are to page numbers in specific editions listed in the front of the book.

CAROLINE GORDON

See C115.

GRAHAM GREENE

C104   Vann, Jerry Don. **Graham Greene: A Checklist of Criticism**. Kent, OH, Kent State University Press, 1970. vii, 69p. LC 70-113763. ISBN 0-87338-101-7.

Almost 700 items are included in 5 lists: Bibliographies, Books about Greene, Chapters about Greene . . . , Articles about Greene, Greene's novels . . . with reviews. There are no annotations or indexes.

GERARD MANLEY HOPKINS

C105   Cohen, Edward H. **Works and Criticism of Gerard Manley Hopkins: A Comprehensive Bibliography**. Washington, DC, Catholic University of America Press, 1969. xv, 217p. LC 68-31683. ISBN 0-8132-0253-1.

Part I, a list of works, includes references to the first appearance in print of the poems in periodicals etc. Part II lists secondary material. 1,522 items, no annotations. Index to critics.

C106   Dilligan, Robert J., and Todd K. Bender, comps. **A Concordance to the English Poetry of Gerard Manley Hopkins**. Madison, University of Wisconsin Press, 1970. xx, 321p. LC 70-10154.

Based on *The Poems of Gerard Manley Hopkins*. 4th ed. Oxford University Press, 1967.

C107   Dunne, Tom. **Gerard Manley Hopkins: A Comprehensive Bibliography**. Oxford, Clarendon Press, 1976. xxvi, 394p. LC 76-357992. ISBN 0-19-818158-2.

Lists 2,460 items in several categories, with annotations. "Comprehensive, but not complete" (Preface). Covers publications up to 1970. Index.

C108   Seelhammer, Ruth. **Hopkins Collected at Gonzaga**. Chicago, Loyola University Press, 1970. xiv, 272p. il. LC 70-108564. ISBN 8-2940-183-0.

Based on the holdings of the Crosby Library at the Gonzaga University, Spokane, WA, this list contains 3,301 books and articles by and about Hopkins. The substantially larger number of items in this list compared to Dunne (C107) and Cohen (C105) is accounted for by the section called "Association Items" consisting of works dealing with his sources and times.

THOMAS MERTON

C109   Breit, Marquita and Robert D. Daggy. **Thomas Merton: A Comprehensive Bibliography**. New ed. New York, Garland, 1986. xiv, 710p. LC 85-31167. ISBN 0-8240-8920-0.

An exhaustive listing of print and audio-visual material by and about Merton. Index.

C110   Dell'Isola, Frank. **Thomas Merton: A Bibliography**. Rev. and Exp. Edition. Kent, OH, Kent State University Press, 1975. 220p. LC 74-79148. ISBN 0-8733-8156-4.

Merton was a prolific writer in several genres and on many topics. These two bibliographies do not overlap each other entirely. Dell'Isola's work is larger, more definitive and concentrates on primary sources. Breit's also covers primary sources, but is chiefly valuable for its listing of nearly 900 critical works.

JOHN HENRY NEWMAN

C111   Blehl, Vincent Ferrer. **John Henry Newman: A Bibliographical Catalog of His Writings**. Charlottesville, Published for the Bibliographical Society of the University of Virginia by the University Press, 1978. xl, 148p. LC 77-12141. ISBN 0-8139-0738-1.

A listing of books, articles, pamphlets, newspaper pieces, etc. Indexes.

C112   British Museum. Department of Printed Books. **John Henry Newman: An Excerpt from the General Catalogue of Printed Books, Revised 1971**. London, British Museum for the British Library Board, 1974. 21p. LC 76-352365, ISBN 0-71410-330-X

A reprinting of the Newman entries in the British Museum Catalog. No Indexes.

C113   Earnest, James David and Gerard Tracey. **John Henry Newman: An Annotated Bibliography of his Tract and Pamphlet Collection**. New York, Garland, 1984. 234p. LC 84-48069. ISBN 0-8240-8958-8

A collection of the "sermons and speeches, broadsides and critiques of friends and enemies in the Oxford Movement and the various controversies of Newman's Catholic years" (Introduction). The 2,178 items are arranged by years with an Author Index and a Subject Index.

C114   Rickaby, Joseph John. **Index to the Works of John Henry Cardinal Newman**. London, Longmans, Green, 1914. viii, 156p.

A subject index to all of his works illustrating the changes in his thought. Based on the Longmans' editions. Entries tend to be for broad rather than narrow categories.

FLANNERY O'CONNOR

C115   Golden, Robert E., and Mary Carmel Sullivan. **Flannery O'Connor and Caroline Gordon: A Reference Guide.** Boston, G. K. Hall, 1977. v, 342p. LC 76-44334. ISBN 0-8161-7845-3.

Contains two separate bibliographies, with separate indexes for these two American Catholic writers. Most annotations are long and quite helpful. Chronological arrangement.

LIAM O'FLAHERTY

C116   Doyle, Paul A. **Liam O'Flaherty: An Annotated Bibliography.** Troy, NY, Whitson Pub. Co., 1972. iii, 68p. LC 71-161085. ISBN 0-8787-5017-7.

Annotations are brief but helpful. Index.

MURIEL SPARK

C117   Tominaga, Thomas T., and Wilma Schneidermeyer. **Iris Murdoch and Muriel Spark: A Bibliography.** Metuchen, NJ, Scarecrow, 1976. xvi, 237p. LC 76-909. ISBN 0-8108-0907-9.

Lists 890 books and articles by and about Spark. Annotations are supplied for critical works. Indexes.

EVELYN WAUGH

C118   **Evelyn Waugh: A Checklist of Primary and Secondary Material.** By Robert Murray Davis and others. Troy, NY, Whitson Pub. Co., 1972. iv, 211p. LC 77-155725. ISBN 0-87875-021-5.

A very comprehensive listing of 2,107 books, articles and reviews. Drawings, book plates and dust jacket designs by Waugh are included. Index.

QUOTATIONS

C119   Chapin, John. **The Book of Catholic Quotations: Compiled from Approved Sources, Ancient, Medieval and Modern.** New York, Farrar, Straus and Cudahy, 1956. x, 1073p.

Unique in coverage among the plethora of quotation books. Scripture is not included, but more than 10,400 quotations drawn from Catholic and non-Catholic sources (if they deal with the Church), from the earliest works to those of the present day, are arranged alphabetically by subjects. The indexes are adequate, but references to sources are not as complete as one might wish. *Critic*, however, termed this work "a splendid collection" (XV [February, 1957], p. 259).

GENRES

DRAMA–BIBLIOGRAPHY

C120   Stratman, Carl Joseph. **Bibliography of Medieval Drama.** 2nd. ed. rev. and enl. New York, Ungar, 1972. 2 v. xv, 1035p. LC 78-163141. ISBN 0-8044-3272-4.

9,000 plays, critical studies and bibliographies are listed in the greatly expanded second edition of this standard work. Manuscripts, books, and articles are included. Liturgical Latin drama, English, Byzantine, French, German, Italian, Spanish and Dutch drama are covered in separate lists. There are no annotations, but important items are starred. A very thorough author, title, subject index appears in volume II.

FICTION–BIBLIOGRAPHY

C121   Brown, Stephen James Meredith. **Novels and Tales by Catholic Writers: A Catalogue.** 8th ed. (rev.) Dublin, Central Catholic Library, 1946. 141p. LC A47-5251.

"Aims to include all fiction, in English and translated into English, by Catholic writers, apart from some forgotten books of little value" (Preface). This is an author list giving only the briefest bibliographical information, with annotations, but no indexes. There are some deliberate omissions of controversial Catholic authors "for which we make no apology."

FICTION–HISTORY AND CRITICISM

C122   Braybrooke, Patrick. **Some Catholic Novelists, Their Art and Outlook.** London, Burns, Oates and Washbourne, 1931. xv, 230p. il. LC 31-20954. Reprinted: Freeport, NY, Books for Libraries, 1966. LC 67-22078. ISBN 6369-1323-X.

Informal studies of seven Catholic writers: Chesterton, Belloc, Ayscough, Benson, Gibbs, Kaye-Smith, and Tynan, with a portrait of each.

C123   Gardiner, Harold Charles. **Fifty Years of the American Novel: A Christian Appraisal.** New York, Scribner, 1951. xiv, 304p. LC 51-14154. Reprinted: New York, Gordian Press, 1968. LC 68-21260.

Covers fourteen twentieth-century writers and a selection of war novelists. The young, unknown Marshall McLuhan was one of the distinguished scholars contributing to this work, along with Anne Fremantle, Francis X. Connolly, and many others, most of whom *America* credited with presenting "striking insights" (LXXXVI [December, 1951], p. 258). Index.

C124   Gardiner, Harold Charles. **Norms for the Novel.** Rev. ed. Garden City, NY, Hanover House, 1960. 166p. LC 60-7872.

Gardiner was for many years the literary editor of *America*, and this work grew out of the controversies that surrounded his usually liberal reviews of the modern novel. The major principles for judging literary works presented in this study first appeared in "Tenets for Readers and Reviewers," a pamphlet published by America Press in 1944. Covering general principles of moral evaluation and realism, and the principles of the function of literature, this work is still a useful guide, especially for young people, to the very adult world of the modern novel.

C125   Kellogg, Jean Defrees. **The Vital Tradition: The Catholic Novel in a Period of Convergence.** Chicago, Loyola University Press, 1970. vi, 278p. LC 74-108375. ISBN 0-8294-0192-X.

Mauriac, Bernanos, Waugh, Greene, Powers and O'Connor are treated in this serious study of Catholic traditions in France, England and America. "Offers important insights into the dialectical relationship between religious belief and social thought and literature" (*Thought*, XLVI [Fall, 1971], p. 472). Bibliography, pp. 249-262. Index.

C126   **The Vision Obscured: Perceptions of Some Twentieth-Century Catholic Novelists.** Ed. by Melvin J. Friedman. New York, Fordham University Press, 1970. 278p. LC 72-1261130. ISBN 0-8232-0890-7.

Thoughtful essays by a number of literary scholars dealing with Powers, O'Connor, Waugh, Spark, Greene, Bernanos, Mauriac, Green Langgässer, Laforet, and Papini. "The Modern Catholic Novel: a Selected Checklist of Criticism" (pp. 241-268) is an extensive bibliography of general works on the Catholic novel and provides separate lists for each of the writers covered. "A failure as a book, but a success as a series of chapters" (*America*, CXXIV [March 27, 1971], p. 325). Index.

POETRY–ANTHOLOGIES

C127   Kilmer, Joyce. **Anthology of Catholic Poets.** With a New Supplement by James Edward Tobin. New rev. ed. Garden City, NY, Image Books, 1955. 398p. LC 55-6322.

Selected poems "written since mid-nineteenth century in English by poets who were Catholics at any period in their lives" (Preface). The supplement more than doubles the size of the collection and includes many minor poets not easily found elsewhere. Author index.

C128   Leslie, Shane. **An Anthology of Catholic Poets.** Rev. and enl. ed. Westminster, MD, Newman Press, 1953. 378p. LC 53-10274.

Selections from the entire span of English literature by poets who "died in communion with the Holy See." Not all the works are religious. No indexes.

C129   Noyes, Alfred. **The Golden Book of Catholic Poetry.** Philadelphia, J. B. Lippincott Co., 1946. xxix, 440p. il. LC 46-3649.

The most complete anthology of this type covering Catholic poetry from the thirteenth century to the present in English and translations from other languages. Some poems by non-Catholics are also included. Not all the poems are religious in theme. Chronological arrangement with author and title indexes.

C130   Walsh, Thomas. **The Catholic Anthology: The World's Great Catholic Poetry**. Rev. ed. New York, Macmillan Co., 1943. xii, 584p. LC 40-1211.

"A selection of Catholic poems written by Catholics and bearing the impress of Catholic dogma, tradition and life" (Preface). The selections are largely English and American, but some translated works are included. A brief biographical dictionary of each of the authors is included (pp. 515-564). Author and title indexes.

BRITAIN

POETRY

Bibliography

C131   Brown, Carleton Fairchild. **A Register of Middle English and Didactic Verse**. Oxford, Bibliographical Society, 1916-20. 2 v. LC 17-6900.

C132   Brown, Carleton Fairchild, and Rossell Hope Robbins. **The Index of Middle English Verse**. New York, Columbia University Press, 1943. xix, 785p. LC 43-16653.

"Completes the work begun by Carleton Brown in the *Register of Middle English and Didactic Verse*" (Preface).

C133   **Supplement**. *The Index of Middle English Verse*. By Russell Hope Robbins and John L. Cutler. Lexington, University of Kentucky Press, 1965. xxix, 551p. LC 43-16653 rev.

The *Register* is an alphabetical author list of 2,273 poems, mostly religious, written between 1200 and 1500 with an index of subjects and titles. Locations and descriptions of the original manuscripts are given as well as references to printed texts.

The *Index* lists 4,365 entries, and the *Supplement* contains 1,500 new entries for works uncovered since 1943. In the latter work the cut-off date of 1500 has been abandoned to include works written up to the early sixteenth century. This work and the index update entries originally contained in previous editions. Each volume contains indexes.

Anthologies

C134   Guiney, Louise Imogen. **Recusant Poets . . . with a Selection from Their Works**. New York, Sheed and Ward, 1939- . v. LC 39-4694.

Each poet is given a scholarly, bio-bibliographical introduction along with the texts of his poems. Editions and criticisms are listed in notes including references to mss. or the original printed versions. Index of first lines, glossary and index of names. Covers many obscure works.

PROSE

Bibliography

C135   **A Manual of the Writings in Middle English, 1050-1500.** By members of
the Middle English Group of the Modern Language Association of America.
New Haven, CT, Academy of Arts and Sciences. Hamden, CT, Shoe String
Press, 1967-73. 4 v. LC 67-7687. ISBN 0-208-00893-4. 0-208-00894-2.
0-208-01220-6. 0-208-01342-3.

The standard work for literature of this period. Commentary and bibliographies are supplied giving evaluation both of the literature and the scholarship. All of the known writings of the time (most of which are religious or
theological) are covered. The commentary is given in narrative form with
bibliography at the end of the volumes. Each volume has its own index.

History and Criticism

C136   Southern, A. C. **Elizabethan Recusant Prose, 1559-1582: A Historical and
Critical Account of the Books of the Catholic Refugees Printed and Pub-
lished Abroad and at Secret Presses in England Together with an Annotated
Bibliography of the Same.** London, Sands, 1950. xxxv, 553p. il. LC A51-417.

(Based on a Ph.D. thesis, University of London.)

Part I treats of the various types of literature produced during this period—
apologetical works, devotional works, and miscellaneous works, as well as
a section on publishers and presses. The annotated bibliography (pp. 367-
536) is arranged by author and followed by a chronological index.

FRANCE

BIBLIOGRAPHY

C137   Sterck, Leo Clement. **Great Books of France: A Catholic Guide.** St. Louis,
Swift, 1941. 74p.

A series of brief essays and bibliographies dealing with nineteen major works
and/or authors. Designed for English speaking students of French literature,
and covering the social, political and religious backgrounds of the authors,
their lives and influence; this work is a useful guide for the general reader.

HISTORY AND CRITICISM

C138   Brémond, Henri. **Manuel de la littérature catholique en France de 1870
à nos jours.** Nouvelle éd. Paris, Éditions Spes, 1939. 493p.

Historical, philosophical and scientific writers are covered as well as purely
literary writers in this "admirable history of literature" (*Catholic World*,
CXXIII [June, 1926], p. 430). The essays are arranged by literary genres
and subject fields and are well documented and indexed.

GERMANY

BIBLIOGRAPHY

C139   Morvay, Karin, and Dagmar Grube. **Bibliographie der deutschen Predigt des Mittelalters: Veröffentlichte Predigten.** München, C. H. Beck, 1974. xxviii, 363p. LC 75-569146.

A bibliography of printed texts of German medieval sermons. The arrangement is chronological with indexes of German and Latin incipits. There is also an index of scriptural quotations. "A well-organized work of some complexity" (*Modern Language Review*, LXXII [January, 1977], p. 231).

C140   Stammler, Wolfgang. **Die deutsche Literatur des Mittelalters: Verfasserlexikon.** Berlin, W. de Gruyter, 1931-35. 5 v. LC 32-22158.

A bio-bibliography of medieval German writers. Most articles tend to be long and are signed by specialists. The fifth volume is a supplement.

BIOGRAPHY

C141   Kehrein, Joseph. **Biographischliterarisches Lexikon der katholischen deutschen Dichter, Volks-und Jugendschriftsteller im 19. Jahrhundert.** Zürich, L. Woerl, 1868. 2 v. in 1. LC 6-25035.

Contains brief biographies of nineteenth century German Catholic poets with exhaustive classified bibliographies of editions and criticism.

LATIN LITERATURE

GUIDES

C142   McGuire, Martin Rawson Patrick, and Hermigild Dressler. **Introduction to Medieval Latin Studies: A Syllabus and Bibliographical Guide.** 2nd. ed. Washington, DC, Catholic University of America Press, 1977. xiii, 406p. LC 77-23238. ISBN 0-8132-0542-5.

In this second edition Dressler has expanded the work to over twice its original size, updated the bibliographies to 1972 and later, and added a subject index. Each chapter contains a brief outline of the period or subject covered and a comprehensive bibliography. Index of medieval works and authors, index of modern authors, subject index. "Invariably the best recent literature and critical editions are listed" (*Theological Studies*, XXV [December, 1964], p. 688).

BIBLIOGRAPHY

C143   Kristeller, Paul Oskar. **Catalogus translationum et commentariorum: Medieval and Renaissance Latin Translations and Commentaries: Annotated Lists and Guides.** Washington, DC, Catholic University of America Press, 1960- . v. LC 60-4006.

"A series that lists and describes the Latin translations of ancient Greek authors and the Latin commentaries on ancient Greek and Latin authors"

(Preface). The first volume contains a list of all the authors to be treated, bibliographies for nine of these authors and an index of translators and commentators. The histories of editions and their influence are traced in the bibliographical essays which treat of each of the authors' works in great detail.

DICTIONARIES

C144   Cappelli, Adriano. **Lexicon abbreviaturarum: dizionario di abbreviature latine ed italiane, usate nelle carte e codici specialmente del Medioevo riprodotte con oltre 14,000 segni incisi.** Milano, Hoepli, 1961. lxxiii, 531p. LC 60-19112.

Contains definitions for signs and symbols as well as abbreviations. Numbers are also covered. Bibliography of works on abbreviations, pp. 517-531.

C145   Pelzer, Auguste. **Abréviations latines médiévales. Supplément au Dizionario di abbreviature latine,** ed. italiane de Adriano Cappelli. 2e éd. Louvain, Publications universitaires; Paris, Beatrice-Nauwelaerts, 1966. vii, 86p. LC 68-114011.

Additional meanings and new symbols are covered.

MUSIC AND HYMNOLOGY

The recent changes in the liturgy have rendered many of the works in this section obsolete since Gregorian chant, Latin hymns and the formerly rigid control over Church music exercised by Rome have all but disappeared. Nevertheless, the student of the history of music will find them useful for research.

BIBLIOGRAPHY

C146   Blume, Clemens. **Repertorium repertorii: Kritischer Wegweiser durch U. Chevalier's Repertorium hymnologicum. Alphabetisches Register falscher mangelhafter oder irreleitender Hymnanfänge und Nachweise mit Erörterung über Plan und Methode des Repertoriums.** Leipzig, O. R. Reisland, 1901. 315p. LC 3-13989.

A supplement of additions and corrections to Chevalier's work (C147).

C147   Chevalier, Cyr Ulysse Joseph. **Repertorium hymnologicum. Catalogue des chants, hymns, proses séquences, tropes en usage dans l'église latine depuis les origines jusqu'à nos jours.** Louvain, 1892-1912; Bruxelles 1920-21. 6 v. (Subsidia hagiographica, n. 4.) LC F-2313.

Contains the titles of Latin hymns, the saint's or feast day on which it was used in the Breviary, its place in the office, the number of strophes, the author, date of composition and a reference to printed texts. This is "the standard bibliography of Latin rhymed texts" (Vincent H. Duckles, *Music Reference and Research Materials* [London, Free Press, 1964], p. 188).

C148   Higginson, J. Vincent. **Handbook for American Catholic Hymnals.** New York, Hymn Society of America, 1976. xxi, 334p. LC 76-13307.

1,100 hymns are listed by subject in three different sections of this work. The first part provides information about the text, the name of the composer and the location of the hymn in various hymnals. The second part provides musical notation and the third section gives a detailed history of the text and melody. An additional section at the end of the book provides biographical information about authors and composers, a bibliography, a list of tune names, and a general index. The coverage is from 1871 to 1964. A very detailed and scholarly work.

C149 Hughes, Andrew. **Medieval Music: The Sixth Liberal Art**. Rev. ed. Toronto, University of Toronto Press, 1980. xiii, 360p. (Toronto Medieval Bibliographies, no. 4.) LC 79-18770. ISBN 0-80202-358-4.

An annotated bibliography of over 2,000 works on medieval music in a classified arrangement with an Index of Authors and Editors and a General Index.

C150 Hughes, Anselm. **Medieval Polyphony in the Bodleian Library: Catalogue**. Oxford, Bodleian Library, 1951. 63p. LC 52-64643.

Descriptions of fifty-one manuscripts with an index of *initia* or first lines.

C151 Münster, Robert. **Katalogue bayerischer Musiksammlungen**. München, G. Henle, 1971- . v.
Vol. 1. *Thematischer Katalog der Musikhandschriften der ehmaligen Klosterkirchen Weyarn, Tegernsee und Benediktbeuern*. 1971. LC 72-329681. Vol. 2. *Thematischer Katalog der Musikhandschriften der Benediktinerinnenabte Frauenwörth und der Pfarrkirchen Indersdorf, Wasserburg*. 1975. LC 75-519985. Vol. 3. *Thematischer Katalog der Musikhandschriften der Fürstlich Oettingen-Wallerstein'shen Bibliothek Schloss Harburg*. 1976. LC 77-461506.

An attempt to list music manuscripts once held in Bavarian monasteries, now scattered in both Church and private collections. For a more complete description of this important series see *Notes*, XXXIII (September, 1976), pp. 72-73.

C152 Verret, Sister Mary Camilla. **A Preliminary Survey of Roman Catholic Hymnals Published in the United States of America**. Washington, DC, Catholic University of America Press, 1964. 165p. LC 64-18590.

Lists over 300 hymnals with locations and descriptive annotations. All editions are given, along with the number of hymns in each. Covers the period 1788-1961. Chronological arrangement with author index.

COLLECTIONS

C153 **Analecta hymnica medii aevi**. Hrsg. von Guido Maria Dreves, S. J., und Clemens Blume. Leipzig, Reisland, 1886-1922. 55 v. Reprinted: New York, Johnson Reprint, 1961.

The most inclusive collection of Latin hymn texts, with historical and bibliographical notes.

C154   **Analecta hymnica medii aevi. Register,** in Zusarb. mit Dorothea Baumann (et al.). Hrsg. von Max Lütolf. Bern, Francke, 1978. 3 v. in 2. LC 80-461615. ISBN 3-77201431-3.

        An index to the main set.

C155   Bryden, John Rennie and David G. Hughes, comps. **An Index of Gregorian Chant.** Cambridge, MA, Harvard University Press, 1969. 2 v. LC 71-91626. ISBN 6-74444-875-8.
Volume I. Alphabetical Index.
Volume II. Thematic Index.

        Provides the incipit of the chant, the type of music (e.g. hymn, antiphon, etc.), printed source, and melodic code. Volume one lists the chants by incipits and volume two by melodic codes.

INDEXES

C156   Mearns, James. **Early Latin Hymnaries: An Index of Hymns in Hymnaries before 1100, With an Appendix from Later Sources.** Cambridge, The University Press, 1913. xx, 107p. LC 14-14173.

        The texts referred to are those reprinted in the *Annalecta hymnica medii aevi* and other sources. The arrangement is alphabetical by first line. Subjects and authors are indicated.

DICTIONARIES AND ENCYCLOPEDIAS

C157   Carroll, Joseph Robert. **Compendium of Liturgical Music Terms.** Toledo, OH, Gregorian Institute of America, 1964. 86p. LC 64-4737.

        Useful for definitions of terms and practices in use before Vatican II.

C158   Hughes, Anselm. **Liturgical Terms for Music Students: A Dictionary.** Boston, McLaughlin and Reilly Co., 1940. iv, 40p. LC 41-18179. Reprinted: St. Clair Shores, MI, Scholarly Press, 1972. LC 70-166236. ISBN 0-403-01363-1.

        Contains concise definitions of musical terms used in the Latin rite, with appended tables outlining the structure of the mass and office.

C159   Julian, John. **A Dictionary of Hymnology Setting Forth the Origin and History of Christian Hymns of All Ages and Nations.** New York, Dover Pub., 1957. 2 v. LC 58-410.

        Covers hymns of all countries and Christian denominations, listing in one alphabet the titles of individual hymns, composers, hymnals and topics in hymnology. Most entries are short, but are signed and contain bibliographies. The emphasis is on English language hymns but other languages are covered, including Latin. Indexes of authors and first lines.

C160   Kornmüller, Utto. **Lexikon der kirchlichen Tonkunst.** 2., verb. und verm. aufl. Regensburg, A. Coppenrath, 1891-95. 2 v. in 1. LC 3-23735.

Volume one is a dictionary of terms used in Catholic Church music and volume two, a biographical dictionary of Church musicians including non-Catholic composers. Volume one has a subject index.

C161   Porte, Jacques, ed. **Encyclopédie\des musiques sacrées.** Paris, Editions Lagergerie, 1968-1970. 4 v. LC 70-211374.

Volume one covers Jewish, Eastern, and Latin American music. Volumes two and three are devoted to Christian music of the West. Volume four contains a discography and eight phonograph records. The contents are arranged geographically without indexes. Articles are substantial with bibliographies. "A well documented source book" (A.J. Walford, *Guide to Reference Material*, 4th ed. [London, Library Association, 1987], v. 4, p. 453).

C162   Weissenbäch, Andreas. **Sacra musica: Lexikon der katholischen Kirchen-musik.** Klosterneuburg bei Wien, Verlag der Augustinus-druckerei, 1937. viii, 419p. il. LC 38-35457.

Includes biographies and technical terms in one alphabet. Organizations and music publishers are also covered. The articles are briefer than Korn-müller's (C160) but contain bibliographies and cover a wider scope of subjects.

HANDBOOKS

C163   Apel, Willi. **Gregorian Chant.** Bloomington, Indiana University Press, 1958. xiv, 529p. LC 57-10729.

A history and analysis of Gregorian chant, covering the structure and development of the liturgy, the texts, notation, tonality and psalmody of the chant, and a stylistic analysis. Ambrosian and Old Roman chants are also treated. Frequent bibliographical notes. Index.

C164   **A Grammar of Plainsong.** By a Benedictine of Stanbrook. 3rd ed. Liverpool, Rushworth and Dreaper, 1934. 106p. il. LC 35-7375.

A general introduction for singers covering pronunciation of Latin, nota-tion, tonality, rhythm, accompaniment and so forth. The history of chant is also explained. Index.

C165   Hayburn, Robert F. **Digest of Regulations and Rubrics of Catholic Church Music.** Rev. ed. Boston, McLaughlin and Reilly Company, 1961. 112p. LC 61-3897.

An excellent source of pre-Vatican II Church law and practice in music. Provides a general summary of Church law on music and individual chapters on the music for specific ceremonies. Index.

C166   Mytych, Joseph F. **Digest of Church Law on Sacred Music.** Toledo, Gre-gorian Institute of America, 1959. 64p. LC 60-237.

Explains approximately 200 laws listed under twenty-two subject headings. References to documents or canons are given. Index.

C167   Rowlands, Leo. **Guide Book for Catholic Church Choirmasters.** Enlarged ed. Boston, McLaughlin and Reilly Company, 1962. 117p. LC 63-25537.

A complete guide to forming and training a choir with detailed directions for what to do at specific ceremonies.

C168   Society of St. Gregory of America. **The White List: With a Selection of Papal Documents and Other Information Pertaining to Catholic Church Music.** Glen Rock, NJ, 1928- . v. Irregular. LC 49-29147. (Imprint varies.) (Fourth ed., 1947 reissued with supplement, 1958).

Contains the texts of selected papal and other documents from the fourteenth century to the present along with an approved list of hymns, masses and organ pieces; a partial "blacklist" is also included. For each item the author, title, publisher and difficulty of performance are indicated. Classified bibliography, pp. 78-85.

C169   Szövérffy, Josef. **Die Annalen der lateinischen Hymnendichtung: ein Handbuch.** Berlin, E. Schmidt, 1964-65. 2 v. LC 66-4938.

A guide to the study of Latin hymnology from the beginnings to the end of the Middle Ages, giving the history and analyses of the poetry of Latin hymns in groups arranged by either author or period. Frequent bibliographies, tables and lists are provided. Index.

HISTORY

C170   Coussemaker, Charles Edmond Henri de, ed. **Scriptorum de musica Medii Aevi novam seriem a Gerbertina alteram collegit.** Paris, Apud A. Durand, 1864--1876. 4 v. Reprinted: Hildesheim, G. Olms, 1963. LC 72-203207.

A continuation of Gerbert (C171) with the same faults and value as that work.

C171   Gerbert, Martin. **Scriptores ecclesiastici de musica sacra potissimum. Exvariis Italiae Galliae et Germaniae codicibus manuscriptis collecti.** n.p. Typis San-Blasianis, 1784. 3 v. Reprinted: Hildesheim, Georg Olms, 1963.

A collection of medieval treatises on music. Index. "Inaccurate and incomplete but still valuable" (Andrew Hughes, *Medieval Music* [Toronto, Univ. Pr., 1980], p. 129.) Continued by Coussemaker (C170).

C172   Nemmers, Erwin Esser. **Twenty Centuries of Catholic Church Music.** Milwaukee, Bruce Pub. Co., 1949. xvii, 213p. LC 49-1798.

A brief history good for definitions, brief accounts and bibliography. Each chapter covers a period with lists of books and music. American church music is included. Glossary. Index.

FINE AND APPLIED ARTS

HANDBOOKS

C173   Hirn, Yrjö. **The Sacred Shrine: A Study of the Poetry and Art of the Catholic Church.** London, Macmillan, 1912. xv, 574p. LC 12-22048.

"Begun as a description of purely aesthetic and literary history, but has developed into a synthetic treatment of the aesthetic characteristics of Catholic mentality" (Introduction). Whatever that might mean, the topics covered include the altar, relics, the mass, the sanctuary, the host, monstrance, tabernacle and Mary. While the text may or may not prove accurate, the bibliographies are at least plentiful.

SYMBOLISM

Christian iconography is the science of the description, history and interpretation of the traditional symbols used in art to represent Christ, the saints, the mass, sacraments, virtues, and other religious themes.

Among the more important works included in this session are those by Kirschbaum (C181), Réau (C185), Didron (C177), Aurenhammer (C175), and Rohault de Fleury (C190, C191, C193, C201). Anna Jameson's four works (C179, C189, C192, C203) should be used with caution; for, although one must be grateful to this tireless collector of obviously unfamiliar facts, anyone conversant with the history of the saints, religious orders, or Mary will surely wish she had limited herself to iconography or at least drawn her information from primary sources.

GENERAL WORKS

C174   Appleton, LeRoy H., and Stephen Bridges. **Symbolism in Liturgical Art.** New York, Scribner, 1959. 120p. il. LC 59-7203.

An alphabetical treatment of symbols used in Catholic and other Christian churches. Brief descriptions, bibliographies, illustrations and citations to the Douay and Authorized versions are provided. "If any criticism is due, it must be for rigid economy rather than lavishness" (*Liturgical Arts*, XXVII [August, 1959], p. 96). Index.

C175   Aurenhammer, Hans. **Lexikon der christlichen Ikonographie.** Wien, Hollinek, 1959- . v.

Saints, Biblical characters, concepts and various objects are covered in one alphabet. Bibliographies and references to works of art appear in each article.

C176   **Dictionnaire du symbolisme.** Par les Religieuses Bénédictines de la rue Monsieur. Paris, Abbaye de Saint-André, Belgium, L'Artisan Liturgique, 1934. 118 col.

A dictionary of brief entries giving definitions and references, where applicable, to the 753 illustrations contained in the back of the book.

C177   Didron, Adolf Napoleon. **Christian Iconography: The History of Christian Art in the Middle Ages.** Trans. from the French by E. J. Millington. New York, F. Ungar Pub. Co., 1965. 2 v. il. LC 65-23577.

"A Standard work in this field" (Mary W. Chamberlain, *Guide to Art Reference Books* [Chicago, A.L.A., 1959], p. 58). Contains studies of the nimbus, aureole, glory, the trinity, angels, devils, the soul and "the Christian schema." Bibliographical footnotes. Index.

C178   Ferguson, George Wells. **Signs and Symbols in Christian Art: With Illustrations from Paintings of the Renaissance.** New York, Oxford University Press, 1954. 346p. il. LC 54-13072.

Well illustrated with black and white and color plates which are included in the index. Covers animals, flowers, the earth, sky, the body, Christ, Mary, and numerous other subjects with an illustration of each object and scriptural or other references. Bibliography pp. 343-46. Index.

C179   Jameson, Anna Brownell (Murphy). **Sacred and Legendary Art.** Boston, Houghton Mifflin, 1911. 2 v. il. LC 12-26198. Reprint of 1896 ed.: New York, AMS Press, 1970. LC 72-145108. ISBN 0-403-01045-4.

Deals with Biblical persons, the angels, patron saints, martyrs, early bishops and hermits, warrior saints, and doctors of the Church. First published in 1848, this work gives short explanations of each item with references to and brief descriptions of works of art. Names of artists, galleries, and churches, are indexed apart from the general subject index.

C180   Künstle, Karl. **Ikonographie der christlichen Kunst.** Freiburg, Herder, 1926-28. 2 v. il.

"A Standard work on Christian Iconography" (Chamberlain, *Guide to Art Reference Books* [Chicago, A.L.A., 1959], p. 59). Volume two is a dictionary of the iconography of the saints giving descriptions of works of art depicting them, biographies, bibliographies and illustrations. The history of Christian symbolism in art is covered in all its aspects in the first volume, with bibliographies for each topic. Index.

C181   **Lexikon der Christlichen Ikonographier.** Hrsg. von Engelbert Kirschbaum, et al. Freiburg, herder, 1968-76. 8 v. LC 71-386111.
Volumes 1-4. Allegemeine Ikonographie.
Volumes 5-8. Ikonographie der Heiligen.

Each article is made up of three parts: a survey of the sources, biblical or literary; a description of the iconography; bibliography. The first four volumes cover biblical and general themes and the last four volumes cover the saints. Subject index, symbol index. "An important contribution to the history of spirituality and of the theology of sacred art, but also to history in the strict sense, philology, cultural anthropology, and ethnology" (*Lumen Vitae*, XXVIII [March, 1973], p. 183).

C182   Mâle, Émile. **L'art religieux de la fin du XVIe siècle du XVIIe siècle et du XVIIIe siècle; étude sur l'iconographie apres le Concile de Trente, Italie-France-Espagne-Flandres.** 2. éd., rev. et corr. Paris, A. Colin, 1951. ix, 532p. il. LC A51-5112.

Protestantism in art is covered as well as the Catholic Counter-Reformation period—martyrs, visions, ecstasies, the new iconography and devotions. Indexed for places, works of art and subjects.

C183   Mâle, Émile. **Religious Art from the Twelfth to the Eighteenth Century.** New York, Pantheon, 1949. 208p. il. LC 49-10882.

An abridged translation of the author's four-volume history of which (C182) is a part. "Though simple and compact, it rests upon an immense amount of erudition" (*Booklist*, XLVI [November 15, 1949], p. 93). Index.

C184   Post, Willard E. **Saints, Signs and Symbols.** 2nd. ed. London, S.P.C.K., 1975. 96p. il. LC 76-350206. ISBN 0-2810-2894-X.

Arranged by subject (e.g. crosses, stars, the Trinity, etc.) with a section on the saints arranged alphabetically. Black and white illustrations accompany the text. Index.

C185   Réau, Louis. **Iconographie de l'art chrétien.** Rev. Paris, Presses Universitaires de France, 1955-59. 3 v. in 6. LC A56-1728.

One of the more recently published comprehensive works in this field. The three major parts are the *Introduction générale*, covering definitions, types of symbols, sources, etc.; *Iconographie de la Bible*, covering characters and stories; and *Iconographie des Saintes*, an alphabetical catalog of saints giving biographies, histories of their cults, descriptions and locations of representations in works of art, and bibliographies. Byzantine and Western, medieval and post-Reformation art are included. Although praised from an artistic point of view, one reviewer pointed out Réau's ignorance of some of the basic laws of the Church regarding the veneration of the saints (*Clergy Review*, XL [September, 1956], p. 567).

C186   Sill, Gertrude Grace. **A Handbook of Symbols in Christian Art.** New York, Macmillan, 1975. 241p. il. LC 75-26560. ISBN 0-02-610920-4.

Arranged alphabetically by broad subject categories giving brief explanations of symbols with illustrations taken from works of art. "For all its compactness, the book is remarkably thorough and clear" (*America*, CXXXV [November 13, 1976], p. 326). Index.

C187   Tiso, Francis. **A Young Person's Book of Catholic Signs and Symbols.** 1st ed. Garden City, NY, Nazareth Books/Doubleday, 1982. ix, 115p. LC 81-43459. ISBN 0-385-17951-0.

Symbols are explained under fourteen categories, e.g., God, Christ, the Holy Spirit, the Church, Mary, the saints, angels, etc. Illustrations are provided but they are not noteworthy. Index.

C188   Webber, Frederick Roth. **Church Symbolism: An Explanation of the More Important Symbols of the Old and New Testament, the Primitive, the Medieval and Modern Church.** 2nd. ed. rev. Cleveland, J. H. Jansen, 1938. ix, 413p. il. LC 38-33530. Reprinted: Detroit, Gale, 1971. LC 79-107627. ISBN 0-8103-3349-X.

Arranged by topic—the Trinity, the Holy Ghost, the Virgin Mary, saints, sacraments—with line drawings and plates. The appendixes include a glossary of common symbols, a list of important saints and a bibliography, pp. 389-394. Index.

CHRIST

C189   Jameson, Anna Brownell (Murphy). **The History of Our Lord as Exemplified in Works of Art: With That of His Types: St. John the Baptist; and Other Persons of the Old and New Testaments.** Continued and completed by Lady Eastlake. 3rd. ed. London, Longmans, Green and Co., 1872. 2 v. il. LC 17-17688. Reprinted: Detroit, Gale, 1976. LC 72-167006. ISBN 0-8103-4304-5.

Includes representatives of Biblical persons, objects and incidents in works of art; with indexes of artists, locations, and subjects.

C190   Rohault de Fleury, Charles. **L'évangile: études iconographiques et archéo-logiques.** Tours, A. Mame et fils, 1874. 2 v. il. LC F-3857.

Concentrates on symbols depicting the life of Christ found in ancient churches and works of art. Index.

THE MASS

C191   Rohault de Fleury, Charles. **La messe: études archéologiques sur ses monu-ments: continuées par son fils.** Paris, V. A. Morel, 1883-89. 8 v. il. LC 13-26016.

"A monumental work on the mass and its iconography" (Chamberlain, *Guide to Art Reference Books* [Chicago, A.L.A., 1959], p. 61). Includes hundreds of plates with detailed descriptions illustrating ancient altars, vestments, sacred vessels, and church furnishings. Bibliographies and indexes are provided in each volume.

MARY

C192   Jameson, Anna Brownell (Murphy). **Legends of the Madonna as Represented in the Fine Arts.** Cor. and enl. ed. Boston, Houghton Mifflin, 1911. xviii, 483p. il. LC 12-26196. Reprint of 1890 ed.: Detroit, Gale, 1972. LC 70-89273. ISBN 0-8103-3114-4.

An "old but still useful" work (Chamberlain, *Guide to Art Reference Books* [Chicago, A.L.A., 1959], p. 59) covering the history of devotion of Mary, her symbols and attributes, and various types of representations of her in art. Index.

C193   Rohault de Fleury, Charles. **La Sainte Vierge: études archéologiques et iconographiques.** Paris, Poussielgue frères, 1878. 2 v. il. LC 14-9632.

"Covers the terrestial and celestial life of Mary in art" including all aspects of her cult. Bibliographical notes and indexes in each volume.

SAINTS

C194   Clement, Clara Erskine. **A Handbook of Christian Symbols and Stories of the Saints As Illustrated in Art.** Boston, Ticknow and Co., 1886. 349p. il. Reprinted: Detroit, Gale, 1971. LC 70-159863. ISBN 0-8103-3288-4.

         A standard work in the field. No bibliography is supplied, but there is an index.

C195   Bles, Arthur de. **How to Distinguish the Saints in Art by their Costumes, Symbols and Attributes.** New York, Art, Culture Publications, 1925. 168p. il. LC 25-21075. Reprinted: Detroit, Gale, 1975. LC 68-18019. ISBN 0-8103-4125-5.

         A classified treatment of 320 saints and general religious symbols according to categories. Coverage extends only to the sixteenth century. More than 400 illustrations. Index.

C196   Drake, Maurice. **Saints and Their Emblems.** Illustrated by 12 plates from photographs and drawings by Wilfred Drake. London, T. W. Laurie, 1916. xiii, 235p. LC 16-25117. Reprinted: Detroit, Gale, 1972. LC 68-18021. ISBN 0-8103-3032-6.

         A dictionary of approximately 5,000 saints indicating their rank, feast day, dates, locality, emblems and symbols used to depict them in art, names of artists and bibliography. A cross-index of symbols is also supplied.

C197   Husenbeth, Frederick Charles. **Emblems of Saints by Which They Are Distinguished in Works of Art.** 3rd. ed., ed. by Augustus Jessapp. Norwich, Norfolk and Norwich Archeological Society, 1882. xiii, 426p. LC 11-28930.

         Not as useful as Drake's work (C196) since it covers only 1,500 saints but has the same features and arrangement.

C198   Milburn, Robert Leslie Pollington. **Saints and Their Emblems in English Churches.** Rev. ed. Oxford, Blackwell, 1957. 283p. il. LC 57-4052.

         An alphabetical listing of saints with biographies and descriptions of symbols. Gives locations of important art works. Not profusely illustrated. Appendix: alphabetical list of emblems.

C199   Post, Willard Ellwood. **Saints, Signs and Symbols.** 2nd. ed. New York, Morehouse-Barlow, 1975. 96p. il. LC 74-191738. ISBN 0-8192-1171-0.

         A small but useful guide to symbols of about 200 saints and religious concepts. Each symbol is illustrated in clear black and white drawings.

C200   Roeder, Helen. **Saints and their Attributes: With a Guide to Localities and Patronage.** Chicago, H. Regnery Co., 1956. xxviii, 391p. LC 56-13630.

         A dictionary arranged by symbols listing all the saints associated with these objects in works of art. Brief biographical information is provided for each saint. Index of saints' names.

C201   Rohault de Fleury, Charles. **Archéologie chrétienne. Les saints de la messe et leurs monuments; études continuées par son fils.** Paris, Librairies-imprimeries réunies, 1893-1900. 10 v. il. LC 14-9621.

Covers only the forty saints formerly named in the canon of the mass. Over 1,000 plates and extensive commentary describe the major churches and shrines of the world dedicated to these saints. A bibliography is provided for each church. Since these names are among the most common for dedications, the coverage of churches and shrines is quite comprehensive. Indexes.

C202   Wimmer, Otto. **Handbuch der Namen und Heiligen, mit einer Geschichte des christlichen Kalenders.** Innsbruck, Tyrolia-Verlag, 1956. 559p. LC 57-21605.

An alphabetical dictionary of saints giving short biographies, symbols used in art works, patrons and bibliography. Geographical and occupational indexes.

RELIGIOUS ORDERS

C203   Jameson, Anna Brownell (Murphy). **Legends of the Monastic Orders As Represented in the Fine Arts Forming the Second Series of Sacred and Legendary Art.** Cor. and enl. ed. Boston, Houghton, Mifflin, 1911. xv, 489p. il. LC 12-26197. Reprinted: New York, AMS Press, 1976. LC 75-41154. ISBN 0-404-14767-4.

Includes the major religious orders—Benedictines, Augustinians, Jesuits, Visitandines, the mendicant orders, and related groups. The monasteries, habits, saints, and symbolism are explained. Index.

ARCHITECTURE

C204   Sharp, Mary. **A Guide to the Churches of Rome.** Philadelphia, Chilton, 1967. xi, 291p. il. LC 66-22875. (Published in London [1967] as *A Traveller's Guide to the Churches of Rome.*)
Describes nearly 500 churches giving their history floor plans and major works of art. Indexes of saints and architects.

VESTMENTS AND ECCLESIASTICAL DRESS

C205   McCloud, Henry J. **Clerical Dress and Insignia of the Roman Catholic Church.** Milwaukee, Bruce Pub. Co., 1948. xiv, 231p. il. LC 48-11997.

Describes all items of clerical dress except the vestments of the mass, explaining when they are worn, by whom, the colors and history. A selection of Church documents is included. Bibliography, pp. 222-23. Index.

C206   Nainfa, John Abel Felix Prosper. **Costume of Prelates of the Catholic Church: According to Roman Etiquette.** Baltimore, J. Murphy, 1909. 211p. il. LC 9-13272.

Scholarly description of the clothing of bishops, archbishops, cardinals, patriarchs, and monsignori. Bibliography, pp. 275-79. Index. Heraldry is also covered.

C207   Norris, Herbert. **Church Vestments: Their Origin and Development.** New York, Dutton, 1950. xv, 190p. il. LC 50-6481.

An expansion of the first volume of the author's *Costume and Fashion* (London, Dent, 1927-38. 3 v.). Treats the history of Church vestments up to the fifteenth century. Illustrations include eight pages of photographs, eight color plates, and hundreds of black and white drawings by the author. Bibliography, pp. XIII-XIV. Index.

C208   Pocknee, Cyril Edward. **Liturgical Vesture: Its Origin and Development.** London, A.R. Mowbray and Company, 1960; Westminster, MD, Newman Press, 1961. 57p. LC 61-16277.

Covers the seven vestments used at mass, episcopal insignia, and the altar. Bibliography.

C209   Roulin, Eugène Augustin. **Vestments and Vesture: A Manual of Liturgical Art.** Trans. by Dom Justin McCann. St. Louis, Herder, 1931. xv, 308p. il. LC 31-20101.

A common sense guide to the selection of modern vestments. Not intended as an historical or artistic treatment. Index.

IV
SOCIAL SCIENCES

GENERAL WORKS

Among the relatively few books listed in this chapter, several important works bear special mention: Herder's *Wörterbuch der Pädagogik* (D20) in education and *Staatslexikon* (D151) in political science are both monumental and scholarly attempts to express a Catholic viewpoint in these fields. The *Dictionnaire de droit canonique* (D172) and Emmerich's *Atlas hierarchicus* (D195) are also important enough in their fields to deserve special attention.

BIBLIOGRAPHY

There are no comprehensive, current or retrospective bibliographical tools covering Catholic contributions to the social sciences. The general bibliographies in Chapter I, however, may be consulted under the appropriate subject headings. The two bibliographies listed here are limited in coverage and out-of-date.

D1   Duval, Frédéric Victor. **Les livres qui s'imposent: vie chrétienne, vie sociale, vie civique.** 4 éd. rev. et augm. Paris, G. Beauchesne, 1913 xiii, 706p. LC 13-1006.

     "A well-annotated Catholic bibliography of the social sciences, especially sociology" (O'Rourke [A74], p. 131). Covers only books in French, arranged by subject with an author-title-subject index.

D2   Laurent, Édouard. **Essai bibliographique autour de "Rerum novarum,"** préparé par Édouard Laurent avec la collaboration de Laval Laurent. Québec, Les Éditions de Culture," 1942. xv, 86p. LC 43-14202.

     Using the famous encyclical *Rerum Novarum* as a point of reference, the author has compiled a comprehensive, classified, critical bibliography of all aspects of Catholic social thought. Books and articles are included in a classified arrangement with an author index.

SOURCES

The major sources of modern Catholic social teachings, in addition to the Gospels, have traditionally been the great social encyclicals issued by the popes, especially Pope Leo XIII, Pius XI and John XXIII.

D3   Abell, Aaron Ignatius, ed. **American Catholic Thought on Social Questions.** Indianapolis, Bobbs-Merrill, 1968. lv, 571p. LC 66-30548. ISBN 0-672-60090-0.

Contains thirty-nine selections from the writings of well known Catholic thinkers from Orestes Brownson to Daniel Callahan. A lengthy introduction is provided along with bibliography and an index.

D4   Harte, Thomas Joseph. **Papal Social Principles: A Guide and Digest.** Milwaukee, Bruce Pub. Co., 1956. ix, 207p. LC 56-11150.

The major papal documents on social problems are arranged under twelve broad subject divisions with an alphabetical index of titles and subjects; for each document an outline, introduction, and bibliography are supplied.

D5   Fremantle, Anne (Jackson). **The Social Teachings of the Church.** New York, New American Library, 1963. 320p. LC 63-23027.

Contains complete texts or selections from thirteen major encyclicals from Leo XIII to John XXIII with introductions and a thorough index of subjects.

D6   **Renewing the Earth: Catholic Documents on Peace, Justice and Liberation.** Ed. by David J. O'Brien and Thomas A. Shannon. Garden City, NY, Image Books, 1977. 598p. LC 76-52008. ISBN 0-385-12954-8.

Fourteen documents, papal, conciliar, United States episcopal and the Medellín documents from Latin America are reprinted along with several introductory essays and a general index.

D7   **Social Justice! The Catholic Position.** Ed. by Vincent P. Mainelli. Washington, DC, Consortium Press, 1975. 1 v., unpaged. ISBN 0-8434-0601-1.

Thirteen documents from Pope John XXIII, Paul VI, the Vatican Council, and the Synod of Bishops are reprinted in this work in numbered paragraphs. A topical index of over 100 subjects indicates which section of the documents deal with which social issues. Ten major social issues are indexed through color tabs. This work was revised and incorporated into *Official Catholic Teachings* (B221)..

D8   **Social Wellsprings: Documents Selected Arranged and Annotated.** By Joseph Husslein. Milwaukee, Bruce Pub. Co., 1940-42. 2 v. LC 41-1099.
     V. 1. Fourteen Epochal Documents by Pope Leo XIII. V. 2. Eighteen Encyclicals of Social Reconstruction by Pope Pius XI.

The documents collected here cover a wide scope of topics ranging from marriage and the family to politics and government. They represent the great social pronouncements of the modern Church—*Rerum novarum, Quadragesimo anno, Mit brennender Sorge,* etc. Each document is preceded by an introduction and a bibliography. Documentation and marginal notes are supplied. Indexes in each volume.

DICTIONARIES AND ENCYCLOPEDIAS

D9   **Dictionnaire de sociologie familiale, politique, économique, spirituelle, générale,** publié sour la direction de G. Jacquement, avec le concours de nombreux collaborateurs. Paris, Letouzey et Ané, 1933- . v. LC 36-32281.

"A Catholic reference work of the first importance" (O'Rourke | [A74], p. 313). Contains long, scholarly articles with bibliographical references throughout, and lists at the end of each article. Covers all aspects of sociology from a Catholic viewpoint. Seems to have been abandoned as of 1939.

D10   Torres Calvo, Angel. **Diccionario de textos sociales pontificios.** 2d ed. Madrid, Cía Bibliográfica Española, 1962. xl, 1948p. (Biblioteca "Fomento social.") LC 63-52926

Quotations from papal documents on social problems are arranged alphabetically by subject. Pertinent documents, references to complete texts, and summaries of contents are also given. Coverage extends from Leo XIII to John XXIII (1961). Indexes.

HANDBOOKS

D11   Cronin, John Francis. **Catholic Social Principles: The Social Teaching of the Catholic Church Applied to American Economic Life.** Milwaukee, Bruce Pub. Co., 1950. xxviii, 803p. LC 50-13609.

Attempts to explain Catholic social principles in the light of American economic life. Each topic or chapter is preceded by a series of excerpts from papal documents stating the principles which the author then explains. A list of "Authoritative References" follows the chapter, and an "Annotated Reading List" appears on pp. 731-69. "An excellent and very valuable book" (*America*, [September 16, 1950], p. 627).

D12   Welty, Eberhard. **A Handbook of Christian Social Ethics.** Trans. by Gregor Kirstein; rev. and adapted by John Fitzsimons. Freiburg, Herder, 1960- . v. LC 59-14568.
       V 1. Man and Society; V 2. The Structure of the Social Order.

A translation of the German work entitled *Herder's Sozialkatechismus.* Consists of questions and brief answers on Catholic social teachings, with quotations from papal documents and other sources and extended commentary. Each volume contains an annotated, critical bibliography and an index. "Altogether the production is of a very high standard" (*Tablet*, CCXIV [October 29, 1960], p. 996).

D13   Williams, Melvin J. **Catholic Social Thought: Its Approach to Contemporary Problems.** New York, Ronald Press Co., 1950. xv, 567p. LC 50-7775.

A bio-bibliography of British and American Catholic social theorists, in the form of a narrative history. Williams is a non-Catholic professor of sociology at the State University of Florida. Classified bibliography, pp. 495-530. Index of names. Criticized for its omissions but generally valued as the only work of its kind (*American Journal of Sociology*, LV [September, 1950], p. 206).

EDUCATION

BIBLIOGRAPHY

The literature of Catholic education encompasses works dealing both with specifically religious education and education in general under Catholic auspices. Again, one must consult the general bibliographies listed in Chapter I as well as the *Education Index* (New York, Wilson, 1929-) which covers the Catholic output rather well.

D14   Barbin, René. **Bibliographie de pédagogie religieuse: introductions et commentaires.** Montréal, Éditions Bellarmin, 1964. 275p. LC 66-85896.

"A tool for religion teachers on the elementary, secondary and university levels" (Preface). The Bible, liturgy, anthropology, psychology, sociology, missiology, art, and catechetics are included in selected annotated bibliographies; audio visual materials and periodicals are also listed. Most items are French, but some English language works are included. For a more up to date listing see (D18).

D15   Centre documentaire catéchétique, Louvain. **Où en est l'enseignement religieux?** Tournai, Éditions Casterman, 1937. xvi, 499p. LC AC39-414.

At one time considered "the fullest and most valuable bibliography of Catholic religious education" (Brown [A16], p. 112). International in coverage with critical annotations and a general index of authors.

D16   Cronin, Lawrence J., comp. **Resources for Religious Instruction of Retarded People.** Boston, Office of Religious Education—CCD, Archdiocese of Boston, 1974. 64p.

A listing with descriptive annotations of books, articles and audio-visual materials for retarded students and for teachers and parents of retarded children. The listings are by type of material and by subject. There is no general index. Not limited to Catholic titles.

D17   Drouin, Edmond Gabriel. **The School Question: A Bibliography on Church-State Relationships in American Education, 1940-1960.** Washington, DC, Catholic University of America Press, 1963. xxi, 261p. LC 62-21859.

"Includes books, pamphlets, periodical articles, book reviews, unpublished dissertations and court decisions" (Preface). The material represents all points of view. Over 12,000 items are listed in classified order with an index of authors and titles. Some descriptive annotations are given.

D18   **The Resource Guide for Adult Religious Education, Revised Edition.** Kansas City, MO, National Catholic Reporter Pub. Co., 1975. 208p.

Designed for catechetical teachers, this guide lists and annotates over 1,000 books, pamphlets and audio-visual items. Complete bibliographical and ordering information is given, but the user must find items through the subject arrangement because there is no author or title index. A very useful tool which should be updated regularly. See also Dalglish (A26).

SOURCES

D19   Kolesnik, Walter Bernard, and Edward J. Power, eds. **Catholic Education: A Book of Readings.** New York, McGraw-Hill, 1965. xi, 512p. LC 65-20975.

An anthology of fifty-four selections reflecting Catholic views on education. The materials span more than a century beginning with an article by Orestes Brownson written in 1862. Brief biographies of authors are given. No index.

DICTIONARIES AND ENCYCLOPEDIAS

D20   **Wörterbuch der Pädagogik.** Hrsg. vom Willmann-Institut München, Wien; Leitung der Herausgabe, Heinrich Rombach. Freiburg, Herder, 1977. 3 v. LC 78-355189. ISBN 3-4511-7641-6. (Formerly *Lexikon der Pädagogik*).

The largest Catholic reference work on education. Now in its fourth edition it is still not widely known in America. Composed of many short articles, each signed and containing a bibliography. The names of schools and universities are not included, but persons, organizations, theories, and national systems of education are covered.

HANDBOOKS

D21   **Catholic Education: A Handbook.** London, Catholic Education Council for England and Wales, 1960- . v. LC 64-2941.

A directory of Catholic schools and educational groups which also contains articles on current topics in Catholic education. "Fills a very great need" (*Clergy Review*, XLVI [September, 1961], p. 571).

D22   National Catholic Educational Association. **Criteria for Evaluation of Catholic Elementary Schools.** Formulated and Ed. by the Criteria Committee, Elementary School Dept. of the National Catholic Educational Association. Washington, DC, Catholic University of America Press, 1965. ix, 246p. il. LC 65-16170.

A series of checklists covering the philosophy, objectives, curriculum, student activities, library, guidance, health and safety, plant, administration, and staff. Some guidelines for calculating statistics are also provided.

D23   United States Catholic Conference. **A National Inventory of Parish Catechetical Programs.** Washington, DC, United States Catholic Conference, 1978. iv, 70p. il. LC 78-109919.

In a series of 30 tables, the personnel, programs, enrollment and finances of parish religious education programs are surveyed.

DIRECTORIES

D24   **Directory of Catholic Schools and Colleges.** London, Paternoster Publications, 1935- . v. Annual. LC 38-17003.

A listing by type of school. Gives information on programs and expenses.

D25   **Directory of Catholic Residential Schools.** Washington, DC, National Catholic Educational Association, 1983. 35p.

Gives basic information for elementary and secondary schools that accept boarders. Arranged by state and diocese. Complete addresses, telephone numbers, enrollment and number of faculty are provided.

D26   National Catholic Educational Association and William Ganley. **NCEA/ Ganley's Catholic Schools in America.** Washington, DC, Curriculum Information Center, Inc./NCEA, 1977- . v. Annual. LC 77-641844.

Contains a wealth of statistical information as well as information about each Catholic elementary and secondary school in the United States and its possessions. Replaces NCEA's *Directory of Catholic Elementary Schools in the United States* and *U. S. Catholic Schools* (NCEA, 1970-1972, 3 vols.).

D27   National Catholic Educational Association. **Directory of Catholic Special Facilities and Programs in the United States for Handicapped Children and Adults.** 5th. ed. Washington, DC, NCEA, 1971. 193p. LC 74-186385.

Lists institutions and programs for the handicapped and maladjusted as well as training centers for work in this field. For each institution basic information and statistics are supplied.

D28   **Official Guide to Catholic Educational Institutions and Religious Communities in the United States.** New York, Catholic Institutional Directory Co., 1936- . v. Annual. LC 38-4126. (Title and imprint vary).

Includes Catholic colleges and universities, junior colleges, schools of nursing, secondary boarding schools, religious orders, houses of study, and diocesan seminaries. Brief statistical information and admission requirements are given along with a special section on how to choose a Catholic college and apply for admission. The most complete and accurate source.

D29   National Catholic Welfare Conference. **A Listing of Catholic Secondary Schools in the U.S.A.** Washington, DC, NCWC, 1965. 62p.

Geographical arrangement with full addresses.

HIGHER EDUCATION

D30   **Catholic Colleges and Universities Directory: A Guide in the Selection of a Catholic College.** Chicago, Catholic College Bureau, 1946- . v. LC 50-31378. Irregular.

Descriptions of 224 colleges and universities in the U. S. are furnished along with indexes for programs of study and professional careers.

D31   Center for Applied Research in the Apostolate. **CARA Seminary Directory, 1978: U.S. Catholic Institutions for the Training of Candidates for the Priesthood.** Washington, DC, Center for Applied Research in the Apostolate, 1978. xxix, 128p.

The Directory section lists 670 seminaries giving the name, address, affiliation, and enrollment statistics. Various tables and figures present an analysis of seminary enrollment trends. Indexes of names.

D32   Congregatio de Seminariis et Studiorum Universitatibus. **Seminaria ecclesiae catholicae.** Romae, Typis Polyglottis Vaticanis, 1963. 1757p.

A guide to all the diocesan seminaries of the world. It does not include, however, the large number of seminaries maintained by religious orders for their members. The information supplied includes history, number of students, curriculum, size of library, and number of graduates. Index of cities and dioceses.

D33   **Directory of Campus Ministry.** Washington, DC, United States Catholic Conference, 1970/71- . v. Annual. LC 73-645269. ISSN 0070-5209.

Gives the names and addresses of Catholic chaplains at colleges and universities in the United States. For each institution basic information is given including the affiliation of the college, number of students, number of Catholic students and a description of the programs sponsored by the chaplain.

D34   **Directory of Departments and Programs of Religious Studies in North America.** Watson E. Mills, editor. 1987 ed. Macon, GA, Council of Societies for the Study of Religion, Mercer University, 1987. xvii, 410p. LC 87-5568. ISBN 0-86554-283-X.

Complete descriptions are given for those colleges, universities and seminaries that responded to a 1986 questionnaire. Other schools of theology are listed in the back of the book with their addresses only. The information provided includes a description of the program, names of chairpersons and faculty, student enrollment, degrees conferred, etc. Indexes.

D35   **Directory of Diocesan Lay Programs and Resources, 1980-81.** Bishops' Committee on the Laity, National Conference of Catholic Bishops. Washington, DC, The Committee, 1981. iv, 95p.

A diocese by diocese listing of training programs and courses for training the laity for ministries in the Church. Officials of the dioceses responsible for those programs are identified. The programs are offered by the dioceses themselves or by colleges and universities. Index.

D36   **Guide to Schools and Departments of Religion and Seminaries in the United States and Canada.** Degree Programs in Religious Studies. New York, Macmillan; London, Collier Macmillan, 1986. 800p. LC 86-21751. ISBN 0-02-921650-8.

Arranged by state and province; gives complete information including a general description of the program, affiliation, environment, accreditation, library holdings, tuition, housing, etc. Denomination Index. Institution Index.

D37   International Federation of Institutes for Social and Socio-Religious Research. **Directory of Centers for Religious Research and Study.** Comp. by Carol van Arnhem. Louvain, 1968. xii, 207p. LC 73-543684.

Covers Christian, Jewish and other non-Christian institutions sponsoring libraries, schools and/or publications devoted to religious research. Arranged geographically, the entries give descriptions of the purposes and activities of each center. No index.

D38   McCarthy, Thomas Patrick. **Guide to the Diocesan Priesthood in the United States.** Washington, DC, Catholic University of America Press, 1959. 180p.

A guide for the candidate to the diocesan priesthood explaining the requirements and training program, in addition to much information on the diocese itself. Index.

HISTORY

Very little by way of reference-type histories of Catholic education exists; for brief histories with bibliographies of Catholic colleges and universities both the *Catholic Encyclopedia* (A89) and *New Catholic Encyclopedia*(A105) should be consulted. Biographies of important figures in Catholic education may also be found in these works.

D39   Burns, James Aloysius, and Bernard J. Kohlbrenner. **A History of Catholic Education in the United States.** New York, Benziger Bros., 1937. xi, 295p. LC 37-11431.

Although criticized for general inadequacy, serious errors, and omissions (*Catholic Historical Review*, XXIII [January, 1938], p. 500), this is the only unified attempt to chronicle the history of American Catholic education with any degree of comprehensiveness and scholarship. The bibliographies at the end of each chapter provide one of the few keys to the rather scarce literature in this field—even if they are outdated.

This work was based on the author's two previous histories which are somewhat more detailed if older.

D40   Burns, James Aloysius, and Bernard J. Kohlbrenner. **The Growth and Development of the Catholic School System in the United States.** New York, Benziger, 1912. 421p. Reprinted: New York, Arno Press, 1969. LC 78-9156.

A continuation of (D41).

D41   Burns, James Aloysius, and Bernard J. Kohlbrenner. **The Principles, Origin and Establishment of the Catholic School System in the United States.** New York, Benziger, 1912. 415p. Reprint: NY, Arno Press, 1969. LC 74-89155.

Each of these works contains a bibliography.

D42   Lee, James Michael. **Catholic Education in the Western World.** Notre Dame, IN, University of Notre Dame Press, 1967. xiv, 324p. LC 67-12120.

Brief histories with bibliographies of Catholic education in France, Germany, Holland, Italy, England, and the United States. Covers organization, finances, curriculum, religious education, staff, and student services. The appendix serves as an index to each section. "All of the essays are good, but two, at least, are outstanding, . . . France and the United States. . . . Remarkable for its mustering of facts and incisive judgments" (*Tablet*, CXXI [September 16, 1967], p. 970-71).

D43   McCluskey, Neil Gerard. **Catholic Education in America, A Documentary History.** New York, Bureau of Publications, Teachers College, Columbia University, 1964. x, 205p. LC 64-23907.

A collection of documents dealing with Catholic education dating from 1792 to 1950. Sources are given but no other bibliography. A brief historical introduction is supplied by the author. No index.

SOCIOLOGY

GENERAL WORKS

BIBLIOGRAPHY

D44 **Bibliographie der Sozialethik**. Ed. by Arthur Utz. Frieburg, New York, Herder, 1964- . v. Biennial. LC 61-2645. (Formerly titled *Grundsatzfragen des Öffentlichen Lebens*.)

A bibliography of books and articles in German, English, French, Italian, and Spanish on the "fundamental questions" of social ethics. Classified arrangement with author indexes in each volume.

D45 Byers, David M., and Bernard Quinn. **Readings for Town and Country Church Workers: An Annotated Bibliography**. Washington, DC, Glenmary Research Center, 1974. 121p. LC 74-77445. ISBN 0-9144-2200-6.

An informative bibliography for rural clergymen as well as anyone with an interest in rural life. The material is not exclusively religious nor Catholic. Annotations are long and descriptive. The arrangement is by topic with indexes for authors and states.

D46 Carrier, Herve. **Sociologie du christianisme: bibliographie internationale. Sociology of Christianity: International Bibliography**. Rome, Presses de l'Université Grégorienne, 1964. 313p. (*Studia Socialia*, 8.) LC 79-220814.

D47 Carrier, Herve. **Sociologie du christianisme: bibliographie internationale. Supplément**, 1962-1966. 1968.

"A first compilation of books and articles in the field of sociology dealing with the Christian Religion" (Preface to 1st. vol.). Arranged by author with no annotations. Geographical and subject index. The *Supplément* is larger than the original compilation.

D48 Klejment, Anne and Alice Klejment. **Dorothy Day and the Catholic Worker: A Bibliography and Index**. New York, Garland, 1986. xxvi, 412p. LC 83-48221. ISBN 0-8240-9045-4.

An exhaustive listing of primary and secondary sources with indexes.

SOURCES

D49 **Die Katholische Sozialdoktrin in ihrer geschichtlichen Entfaltung**. Aachen, Scientia Humana Inst., 1976. 4 v. xxxii, 3296p. LC 78-372475.

Texts of papal and other Church documents bearing on social issues. Coverage is from 1431 (Pope Eugene IV) to 1976 (Paul VI). The documents are reprinted both in Latin and German. The arrangement is by subject categories with indexes of names and subjects and a chronological list of documents.

DICTIONARIES AND ENCYCLOPEDIAS

D50   Fappani, Antonio. **Dizionario sociale.** Ed. riv. ed. ampliata. Roma, Edizioni ACLI, 1960. 668p. LC A62-2620.

A brief-entry encyclopedia of sociology based on Christian principles. Although it has no introduction, index or bibliography, it was praised by *Civiltà* for being accurate, if not exhaustive (CXII [February, 1961], p. 289).

D51   **Katholisches Soziallexikon.** Hrsg. im Auftrag der Katholischen Sozialakademie Österreichs. Schriftleitung: Alfred Klose. Innsbruck, Tyrolia-Verlag, 1964. Col. 1426. LC 66-87633.

Contains long, signed articles by more than 100 contributors. Bibliographies and cross references are supplied. The topics cover all aspects of the social sciences as well as biographies of important persons.

SOCIAL WORK

While every diocese has its office of Catholic charities or an equivalent, the National Conference of Catholic Charities (NCCC) has been the central coordinating agency since 1910 and has produced most of the directories and handbooks listed here.

D52   **Catholic Social Year Book.** Ed. by the Central Executive of The Catholic Social Guild. London, the Guild, 1910- . v. Annual. LC 14-17248. (Title and imprint vary.)

Begun by Father Charles Plater, the first six volumes of this series were composed of essays recounting the activities of the Guild and other charitable organizations in Britain and the U. S., and an annual diary of the events of the previous year. In 1916, the work was transformed into volumes centered on a single theme. Some of the better known titles are *A Social Crusade* (1918), *The Community and the Criminal* (1926), *Catholics and Public Medical Services* (1930), *Quadragesimo Anno* (1934), *Usury in Catholic Theology* (1945), and the 1960 edition, *Catholic Social Action in Britain, 1909-59*, a history of the Guild with a complete bibliography.

D53   McGrath, John Joseph. **Catholic Institutions in the United States: Canonical and Civil Law Status.** Washington, DC, Catholic University of America Press, 1968. ix, 48p. LC 67-31752.

A handbook for administrators of Catholic hospitals, schools, and similar institutions, explaining both the civil and canon laws applicable to them. "Highly recommended for anyone affiliated with Catholic institutions in the United States" (*American Ecclesiastical Review*, CLVIII [May, 1968], p. 354). Should be updated for the *New Code of Canon Law*.

HANDBOOKS

D54   National Conference of Catholic Charities. **Guides for Catholic Day Care Centers.** By Marie E. Costello. Washington, DC, NCCC, 1965. xi, 37p. LC 65-28316.

This manual and the three following are administrative guides compiled by committees of the National Conference of Catholic Charities. Each has a bibliography.

D55   National Conference of Catholic Charities. **Guides for Facilities for the Aging.** Washington, DC, NCCC, 1969. 28p.

D56   National Conference of Catholic Charities. **Guides for Services to Children in Catholic Institutions.** Washington, DC, NCCC, 1964. vii, 44p. LC 64-8291.

D57   National Conference of Catholic Charities. **Guidelines to Personnel Practices and Salary Scales.** Washington, DC, NCCC, 1966. iv, 30p. LC 66-29415.

DIRECTORIES

D58   Catholic Hospital Association. **Guidebook.** St. Louis, MO, 1974- . v. LC 74-648900.

Contains a list of Catholic hospitals, long-term care facilities, personal and associate members of the Association, and religious orders engaged in health care. The information given for each hospital includes address, telephone, bed capacity, types of facilities, and the name of the administrator.

D59   De Bettencourt, F. G. **The Catholic Guide to Foundations.** 2nd. edition. Washington, DC, Guide Publishers, 1973. iii, 170p. LC 73-865663. ISBN 0-9141-5001-4.

336 foundations "whose grants suggest some preference for activities carried out under Catholic auspices" are described in this directory. For each foundation the name, net worth, sample grants, special interests and names of officials are given. An introductory section analyses the general activities of these foundations.

D60   **Directory of Catholic Camps.** Washington, DC, National Catholic Camp Association, 1965- . v. Annual. LC 65-2862.

A geographical listing of camps indicating the cost, length of season, sponsoring body, activities, and so forth.

D61   National Conference of Catholic Charities. **Directory of Catholic Institutions in the U. S., 1960.** Sponsored by the Conference of Religious. 2nd. ed. Washington, DC, NCCC, 1960. 140p.

Lists homes for the aged, mothers and children; protective institutions; and schools for exceptional children. Basic information, including statistics, is supplied for each institution. Geographical arrangement with an index. This work has been updated in sections by the following directories:
    1. *Catholic Day Care Centers.* Washington, 1969. 28p.
    2. *Directory of Residences for Unwed Mothers.* Washington, 1969. 79p.

D62   National Conference of Catholic Charities. **Directory: Diocesan Agencies of Catholic Charities: United States, Puerto Rico and Canada.** Washington, DC, National Conference of Catholic Charities, 1964- . v. Irregular. LC 73-642569. ISSN 0091-1003.

Gives NCCC staff and affiliated organizations and a geographical listing of diocesan agencies, with addresses, telephone numbers, and names of personnel. A list of Catholic schools of social work is also included.

D63   O'Grady, John. **Directory of Catholic Charities in the United States.** Washington, DC, National Conference of Catholic Charities, Catholic University, 1922. iv, 365p. LC 22-15897.

The predecessor of (**D62**).

CHILDREN AND YOUTH

D64   Fullam, Raymond B. **The Popes on Youth: Principles for Forming and Guiding Youth from Popes Leo XIII to Pius XII.** New York, D. McKay Co., 1956. 442p. LC 57-4398.

A subject arrangement of selections from papal statements on youth. References to complete texts in English and the original language are supplied as well as an index of titles and subjects.

ETIQUETTE AND CUSTOMS

D65   Broderick, Robert C. **The Catholic Layman's Book of Etiquette.** St. Paul, Catechetical Guild Educational Society, 1957. 320p. il. LC 57-29531.

An introduction to practices and customs of the American Catholic Church covering liturgical, social, legal, and other matters. Now largely outdated.

D66   Fenner, Kay Toy. **American Catholic Etiquette.** Westminster, MD, Newman Press, 1961. 402p. LC 61-16569.

The most complete and reasonably up-to-date handbook for the Laity. Participation in funerals, weddings and other sacraments and ceremonies is covered, along with forms of address, duties of parishioners, behavior at mass, and Catholic home life. Both the social and religious aspects are treated; and some information on similar non-Catholic functions is given. Index. "Eminently practical" (*America*, CVI [March 3, 1962], p. 728).

D67   Frederic, Mary Catherine, Sister. **The Handbook of Catholic Practices.** New York, Hawthorn Books, 1964. 319p. LC 64-10670.

Not so much a book of etiquette as a guide to understanding traditional Catholic devotions, beliefs and ceremonies. Contains an annotated bibliography, pp. 303-308, and an index.

D68   Henry, Hugh Thomas. **Catholic Customs and Symbols: Varied Forms and Figures of Catholic Usage, Ceremony and Practice Briefly Explained.** New York, Benziger Brothers, 1925. xvii, 322p. LC 25-6436.

Brief explanations of Catholic symbolism; church architecture and furnishings; vestments; liturgical colors, seasons, and ceremonies; and various Catholic customs. Bibliography, glossary and index.

D69   Sullivan, John Francis. **The Externals of the Catholic Church. A Handbook of Catholic Usage.** Completely rev. by John C. O'Leary. 2nd. ed. New York, Kenedy, 1959. 403p. il. LC 60-2489.

Covers the government of the church; the religious orders; the apostolate; the sacraments; the mass; the liturgical books and seasons; the Bible and devotions. Designed for the average layman, explaining each topic in clear, simple terminology. No bibliography. "Succinct and clear explanations" (*Critic*, XVIII [January, 1960], p. 57). Index.

STATISTICS

GENERAL YEARBOOKS AND DIRECTORIES

Much more information than mere statistics is included in the yearbooks and compendiums listed here—some verge on being encyclopedic in content, containing basic information on the Church's government, teachings, and activities in a variety of fields.

Only international and national works are included. Most dioceses, however, publish a yearbook or directory of their own.

D70   **L'année de l'église.** Paris, Libraire V. Lecoffre, 1898-1900. 3 v. Annual.

A review of the activities of the Church in every country of the world including missionary territories. Index.

D71   **Annuaire pontificale catholique.** Paris, La Bonne Presse, 1897-1948. 41 v. il. LC 7-16321.

D72   **Annuaire pontificale catholique. Tables générales de 20 premiers volumes (1898-1917).** 1921. LC 7-16321x.

Contains lists of popes, cardinals, archbishops, bishops, and monsignori from all over the world. Arranged by residential sees and titular sees with a general alphabetical index.

D73   **Annuario pontificio per l'anno.** Roma, Tipografia Poliglotta Vaticana, 1716- . v. Annual. LC 20-5316.

The official, universal yearbook of the Church issued by the Vatican. Statistical and historical information on the popes, cardinals, patriarchs, bishops, religious orders, the Curia and Vatican diplomats is provided. A very detailed "Indice Alfabetico dei nomi delle Persone e delle Materies" makes the work easy to use. Complete coverage is given for the diocese of Rome.

D74   **Annuarium statisticum ecclesiae. Statistical Yearbook of the Church. Annuaire statistique de l'église.** Secretaria Status, Rationarium Generale Ecclesiae. Civitas Vaticana, Typis Polyglottis Vaticanis, 1977- . v. Biennial.

An important source of international statistics gathered by the Vatican every year and published every other year. Topics include general population, dioceses, parishes, institutions, bishops, priests, seminarians, and nuns. Figures include numbers of clergy, new ordinations, deaths, defections and total changes for the year. Each table is arranged by continent and then by country. Some of the information contained in this work is unavailable anywhere else.

D75   **L'Attività della Santa sede.** Roma, Tipografia Poliglotta Vaticana, 1716- .
        v. Annual. LC 20-5316.

        This "publicazione non-ufficiale" chronicles the activities of the various
        Vatican curial bodies, and charitable, cultural, artistic, and scientific organ-
        izations. Reprints some of the major addresses given by the Pope in the
        previous year. Appendixes and indexes.

D76   **Bilan du monde.** 2d éd. Publié par le Centre "Église Vivante" (Louvain) et la
        Féderation Internationale des Institutes de Recherches Sociales et Socio-
        religieuses. Tournai, Casterman, 1964. 2 v. il. LC 65-87638.

        A comprehensive attempt at a continuing statistical compendium for the
        universal Church. Published every few years in two volumes, it contains
        general, political, social, historical, and statistical information for each
        country in addition to the specifically Catholic Church information. The
        state of other religious groups is also reported. Sources of information are
        given. Would probably be more useful if it concentrated more on specifi-
        cally religious information.

D77   **Churches and Church Membership in the United States, 1980: An Enumeration**
        by Region, State and County, based on Data Reported by 111 Church Bodies.
        [Ed. by] Bernard Quinn [et al.]. Atlanta, Glenmary Research Center, 1982. 321p.
        LC 82-81978. ISBN 0-914422-12-X.

        Membership and numbers of churches (or parishes) are given for 121
        denominations in the U.S. Four tables give figures for the nation, by region, by
        state and by county respectively. In addition to the number of members and
        churches, each table indicates what percentage the membership represents of the
        total population of the geographic area in question and what percentage of total
        church membership each sect is in that area.

D78   **Mondo cattolico.** Roma, Domani, 1952- . v. LC A52-8251.

        (No longer published.)

        Contains a "Who's Who" section along with almost the same features found
        in the *Annuario pontificio* (D73). The work could have served a purpose as
        a vernacular edition, but was criticized for its poor arrangement and lack of
        international perspective (*Catholic Library World*, XXIV [November, 1952],
        pp. 69-70).

D79   **Orbis catholicus.** London, Burns, Oates and Washbourne, 1938- . v. LC
        38-33188.

        (No longer published.)

        An English language version of the *Annuario pontificio* (D73), covering the
        entire Catholic world with no special emphasis on England or any other
        country. Lists all dioceses, vicariates, titular sees, religious orders, rites,
        and the government of the Church. "As a whole the book represents an
        amount of work and degree of accuracy worthy of the editor's high repu-
        tation" (*Catholic World*, CXLVII [August, 1938], p. 147).

NATIONAL YEARBOOKS AND DIRECTORIES

AFRICA

D80   **Annuaire de l'Église catholique à Madagascar.** Tanarive, Impr. Catholique, 1971- . v. Annual? LC 73-643097.

Contains information on the clergy and institutions as well as religious orders serving in Madagascar.

D81   **Annuaire de l'Église catholique au Zäire.** Kinshasa-Combé, Édition du Secrétariat-Général, 1974/75- . v. Annual? LC 76-645895.

Contains general statistical information for the Diocese, the names and addresses of each parish and institution and a list of medical centers and schools.

D82   **Annuaire ecclésiastiques: Burundi et Rwanda.** Bujumbura, Secrétariat de la Conférence des Ordinaires du Rwanda et du Burundi, 19??- . v. Annual? LC 70-616984.

Replaces *Katoliek Jaarboek voor Kongo, Ruanda en Urundi* (D87).

D83   **Catholic Directory of Eastern Africa.** Tabora, Tanzania, T.M.P. Book Dept., 1950- . v. LC 70-618053. (Title and imprint vary).

Includes the Church in Kenya, Malawi, Seychelles, Tanzania, Ugandi and Zambia. For each Diocese, the name and biography of the bishop, the number of clergy and nuns, and the name and address of each parish and institution are given.

D84   **Catholic Directory of Ethiopia.** Addis Ababa?, 196?- . v. Annual?

Contains a list of clergy as well as information on Catholic parishes, institutions and diocesan officials.

D85   **The Catholic Directory of Southern Africa.** Capetown, Salesian Press, 1904- . v. LC 75-642049.

D86   **The Catholic Directory of Southern Africa. Supplement.** Capetown, Salesian Press, 19??- . v. LC 75-642048.

Gives names of individual clergymen as well as other information. The Supplement covers Zambia, Malawi and Nairobi.

D87   **Katoliek Jaarboek voor Kongo, Ruanda en Urundi. Annuaire catholique du Congo, du Ruanda et de l'Urandi.** Brussel, Pauselijke Missiewerken, 19??- . v. LC 63-47269.

Contains basic information about the government and hierarchy of the universal Church as well as the history and statistics of the dioceses and mission territories of the Congo, Ruanda and Urundi. Religious orders, charitable services, organizations and schools are also covered. Alphabetical list of clergy.

D88 **The Official Nigeria Catholic Directory.** Lagos, African Universities Press, 19??- . v. LC 73-5726.

A complete list of priests and brothers serving in the area is provided along with the standard information.

AMERICA

D89 **The Book of Catholic Names and Numbers.** Piermont, NY, Catholic Heritage Press; distributor, Minneapolis, Winston Press, 1980. 168p. LC 79-54375. ISBN 0-89958-025-4.

A directory of "institutions, services and resources of the American Catholic Community" (Preface). The arrangement is alphabetical by subject. Complete names, addresses and telephone numbers are given. *The Official Catholic Directory* (D99) is much more complete.

D90 **Catholic Almanac.** Huntington, IN, Our Sunday Visitor, Inc., 1904- . v. Annual. LC 43-2500. (Title and imprint vary).

Published since 1904 in more or less the same form but with various titles and publishers, it is an annual collection of basic information on the universal Church and especially the Church in the United States. From the years 1904 to 1940 the title alternated between *St. Anthony's Almanac* and the *Franciscan Almanac.* From 1940 to 1969 it was called *The National Catholic Almanac.* The current issue contains sections on Church history, current affairs, biography, statistics, the government of the Church, Church teachings, worship, the Church in the U. S., texts of current documents, a list of Catholic publishers, a Catholic bibliography for the year, and a list of Catholic periodicals and newspapers. A detailed index makes all this information easy to find.

D91 **The Clergyman's Fact Book.** New York, M. Evans, 1963/64- . v. LC 63-19658.

An interfaith almanac or guide for the Clergy to basic religious and general information and statistics. Sources of information are cited. Index.

D92 Deedy, John G. **The Catholic Fact Book.** Chicago, Thomas More Press, 1986. 412p. LC 86-215323. ISBN 0-88347-186-8.

Intends to provide "a certain amount of information to convey something of the flavor of Roman Catholicism, what it is and how it is understood and run from official levels" (Foreward). Composed of seven sections: History, Basic Tenets of Belief; The Teaching Church; Movements, Artifacts, Institutions, Orders, Organizations, Communications; Saints; Famous Catholics of History; Miscellanea. An extensive index adds to the reference value of this up-to-date work.

D93 **Ecumenical Directory of Retreat and Conference Centers.** Philip Deemer, ed. San Francisco, Jarrow Press, 1974- . v. LC 76-640121. ISSN 0361-2236. Irregular.

Brief descriptions of the facilities, mailing addresses and other pertinent information are supplied for U.S. and Canadian, Catholic and Protestant retreat or conference centers. A third edition appeared in 1984.

D94   Foy, Felician A. and Rose M. Avato. **A Concise Guide to the Catholic Church.**
       Huntington, IN, Our Sunday Visitor, Inc., 1984-86. 2 v. LC 83-63170. ISBN
       0-8797-3616-X.

       Another useful, up-to-date compilation on the contemporary Church, covering
       history, doctrines, practices, organization, and a wealth of miscellaneous
       information. Index.

D95   Halvorson, Peter L. and William M. Newman. **Atlas of Religious Change in
       America, 1952-1971.** Cartography by Mark C. Nielson. Washington, DC,
       Glenmary Research Center, 1978. 95p. Maps. LC 78-67653. ISBN 0-914422-09-X.

       For each of 35 major denominations, a series of four maps depicts patterns of
       distribution and change for the years 1952 and 1971. A written analysis is
       provided for each series of maps.

D96   Hassan, Bernard. **The American Catholic Catalog.** 1st ed. New York, Harper and
       Row, 1980. 274p. LC 80-129756. ISBN 0-06-063735-8.

       A basic introduction to Catholicism covering the sacraments, liturgy, Mary,
       spirituality, and Church music. Also contains a directory of Catholic
       organizations and services called "The Yellow Pages." Index.

D97   **The Illustrated Catholic Family Annual.** New York, The Catholic Publication
       Society, 1869?-1897? v. LC 25-823.

       A predecessor of the *Catholic Almanac* (D90) containing historical, bio-
       graphical, devotional and Catholic-interest articles in addition to a liturgical
       calendar and other information.

D98   Johnson, Douglas W. **Churches and Church Membership in the United States:
       An Enumeration by Region, State, and County, 1971.** Washington, DC,
       Glenmary Research Center, 1974. xiv, 237p. maps. LC 73-94224. ISBN
       0-914422-01-4.

       Consists of three tables: "Churches and Church Membership by Denomina-
       tion in the U. S.," ". . . by Region, State, and Denomination," and ". . . by
       State, County, and Denomination." The survey is incomplete in that only
       53 sects are listed (80% of Christians). Black churches and oriental religions
       are not included. A fold out map uses color codes to identify the major sect
       in each county of the U. S. The Glenmary Research Center was established
       in 1966 to serve the research needs of the Catholic Church in rural America.
       In 1971, in cooperation with the National Council of Churches and the
       Missouri Synod, the Center sponsored a nationwide study of religious activity.
       This work, (D101)and (D102) came out of that study.

D99   **Official Catholic Directory.** New York, P. J. Kenedy, 1886- . v. Annual.
       LC 1-30961. (Title and imprint vary).

       The chief source of up-to-date information on the Catholic Church in the
       U. S. Issued every year in May, it contains the name and address of every
       priest in the U. S. and of every Catholic Church and institution, along with
       basic statistical information, such as numbers of students and teachers in

schools, etc. General and diocesan statistics are also given as well as information on the hierarchy and the missions. Briefer coverage is provided for Canada, Mexico, Cuba, Puerto Rico, the Canal Zone, the Virgin Islands, Bermuda, Jamaica, the Marshalls, the Phillippines, Ireland, Great Britain, Oceana, Australia, and New Zealand. The previous titles by which this work was known are as follows:

1. *Hoffman's Catholic Directory, Almanac and Clergy List*. Milwaukee, Hoffman Bros., 1886-99.
2. Wiltzius, M. H. *Official Catholic Directory*. Milwaukee, Wiltzius, 1900-11.

The P. J. Kenedy Company began publishing it in 1912.

D100　**The Official Catholic Year Book: A Comprehensive Summary of the History, Activities and Accomplishments of the Roman Catholic Church in the United States of America.** New York, P. J. Kenedy, 1928. LC 28-29791.

(No more volumes published.)

Contains the usual yearbook information with a brief history of the Church in the U. S., the texts of Church documents, lists of the hierarchy, Catholic institutions, and organizations. Index. Much of the information contained here could also be found in the *Catholic Almanac* (D90) and the *Official Catholic Directory* (D99).

D101　Quinn, Bernard, and John Feister. **Apostolic Regions of the United States, 1971.** Washington, DC, Glenmary Research Center, 1978. iv, 53p. map. LC 78-67012. ISBN 0-914422-08-1.

Describes both in text and tables the strength of the Catholic Church in nine regions of the United States. Alaska and Hawaii are treated separately. A large, color coded, fold out map is also supplied.

D102　Quinn, Bernard, and John Feister. **Distribution of Catholic Priests in the United States, 1971.** Washington, DC, Glenmary Research Center, 1975. v, 35p. map. LC 75-326803. ISBN 0-914422-0-49.

"The purpose of this study is to compare Catholic Dioceses in the United States according to their ratio of priests to Catholics, other Christians and the unchurched" (Preface). This is achieved through 7 tables and a large, color coded fold out map.

D103　Shuster, George and Robert M. Kearns. **Statistical Profile of Black Catholics.** Washington, DC, Josephite Pastoral Center, 1976. vii, 42p. LC 76-363302.

A series of ten tables ranking dioceses by the percentage of black Catholics present. The changes in the black Catholic population from 1960 to 1970 and 1940 to 1975 are also presented.

D104　U. S. Bureau of the Census. **Religious Bodies: 1936. Selected Statistics for the United States by Denominations and Geographic Divisions.** Washington, GPO, 1941. iv, 185p. LC 41-50480.

Formerly published every ten years, this project was abandoned after 1936 when the Government decided to discontinue the census of religious bodies. It was, however, one of the few sources of information on the finances of the churches as well as of other statistics, history, and statements of belief.

ARGENTINA

D105   **Annuario católico argentino.** Buenos Aires, Junta Nacional de la Acción Católica Argentina 1932- . v. Annual. LC 34-31880.

Lists dioceses, the hierarchy, parishes, Catholic organizations; and reports apostolic activities of the previous year. No index.

ASIA

D106   **Catholic Directory of India, Pakistan, Burma, and Ceylon.** Madras, Good Pastor Press, 18??- . v.

General information on the teachings and organization of the Church is provided, along with listings of local parishes, clergy, institutions and organizations by diocese. Educational statistics are given as well as a general alphabetical clergy list.

AUSTRALIA

D107   **Official Directory of the Catholic Church of Australia and Papua-New Guinea, New Zealand and the Pacific Islands.** Sydney, 19??- . v. Annual. LC 76-617503. (Title varies).

Contains liturgical instructions for the feasts of the year in addition to the standard information on parishes, institutions, organizations, etc. Alphabetical clergy list.

BELGIUM

D108   Interdiocesaan Centrum. **Basisstatisieken over de decanaten en bisdommen van de Belgische kerkprovincie.** Brussel, Guimardstr. 5, 1974. xii, 116p. il. LC 77-462033.

Covers Catholic population, clergy and institutions.

D109   Interdiocesaan Centrum. **Bevolking en misvierenden in de decanaten en bisdommen van de Belgische kerkprovincie.** Brussel, Dienst voor Godsdienststatistiek, Guimardstr. 5, 1972. xxviii, 119p. il. LC 73-305631.

Illustrates with maps and tables the numbers of active Catholics in Belgium from 1962 to 1968. Arranged by Diocese and Deanery.

D110   **Katoliek Jarrboek voor Belgie: Annuaire catholique de Belgique.** Brussel, Interdiocesaan Centrum, 1946- . v. Annual. LC 57-38872.

Covers Rome and the universal Church, the Belgian hierarchy, parishes, religious orders, education, army chaplains, organizations, and has an alphabetical list of clergy.

BRAZIL

D111   **Anuário católico do Brasil**. Petropolis, Editôra Vozes Limitada. 19??-. v. Annual. LC 65-32048.

A comprehensive work covering the universal Church as well as the dioceses, hierarchy, organizations, institutions of Brazil by region with an alphabetical clergy list.

BRITAIN

D112   **Catholic Directory, Ecclesiastical Register and Almanac**. London, Burns and Oates, 1838-1970. 132 v. Annual. LC 12-774.

"The Official Handbook of the Catholic Church in England and Wales" (Preface). Covers the British hierarchy, clergy, parishes, institutions, etc., as well as material on the universal Church. Indexes. Continued by (D114).

D113   **The Catholic Directory for Scotland**. Glasgow, J. S. Burns, 19??- . v. LC 74-644568.

Covers world wide and local Church government, dioceses of Scotland, organizations, institutions, and an alphabetical clergy list.

D114   **Catholic Directory of England and Wales**. Liverpool, Published for the Hierarchy by The Universe, 1973- . v. Annual. LC 82-641835.

Replaces *Catholic Directory, Ecclesiastical Register and Almanac* 1838-1970 (D112). 1971, 1972 not published.

D115   **The Catholic Year Book**. London, Burns, Oates and Washbourne, 1950- . v. Annual. LC 52-18339. (Title varies).

Resembles the *Catholic Almanac* (D90) in some respects. Basic information for each country of the world is provided along with an ecclesiastical calendar, a review of the year and general information on the Church. Index.

CANADA

D116   **Le Canada ecclésiastique. Catholic Directory of Canada**. Montréal, Beauchemin, 1887- . v. Annual. LC 35-22140.

English and French speaking areas are treated in their respective languages. Arranged by diocese, giving complete information, both secular and religious. Religious orders are covered in a special section. Index of clergy. Index of parishes.

CARIBBEAN

D117   **The Catholic Directory of the British Caribbean**. Kingston, Jamaica, Catholic Opinion Press, 1958- . v. Annual. LC 60-23556.

Trinidad, Belize, Castries, Georgetown, Kingston, Roseau, St. George's in Grenada and the Bahamas are included with lists of parishes, institutions, religious orders and an alphabetical list of clergy.

CHILE

D118   **Guía eclesiastica de Chile.** Santiago de Chile, Officina Nacional de Estadística de la Acción Católica Chilena, 1944- . v. LC 46-20729.

Contains brief biographies of the popes and members of the hierarchy, lists of clergy and parishes and Catholic organizations. Arranged by diocese.

CUBA

D119   **Directorio católico de Cuba.** La Habana, 19??- . v. Annual. LC 56-26683.

Contains an ecclesiastical calendar, information on the hierarchy, Church government, dioceses and a list of Catholic families.

FRANCE

D120   **Almanach catholique français.** Paris, Bloud, 1920-36. 17 v. Annual.

Contains a Catholic calendar for the year, articles on the religious, social, artistic, scientific and literary events of the past year in addition to basic information on the dioceses of France, biographies of famous Catholics and information on the Catholic press. No index.

D121   **Annuaire-agenda catholique: livre d'annonces paroissiales.** Paris, P. Lethielleux, 1938- . v. Annual?

Replaced *Annuaire générale du clerge* (D124) and supplies the same information.

D122   **Annuaire catholique de France.** Paris, Les Presses Continentales, 1952- . v. LC 61-23178. ISSN 0066-2488. (Title varies).

Replaces *Guide de la France chrétienne et missionnaire* (D125) and contains essentially the same information.

D123   **Annuaire de l'Église catholique.** Paris, Office National de Publications Catholiques, 1970/71- . v. Annual. LC 70-649892. (Title varies: title 1970-71: *Annuaire de l'Église catholique en Afrique francophone, îsles de Océan indien, D. O. M. et T. O. M.*).

Contains information and statistics on French missions and missionaries in 30 African and Indian Ocean countries.

D124   **Annuaire générale du clerge, de l'ensiegnement et des oeuvres catholiques en France.** Paris, P. Lethielleux, 1934-38. 6 v. LC 34-20014.

The Catholic directory for the dioceses of France, covering diocesan administration, activities, religious orders, schools, churches, and statistics. General information on the Holy See and the French hierarchy is also given.

Now replaced by the *Annuaire-agenda catholique* (D121).

D125   **Guide de la France chrétienne et missionnaire.** Paris, Centre Catholique International de Documentation et Statistiques, 1948/49- . v. Annual. LC 51-17958.

Treats the liturgy, canon law, the structure of the Church, French seminaries, dioceses, parishes, and schools; with sections on motion pictures, booksellers, printers, sacred art and so forth. French missionaries overseas are listed. Indexes of churches and clergy.

GERMANY

D126   **Adressbuch für das katholische Deutschland.** Köln, Benziger, 1965- . v. Annual? LC 74-314441.

Contains a section on the Church in general as well as diocesan information for German parishes, religious orders, Catholic organizations and institutions. Name and subject indexes.

D127   **Das katholische Jahrbuch.** Heidelburg, Verlag Kemper, 1948/49- . v. LC 50-18789.

Supplies essentially the same information in the same format as the previous work.

D128   **Kirchliches Handbuch: amtliches statistisches Jahrbuch der katholischen Kirche Deutschland.** Köln, J. P. Bachem, 1908-1944/51. v. Annual. LC 9-22957. (Title and imprint vary).

Covers the universal Church as well as detailed information on the Church in Germany and on German-speaking Catholics in other lands. No indexes.

Replaced by (D127).

INDIA

D129   **Catholic Directory of India.** Bombay, St. Paul Publications. v. LC 73-902893.

Contains photographs of the hierarchy along with the standard information.

IRELAND

D130   **Irish Catholic Directory.** Dublin, J. Duffy, 19??- . v. Annual. LC 8-2966.

Contains an "Irish Catholic Calendar," list of Roman officials, the Irish hierarchy, parishes, institutions, religious orders and lists of regular and secular clergy. Index.

ITALY

D131   **Annuario cattolico d'Italia.** Roma, Treveri, 19??- . v. Annual. LC 62-67073.

The parishes, schools, and seminaries of Italy are covered by city, with information on the hierarchy, religious orders, Catholic Action, the Catholic press and various organizations. Larger and more detailed than most national yearbooks.

JAPAN

D132   **Catholic Directory of Japan.** Tokyo, National Catholic Committee of Japan, 1950- . v. LC 62-27223.

Arranged by diocese giving the usual information on churches, institutions, and organizations with indexes of clergy, etc.

LATIN AMERICA

D133   **Guiá eclesiastica latinoamericana.** Bogota, Colombia, Consejo Episcopal Latinoamericano, Secretariado General, 1977- . v. LC 77-641657.

Gives membership of CELAM and the name, address, and telephone number of every bishop in Latin America. Arranged by diocese with a general index.

MEXICO

D134   **Directorio de la Iglesa en México.** México, Buena Prensa, 1952. 471p. il.

Contains complete lists of all the former bishops and archbishops of each diocese, lists of churches, seminaries, clergy, religious orders and so forth. Mission territories, organizations and Catholic publications are also covered. No indexes.

D135   González Ramírez, Manuel R. **La Iglesia mexicana en cifras.** 1. ed. México, Centro de Investigación y Acción Social, 1969. 200p. il. LC 72-339932.

A general historical and statistical survey of Mexico's Catholic population, dioceses, parishes, clergy, seminaries and religious orders. Tables. No index.

MIDDLE EAST

D136   **Annuaire de L'Église catholique en Terre sainte.** Jerusalem, Franciscan Printing Press, 1972- . v. Annual. LC 72-955579.

Provides information on the Church in Israel, Jordan, and Cyprus.

NETHERLANDS

D137   Katholiek Documentatie Centrum. **Jaarboek van het Katholiek Documentatie Centrum.** Nijmegen, Katholiek Documentatie Centrum, 1971- . v. LC 75-642877.

The KDC is a Catholic information organization which operates an archives and library. The yearbook summarizes its activity, lists publications and important additions to the archives and library.

PHILIPPINES

D138   **Catholic Directory of the Philippines.** Manila, Catholic Trade School, 19??- . v. LC 55-34466.

Arranged by diocese with complete lists of churches and institutions.
Organizations, Church government and religious orders are covered.
Alphabetical list of clergy.

PORTUGAL

D139　**Anuário católico de Portugal.** Lisboa, Oficinas gráficas da Rádio renascenca,
1947- . v. Annual. LC A53-6963.

Contains basic statistics and information on the clergy, organizations,
institutions, etc., but does not give addresses and statistics for each parish.
Indexes.

SPAIN

D140　**Anuario católico español.** Madrid, 1953- . v. Annual. LC 65-38660.

Surveys the history and activities of the universal Church and especially
the Spanish Church; both narrative accounts and documents are presented.
Some editions cover more than one year.

D141　**Guía de la Iglesia en España: oficina general de information y estadística
de la Iglesia en España.** Madrid, Secretariade del episcopado español, 1954- .
v. LC A54-6320.

Part one presents summary tables of statistics from all the dioceses of
Spain but does not list each church, school, etc. Part two deals with the
Church in general, the Spanish hierarchy, and Catholic events of the past
year.

URUGUAY

D142　**Anuario Católico del Uruguay.** Montevideo, 19??- . v.

Contains a liturgical calendar; lists of churches, religious orders, and clergy
for each diocese; Catholic Action activities; and classification of motion
pictures. No index or table of contents.

VENEZUELA

D143　**Anuario eclesiástico venezolano.** Caracas, 1953- . v. Annual. LC 54-34139.

In addition to the usual information, the history of each diocese is presented.

ECONOMICS

BIBLIOGRAPHY

D144　Fitzpatrick, Paul Joseph, and Cletus F. Dirksen. **Bibliography of Economic
Books and Pamphlets by Catholic Authors, 1891-1941.** Washington, DC,
The Catholic University of America Press, 1941. xi, 55p. LC A42-1661.

An author list chronicling the Catholic contribution in this field. No annotations or indexes are supplied, but full bibliographical entries are given.

SOURCES

D145   Cave, Roy Clinton, and Herbert H. Coulson. **A Source Book for Medieval Economic History.** Milwaukee, Bruce Pub. Co., 1936. xx, 467p. LC 36-3938.

Contains a collection of English translations of medieval documents bearing on economics. Much of the material deals with the economic history of the Church. Bibliography, pp. 435-45.

POLITICAL SCIENCE

BIBLIOGRAPHY

D146   Dahlin, Therrin C., Gary P. Gillum, and Mark L. Grover. **The Catholic Left in Latin America: A Comprehensive Bibliography.** Boston, G.K. Hall, 1981. xivi, 410p. LC 81-778. ISBN 0-8161-8396-1.

Lists almost 4,000 books and articles published from 1960 to 1978. The works are listed for Latin America in general and then for each country. Author Index. Title Index.

D147   Menendez, Albert J. **Church-State Relations: An Annotated Bibliography.** New York, Garland, 1976. x, 126p. LC 75-24894. ISBN 0-8240-9956-7.

Not limited to the Catholic Church but many specifically Catholic topics are included; e.g. "The Vatican in Church-State Relations," "Conversion to and from Catholicism," "Parochial Education." Includes only books in English published after 1875. Index.

D148   Pogany, Andras H., and Hortenzia Lers Pogany. **Political Science and International Relations: Books Recommended for Use of American Catholic College and University Libraries.** Metuchen, NJ, Scarecrow Press, 1967. xvii, 387p. LC 67-10196.

"The primary aim of this bibliography is to help the small or medium sized college library in book selection, procedure, and purchasing" (Introduction). While not limited to Catholic authors, the selection leans heavily on Catholic authorities in the various fields covered. Classified arrangement with author and subject indexes.

SOURCES

D149   Powers, Francis Joseph. **Papal Pronouncements on the Political Order.** Westminster, MD, Newman Press, 1952. xii, 245p. LC 52-6807.

Contains selected excerpts from papal addresses and documents issued from 1878 to 1951 grouped under subject headings in classified order. The citizen, the state, Church and state, liberty and law, and international order are examples of the areas covered. Bibliography, pp. 221-25. Index.

D150   Ehler, Sidney Z., and John B. Morrall, eds. **Church and State through the Centuries: A Collection of Historic Documents with Commentaries.** Westminster, MD, Newman Press, 1954. 625p. LC 54-12446.

The selections range in date from Trajan's *Letter to Pliny* on the Treatment of Christians (113) to the Czechoslovakian Law on church affairs of 1949. The arrangement is chronological with introductions for each period and document. References to original language editions are supplied. Index.

DICTIONARIES AND ENCYCLOPEDIAS

D151   **Staatslexikon. Recht, Wirtschaft, Gesselschaft.** Hrsg. von der Görres-Gesellschaft. 6. völlig neubearb. und erweiterte Aufl. Freiburg, Herder, 1957-63. 8 v. LC A59-49.

This work originated in the program drawn up by Georg Freiher von Hertling, the chief founder of the *Görres-Gesellschaft* and the Imperial Chancellor in the last years of the German Empire (1917-18). The first edition, in five volumes, appeared from 1887 to 1897; the present edition is "not so much a revision of the fifth edition as an entirely new work, wider is scope and greatly enlarged" (*Catholic Historical Review*, L [October, 1964], p. 412). The purpose of the work is to deal with the concepts of the state, law, society and social problems, historically and descriptively from a Catholic philosophical and theological point of view. Planned by the specialists of the *Görres-Gesellschaft* in scope and emphasis primarily for the German-speaking world, it is, nevertheless, "Universal in its coverage, and highly recommended to all historians as an indispensable scholarly work of reference" (*Ibid.*, p. 415).

The articles tend to be long, are signed and contain full bibliographies. Index.

CANON LAW

The laws, decrees, definitions, and instructions coming from the councils, popes, and curial bodies of the Church have been codified into a body of laws known as the *Codex iuris canonici*. From 1963 until 1983, a Pontifical Commission for the Review of the *Code of Canon Law* worked on a complete, radical revision of the *Code* as called for by the Second Vatican Council. The final official version is contained in D162. English translations may be found in D159, D160, and D161. The previous codification (D163) was done in 1917 and remains an important document for the study of twentieth-century Catholicism.

BIBLIOGRAPHY

The literature of canon law is also indexed in most of the general and theological bibliographies mentioned in Chapters I and II.

D152   **Canon Law Abstracts: A Half-Yearly Review of Periodical Literature in Canon Law.** Edinburgh, Canon Law Society of Great Britain, 1959- . v. Semi-annual. LC 87-8398. ISSN 0008-5650.

Lists articles and books in an arrangement corresponding to the *Code*. Abstracts are long and helpful. No Indexes.

D153   Cunningham, Richard G. **An Annotated Bibliography of the Works of the Canon Law Society of America, 1965-1980.** Washington, DC, Canon Law Society of America, 1982. v, 121p. LC 82-151848. ISBN 0-943626-06-9.

An annotated bibliography of over 400 items covering the years of the revision of the Code of Canon Law. A most useful work for scholars of this process. Main entries, cross references and subject headings are all listed in one alphabetical sequence.

D154   Ferreira-Ibarra, Darbo C. **The Canon Law Collection of the Library of Congress: A General Bibliography with Selective Annotations.** Washington, DC, Library of Congress, 1981. xiii, 210p. LC 81-607964. ISBN 0-8444-0367-9.

The first three sections of the bibliography deal with the three early editions of the Code. The remaining sections are divided according to the sections of the 1917 Code. Bibliographies contained in books are noted. Name Index. Subject Index.

D155   Schulte, Johann Friedrich, Ritter von. **Die Geschichte der Quellen und Literatur des canonischen Rechts von Gratian bis auf die Gegenwart.** Stuttgart, F. Enke, 1875-80. 3 v. in 4. LC 5-10346.

A comprehensive retrospective bio-bibliography of canon law covering canonists and commentators up to the end of the nineteenth century. Indexes in each volume.

D156   **Sheridan, Leslie W. Bibliography on Canon Law, 1965-1971.** Austin, TX, University of Texas, School of Law, 1971. v, 80l. (Tarlton Law Library Legal Bibliography, no. 6.) LC 80-621919.

Lists articles and books in a classified arrangement. No indexes.

D157   Zimmerman, Marie. **Revision of Canon Law: International Bibliography, 1965-June 1977. Indexed by Computer/Revision de droit canonique: Bibliographie internationale, 1965-June 1977, etablier par ordinateur.** Strasbourg, CERDIC Publications, 1977. 46p. (RIC Supplément, no. 29.)

Contains two alphabetical lists of periodical articles: "Reforme du code droit canonique" and "Lex fundamentalis." The articles are in all major languages. No indexes.

TEXTS AND SOURCES

D158   Bouscaren, Timothy Lincoln. **The Canon Law Digest: Officially Published Documents Affecting the Code of Canon Law.** Milwaukee, Bruce Pub. Co., 1934- . v. LC 34-17255.

(Published every five years with intermediate supplements.)

Contains English translations of new documents with commentary and bibliographies. References are given to the canons of the 1917 Code which the documents affect. Volume VII of this series appeared in 1975 under the editorship of James I. O'Connor (Chicago, Chicago Province of the Society of Jesus).

D159   **The Code of Canon Law: A Text and Commentary.** Commissioned by the Canon Law Society of America, edited by James A. Coriden, Thomas J. Green, Donald E. Heintschel. New York, Paulist Press, 1985. xxvi, 1152p. LC 84-62582. ISBN 0-8091-0345-1.

This huge work contains the new text and a commentary on each canon, bibliographies for each book or section of canons, notes and introductions to each section of the Code. A 55 page index makes this edition of the Code the most useful for reference work. "This commentary is definitely a success and is not likely to be displaced in the English speaking world for at least a decade" (*New Blackfriars*, LXVII [February, 1986], p. 99).

D160 **Code of Canon Law in English Translation.** Prepared by the Canon Law Society of Great Britain and Ireland in association with the Canon Law Society of Australia and New Zealand and the Canadian Canon Law Society. London, Collins; Grand Rapids, MI, Eerdmans, 1983. xv, 319p. LC 83-212404. ISBN 0-8028-1978-8.

The approved translation of the New Code for English speaking Catholics. A brief glossary, but no other commentary, is included. No index.

D161 **Code of Canon Law, Latin-English Edition.** Translation prepared under the auspices of the Canon Law Society of America. Washington, DC, Canon Law Society of America, 1983. xlii, 668p. LC 84-115664. ISBN 0-9436-1620-4.

The English translation contained in this work is different from that in D160. "This work took more time to prepare than did the British translation and thus has fewer mistakes in translation" (*Louvain Studies*, X [Spring, 1984], p. 84). The index is useful, but not nearly as extensive as that in D159.

D162 **Codex iuris canonici.** Auctoritate Joannis Pauli PPII promulgatis. Vatican City Libreria Editrice Vaticana, 1983. xxx, 317p. LC 83-126300. ISBN 88-209-1418-2.

The newly revised Code of Canon Law in the official Vatican Latin text edition. "The only official and binding version of the Code is the Latin text" (*Code of Canon Law in English Translation* [D160] p. vii). The laws or canons are presented in eight books which are subdivided into parts, titles, and chapters. The canons are numbered consecutively from 1 to 1,752. This edition contains no index.

D163 **Codex juris canonici Pii X pontificis maximi iussu digestus, Benedicti papae XV auctoritate promulgatus.** Romae, Typis Polyglottis Vaticanis, 1917. 593p. LC 19-4454.

The official text of the previous revision of the Code as compiled by Cardinal Gasparri and his commission in 1917 by the order of Pope Pius X and later of Benedict XV. The laws or canons are arranged in a numbered sequence (1-2414), and an analytical index is provided along with footnotes to sources referring to the records of the Council of Trent, the *Corpus iuris canonici* (D164). Changes in the Code were reported in *Acta Apostolicae Sedis* (E121) and Bouscaren's *Canon Law Digest* (D158) in English translation.

D164 **Corpus juris canonici.** Editio lipsiensis secunda: post Aemilii Ludovici Richteri curas ad librorum manu scriptorum et editionis romanae fidem recognovit et adnotatione critica instruxit Aemilius Freidberg. Lipsiae, Tauchnitz, 1879-81. 2 v. LC 9-3770. Reprint: Graz, 1955.

Contains the early canons and decrees on which much of the 1917 Code (D163) is based. It is made up of six different collections of laws promulgated at various times in the history of the Church: Gratian's Decree, the Decretals of Gregory IX, the *Liber sextus* promulgated by Boniface VIII, the Constitutions of Clement V, the *Extravagentes* of John XXII, and the *Extravagantes Communes*.

D165   Gasparri, Pietro, Cardinal. **Codicis juris canonici fontes**. Romae, Typis Polyglottis Vaticanis, 1923-39. 9 v. LC 25-25468.

A collection of documents on which the 1917 Code of Canon Law (D163) is based but which had never hitherto appeared in any one source. Conciliar documents, and those of various popes and curial bodies, are reprinted and thoroughly indexed. The work was begun by Cardinal Gasparri, but the last three volumes were edited by Cardinal Seredi.

D166   Sartori, Cosmas. **Enchiridion canonicum seu Sanctas Sedis responsiones**. Ed. xi. Romae, Pontificium Athenaeum Antonianum, 1963. x, 503p.

Contains the decisions of the Holy See affecting canon law since the Code of 1917 up to 1963. The arrangement of texts by canon number in one sequence makes this work more convenient to use than the *Canon Law Digest* (D158). Subject index.

INDEXES

D167   Canon Law Society of Great Britain and Ireland. **Index to the Code of Canon Law in English Translation**. London, Collins, 1984. v, 98p. GB 85-15230. ISBN 0-00-599802-6.

A companion volume to the *Code of Canon Law in English Translation* (D160), but may be used with any translation since the references are to canon, not to pages. A very detailed index.

D168   Courville, Robert W. **Index to the Code of Canon Law**. Lafayette, LA, Boanerges Pub. Co., 1984. 133p. LC 84-142553.

A useful index to the new *Code*. References are to canon numbers. An introduction or preface and more cross references would be helpful.

D169   Lauer, Artur. **Index verborum Codicis iuris canonici**. Rome, Typis Polyglottis, Vaticanis, 1941. xxv, 936p. LC 54-51005.

A concordance to the Code of Canon Law, 1917 edition, arranged in sections by part of speech rather than in a straight alphabetical list. The use of the word in a phrase or sentence is not quoted; rather, through a complex system of symbols, the grammatical and syntactical use only is given. No words are omitted. "The impression is inevitable that all the complicated and refined work of grammatical analysis performed by Lauer gives too much, and does not give enough. . . . The need of the student to obtain semasiological information has been completely ignored" (*Jurist*, III [April, 1943], pp. 270-79).

D170   Ochoa Sanz, Javier. **Index verborum ac locutionum Codicis iuris canonici**. 2 ed. Cittá del Vaticano, Libreria Editrice Lateranense, 1984. xv, 592p. ISBN 84-499-7498-4

A concordance to the Latin version of the new *Codex* (D162). Words are given in context with a reference to the canon they appear in.

D171 Turner, Cuthbert Hamilton. **Ecclesiae occidentalis monumenta iuris antiquissima.** Canonum et conciliorum graecorum interpretationes latinae. Post Christophorum Iustel, Paschasium Quesnel, Petrum et Hieronymum Ballerini, Ioannem Dominicum Mansi, Franciscum Antonium Gonzales,

Fridericum Maassen edidit Cuthbertus Hamilton Turner. Oxonii, et typographeo Clarendoniano, 1899-1913. 2 v. in 5 pts. LC 24-28222.

Indexes the canons of the ecumenical councils up to the Council of Antioch (431) as they appear in the major collections of council documents such as Mansi's (E146).

DICTIONARIES AND ENCYCLOPEDIAS

D172 **Dictionnaire de droit canonique, contenant tous les termes du droit canonique, avec un summaire de l'histoire et des institutions et de l'état actuel de la discipline;** publié sous da direction de R. Naz avec le concours d'un grand nombre de collaborateurs. Paris, Letouzey et Ané, 1935- . v. LC 25-20238.

When completed this will be the largest reference work on canon law. Based on the 1917 Code (D163), the work contains long signed articles on historical topics, biographies, terms, and practices mentioned in canon law showing their origin and development in the earlier codes. Longer articles are subdivided, as are their bibliographies, with introductions showing the bases of the divisions. Biographies cover the life, works, and influence of the subject. Bibliographies follow every article.

D173 Köstler, Rudolf. **Wörterbuch zum Codex juris canonici.** München, J. Kösel and F. Pustet, 1927-29. 379p. LC 29-25987.

A dictionary of the Latin terms commonly used in canon law giving definitions in German and Latin. References to the canons in which the term is used and a summary of the law are also supplied. May be used as an index to the Code.

D174 Roussos, E. **Lexilogion ekklēsiastikou dikaiou.** Athens, 1948-49. 2 v. LC A52-10096.

A polyglot dictionary of the vocabulary of Eastern and Western canon law giving French, Latin, and English definitions of Greek terms in volume one, and of Latin terms in volume two. References to canons in which the term appears are given.

D175 Trudel, P. **A Dictionary of Canon Law.** St. Louis, Herder, 1919. 242p. LC 20-2135.

"A concise summary of the 1917 Code arranged alphabetically by subjects" (*Catholic World*, CXI [May, 1920], p. 256). Under each subject heading, lists the provisions of the Code that apply and their numbers. 606 entries.

HANDBOOKS AND COMMENTARIES

D176   Abbo, John A., and Jerome D. Hannon. **The Sacred Canons: A Concise Presentation of the Current Disciplinary Norms of the Church.** 2nd. ed. rev. St. Louis, Herder, 1960. 2 v. LC 60-14967.

"The most comprehensive commentary in English" (*Jurist*, XXI [April, 1961], p. 281). Explains each canon in numerical order, in clear and simple terms. The actual texts of the canons are not reprinted, but background and historical information along with bibliographical references are given. General bibliography, pp. 873-90. Index.

D177   Bouscaren, Timothy Lincoln, Adam C. Ellis, and Francis K. North. **Canon Law: A Text and Commentary.** 4th rev. ed. Milwaukee, Bruce Pub. Co., 1966. xvi, 1011p. LC 66-16640.

English translations of the text of the 1917 canons are given with commentary and background. Sample cases and questions with bibliographies are contained in each section. "The fourth edition of a very popular work; a good revision, particularly apt and serviceable for Americans" (*Theological Studies*, XXV [June, 1964], p. 319). Index.

D178   Orsy, Ladislas M. **Marriage in Canon Law: Texts and Comments, Reflections and Questions.** Wilmington, DE, M. Glazier, 1986. 328p. LC 86-80421. ISBN 0-89453-582-X.

Book IV, Title VIII, canons 1055-1165 of the new Code, contain the Church's legislation on marriage and are of more concern to the laity than most other canons. This work presents an introduction to each chapter of this section of the Code and a commentary on each canon. There is a "Selected and Annotated Bibliography," an "Index of Persons," and an "Index of Structures and Topics in the Law of Marriage." "This is much more than a purely juridical commentary" (*America*, CLVI [March 7, 1987], p. 203).

D179   Rocca, Fernando della. **Manual of Canon Law.** Trans. by Anselm Thatcher. Milwaukee, Bruce Pub. Co., 1959. 624p. LC 59-13650.

Contains a history of the sources of canon law in addition to a law-by-law explanation of the 1917 Code in numerical order. "A successful reference manual, but offers no bibliography" (*Jurist*, XX [April, 1960], p. 232). General index.

D180   Van Hove, Alphonse. **Commentarium lovaniense in Codicem iuris canonici.** Mechliniae, Dessain, 1928-39. 5 v. 2d. ed., 1942.

"Possibly the best commentary on the canons" (*American Ecclesiastical Review*, CII [January, 1940], p. 88). Each of the five volumes is devoted to a different section of the 1917 Code, covering in great detail the history of every canon with many bibliographical references. Index.

D181   Vermeersch, Arthur, and I. Creusen. **Epitome iurius canonici cum commentariis ad scholas et ad usum privatim.** Mechliniae, H. Dessain, 1940-49. 3 v. (8th ed. 1962-? .) LC 50-33767.

The text and commentary on the 1917 Code of Canon law with bibliographies for each section and many bibliographical footnotes. Indexes of canons in each volume and a general index in volume three. "A well-known, classic commentary . . . in a new and extensively revised edition" (*American Ecclesiastical Review*, CLI [October, 1964], p. 283).

D182   Wernz, Franz Xaver. **Ius decretalium ad usum praelectionem in scholis textus canonici sive iuris decretalium.** Romae: Giachetti, 1913. 7 v. in 8.

A monumental commentary on the canons as they existed before the codification of 1917; still useful for historical research. When it first appeared, it received high praise for its comprehensiveness and completeness (*America*, X [December 6, 1913], p. 211). Index in each volume.

D183   Woywood, Stanislaus. **A Practical Commentary on the Code of Canon Law.** Rev. and Aug. by C. Smith. New York, Wagner, 1962. 2 v. in 1.

A standard commentary giving more emphasis to books IV and V of the Code than most other English commentaries, but the latest revision was criticized for its lack of updating of the text (*Jurist*, XVIII [April, 1958], p. 249). Bibliography, v. 2, pp. 943-47. Index.

HISTORY

D184   Stickler, Alfonso Maria. **Historia juris canonici latini institutiones academicae.** Torino, Libreria Pontif. Athenaei Salesiani, 1950- . v. LC A51-8486.

The first and only volume of this work to appear to date covers the history of the various compilations of canon law that had been used in the past, with descriptions of their contents and accounts of their influence on the 1917 code. *Jurist* described the work as "admirable," but criticized its poor Latinity (XI [July, 1951], p. 442).

EASTERN CANON LAW

D185   Pitra, Jean Baptiste, Cardinal. **Iuris ecclesiastici graecorum historia et monumenta iussu Pii IX pont. max.** Romae, Typis Collegii Urbani, 1864-68. 2 v. LC 14-22037.

Contains the text and a commentary on Greek canon law. The texts are given in Greek and Latin, and bibliographies are supplied along with the historical and explanatory commentary. Both canons and subjects are indexed in volume two.

TREATIES

D186   Mercati, Angelo. **Raccolta di concordati su materie ecclesiastiche tra la Sante Sede e le autorita civili.** Città del Vaticano, Tipografia Poliglotta Vaticana, 1954. 2 v. LC A55-3900.

Contains the complete texts of all the concordats or treaties made by the Church with secular governments from 1098 to 1954 in chronological order. Indexes of subjects, popes, and countries.

GEOGRAPHY

GUIDEBOOKS

D187   Cartwright, John Keating. **The Catholic Shrines of Europe.** Photos by
Alfred Wagg. Foreword by Martin J. O'Connor. New York, McGraw-Hill,
1955. 212p. il. LC 54-11259.

Arranged by countries, this work covers churches, convents, monasteries,
tombs, etc., giving pictures and brief historical material in narrative form.
Only selected shrines are covered. No index.

D188   *Extension Magazine.* **The Catholic Traveler's Guide.** Comp. by Eileen
O'Hayer. Chicago, Extension, 1954. 168p. LC 54-1975.

Now very much out of date but contains the names and addresses of all
U. S. cathedrals and about 13,000 churches giving the times of masses,
confessions, and other services. Some listings are given for Canada and
Mexico.

D189   McNaspy, Clement Joseph. **A Guide to Christian Europe.** New York,
Hawthorn Books, 1963. LC 63-8021.

An informal guide to the major shrines stressing their historical and artistic importance. Does not cover the Scandinavian countries. Index. Glossary.
Bibliography, pp. 241-46.

D190   **Guide to Catholic Italy: With a Dictionary of Church Terminology.** Washington, DC, Catholic War Veterans of the U.S.A., 1950. 1373p.

A general handbook on the Church as well as a guide to Catholic shrines
and works of art.

D191   Sharp, Mary. **A Traveller's Guide to Saints in Europe.** London, H. Evelyn,
1964. xv, 251p. LC 64-7696.

Arranged by names of saints, gives brief biography, symbols in art and
location of churches, shrines and relics. Index.

D192   Sullivan, Kay. **The Catholic Tourist Guide.** New York, Meredith Press,
1967. ix, 326p. LC 67-24430.

Covers only the United States and Canada. For each state or province a
brief introduction and Catholic history is given followed by listings of
major churches, shrines, institutions and historical sites. Contains much
information not readily available elsewhere. Index.

ATLASES

D193   **Atlas zur Kirchengeschichte: die christlichen Kirchen in Geschichte und
Gegenwart. 257 mehrfarbige Karten und schematische Darstellungen,
Kommentare, ausführliches Register.** Hrsg. von Hubert Jedin, Kenneth
Scott Latourette und Jochen Martin. Unter Mitwirkung zahlreicher
Fachgelehrter bearb. von Jochen Martin. Freiburg, Herder, 1970. 83+152,
xxxviiip. il. maps. LC 70-654350.

An ecumenical work by an American Protestant and a German Catholic covering the history of all major Christian faiths. The 257 maps and charts are divided by period: early, medieval, and modern. The maps show the spread of the various faiths, diocesan and other boundaries, plans of important cities, religious orders, church governing bodies, etc. The first 83 pages of the work supply commentary and bibliography on the maps. "By far the best general atlas of ecclesiastical history in existence" (*Catholic Historical Review*, LVIII [October, 1972], p. 464). Index.

D194   Freitag, Anton. **The Twentieth Century Atlas of the Christian World: The Expansion of Christianity Through the Centuries.** Rev. and updated translation. New York, Hawthorn Books, 1964. xi, 199p. LC 63-17035.

Contains twenty-nine colored maps and 612 photographs. The text covers the history of Catholic missions and of some Protestant ones. The maps illustrate the spread of Christianity at various periods of history.

D195   Emmerich, Heinrich. **Atlas hierarchicus: descriptio geographica et statistica ecclesiae catholicae tum occidentis tum orientis.** Hanc ed. anno sacro 1975. Mödling bei Wien, St. Gabriel-Verl.; Aachen, Missionswissenschaftl. Inst., Mission e. v., 1976. 126+107p. Maps. LC 76-481191 MAP.

Composed of two parts: maps showing the establishment of the Church in each country, and text in five languages—English, French, German, Italian, and Spanish. Statistical information is contained in the supplement listed below. The most complete and carefully done work of its type. Indexes.

D196   Emmerich, Heinrich. **Atlas hierarchicus: descriptio geographica et statistica ecclesiae catholicae tum occidentis tum orientis. Praecipua indicia statistica de ecclesiasticis dicionibus die XXXI mensis Decembris MCMLXXIII. (Principal Statistical Data of the Ecclesiastical Territories on 31 December 1973.)** Vatican City, Typis Polyglottis Vaticanis, 1975. 50p.

Published as a supplement to, and inserted in the *Atlas hierarchicus*. Contains an index.

V
HISTORY

GENERAL CHURCH HISTORY

Among the more important works listed here are the *Bibliographie* (E2), published at the University of Louvain, the most inclusive bibliography for the field; the manuals or handbooks of Church history (E12-24) which cover all periods and countries in brief documented articles; and the dictionaries of Baudrillart (E8) and Cabrol (E27) covering history and archeology respectively.

BIBLIOGRAPHY

E1   Case, Shirley Jackson. **A Bibliographical Guide to the History of Christianity.** New York, Peter Smith, 1951. 256p.

An adequate, if somewhat outdated, critical bibliography of Catholic and other historical sources. Index.

E2   *Revue d'histoire ecclésiastique.* **"Bibliographie."** Louvain, Université Catholique de Louvain, 1900- . v. Annual. LC 60-20389.

A "comprehensive and detailed" (Case [E1], p. 21) listing of over 7,000 periodical articles and books on Church history and related topics with some contents notes and references to book reviews. International coverage; classified arrangement with author index. The largest bibliography in the field.

SOURCES

E3   Barry, Coleman James. **Readings in Church History.** Westminster, MD, Newman Press, 1960-65. 3 v. LC 59-14755.

A selection of important documents illustrating the history of the Church from its founding up to the present. References to sources are given. No indexes.

E4   Kidd, Beresford James. **Documents Illustrative of the History of the Church.** London, Society for Promoting Christian Knowledge, 1920-41. 3 v. LC 20-17806.

Covers up to the year 1500, giving excerpts from conciliar documents, laws, letters and so forth. References to sources are given. Index in each volume.

E5   **Records of Christianity.** By David Ayerst and A. S. T. Fisher. New York,
      Barnes and Noble, 1971- . v. il. LC 70-28480. ISBN 0-389-01345-5, v. 1;
      0-06-490255-2, v. 2.

      Contains excerpts from selected documents chosen to illustrate the early
      history of the Church. Each volume has an index of persons and an index
      of subjects.

BIBLIOGRAPHY OF SOURCES

E6   Fink, Karl August. **Das Vatikanische Archiv: Einführung in die Bestände und
      Ihre Erforschung.** 2. Aufl. Rome, W. Regensberg, 1951. ix, 185p.

      Treats each section of the Archives, describing the contents and listing published
      works dealing with them. Index. "Necessary tool for anyone proposing to work
      on the Vatican Archives" (A.J. Walford, *Guide to Reference Material*, 4th ed.
      [London, The Library Association, 1982], v. 2, p. 655). See also Boyle (E37).

E7   Vatican. Archivio vaticano. **Bibliografia dell' Archivio vaticano. A cura
      della Commissione internazionale per la bibliografia dell' Archivio vaticano.**
      Città del Vaticano, Presso l' Archivio vaticano, 1962- . v. LC 74-418214.

      An extensive bibliography of works about the contents of the Vatican
      Archives. Arranged by author and by document, this list includes books
      and articles in all languages treating the many important items in this
      unique collection.

DICTIONARIES AND ENCYCLOPEDIAS

E8   Baudrillart, Alfred, Cardinal. **Dictionnaire d'histoire et de géographie
      ecclésiastiques,** publié sous la direction de mgr. Alfred Baudrillart, avec
      le concours d'un grand nombre de collaborateurs. Paris, Letouzey et Ané,
      1912- . v. il. LC 9-26333.

      The most comprehensive reference work in Church history; an encyclopedia
      of mostly brief articles on terms, persons, places, events, movements and
      periods significant in Church history. All articles have full bibliographies.
      The entries for each country are usually very long and include maps. *Cath-
      olic Historical Review* praised it for its completeness and scholarship
      (XVII [October, 1932], p. 410), and *Month* declared it "a colossal work—
      the most important treatise on ecclesiastical history" (CXVI [July, 1910],
      p. 103). The fact that the nineteen volumes issued so far cover only up
      to the letter G in the alphabet gives some idea of the projected scope of
      the work.

E9   **Diccionario de Historia Eclesiástica de España.** Dirigido por Quintín Aldea
      Vaquero, Tomás Marín Martínez, José Vives Gatell . . . Madrid, Instituto
      Enrique Flóres, Consejo Superior de Investigaciones Científicas, 1972-75.
      4 v. il. LC 73-342083.

      A major work covering the entire history of Spanish Catholicism. The
      articles include biographies, events, geographical areas, and numerous
      related topics. Most articles are rather lengthy; each is signed and contains
      a bibliography.

E10 **Dictionnaire des Eglises de France, Belgique, Luxembourg, Suisse.** Paris, R. Laffont, 1966- . v. (Histoire générale des Églises de France, Belgique, Luxembourg, Suisse, v. 2- .) LC 67-73940.

Arranged geographically giving brief histories and descriptions with pictures and floor plans of churches and monasteries. Beautifully printed. Bibliographies are given for each church. "A dictionary that gives one pleasure to glance through and profit to consult" (*Études*, CCCXXVI [February, 1968], p. 299).

E11 **Westminster Dictionary of Church History.** Editor, Jerald C. Brauer. Associate editors, Brian Gerrish et al. Philadelphia, Westminster Press, 1971. xii, 887p. LC 69-11071. ISBN 0-664-21285-9.

An ecumenical effort "to give an immediate, accurate, introductory definition and explanation concerning the major men, events, facts, and movements in the history of Christianity" (Preface). Most articles are short; longer articles include bibliographies. "Brauer's effort, unfortunately, is not of the caliber to be helpful to scholars or serious students" (*Theological Studies*, XXXIV [December, 1973], p. 761).

HANDBOOKS

E12 Albers, Petrus Henrícus. **Manuel d'histoire ecclésiastique**; adaptation de la seconde édition hòllandiase par le R. P. René Hedde, O. P. Nouv. éd., rev. et mise à jour par le R. P. Paulin Jouet, O. P. Paris, Gabalda, 1939. 2 v.

Originally published in Dutch; covers the entire span of Church history providing a bibliography for each chapter or period with many bibliographical footnotes and a "Supplément bibliographique," v. 2., p. 609-611. "A comprehensive, clear, accurate, scientific history of the Church" (*Catholic World*, XCI [July, 1010], p. 542).

E13 Alzog, Johannes Baptist. **Manual of Universal Church History.** Trans. with additions from the ninth and last German ed. by F. J. Pabisch and Rt. Rev. Thomas S. Byrne. Cincinnati, R. Clarke Co., 1902-04. 3 v. LC 2-20069.

Divided into three epochs covering from the birth of Christ to the end of the 19th century with individual bibliographies for each epoch and subdivision therein. Contains many chronological tables, charts, etc., and a section on the science of history. "Often reprinted and much used; a substantial product of Roman Catholic scholarship" (Case [E1], p. 7). General index in v. 3.

E14 Bilhmeyer, Karl. **Church History.** Rev. by Hermann Tüchle. Trans. from the 13th ed. by Victor E. Mills. Westminster, MD, Newman Press, 1958-66. 3 v. LC 58-8753.

Based on an older history by F. X. Funk, this work is especially rich in bibliography—each chapter containing several lists. Indexes in each volume.

E15 Boulenger, Auguste. **Histoire générale de l'Église.** Lyon, E. Vitte, 1931-50. 3 v. in 9. LC 38-23666.

Clearly arranged with outlines of each section and many bibliographies in
every chapter. A "very rich" source of references (Louise Noëlle Malclès,
Les Sources du travail bibliographique [Geneve, E. Droz, 1950-58], v. 2,
p. 443).

E16   Dufourcq, Albert. **L'avenir du Christianisme.** Paris, Plon, 1905-20. 9 v.
           V1. Les religions païennes et la religion juive comparées. 1924. LC
           38-14288; V2. La révolution religieuse: Jésus. 1927. LC 38-1233;
           V3. Le christianisme primitif. 1929. LC 38-4234; V4. Le christianisme
           et l'empire (200-700). 1930. LC 30-255513; V5. Le christianisme et
           les barbares (395-1049). 1931. LC 38-31522; V6. Le christianisme et
           l'organization féodale (1049-1294). 1932. LC 38-4230; V7. Le christian-
           isme et la désorganisation individualiste (1294-1527). LC 38-4232;
           V8. Le christianisme et la réorganisation absolutiste. 1933-36. 2 v.
           LC 38-4229.

"This monumental work comprises a history of Christianity preceded by a
comparative study of the pagan religions and Judaism. His grasp of the data
is masterful and his criticism unprejudiced and serene" (*Catholic World*,
XCI [April, 1910], p. 116). Provides a bibliography for each chapter. No
index, but concise treatment and clarity of arrangement make the work
easy to consult.

E17   Eberhardt, Newman C. **A Summary of Catholic History.** St. Louis, Herder,
           1961-62. 2 v. LC 61-8059.

An almost decade-by-decade treatment of the history of the Church. Volume
1 ends with the year 1453 and volume 2 covers events up to the 1950's. "If
any negative criticism is in order it concerns the arrangement of the material."
However, it is "an accurate readable and comprehensive survey" (*Catholic
Historical Review.* LXIX [April, 1963], p. 100). Each volume has a detailed
subject index, and volume 2 contains an extensive bibliography. Various
appendixes in each volume list popes, councils, patriarchs, and the like.

E18   **Histoire de l'Église, depuis les origines jusqu'à nos jours.** Publiée sous la
           direction de Augustin Fliche et Victor Martin. Paris, Bloud et Gay, 1934-49.
           20 v. LC 63-56855.

A monumental work "high on the list of the excellent studies in historiography coming out of the renaissance of French Catholicism" (*Catholic
Historical Review*, XXXVI [October, 1950], p. 312). Covers up to the middle
of the nineteenth century with bibliographies for each chapter. No indexes.

E19   Jedin, Hubert. **Handbook of Church History.** Edited by Hubert Jedin and John
           Dolan. New York, Herder, 1965-1981. 10 v. LC 64-15929.

Planned as an introduction to the literature and sources as well as an actual
history of the Church. Each chapter contains a full bibliography stressing
the important older sources and the most recent works. "Written by a small
number of prominent German historians to give certain and precise information about the main events and persons in the history of the Church . . .
copious and up-to-date information" (*Catholic Historical Review*, L
[April, 1964], p. 71). Indexes in each volume.

E20   Jong, Jan de. **Handboek der kerkgeschiedenis.** 3 druk, herzien en verbeterd
       onder medewerking van dr R. R. Post. Utrecht-Nijmegen, Dekker, van de
       Vegt, 1936-37. 4 v. LC 39-11875.

       Described by Malclès as being "One of the better Catholic manuals for its
       richness, fullness, and impartiality" (*Les sources du travail bibliographique*
       [Geneve, E. Droz, 1950-58], v. 2, p. 444). Along with its many biblio-
       graphies, this work gives frequent quotations and excerpts from original
       sources and contains many helpful tables, charts and lists. Index, v. 4.

E21   Kirsch, Johann Peter. **Kirchengeschichte.** Unter Mitwirkung von Andreas
       Bigelmair, Joseph Greven, und Andreas Veit. Freiburg, Herder, 1930- .
       v. LC 31-21953.

       A widely respected history of the Catholic Church with some coverage of
       Protestantism and Orthodoxy. Praised by the *Catholic Historical Review*
       for its "astonishing erudition" and complete bibliographies (XVII [July,
       1931], p. 199). Each volume is by a different author; four volumes pro-
       jected. Indexes in each volume.

E22   McSorley, Joseph. **An Outline History of the Church by Centuries from
       St. Peter to Pius XII.** 11th ed. St. Louis, Herder, 1961. xxxi, 1174p.

       Each chapter covers a period of about 100 years in two sections: "Political
       background" and "The Church." Each of these is subdivided by certain
       general topics such as Catholic life, doctrine, discipline, practice and by
       other topics suitable to the period. It has been praised for its "excellent
       bibliographies by periods of largely Catholic sources" (American Historical
       Association, *Guide to Historical Literature* [New York, Macmillan, 1961],
       p. 67). Many appendixes and a detailed index add to its reference value.

E23   Mourret, Fernand. **A History of the Catholic Church.** Trans. by Rev.
       Newton Thompson. St. Louis, B. Herder Book Co., 1930-45. 9 v. LC 31-507.

       Although it was praised highly in *Catholic World* for its reference features
       (CXLIII [June, 1936], p. 380), Malclès describes it as being more apologetic
       than historic, with errors in details and inadequate bibliography (*Les
       sources du travail bibliographique* [Genève, E. Droz, 1950-58], v. 2, p. 443).
       Indexes in each volume.

E24   Rice, Edward E. **The Church: A Pictorial History.** New York, Farrar, Straus
       & Cudahy, 1961. 268p. il. LC 61-6989.

       250 illustrations drawn from works of art and manuscripts as well as
       photographs make up this collection. The arrangement is chronological,
       but a subject and name index help locate the illustrations. The accompany-
       ing text is selective in the events covered, but clear and readable.

BIOGRAPHY

E25   **Church Historians: Including Papers on Eusebius, Orosius, St. Bede the
       Venerable, Ordericus Vitalis, Las Casas, Baronius, Bollandus, Muratori,
       Moehler, Lingard, Hergenroether, Janssen, Denifle, Ludwig von Pastor.**

New York, P. J. Kenedy, 1926. vii, 430p. LC 27-6831. Reprinted: New York, Burt Franklin, 1968. ISBN 0-8337-4144-6.

Biographies and commentary on the works of fifteen Church historians are provided along with critical bibliographies of works by and about them. Each essay is by a different member of the American Catholic Historical Society. Index.

ARCHEOLOGY

BIBLIOGRAPHY

E26   De Marco, Angelus A. **The Tomb of St. Peter: A Representative and Annotated Bibliography of the Excavations.** Leiden, E.J. Brill, 1964. 261p. (Supplements to Novum Testamentum, v. 8.) LC 66-1271.

A listing of 870 books and articles in a classified arrangement with an author index.

DICTIONARIES AND ENCYCLOPEDIAS

E27   Cabrol, Fernand. **Dictionnaire d'archéologie chrétienne et de liturgie,** publié par le r. p. dom Fernand Cabrol, avec le concours d'un grand nombre de collaborateurs. Paris, Letouzey et Ané, 1907-53. 15 v. il. LC 3-15097.

This work is described in the liturgy section of Chapter II (**B382**). Here it is sufficient to point out that it also covers early Christian institutions, morals, customs, social and private life, through the investigation of Christian epigraphy, paleography and numismatics. *Month* emphasized its value in dealing with "aspects of the history of the Church too largely ignored hitherto or touched upon only incidentally" (CI [June, 1903], p. 204). O'Rourke lists it as "the most complete and scholarly work for Catholic archeology" ([A74], p. 119).

HANDBOOKS

E28   Leclercq, Henri. **Manuel d'archéologie chrétienne depuis les origines jusqu'au VIIIᵉ siècle.** Paris, Letouzey et Ané, 1907. 2 v. il. LC 12-15928.

A handbook of archeological studies covering catacombs, buildings, monuments and related minor arts, containing many subject bibliographies and a general bibliography. Index in vol. 2.

HISTORY BY PERIODS

ANCIENT

SOURCES

E29   Ayer, Joseph Cullen. **A Source Book for Ancient Church History from the Apostolic Age to the Close of the Conciliar Period.** New York, C. Scribner's Sons, 1913. xxi, 707p. LC 13-23627. Reprinted: New York, AMS Press, 1970. LC 70-113546. ISBN 0-404-00436-9.

A collection of standard source material for early Church history down to the year 787 arranged by subject. Each text or excerpt is prefaced by a reference to a printed version in the original language and by a short annotation on its accuracy and authority. Index.

E30 Stevenson, James. **Creeds, Councils and Controversies: Documents Illustrative of the History of the Church A.D. 337-461.** Rev. ed. with additional documents by W.H.C. Frend. London, SPCK, 1988. 448p. GB 88-275. ISBN 0-28104-327-2.

This work and the one following are based on the older Kidd collection (E4) omitting some items and adding others. Sources are given for each text along with a brief commentary on the context or authenticity of the text. "Notes on Sources" (i.e. biographical), "Chronological Tables," and index.

E31 Stevenson, James. **A New Eusebius: Documents Illustrative of the History of the Church to A.D. 337.** Rev. ed. with additional documents by W.H.C. Frend. London, SPCK, 1987. xxii, 404p. GB 87-20. ISBN 0-28104-268-3.

Same format as E30.

DICTIONARIES AND ENCYCLOPEDIAS

E32 Smith, William, and Samuel Cheetham, eds. **A Dictionary of Christian Antiquities: Being a Continuation of the Dictionary of the Bible.** Hartford, The J. B. Burr Pub. Co., 1880. 2 v. Reprinted: New York, Kraus, 1968. ISBN 0-527-84150-1.

Covers the "history, institutions, and antiquities" of the Church up to the age of Charlemagne. Impartial in most articles, this work is valuable for its bibliographical references which usually are to primary sources. A companion set to the *Dictionary of Christian Biography* (A177).

HANDBOOKS

E33 Batiffol, Pierre Henri. **Le Catholicisme des origines à saint Léon.** Paris, Gabalda, 1924-29. 4 v.

An apologetic study of the origin and history of the Church to the year 451. Volume one was published in English as *Primitive Catholicism* (London, Longmans, 1911), but no other sections have been translated. It is a clearly written work with much documentation and bibliography but not as useful as the general handbooks listed above.

E34 Prümm, Karl. **Religionsgeschichtliches Handbuch für den Raum der altchristlichen Umwelt; hellenistische-römische Geistesströmungen und Kulte mit Beachtung des Eigenlebens der Provinzen.** Rom, Päpstliches Bibelinstitut, 1954. xvi, 921p. LC A56-4854.

Covers the complete religious background of the classical world. Roman and Hellenic culture and the life of the provinces are treated in brief, clear chapters with copious notes and bibliographies. The author index includes the bibliographies; there is also a subject index.

ATLASES

E35   Meer, Frederik van der, and Christine Mohrmann. **Atlas of the Early Christian World.** Trans. and Ed. by Mary F. Hedlund and H. H. Rowley. London, Nelson, 1958. 215p. il. LC Map 58-7.

Originally issued in Dutch as a companion to Grollenberg's *Atlas of the Bible* (B131). Forty-two colored maps and 620 plates illustrate the history of Christianity from apostolic times to the year 600. This work also contains a section on the Fathers of the Church and early Christian literature. Full indexes are supplied.

MEDIEVAL

GUIDES

E36   Boyce, Gray Cowan, comp. **Literature of Medieval History, 1930-1975: A Supplement to Louis John Paetow's "Guide to the Study of Medieval History."** Sponsored by the Medieval Academy of America. Milwood, NY, Kraus International Publications,1981. 5 v. LC 80-28773. ISBN 0-5271-0462-0.

Continues Paetow (E39) but with more emphasis on advanced materials. A listing of books and articles in a classified arrangement. Volume 5 is an author and personal name index. The emphasis is on Western Europe not Eastern, Northern not British. References to reviews are provided for book entries.

E37   Boyle, Leonard E. **A Survey of the Vatican Archives and Its Medieval Holdings.** Tornoto, Pontifical Institute of Medieval Studies, 1972. iv, 250p. (Subsidia Mediaevalia, 1.) LC 73-159977. ISBN 0-8884-4350-1.

A survey of the Archives arranged by Vatican departments. Extensive "General Bibliography" and "General Index to Text and Bibliography." "This is likely to remain the indispensable standard work. The best in any language" (*English Historical Review*, LXXXIX [October, 1974], p. 871).

E38   Paetow, Louis John. **A Guide to the Study of Medieval History.** Rev. ed. Prepared under the Auspices of the Medieval Academy of America. New York, F. S. Crofts and Co., 1931. xii, 643p. LC 31-14070. Reprinted: New York, Kraus, 1959. LC 73-9705. ISBN 0-527-69100-3.

"The most useful general guide to the literature of medieval history" (Winchell, Constance M., *Guide to Reference Books* [Chicago, A.L.A., 1967] , p. 471). A critical study of over 1,000 general and specific reference books and the literature of individual subject areas. The text is minimal and in outline form; almost the entire work is devoted to bibliography. Index. Continued by Boyce (E36).

BIBLIOGRAPHY

E39   Atiya, Aziz Suryal. **The Crusade: Historiography and Bibliography.** Bloomington, Indiana University Press, 1962. 107p. LC 62-18368.

A guide to the great library collections on the crusades as well as a bibliography of books and articles. Not so comprehensive as Mayer's work (E46).

E40   Berkhout, Carl T. and Jeffrey B. Russell. **Medieval Heresies: A Bibliography, 1960-1979.** Tornoto, Pontifical Institute of Medieval Studies, 1981. 201p. LC 81-159998. ISBN 0-8884-4360-9.

Supplements Herbert Grundmann's *Bibliographie zur Ketzergeschichte des Mittelalters* (Rome, Ed. di Storia e Letterature, 1967). Over 2,000 books and articles published between 1960 to 1979 are listed in subject order. There are extensive author, subject, and manuscript indexes.

E41   Chevalier, Cyr Ulysse Joseph. **Répertoire des sources historiques du moyen âge.** Paris, Picard, 1894-1907. 2 v. in 4. LC 5-9616. Reprinted: New York, Kraus, 1959. LC 75-77037. ISBN 0-527-1670-2, v. 1, 0-527-16710-X, v. 2. Pt. 1. Bio-bibliographie. 2 v. (See A141). Pt. 2. Topo-bibliographie. 2 v. An alphabetical subject bibliography covering the place names and subjects, giving brief descriptions or explanations of the terms and full bibliographies, but subject to the same reservations about ease of consultation and selectivity of titles expressed in Chapter 1 (A170).

E42   Farrar, Clarissa Palmer, and Austin P. Evans. **Bibliography of English Translations from Medieval Sources.** New York, Columbia University Press, 1946. xiii, 534p. LC A46-1541.

Lists almost 4,000 translations of medieval documents, both Eastern and Western, in alphabetical order by author supplying full bibliographical information and historical notes. Index.

E43   Ferguson, Mary Ann. **Bibliography of English Translations from Medieval Sources, 1943-1967.** New York, Columbia University Press, 1974. x, 274p. (Records of Civilization: Sources and studies, no. 88.) LC 73-7751. ISBN 0-2310-3435-0.

A supplement to Farrar (**E42**), but expanded in time coverage, types of material and bibliographical technique. 1,980 items are listed including books and translations appearing in periodicals. The arrangement is by author with an author-subject index. "A work demanding the attention of librarians, scholars and students." (*Review for Religious*, XXXIV [March, 1975], p. 345).

E44   García y García, Antonio. **Catálogo de los manuscritos e incunables de la Catedral de Córdoba.** Salamanca, Universidad Pontificia, 1976. lxxx, 746p. (Bibliotheca salmanticensis, 6.) LC 77-473902. ISBN 84-7299044-3.

Lists 171 manuscripts and 500 incunabula giving a descriptive annotation for each. "An essential tool for students of the intellectual and legal history of the later Middle Ages" (*English Historical Review*, XCII [April, 1977], p. 415). Index of incipits; index of incunabula; author, title indexes.

E45   Kennedy, James Francis. **The Sources for the Early History of Ireland: Ecclesiastical.** New York, Columbia University Press, 1929. xvi, 807p. (*Records of Civilization: Sources and Studies*, no. 11.) Reprinted: New York, Octagon Books, 1966. LC 66-15998.

Lists 695 sources with annotations, bibliography and references to printed editions. The documents deal with the early history of the Church in Ireland, religious orders and monasteries and lives of early Irish saints. "Offers the first comprehensive scientific survey of modern research in early Irish Christian history" (*Catholic Historical Review*, XVII [July, 1929], p. 180).

E46   Mayer, Hans Eberhard. **Bibliographie zur Geschichte der Kreuzzüge.** Hanover, Hahnsche Buchhandlung, 1960. xxxii, 272p. LC A61-2628.

A classified list of over 5,400 items on the crusades and related topics. Covers to the year 1453.

E47   Pontifical Institute of Medieval Studies. **Dictionary Catalog of the Pontifical Institute of Medieval Studies.** Boston, G.K. Hall and Co., 1972. 5 v. LC 74-152760. ISBN 0-816-10970-2.

A reproduction of the author-title-subject catalog of this impressive collection of over 40,000 titles.

E48   Potthast, August. **Bibliotheca historica medii aevi. Wegweiser durch die Geschichtswerke des europäischen Mittelalters bis 1500. Vollständiges Inhaltsverzeichniss zu 'Acta sanctorum' Boll.–Bouquet–Migne, Monum. germ. hist. Muratori–Rerum britann. scriptores etc.; Anhang; Quellenkunde für die Geschichte der europäischen Staaten während des Mittelalters.** 2. verb. und verm. Aufl. Berlin, W. Weber, 1896. 2 v. LC 2-5027. Reprinted: Graz, 1954.

"A stupendous undertaking devoted to the classification of the primary sources of medieval history" (Paetow [E38], p. 7). Made up of two parts: 1) an index to printed texts of the documents written between A. D. 375 and 1500; and 2) an alphabetical list of medieval authors giving an identifying phrase, references to biographies, and a list of written works indicating manuscripts, translations, editions and commentaries. August Potthast was the Librarian at the Royal Library in Berlin and compiled this list singlehandedly; therefore, it is not surprising that there are some inaccuracies and omissions. A thorough revision of his work was begun in 1962 by an international group of historians (E49).

E49   **Repertorium fontium historiae medii aevi: primum ab Augusto Potthast digestum, nunc cura coleggii historicorum e pluribus nationibus emendatum et auctum.** Romae, apud Istituto storico italiano peril medio evo, 1962- . v.

A revision of the previous work including additions and corrections, improved typography and expanded treatment of oriental sources.

SOURCES

E50   Jones, Putnam Fennell. **A Concordance to the Historia ecclesiastica of Bede.** Cambridge, MA, Medieval Academy of America, 1929. ix, 585p. LC 29-29389.

A concordance "to every instance of every significant word in the historia." Omissions are noted in their alphabetical place. Each word is listed under its first grammatical form. A generous amount of text is quoted to identify the usage, making this as much an index as a concordance.

E51 **Monumenta germanica historica.** Berlin etc., 1826- . v. Reprint: Weimar, H. Bohlaus Nachfolger, 1949- . v. LC 67-34727.

E52 **Monumenta germanica historica. Indices.** 1890. LC 2-14612.

E53 **Monumenta germanica historica. Inhaltsverzeichnisse der zehn ersten Bände.** 1848. LC AC37-1810.

Contains complete texts of medieval authors, documents of chapters, councils, and numerous Church and civil documents for the years 500-1500.

E54 **Recueil des historiens des Gaules et de France.** Nouvelle éd. Publiée sous la direction de M. Lépold Delisle. Farnborough, Gregg, 196?- . v. LC 78-423788.

First published, 1738- , as *Rerum gallicarum et franciscarum scriptores.*

E55 **Rerum britanicarum medii aevi scriptores: or Chronicles and Memorials of Great Britain and Ireland during the Middle Ages.** London, Longmans, 1858-96. 253 v. LC 58-52651.

Known as the "Rolls Series," this collection contains documents—mostly from the popes, monasteries, and other ecclesiastical sources—and provides introductions on the lives of the authors and sources of the texts. The work covers from the Roman invasion to the reign of Henry VIII. All texts are indexed.

E56 **Rerum Italicarum scriptorum, 500-1500.** Milan, etc., 1723- . v. LC AC35-2821.

A collection for Italy similar to (E55).

E57 Silva-Tarouca, Carlo. **Fontes historiae ecclesiasticae medii aevi in usum scholarum.** Romae, Universitatis Gregorianae, 1930- . v. LC 31-33816.

"A useful complement to the well-known standard bibliographies such as those of Paetow and Potthast." (Brown [A78], v. 1, p. 111). Chronologically arranged excerpts from various authors and other sources with references to full, printed texts. Index of names.

DICTIONARIES AND ENCYCLOPEDIAS

E58 **Dictionary of the Middle Ages.** Joseph R. Strayer, ed. in chief. New York, Scribner, 1982- . v. LC 82-5904. ISBN 0-68416-760-3.

Sponsored by the American Council of Learned Societies, this major work is the labor of mostly American and Canadian scholars. 5,000 articles are projected ranging in length from 50 words to 10,000. All articles are signed and only the briefest do not contain a bibliography of mostly English language works. The period covered is roughly 500-1500 A.D. Geographically it covers the Latin West, the Slavic lands, the Byzantine Empire, and the Islamic world as far east as Iran. In 1985 an *Interim Index* was published for the first 5 volumes. After the 12th and final volume of text a final cumulative index volume will be published.

"There is nothing in English to which this can be compared. Its usefulness and merit must therefore be measured against the virtual absence of alternatives" (*RQ*, XXII [Spring, 1983], p. 304). The reviewer does, however, point some problems in cross referencing and terminology.

E59   **A Handlist of Medieval Ecclesiastical Terms.** Comp. by F. R. H. DuBoulay. London, The Council for the Standing Conference for Local History, 1952. 31p.

Defines about 500 elementary terms for the benefit of "beginners and amateurs who wish to search into the records of their parish or diocese" (Foreword).

E60   Latham, Ronald E., ed. **Revised Medieval Latin Word-List from British and Irish Sources.** London, Oxford University Press for the British Academy, 1965. xxiii, 524p. LC 65-28937.

"Includes in principle all words collected to date from British and Irish sources insofar as they are non-Classical either in form or meaning" (Preface). Gives definitions and dates of first use.

E61   **Lexikon des Mittelalters.** Hrsg. von Robert Auty, et al. München; Zürich, Artimus Verlag, 1977- . v. LC 79-390542.

A very large work. Volumes I-III cover A-Erz. Articles are signed, of moderate length, and contain bibliographies.

HANDBOOKS

E62   **The Cambridge Medieval History.** Planned by J. B. Bury; ed. by H. M. Gwatkin and J. P. Whitney. New York, Macmillan, 1911-36. 8 v. LC 11-20851. (2nd. ed. 1966- . v. LC 66-4537).

Little need be said here about this well-known series as a source of information for this period. The wide scope of its coverage, impartiality in the selection of contributors and the richness of its bibliographies are bywords in reference work. There are few medieval topics that cannot be found in this series through its indexes.

MODERN

BIBLIOGRAPHY

E63   Bruggeman, J. **Inventaire des piéces d'archives françaises se rapportant à l'abbaye de Port-Royal des Champs et son cercle et à la résistance contre la Bulle Unigenitus et à l'appel (ancien fonds d'Amersfoort).** La Haye, M. Nijhoff, 1972. xxvii, 450p. (*Archives internationales d'histoire des idées,* 54.)

Contains 7,156 numbered items to be found in the *Fonds d'Amersfoort* archives relating to the Jansenist heresy and the papal bull *Unigenitus* which condemned the doctrine. Indexes of authors and names are included.

E64   Pollen, John Hungerford, ed. **Sources for the History of Roman Catholicism in England, Ireland and Scotland from the Reformation Period to the**

Emancipation, 1533-1795. New York, Macmillan Co.; London, SPCK, 1921. 47p. (Helps for Students of History, no. 39.) LC 21-9804.

A bibliographical essay written in chronological order. No index. Chapter 16, "A Few Hints on Books and Authors" presents a more or less comprehensive list of titles.

E65 Szeplaki, Joseph. **Bibliography on Cardinal Mindszenty.** Youngstown, OH, Catholic Hungarians Sunday, 1977. 31p. LC 77-80152.

Provides a brief biography and lists 347 books, articles, newsletters, and A. V. materials in separate lists. No indexes.

E66 Vekene, Emil van der. **Bibliotheca bibliographica historiae sanctae inquistitionis. Bibliographisches Verzeichnis der gerdruckten Schrifttums zur Geschichte und Literatur der Inquisition.** Vaduz, Topas Verlag, 1982-83. 2 v. LC 83-183742. ISBN 3-289-00272-1.

A list of primary and secondary literature on the Inquisition with library locations given. The arrangement is classified. Index.

SOURCES

E67 Olin, John C., comp. **The Catholic Reformation: Savanarola to Ignatius Loyola: Reform in the Church, 1495-1540.** New York, Harper and Row, 1969. xxvi, 220p. il. LC 69-17021. Reprinted: Westminster, MD, Christian Classics, 1978. ISBN 0-87061-001-5.

Contains the texts of 15 documents, a "Bibliographical Postscript," and an index of names. The selection of documents is from an interesting variety of sources.

E68 Szczesniak, Boleslaw. **The Russian Revolution and Religion: A Collection of Documents Concerning the Suppression of Religion by the Communists, 1917-1925: With Introductory Essays, Appendices, and a Selective Bibliography.** Notre Dame, IN, University of Notre Dame Press, 1959. xx, 289p. LC 58-14180.

The resolutions, decrees, laws and speeches documenting the Russian suppression of religion, especially Roman Catholicism, are collected and translated in this work. The sources of the documents are supplied along with a "Selective Bibliography," pp. 253-69.

E69 Wyszynski, Stephan, Cardinal. **Listy pasterskie prymasa Polski, 1946-1974.** Paris, Editions du Dialogue, 1975. 693p. LC 76-526482. ISBN 2-85316-009-2.

A collection of the pastoral letters of Cardinal Wyszynski.

DICTIONARIES AND ENCYCLOPEDIAS

E70 Avery, Catherine B., ed. **The New Century Italian Renaissance Encyclopedia.** Editorial consultants: Marvin B. Becker and Ludovico Borgo. New York, Appleton-Century-Crofts, 1972. xiii, 978p. LC 76-181735. ISBN 0-3906-6950-X.

"The emphasis ... is on men and events in Italy" (Peface). But many non-Italian figures are also included. Made up of brief, non-signed articles without bibliographies. "Here in one handy volume, can be found at least basic information on over 4,000 people and events connected with this period" (*RQ*, XII [Fall, 1972], p. 85).

HANDBOOKS

E71   Imbart de la Tour, Pierre. **Les origines de la Réforme**. Paris, Hachette, 1905-35. 4 v. LC 18-15175. (2ᵉ éd. Melun, Librairie D'Argences, 1948- .v.).

Treats the entire Reformation but from the point of view of France. Luther and other non-French reformers are grouped in volume three. Each volume of the new edition contains a critical bibliography of the period and subjects covered. No indexes.

AMERICAN CHURCH HISTORY

In keeping with the general limitations of this bibliography, most reference books dealing with specific countries have been excluded with the exception of the United States, which may serve as an example of the types of material available for most other countries.

American Catholic Church history has been well-covered bibliographically by John Tracy Ellis (E73) and Edward Vollmar (E81) but is weak in dictionaries and handbooks.

GUIDES

E72   Cadden, John Paul. **The Historiography of the American Catholic Church: 1785-1943**. Washington, DC, The Catholic University of America Press, 1944. xi, 122p. LC A44-2782.

Part of a projected guide to the literature of American Catholic History. It covers "the development that has taken place in this field with particular attention directed to the outstanding critical historians of the period" (Preface). The other parts of the series—a study of the literature of American Catholic Church history and a "select catalogue" of American Catholic Church literature—have never appeared, perhaps because the *Guide* by Ellis (E73) and Vollmar's *Bibliography* (E81) filled this need.

E73   Ellis, John Tracy, and Robert Trisco. **A Guide to American Catholic History**. 2nd. ed. Santa Barbara, CA, ABC-Clio, 1982. xiii, 265p. LC 81-17585. ISBN 0-87436-318-7.

Formerly a professor of Church history at Catholic University, Ellis developed this work for his students of American Church history. Arranged by subject, it points out strengths and weaknesses in the literature, and lists and evaluates the most important works in each field. Over 1,200 works are covered in the 2nd edition. Index. "A book conceived and arranged with a view to its usefulness and convenience" (*Catholic Historical Review*, LXIX [January, 1983], p. 93).

BIBLIOGRAPHY

E74   Academy of American Franciscan History. **United States Documents in the Propaganda Fide Archives: A Calendar.** By Finbar Kenneally. Washington, DC, Academy of Franciscan History, 1966- . v. LC 66-8979. (V. 7, 1977)

An immense catalog of all extant documents contained in the Propagation of the Faith Archives. These include papal bulls and other documents, as well as letters to and from Rome regarding American ecclesiastical history. For each item, the archive volume and page numbers are given as well as a summary of the contents. "A most valuable aid for historians of the American Catholic Church" (*Catholic Historical Review*, LV [July, 1969], p. 230). Each volume contains an index.

E75   **Catholicism and Anti-Catholicism: A Title List from the Microfiche Collection, Pamphlets in American History, Group IV.** Ed. by Michael J. Matochik. Sanford, NC, Microfilming Corporation of America, 1982. v, 127p. 83-103691. ISBN 0-6670-0702-4.

1,340 titles are listed in no apparent order. Complete bibliographical citations are supplied. A separate author, title, subject index is available with the purchase of the microfiche collection. The materials listed include sermons, pastoral letters, missionary reports, etc.

E76   Ellis, John Tracy. **A Select Bibliography of the History of the Catholic Church in the United States.** New York, The Declan X. McMullen Co., 1947. 96p. LC 47-4369.

An earlier version of his *Guide* (E73) but with a broader scope and fewer entries. Includes books on American history in general as well as American Catholic history.

E77   Liebman, Seymour B. **The Inquisitors and the Jews in the New World: Summaries of Procesos: 1500-1810: and Bibliographical Guide.** Coral Gables, FL, University of Miami Press, 1975. 224p. il. LC 72-85110. ISBN 0-87024-245-8.

An alphabetical listing (by the name of the accused) under four geographic areas. Each entry contains a brief summary of the case and locations of pertinent documents. "An important archival guide to Jewish Inquisitional materials" (*Catholic Historical Review*, LXIII [July, 1977], p. 480).

E78   McCoy, James Comly. **Jesuit Relations of Canada, 1632-1673: A Bibliography.** Paris, A. Rau., 1937. xv, 310p. il. LC 37-22522. Reprinted: New York, Burt Franklin, 1972. LC 76-153038. ISBN 0-8337-2314-6.

A list of 132 items in the Jesuit Relations indicating the first printed editions and giving careful bibliographical descriptions, reproductions of title pages, locations in libraries, and a reference to the English translations printed in the Thwaites edition (E88).

E79   Steck, Francis Borgia. **A Tentative Guide to Historical Materials on the Spanish Borderlands.** Philadelphia, Catholic Historical Society of Philadelphia, 1943. 106p. LC 44-809. Reprinted: New York, Burt Franklin, 1971. LC 71-143659. ISBN 0-8337-3379-6.

A bibliography of scholarly books and articles on the lands now in the U. S. which Spain once ruled—Florida to 1814, Louisiana to 1803, Texas to 1836, New Mexico and Arizona to 1846, and California to 1846. Annotations are given, but there are no indexes.

E80   Tomasi, Silvano and Edward C. Stabili. **Italian Americans and Religion: An Annotated Bibliography.** New York, Center for Migration Studies, 1978. xiii, 222p. LC 76-44921. ISBN 0-913-25625-0.

Lists 1,158 books and articles, primary and secondary materials by format, e.g., manuscripts, books, articles, etc. Index.

E81   Vollmar, Edward R. **The Catholic Church in America: An Historical Bibliography.** 2nd. ed. New York, Scarecrow Press, 1963. 399p. LC 63-7466.

An author list of books and articles including doctoral and masters' theses dealing with the American Church from 1850 to 1961. Subject index. No annotations.

E82   Weber, Francis J., comp. **A Select Bibliography to California Catholic Literature, 1856-1974.** Los Angeles, Dawson's Book Shop, 1974. x, 70p. LC 73-76146.

Lists 500 books and pamphlets dealing with the Church in California. Twentieth century material makes up the bulk of the listings. Annotated.

E83   Weigle, Marta, comp. **A Penitente Bibliography.** Albuquerque, University of New Mexico Press, 1976. 162p. LC 75-40839. ISBN 0-8263-0401-X.

The Penitentes were flagellant societies that figure in the Catholic history of the Southwest. This exhaustive bibliography lists books, articles and ephemera, published and unpublished, alphabetically in five different lists by type of material. Each item is annotated, and locations are given. There is no general index.

SOURCES

E84   **Concilium plenarium totius Americae Septentrionalis Foederatae.** Baltimori habitum anno 1852. Baltimori, J. Murphy, 1853. 72p. LC 40-24396.

E85   **Concilii plenarii baltimorensis II in ecclesia metropolitana baltimorensi a die vii ad diem xii octobris a. d. MDCCCLXVI habiti et a Sede apostolica recogniti acta et decreta.** Editio altera mendis expurgata. Baltimorae, J. Murphy, 1877. lxxv, 311p. LC 40-21540.

E86   **Decreta Concilii plenarii baltimorensis tertii.** A. D. MDCCCLXXIV. Praeside illmo. ac revmo. Jacobo Gibbons. Baltimorae, J. Murphy, 1894. vii, 189p. LC 40-21543.

The decrees of the three plenary councils of Baltimore are an important source for American Church history since at these meetings the legislation responsible for the present day parochial school system, diocesan seminary education, the Catholic University, the Baltimore Catechism, and many other characteristics of the Church in the U. S. was passed.

The three collections listed here contain all the pertinent decrees and other documents and are indexed.

E87   **Documents of American Catholic History.** Ed. by John Tracy Ellis. Wilmington, DE, M. Glazier, 1987. 3 v. LC 86-80801. ISBN 0-89453-611-7.

Selected from all sources, ecclesiastical, lay, and non-Catholic, these documents attempt to illustrate American Catholic history from 1493 to 1986. Ellis's definition of a document is "any written record that would illustrate an event from a contemporary point of view" (Preface). Each volume has an index. See also *Pontificia americana: A Documentary History of the Catholic Church in the United States* (E112).

E88   **The Jesuit Relations and Allied Documents, Travels and Explorations of the Jesuit Missionaries in New France, 1610-1791: the Original French, Latin, and Italian texts with English Translations and Notes.** Ed. by Reuben Gold Thwaites. New York, Pageant Book Co., 1959. 73 v. in 36. il. LC A62-8676.

An indispensable collection of sources for early American and Canadian, general, as well as Church history. The "Relations" are letters, reports and other documents written by the early Jesuit missionary explorers. This edition also includes material not part of the *Relations* as such but bearing on the history of Jesuit missions in New France. Introductions and bibliographical notes are supplied for each of the documents as well as English translations. Reuben Thwaites, former secretary of the State Historical Society of Wisconsin, prepared this edition in collaboration with several Jesuits and others knowledgeable of these documents. For other editions see *Jesuit Relations and Other Americana in the Library of James F. Bell: A Catalogue Compiled by Frank Walter and Virginia Donaghy* (Minneapolis University of Minnesota Press, 1950).

E89   **National Pastorals of the American Hierarchy, 1792-1919.** Foreword, Notes and Index by Peter Guilday. Westminster, MD, Newman Press, 1954. xi, 358p. LC 54-11373.

Contains thirteen pastoral letters, all but one of which were written by the bishops of the U. S. assembled, as has become the custom in America. They deal with the religious and social problems of the day and the decisions reached by the bishops at their meetings. Notes and index by the editor.

E90   **Origins, N(ational) C(atholic) Documentary Service.** Washington, DC, National Catholic News Service, 1971- . v. Weekly. ISSN 0093-609X.

American ecclesiastical documents of all kinds as well as Papal and other Roman documents are reprinted in this periodical along with brief documented surveys of current issues affecting the Church. Quarterly author and subject indexes are issued and cumulated annually. This work was preceded by *Documentary Service* (Washington, DC, National Catholic Welfare Conference, 1965?-1971).

E91   O'Toole, James M. **Guide to the Archives of the Archdiocese of Boston.** New York, Garland, 1982. 328p. Index. LC 80-8989. ISBN 0-8240-9359-3.

Arranged in two parts: 1. An overview and description of the entire collection as well as the more than 200 series of records in the Archives; 2. A detailed description of the papers of the first four bishops of Boston covering the years 1797-1907. Glossary. Index.

E92   **Our Bishops Speak: National Pastorals and Annual Statements of the Hierarchy of the United States, Resolutions of Episcopal Committees and Communications of the Administrative Board of the National Catholic Welfare Conference, 1919-1951.** Milwaukee, Bruce Pub. Co., 1952. xxxiii, 402p. LC 56-6477.

A continuation of the pastoral letters, but also contains the resolutions of the various episcopal committees and communications of the administrative board of the National Catholic Welfare Conference, and resolutions and letters of the hierarchy sent to individuals. Notes and index.

E93   **Pastoral Letters of the American Hierarchy, 1792-1970.** Hugh J. Nolan, ed. Huntington, IN, Our Sunday Visitor, 1971. xiv, 785p. LC 74-160366.

This compilation contains all of the Pastoral Letters found in Guilday (E89) and *Our Bishops Speak* (E92), but Guilday has a more thorough index for the first thirteen letters and *Our Bishops Speak* contains some peripheral documents not reprinted here. This work, however, is a convenient grouping of all the pastorals and statements "that had the approval of the entire American hierarchy. Only when this general approval could be ascertained . . . were statements included in this volume." A general index, introductory essays on each period and a chronology of American Catholic Church history are supplied.

E94   **Pastoral Letters of the United States Catholic Bishops, 1792-1983.** Hugh J. Nolan, editor. Washington, DC, National Conference of Catholic Bishops, United States Catholic Conference, 1983-84. 4 v. il. LC 84-173104.

This latest compilation of national pastorals is a monumental work and includes all documents found in previous collections. Each volume has its own index. Documents are presented chronologically and in numbered paragraphs. Introductions precede each major historical period. Lacks a single cumulative index.

DICTIONARIES AND ENCYCLOPEDIAS

E95   **American Catholic Historical Society of Philadelphia. Records. Index vols. 1-31, 1884-1920.** Philadelphia, the Society, 1924. iii, 515p. LC 8-20408-10x.

Because of the brief explanatory information given for each term and name listed, this work is more like a dictionary or encyclopedia than an index. (The second index volume, 1921-30, gives page references only.)

HANDBOOKS

E96   Eberhardt, Newman C. **A Survey of American Church History.** St. Louis, Herder, 1964. ix, 308p. LC 64-7636.

Based on the author's *Summary of Catholic History* (E17), this work treats North and South America chronologically and provides bibliography and a detailed subject index.

E97   Putz, Louis J. **The Catholic Church, U. S. A.** Contributors: John J. Wright and others. Chicago, Fides Pub. Assoc., 1956. xxiii, 415p. LC 56-11629.

The lack of bibliographies makes this work less valuable as a reference source than it could have been. It does contain, however, clear and concise statements by recognized authorities on a wide variety of topics ranging from regional histories of the Church in the U. S. to the financial structure of the Church in general—something one does not often come across.

THE PAPACY

BIBLIOGRAPHY

In addition to the two works listed below, many of the general bibliographies listed in Chapters I and II contain sections on the Papacy.

E98   **Les Actes pontificaux originaux des Archives nationales de Paris.** Città del Vaticano, Biblioteca Apostolica Vaticana, 1975- . v. il. LC 76-461354. (Index actorum Romanorum pontificum ab Innocentio III ad Martinum V electum).

This work represents the French part of a project to catalog every papal document issued from 1198 to 1417. While it may not be complete, it is more so than Potthast (E107) or most other sources usually consulted (*English Historical Review*, XCII [July, 1977], p. 642-23). For each item an abstract in Latin, signatures and notes are given. Indexes of scribes, distributors, proctors, incipits, and persons, places, subjects.

E99   **Archivum historiae pontificiae.** Romae, Pontificia Università gregoriana, 1963- . v. Annual. LC 65-55675.

Each volume contains a series of articles on the papacy; book reviews, and a thorough bibliography of books and articles citing reviews of the books listed. List of periodicals indexed. Author index.

SOURCES

Because of their wide scope and frequently brilliant contents, the encyclical letters of the modern popes from about the middle of the nineteenth century have been the subject of much study and publication. Texts of these documents may be found in *Acta Sanctae Sedis* (E121) and its successor *Acta Apostolicae Sedis* (E120). English translations have always been available in pamphlet form and in numerous collections, some of which are listed here.

Sister Claudia Carlen has done English-speaking papal scholars a great service by compiling her five-volume collection of modern encyclicals (E114). Here for the first time is a comprehensive and detailed index to these important documents.

E100   **Bibliothèque des écoles françaises d'Athènes et de Rome.** Paris, E. Thorin (1ᵉ série), 1877- ; (2ᵉ série), 1884- ; (3ᵉ série), 1882- . v.

Contains the *regestae* of thirteenth and fourteenth century popes including a fine edition of the *Liber pontificalis* (E110).

E101   **Acta pontificium romanorum inedita.** Gesammelt und hrsg. von J. von Pflugk-Harttung. Tübingen, F. Fues, 1881-88. 3 v. Reprint: Graz, 1958. LC 2-20750.

A supplement to the larger collections of papal documents giving the texts of unpublished letters and documents for the period 97-1191. Indexes of names, places and subjects in each volume.

E102   **Bullarum, diplomatum et privilegiorum sanctorum romanorum pontificum taruinensis editio locupletior facta collectione novissima plurium brevium, epistolarum, decretorum actorumque S. Sedis a S. Leone Magno usque ad praesens cura et studio collegii adlecti Romae virorum S. theologiae et ss. canonum peritorum quam ss. d. n. Pius papa IX apostolica benedictione exexit auspicante emo ac revmo dno S. R. E. cardinale Francisco Gaude.** Augustae Taurinorum. Seb. Franco et Henrico Dalmazzo editoribus. 1857-72. 25 v. LC 8-857.

Continued by E103.

E103   **Bullarium Benedicti (et) Bullarii romani continuatio.** Prati, In Typographia Aldine 1845-57. 9 v. in 14.

The Tomassetti, or "Turin Bullarium" as it is called, was undertaken to replace the Mainardi edition with better printing, arrangement, and fuller inclusion of documents, but according to Herbert Thurston, "the additions are insignificant and the typographical errors are numerous. Moreover, among the documents added are included some whose authenticity is more than doubtful. . . . Mainardi's *Magnum Bullarium* (E104) still remains the most accurate and practically useful" ("Bullarium," *Catholic Encyclopedia*, III, p. 50).

E104   **Magnum bullarium Romanum; bullarum, privilegiorum ac diplomatum Romanorum Pontificium amplissima collectio.** Graz, Akademische Druck-u. Verlagsanstalt, 1964-66. 18 v. in 13.

E105 **Magnum bullarium Romanum; bullarum, privilegiorum ac diplomatum Romanorum Pontificium amplissima collectio. Continuatio.** 1963- . v. LC 65-85583.

A reprint of the Mainardi edition of 1733-62. The documents in this collection are mostly papal bulls, i.e. official letters carrying a certain type of seal and usually dealing with administrative or diplomatic topics. They are reprinted here beginning with the reign of Leo the Great (440) and ending with Clement XII (1740). The continuation was done in the nineteenth century and covers up to Pius VIII (1830).

E106 **Regesta pontificum romanorum ab condita ecclesia ad annum post Christum natum MCXCVIII,** edidit Philippus Jaffe. Editionem secundam correctam et auctam auspiciis Guiliemi Wattenbach. Lipsiae, Viet, 1885-88. 2 v. Reprinted: Graz, 1956. LC 2-17748.

A list of papal letters and documents arranged chronologically by popes giving the date, place of issue, the addressee, topic, opening words and sources of the text. An "Index initiorum" and appendix treating of spurious documents are added features.

E107 **Regesta pontificum romanorum inde ab a. post Christum natum MCXCVIII ad a. MCCCIV,** edidit Augustus Potthast. Opus ab Academia litterarum berolinensi duplici praemio ornatum eiusque subsidiis liberalissime concessis editum. Berolini, R. Decker, 1874-75. 2 v. LC 2-17749.

A continuation of Jaffe's list (E106) up to the year 1304 but without an "Index initiorum."

E108 **Regesta pontificium romanorum.** Iubente Regia societate gottingensi opes porrigentibus euratoribus Legati wedekindiani congessit Albertus Brackmann. Berolini, Weidmannos, 1906- . v.
　　Italia pontificia, 1906- . v. LC AC35-2939.
　　Germania pontificia, 1910- . v. LC AC35-2938.

An expansion and re-arrangement of the material in Jaffe (E106) and Potthast (E107). More documents are listed with longer annotations, but only two countries have been covered to date.

E109 **The Book of the Popes. Liber pontificalis.** Trans. with an intro. by Louis Ropes Loomis. New York, Octagon Books, 1965- . v. LC 65-9020.

The *Liber pontificalis* is one of the oldest sources for the history of the papacy. Written by various biographers from the seventh century to the fifteenth, it contains brief biographies and lists of accomplishments of the popes beginning with St. Peter.

E110 **Liber pontificalis.** Texte, introduction et commentaire par l'abbé Duchesne. Paris, E. Thorin, 1886-92. 2 v. LC A14-154.

The "best complete edition" (Paetow [E38], p. 125).

E111 Mirbt, Karl. **Quellen zur Geschichte des Papsttums und des römischen Katholizismus.** 3 verb. und verm. Aufl. Tübingen, Mohr, 1911. xxiv, 514p. LC 11-24704.

A "convenient, well selected, scholarly collection giving the Latin texts of some of the most important sources for the history of the papacy and of Catholic doctrine" (George M. Dutcher, *Guide to Historical Literature* [New York, Macmillan, 1936] , p. 240). Sources are indicated. Index.

E112   **Pontificia americana: A Documentary History of the Catholic Church in the United States (1784-1884).** By Reverend Donald C. Shearer. Washington, DC, The Catholic University of America Press, 1933. xi, 413p. LC 33-30687.

A collection of papal documents dealing with the Church in America from 1784 to 1884. Introductions and brief summaries in English are given for each document, but the texts are in Latin. Index. *See also United States Documents in the Propagande Fide Archives* (E74).

MODERN COLLECTIONS

E113   **Colección completa Enciclicas Pontificias, 1832-1965.** 4ª ed. corr. y aum. Por el P. Federico Hoyos, S. V. D. Buenos Aires, Editorial Guadalupe, 1965. 2 v.

One of the more complete collections of modern encyclicals. A full subject index (523pp.) is perhaps its most useful feature. Also contains indexes of sacred scripture, popes, persons and places, and a chronological list of documents.

E114   **The Papal Encyclicals, 1740-1981.** Compiled by Claudia Carlen. Wilmington, NC, McGrath, 1981. 5 v. LC 81-84885. ISBN 0-8434-0765-4.

The first comprehensive collection of Papal Encyclicals in English. Contains the complete texts of 280 encyclicals from Benedict XIV to John Paul II. Each document is followed by a citation to the original (usually Latin) text, reference notes from the document and a bibliography of commentaries on the text. Of special value is the 82-page subject index in vol. 5. "A reference work that will be put to use by students and scholars for generations to come ... truly one of its kind and is not likely to be surpassed" (*Theological Studies*, XLIII [September, 1982], p. 529).

E115   **Papal Teachings.** Boston, St. Paul Editions, 1958-63. 9 v.

Each of the volumes in this series is composed of documents or excerpts on one subject, such as peace, education, the liturgy, women, the Church, the laity, the human body, marriage, and Mary. Classified and alphabetical indexes are supplied along with references to texts in the original languages.

E116   **Social Wellsprings.** Selected, arr. and ann. by Joseph Husslein. Milwaukee, Bruce Pub. Co., 1940-42. 2 v. LC 41-1099.

Contains the complete texts of thirty-two of the most significant social encyclicals of Leo XIII and Pius XI with an index in each volume.

E117   Pius XII. Pope. 1939-58. **Discoursi e radiomessaggi di sua santiti Pio XII.** Romae, Tipografia Poliglotta Vaticana, 1940-66. 21 v. LC A52-32.
        V. 21 Indice analitico delle materie contenute nell'opera completa del P. Igino Tubaldo.

The collected speeches of Pius XII who was renowned for his ability to speak meaningfully to people from all walks of life.

E118   John XXIII, Pope. 1958-63. **Discoursi, messaggi, coloqui del santo padre Giovanni XXIII.** Romae, Tipografia Poliglotta Vaticana, 1960-67. 6 v.
  V. 6. Indice delle materie contenute nei cinque volumi die discoursi, messaggi, colloqui del Santo Padre Giovanni XXIII.

John XXIII's complete speeches.

E119   Paul VI, Pope, 1963- . **Insegnamenti di Paolo VI.** Romae, Tipografia Poliglotta Vaticana, 1963- . v.

(Indice analitico delle materie contenute nei primi cinque volumi del P. Igino Tubaldo. 1969).

Speeches of Paul VI.

CURRENT

E120   **Acta Apostolicae Sedis: commentarius officiale.** Città del Vaticano, Typis Polyglottis Vaticanis, 1909- . v. Frequency varies. LC 51-35381. ISSN 0001-5199.

Contains most of the documents and speeches of the popes, the acts and decisions of the congregations and other curial bodies, and the decrees of the recent council in their official versions. Issues appear about thirteen to fourteen times per year along with an annual index. The language of the documents is Latin or, in the case of speeches, that in which they were given. Documentation and cross references to other documents in the series are given.

E121   **Acta Sanctae Sedis: ephemerides romanae a SSMO D.M. Pio PP. X authenticae et officiales Apostolicae Sedis actis publice evulgandis declaratae.** Romae, Ex Typographia Polyglotta S. C. de Propaganda Fide, 1865-1908. 41 v. Reprinted: New York, Johnson Reprint, 1970- . LC 51-53035.

An unofficial journal for most of its life, it served the same purpose as the *Acta Apostolicae Sedis* which succeeded it.

E122   **Catholic Documentation: A Quarterly Periodical Devoted to the Publication in Australia and New Zealand of Papal, Ecclesiastical, and Other Authoritative Statements on Matters of General Interest.** Sydney, Catholic Press Newspaper Co., 1955- . v. ISSN 0008-8005.

In addition to papal documents, contains those of the Roman Curia and selected sources all over the world. Indexes.

E123   **Catholic Documents: Containing Recent Pronouncements and Decisions of His Holiness.** London, Pontifical Court Club, 1950-56. 20 v. Quarterly. LC 55-23526.

Published quarterly with two cumulative indexes for volumes 1-10 and 11-20.

E124   **L'Osservatore romano, Weekly Edition in English.** Vatican City, 1968- .
v. il.

Contains virtually all Papal documents and speeches as well as Church documents from all over the world. Roman Curial documents are also reprinted.
Articles of general interest and book reviews are also provided along with
the daily schedule of the pope.

E125   **The Pope Speaks: The Church Documents Quarterly.** Washington, DC,
1954- . v. Quarterly. LC 57-58247. ISSN 0032-4353.

Contains selected papal documents in English translation. "News and Notes"
of papal activities, "Brief Messages and Excerpts" of speeches and letters,
and a continuing bibliography of all papal documents for the preceding
quarter. The "T.P.S. Log," as it is called, is arranged chronologically by
date of publication and gives the title, subject, type of document, number
of words and references to the original text and translations. Annual
indexes. *See also Origins* (E90) for weekly publication of Papal and Roman
documents.

DICTIONARIES

E126   Bacci, Antonio, Cardinal. **Varia latinitatis scripta.** Ed. 4. Romae, Societas
Libaria "studium," 1963- . v. LC 65-82537.

V. 1. Lexicon vocabularum quae difficilius Latine reduntur.
V. 2. Inscriptiones, orationes, epistulae.

The first volume of this work is especially helpful to those who have to
translate Latin texts of modern papal documents since it lists Latin equivalents for modern words.

GUIDES

E127   Carlen, Sister Mary Claudia. **Dictionary of Papal Pronouncements, Leo XIII
to Pius XII, 1878-1957.** New York, P. J. Kenedy, 1958. 216p. LC 58-12095.

A guide to papal documents and a bibliography of texts and translations.
Nearly 800 encyclicals, speeches and other documents are arranged alphabetically by opening words (i.e. their titles), giving date, addressee, topic,
a brief resume, and references to full texts. For documents after 1958 see
The Pope Speaks (E125) or *The Catholic Periodical and Literature Index*
(A160).

E128   Carlen, Sister Mary Claudia. **Guide to the Documents of Pius XII, 1939-
1949.** Westminster, MD, Newman Press, 1951. xxviii, 229p. LC 51-11369.

Replaced by *Dictionary of Papal Pronouncements* (E127) except that it
lists more documents and more translations.

E129   Carlen, Sister Mary Claudia. **A Guide to the Encyclicals of the Roman Pontiffs from Leo XIII to the Present Day (1878-1937).** New York, H.W.Wilson,
1939. 247p. LC 39-13091. Reprinted: New York, Scolarly Press, 1977.
ISBN 0-403-07171-2.

An earlier version of the *Dictionary of Papal Pronouncements* (E127); still valuable for references to commentaries on documents not included in the later work.

E130   **The Papal Encyclicals in their Historical Context.** By Anne Fremantle. New York, New American Library, 1963. 448p. LC 64-2656.

Contains texts or excerpts of many of the better known encyclicals along with a history of papal letter writing from St. Peter to Pius XII. Introductions to the texts provide the historical background of the pronouncements in clear, readable style. Index.

DICTIONARIES AND ENCYCLOPEDIAS

E131   Attwater, Donald. **A Dictionary of the Popes from Peter to Pius XII.** London, Burns, Oates and Washbourne, 1939. vi, 336p. LC 40-5687.

A biographical dictionary devoting several pages to the more famous popes and only a paragraph or two to the lesser known. Each pope is represented by a picture or engraving. Chronological arrangement with index.

E132   John, Eric, ed. **The Popes: A Concise Biographical History.** London, Burns and Oates, 1964. 496p. il. LC 64-12422.

Arranged chronologically with general introductions to various periods followed by a name-by-name biographical section. Each pope is the subject of at least one illustration. No bibliographies. Index.

E133   Kelly, John Norman Davidson. **The Oxford Dictionary of Popes.** Oxford, Oxford University Press, 1986. xiii, 347p. LC 85-15599. ISBN 0-19-213964-9.

Well written, candid biographies of all the popes from Peter to John Paul II. Bibliographies are supplied for all entries. The arrangement is chronological but an "Alphabetical List of Popes and Antipopes" and a detailed name and subject index are given. "The book is thoroughly researched, entertainingly written and attractively produced" (*Tablet*, CCXL [May 17, 1986], p. 514).

E134   Kühner, Hans. **Encyclopedia of the Papacy.** Trans. from the German by Kenneth J. Northcott. New York, Philosophical Library, 1958. 249p. LC 58-4521.

Very brief biographies with dates and some historical background.

HISTORY

The most scholarly and detailed papal histories are Mann's (E138) and Pastor's (E139), which together cover the period from 590 to 1799 fairly objectively. They are unsurpassed in the amount of research involved in their composition.

E135   Brusher, Joseph Stanislaus. **Popes through the Ages: Photos.** Coll. and Ed. by Emanual Borden. Princeton, NJ, Van Nostrand, 1959, xiii, 530p. il. LC 59-14622.

A pictorial history of the popes containing little more than the 259 portraits of popes from St. Peter to John XXIII.

E136   Coffin, Joseph. **Coins of the Popes**. New York, Coward-McCann, 1946. 169p.
         LC 46-3783.

         477 coins are described in a list arranged alphabetically by inscriptions. 84 of the
         coins are illustrated in plates. Indexes are provided for persons mentioned on the
         coins and engravers. Bibliography. Index of Plates.

E137   Galbreath, Donald Lindsay. **Papal Heraldry**. 2nd. ed. rev. by G. Briggs.
         London, Heraldry Today, 1972 (Dist. by Gale). xix, 135p. il. LC 73-155728.
         ISBN 0-90045522-5.

         Covers 9 centuries of the papacy (Innocent III-Paul VI) with additional
         material for earlier popes and the papacy in general. For each pope a brief
         family history, a description of his coat of arms and an illustration are
         provided. There are 206 illustrations and 8 color plates. A list of popes and
         an index are also included.

E138   Mann, Horace Kinder. **The Lives of the Popes in the Early Middle Ages**.
         London, K. Paul, Trench, Trubner and Co., 1902-32. 18 v. in 19. il. LC
         4-16966.

         Covers the lives and times of the popes from Gregory the Great (590) to
         Benedict XI (1304). Each biography is prefaced by a short critical intro-
         duction on the sources used and a list of the contemporary civil rulers of
         the world. The biographies are documented with bibliographical and ex-
         planatory notes, and the appendixes contain the texts of many important
         documents. Each volume is indexed, and later volumes contain some illus-
         trations. This work, one of the two great histories of the popes (*see* Pastor
         [E139]), was written by "the leading English R. C. authority in this field"
         (George M. Dutcher, *Guide to Historical Literature* [New York, Macmillan,
         1936], p. 269). *Catholic World* described it as well-written, scholarly, and
         honest in its criticism (CXXVI [March, 1933], pp. 760-62).

E139   Pastor, Ludwig, Freiherr von. **The History of the Popes from the Close of
         the Middle Ages: Drawn from the Secret Archives of the Vatican and Other
         Original Sources**. London, J. Hodges, 1891-1940. 32 v. LC 24-12249.

         Begun before Mann's history, this work, nevertheless, follows his chrono-
         logically, starting with Pope Clement V (1305) and ending with Pius VI
         (1799). It contains longer biographies than Mann in most cases—sometimes
         devoting more than one volume to one pope and at others grouping a whole
         series in one volume (e.g., "The Avignon Popes"). Frequent and lengthy
         bibliographies appear throughout the work, along with an index in each
         volume and many useful appendixes. As *America* pointed out, this is the
         first history of the popes based on the original sources in the Vatican Ar-
         chives, which were not previously open to scholars (XXV [June 18, 1921],
         p. 208). The work has been very favorably reviewed in *Catholic World* and
         America, almost volume by volume as they appeared. (*See Guide to Catholic
         Literature* [A56], v. 1, pp. 736 and 900.) The *American Historical Review*,
         however, criticized Pastor for his "ultramontanism, excessive caution and
         half apologetic tone," but also credited him with a balanced sense of criti-
         cism and abundant erudition (XXXIV [January, 1929], p. 407).

E140   **The Popes through History.** Ed. by Raymond H. Schmandt. London, Burns and Oates, 1961- . v.

"A series consisting of the biographies of the most important popes who reigned in the times of particular crisis for the Church" (Intro., v. 1). Three volumes have appeared so far: *Eugenius IV: Pope of Christian Union* by Joseph Gill (1961), *The Ancient Popes* by Edward G. Welton (1964) which treats the forty-four popes prior to Leo I, and *Alexander III and the Twelfth Century* by Marshall Baldwin (1968). Each volume contains a bibliographical essay on the sources used and an index.

E141   Seppelt, Franz Xaver. **Geschichte der Päpste von den Abfängen bis zur Mitte des zwanzigsten Jahrhunderts.** 2. neubearb. Aufl. München, Kosel, 1954- . v. LC A55-1064.

A five-volume work covering the entire span of papal history down to the year 1799 (despite the title). Each volume contains an extensive bibliography and an index. *American Catholic Historical Review* praised this work for its dispassionate treatment of controversial issues, its scholarliness and clearly envisaged plan (XVIII [September, 1932] , p. 369). An English adaptation of the first edition appeared as *A Short History of the Popes: Authorized Adaptation from the German.* By Horace A. C. Frommelt (St. Louis, B. Herder Book Co., 1932. vi, 567p.).

COUNCILS

The largest collection of conciliar documents, Mansi's (E145), has recently been reprinted. In 1977, the Vatican completed publication of the *Acta* of Vatican II (E151).

Among the other significant works in this section are Palazzini's *Dizionario dei Concili* (E167), an index to all ecumenical and local councils; Deretz's *Dictionary of the Council* (E164), a subject arrangement of the decrees of Vatican II; and the *Commentary on the documents of Vatican II* (E152), containing both the texts and expert analysis.

SOURCES

E142   **Acta conciliorum oecumenicorum.** Societas Scientiarum Argentoratensis. Ed. Eduardus Schwartz. Berlin, de Gruyter, 1914-40. 4 v. in 25.

Probably the most useful collection of conciliar documents because of its completeness and full indexing. Unfortunately only the third, fourth and fifth ecumenical councils (Ephesus, Chalcedon and Constantinople) had been covered by 1940 when work on the project was abandoned. Nevertheless, for the councils included, this series, which had already reached 25 volumes, is the "most important work on the sources of the councils" (Hubert Jedin, *Ecumenical Councils of the Catholic Church* [E168], p. 224).

E143   **Conciliorum oecumenicorum decreta.** Bologna, Freiburg, Herder, 1962. 729+72p.

Contains the decrees in Latin of the twenty ecumenical councils prior to Vatican II printed in chronological order with documentation and a series of detailed indexes to scriptural passages, canon law, sources, names, and subjects. ([E144] contains English translations of much the same material.)

E144 **Disciplinary Decrees of the General Councils.** Text, trans., and comm. by Rev. H. J. Schroeder. St. Louis, MO, Herder Book Co., 1937. viii, 669p. LC 37-14731.

Original texts and English translations of the disciplinary decrees of all ecumenical councils except for Trent and Vatican I. The same translator issued a separate collection for Trent (E146), and the First Vatican Council did not issue any disciplinary decrees. Index.

E145 **Sacrorum conciliorum, nova et amplissima collectio.** Graz, Akademische Druck-u Verlagsanstalt, 1960-61. 53 v. in 60.

This collection, first edited by Giovanni Domenico Mansi in 1757-98 and continued by Petit and Martin of Paris from 1889 to 1927, is the largest source of conciliar documents and the "standard collection" (Jedin [E168], p. 242). Contains, in addition to the documents of the general or ecumenical councils, those of many local councils. Decrees, letters, and other related documents are included in Latin and Greek with Latin translations. Although universally recognized as the most exhaustive collection, this work has been criticized for being too inclusive and difficult to use because of its lack of indexes (A. Boudinhon, "Mansi," *Catholic Encyclopedia*, IX, p. 610), no small defect in a 60 volume work. For documents of the Second Vatican Council see E153.

COUNCIL OF TRENT (1545-63)

E146 **Canons and Decrees of the Council of Trent: Original Text with English Translation.** By the Rev. H. J. Schroeder. St. Louis, MO, Herder Book Co., 1941. xxxiii, 608p. LC 41-21651.

A companion to the translator's *Disciplinary Decrees of the General Councils* (E144) containing the original Latin text and an English translation of the legislation passed by the Council with subject indexes.

E147 **Catechism of the Council of Trent for Parish Priests.** Issued by Order of Pope Pius V. Trans. into English with notes by John A. McHugh and Charles J. Callan. New York, Joseph F. Wagner, 1923. LC 23-6519.

The standard source of Catholic instruction on which other catechisms were based including the American Baltimore Catechism. It answers basic questions on the creed, the sacraments, the commandments and prayer. Frequent references to scripture and St. Thomas are given.

E148 **Concilium Tridentinum: diariorum, actorum, epistolarum, tractatum, nova collectio.** Societas Goerresiana. Freiburg, Herder, 1901-24. 10 v.

"The definitive source collection for the Council of Trent" (*Dublin Review*, CLII [April, 1963], p. 198), which Council largely determined the course of Post-Reformation Catholicism. Contains all the decrees as well as debates and related documents with indexes.

VATICAN COUNCIL I (1869-70)

E149   MacGregor, Geddes. **The Vatican Revolution**. Boston, Beacon Press, 1957.
xiv, 226p. LC 57-6524.

"The Text of the Vatican Decrees with an English Translation and Notes,"
pp. 165-197. The first part of the book covers the history and background
of the Council. Bibliography, pp. 205-216.

VATICAN COUNCIL II (1962-65)

BIBLIOGRAPHY

E150   Dollen, Charles. **Vatican II: A Bibliography**. Metuchen, NJ, Scarecrow
Press, 1969. 208p. LC 70-8394.

A listing of over 2,500 books and articles in English arranged by author
with a subject index. No annotations.

SOURCES

E151   **Acta synodalia Sacrosancti Concilii Oecumenici Vaticani II**. Vatican City,
Typis Polyglottis Vaticanis, 1970-77. 4 v. in 20. LC 74-302310.

The official *Acta* for Vatican II, this work contains the text of every speech
given and every document promulgated at the Council. Supporting documents and a record of each vote are also provided. Each volume contains
its own indexes.

E152   **Commentary on the Documents of Vatican II**. Herbert Vorgrimler, gen. ed.
New York, Herder and Herder, 1967-69. 5 v. LC 67-22928.

Contains a general introduction to each document, the text, and a commentary on each article of the document. Although criticized for errata and
omissions, the work is quite generally regarded as a "standard work for
reference, research, and reflection" (*Journal of Ecumenical Studies*, V
[Fall, 1968], p. 763).

E153   **The Conciliar and Post Conciliar Documents**. Austin Flannery, gen. ed.
Wilmington, DE, Scholarly Resources, Inc., 1975. xxiv, 1062p. LC 76-3401.
ISBN 0-8420-2079-9.

Contains the 16 original documents of the Council and 49 documents issued
subsequently by Pope Paul VI and various curial bodies. A list of 250 additional "More Important Postconciliar Documents" is contained in an appendix
with references to the texts. An index of subjects and initial words is supplied.

E154   **Constitutiones, decreta, declarationes, cura et studio Secretariae generalis
Concilii oecumenici Vaticani II.** Romae, Typis Polyglottis Vaticanis, 1966.
xxiv, 292p.

The official Latin texts of the sixteen decrees of the Council. Index.

E155   **The Documents of Vatican II: Introductions and Commentaries by Catholic Bishops and Experts: Responses by Protestant and Orthodox Scholars.** Walter M. Abbott, gen. ed. Joseph Gallagher, trans. editor. New York, Guild Press, 1966. xxi, 794p. LC 66-20201.

Contains translations of the sixteen documents and many other important documents and speeches related to the Council, with commentary by well known Catholic and non-Catholic authorities on each decree. Contains the best index available to all the documents in English.

E156   **Documents of Vatican II: The Conciliar and Post Conciliar Documents.** Austin P. Flannery, editor. Grand Rapids, MI, Eerdmans, 1975-82. 2 v. LC 75-18840. ISBN 0-8028-1623-1.

Volume one is a reprint of E153. Volume two, titled *Vatican Council II, More Postconciliar Documents*, contains fifty-six additional papal and curial documents arranged in seven categories. Name and subject indexes.

E157   Hastings, Adrian. **A Concise Guide to the Documents of the Second Vatican Council.** London, Darton, Longman and Todd, 1968. 2 v. LC 70-381885. ISBN 0-2325-0943-3.

For each of the major documents there is a summary, an explanation, a history of the text, a bibliography, and questions for classroom use. Index.

E158   **The Sixteen Documents of Vatican II and the Instruction on the Liturgy: With Commentary by the Council Fathers.** Boston, St. Paul Editions, 1967. 760p. LC 66-19616.

Contains no index.

E159   **The Teachings of the Second Vatican Council: Complete Texts of the Constitutions, Decrees and Declarations.** Intro. by Gregory Baum. Westminster, MD, Newman Press, 1966. xi, 676p. LC 66-19960.

Most of the translations are those done by the National Catholic Welfare Conference. An appendix contains a selection of related papal documents and the same index to the Council documents to be found in the Abbot edition (E155).

INDEXES

E160   **Indices verborum et locutionum decretorum Concilii Vaticani II.** Firenze, Vallecchi, 1968- . v. LC 70-389280.

The most complete index and concordance to Vatican II documents available. Each volume is devoted to one or more documents, giving the complete text in Latin, a concordance of words used in the documents (given in context), and indexes of papal, conciliar, and patristic quotations found in the documents.

E161   Spiecker, Rochus. **Register zu den Konzilsdokumenten und Uebersichtsschemata verwendbar für alle Ausgaben.** Luzern, Rex-Verlag, 1966. 190p. LC 68-40473.

An alphabetical subject index to the documents of Vatican II.

E162   Tardif, H., and G. Pelloquin, eds. **Index et concordance, Vatican II.** Paris, Les Editions Ouvrières, 1969. 252p. LC 78-473110.

The first part is made up of indexes to citations from the Old and New Testaments, former councils, the Fathers, and recent popes. Part II is a "concordance of words" in Latin listing nouns, adjectives, verbs (except *sum*), and important adverbs. The reference is to the article of the document in which the word appears.

DICTIONARIES

E163   **Dizionario del Concilio ecumenico Vaticano secondo.** In collaborazione. Direttore Salvatore Garofalo, redattore capo Tommaso Federici. Roma, UNEDI, 1969. xv, 2034 col. LC 77-463610.

Contains the texts of the Council documents and an alphabetical dictionary of topics treated by the Council. The articles are of moderate length, are signed, contain references to and quotes from the documents, and some provide a bibliography.

E164   Deretz, Jacques, and A. Nocent, eds. **Dictionary of the Council.** Washington, DC, Corpus Books, 1968. 506p. LC 69-14374.

Contains excerpts from the documents of Vatican II arranged by subject under nearly 500 headings with cross references. "For the professor . . . for the student . . . and for the general reader this book is simply a necessity" (*Theological Studies*, XXX [June, 1969], p. 382).

An abridged version of *Synopse des textes conciliares* (Paris, Editions Universitaires, 1966).

E165   Molina Martínez, Miguel Angel. **Diccionario del Vaticano II.** Madrid, Editorial Católica, 1969. xiii, 651p. LC 72-230844.

An index to the documents giving quotations from the texts under subject headings.

E166   Torres Calvo, Angel. **Diccionario de los textos conciliares (Vaticano II).** Madrid, Compañía Bibliografica Española, 1968. 2 v. 2145p. LC 76-406497.

A thorough index to the Council documents. Excerpts from the documents are quoted under alphabetically arranged subject headings.

DICTIONARIES

E167   **Dizionario dei concili.** Diretto da Pietro Palazzini. Roma, Città Nuova Editrice, 1963-67. 6 v.

An alphabetical listing of all the councils of the Church, local and general, giving their dates, a brief summary of their major accomplishments and references to histories and printed sources.

HANDBOOKS

E168   Jedin, Hubert. **Ecumenical Councils of the Catholic Church: An Historical Outline.** Trans. by Ernest Graf. New York, Herder and Herder, 1960. 253p. LC 59-15483.

A brief, handy work by an expert on the subject containing the histories of twenty ecumenical councils with Trent and Vatican I receiving the fullest treatment. Conciliarism is also covered. A critical bibliography on the history and sources of councils in general and each council in particular appears on pp. 240-250.

E169   Raab, Clement. **The Twenty Ecumenical Councils of the Catholic Church.** Westminster, MD, Newman Press, 1959. 226p. LC 60-2894.

A source of basic information on each council—dates, reasons for its convocation, historical background and the proceedings of the council by session. Index.

RELIGIOUS ORDERS

The reference books listed under "General Works" include a number of directories and dictionaries listing religious orders by name with brief information. Some of them were compiled for prospective candidates and others as reference works. Kapsner's *Catholic Religious Orders* (E189) is easily the most complete source of brief information in English in this field. The *Dizionario degli istitute di perfezione* (E181), which began publication in 1974, is the most important new work to appear since the 1930s.

Under the names of individual religious orders are reference works, mostly bio-bibliographies of a comprehensive nature, i.e. covering the order as a whole or one province of the order for a long period of time. Where one work has replaced many smaller collections as in the case of the Jesuits, the smaller works are not listed. The Jesuits, Franciscans, and Carmelites have the best bibliographical control of all the orders listed—even to the point of issuing annual bibliographies.

GENERAL WORKS

BIBLIOGRAPHY

E170   **Checklist of Manuscripts Microfilmed for the Monastic Manuscript Microfilm Library.** Collegeville, MN, St. John's University Library, 1967- . v.

Vol. 1, pts. 1 and 2 cover Austrian monasteries. Consists only of a list of manuscript codex numbers and the project number of the microfilm.

E171   Constable, Giles. **Medieval Monasticism: A Select Bibliography.** Toronto, University of Toronto Press, 1976. xx, 171p. LC 75-42284. (*Toronto Medieval Bibliographies*, 6). ISBN 0-8020-2200-6.

Lists and annotates 1,036 books and articles in broad subject categories—history, economics, clothing, rules, education, works, vows, governance, etc. Concentrates on the cloistered orders and covers books in Western languages. The material is selected to provide a comprehensive view of monasticism rather than histories of individual houses or monks. "Reliable, intelligently planned and carefully cross-referenced" (*RQ*, XVII [Fall, 1977], p. 74).

E172   Cottineau, L. H. **Répertoire topo-bibliographique des abbayes et prieurés.** Mâcon, Protat Frères, 1935-70. 3 v. LC 37-20490.

Both a dictionary and a bibliography; lists by place all the religious houses of the rank of abbey or priory giving a brief history of each and an extensive bibliography. Medieval houses and benefices no longer in existence are included as are modern houses in all countries, including America. This is an important reference source for both medievalists and historians of religious orders.

E173   Molette, Charles. **Guide des sources de l'histoire des congregationes féminines françaises de vie active.** Paris, Éditiones de Paris, 1974. 475p.

396 active (non-cloistered) congregations for women in France are described. Basic information is given, as well as a brief description of their archival holdings and bibliography of published works about them. Indexes.

E174   Morgan, John H. **Aging in the Religious Life: A Comprehensive Bibliography, 1960-75.** Wichita, KS, Institute on Ministry and the Elderly, 1977. xii, 34p.

Lists books and articles dealing with the problems of aging in religious orders as well as some general works on aging.

E175   Ravasi, Ladislaus R. **Fontes bibliographia de vocatione religioso et sacerdotali.** Mediolani, Edizioni Fonti vive, 1961. 139p.

A classified bibliography of books and articles on religious vocations. The lack of an index and paucity of English language titles make this work less useful than it could have been.

SOURCES

E176   **Women Religious History Sources: A Guide to Repositories in the United States.** Ed. by Evangeline Thomas with the assistance of Joyce L. White and Lois Sachtel. New York, Bowker, 1983. xxvii, 329p. LC 82-22648. ISBN 0-8352-1681-0.

Describes the archives of 569 religious orders of women in the United States, Catholic, Protestant, and Orthodox. For each order, there is a brief history, a description of the holdings of their archives and references to a general bibliography of published works. Appendices include a Glossary, Table of U.S. Founding Dates, a Biographical Register of Foundresses and Major Superiors. There is an extensive index.

INDEXES

E177   Clément, Jean Marie. **Lexique des anciennes règles monastique occidentales.** Steenbrugis, in Abbatia S. Petri, 1978. 2 v. (Instrumenta patristica, 7 A-B.) LC 78-387194.

A concordance to the Latin texts of thirty-one medieval monastic rules. A list of the editions used may be found in the front of volume one.

DICTIONARIES AND DIRECTORIES

E178   **Annuaire des instituts de religieuses en France.** Paris, Centre National des Vocations Français, 1959- . v. Irregular. ISSN 0066-2860.

Gives addresses of motherhouses and other foundations as well as brief descriptions of the work of each order.

E179   Anson, Peter Frederick. **The Religious Orders and Congregations of Great Britain and Ireland.** Worcester, Stanbrook Abbey Press, 1949. 413p. LC 50-37473.

Now superseded by the annual *Directory* (E180). Gives details of history, activities, habit, locations, etc. Index.

E180   **Directory of Religious Orders, Congregations and Societies of Great Britain and Ireland.** Glasgow, J. S. Burns, 1955- . v. Annual. LC 56-23821.

An alphabetical list of orders giving brief sketches of their histories and activities with indexes of activities and types of institutions.

E181   **Dizionario degli instituti de perfezione.** Diretto da Guerrino Pelliccia e da Giancarlo Rocca. Roma, Edizioni Paoline, 1974-1983. 7 v. LC 77-576428.

An immense work "in the tradition of the multi-volume encyclopedia-dictionaries like the *Dictionnaire d'histoire et de géographie ecclésiastiques*" (*Catholic Historical Review*, LXIII [January, 1977], p. 69). Entries are under names of orders, founders, famous monasteries, geographical areas and various aspects of the religious life. The bibliographies are extensive and list publications of orders as well as books about them. Authorities from all over the world have contributed articles. In the planning stages since 1950, this work replaces Hélyot (E187), and supplies more up to date and detailed information than may be found in most of the works listed in this section. Cross references; index volume forthcoming.

E182   Dehey, Elinor Tong. **Religious Orders of Women in the United States: Catholic. Accounts of Their Origin, Works and Most Important Institutions, Interwoven with Histories of Many Famous Foundresses.** Rev. ed. Hammond, IN, W. B. Conkey Co., 1930. xxxi, 908p. il. LC 30-22058.

Concentrates on the larger groups from which smaller orders have broken away, e.g., Sisters of Charity, Sisters of St. Joseph. Some 200 orders, however, are covered. A good source for history and lives of foundresses. Many portraits and photographs of convents and institutions. Now considerably out-of-date for current information.

E183   **Guide to Religious Communities for Women.** Edited by Deborah Barrett. Chicago, National Sisters Vocation Conference, 1983. viii, 445p. LC 83-60424.

Brief one-page descriptions of over 700 religious communities for women in the United States. Emphasis is placed on how these communities have changed since Vatican II. Arranged by broad categories, e.g. Benedictines, Franciscans, etc. Index.

E184   **A Guide to Religious Ministries for Catholic Men and Women.** New Rochelle, NY, Catholic News Publishing Co., 1987, 192p. il.

(Previous editions published as *A Guide to Religious Careers for Catholic Men and Women.*)

Contains a "Suggested Reading List," a directory of religious orders of men and women, a list of diocesan vocation directors and "profiles" or advertisements for selected orders.

E185   **The Guidepost: Religious Vocation Manual for Young Men.** Comp. by the Catholic University Conference of Clerics and Religious. 4th ed. Washington, DC, 1964. xxvii, 244p. il. LC 64-19577.

Illustrations of the work, dress, and institutions of the orders accompany a brief account of their history and work. Designed for interested candidates, this work also provides the address of the motherhouse or headquarters. This work is now replaced by (E193) but is retained here for historical reference with respect to former institutions and manners of dress.

E186   Heimbucher, Max Josef. **Die Orden und Kongregationen der katholischen Kirche.** 3. grossenteils neubearb. Aufl. Paderborn, F. Schöningh, 1933-34. 2 v. LC 35-820.

A good source of bibliography but covers fewer orders than Kapsner (E189), Hélyot (E187), or the *Dizionario* (E181). An historical treatment of individual religious orders giving some statistical information, biographies of famous members and so forth. Malclès describes it as "a capital work abounding in bibliographies."

E187   Hélyot, Pierre. **Dictionnaire des ordres religieux: ou Histoire des ordres monastiques, religieux et militaires, et des congrégations séculières de l'un et de l'autre sexe, qui ont été établies jusqu'à présent; contenant les vies de leurs fondateurs et de leur réformateurs. Avec des figures qui représentent les différents habillements de ces ordres et de ces congrégations.** Mise par ordre alphabétique, cor. et augm. d'une introduction. d'une notice sur l'auteur, d'un grande nombre d'articles ou parties d'articles, et d'un supplément où l'on trouve l'histoire des congrégations omises par Hélyot et l'histoire des sociétés religieuses établies depuis que cet auteur a publié son ouvrage, par Marie Léandre Badiche. Paris, Migne, 1859-63. 4 v. il. LC 17-22659.

Contains rather long histories of the major religious orders up to the middle of the nineteenth century. Weak in bibliography. "Catalogue" of books consulted by the author, v. 1, pp. 58-105.

E188   **Images of Women in Mission: Resource Guide and National Directory of Catholic Church Vocations for Women**. Ramsey, NJ, Paulist Press, 1981. vi, 186p. LC 81-119044. ISBN 0-80912-350-7.

Describes 180 religious congregations for women located in the United States. Index.

E189   Kapsner, Oliver Leonard. **Catholic Religious Orders: Listing Conventional and Full Names in English, Foreign Language, and Latin, Also Abbreviations, Date and Country of Origin and Founders**. 2nd. ed., enl. Collegeville, MN, St. John's Abbey Press, 1957. xxxviii, 594p. LC 57-1997.

A comprehensive and useful dictionary. "Primarily this is a list of religious orders intended for the use of library cataloguers" (Preface). All kinds of religious orders, societies, congregations, tertiaries, and military orders, surviving and extinct, are included with cross references from various forms of their names. A glossary of the terminology of religious orders is included along with an index of founders.

E190   Lexau, Joan M. **Convent Life: Roman Catholic Religious Orders for Women in North America**. New York, Dial Press, 1964. xviii, 398p. LC 64-15224.

A series of essays on contemporary American convent life and activities with a detailed "Index of Orders" (pp. 207-398) giving basic information and addresses of motherhouses.

E191   McCarthy, Thomas Patrick. **Guide to the Catholic Sisterhoods in the United States**. 5th ed. rev. and enl. Washington, DC, Catholic University of America Press, 1964. xii, 404p. il. LC 64-15336.

Companion volume to *The Guidepost* (E185) illustrating the activities and dress of about 380 religious orders of women in the U. S., each order being allotted one page for an illustration and brief description including statistics, history, and apostolic works. Indexes of variant forms of names, initials and affiliated houses. This work and *The Guidepost* are both very much out of date especially with regard to religious dress and other practices that have been reformed in the wake of Vatican II. Nevertheless, they are valuable sources of historical information since little was changed in these orders from the dates of their founding until the 1960s.

E192   McCarthy, Thomas Patrick. **Total Dedication for the Laity: A Guidebook to Secular Institutes**. Boston, St. Paul Editions, 1964. 103p. il. LC 63-23366.

Secular institutes are "societies composed of priests, laymen or laywomen who have bound themselves under vows, oaths or promises to practice the evangelical counsels of poverty, chastity and obedience for their own personal sanctification while exercising an apostolate of love for Christ within the world" (Preface). This directory explains the history, purposes, spiritual life, formation and entrance requirements for over twenty of these institutions established in the United States. A more up to date but less detailed listing may be found in (E194).

E193 **Ministries for the Lord: A Resource Guide and Directory of Church Vocations for Men**. 3rd. ed. New York, Paulist Press, 1985. 127p. LC 85-60418. ISBN 0-8091-2724-5.

Presents the history, ministry, training program and miscellaneous information for nearly 100 religious orders of men. General information on religious vocations is also supplied. Indexes.

E194 National Center for Church Vocations. **Directory of Secular Institutes with Foundations in the U. S. A.** Washington, DC, United States Catholic Conference, 1975. 12p.

This directory briefly describes 15 institutes who have members in the United States. For more detailed information see (E192).

E195 Ooms, Herwig. **Repertorium universale siglorum ordinum et institutum religiosorum in Ecclesia Catholica**. Bruxelles, Commission Belge de Bibliographie, 1959. 303p. (Bibliographia Belgica, 45.) LC 60-24977.

Members of religious orders usually affix the initials of their order to their names. These initials are frequently confusing because they may represent the Latin form of the name, a lesser known official form, or a foreign language form. Some of the works listed above contain indexes of initials, but this is the most useful source since it gives the name in Latin and all other languages in which the order is known. Dates and places of founding and the name of the founder are also supplied.

E196 Thérlault, Michel. **Les instituts de vie consacrée au Canada depuis les débuts de la Nouvelle-France jusqu'à aujourd'hui: notes historiques et références. The Institutes of Consecrated Life in Canada from the Beginning of New France up to the Present: Historical Notes and References**. Ottawa, Bibliotheque Nationale de Canada, 1980. 295p. LC 81-117842. ISBN 0-660-50453-7.

A thorough listing of all of the religious orders that have existed in Canada. Undertaken originally as a project of the National Library of Canada, Cataloguing Branch. For eacn order, there is a brief history of its origins and its presence in Canada, a list of all the names it is known by, and the standard abbreviation of its name. Alphabetical and other indexes are supplied.

HISTORY

E197 Braunfels, Wolfgang. **Monasteries of Western Europe: The Architecture of the Orders**. 3rd. ed. Princeton, NJ, Princeton University Press, 1973. il. LC 73-2472. ISBN 0-691-03896-1.

A lavishly illustrated treatment of monastic architecture, with floor plans and photographs. The arrangement is by broad subject category, e.g., major orders, types of orders, periods, etc. Selected documents are presented in the original Latin with translation. "If the book has a weakness, it lies in . . . Professor Braunfels' occasionally over-ready characterization of the various orders" (*Catholic Historical Review*, LXI [October, 1975] , p. 650).

E198 Dugdale, William. **Monasticon anglicanum; A History of the Abbies and other Monasteries, Hospitals, Frieries, and Cathedral and Collegiate Churches with Their Dependencies, in England and Wales; Also of All Such Scotch, Irish, and**

French Monasteries as Were in Any Manner Connected with Religious Houses in England. New ed. Westmead, Eng., Gregg International Publishers, 1970. 6 v. in 8.

Reprints all original documents; lists names of abbots, priors and other officers. Index. "An essential sourcebook that details the charters of foundations and other deeds of monasteries and religious houses, with a historical summary of each" (A.J. Walford, *Guide to Reference Material*, 4th ed. [London, The Library Association, 1982], v. 2, p. 59).

E199   Knowles, David, and R. Neville Hadcock. **Medieval Religious Houses: England and Wales.** New York, St. Martin's Press, 1972. xv, 565p. il. LC 76-167756. ISBN 0-312-52780-2.

This is a greatly expanded new edition of the 1953 work of the same title. Several thousands of monasteries, hospitals and secular colleges are identified. A brief history with references to documents and books is given along with numbers of monks or nuns and incomes at various times during the history of the house. The arrangement is alphabetical by the name of the house under the generic name of the religious order. There is a general index of monasteries as well as numerous appendices and a scholarly introduction by the author. (E201) and (E201) were undertaken to complete a definitive list of monastic establishments in the British Isles during the Middle Ages.

E200   Gwynn, Aubrey Osborn, and Richard Neville Hadcock. **Medieval Religious Houses: Ireland.** With an appendix to early sites. Harlow, Longmans, 1970. xii, 479p. map. LC 70-494769. ISBN 582-11229-X.

Part of the Knowles and Hadcock project. Lists over 1,000 houses, cathedrals, hospitals, colleges and military orders for the period 1111-1600. Pre 1111 houses are listed in a separate section. The arrangement is by order and then by geographical area. "Completes in a masterly way the trilogy begun in 1953 to survey all the Medieval monastic establishments of England, Wales, Scotland and Ireland" (*Review for Religious*, XXX [March, 1971], p. 340).

E201   Cowan, Ian Borthwick, and David E. Easson. **Medieval Religious Houses, Scotland: With an Appendix on the Houses in the Isle of Man.** 2nd. ed. London, New York, Longman, 1976. xxviii, 246p. map. LC 75-42083. ISBN 0-5821-2069-1.

(1957 edition by David E. Easson.)

Contains the same type of information as Knowles' work (E199) with a long scholarly introduction on the development of monasticism in Scotland. This edition is expanded and revised considerably.

E202   Knowles, David. **The Monastic Order in England: A History of its Development from the Times of St. Dunstan to the Fourth Lateran Council, 940-1216.** 2nd. edition. Cambridge, University Press, 1963. xxi, 780p. il. LC 64-29. ISBN 0-521-05479-6.

E203   Knowles, David. **The Religious Orders in England.** Cambridge, University
         Press, 1948-59. 3 v. LC 48-10465.
         V. 1. The Old Orders, The Friars, The Monasteries and their World. 1216-
         1304; V. 2. The End of the Middle Ages; V. 3. The Tudor Age.

         Dom David Knowles, an English Benedictine, has written a "balanced and
         penetrating interpretation of men and institutions" (*Catholic Historical
         Review*, XXVI [January, 1941], p. 500) in this series of books on the
         history of religious orders in England. This work and (E202) together span
         the years from 943 to 1536. "A full account based at every point on the
         sources" (*Ibid.*). Sometimes "magisterial" (*Ibid.*, XXV [July, 1949], p.
         178), the work is uniformly scholarly. Each volume is thoroughly indexed
         and contains a bibliography and numerous bibliographical notes.

BIOGRAPHY

E204   Code, Joseph Bernard. **Great American Foundresses.** Freeport, NY, Books
         for Libraries Press, 1968. xviii, 512p. il. LC 68-20291.

         A reprint of the 1929 edition of (E205).

E205   Code, Joseph Bernard. **The Veil Is Lifted.** Milwaukee, Bruce Pub. Co., 1932.
         161p. LC 32-7804.

         The lives of sixteen distinguished foundresses of American religious orders
         with bibliographies for each foundress. Contains no bibliography.

E206   **The Directory of Women Religious in the United States, 1985.** Ed. dir.,
         Magdalen O'Hara. Wilmington, DE, M. Glazier, 1985. xlvii, 987p. LC 85-47752.
         ISBN 0-89453-528-5.

         A listing of residences of religious women by Diocese, listing all the inhabitants
         by name, followed by an index of names. Also contains a list of religious orders,
         vicars for religious and national organizations for women religious.

E207   Knowles, David, and C. N. L. Brooke. **Heads of Religious Houses: England
         and Wales, 940-1216.** Cambridge, University Press, 1972. xlviii, 277p.
         LC 79-171676. ISBN 0-521-08367-2.

         An extensive, scholarly introduction precedes the listing of abbots, priors,
         etc. who are grouped first by order and then alphabetically by house.
         A separate section lists heads of houses of women. There is a bibliography
         of manuscripts, books and articles, and "pre-Conquest" charters. Separate
         indexes are provided for names and houses.

INDIVIDUAL ORDERS

AUGUSTINIANS

E208   Cěrnik, Berthold Otto, et al. **Die Schriftsteller der noch bestehenden
         Augustinerchorherrenstifte Österreichs von 1600 bis auf den heutigen Tag.**
         Wien, H. Kirsch, 1905. xiv, 397p. LC 5-20617.

Bio-bibliographies of Augustinians in the Austrian Empire. Chronological arrangement with indexes of persons and subjects.

E209　Ossinger, Joannes Felix. **Bibliotheca Augustiana, historica, critica et chronologica, in qua mille quadringenti Augustiniani Ordinis Scriptores, eorumque opera tam scripta, quam typis edita inveniuntur, simulque reperitur, quo saeculo vixerint, et de plurimus, quo anno obierint.** Vindelicorum, Ingolstadii et Augustae, 1768. 1002p. Reprinted: Torino, Bettega D'Erasmo, 1963.

An alphabetical catalog giving short biographies and lists of works as well as sources of biographical information.

E210　Perini, Davide Aurelio. **Bibliographia Augustiniana, cum notis biographicis.** Scriptores itali. Firenze, Tipografia Sordomuti, 1929-38. 4 v. LC A53-5823.

Covers Italian members of the order who were authors giving a short biographical sketch and a list of mss. and printed works. Arranged in alphabetical order.

E211　Santiago Vela, Gregorio de. **Ensayo de una biblioteca ibero-americana de la Orden de San Agustin: Obra basada en el catálogo bio-bibliográfico augustiano del p. Bonifacio Moral.** Pub. á expensas de la expresada Provincia de Filipinas. Madrid, Impr. del Asilo de huerfános del S. C. de Jesús, 1913-31. 8 v. LC 15-3472.

A bio-bibliography of Latin American Augustinians, i.e. those who were born or who served there. Detailed treatment.

AUGUSTINIAN RECOLLECTS

E212　Hugolin, Père. **Notes bibliographiques pour servir à l'histoire des Récollets du Canada.** Montréal, Imp. des Franciscains, 1932- . v. LC 33-29331.

Recollects are a branch of the Augustinians.

BARNABITES

E213　Boffito, Giuseppe. **Scrittori barnabiti o della Congregazione dei chierici regolari di San Paolo (1533-1933):** Biografia, Bibliografia Iconografia. Firenze, L. S. Olschki, 1933-37. 4 v. il. LC 41-23223.

An annotated bio-bibliography carefully done and well-illustrated with portraits and facsimiles.

BENEDICTINES

E214　Albareda, Anselmo Mariá. **Bibliografia de la Regla benedictina.** Monestir de Montserrat, Imprenta del Monestir de Montserrat, 1933. xviii, 660p. il. LC 34-16015.

A finely printed bibliography with an extensive introduction giving the history of the rule, a bibliography of literature inspired by the rule, and many facsimiles of title pages. The bibliography itself is a chronological listing of 902 editions printed from 1489 to 1929, with locations. Indexes of translators, commentators, editors, printers and booksellers.

E215 François, Jean. **Bibliothèque générale des écrivains de l'Ordre de Saint Benoît.** Bouillon, 1777-78. Reprinted: Louvain, Bibliothéque S. J., 1961. 4 v.

A bio-bibliography continued by the following work:

E216 Kapsner, Oliver Leonard. **A Benedictine Bibliography.** Comp. for the Library Section of the American Benedictine Academy. Collegeville, MN, St. John's Abbey, 1949-50. 2 v. LC 50-726.

This bibliography is in reality a union list of the contents of Benedictine monastery libraries in the U. S. and Canada—books, manuscripts, theses, music and serials by Benedictines. 13,428 items are listed in two sections, by author and by subject. Locations are given, as are analyses of large series.

E217 Kapsner, Oliver L. **A Benedictine Bibliography: An Author-Subject Union List. First Supplement: Author and Subject Part.** St. John's Abbey, Collegeville, MN, Liturgical Press, 1982. 807p. Index. LC 81-20790. ISBN 0-8146-1258-X.

7,833 items are listed in an author list and a classified subject list. Author and subject indexes. See also Kapsner's *Benedictine Liturgical Books in American Benedictine Libraries* (B331).

E218 Lama, Carl von. **Bibliothèque des écrivains de la Congrégation de Saint-Maur, order de Saint-Benoît en France.** Ouvrage publié avec le concours d'un Bénédictin de la Congrégation de France de l'abbaye de Solesmes. 2ᵉ éd. Munich, C. de Lama; Paris, V. Palmé, 1882. 261p. LC 2-20948.

A bio-bibliography of the Benedictines of the Congregation of St. Maure of France covering the years 1620 to 1830. For earlier writers see the bibliography by Le Cerf de la Viéville (E219).

E219 Le Cerf de la Viéville, Philippe. **Biblioteque historique et critique des auteurs de la Congrégation de St. Maur.** Où l'on fait voir quel a été leur caractère particulier, ce qu'ils ont fait de plus remarquable: et où l'on done un catalogue exact de leurs ouvrages et une idée générale de ce qui'ls contiennent. La Haye, P. Grosse, 1726. 1+492p. LC F-788.

The articles on each author tend to be longer than usual in this type of work, but the arrangement and typography make it difficult to use.

E220 Monte Cassino (Benedictine Monastery). **I registi dell'archivo**, a cura di Tommasso Leccisotti. Roma, Ministero dell'Interno, 1964- . v. LC 71-417322. (Vol. 10, 1974).

A classified list of the contents of the archives of Monte Cassino. Each entry gives the location of the item and a description of the contents. Indexes are supplied for each volume.

CARMELITES

E221   Ambrosius a Sancta Teresia. **Bio-bibliographia missionaria ordinis carmelitarum discalceatorum (1584-1940).** Rome, Apud Curiam Generalitiam, 1940. 495p.

1,697 items are listed chronologically. Books and articles are included. Subject index.

E222   Bartolommeo da S. Angelo. **Collectio scriptorum ordinis Carmelitarum excalceatorum utriusque congregationis et sexus; cui accedit Supplementum scriptorum ordinis qui aut obliti fuerunt aut recentius vixerunt,** auctore et collectore P. F. Henrico M. a SS. Sacramento. Accedunt insuper Catalogus episcoporum, index praepositorum generalium et prospectus provinciarum et coenobiorum ordinis. Savonae, A. Ricci, 1884. 2 v. in 1. LC 5-39538.

Bio-bibliographies of men and women Carmelites up to the year 1884. Arranged by first names. Lists unpublished mss. as well as books.

E223   Villiers de St. Étienne, Cosme de. **Bibliotheca carmelitana: notis criticis et dissertationibus illustrada.** Aurelianis, Rouzeau-Montau, 1752. 2 v. Repr. with a preface and supplement by Gabriel Wessles. Roma, Collegii S. Alberti, n. d.

An annotated bio-bibliography with a supplement covering seventy later writers.

E224   **Catalog of the Carmelitana Collection, Whitefriars Hall.** Comp. by Joachim Smet and Gervase Toelle. Washington, DC, 1959. 381p.

A bio-bibliography of Dominican authors who died during the years 1701 to 1749, giving brief biographical accounts and a list of their works. Chronological order with no indexes.

A classified bibliography of 237 items by or about Carmelites. Author index.

Current

E225   **Archivum bibliographicum carmelitanum.** Romae, 1955- . v. Annual. (Ephemerides carmeliticae supplementum).

An annual listing of books, articles and music pertaining to the Discalced Carmelites, giving references to book reviews and some annotations. Classified arrangement with author index.

E226   Benno, A. S. Joseph. **Bibliographia carmelitana recentior.** Romae, Ephemerides carmeliticano, 1946-49. 3 v.

A predecessor of (E225).

CISTERCIANS

E227   Bouton, Jean de la Croix. **Bibliographie bernardine, 1891-1957.** Paris, P. Lethielleux, 1958. xiv, 164p. LC 59-24283.

A continuation of Janauschek's work (E228) listing 1,075 books and articles in chronological order with geographical and author indexes.

E228   Janauschek, Leopold. **Bibliographia bernardina; qua Sancti Bernardi, primi abatis claravallensis, operum cum omnium tum singulorum, editiones ac versiones, vitas et tractatus de eo scriptos quotquot usque ad finem anni MDCCCXC reperire potuit collegit et adnotavit.** Vindobonae, A. Hölder, 1891. 558p. LC 1-17090.

A chronological listing with indexes of 2,701 books and articles.

CONGREGATION OF THE IMMACULATE HEART OF MARY (BELGIUM)

E229   Grootaers, Willem A. **Proeve eener bibliographie van de missionarissen van Scheut** (Congregatio Immaculati Cordis Mariae) door Willem A. Grootaers en Dries van Coillie. Brussel, 1939. 115p.

E230   Grootaers, Willem A. **Proeve eener bibliographie van de missionarissen van Scheut. Aanvullingen en verbeteringen.** Peking, Drukkerij der Lazaristen, 1941- . v. LC 50-44260.

(No more published?)

A bio-bibliography of the Congregation of the Immaculate Heart of Mary, a Belgian missionary order. Arranged by author, listing books and articles, with a classified index.

DOMINICANS

E231   Quétif, Jacques. **Scriptores Ordinis Predicatorum recensiti notisque historicis et criticis illustrati.** Inchoavit Jacobus Quétif absolvit Jacobus Echard. New York, Burt Franklin, 1959-61. 2 v. in 4. il. LC 60-1099.

FRANCISCANS AND CAPUCHINS

Bibliography

E232   Adams, Eleanor Burnham. **A Bio-bibliography of Franciscan Authors in Colonial Central America.** Washington, DC, Academy of American Franciscan History, 1953. xxi, 97p. LC 53-3645.

Covers the Spanish colonial period. Descriptive annotations.

E233   Asencio, José. **Cronistas franciscanos.** Guadalajara, Impr. "Gráfica," 1944. 38p. LC 47-5373.

A bio-bibliography of the Franciscans and Capuchins in Mexico. Geographical arrangement by province with author index.

E234   Adasiewicz, Leo, and Donald Bilinski, comps. **Catalog of Books in the Academy of American Franciscan History Library.** Pulaski, WI, Provincial Library, 1951. 87p. LC 54-24771.

Contains many titles by Franciscans in New Spain. No annotations.

E235   Dirks, Servatius. **Histoire littéraire et bibliographiques des Frères Mineurs de l'observance de St. François en Belgique et dan les Pays-Bas,** Par le P. F. Servais Dirks. Anvers, Typographie van Os de Wolf 1886. xxiv, 456p. LC 3-5138.

Bio-bibliographies arranged chronologically by date of death covering the years 1473 to 1886. Index of authors.

E236   Donato da S. Giovanni in Persiceto, Father. **Biblioteca dei Frati minori cappuccini della provincia di Bologna (1535-1946).** Budrio, Montanari fratelli, 1949. xxxix, 479p. il. LC 51-30082.

An annotated bio-bibliography with some portraits. Gives locations as well as full bibliographical information. Indexes of authors, editors, and secular names.

E237   Felice da Mareto, Father. **Biblioteca dei Frati minori cappuccini della Provincia parmense.** A cura del p. Felice da Mareto, sotto gli auspici della Deputazione di Storia patria per le provincie parmensi. Modena, Società tip. Modenese, 1951. xxxv, 451p. il. LC A52-10314.

Gives brief biographical sketches, portraits and detailed bibliography of work by and about the authors. Locations are indicated. Arranged by religious names with indexes.

E238   Golubovich, Gerolamo. **Biblioteca bio-bibliografice della Terra Santa e dell' Oriente francescano.** Quaracchi, Collegio di S. Bonaventura: Le Caire, Centre d'études Orientales de la Custodie franciscaine, 1906- . v.

Four series:
1. Annals, 1906- . LC 8-29911; 2. Documents, 1921- . LC 27-4870; 3. Documents, 1928- . LC 30-9659; 4. Studies, 1954- . LC 61-32477.

Chronological listings of the lives and works of Franciscans in the Middle East.

E239   Marcellino da Civezza. **Saggio di bibliografia, geografica storica, etnografica, sanfrancescana.** Prato, R. Guasti, 1879. xiv, 698p. LC 3-4750.

A bio-bibliography of 819 Franciscan writers many of whose works concern the early history of Spanish America. Contains excerpts and reprints of numerous works.

E240   Troeyer, Benjamin de. **Bio-bibliographia franciscana neerlandica saeculi XVI.** Nieuwkoop, B. DeGraaf, 1969. 2 v. LC 69-16190.
    V. 1. *Pars biographica. De auteurs van de uitgevenwerken.*
    V. 2. *Pars bibliographica. De edite.*

Biographies as well as bibliographies of secondary sources are included in volume one. Indexes in each volume.

E241   Troeyer, Benjamin de, and Leonide Mees. **Bio-bibliographia franciscana neerlandica ante saeculum XVI.** Nieuwkoop, B. DeGraaf, 1974. 3 v. LC 73-77817.

V. 1. *Auctores editionum qui scripserunt ante saeculum XVI*, by B.
DeTroeyer. V. 2. *Incunabula*, by L. Mees. V. 3. *Illustrationes incuna-
bularum*, by L. Mees.

Provides complete bibliographical description including locations and bibliographies of secondary sources. Both of the above works are carefully done
and finely printed.

E242   Wadding, Luke. **Scriptores Ordinis minorum quibus accessit syllabus illorum
qui ex eodem ordine pro fide Christe fortiter occubuerunt. Priores atramento,
posteriores sanguine christianam, religionem asseruerunt.** Edito-novissima.
Romae, A. Nardecchia, 1906. 243p. (Bibliotheca historico-bibliographia. I).

E243   Wadding, Luke. **Scriptores Ordinis minorum quibus accessit syllabus illorum
qui ex eodem ordine pro fide Christe fortiter occubuerunt. Supplementum
et castigatio ad scriptores trium ordinum S. Francisci a Waddingo, aliisve
descriptos,** posthuman fr. Jo. Hyacinthi Ebaraleae. Editio nova variis
additamentis et indice scriptorum chronologico locupletata. 1908-36. 3 v.
(Bibliotheca historico-bibliographica. II.) LC 9-7934.

The first part of this work was originally published in 1650: the supplement
covers up to the year 1806 with bio-bibliographies of notable Franciscans.

E244   Zulaica Garate, Román. **Los franciscanos y la imprenta en México en el
siglo XVI: Estudio bio-bibliografico México,** D. F. P. Robredo, 1939. 373p.
il. LC 40-12909.

A chronologically arranged bio-bibliography with long descriptive annotations.
Author index.

E245   **Bibliographia franciscana.** Roma, Istituto Storico dei Fr. Minori Cappuccini,
1931- . v. Annual. LC 76-644593.

An annotated, classified bibliography with indexes for persons and places.

Dictionaries

E246   **Lexicon capuccinum, promptuarim historico bibliographicum Ordinis
fratrum minorum capuccinorum (1515-1950).** Romae, Bibliotheca Collegii Internationalis S. Laurentii Brundusini, 1951. 1868 col. il.

An encyclopedia of notable Capuchins, provinces, monasteries, missions,
publications, events and so forth. Each article is followed by a detailed
bibliography.

JESUITS

Bibliography

E247   Backer, Augustin. **Bibliothèque de la Compagnie de Jésus.** Nouv. éd. par
Carlos Sommervogel, S. J. Bruxelles, O. Schepens. Paris, A. Picard, 1890-
1932. 10 v. LC 1-10185.

E248   Backer, Augustin. **Bibliothèque de la Compagnie de Jésus. Corrections et additions à la Bibliothèque de la Compagnie de Jésus.** Supplément au "De Backer-Sommervogel." Toulouse, L'auteur, 1911- .

A monumental work giving brief biographies and historical sidelights on issues and events with complete lists of works. Volumes one through eight contain the main author list; volume nine, anonymous works; volume ten, a classified index; volume 11, the supplement and volume 12, a separate bibliography of the history of the Jesuits by Pierre Bliard.

E249   Bangert, William V. **A Bibliographical Essay on the History of the Society of Jesus: Books in English.** St. Louis, MO, Institute of Jesuit Sources, 1976. xiv, 75p. (*Study Aids on Jesuit Topics*, no. 6.) LC 76-12667. ISBN 0-912422-05-X.

Treats in essay form some 400 titles dealing only with the history of the Jesuits. Polgár's work (E250) is more comprehensive. Index of authors and names.

E250   Polgár, László. **Bibliography of the History of the Society of Jesus . . . .** Rome, Jesuit Historical Institute; St. Louis, MO, St. Louis University, 1967. 207p. (*Sources and Studies for the History of the Jesuits*, no. 1.) LC 75-443884.

A useful selection of items from a vast body of literature. Arranged in chronological order with an index.

E251   Sommervogel, Carlos. **Dictionnaire des ouvrages anonymes et pseudonymes publié par des religieux de la Compagnie de Jésus depuis sa fondation jusqu'à nos jours.** Paris, Librairie de la Société bibliographique, 1884. iii, 1398p. LC 2-23892.

Arranged by title giving complete bibliographical information and the name of the author if known.

Current

E252   **Index bibliographicus Societatis Iesu.** Romae, 1937- . v. Annual. LC 40-24556.

An annual listing of books and articles by Jesuits of all provinces. Arranged by author with subject indexes. No annotations.

Ignatius Loyola

E253   Gilmont, Jean Francois, and Paul Daman. **Bibliographie ignatienne, 1894-1957: classement méthodique des livres et articles concernant saint Ignace de Loyola, sa vie, les Exercices spirituels, les Constitutions, ses autres écrits et sa spiritualité.** Paris, Desclées de Brouwer, 1958. xxviii, 251p. LC A59-5984.

Intended to continue the Ignatian bibliography begun in **Monumenta Historica Societatis Iesu** (1894), an eighty volume work which reprinted all the original documents pertaining to the life of St. Ignatius. This bibliography covers his life, his writings and his teachings on spirituality. 2,872 books and articles arranged by subject. No annotations. Subject and author indexes.

Dictionaries and Biographies

E254   Koch, Ludwig. **Jesuiten-lexikon: die Gesellschaft Jesu einst und jetzt.** Paderborn, Verlag Bonifacius-druckerie, 1934. 1878 col. Reprinted with corrections and a supplement: Leiden, 1962. 2 v. LC 34-38701.

"A model of conciseness and precision" (*American Catholic Historical Review*, XXI [January, 1936], p. 493) covering the history activities and institutions of the order with numerous biographies. Each article is supplied with bibliographical references. 2,211 articles.

E255   Tylenda, Joseph N. **Jesuit Saints and Martyrs: Short Biographies of the Saints, Blessed, Venerables and Servants of God of the Society of Jesus.** Chicago, Loyola University Press, 1984. xxvi, 503p. LC 83-19907. ISBN 0-8294-0447-3.

Arranged by feastday with indexes, this work provides brief, well-written biographies of 323 Jesuits including 38 canonized saints. No bibliography is supplied.

MARIANISTS

E256   Frederick, Brother Anthony. **This They Wrote: A Bibliography Compiled during the Centenary Year of the Society of Mary in Texas.** San Antonio, St. Mary's University, 1953. 80p. LC A53-8706.

A bibliography of Marianist authors listing books, articles, theses and pamphlets. No annotations.

MERCEDARIANS

E257   Garí y Siumell, José Antonio. **Biblioteca Mercedaria, ó sea Escritores de la celeste real y militar Órden de la merced, redencion de cautivos, con indicacion de sus obras, tanto impresas como manuscritas, su patria, títulos, dignidades, hechos memorables, época y provincia en que florecieron y murieron, y dos copiosus índices uno de excritores y otro de las obras y excritos.** Barcelona, Impr de los herederos de la viuda Pla, 1875. vii, 395p. LC 14-21343.

A bio-bibliography listing printed works and manuscripts with classified indexes.

NORBERTINES

E258   Goovaerts, André Léon. **Écrivains, artistes et savants de l'ordre de Prémontré. Dictionnaire bio-bibliographique.** Bruxelles, Société belge de librairie, 1899-1920. 4 v. LC 7-20499.

A detailed bio-bibliography listing works by and about the members in two series, the second of which contains mostly additions to and some corrections of the first.

OBLATES OF MARY IMMACULATE

E259   Bernad, Marcel. **Bibliographie des missionnaires oblats de Marie Immaculée.** Liege, H. Dessain, 1922- . v. LC 35-25992. V. 1. *Écrits des missionaires oblats 1816-1915.*

      (No more volumes published.)

      Gives the dates and places of birth and death and lists of books and articles with a geographical index.

ORATORIANS

E260   Ingold, Augustin Marie Pierre. **Essai de bibliographie oratorienne.** Paris, Pouisielgue, 1880-82. viii, 200p.

      Lists the works by and about 30 priests of the Oratory with biographies.

REDEMPTORISTS

E261   Meulemeester, Marice de. **Bibliographie générale des écrivains rédemptoristes,** par M. de Meulemeester avec la collaboration de Ern. Collet et Cl. Henze. Louvain, Imprimerie Saint-Alphonse, 1933-39. 3 v. LC 33-24971.
      V. 1. Bibliographie de S. Alphonse de Liguori; V. 2. Auteurs rédemptoristes, A-Z; V. 3. Anonymes, Périodiques, Supplément, Tables.

      The first volume lists works by and about St. Alphonsus; the second is a bio-bibliography, and the third contains, in addition to other material, an index to the entire work.

SULPICIANS

E262   Bertrand, Louis. **Bibliothèque sulpicienne: ou Histoire littéraire de la Compagnie de Saint-Sulpice.** Paris, A. Picard, 1900. 3 v. LC 1-25341.

      A chronological listing covering from the seventeenth to the end of the nineteenth century. Biographies are long, and bibliographies include published and unpublished works. Volume three contains a supplement. Index in each volume.

TEMPLARS

E263   Dessubré, M. **Bibliographie de l'Ordre des Templiers: imprimés et manuscrits.** Réimpression de l'édition. Paris, 1928. Nieuwkoop, B. DeGraaf, 1966. xix, 324p. LC 72-350204.

      An annotated author list covering the written works of Templars from all countries.

TRINITARIANS

E264   Antonio de la Asunción, fray. **Diccionario de escritores trinitarios de España y Portugal.** Roma, Impr. de F. Kleinbub, 1898-99. 2 v. LC 2-26481.

Bio-bibliographies of Spanish and Portuguese Trinitarians including those who served in other countries. Published works and manuscripts are listed.

APPENDIX 1
Diocesan
Reference Publications

The following works for the Archdiocese of Detroit are listed as an example of reference works typically available in most American dioceses.

F1 **Order of Prayer in the Liturgy of the Hours and the Celebration of the Eucharist.** Prepared expressly for the Archdiocese of Detroit. Ramsey, NJ, Paulist Press, 1969- . v.

A daily liturgical guide (*See* B398, 399, 400) for the proper celebration of Mass and the Office in the Diocese. A necrology of clergy is also provided.

F2 **Catholic Directory and Guide for the Archdiocese of Detroit.** Detroit, Michigan Catholic, 1949- . v. Annual. (Title and publisher vary).

Provides much the same information contained in the Official Catholic Directory but with a little more detail—churches with times of services and other information, institutions, religious orders and their houses, a clergy list, Archdiocesan officials, Catholic organizations, regulations for marriages, and so forth.

F3 **School Directory for the Archdiocese of Detroit.** Detroit, The Archdiocese, 1947-. v. Annual.

A geographical listing of diocesan and private Catholic schools in the Archdiocese giving basic statistics, addresses and names of principals.

F4 **1969 Synod-Archdiocese of Detroit.** Celebrated by the Most Reverand John F. Dearden, Archbishop of Detroit, together with the Church of Detroit. Cobo Hall, Detroit, Michigan, March 30, 1969. Detroit, The Archdiocese, 1969. 80p.

Contains both the statutes of the Archdiocese and explanations of why they were decided upon by the Synod. A brief history of the Synod is also given. The 1969 Synod was the tenth held in Detroit, and its statutes supersede those of all previous synods.

F5 Paré, George. **The Catholic Church in Detroit, 1701-1888.** Detroit, Gabriel Richard Press, 1951. xv, 717p. il. LC 51-32288.

An "official history" of the Archdiocese in that it was commissioned by Bishop Gallagher and published by the Chancery of the Archdiocese. It traces the Catholic history of the area from early missionary times down to 1888. Well-documented. Index.

APPENDIX 2
Bibliographies Consulted

Rather than repeat all the titles listed in Chapter I, I have limited this list to those works containing essays or studies of Catholic reference works and to those containing special lists.

American Reference Books Annual. Littleton, CO, Libraries Unlimited, 1970- .

Bernard, Jack J., and John Delaney. *A Guide to Catholic Reading.* Garden City, NY, Doubleday, 1966. (Esp. "Reference Books," pp. 290-302).

Barrow, John Graves. *A Bibliography of Bibliographies in Religion.* Ann Arbor, MI, Edwards Bros., 1955. (Esp. "The Catholic Church," pp. 207-59).

"Bibliographical Abbreviations." *New Catholic Encyclopedia.* New York, McGraw-Hill, 1967. v.15, 207-26. A list of reference works most frequently referred to in this work.

Brown, Stephen James Meredith, S.J. *An Introduction to Catholic Booklore.* London, Burns, Oates, 1933. (Esp. "Catholic Bibliographies," pp. 9-17; "Other Catholic Bibliographical Sources," pp. 18-23; "Catholic Reference Books," pp. 39-47 and 48-55; and many other helpful chapters.)

Carlen, Sister Mary Claudia, I.H.M. "Catholic Encyclopedias and Dictionaries." *New Catholic Encyclopedia.* New York, McGraw-Hill, 1967. v.2, 333-34.

_____. "Bibliography of Catholic Bibliographies." Unpublished bibliography in the Archives of Marygrove College Library, Detroit, Michigan.

Catholic Library Association. *Booklist,* 1941- . Haverford, PA, C.L.A., 1941- . Each edition contains a list for "Bibliography, Reference, and Library Science."

_____. *C.L.A. Basic Reference Books for Catholic High School Libraries.* Haverford, PA, C.L.A. 1963.

Catholic Library World. Haverford, PA, C.L.A., 1930- . An annual list of C.L.A. publications is contained in the October issue.

Fitzmyer, Joseph A. *An Introductory Bibliography for the Study of Scripture.* Rev. ed. Rome, Biblical Institute Press, 1981.

Freudenberger, Elsie. *Reference Works in the Field of Religion, 1977-1985. A Selective Bibliography.* Haverford, PA, C.L.A., 1986.

Glanzman, George S., S.J. *Introductory Bibliography for the Study of Scripture.* Westminster, MD, Newman, 1961. Lists bibliographies and reference tools.

Gorman, G. E., and Lyn Gorman. *Theological and Religious Reference Materials.* Westport, CT, Greenwood Press, 1984- . v.

Grace, Sister Melania, and Gilbert C. Peterson. *Books for Catholic Colleges.* Chicago, ALA, 1948 and supplements. Special lists of reference books are given under each subject heading.

Guide to Catholic Literature, 1888- . Haverford, PA, C.L.A., 1940- . Reference books listed under various headings in different volumes — "Dictionaries,""Encyclopedias," "Reference Books."

The Library of Congress Main Reading Room Reference Collection Subject Catalog. Washington, GPO, 1975.

Malclès, Louise Noëlle. *Les sources du travail bibliographique.* Genève, E. Droz, 1950-58. (Esp. "Sciences religieuses," v.2, 434-79).

Martin, Brother David. *Catholic Library Practice.* Portland,OR, Univ. of Portland Press, 1947-50. (Esp. "Catholic Bibliography," v.1, 97-119; "Catholic Reference Tools," v.2, 187-208).

Murphey, Robert W. *How and Where to Look It Up.* New York, McGraw-Hill, 1958. (Esp. "Religion," pp. 586-90; "Roman Catholic Church," pp. 592-94).

O'Rourke, William Thomas. *Library Handbook for Catholic Readers.* Milwaukee, Bruce Pub. Co., 1937. (Esp. "General Reference Works," pp. 27-34; "Special Reference Works," pp. 42-105; Appendix: "Some Foreign Language Catholic Reference Works," pp. 117-32).

Parsons, Wilfred, S.J. *Early Catholic Americana.* New York, Macmillan, 1939. (Esp. "Introduction," pp. ix-xxv).

Readers' Advisor. 13th ed. New York, Bowker, 1986- . v.

Reference and Subscription Books Reviews. Chicago, ALA, 1970- .

Reference Services Review: A Quarterly Guide to the World of Reference. Ann Arbor, MI, The Pierian Press, 1972- .

Regis, Sister Mary, I.H.M. *The Catholic Bookman's Guide.* New York, Hawthorn, 1962. (Esp. "Bibliographical Sources," pp. 35-71).

Sheehy, Eugene Paul. *Guide to Reference Books.* 9th ed. Chicago, ALA, 1979. (Esp. "Religion," pp. 252-77).

_____. *Guide to Reference Books.* 10th ed. Chicago, ALA, 1986. (Esp. "Religion," pp. 340-91).

Sloane, Charles O'Conner. "Biblical Concordances, Dictionaries, and Encyclopedias." *New Catholic Encyclopedia,* New York, McGraw-Hill, 1967. v.2, 537-39.

Walford, Albert John. *Guide to Reference Materials.* London, Library Assoc., 1959 and supplement, 1963. (Esp. "Religion," pp. 69-89; Supplement, pp. 37-45).

_____. *Guide to Reference Materials*. 3rd edition. Vol. 2: Social and Historical Sciences, Philosophy and Religion. London, Library Assoc., 1975. (Esp. "Religion," "Christianity," pp. 28-62).

_____. *Guide to Reference Material*. 4th edition. London, Library Assoc., 1982. Vol. 2: Social and Historical Sciences, Philosophy and Religion. (Esp. "Religion, Christianity," pp. 38-69).

Winchell, Constance M. *Guide to Reference Books*. 8th ed. Chicago, ALA, 1967. (Esp. "Religion," pp. 203-28).

AUTHOR/TITLE/SUBJECT INDEX

References are to item number, not page number. Subject entries are in capital letters.

ABC of the Bible/H. J. Richards, B108

Abbo, J. A./Sacred Canons, D176

Abbott, W. M./Documents of Vatican II, E155

Abell, A. I./American Catholic Thought on Social Questions, D3

Abortion Bibliography/M. K. Floyd, B258

Abortion in Context/C. Dollen, B259

Abréviations latines médiévales/ A. Pelzer, C145

Abridged Catholic Periodical and Literature Index, A161

Academy of American Franciscan History/U.S. Documents in the Propaganda Fide Archives, E74

Achievement of Jacques and Raïssa Maritain/D. Gallagher, C48

Acta Apostolica Sedis, E120

Acta conciliorum oecumenicorum/E. Schwartz, E142

Acta pontificium romanorum medita/ J. von Pflugk-Harttung, E101

Acta Sanctae Sedis, E121

Acta sanctorum, A205

Acta synodalia Sacrosancti Concilii Oecumenici Vaticani II, E151

Actes pontificaux, E98

Acton Collection, A2

Acts of the Christian Martyrs, A216

Adams, C. J./Encyclopedia of Religion, A100

Adams, E. B./Bio-bibliography of Franciscan Authors, E232

Adasiewicz, L./Catalog of Books in the Academy of American Franciscan History, E234

Addis, W. E./Catholic Dictionary, A85

Addressbuch für das Katholische Deutschland, D126

Aelfric/L. M. Reinsma, C101

AELFRIC THE GRAMMARIAN, C101

Agenzia Internationale Fides/Le missioni cattoliche, B297

Aging in the Religious Life/J. H. Morgan, E174

Aherne, C. M./Encyclopedic Dictionary of Religion, A101

Albareda, A. M./Bibliografia de la Regla benedictina, E214

Albers, P. H./Manuel d'histoire ecclésiastiques, E12

ALBERT THE GREAT, C33

Aldea Vaquero, Q./Diccionario de Historia Eclesiástica de España, E9

Alexander, C./Catholic Literary Revival, C97

Alfaro, D./Guiá apostolicá latinamericana, A162

Algermisson, K./Christian Denomina- tions, B1

_____. Lexikon der Marienkunde, B243

Alhadef, J. J./National Bibliography of Theological Titles in Catholic Libraries, B21

Allenbach, J./Biblia patristica, B152

Allison, A. F./Catalogue of Catholic Books Printed in English, A11

Almanach catholique français, D120

Altaner, B./Patrology, B135

Alternative Classification for Catholic Books/J. M. Lynn, A82

Alzog, J. B./Manual of Universal Church History, E13

Ambrosius a Sancta Teresia/Bio-bibliographia missionaria, E221

American Bishops, 1964-1970/J. B. Code, A186

American Catholic Catalog/B. Hassan, D96

American Catholic Catechism/G. J. Dyer, B199

American Catholic Convert Authors/ D. Martin, C92

American Catholic Etiquette/K. T. Fenner, D66

American Catholic Historical Society Records/Index, E95

American Catholic Philosophical Society/Directory of Members, C31

American Catholic Thought on Social Questions/A. I. Abell, D3

American Catholic Who's Who, A196

AMERICAN CHURCH HISTORY, E72-E97

America's Thousand Bishops/C. A. Liederbach, A190

Amiet, R./Repertorium liturgicum Augustanum, B330

Analecta Bollandiana, A208

Analecta hymnica medii aevi/G. M. Dreves, C152

Analecta sacra spicilegio solesmensi parata/J. B. Pitra, B175

Anchor Bible, B116

Ancient Christian Writers, B153

ANCIENT CHURCH HISTORY, E29-E36

Ancilli, E./Dizionario enciclopedico di spiritualitá, B317

Andresen, C./Bibliographia Augustiniana, C35

Annalen der lateinischen Hymnendichtung: ein Handbuch/J. Szövérffy, C169

Année de l'église, D70

Annotated Bibliography in Religion and Psychology/W. W. Meissner, C74

Annotated Bibliography of Philosophy in Catholic Thought/G. F. McLean, C3

Annotated Bibliography of the Works of the Canon Law Society of America, R. G. Cunningham, D153

Annuaire-agenda catholique, D121

Annuaire catholique de Belgique, D110

Annuaire catholique de France, D122

Annuaire de l'Église catholique, D123

Annuaire de l'Église catholique à Madagascar, D80

Annuaire de l'Église catholique au Zäire, D81

Annuaire de l'Église catholique en Terre sainte, D136

Annuaire des instituts de reliqieuses en France, E178

Annuaire ecclésiastique: Burundi et Rwanda, D82

Annuaire général du clerge, D124

Annuaire pontificale catholique, D71

Annuaire statistique de l'église/ Secretaria Status, D74

Annuario católico argentino, D105

Annuario cattolico d'Italia, D131

Annuario pontificio, D73

Annuarium statisticum ecclesiae/ Secretaria Status, D74

ANSELM, SAINT, C34

Anson, P. F./Religious Orders and Congregations of Great Britain and Ireland, E179

Ante-Nicene Fathers/A. Roberts, B154

ANTHOLOGIES, C80-C86, C127-C133

Anthology of Catholic Poets/J. Kilmer, C127

Anthology of Catholic Poets/ S. Leslie, C128

Anthology of Mysticism, P. de Jaegher, B313

Antonio de la Asunción/Diccionario de escritores trinitarios, E264

Anuário católico de Portugal, D139

Anuario Católico del Uruguay, D142

Anuário catolico do Brasil, D111

Anuario católico español, D140

Anuario eclesiástico venezolano, D143

Anwander, A./Die Religionen der
  Menscheit, B13
_____. Wörterbuch der Religion, B18
Apel, W./Gregorian Chant, C163
APOLOGETICS, B214-B215
Apostolic Regions of the U.S./B.
  Quinn, D101
Appleton, L. H./Symbolism in
  Liturgical Art, C174
Archéologie chrétienne/C. Rohault
  de Fleury, C201
ARCHEOLOGY, E26-E28
L'Archevêque, P./Teilhard de
  Chardin, C53
ARCHITECTURE, C204
Archivio vaticano/Bibligrafia
  dell'Archivio vaticano, E7
Archivum bibliographicum
  Carmelitanum, E225
Archivum historiae pontificiae, E99
Armorial des évêques du Canada/
  G. Brassard, A245
Armorial of the American Hierarchy/
  G. Brassard, A246
Arnold, F. X./Handbuch der
  Pastoraltheologie, B283
Arnold, T. A./Catholic Dictionary,
  A85
ART, C173-C209
L'Art religieux/É.Mâle, C182
Ascencio, J./Cronistas Franciscanos,
  E233
ASCETICAL THEOLOGY,
  B302-B324
Atiya, A. S./Crusades, E39
Atlas biblique/P. Lemaire, B133
Atlas hierarchicus/H. Emmerich,
  D195
Atlas of the Bible/L. J. Grollenberg,
  B131
Atlas of Religious Change in America,
  1952-1971/P. L. Halvorson,
  D95
Atlas of the Early Christian World/
  F. van der Meer, E35
Atlas zur kirchengeschichte/H. Jedin,
  D193
ATLASES, B232, B301, D193-D196,
  E35

ATLASES, BIBLICAL, B131-B134
Attività della Santa sede, D75
Attwater, D./Catholic Dictionary,
  A86
_____. Christian Churches of the
  East, B8
_____. Dictionary of Mary, B241
_____. Dictionary of Saints, A217
_____. Dictionary of the Popes, E131
_____. List of Books about Eastern
  Churches, B9
_____. Lives of the Saints, A226,
  A227
_____. Martyrs, A218
_____. Names and Name Days, A247
_____. Penguin Dictionary of Saints,
  A219
_____. Saints of the East, A239
AUGUSTINE, SAINT, C35-C41
Augustine Bibliography/Institut des
  Études Augustiniennes, C37
Augustinian Bibliography, 1970-1980/
  T. L. Miethe, C39
AUGUSTINIANS, E208-E212
Augustinus/M. F. Sciacca, C41
Aurenhammer, H./Lexikon der
  christlichen Ikonographie,
  C175
AUTHORS, C88-C118
Auty, R./Lexikon des Mittelalters,
  E61
Avato, R. M./Concise Guide to the
  Catholic Church, D94
Avenir due Christianisme/A.
  Dufourcq, E16
Avery, C. B./New Century Italian
  Renaissance Encyclopedia, E70
Ayer, J. C./Source Book for Ancient
  Church History, E29
Ayerst, D./Records of Christianity,
  E5
Axtell, J./Indian Missions, B291

Bacci, A./Varia latinitatis scripta,
  E126
Backer, A./Bibliothèque de la
  Compagnie de Jésus, E247
Baers, J./Lectuur-repertorium, A30

Baker, K./Philosophical Dictionary, C16

Baldi, D./Atlas biblique, B133

Baltimore Councils, E84-E86

Balz, H./Exegetisches Worterbuch zum Neuen Testament, B99

Bangert, W. V./Bibliographical Essay on the History of the Society of Jesus, E249

Baptismal and Confirmation Names/ E. F. Smith, A249

Bar, J. R./Polska bibliografia teologiczna, A67

———. Polska bibliografia teologii, A68

Barbin, R./Bibliographie de pédagogie religieuse, D14

Bardenhewer, O./Geschichte der altkirchlichen Literatur, B136

———. Patrology, B137

Bardy, G./Enciclopedia cristologica, B237

Baring-Gould, S./Lives of the British Saints, A241

———. Lives of the Saints, A220

BARNABITES, E213

Barrett, D./Guide to Religious Communities for Women, E183

Barrow, J. G./Bibliography of Bibliographies in Religion, A1

Barry, C. J./Readings in Church History, E3

Barry, M. I./Complete Index of the Summa of St. Thomas Aquinas, C63

———. Lexicon of St. Thomas Aquinas, C67

Bartolommeo da S. Angelo/Collectio scriptorum ordinis Carmelitarum, E222

Basdekis, A./Ökumene Lexikon, B329

Basic Teachings for Catholic Religious Education/National Conference of Catholic Bishops, B204

Basic Tools of Biblical Exegesis/ S. B. Marrow, B69

Basisstatistieken over de decanaten en bisdommen van de Belgische Kerkprovincie/Interdiocesaan Centrum, D108

Batiffol, P. H./Catholicisme, E33

———. History of the Roman Breviary, B367

Baudrillart, A./Dictionnaire d'histoire et de géographie ecclésiastiques, E8

Bauer, J. B./Encyclopedia of Biblical Theology, B94

———. Sacramentum verbi, B94

Baumann D./Analecta hymnica medii aevi, C154

Baumeister, E. J./Booklist of the Marian Library, B239

Baumstark, A./Comparative Liturgy, B407

Bavel, T. J. van/Répertoire bibliographique de saint Augustin, C36

Bechis, M./Repertorium biblicum, B81

Becker, U./Der Neue Herder, A125

Beeson, C. H./Primer of Medieval Latin, C84

Behavior Patterns in Children's Books/C. J. Kircher, A37

Bender, T. K./Concordance to the English Poetry of Gerard Manley Hopkins, C106

Benedictine Bibliography/O. L. Kapsner, E216

Benedictine Bibliography, First Supplement/O. L. Kapsner, E217

Benedictine Liturgical Books in American Benedictine Librar-ies/O.J. Kapsner, B331

BENEDICTINES, E214-E220

Benno, A. S. J./Bibliographia Carmelitana recentior, E226

Bentley, J./Calendar of Saints, A221

Benziger Bros./Catalogue of All Catholic Books in English, A53

Berger, F. E./Cooking for Christ, B404

Berger, R./Kleines Liturgisches
    Wörterbuch, B378
Berkhout, C. T./Medieval Heresies,
    E40
Bernad, M./Bibliographie des
    missionnaires oblats de Marie
    Immaculée, E259
Bernard, J. F./Guide to Catholic
    Reading, A15
Bernareggi, A./Enciclopedia
    ecclesiastica, A134
BERRIGAN, D., P., AND E., C102
Berrigans/A. Klejment, C102
Bertrand, L. Bibliothèque sulpicienne,
    E262
Best Sellers, A20
Besutti, G. M./Bibliografia Mariana,
    B238
Bevolking en misvierender in de
    decanaten en bisdommen van
    de Belgische Kerkprovincie/
    Interdiocesaan Centrum,
    D109
Bibel-Lexikon/H. Haag, B101
BIBLE, B44-B134
Bible in Order/J. Rhymer, B55
Bible Themes/T. Maertins, B287
Biblia patristica/J. Allenbach,
    B152
Biblia Sacra iuxta latinam vulgatam/
    A. Gasquet, B44
Biblica: Elenchus bibliographicus,
    B60
Biblical Subject Index/Kiefer, W. J.,
    B85
Bibliografía de la devoción al
    Carazón de Jesús/J. M. Sáenz
    de Tejada, B310
Bibliografia de la Regla benedictina/
    A. M. Albareda, E214
Bibliografia dell'Archivio vaticano, E7
Bibliografía filosofica española e
    hispano-americana/L. Martínez
    Gómez, C15
Bibliografia filosofica italiana, C12
Bibliografia mariana/G. M. Besutti,
    B238
Bibliografia missionaria/G.
    Rommerskirchen, B290

Bibliografia ragionata delle reviste
    filosofiche italiane/Istituto di
    studi filosofici, C14
Bibliografía teologica, A70
Bibliografie ceské Katolické/J.
    Tumpach, A62
Bibliographia academica/G. Dreesen,
    B27
Bibliographia Augustiniana/C.
    Andresen, C35
Bibliographia augustiniana/E.
    Nebreda del Cura, C40
Bibliographia Augustiniana/D. A.
    Perini, E210
Bibliographia bernardina/L.
    Janauschek, E228
Bibliographia carmelitana recentior/
    A. S. J. Benno, E226
Bibliographia catholica Americana/
    J. M. Finotti, A49
Bibliographia de vita, operibus et
    doctrina, Iohannis Duns
    Scoti/O. Schäefer, C42
Bibliographia franciscana, E245
Bibliographia internationalis
    spiritualitatis, B302
Bibliographia liturgica/W. H. J.
    Weale, B356
Bibliographia patristica/W.
    Scheemelcher, B144
Bibliographica philosophica/G. A.
    Brie, C1
Bibliographical Account of Catholic
    Bibles, Testaments and Other
    Portions of the Scripture/
    J. D. G. Shea, B75
Bibliographical Dictionary of the
    English Catholics/J. Gillow,
    A198
Bibliographical Essay on the History
    of the Society of Jesus/W. V.
    Bangert, E249
Bibliographical Guide to the History
    of Christianity/S. J. Case,
    E1
Bibliographical Index of Five English
    Mystics/M. E. Sawyer, B311
Bibliographie/Revue d'histoire
    ecclésiastique, E2

Bibliographie bernardine/J. Bouton, E227

Bibliographie biblique, B61

Bibliographie biblique/P. E. Langevin, B67

Bibliographie catholique, A21

Bibliographie chronologique de la littérature spiritualité/ J. Dagens, B305

Bibliographie critique d'Origène/H. Crouzel, B147

Bibliographie de L'Ordre des Templiers/M. Dessubré, E263

Bibliographie de pédagogie religieuse/ R. Barbin, D14

Bibliographie der breviere/H. Bohatta, B363

Bibliographie der deutschen Predigt/ K. Morvay, C139

Bibliographie der livres de'heures/ H. Bohatta, B364

Bibliographie der modern devotie/ J. M. E. Dols, B306

Bibliographie der Sozialethik/A. Utz, D44

Bibliographie des missionnaires oblats de Marie Immaculée/M. Bernad, E259

Bibliographie générale des écrivains rédemptoristes/M. de Meulemeester, E261

Bibliographie génerale des oeuvres et articles sur Pierre Teilhard de Chardin/J. E. Jarque i Jutglar, C49

Bibliographie ignatienne/J. F. Gilmont, E253

Bibliographie internationale sur le sacerdoce et le ministère/A. Guitard, B251

Bibliographie Karl Rahner: 1924-1969/ R. Bleistein, B22

Bibliographie Karl Rahner: 1969-1974/ R. Bleistein, B23

Bibliographie philosophique de Saint Albert le Grand (1931-1960)/ M. Schooyans, C33

Bibliographie thomiste/P. F. Mandonnet, C58

Bibliographie zur Geschichte der Kreuzzüge/H. E. Mayer, E46

Bibliographie zur Ketzergeschichte des Mittelalters/H. Grundmann, E40

Bibliographies and Bulletins in Theology/W. H. Principe, B35

BIBLIOGRAPHIES OF BIBLIOGRAPHY, A1

Bibliographisches Verzeichnis der gerdruckten Schrifttums zur Geschichte und Literatur der Inquistion/E. Vekene, E66

Bibliography for Christian Formation in the Family/M. A. Carey, A24

Bibliography for the Gospel of Mark, 1954-1980/H. Humphrey, B66

BIBLIOGRAPHY, GENERAL, A2-A31

Bibliography of Bibliographies in Religion/J. G. Barrow, A1

Bibliography of Bioethics, B257

Bibliography of Catholic Books Published during 1948/J. G. Maddrell, A57

Bibliography of Christian Philosophy and Contemporary Issues/ G. F. McLean, C4

Bibliography of Economic Books and Pamphlets by Catholic Authors/P. J. Fitzpatrick, D144

Bibliography of English Translations from Medieval Sources/C. P. Farrar, E42, E43

Bibliography of Fr. Richard's Press in Detroit, A9

Bibliography of French Bibles/B. T. Chambers, B62

Bibliography of Interchurch and Interconfessional Dialogues/ J. F. Puglisi, B327

Bibliography of Medieval Drama/ C. J. Stratman, C120

Bibliography of the Catholic Church, National Union Catalog, A3

Bibliography of the History of the Society of Jesus/L. Polǵar, E250

Bibliography on Canon Law, 1965-1971/L. W. Sheridan, D156

Bibliography on Cardinal Mindszenty/ J. Szeplaki, E65

Biblioteca bio-bibliografice della Terra Santa e dell'Oriente francescano/G. Golubovich, E238

Biblioteca dei Frati minori cappuccini (Bologna)/Donato da S. Giovanni, E236

Biblioteca dei Frati minori cappuccini (Parma)/Felice da Mareto, E237

Biblioteca Mercedaria/J. A. Gari y Siumell, E257

Biblioteca vaticana/Catalogo delle pubblicazioni periodiche, A158

Biblioteca vaticana/Rules for the Catalog of Printed Books, A80

Biblioteque historique et critique des auteurs de la Congregation de St. Maur/P. Le Cerf de la Viéville, E219

Bibliotheca Augustiana/J. F. Ossinger, E209

Bibliotheca bibliographica historiae sanctae inquisitionis/E. Vekene, E66

Bibliotheca carmelitana/E. de Villiers de St. Étienne, E223

Bibliotheca Catholica Neerlandica, B303

Bibliotheca Erasmiana/F. van der Haeghen, C43

Bibliotheca hagiographica graeca, A210

Bibliotheca hagiographica latina, A211

Bibliotheca hagiographica orientalis, A213

Bibliotheca historica medii aevi/A. Potthast, E48

Bibliotheca Janseniana Belgica/L. Willaert, B41

Bibliotheca missionum/R. Streit, B292

Bibliotheca sanctorum, A222

Bibliothèque de la Compagnie de Jésus/A. Backer, E247

Bibliothèque des écoles francaises d'Athènes et de Rome, E100

Bibliothèque des écrivains de la Congrégation de Saint-Maur/C. von Lama, E218

Bibliothèque générale des écrivains de l'Ordre de Saint Benoit/ J. Francois, E215

Bibliothèque sulpicienne/L. Bertrand, E262

Bilan de la théologie du XXe siecle, B210

Bilan du monde, D76

Bilhmeyer, K./Church History, E14

Bilinski, D./Catalog of books in the Academy of American Franciscan History Library, E234

Bio-bibliografía eclesíastica mexicana/ T.E. Valverde, A204

Bio-bibliographia franciscana neerlandica ante saeculum XVI/B. de Troeyer, E241

Bio-bibliographia franciscana neerlandica saeculo XVI/ B. de Troeyer, E240

Bio-bibliographia missionaria/ Ambrosius a Sancta Teresia, E221

Bio-bibliography of Franciscan Authors/E. B. Adams, E232

Biographica catholica/H. Korff, A202

Biographical Cyclopedia of the Catholic Hierarchy/F. X. Reuss, A194

Biographical Dictionary of the Saints/F. G. Holweck, A232

Biographical Register of Paris Doctors of Theology, 1500-1536/J. K. Farge, B212

Biographical Studies, A197

Biographies of English Catholics in the Eighteenth Century/J. Kirk, A199

Biographischliterarisches Lexikon der katholischen deutschen Dichter/J. Kehrein, C141

BIOGRAPHY, A169-A244

Bishops' Committee on the Laity/ Directory of Diocesan Lay Programs and Resources, D35

Blaise, A./Dictionnaire latin francais des auteurs chretiens, B177

———. Lexicon latinitatis medii aevi, B178

———. Vocabulaire latin des principaux themes liturgiques, B380

Blehl, V. F./John Henry Newman, C111

Bleistein, R./Bibliographie Karl Rahner: 1924-1969, B22

———. Bibliographie Karl Rahner: 1969-1974, B23

Bles, A. de/How to Distinguish the Saints in Art, C195

Blume, C./Analecta hymnica medii aevi, C152

———. Repertorium repertorii, C146

Boffito, G./Scrittori barnabiti, E213

Bohatta, H./Bibliographie der breviere, B363

———. Bibliographie der livres de'heures, B364

———. Katalog der liturgis 'chen Drucke, B340

———. Liturgische Bibliographie des XV Jahrhunderts, B341

Bolland, J./Acta sanctorum, A205

Bollettino bibliografica internazionale, A22

Book of Catholic Authors/W. Romig, C93

Book of Catholic Names and Numbers, D89

Book of Catholic Quotations/J. Chapin, C119

Book of Ceremonies/L. J. O'Connell, B402

Book of the Popes/L. R. Loomis, E109

Book of the Saints, A223

BOOK SELECTION AIDS, A15-A19

Booklist of the Marian Library/ E. J. Baumeister, B239

Books by Catholic Authors in the Cleveland Public Library/ E. L. Haley, A23

Books for Catholic Colleges/ M. Grace, A41

Books for Catholic Elementary Schools/E. F. Noonan, A35

Books for Religious Education in Catholic Secondary Schools/ E. F. Noonan, A36

Books for Religious Sisters/M. F. Harmer, A48

Book of the Latin Liturgy/F. Cabrol, B345

Books Published by the Vatican Library, A5

Born, A. van den/Bibel-Lexikon, B101

———. Encyclopedic Dictionary of the Bible, B98

Boulenger, A./Histoire générale de l'Église, E15

Bourke, V. J./Thomistic Bibliography, 1920-1940, C56

———. Thomistic Bibliography, 1940-1978, C60

Bouscaren, T. L./Canon Law, D177

———. Canon Law Digest, D158

Bouton, J./Bibliographie bernardine, E227

Bouyer, L./Dictionary of Theology, B182

———. History of Christian Spirituality, B322

Bouyer, M. D./Table Prayer, B412

Bowden, J. S./Westminster Dictionary of Christian Theology, B198

Bowe, F./List of Additions and Corrections to Early Catholic Americana, A52

Bowman, M. A./Western Mysticism, B304

Boyce, G. C./Literature of Medieval History, E36

Boyle, L. E./Survey of the Vatican Archives, E37

Brackmann, A./Regesta pontificium romanorum, E108

Bradley, J. P./Encyclopedic Dictionary of Christian Doctrine, B183

Bradley, R./14th Century English Mystics, B307

Brassard, G./Armorial des évêques du Canada, A245

———. Armorial of the American Hierarchy, A246

Brauer, J. C./Westminster Dictionary of Church History, E11

Braun, J./Liturgisches Handlexikon, B379

Braunfels, W./Monasteris of Western Europe, E197

Braybrooke, P./Some Catholic Novelists, C122

———. Some Victorian and Georgian Catholics, C98

Breit, M./Thomas Merton, C109

Bremond, H./Manuel de la litterature catholique en France, C138

Brevarium romanum, B357

Breve diccionario de la Biblia/ H. Haag, B101

BREVIARY, B357-B367, B411

Breviary Explained/P. Parsch, B411

Brevior synopsis theologiae dogmaticae/A. Tanquerey, B232

Brevior synopsis theologiae moralis et pastoralis/A. Tanquerey, B281

Bricourt, J./Dictionnaire practique des connaissances religieuses, A118

———. Ou en est l'histoire de religións, B14

Bridges, S./Symbolism in Liturgical Art, C174

Brie, G. A./Bibliographia philosophica, C1

Brinkoff, L./Liturgisch woordenboek, B381

British Museum/John Henry Newman, C112

Britt, M./Dictionary of the Psalter, B365

———. Hymns of the Breviary and Missal, B361

Broderick, R. C./Catholic Concise Dictionary, A87

———. Catholic Encyclopedia, A88

———. Catholic Layman's Book of Etiquette, D65

Brooke, C. N. L./Heads of Religious Houses, E207

Brown, C. F./Register of Middle English and Didactic Verse, C131

Brown, R. E./Jerome Biblical Commentary, B117

Brown, S. J. M./International Index of Catholic Biographies, A169

———. Introduction to Catholic Booklore, A16

———. Novels and Tales by Catholic Writers, C121

———. Survey of Catholic Literature, C99

Bruggeman, J./Inventaires des pièces d'archives françaises, E62

Brugger, W./Philosophical Dictionary, C16

Brusher, J. S./Popes through the Ages, E135

Bryden, J. R./Index of Gregorian Chant, C155

Buchberger, M./Lexikon für Theologie und Kirche, B193

Bücherkunde des katholischen Lebens/F. Rennhofer, A65

Bujanda, J. Mide/Index des livres interdits, A43

Bullarium/H. Mainardi, E104

Bullarium Benedicti, E103

Bullarum/L. Tomassetti, E102

Bulletin d'ancienne littérature chrétienne latine, B146

Bulletin de théologie ancienne et médiéval, B24

Bulletin thomiste/*see* Rassegna di letteratura tomistica, B36, C6, C59

Bulteau, M. G./Bibliographie intertnationale sur le sacerdoce et le ministère, B251

Burke, R. A./What is the Index?, A44

Burns, J. A./Growth and Development of the Catholic School System in the U.S., D40

———. History of Catholic Education in the U.S., D39

———. Principles, Origin and Establishment of the Catholic School System in the U.S., D41

Bury, J. B./Cambridge Medieval History, E62

Busa, R./Index Thomisticus, C64

Butler, A./Butler's Lives of the Saints Concise Edition ed. by M. Walsh, E224

———. Lives of the Saints, A224-A227

Butler's Lives of the Saints, Concise Edition, ed. by M. Walsh, E224

Byers, D. M./Readings for Town and Country Church Workers, D45

Byrns, L./Recusant Books in America, A12

C.L.A. Basic Reference Books for Catholic High School Libraries, A47

C.L.A. Booklist/Catholic Library Association, A25

Cabrol, F./Books of the Latin Liturgy, B345

———. Dictionnaire d'archéologie chrétienne et de liturgie, B382, E27

Cacciatore, G./Encyclopedia del sacerdozio, B256

Cadden, J. P./Historiography of the American Catholic Church, E72

Calendar of Saints/J. Bentley, A221

Callan, C. J./Moral Theology, B271

Cambridge Medieval History, E62

Campbell, T. J./Pioneer Laymen of North America, A182

———. Pioneer Priests of North America, A183

Canada ecclésiastique, D116

Canada's Bishops/C. A. Liederbach, A201

CANON LAW, D152-D186

Canon Law/T. L. Bouscaren, D177

Canon Law Abstracts, D152

Canon Law Collection of the Library of Congress/D. C. Ferreira-Ibarra, D154

Canon Law Digest/T. L. Bouscaren, D158

Canon Law Society of America/Code of Canon Law, D159

———. Code of Canon Law, Latin-English Edition, D161

Canon Law Society of Great Britain and Ireland/Code of Canon Law in English Translation, D160

———. Index to the Code of Canon Law, D167

Canons and Decrees of the Council of Trent/H. J. Schroeder, E146

Capelli, A./Lexicon abbreviaturarum, C144

Caponigri, A. R./Modern Catholic Thinkers, C80

CAPUCHINS, E232-E246

CARA Seminary Directory/Center for Applied Research in the Apostolate, D31

Carey, M. A./Bibliography for Christian Formation in the Family, A24

Carlen, C./Papal Encyclicals, E114

———. *See also* Carlen, M. C.

Carlen, M. C./Dictionary of Papal Pronouncements, E127
_____. Guide to the Documents of Pius XII, E128
_____. Guide to the Encyclicals, E129
CARMELITES, E221-E226
Carnandet, J./Acta Sanctorum, A205
Carol, J. B./Mariology, B246
Carrier, H./Sociologie du christianisme, D46
Carroll, J. R./Compendium of Liturgical Music Terms, C157
Cartwright, J. K./Catholic Shrines of Europe, D187
Casati, G./Scritorri cattolici italiani viventi, C95
Case, S. J./Bibliographical Guide to the History of Christianity, E1
Catalog and Basic List of Essential First-Purchase Books/Catholic Library Service, A17
Catalog of Books in the Academy of American Franciscan History/L. Adasiewicz, E234
Catalog of Catholic Paperback Books/E. P. Willging, A60
Catalog of the Carmelitana Collection/J. Smet, E224
CATALOGING AND CLASSIFICATION, A80-A84
Catálogo de los manuscritos/A. García y García, E44
Catalogo delle pubblicazioni periodiche/Biblioteca Vaticana, A158
Catalogo delle publicazioni periodiche/Istituto per le Scienze Religiose, A151
Catalogo generale del libro cattolico in Italia, A66
Catalogue collectif des livres de culture religieuse en langue française, A64
Catalogue collectif des livres religieux, A63
Catalogue of All Catholic Books in English/Benziger Bros., A53

Catalogue of Catholic Books Printed in English/A. Allison, A11
Catalogue of Renaissance Philosophers/J. O. Riedl, C32
Catalogue of the Bible Collections in the Library at St. Mary's Oscott/G. F. Pullen, B73
Catalogue sélectif de publications religieuses françaises et des inspiration, A142
Catalogus translationum et commentariorum/P. O. Kristeller, C143
Catechism Explained/F. Spirago, B208
Catechism of the Council of Trent for Parish Priests, E147
Catholic Almanac, D90
Catholic Anthology/T. Walsh, C130
Catholic Apologetical Literature in the United States/R. Gorman, B214
Catholic Authors/M. Hoehn, C91
Catholic Authors in Modern Literature, C88
Catholic Authorship in the American Colonies before 1874/W. S. Merrill, A50
Catholic Biblical Encyclopedia/ J. E. Steinmueller, B95
Catholic Book in Poland/M. Pszczólkowska, A69
Catholic Book Merchandiser, A58
Catholic Bookman, A54
Catholic Bookman's Guide/M. Regis, A19
Catholic Bookseller and Librarian, A58
Catholic Builders of the Nation, A184
Catholic Catechism/J. A. Hardon, B201
Catholic Church in America/E. R. Vollmar, E81
Catholic Church in Detroit/G. Paré, F5
Catholic Church, U.S.A./L. J. Putz, E97
Catholic Colleges and Universities Directory, D30

Catholic Companion to the Bible/
R. L. Woods, B130
Catholic Concise Dictionary/ R. C.
Broderick, A87
Catholic Cookbook/W. I. Kaufman,
B405
Catholic Customs and Symbols/H. T.
Henry, D68
Catholic Day Care Centers/N.C.C.C.,
D61
Catholic Dictionary/W. E. Addis,
A85
Catholic Dictionary/D. Attwater, A86
Catholic Dictionary of Theology, B184
Catholic Directory/Ecclesiastical
Register and Almanac, D112
Catholic Directory and Guide for the
Archdiocese of Detroit, F2
Catholic Directory for Scotland, D113
Catholic Directory of Canada, D116
Catholic Directory of Eastern
Africa, D83
Catholic Directory of England and
Wales, D114
Catholic Directory of Ethiopia, D84
Catholic Directory of India, D129
Catholic Directory of India, Pakistan,
Burma and Ceylon, D106
Catholic Directory of Japan, D132
Catholic Directory of Southern
Africa, D85
Catholic Directory of the British
Caribbean, D117
Catholic Directory of the Philippines,
D138
Catholic Documentation, E122
Catholic Documents, E123
Catholic Education/W. B. Kolesnik,
D19
Catholic Education: A Handbook,
D21
Catholic Education in America/N. G.
McCluskey, D43
Catholic Education in the Western
World/J. M. Lee, D42
Catholic Encyclopedia (1905), A89
Catholic Encyclopedia (1936), A93
Catholic Encyclopedia/R. C.
Broderick, A88

Catholic Encyclopedia and Its Makers,
A179
Catholic Encyclopedia Dictionary,
A94
Catholic Encyclopedia for School and
Home, A95
Catholic Fact Book/J. G. Deedy,
D92
Catholic Guide to Foundations/
F. G. DeBettencourt, D59
Catholic Hierarchy in the U.S./
J. H. O'Donnell, A192
Catholic Hospital Association/
Guidebook, D58
Catholic Institutions in the U.S.,
Canonical and Civil Law
Status/J. J. McGrath,
D53
Catholic Layman's Book of Etiquette/
R. C. Broderick, D65
Catholic Left in Latin America/T. C.
Dahlin, D146
Catholic Library Association/C.L.A.
Basic Reference Books for
Catholic High School
Libraries, A47
_____. C.L.A. Booklist, A25
_____. Handbook and Membership
Directory, A71
_____. Parish Library Manual, A75
_____. Parish Library Manual:
Suggested Books, A76
Catholic Library Practice/D. Martin,
A78
Catholic Library Service/Catalog and
Basic List of Essential First-
Purchase Books, A17
Catholic Library World/Handbook
and Membership Directory,
A71
Catholic Literary Revival/C.
Alexander, C97
Catholic Magazine Index, A159
Catholic Mission History/J.
Schmidlin, B299
Catholic Mission Theory/J.
Schmidlin, B300
Catholic Periodical and Literature
Index, A160

Catholic Picture Dictionary/H. A.
Pfeiffer, A111
Catholic Press Directory, A143
Catholic Press in India: Directory,
A145
Catholic Priesthood According to
the Teaching of the Church/
P. Veuillot, B254
Catholic Reference Encyclopedia,
A98
Catholic Reformation/J. C.
Olin, E67
Catholic Religious Orders/O. L.
Kapsner, E189
Catholic Schools in America/
N.C.E.A., D26
Catholic Serials of the Nineteenth
Century/E. P. Willging, A155
Catholic Shrines of Europe/J. K.
Cartwright, D187
Catholic Social Principles/J. F.
Cronin, D11
Catholic Social Thought/M. J.
Williams, D13
Catholic Social Yearbook, D52
Catholic Subject Headings/O. L.
Kapsner, A84
Catholic Tourist Guide/K. Sullivan,
D192
Catholic Tradition/C. J. Dolan, C81
Catholic Traveler's Guide/Extension
Magazine, D188
Catholic University of America/
Theses and Dissertations,
A55
Catholic Who's Who, A200
Catholic Writer Yearbook/E.
Marolla, A145
Catholic Writer's Magazine Market,
A154
Catholic Year Book, D115
Catholicism/R. P. McBrien, B203
Catholicism and Anti-Catholicism/
M. J. Matochik, E75
Catholicisme/P. H. Batiffol, E33
Catholicisme: hier, aujourd'hui,
demain/G. Jacquement, A117
Catholics in Psychology/H. Misiak,
C76

Cavallera, F./Thesaurus doctrinae
catholicae, B216
Cave, R. C./Source Book for
Medieval Economic History,
D145
Cayre, F./Patrologie et histoire
de la théologie,
B138
Ceccaroni, A./Piccola enciclopedia
ecclesiastica, A129
Ceillier, R./Histoire générale des
auteurs sacrés et
ecclésiastiques, A171
Center for Applied Research in the
Apostolate/CARA Seminary
Directory, D31
Center for Reformation Research/
Early Sixteenth Century
Roman Catholic Theologians,
B25
Centre documentaire catéchétique/
Où en est l'ensiegnement
religieux?, D15
CEREMONIES, B401-B403
Ceremonies of the Roman Rite
Described/A. Fortescue,
B401
Černik, B. O./Schriftsteller der
noch bestehenden
Augustinerchorherrenstifte,
E208
Chabot, I. B./Corpus scriptorum
christianorum orientalium,
B163
Chambers, B. T./Bibliography of
French Bibles, B62
Chapin, J./Book of Catholic
Quotations, C119
_____. Treasury of Catholic
Reading, C82
Checklist of Manuscripts, E170
Check-List of Middle English
Prose Writings of Spiritual
Guidance/P. S. Jolliffe,
A6
Cheetham, S./Dictionary of
Christian Antiquities,
E32
CHESTERTON, G. K., C103

Chevalier, C. U. J./Répertoire des sources historiques du moyen âge, E41
_____. Répertoire des sources historiques du moyen âge: Bio-bibliographie, A170
_____. Repertorium hymnologicum, C147
Chicago Area Theological Library Association/Union List of Serials, A156
CHILDREN'S BOOKS, A32-A39
Children's Catalog: Catholic Supplement/M. Fidelis, A32
Childress, J. F./Westminster Dictionary of Christian Ethics, B270, C19
CHRIST, SYMBOLS, C189-C190
Christian Churches of the East/ D. Attwater, B8
Christian Communication Directory Africa/F.-J. Eilers, A148
Christian Communication Directory Asia/F.-J. Eilers, A149
Christian Denominations/K. Algermisson, B1
Christian Faith in the Doctrinal Documents of the Catholic Church/J. Neuner, B220
Christian Iconography/A. N. Didron, C177
Christian Spirituality/P. Pourrat, B324
CHRISTOLOGY, B234-B237
Christus: manuel d'histoire des religions/P. Rousselot, B17
Chronicles and Memorials of Great Britain and Ireland during the Middle Ages, E55
Chronological Harmony of the Gospels/S. J. Hartdegen, B57
CHURCH (THEOLOGY OF), B249
Church: a Bibliography/A. Dulles, B249
Church, A Pictorial History/E. E. Rice, E24

Church and State through the Centuries/S. Z. Ehler, D150
Church at Prayer/A. G. Martimort, B390
Church Historians, E25
Church History/K. Bilhmeyer, E14
Church State Relations/A. J. Menendez, D147
Church Symbolism/F. R. Webber, C188
Church Teaches/J. F. Clarkson, B217
Church Vestments/H. Norris, C207
Churches and Church Membership in the U.S./D. W. Johnson, D98
Churches and Church Membership in the United States, 1980/B. Quinn, D77
Church's Year of Grace/P. Parsch, B395
Cirlot, J. E./Dictionary of Symbols, C75
CISTERCIANS, E227-E228
Clancy, T. H./English Catholic Books, A13
Clarke, R. H./Lives of the Deceased Bishops, A185
Clarkson, J. F./The Church Teaches, B217
Classics of Western Spirituality, B312
Clavis patrum apostolicorum/H. Kraft, B151
Clavis patrum graecorum/M. Geerard, B150
Clavis patrum latinorum/E. Dekkers, B149
Clement, C. E./Handbook of Christian Symbols, C194
Clément, J. M./Lexique des anciennes règles, E177
Clergyman's Fact Book, D91
Clerical Dress and Insignia of the Roman Catholic Church/H. J. McCloud, C205

Code, J. B./American Bishops, 1964-1970, A186

_____. Dictionary of the American Hierarchy, A187

_____. Great American Foundresses, E204

_____. The Veil is Lifted, E205

Code of Canon Law/Canon Law Society of America, D159

Code of Canon Law in English Translation/Canon Law Society of Great Britain and Ireland, D160

Code of Canon Law, Latin-English Edition/Canon Law Society of America, D161

Codex iuris canonici (1917), D163

Codex iuris canonici (1983), D162

Codices manuscripti operum Thomae de Aquino/H. F. Dondaine, C57

Codicis iuris canonici fontes/P. Gasparri, D165

Coffin, J./Coins of the Popes, E136

Cohen, E. H./Works and Criticism of Gerard Manley Hopkins, C105

Coins of the Popes/J. Coffin, E136

Coleccion completa Enciclicas/ Hoyos, F., E113

Collectio scriptorum ordinis Carmelitarum/Bartolommeo de S. Angelo, E222

COLLEGE READING, A40-A42

COLLEGES AND UNIVERSITIES, DIRECTORIES, D30-D38

Collins, J. D./History of Modern European Philosophy, C23

Collins, M./New Dictionary of Theology, B194

Combined Biblical Dictionary and Concordance for the New American Bible, B82

Commentarium lovaniense in Codicem iuris canonici, D180

Commentary on the Documents of Vatican II/H. Vorgrimler, E152

Commentary on the New Lectionary/ G. S. Sloyan, B355

Committee for the Responsible Election of the Pope/The Inner Elite, A180

Common Catechism/J. Feiner, B200

Companion to Scripture Studies/ J. E. Steinmuller, B77

Companion to the Summa/W. Farrell, C70

Comparative Liturgy/A. Baumstarck, B407

Compendium of Liturgical Music Terms/J. R. Carroll, C157

Complete Concordance to the Bible/ N. W. Thompson, B91

Complete Index of the Summa of St. Thomas Aquinas/R. J. Deferrari, C63

Conciliar and Post Conciliar Documents/A. Flannery, E153

Concilii plenarii baltimorensis II, E85

Conciliorum oecumenicorum decreta, E143

Concilium plenarium totius Americae Septentrionalis Foederatae, E84

Concilium Tridentinum, E148

Concise Dictionary of Christian Ethics/B. Stoeckle, B263

Concise Dictionary of the Christian World Mission/S. C. Neill, B296

Concise Guide to the Catholic Church/F. A. Foy, D94

Concise Guide to the Documents of the Second Vatican Council/ A. Hastings, E157

Concise Sacramentum mundi/K. Rahner, B196

Concordance of the Proper Names in the Holy Scriptures/T. D. Williams, B93

Concordance to the English Poetry of Gerard Manley Hopkins/ R. J. Dilligan, C106

Concordance to the Historia ecclesiastica of Bede/P. F. Jones, E50

Concordance to the Works of St. Anselme/G. R. Evans, C34

Concordantiae Biblorum sacrorum vulgatae etitionis/F. P. Dutripon, B83

Concordantiarum universae sacrae Scripturae thesaurus/E. Peaultier, B89

Congregatio de Seminariis et Studiorum Universitatibus/ Seminaria ecclesiae catholicae, D32

Congregatio pro Causis Sanctorum/ Index ac status causarum beatificationis servorum Dei, A238

CONGREGATION OF THE IMMACULATE HEART OF MARY, E229-E230

Connelly, J./Hymns of the Roman Liturgy, B362

Constable, G./Medieval Monasticism, E171

Constitutiones, decreta, declarationes ... Vaticani II, E154

Contemporary Catholic Thought/ B. Ulanov, C86

Contemporary Church, A97

Contemporary Theology/U. J. Steiner, B40

Convent Life/J. M. Lexau, E190

Conway, J. D./What They Ask about Morals, B272

Cooking for Christ/F. E. Berger, B404

Copleston, F./History of Philosophy, C24

Coriden, J./Code of Canon Law, D159

Corpus Christianorum, B158

Corpus Dictionary of Western Churches/T. C. O'Brien, A99

Corpus juris canonici/A. L. Richter, D164

Corpus scriptorum christianorum orientalium/I. B. Chabot, B163

Corpus scriptorum ecclesiasticorum latinorum, B164

Correct Pronunciation of Latin According to Roman Usage/ M. DeAngelis, B384

Corrigan, J. T./Guide for the Organization and Operation of a Religious Resource Center, A77

_____. Periodicals for Religious Education Resource Centers, A146

Costello, M./Guides for Catholic Day Care Centers, D54

Costumes of Prelates of the Catholic Church/J. A. Nainfa, C206

Cottineau, L. H./Répertoire topo-bibliographique des abbayes et prieurés, E172

Coulson, H. H./Source Book for Medieval Economic History, D145

Coulson, J./Saints, A233

COUNCIL OF TRENT, E146-E148

COUNCILS, E142-E169

Courville, R. W./Index to the Code of Canon Law, D168

Coussemaker, C. E. H. de/Scriptorum de musica Medii Aevi, C170

Cowan, I. B./Medieval Religious Houses: Scotland, E201

Creeds, Councils and Controversies/ J. Stevenson, E30

Creusen, I./Epitome iuris canonici, D181

Criteria for Evaluation of Catholic Elementary Schools/N.C.E.A., D22

Critical Bibliography of Ecumenical Literature/J. F. Lescrauwaet, B326

Critical Bibliography of Liturgical Literature/T. A. Vismans, B333

Critical Bibliography of Missiology/ L. Vriens, B293

Cronin, J. F./Catholic Social
Principles, D11
Cronin, L. J./Resources for Religious
Instruction of Retarded
People, D16
Cronistas franciscanos/J. Ascencio,
E233
Crouzel, H./Bibliographie critique
d'Origène, B147
Crusades/A. S. Atiya, E39
Cuénot, C./Nouveau lexique
Teilhard de Chardin, C54
Culkin, H. M./Guide to Current
Catholic Diocesan Newspapers
in Microform, A147
Cunningham, R. G./Annotated
Bibliography of the Works
of the Canon Law Society
of America, D153
CUSTOMS, B404-B406, D65-D69
Cutler, J. L./Index of Middle English
Verse: Supplement, C132
Cuypers, H./Vocabulaire Teilhard de
Chardin, C55

Dąbrowskiego, E./Podręczna
encyklopedia biblijna, B107
Dagens, J./Bibliographie
chronologique de la
littérature spiritualité, B305
Daggy, R. E./Thomas Merton, C109
Dahlin, T. C./Catholic Left in
Latin America, D146
D'Ales, A./Dictionnaire apologétique
de la foi catholique, B215
Dalglish, W. A./Media for Christian
Formation, A26
Daman, P./Bibliographie ignatienne,
E253
Danielou, J./Sources chrétienne,
B176
Daniel-Rops, H./Twentieth Century
Encyclopedia of Catholicism,
A112
Darton, M./Modern Concordance to
the New Testament, B87
Davies, J. G./Dictionary of Liturgy
and Worship, B383

_____. New Westminster Dictionary
of Liturgy and Worship,
B388
Davis, H./Moral and Pastoral
Theology, B273
Davis, R. M./Evelyn Waugh: A
Checklist, C118
Day, P. D./Eastern Christian
Liturgies, B420
Dayton University, Marian Library/
Booklist of the Marian
Library, B239
Dead Sea Scrolls/J. A. Fitzmyer, B64
DeAngelis, M./Correct Pronunciation
of Latin According to Roman
Usage, B384
Death and Dying/J. H. Morgan, B282
DeBettencourt, F. G./Catholic Guide
to Foundations, D59
Decreta Concilii plenarii Baltimorensis
III, E85
Deedy, J. G./Catholic Fact Book, D92
Deemer, P./Ecumenical Directory of
Retreat and Conference
Centers, D93
Deferrari, R. J./Complete Index of
the Summa of St. Thomas
Aquinas, C63
_____. Latin-English Dictionary of
St. Thomas Aquinas, C67
_____. Lexicon of St. Thomas
Aquinas, C67
DeFiores, S./Dictionnaire de la vie
spirituelle, B315
Dehey, E. T./Religious orders of
Women in the U.S., E182
Dekkers, E./Clavis patrum latinorum,
B149
Delaney, J. J./Dictionary of American
Catholic Biography, A188
_____. Dictionary of Catholic
Biography, A172
_____. Dictionary of Saints, A228
_____. Guide to Catholic Reading,
A15
Delehaye, H./Martyrologium
romanum, B375
_____. Work of the Bollandists
through Three Centuries, A214

Delisle, L./Recueil des historiens des Gaules et de France, E54

Dell'Isola, F./Thomas Merton, C110

DeLubac, H./Sources chrétienne, B176

DeMarco, A. A./Tomb of St. Peter, E26

Denzinger, H. J. D./Enchiridion symbolorum, B218

_____. Sources of Catholic Dogma, B219

Deretz, J./Dictionary of the Council, E164

Despont, J./Nouvel atlas des missions, B301

Dessubré, M./Bibliographie de l'Ordre des Templiers, E263

Destrez, J./Bibliographie thomiste, C58

Deutschen Literatur des Mittelalters/ W. Stammler, C140

Dheilly, J./Dictionnaire biblique, B96

Diamond, W. J./Dictionary of Liturgical Latin, B385

DiBerardino, A./Dizionario patristico ed: antichità cristiane, B179

_____. Patrology, B143

Diccionario de escritores trinitarios/ Antonio de la Asunción, E264

Diccionario de Historia Eclesiástica de España, E9

Diccionario de los textos conciliares/ A. Torres Calvo, E166

Diccionario de textos sociales pontificios/A. Torres Calvo, D10

Diccionario del hogar católico, A140

Diccionario del Vaticano II/M. A. Molina Martinez, E165

DICTIONARIES AND ENCYCLO- PEDIAS, GENERAL, A85-A141

Dictionarium morale et canonicum/ P. Palazzini, B267

Dictionary Catalog of the Pontifical Institute of Medieval Studies, E47

Dictionary of American Catholic Biography/J. J. Delaney, A188

Dictionary of Biblical Theology/ X. Léon-Dufour, B102

Dictionary of Canon Law/P. Trudel, D175

Dictionary of Catholic Biography/ J. J. Delaney, A172

Dictionary of Christian Antiquities/ W. Smith, E32

Dictionary of Christian Biography/ W. Smith, A177

Dictionary of Christian Biography and Literature to the End of the Sixth Century/H. Wace, A178

Dictionary of Dogmatic Theology/P. Parente, B225

Dictionary of Hymnology/J. Julian, C158

Dictionary of Liturgical Latin/W. J. Diamond, B385

Dictionary of Liturgy and Worship/ J. G. Davies, B383

Dictionary of Mary/D. Attwater, B241

Dictionary of Moral Theology/F. Roberti, B268

Dictionary of Papal Pronouncements/ M. C. Carlen, E127

Dictionary of Proper Names and Places in the Bible/O. Odelain, B106

Dictionary of Saintly Women/A. B. C. Dunbar, A237

Dictionary of Saints/D. Attwater, A217

Dictionary of Saints/J. J. Delaney, A228

Dictionary of Scholastic Philosophy/ B. Wuellner, C20

Dictionary of Secret and Other Societies/A. Preuss, A165

Dictionary of Symbols/J. E. Cirlot, C75

Dictionary of the American Hierarchy/J. B. Code, A187

Dictionary of the Bible/J. L. McKenzie, B104

Dictionary of the Council/J.
  Deretz, E164
Dictionary of the Middle Ages/J. R.
  Strayer, E58
Dictionary of the New Latin Psalter/
  W. J. Konus, B366
Dictionary of the New Testament/
  X. Leon-Dufour, B103
Dictionary of the Popes/D. Attwater,
  E131
Dictionary of the Psalter/M. Britt,
  B365
Dictionary of Theology/L. Bouyer,
  B182
Dictionary of Theology/K. Rahner,
  B195
Dictionnaire apologétique de la foi
  catholique/A. D'Ales, B215
Dictionnaire biblique/J. Dheilly, B96
Dictionnaire d'archéologie chrétienne
  et de liturgie/F. Cabrol,
  B382, E27
Dictionnaire de bibliographie
  catholique/F. M. Pérennès, A4
Dictionnaire de droit canonique/R.
  Naz, D172
Dictionnaire de théologie catholique/
  A. Vacant, B185
Dictionnaire de la Bible/F. G.
  Vigourouz, B113
Dictionnaire de la foi catholique/
  O. LaBrosse, B191
Dictionnaire de la vie spirituelle/
  S. DeFiores, B315
Dictionnaire de sociologie/G.
  Jacquement, D9
Dictionnaire de spiritualité ascétique
  et mystique/M. Viller, B316
Dictionnaire des Églises de France,
  Belgique ..., E10
Dictionnaire des ordres religieux/P.
  Hélyot, E187
Dictionnaire des ouvrages anonymes
  et pseudonymes (Jesuit)/C.
  Sommervogel, E251
Dictionnaire d'histoire et de géographie
  ecclésiastiques/A. Baudrillart,
  E8
Dictionnaire du foyer catholique, A119

Dictionnaire du symbolisme, C176
Dictionnaire latin francais des
  auteurs chrétiens/A. Blaise,
  B177
Dictionnaire pratique de liturgie
  romaine/R. Lesage, B387
Dictionnaire practique des connais-
  sances religieuses/J.
  Bricourt, A118
Didron, A. N./Christian Iconography,
  C177
Diener, R. E./Bibliographies and
  Bulletins in Theology,
  B35
Digest of Church Law on Sacred
  Music/J. F. Mytych, C166
Digest of Regulations and Rubrics
  of Catholic Church Music/
  R. F. Hayburn, C165
Dilligan, R. J./Concordance to the
  English Poetry of Gerard
  Manley Hopkins, C106
Dindinger, J./Bibliotheca missionum,
  B292
DIRECTORIES, D65-D143
Directorio católico de Cuba,
  D119
Directorio de la Iglesia en México,
  D134
Directory: Diocesan Agencies of
  Catholic Charities/N.C.C.C.,
  D62
Directory of Campus Ministry, D33
Directory of Catholic Camps, D60
Directory of Catholic Charities in the
  U.S./J. O'Grady, D63
Directory of Catholic Institutions in
  the U.S./N.C.C.C.,
  D61
Directory of Catholic Residential
  Schools, D25
Directory of Catholic Schools and
  Colleges, D24
Directory of Catholic Special
  Facilities in the U.S. for
  Handicapped Children and
  Adults/N.C.E.A., D27
Directory of Centers for Religious
  Research and Study, D27

Directory of Departments and Programs of Religious Studies in North America/W. E. Mills, D34

Directory of Diocesan Lay Programs and Resources, 1980-81/ Bishops' Committee on the Laity, D35

Directory of Members/American Catholic Philosophical Society, C31

Directory of Religious Orders (Great Britain), E180

Directory of Religious Organizations in the United States, A163

Directory of Residences for Unwed Mothers/N.C.C.C., D61

Directory of Secular Institutes, E194

Directory of Women Religious in the United States, 1985/M. O'Hara, E206

Dirks, S./Histoire littéraire et bibliographique des Frères Mineurs, E235

Dirksen, C. F./Bibliography of Economic Books and Pamphlets by Catholic Authors, D144

Disciplinary Decrees of the General Councils/H. J. Schroeder, E144

Discoursi e radiomessaggi/Pius XII, E117

Discoursi, messaggi, coloqui/John XXIII, E118

Dissertationen der Katholische Theologischen der Fakultät der Universität Wien, 1831-1965/F. Loidl, B32

Distribution of Catholic Priests in the U.S., D102

Divine Armory of Holy Scripture/ K. Vaughan, B223

DIVINE OFFICE, B357-B367, B411

Dizionario biblico/F. Spadafora, B111

Dizionario degli istituti di perfezione/ G. Pelliccia, E181

Dizionario dei concili/P. Palazzini, E167

Dizionario del Concilio ecumenico Vaticano secondo/S. Garofalo, E163

Dizionario di erudizione storico-ecclesiastica/G. Moroni, A135

Dizionario di mariologia/G. M. Roschini, B245

Dizionario ecclesiastico/A. Mercati, A130

Dizionario enciclopedico di spiritualitá/E. Ancilli, B317

Dizionario enciclopedico di teologia morale/L. Rossi, B269

Dizionario patristico e di antichità cristiane/A. DiBerardino, B179

Dizionario sociale/A. Fappani, D50

Doble, G. H./Lives of the Welsh Saints, A242

————. Saints of Cornwall, A243

Documents Illustrative of the History of the Church/B. J. Kidd, E4

Documents of American Catholic History/J. T. Ellis, E87

Documents of Vatican II/W. M. Abbott, E155

Documents of Vatican II; The Conciliar and Post Conciliar Documents/A. P. Flannery, E156

Documents on the Liturgy, 1963-1979/ International Commission on English in the Liturgy, B335

Dogma/M. Schmaus, B229

DOGMATIC THEOLOGY, B216-B256

Doheny, W. J./Papal Documents on Mary, B240

Dolan, C. J./Catholic Tradition, C81

Dollen, C./Abortion in Context, B259

————. Vatican II: A Bibliography, E150

Dols, J. M. E./Bibliographie der moderne devotie, B306

DOMINICANS, E231

Donaldson, J./Ante-Nicene Fathers, B154

Donato da S. Giovanni/Biblioteca dei Frati minori cappuccini (Bologna), E236

Dondaine, H. F./Codices manuscripti operum Thomae de Aquino, C57

Doohan, L./Laity: a Bibliography, B26

Dorneich, M./Vaterunser Bibliographie, B419

Dorothy Day and the Catholic Worker/A. Klejment, D48

Douay Version, Holy Bible, B47

Douze années de bibliographie érasmienne/J. C. Margolin, C45

Doyle, P. A./Liam O'Flaherty, C116

Drake, M./Saints and Their Emblems, C196

DRAMA, C120

Dreesen, G./Bibliographia academica, B27

Dressler, H./Introduction to Medieval Latin Studies, C142

Dreves, G. M./Analecta hymnica medii aevi, C152

Drouin, E. G./School Question: A Bibliography, D17

DeBoulay, F. R. H./Handlist of Medieval Ecclesiastical Terms, E59

Duchesne, L. M./Liber pontificalis, E110

Dufourcq, A./Avenir du Christianisme, E16

Dugdale, W./Monasticon anglicanum, E198

Dulles, A./The Church, A Bibliography, B249

DuManoir de Juaye, H./Maria, B247

Dunbar, A. B. C./Dictionary of Saintly Women, A237

Dunne, T./Gerard Manley Hopkins, C107

DUNS SCOTUS, J./C42

Dupuis, J./Christian Faith in the Doctrinal Documents of the Catholic Church, B220

Dutch Catechism, B205

Dutripon, F. P./Concordantiae Biblorum sacrorum vulgatae editionis, B83

Duval, F. V./Livres qui s'imposent, D1

Dwight, H. O./Encyclopedia of Missions, B295

Dyer, G. J./American Catholic Catechism, B199

Early Catholic Americana/W. Parsons, A51

Early Latin Hymnaries/J. Mearns, C156

Early Sixteenth Century Roman Catholic Theologians/Center for Reformation Research, B25

Earnest, J. D./John Henry Newman, C113

Easson, D. E./Medieval Religious Houses: Scotland, E201

Eastern Christian Liturgies/ P. D. Day, B420

EASTERN CHURCHES, B8-B12

EASTERN RITES, B420-B422

Eberhardt, N. C./Summary of Catholic History, E17

———. Survey of American Church History, E96

Ecclesiae occidentalis monumenta iuris antiquissima/C. H. Turner, D171

Ecclesiastical Japanese/Satō Seitaro, A137

Ecclesiastical Prohibition of Books/ J. M. Pernicone, A46

ECONOMICS, D144-D145

Écrivains, artistes et savants de l'ordre de Prémontré/A. L. Goovaerts, E258

ECUMENICAL COUNCILS, E142-E169

Ecumenical Councils/H. Jedin, E168

Ecumenical Directory of Retreat and Conference Centers/P. Deemer, D93

ECUMENISM, B325-B329

Ecumenism Around the World: a
    Directory of Ecumenical
    Institutes, Centers and
    Organizations, A164
EDUCATION, D14-D43
Egger, C./Lexicon nominorum
    virorum et mulierum, A248
Église en prière/A. G. Martimort,
    B393
Ehler, S. Z./Church and State through
    the Centuries, D150
Eilers, F.-J./Christian Communication
    Directory Africa, A148
————. Christian Communication
    Directory Asia, A149
Eisenhofer, L./Liturgy of the Roman
    Rite, B391
Elenchus bibliographicus/Biblica,
    B60
Elenchus bibliographicus/
    Ephemerides theologicae
    lovaniensis, B28
Eliade, M./Encyclopedia of Religion,
    A100
Elizabethan Recusant Prose/A. C.
    Southern, C136
Ellis, J. T./Documents of American
    Catholic History, E87
————. Guide to American Catholic
    History, E73
————. Select Bibliography of the
    Catholic Church in the U.S.,
    E76
Emblems of Saints/F. C. Husenbeth,
    C197
Emmerich, H./Atlas hierarchicus,
    D195
Enchiridion asceticum/M. J. Rouët
    de Journel, B314
Enchiridion canonicum/C. Sartori,
    D166
Enchiridion clericorum, B255
Enchiridion de Verbo Incarnato/
    B. M. Xiberta y Roqueta, B236
Enchiridion documentorum
    instaurationis liturgicae/
    R. Kaczynski, B336
Enchiridion indulgentiarum, B413
Enchiridion liturgicum/P. Radó, B396

Enchiridion patristicum/M. J. Rouët
    de Journel, B222
Enchiridion symbolorum/H. J. D.
    Denzinger, B218
Enciclopedia Biografica/G. G.
    Roschini, A176
Enciclopedia cattolica, A131
Enciclopedia cristologica/G. Bardy,
    B237
Enciclopedia de la Biblia, B109
Enciclopedia de la Iglesia Católica
    en México/J. Rogelio Alvarez,
    A138
Enciclopedia de la religión cathólica,
    A141
Enciclopedia de orientación
    bibliografica/T. Zammariego,
    A27
Enciclopedia del cattolico, A132
Enciclopedia del Cristianismo/S.
    Romani, A133
Enciclopedia del sacerdozio/G.
    Cacciatore, B256
Enciclopedia della Bibbia/A.
    Rolla, B109
Enciclopedia delle religione, B19
Enciclopedia ecclesiastica/A.
    Bernareggi, A134
Enciclopedia filosofica, C17
Enciclopedia Mariana "Theotócos",
    B242
Encyclopaedie van het Katholicisme/
    E. Hendrikx, A115
Encyclopedia katolika/W. Granat,
    A139
Encyclopedia of Biblical Theology/
    J. B. Bauer, B94
Encyclopedia of Bioethics/W. T.
    Reich, B264
Encyclopedia of Catholic Saints, A229
Encyclopedia of Missions/H. O.
    Dwight, B295
Encyclopedia of Mysticism and
    Mystery Religions/J.
    Ferguson, B318
Encyclopedia of Religion/M. Eliade,
    A100
Encyclopedia of the Bible/P. A.
    Marijnen, B97

Encyclopedia of the Papacy/
H. Kühner, E134
Encyclopedia of Theology: The
concise Sacramentum mundi/
K. Rahner, B196
Encyclopedic Dictionary of Christian
Doctrine/J. P. Bradley,
B183
Encyclopedic Dictionary of Religion/
P. K. Meagher, A101
Encyclopedic Dictionary of the
Bible/A. van den Born, B98
Encyclopedie des musiques sacrées/
J. Porte, C161
Encyclopédie des sciences religieuses,
A120
Encyclopédie théologique/J. P.
Migne, A122
Encyklopedia Katolika/W. Granat,
A139, B190
Englebert, O./Lives of the Saints,
A230
English Catholic Books/T. H.
Clancy, A13
English Versions of the Bible/H.
Pope, B72
Ensayo de una biblioteca/G. de
Santiago Vela, E211
Ephemerides theologicae lovaniensis,
Elenchus bibliographicus,
B28
Episcopal Lineage of the Hierarchy in
the U.S./J. W. Lonsway, A191
Epitome iuris canonici/A. Vermeersch,
D181
ERASMUS, D./C43-C46
Essai bibliographique autour de
"Rerum novarum"/É. Laurant,
D2
Essai de bibliographie oratorienne/
A. M. P. Ingold, E260
ETIQUETTE, D65-D69
L'Étude comparée des religions/H.
Pinard de La Boullaye,
B16
Eubel, C./Hierarchia catholica medii
et recentioris aevi, A173
Euthanasia Controversy/C. W.
Triche, B261

Evans, A. P./Bibliography of English
Translations from Medieval
Sources, E42
Evans, G. R./Concordance to the
Works of St. Anselme, C34
Evans, I./New Library of Catholic
Knowledge, A109
L'évangile: études iconographiques et
archéologique/C. Rohault de
Fleury, C190
Evelyn Waugh: A Checklist/R. M.
Davis, C118
Exegetisches Worterbuch zum Neuen
Testament/H. Balz, B99
Exeler, A./Glaubersinformation, B188
Extension Magazine/Catholic
Traveler's Guide, D188
Externals of the Catholic Church/
J. F. Sullivan, D69

Fappani, A./Dizionario Sociale, D50
Farge, J. K./Biographical Register
of Paris Doctors of Theology,
1500-1536, B212
Farmer, D. H./Oxford Dictionary
of Saints, A231
Farrar, C. P./Bibliography of English
Translations from Medieval
Sources, E42
Farrell, E./Moral Theology, B271
Farrell, W./Companion to the
Summa, C70
FATHERS OF THE CHURCH,
B135-B181
Fathers of the Church, B155
Federici, T./Dizionario del
Concilio ecumenico Vaticano
secondo, E163
Feiner, J./Common Catechism, B200
Feister, J./Apostolic Regions of the
U.S., D101
_____. Distribution of Priests in the
U.S., D102
Felice da Mareto/Biblioteca dei Frati
minori cappuccini (Parma),
E237
Fenner, K. T./American Catholic
Etiquette, D66

Ferguson, G. W./Signs and Symbols in Christian Art, C178

Ferguson, J./Encyclopedia of Mysticism and Mystery Religions, B318

Ferguson, M. A./Bibliography of English Translations from Medieval Sources, E43

Fernandez-Garcia, M./Lexicon scholasticum philosophico-theologicum, C18

Ferreira-Ibarra, D. C./Canon Law Collection of the Library of Congress, D154

Fichier augustinien/Institut des Études Augustiniennes, C37

FICTION, C121-C126

Fidelis, M./Children's Catalog: Catholic Supplement, A32

Fifteenth Century English Prayers and Meditations/P. Revell, A8

Fifty Years of the American Novel/ H. C. Gardiner, C123

Fink, K. A./Vatikanische Archiv, E6

Finn, B. A./Twenty-four American Cardinals, A189

Finnegan, E. G./New Catholic People's Encyclopedia, A108

Finotti, J. M./Bibliographia catholica americana, A49

Fischer, B./Novae concordantiae biblorum sacrorum iuxta vulgatam versionem, B84

Fischl, J./Geschicte der Philosophie, C25

Fisher, A. S. T./Records of Christianity, E5

Fisher, J./Lives of the British Saints, A241

Fitzgerald, C. A./Union List of Catholic Periodicals, A157

FitzGerald, J. A./List of 5,000 Catholic Authors, C89

Fitzmyer, J. A./Dead Sea Scrolls, B64

_____. Introductory Bibliography for the Study of Scripture, B63

Fitzpatrick, P. J./Bibliography of Economic Books and Pamphlets by Catholic Authors, D144

Flannery, A./Conciliar and Post Conciliar Documents, E153

Flannery, A. P./Documents of Vatican II: The Conciliar and Post Conciliar documents, E156

_____. Vatican Council II, More Post Conciliar Documents, E156

Flannery O'Connor and Caroline Gordon: A Reference Guide/ R. E. Golden, C115

Fliche, A./Histoire de l'Église, E18

Floyd, M. K./Abortion Bibliography, B258

Focus/D. Smyth, A40

Follain, J./Petit glossaire de l'argot écclésiastique, A121

Fontes bibliographia de vocatione/ L. R. Ravasi, E175

Fontes historiae ecclesiasticae/C. Silva-Tarouca, E57

Fortescue, A./Ceremonies of the Roman Rite Described, B401

_____. Lesser Eastern Churches, B10

_____. Orthodox Eastern Churches, B11

_____. Uniate Eastern Churches, B12

14th Century English Mystics/V. M. Lagorio, B307

Foy, F. A./Concise Guide to the Catholic Church, D94

Franciscanos y la imprenta en México/ R. Zulaica Garate, E244

FRANCISCANS, E232-E246

Francois, J./Bibliothèque générale des écrivains de l'Ordre de Saint Benoît, E215

Frederick, M. C./Handbook of Catholic Practices, D67

Frederick, A./This They Wrote, E256

Free and Faithful in Christ/B. Haring, B275

Freemantle, A./Papal Encyclicals in Their Historical Context, E130
_____. Social Teachings of the Church, D5
Freitag, A./Twentieth Century Atlas of the Christian World, D194
French Devotional Texts of the Middle Ages/K. V. Sinclair, B416
Freudenberger, E./Reference Works in the Field of Religion, 1977-1985, A18
Friedman, M. J./Vision Obscured, C126
Fries, H./Handbuch theologischer Grundbegriffe, B189
Fullam, R. B./Popes on Youth, D64
_____. Spiritual Books for Catholic Youth, A33
Fundamentals of Catholic Dogma/L. Ott, B227

Gabriel Marcel and His Critics/F. Lapointe, C47
Gagné, A./Répertoire des thèses des facultiés ecclésiastiques de l'Université Laval, 1935-1960, B29
Gaines, S. J./Publishers Guide: Catholic Journals, A150
Galbraeth, D. L./Papal Heraldry, E137
Gallagher, D./Achievement of Jacques and Raïssa Maritain, C48
Gallery of Living Catholic Authors/ Sr. Mary Joseph, C90
Gams, P. B./Series episcoparum Ecclesiae catholicae, A175
Ganley, W./Catholic Schools in America, N.C.E.A., D26
García y García, A./Catálogo de los manuscritos, E44
Gardiner, H. C./Fifty Years of the American Novel, C123
_____. Norms for the Novel, C124
_____. The Great Books: A Christian Appraisal, C100

Gari y Siumell, J. A./Biblioteca Mercedaria, E257
Garofalo, S./Dictionary of Dogmatic Theology, B225
_____. Dizionario del Concilio ecumenico Vaticano secondo, E163
Gasparri, P./Codicis iuris canonici fontes, D165
Gasquet, A./Biblia Sacra iuxta latinam vulgatam, B44
Gautier, J./Some Schools of Catholic Spirituality, B323
Geddes, L. W./Moral and Pastoral Theology, B273
Geerard, M./Clavis patrum graecorum, B150
GENEALOGY, A245-A249
General Catechetical Directory/Sacred Congregation for the Clergy, B207
General Intercessions/A. J. Nevins, B352
GEOGRAPHY, D187-D196
Gerard Manley Hopkins: A Comprehensive Bibliography/T. Dunne, C107
Gerbert, M./Scriptores ecclesiastici de musica sacra potissimum, C171
Germania pontificia, E108
Geschichte der altkirchlichen Literatur/O. Bardenhewer, B136
Geschichte der Päpst/F. X. Seppelt, E141
Geschichte der Philosophie/J. Fischl, C25
Geschichte der Quellen und Literatur des canonischen Rechts/J. F. Schulte, D155
Gillow, J./Literary and Biographical History, A198
Gillum, G. P./Catholic Left in Latin America, D146
Gilmont, J. F./Bibliographie ignatienne, E253

Gilson, É. H./History of Christian Philosophy in the Middle Ages, C26
_____. History of Philosophy, C27
Gini, P./I Grandi del Cattolicesimo, A176
Gla, D./Systematisch geordnetes Repertorium der katholisch-theologischen Litteratur, B30
Glaubersinformation/A. Exeler, B188
Glenn, P. J./Tour of the Summa, C71
Glorieux, P./Pour revaloriser Migne, B165
_____. Répertoire de maîtres en théologie, B31
Glossary of Later Latin to 600 A.D./ A. Souter, B181
Golden Book of Catholic Poetry/ A. Noyes, C129
Golden Legend/J. de Voragine, A215
Golden, R. E./Flannery O'Connor and Caroline Gordon, C115
Golubovich, G./Biblioteca bio-bibliografice della Terra Santa e dell'Oriente francescano, E238
Gonzáles Ramírez, M. R./La Iglesia mexicana en cifrus, D135
Goovaerts, A. L./ Écrivains, artistes et savants de l'ordre de Prémontré, E258
GORDON, C., C115
Gorman, R./Catholic Apologetical Literature in the United States, B214
Görres Gesellschaft/Staatslexikon, D151
Gospel Harmony/J. E. Steinmueller, B59
Grabner-Haider, A./Praktisches Bibellexikon, B100
Grace, M./Books for Catholic Colleges, A41
Gradual romain, B351
Graffin, R./Patrologia orientalis, B166
_____. Patrologia syriaca, B167

Graham Greene: A Checklist of Criticism/J. D. Vann, C103
Grammar of Plainsong, C164
Granat, W./Encyklopedia Katolika, A139, B190
Grandi del cattolicesimo/G. G. Roschini, A176
Granfield, P./The Church: A Bibliography, B249
Great American Foundresses/ J. B. Code, E204
Great Books: A Christian Appraisal/ H. C. Gardiner, C100
Great Books of France/L. C. Sterc, C137
GREENE, G., C104
Greenly, A. H./Bibliography of Fr. Richard's Press in Detroit, A9
Gregorian Chant/W. Apel, C163
Grieschischen christlichen Schriftsteller der ersten drei Jahrhunderte, B168
Grisez, G. G./Way of the Lord Jesus, B274
Grollenberg, L. H./Atlas of the Bible, B131
_____. Shorter Atlas of the Bible, B132
Grootaers, W. A./Proeve eener bibliographie van de missionarissen, van Scheut, E229
Grosse Herder, A123
Grover, M. L./Catholic Left in Latin American, D146
Growth and Development of the Catholic School System in the U.S./J. A. Burns, D40
Grube, D./Bibliographie der deutschen Predigt, C139
Grundler, J./Lexikon der Christlichen Kirchen, B2
Grundmann, H./Bibliographie zur Ketzergeschichte des Mittelalters, E40
Guiá apostolicá latinoamericana/C. Alfaro, A162
Guiá de la Iglesia en España, D141
Guiá eclesiastica de Chile, D118

Guiá eclesiastica latinoamericano, D133

Guide Book for Catholic Church Choirmasters/L. Rowlands, C167

Guide de la France chretienne et missionaire, D125

Guide des sources de l'histoire des congregationes féminines francais de vie active/C. Molette, E173

Guide for the Organization and Operation of a Religious Resource Center, A77

Guide to American Catholic History/ J. T. Ellis, E73

Guide to Bibles in Print/G. Hester, B65

Guide to Catholic Italy, D190

Guide to Catholic Literature/C. M. Pilley, A56

Guide to Catholic Reading/J. F. Bernard, A15

Guide to Christian Europe/C. J. McNaspy, D189

Guide to Current Catholic Diocesan Newspapers in Microform/ H. M. Culkin, A147

Guide to Religious Careers for Catholic Men and Women, E184

Guide to Religious Communities for Women/D. Barrett, E183

Guide to Religious Ministries for Catholic Men and Women, E184

Guide to Schools and Departments of Religion and Seminaries in the United States and Canada, D36

Guide to the Archives of the Archdiocese of Boston/J. M. O'Toole, E91

Guide to the Bible/A. Robert, B126

Guide to the Catholic Sisterhoods in the U.S./T. P. McCarthy, E191

Guide to the Churches of Rome/M. Sharp, C204

Guide to the Diocesan Priesthood in the U.S./T. P. McCarthy, D38

Guide to the Documents of Pius XII/M. C. Carlen, E128

Guide to the Encyclicals/M. C. Carlen, E129

Guide to the Study of Medieval History/L. J. Paetow, E38

Guidebook/Catholic Hospital Association, D58

Guidelines to Personnel Practices and Salary Scales/N.C.C.C., D57

Guidepost, E185

Guides for Catholic Day Care Centers/ N.C.C.C., D54

Guides for Facilities for the Aging/ N.C.C.C., D55

Guides for Services to Children in Catholic Institutions/ N.C.C.C., D56

Guilday, P./National Pastorals of the American Hierarchy, E89

Guiney, L. I./Recusant Poets, C134

Guitard, A./Bibliographie internationale sur le sacerdoce et le ministère, B251

Gwynn, A. O./Medieval Religious Houses: Ireland, E200

Haag, H./Bibel-Lexikon, B101
_____. Breve diccionario de la Biblia, B101

Habig, M. A./Saints of the Americas, A240

Hadcock, R. N./Medieval Religious Houses: England, E199
_____. Medieval Religious Houses: Ireland, E200

Haeghen, F. van der/Bibliotheca Erasimiana, C43

Haley, E. L./Books by Catholic Authors in the Cleveland Public Library, A23

Halkin, F./Bibliotheca hagiographica graeca, A210

Halvorson, P. L./Atlas of Religious Change in America, 1952-1971, D95

Handboek der kerkgeschiedenis/J. deJong, E20

Handbook and Membership Directory/Catholic Library Association, A71

Handbook for American Catholic Hymnals/J. V. Higginson, C148

Handbook of American Catholic Societies/E. P. Willging, A168

Handbook of Catholic Practices/ M. C. Frederic, D67

Handbook of Christian Feasts and Customs/F. X. Weiser, B406

Handbook of Christian Social Ethics/E. Welty, D12

Handbook of Christian Symbols/ C. E. Clement, C194

Handbook of Church History/H. Jedin, E19

Handbook of Moral Theology/D. M. Prümmer, B279

Handbook of Secret Organizations/ W. J. Whalen, A167

Handbook of Symbols in Christian Art/G. G. Sill, C186

Handbook, U.S. Catholic Mission Council, B298

Handbuch der Namen und Heiligen/ O. Wimmer, C202

Handbuch der Pastoraltheologie/ F. X. Arnold, B283

Handbuch theologischer Grundbegriffe/H. Fries, B189

Handlist of Medieval Ecclesiastical Terms, E59

Hannon, J. D./Sacred Canons, D176

Hardon, J. A./Catholic Catechism, B201

_____. Modern Catholic Dictionary, A102

_____. Pocket Catholic Dictionary, A103

_____. Protestant Churches of America, B3

_____. Religions of the World, B4

_____. Spirit and Origins of American Protestantism, B5

Häring, B./Free and Faithful in Christ, B275

_____. Law of Christ, B276

Harmer, M. F./Books for Religious Sisters, A48

Harmony of the Gospels in the Knox Translation/L. Johnston, B58

Harrington, W./New Testament Message, B122

Hartdegen, S. J./Chronological Harmony of the Gospels, B57

_____. Nelson's Complete Concordance to the New American Bible, B88

Harte, T. J./Papal Social Principles, D4

Hartman, L. F./Encyclopedic Dictionary of the Bible, B98

Hassan, B./American Catholic Catalog, D96

Hastings, A./Concise Guide to the Documents of the Second Vatican Council, E157

Hayburn, R. F./Digest of Regulations and Rubrics of Catholic Church Music, C165

Heads of Religious Houses/D. Knowles, E207

Hebrew-Ugaritic Index/E. R. Martinez, B86

Heimbucher, M. J./Orden und Kongregationen, E186

Hélyot, P./Dictionnaire des ordres religieux, E187

Hendrikx, E./Encyclopaedie van het Katholicisme, A115

Henry, A. M./Dictionnaire de la foi catholique, B191

_____. Theology Library, B209

Henry, H. T./Catholic Customs and Symbols, D68

Henschenius G./Acta Sanctorum, A205

HERALDRY, A245-A246

Herrera Oria, A./Preacher's Encyclopedia, B286

Hester, G./Guide to Bibles in Print, B65

Hierarchia catholica medii et recentioris aevi/C. Eubel, A173
Higginson, J. V./Handbook for American Catholic Hymnals, C148
Hirn, Y./Sacred Shrine, C173
Histoire de la littérature grecque chrétienne/A. Peuch, B142
Histoire de la littérature latine chrétienne/P. C. de Labriolle, B139
Histoire de la philosophie: period chrétienne/F. van Steenberghen, C29
Histoire de la théologie au XIXe siècle/E. Hocedez, B211
Histoire de l'Église/A. Fliche, E18
Histoire générale de l'Eglise/A. Boulenger, E15
Histoire générale des auteurs sacrés et ecclésiastiques, A171
Histoire littéraire et bibliographique des Frères Mineurs/S. Dirks, E235
Historia juris canonici/A. M. Stickler, D184
Historiography of the American Catholic Church/J. P. Cadden, E72
HISTORY, E1-E98
History and literature of Christianity from Tertullian to Boethius/ P. C. deLabriolle, B140
History of Catholic Education in the U.S./J. A. Burns, D39
History of Christian Philosophy in the Middle Ages/É. H. Gilson, C26
History of Christian Spirituality/ L. Bouyer, B322
History of Medieval Philosophy/ M. M. Wulf, C30
History of Modern European Philosophy/J. D. Collins, C23
History of Our Lord as Exemplified in Works of Art/A. B. Jameson, C189

History of Philosophy/F. Copleston, C24
History of Philosophy/É. H. Gilson, C27
History of the Catholic Church/F. Mourret, E23
History of the Popes/L. F. von Pastor, E139
History of the Roman Breviary/P. Batiffol, B367
Hocedez, E./Histoire de la théologie au XIXe siècle, B211
Hoehn, M./Catholic Authors, C91
Holweck, F. G./Biographical Dictionary of the Saints, A232
Holy Bible, Confraternity Edition, B48
Holy Bible, Douay Version, B47
Holy Bible, R. A. Knox, tr., B46
Holy Bible, RSV Catholic Edition, B45
HOLY ORDERS, B251-B256
HOMILETICS, B286-B289
HOPKINS, G. M., C105-C108
Hopkins Collected at Gonzaga/K. Seelhammer, C108
Horae Beatae Mariae Virginis/E. Hoskins, B342
Horman, K./Lexikon der christlichen Moral, B265
Hoskins, E./Horae Beatae Mariae Virginis, B342
How to Distinguish the Saints in Art/A. deBles, C195
Hoyos, F./Coleccion completa Enciclicas, E113
Hughes, A./Liturgical Terms for Music Students, C158
_____. Medieval Music, C149
_____. Medieval Polyphony in the Bodleian Library, C150
Hughes, D. C./Index of Gregorian Chant, C155
Hugolin, P./Notes bibliographiques, E212
Humphrey, H./Bibliography for the Gospel of Mark, 1954-1980, B66

Hurter, H./Nomenclator literarius
theologiae catholicae theologos,
B213
Husenbeth, F. C./Emblems of Saints,
C197
Husslein, J./Social Wellsprings,
D8, E116
HYMNOLOGY, C146-C172
Hymns of the Breviary and Missal/
M. Britt, B361
Hymns of the Roman Liturgy/J.
Connelly, B362

Iconographie de l'art chrétien/L.
Réau, C185
ICONOGRAPHY, C174-C203
Iglesia mexicana en cifras/M. R.
Gozáles Ramírez,
D135
IGNATIOUS LOYOLA, E253
Ikonographie der christlichen Künst/
K. Künstle, C180
Illustrated Catholic Family Annual,
D97
Images of Women in Mission, E188
Imbart de la Tour, P./Origines de
la Réforme, E71
In Pursuit of Values/M. E. Kelley,
A34
Index ac status causarum
beatificationis servorum
Dei, A238
Index bibliographicus Societatis
Iesu, E252
Index des livres interdits/J. M. de
Bujanda, A43
Index et concordance, Vatican II/H.
Tardif, E162
Index librorum prohibitorum, A45
Index of Gregorian Chant/J. R.
Bryden, C155
Index of Middle English Verse/R. H.
Robbins, C132
Index Thomisticus/R. Busa, C64
Index to Catholic Pamphlets/E. P.
Willging, A61
Index to G. K. Chesterton/J. W.
Sprug, C103

Index to the Code of Canon Law/
Canon Law Society of Great
Britain and Ireland, D167
Index to the Code of Canon Law/
R. W. Courville, D168
Index to the New Testament and The
Topical Analysis of the New
Testament/A. H. Seubert, B90
Index to the Records of the American
Catholic Historical Society,
E95
Index to the Works of John Newman/
J. J. Rickaby, C114
Index verborum ac locutionum Codicis
iuris canonici/J. Ochoa
Sanz, D170
Index verborum Codicis iuris
canonici/A. Lauer, D169
Indian Missions/J. P. Ronda, B291
Indices verborum et locutionum
decretorum Concilii Vaticani
II, E160
Ingold, A. M. P./Essai de bib-
liographie oratorienne, E260
Inner Elite/G. MacEoin, A180
Inquisitors and the Jews/S. B.
Liebman, E77
Insegnamenti/Paul VI, E119
Institute des Études Augustiniennes/
Fichier augustinien, C37
Institutiones systematico-historicae in
sacram liturgiam/P.
Oppenheim, B408
Instituto Nacional del Libro
Español/Libros de religion,
A29
_____. Selección de libros católicos
españoles, A28
Instituts de vie consacrée au Canada/
M. Thériault, E196
Interdiocesaan Centrum/
Basisstatistieken over de
decanaten en bisdommen
van de Belgische Kerkprovincie,
D108
_____. Bevolking en misvierenden
in de decanaten en bisdommen
van de Belgische Kerkprovincie,
D109

International Bibliography on the Priesthood and the Ministry/ A. Guitard, B251

International Commission on English in the Liturgy/Documents on the Liturgy, 1963-1979, B335

International Directory of Religious Information Systems/D. O. Moberg, A72

International Ecumenical Bibliography, B325

International Federation of Institutes for Social and Socio-Religious Research/Directory of Centers for Religious Research and Study, D37

International Index of Catholic Biographies/S. J. M. Brown, A169

International Review of Biblical Studies, B78

Internationale ökumenische bibliographie, B325

Internationale Teilhard-Bibliographie/ L. Polgár, C51

Internationale Zeitschriftenschau für Biblewissenschaft und Grenzgebiete, B78

Introductio in liturgiam occidentalem/ H. Schmidt, B397

Introductio in liturgiam orientalum/ A. Raes, B422

Introduction à la philosophie/L. de Raeymaker, C21

Introduction to American Catholic Magazines/W. L. Lucey, A152

Introduction to Catholic Booklore/ S. J. M. Brown, A16

Introduction to Medieval Latin Studies/M. R. P. McGuire, C142

Introduction to the New Testament/ A. Robert, B127

Introduction to the Old Testament/ A. Robert, B128

Introductory Bibliography for the Study of Scripture/J. A. Fitzmyer, B63

Inventaires des pièces d'archives françaises/J. Bruggeman, E62

Iris Murdoch and Muriel Spark; A Bibliography/T. T. Tominaga, C117

Irish Catholic Directory, D130

Istituto di studi filosofici/ Bibliografia ragionata delle reviste filosofiche italiane, C14

Istituto per le Scienze Religiose di Bologna, Biblioteca/Catalogo della publicazioni periodiche, A151

Italia pontificia, E108

Italian Americans and Religion/ S. Tomasi, E80

Iuris ecclesiastici graecorum/ J. B. Pitra, D185

Ius decretalium/F. X. Wernz, D182

Jaarboek van het Katholiek Documentatie Centrum, D137

Jacquement, G./Catholicisme: hier, aujourd'hui, demain, A117

_____. Dictionnaire de Sociologie, D9

Jaegher, P. de/Anthology of Mysticism, B313

Jaffe, P./Regesta pontificium, E106

Jameson, A. B./History of Our Lord, C189

_____. Legends of the Madonna, C192

_____. Legends of the Monastic Orders, C203

_____. Sacred and Legendary Art, C179

Janauschek, L./Bibliographia bernardina, E228

Jarque i Jutglar, J. E./Bibliographie générale des oeuvres et articles sur Pierre Teilhard de Chardin, C49

Jedin, H./Atlas zur kirchengeschichte, D193

_____. Ecumenical Councils, E168

_____. Handbook of Church History, E19

Jerome Biblical Commentary/R. E. Brown, B117
Jerusalem Bible, B49
Jesuit Relations/R. G. Thwaites, E88
Jesuit Relations of Canada/J. C. McCoy, E78
Jesuit Saints and Martyrs/J. N. Tylenda, E255
Jesuiten-lexicon/L. Koch, E254
JESUITS, E247-E255
Jesus Christ/F. Prat, B234
Jochi Daigaku/Katorikku Daijiten, A136
John, C. R./Penguin Dictionary of Saints, A219
John, E./The Popes, E132
John Henry Newman/V. F. Blehl, C111
John Henry Newman/British Museum, C112
John Henry Newman/J. D. Earnest, C113
John XXIII/Discoursi, E118
Johnson, D. W./Churches and Church Membership in the U.S., D98
Johnston, L./Harmony of the Gospels in the Knox Translation, B58
Jolliffe, P. S./Check-List of Middle English Prose Writings of Spiritual Guidance, A6
Jone, H./Moral Theology, B277
Jones, C./The Study of Spirituality, B320
Jones, P. F./Concordance to the Historia ecclesiastica of Bede, E50
Jong, J. de/Handboek der kerkgeschiedenis, E20
Joseph, Sr. M./Gallery of Living Catholic Authors, C90
Julian, J./Dictionary of Hymnology, C158
Jungmann, J. A./Mass of the Roman Rite, B410

Kaczynski, R./Enchiridion documentorum instaurationis liturgicae, B336

Kapsner, O. L./Benedictine Bibliography, E216
———. Benedictine Bibliography. First Supplement, E217
———. Benedictine Liturgical Books in American Benedictine Libraries, B331
———. Catholic Religious Orders, E189
———. Catholic Subject Headings, A84
———. Manual of Cataloging Practice for Catholic Author and Title Entries, A81
Kataloge bayerischer Musiksammlungen/R. Münster, C151
Katalog der liturgischen Drücke/H. Bohatta, B340
Katechetisches Wörterbuch/L. Lentner, B285
Katholiek Documentatie Centrum/Jaarboek, D137
Katholieke encyclopaedie/P. van der Meer, A116
Katholisch-theologische bücherkunde/M. S. Tavagnutti, A31
Katholische Deutschland/W. Kosch, A203
Katholische Jahrbuch, D127
Katholische Marienkunde/P. Sträter, B248
Katholische Sozialdoktrin in ihrer geschichtlichen, D49
Katholischen Sozialakademie Österreichs/Katholisches Soziallexikon, D51
Katholischer literaturkalender, C96
Katholisches Soziallexikon, D51
Katoliek Jaarboek voor Belgie, D110
Katoliek Jaarboek voor Kongo, Ruanda en Urundi, D87
Katorikku Daijitan/Jōchi Daigaku, A136
Kaufman, W. I./Catholic Cookbook, B405
Kearns, R. M./Statistical Profile of Black Catholics, D103

Kehrein, J./Biographischliterarisches Lexikon der katholischen deutschen Dichter, C141

Kelley, M. E./In Pursuit of Values, A34

Kellogg, J. D./Vital Tradition, C125

Kelly, J. A./Maps of the Land of Christ, B134

Kelly, J. N. D./Oxford Dictionary of Popes, E133

Kelly, J. P./Papal Documents on Mary, B240

Kenneally, F./U.S. Documents in the Propagande Fide Archives, E74

Kenney, J. F./Sources for the Early History of Ireland, E45

Kidd, B. J./Documents Illustrative of the History of the Church, E4

Kiefer, W. J./Biblical Subject Index, B85

Kilmer, J./Anthology of Catholic Poets, C127

King, A. A./Rites of Eastern Christendom, B421
_____. Rites of Western Christendom, B392

Kirchengeschichte/J. P. Kirsch, E21

Kirchenlexikon/H. J. Wetzel, A127

Kircher, C. J./Behavior Patterns in Children's Books, A37

Kirchliches Handbuch, D128

Kirishtan bunko/J. Laures, B294

Kirk, J./Biographies of English Catholics in the Eighteenth Century, A199

Kirsch, J. P./Kirchengeschichte, E21

Kirschbaum, E./Lexikon der Christlichen Ikonographier, C181

Kleines Liturgisches Wörterbuch/ R. Berger, B378

Klejment, A./Berrigans, C102
_____. Dorothy Day and The Catholic Worker, D48

Klinger, E./Bibliographie Karl Rahner: 1924-1969, B22

Knowles, D./Heads of Religious Houses, E207
_____. Medieval Religious Houses: England, E199
_____. Monastic Order in England, E202
_____. Religious Orders in England, E203

Knox, R. A./Holy Bible, B46
_____. New Testament Commentary for English Readers, B118

Koch, L./Jesuiten-lexikon, E254

Kohlbrenner, B. J./Growth and Development of the Catholic School System in the U.S., D40
_____. History of Catholic Education in the U.S., D37
_____. Principles, Origin and establishment of the Catholic School System in the U.S., D41

Kolesnik, W. B./Catholic Education, D19

Komonchak, J. A./New Dictionary of Theology, B194

Konig, F./Religionswissenschaftliches Wörterbuch die Grundbegriffe, B20

Konus, W. J./Dictionary of the New Latin Psalter, B366

Koren, H. J./Research in Philosophy, C2

Korff, H./Biographica catholica, A202

Kornmüller, U./Lexikon der kirchlichen Tonkunst, C160

Kosch, W./Catholische Deutschland, A203

Köstler, R./Wörterbuch zum Codez juris canonici, D173

Kraft, H./Clavis patrum apostolicorum, B151

Kristeller, P. O./Catalogus Translationum, C143
_____. Latin Manuscript Books Before 1600, A7

Kühner, H./Encyclopedia of the Papacy, E134

Künstle, K./Ikonographie der christlichen Kunst, C180

Labriolle, P. C. de/Histoire de la
littérature latine chrétienne,
B139
_____. History and Literature
of Christianity from
Tertullian to Boethius,
B140
LaBrosse, O./Dictionnaire de la foi
catholique, B191
Lacombe, P./Livres d'heures, B343
Lagorio, V. M./14th Century English
Mystics, B307
Laity: a Bibliography/L. Doohan,
B26
Lama, C. von/Bibliotèque des
écrivains de la Congrégation
de Saint-Maur, E218
Lampe, G. W. H./Patristic Greek
Lexicon, B180
Lane, D./New Dictionary of
Theology, B194
Langevin, P. É./Bibliographie
biblique, B67
Lapointe, F./Gabriel Marcel and His
Critics, C47
Latham, R. E./Revised Medieval
Latin Word-List, E60
Latin-English Dictionary of St.
Thomas Aquinas/R. J.
Deferrari, C67
Latin Manuscript Books Before 1600/
P. O. Kristeller, A7
Lauer, A./Index verborum Codicis
ivuris canonici, D169
Laurent, É./Essai bibliographique
autour de "Rerum novarum,"
D2
Laures, J./Kirishtan bunko, B294
Law of Christ/B. Häring, B276
Lawler, R. D./Teachings of Christ,
B202
Leccisotti, T./I registi dell'archivo
(Monte Cassino), E220
Le Cerf de la Viéville, P./Biblioteque
historique et critique des
auteurs de la Congrégation
de St. Maur, E219
Lechner, J./Liturgy of the Roman
Rite, B391

Leclercq, H./Manuel d'archéologie
chrétienne, E28
Lectionary for Mass (Jerusalem
Bible), B347
Lectionary for Mass (New American
Bible), B349
Lectionary for Mass (R.S.V.C.E.),
B348
Lector's Guide to Biblical Pronuncia-
tions/J. M. Staudacher,
B112
Lectuur-repertorium/J. Baers, A30
Lee, J. M./Catholic Education in
the Western World, D42
Legenda sanctorum/J. deVoragine,
A215
Legends of the Madonna as Repre-
sented in the Fine Arts/A. B.
Jameson, C192
Legends of the Monastic Orders As
Represented in the Fine Arts/
A. B. Jameson, C203
Lemaire, P./Atlas biblique, B133
Lentner, L./Katechetisches
Wörterbuch, B285
Léon-Dufour, X./Dictionary of
Biblical Theology, B102
_____. Dictionary of the New Testa-
ment, B103
Lercaro, G./Small Liturgical Dic-
tionary, B386
Lesage, R./Dictionnaire pratique
de liturgie romaine, B387
Lescrauwaet, J. F./Critical Bibliog-
raphy of Ecumenical Literature,
B326
Leslie, S./Anthology of Catholic
Poets, C128
Lesser Eastern Churches/A.
Fortescue, B10
Lessico biblico/G. Nolli, B105
Lexau, J. M./Convent Life, E190
Lexicon abbreviaturarum/A.
Capelli, C144
Lexicon cappuccinum, E246
Lexicon latinitatis medii aevi/A.
Blaise, B178
Lexicon nominorum virorum et
mulierum/C. Egger, A248

Lexicon of St. Thomas Aquinas/
R. J. Deferrari, C67
Lexicon scholasticum philosophico-
theologicum/M. Fernandez-
Garcia, C18
Lexikon der christlichen Ikonographie/
H. Aurenhammer, C175
Lexikon der Christlichen
Ikonographier/E. Kirschbaum,
C181
Lexikon der Christlichen Kirchen/
J. Grundler, B2
Lexikon der Christlichen Moral/
K. Hörman, B265
Lexikon der kirchlichen Tonkunst/
U. Kornnüller, C160
Lexikon der Marienkunde/K.
Algermissen, B243
Lexikon des katholischen Lebens/
W. Rauch, B266
Lexikon des Mittelalters/R. Auty,
E61
Lexikon für Theologie und Kirche/
M. Buchberger, B193
Lexilogion ekklēsiaskikou dikaiou/
E. Roussos, D174
Lexique biblique/A. L. Vincent, B115
Lexique des anciennes règles/J. M.
Clèment, E177
Liam O'Flaherty: An Annotated
Bibliography/P. A. Doyle,
C116
Liber pontificalis/L. M. Duchesne,
E110
Liber pontificalis/R. L. Loomis,
E109
LIBRARY DIRECTORIES, A71-A73
Library Handbook for Catholic
Readers/W. T. O'Rourke, A74
LIBRARY HANDBOOKS, A63-A79
Library Index to Biblical Journals/
Saint John's University, B74
LIBRARY SCIENCE, A75-A84
Libros de religiòn/Instituto Nacional
del Libro Español, A29
Liebman, S. B./Inquisitors and
the Jews, E77
Liederbach, C. A./America's
Thousand Bishops, A190

_____. Canada's Bishops, A201
List of Additions and Corrections to
Early Catholic Americana/
F. Bowe, A52
List of Books About the Eastern
Churches/D. Attwater, B9
List of Editions of the Holy Scriptures/
E. B. O'Callaghan, B71
List of 5,000 Catholic Authors/
J. A. FitzGerald, C89
Listing of Catholic Secondary Schools
in the U.S.A./N.C.W.C.,
D29
Listy pasterskie/S. Wyszynski, E69
Literary and Biographical History/
J. Gillow, A198
LITERATURE, C77-C145
Literature of Medieval History/
G. C. Boyce, E36
Little Office of the Blessed Virgin
Mary, B360
Liturgicae orationis concordantia
verbalia/A. Pflieger, B353
LITURGICAL BOOKS, B340-B377
Liturgical Calendar and Ordo:
U.S.A., B399
Liturgical Terms for Music Students/
A. Hughes, C158
Liturgical Vesture/C. E. Pocknee,
C208
Liturgical Year/A. Nocent, B394
Liturgiesgeschichtliche Quellen
und Forschungen, B337
Liturgisch woordenboek/L.
Brinkhoff, B381
Liturgische Bibliographie des XV
Jahrhunderts/H. Bohatta, B341
Liturgische Zeitschriften/U. I. Rupke,
B332
Liturgisches Handlexikon/J. Braun,
B379
LITURGY, B330-B421
Liturgy of the Hours, B359
Liturgy of the Roman Rite/L.
Eisenhofer, B391
Lives of the British Saints/S. Baring-
Gould, A241
Lives of the Deceased Bishops/R. H.
Clarke, A185

Lives of the Irish Saints/J. O'Hanlon, A244

Lives of the Popes/H. K. Mann, E138

Lives of the Saints/S. Baring-Gould, A220

Lives of the Saints/A. Butler, A224-A227

Lives of the Saints/O. Englebert, A230

Lives of the Welsh Saints/G. H. Doble, A242

Livres d'heures/P. Lacombe, B343

Livres qui s'imposent/F. V. Duval, D1

Lohr, C. H./Thomas Aquinas. Scriptum super Sententiis, C65

Loidl, F./Dissertationen der Katholische Theologischen Fakultät der Universität Wien, 1831-1965, B32

Lonsway, J. W./Episcopal Lineage of the Hierarchy in the U.S., A191

Loomis, L. R./Book of the Popes, E109

Lucey, W. L./Introduction to American Catholic Magazines, A152

Lynn, D. E./Handbook of American Catholic Societies, A168

Lynn, J. M./Alternative Classification for Catholic Books, A82

MacEoin, G./The Inner Elite, A180

MacGregor, G./Vatican Revolution, E149

Macquarrie, J./Westminster Dictionary of Christian Ethics, B270, C19

Maddrell, J. G./Bibliography of Catholic Books Published during 1948, A57

Maertins, T./Bible Themes, B287

Magill, F. N./Masterpieces of Catholic Literature, C87

Magnum bullarium Romanum/H. Mainardi, E104

Mainardi, H./Magnum bullarium Romanum, E104

Mainelli, V. P./Social Justice, D7

Malatesta, E./St. John's Gospel, B68

Mâle, É./L'art religieux, C182

_____. Religious Art, C183

Mandonnet, P. F./Bibliographie thomiste, C58

Mangenot, E./Dictionnaire de Théologie catholique, B185

Mann, H. K./Lives of the Popes, E138

Mansi, G. D./Sacrorum conciliorum, E145

Manual of Canon Law/F. Rocca, D179

Manual of Cataloging Practice for Catholic Author and Title Entries, A81

Manual of Dogmatic Theology/A. Tanquerey, B233

Manual of Episcopal Ceremonies/ A. Stehle, B373

Manual of the Writings in Middle English/M. L. A., C135

Manual of Universal Church History/ J. B. Alzog, E13

Manuale di storia liturgica/M. Righetti, B409

Manuale theologiae moralis/D. M. Prümmer, B279

Manuel d'archéologie chrétienne/ H. Leclercq, E28

Manuel de la littérature catholique en France/H. Brémond, C138

Manuel d'histoire ecclésiastiques/ P. H. Albers, E12

Manuscritos pretridentinos hispaños de ciencias sagradas en la Biblioteca Universitaria de Salamanca/F. Marcos Rodríguez, B33

Maps of the Land of Christ/E. W. Seraphin, B134

MARCEL, G., C47

Marcellino da Civezza/Saggio di bibliografia, E239

Marcos Rodríguez, F./Manuscritos pretridentinos hispaños de ciencias sagradas en la Biblioteca Universitaria de Salamanca, B33

Maréchal, J./Précis d'histoire de la philosophie moderne, C28

Margolin, J. C./Douze anneés de bibliographie érasmienne, C45

————. Neuf anneés de bibliographie érasmienne, C46

————. Quatorze anneés de bibliographie érasmienne, C44

Maria/H. Du Manoir de Juaye, B247

MARIANISTS, E256

Marijnen, P. A./Encyclopedia of the Bible, B97

MARIOLOGY, B238-B248

Mariology/ J. B. Carol, B246

MARITAIN, J., C48

Marolla, E./Catholic Writer Yearbook, A145

Marriage in Canon Law/L. M. Orsy, D178

Marrow, S. B./Basic Tools of Biblical Exegesis, B69

Martimort, A. G./Church at Prayer, B390

————. L'Église en prière, B393

Martin, D./American Catholic Convert Authors, C92

————. Catholic Library Practice, A78

Martin, V./Histoire de l'Église, E18

Martinez, E. R./Hebrew-Ugaritic Index, B86

Martínex Gómez, L./Bibliografía filosofica española e hispano-americana, C15

Martyrologium romanum, B374

Martyrologium romanum/H. Delehaye, B375

MARTYROLOGY, B374-B377

Martyrology Pronouncing Dictionary/ A. I. Russo-Alesi, B377

Martyrs/D. Attwater, A218

MARY, SYMBOLS, C192-C193

Maryknoll Catholic Dictionary/ A. J. Nevins, A104

Mass of the Roman Rite/J. A. Jungmann, B410

Masterpieces of Catholic Literature/ F. N. Magill, C87

Matczak, S. A./Philosophy: A Select, Classified Bibliography, C5

Matochik, M. J./Catholicism and Anti-Catholicism, E75

Matters Liturgical/J. Wuest, B403

Matthews, S. G./Recommended Spiritual Reading Books, B308

Mayer, H. E./Bibliographie zur Geschichte der Kreuzzüge, E46

McBrien, R. P./Catholicism, B203

McCarthy, J. M./Pierre Teilhard de Chardin: A Comprehensive Bibliography, C50

McCarthy, T. P./Guide to the Catholic Sisterhoods in the U.S., E191

————. Guide to the Diocesan Priesthood in the U.S., D38

————. Total Dedication for the Laity, E192

McCloud, H. J./Clerical Dress, C205

McCluskey, N. G./Catholic Education in America, D43

McCoy, J. C./Jesuit Relations of Canada, E78

McDermott, T./Survey of Catholic Literature, C99

McEleney, N. J./Pamphlet Bible Series, B119

McGrath, J. J./Catholic Institutions in the U.S., D53

McGuire, C. E./Catholic Builders of the Nation, A184

McGuire, M. R. P./Introduction to Medieval Latin Studies, C142

McKenzie, J. L./Dictionary of the Bible, B104

————. New Testament for Spiritual Reading, B120

McLean, G. F./Annotated Bibliography of Philosophy in Catholic Thought, C3
———. Bibliography of Christian Philosophy and Contemporary Issues, C4
McNamara, M./Old Testament Message, B123
McNaspy, C. J./Guide to Christian Europe, D189
McSorley, J./Outline History of the Church, E22
Meagher, P. K./Encyclopedic Dictionary of Religion, A101
Mearns, J./Early Latin Hymnaries, C156
Media for Christian Formation/ W. A. Dalglish, A26
Media Three/W.A. Dalglish, A26
Media Two/W.A. Dalglish, A26
MEDIEVAL CHURCH HISTORY, E36-E62
Medieval Heresies/C. T. Berkhout, E40
Medieval Latin Liturgy/R. W. Pfaff, B344
Medieval Monasticism/G. Constable, E171
Medieval Music/A. Hughes, C149
Medieval Polyphony in the Bodleian Library/A. Hughes, C150
Medieval Religious Houses: England/ D. Knowles, E199
Medieval Religious Houses: Ireland/ A. O. Gwynn, E200
Medieval Religious Houses: Scotland/ I. B. Cowan, E201
Meer, F. van der/Atlas of the Early Christian World, E35
Meer, P. van der/Katholicke encyclopaedie, A116
Mees, L./Bio-bibliographia franciscana neerlandica ante saeculum XVI, E241
Meissner, W. W./Annotated Bibliography in Religion and Psychology, C74
Melsheimer, L./Who's Who in the Catholic World, A181

Menendez, A. J./Church-State Relations, D147
———. Road to Rome, C77
Mercati, A./Dizionario ecclesiastico, A130
———. Raccolta di concordati, D186
MERCEDARIANS, E257
Merk, A./Novum testamentum graece et latine, B50
Merrill, W. S./Catholic Authorship in the American Colonies before 1784, A50
MERTON, T., C109-C110
Messe: études archéologiques sur ses monuments/C. Rohault de Fleury, C191
Metodio da Nembro, C. M./Quatrocento scrittori spirituali, B309
Meulemeester, M. de/Bibliographie générale des écrivains rédemporistes, E261
Mierzwinski, T. T./What Do You Think of the Priest?, B252
Miethe, T. L./Augustinian Bibliography, 1970-1980, C39
———. Thomistic Bibliography, 1940-1978, C60
Migne, J. P./Encyclopédie théologique, A122
———. Patrologiae, B169
Mihanovich, C. S./Papal Pronouncements on Marriage and the Family, B262
Milburn, R. L. P./Saints and Their Emblems, C198
Mills, W. E./Directory of Departments and Programs of Religious Studies in North America, D34
Ministries for the Lord, E193
Minority Religions in America/ W. J. Whalen, B6
Mirbt, K./Quellen zur Geschichte des Pappsttums, E111
Misiak, H./Catholics in Psychology, C76
MISSAL, B346-B356
Missale romanum, B346

Missioni cattoliche/Agenzia Internationale Fides, B297
MISSIONS, B290-B301
Mitros, J. F./Religions: A Select, Classified Bibliography, B15
Moberg, D. O./International Directory of Religious Information Systems, A72
Modern Catholic Dictionary/J. A. Hardon, A102
Modern Catholic Thinkers/A. P. Caponigri, C80
MODERN CHURCH HISTORY, E63-E71
Modern Concordance to the New Testament/M. Darton, B87
Modern Language Association of America/Manual of the Writings in Middle English, C135
Modification and Expansion of the Dewey Decimal Classification in the 200 Class, A83
Mohrmann, C./Atlas of the Early Christian World, E35
Molette, C./Guide des sources de l'histoire des congregationes fémines françaises de vie active, E173
Molina Martinez, M. A./Diccionario del Vaticano II, E165
MONASTERIES, E197-E203
Monasteries of Western Europe/W. Braunfels, E197
Monastic Order in England/D. Knowles, E202
Monasticon anglicanum/W. Dugdale, E198
Mondo cattolico, D78
Monte Cassino/I registi dell'archiva, E220
Monumenta eucharistica et liturgica/ J. Quasten, B250
Monumenta germanica historica, E51
Moral and Pastoral Theology/H. Davis, B273
MORAL THEOLOGY, B257-B281
Moral Theology/C. J. Callan, B271
Moral Theology/H. Jone, B277

Morall, J. B./Church and State Through the Centuries, D150
Morel, R./Encyclopedia of Catholic Saints, A229
Morgan, J. H./Aging in the Religious Life, E174
_____. Death and Dying, B282
_____. Ordination of Women, B253
Moroni, G./Dizionario di erudizione storico-ecclesiastica, A135
Morvay, K./Bibliographie der deutschen Predigt, C139
Mourret, F./History of the Catholic Church, E23
Münster, R./Kataloge bayerischer Musiksammlungen, C151
MUSIC, C146-C172
Musurillo, H. A./Acts of the Christian Martyrs, A216
MYSTICAL THEOLOGY, B302-B324
Mytych, J. F./Digest of Church Law on Sacred Music, C166

Nainfa, J. A./Costumes of Prelates, C206
NAMES, A247-A249
Names and Name Days/D. Attwater, A247
Names and Titles of Jesus/L. Sabourin, B235
NATIONAL BIBLIOGRAPHIES, A49-A70
National Bibliography of Theological Titles in Catholic Libraries/ J. J. Alhadef, B21
National Catholic Almanac, D90
National Catholic Educational Association/Catholic Schools in America, D26
_____. Criteria for Evaluation of Catholic Elementary Schools, D22
_____. Directory of Catholic Special Facilities and Programs in the U.S. for Handicapped Children and Adults, D27

National Catholic Welfare
Conference/A Listing of
Catholic Secondary Schools
in the U.S.A., D29
National Center for Church Voca-
tions/Directory of Secular
Institutes, E194
National Conference of Catholic
Bishops/Basic Teachings for
Catholic Religious Education,
B204
National Conference of Catholic
Charities/Catholic Day Care
Centers, D61
_____. Directory: Diocesan Agencies
of Catholic Charities,
D62
_____. Directory of Catholic Institu-
tions in the U.S., D61
_____. Directory of Residences for
Unwed Mothers, D61
_____. Guidelines to Personnel
Practices and Salary Scales,
D57
_____. Guides for Catholic Day
Care Centers, D54
_____. Guides for Facilities for
the Aging, D55
_____. Guides for Services to
Children in Catholic
Institutions, D56
National Inventory of Parish
Catechetical Programs/
U.S.C.C., D23
National Pastorals of the American
Hierarchy/P. Guilday,
E89
National Union Catalog, A
Bibliography of the Catholic
Church, A3
Naz, R./Dictionnaire de droit
canonique, D172
Nebreda del cura, E./Bibliographia
augustiniana, C40
Negro Catholic Writers/M. A. Scally,
C93
Neill, S. C./Concise Dictionary of
the Christian World Mission,
B296

Nelson's Complete Concordance to
the New American Bible/S. J.
Hartdegen, B88
Nemmers, E. E./Twenty Centuries
of Catholic Church Music,
C172
Neue Herder/U. Becker, A125
Neuf années de bibliographie
érasmienne/J. C. Margolin,
C46
Neuner, J./Christian Faith in the
Doctrinal Documents of the
Catholic Church, B220
Nevins, A. J./General Intercessions,
B352
_____. Maryknoll Catholic Dic-
tionary, A104
New American Bible, B51
New Catechism: Catholic Faith for
Adults, B151
New Catholic Commentary on Holy
Scripture, B121
New Catholic Encyclopedia, A105
New Catholic People's Encyclopedia,
A108
New Century Italian Renaissance
Encyclopedia/C. B. Avery,
E70
New Dictionary of the Liturgy/G.
Podhradsky, B389
New Dictionary of Theology/J. A.
Komonchak, B194
New Eusebuis/J. Stevenson, E31
New Jerusalem Bible, B52
New Library of Catholic Knowledge/
I. Evans, A109
New Liturgy/R. K. Seasoltz, B339
New Oxford Annotated Bible, B53
New Testament Abstracts, B79
New Testament Commentary for
English Readers/R. A. Knox,
B118
New Testament for Spiritual
Reading/J. L. McKenzie, B120
New Testament Introduction/A.
Wikenhauser, B129
New Testament Message/W.
Harrington, B122
New Testament Reading Guide, B124

New Titles in Bioethics, B260

New Westminster Dictionary of Liturgy and Worship/J. G. Davies, B388

NEWMAN, J. H., C111-C114

Newman, W. M./Atlas of Religious Change in America, 1952-1971, D95

Nickels, P./Targum and New Testament, B70

1969 Synod—Archdiocese of Detroit, F4

Nocent, A./Dictionary of the Council, E164

———. Liturgical Year, B394

Nolan, H. J./Pastoral Letters of the American Hierarchy, 1792-1970, E93

———. Pastoral Letters of the United States Catholic Bishops, 1792-1983, E94

Nolan, J. G./Handbook of Moral Theology, B278

Nolli, G./Lessico biblico, B105

Nomenclator literarius theologiae catholicae theologos/H. Hurter, B213

Noonan, E. F./Books for Catholic Elementary Schools, A35

———. Books for Religious Education in Catholic Secondary Schools, A36

NORBERTINES, E258

Norms for the Novel/H. C. Gardiner, C124

Norris, H./Church Vestments, C207

Notes bibliographiques/P. Hugolin, E212

Notitiae, B338

Nouveau lexique Teilhard de Chardin/ C. Cúenot, C54

Nouvel atlas des missions/J. Despont, B301

Nova Vulgata Biblorum Sacrorum, B54

Novae concordantiae biblorum sacrorum iuxta Vulgatam versionem, B84

Novels and Tales by Catholic Writers/S. J. M. Brown, C121

Novum testamentum graece et latine/A. Merk, B50

Noyes, A./Golden Book of Catholic Poetry, C129

OBLATES OF MARY IMMACULATE, E259

O'Brien, D. J./Renewing the Earth, D6

O'Brien, E./Theology in Transition, B34

O'Brien, T. C./Corpus Dictionary of Western Churches, A99

———. Encyclopedic Dictionary of Religion, A101

O'Callaghan, E. B./List of Editions of the Holy Scriptures, B71

O'Carroll, M./Theotokos, B244

———. Trinitas, B226

Ochoa Sanz, J./Index verborum ac locutionnum Codicis iuris cononici, D170

O'Connell, J. B./Ceremonies of the Roman Rite Described, B401

———. Roman Martyrology, B376

O'Connell, L. J./Book of Ceremonies, B402

O'CONNOR, F./C115

O'Connor, J. I./Canon Law Digest, D158

Odelain, O./Dictionary of Proper Names and Places in the Bible, B106

O'Donnell, J. H./Catholic Hierarchy in the U.S., A192

Official Catholic Directory, D99

Official Catholic Teachings, B221

Official Catholic Yearbook, D100

Official Directory of the Catholic Church of Australia and Papua-New Guinea, New Zealand and the Pacific Islands, D107

Official Guide to Catholic Educational Institutions and Religious Communities in the U.S., D28

Official Nigeria Catholic Directory,
D88
O'FLAHERTY, L., C116
O'Grady, J./Directory of Catholic
Charities in the U.S., D63
O'Hanlon, J./Lives of the Irish
Saints, A244
O'Hara, M./Directory of Women
Religious in the United
States, 1985, E206
O'Hayer, E./Catholic Traveler's
Guide, D188
Ökumene Lexikon/A. Basdekis, B329
Old Testament Abstracts, B80
Old Testament Message/C.
Stuhlmueller, B123
Old Testament Reading Guide, B125
Olin, J. C./Catholic Reformation,
E67
O'Malley, C. D./Sutro Library
Catalogue, A10
Ooms, H./Repertorium universale
siglorum ordinum, E195
Oppenheim, P./Institutiones
systematico-historicae in
sacram liturgiam, B408
ORATORIANS, E260
Orbis catholicus, D79
Orden und Kongregationen/M. J.
Heimbucher, E186
Order of Prayer in the Liturgy of
the Hours and the Mass, F1
Ordination of Women/J. H. Morgan,
B253
Ordo, B398
Organisations internationales
catholique/R. Sugranyes
de Franch, A166
Origines de la Réforme/P. Imbart
de la Tour, E71
Origins, E90
O'Rourke, W. T./Library Handbook
for Catholic Readers, A74
Orsy, L. M./Marriage in Canon Law,
D178
Orthodox Eastern Church/A.
Fortescue, B11
Ortiz de Urbina, I./Patrologia Syriaca,
B141

Osservatore romano, E124
Ossinger, J. F./Bibliotheca
Augustiana, E209
O'Toole, James M./Guide to the
Archives of the Archdiocese
of Boston, E91
Ott, L./Fundamentals of Catholic
Dogma, B227
Où en est l'enseignement religieux?,
D15
Où en est l'histoire des religions/J.
Bricout, B14
Our American Princes/F. B.
Thornton, A195
Our Bishops Speak, E92
Our Lady's Daily Hours, B360
Outline History of the Church/J.
McSorley, E22
Oxford Annotated Bible, B53
Oxford Dictionary of Popes/J. N. D.
Kelly, E133
Oxford Dictionary of Saints/D. H.
Farmer, A231

Pace, E. A./Universal Knowledge,
A114
Paetow, L. J./Guide to the Study of
Medieval History, E38
Palazzini, P./Dictionarium morale et
canonicum, B267
_____. Dizionario dei Concili, E167
Palmer, P. F./Sources of Christian
Theology, B42
Pamphlet Bible Series/N. J.
McEleney, B119
PAPACY, E98-E141
Papal Documents on Mary/W. J.
Doheny, B240
Papal Encyclicals/C. Carlen, E114
Papal Encyclicals in their Historical
Context/A. Freemantle, E130
Papal Heraldry/D. L. Galbraeth,
E137
Papal Pronouncements on Marriage
and the Family/A. Werth, B262
Papal Pronouncements on the
Political Order/F. J. Powers,
D149

Papal Social Principles/T. J. Harte, D4

Papal Teachings, E115

Paré, G./Catholic Church in Detroit, F5

Parente, P./Dictionary of Dogmatic Theology, B225

Parish and Catholic Lending Library Manual/V. P. Schneider, A79

Parish Library Manual/Catholic Library Association, A75

Parish Library Manual: Suggested Books/Catholic Library Association, A76

Parsch, P./Breviary Explained, B411

———. Church's Year of Grace, B395

Parsons, W./Early Catholic Americana, A51

———. List of Additions and Corrections to Early Catholic Americana, A52

Pastor, L. F. von/History of the Popes, E139

Pastoral Letters of the American Hierarchy, 1792-1970/ H. J. Nolan, E93

Pastoral Letters of the United States Catholic Bishops, 1792-1983/H. J. Nolan, E94

PASTORAL THEOLOGY, B282-B301

Patristic Greek Lexicon/Lampe, G. W. H., B180

Patrologia orientalis/R. Graffin, B166

Patrologia syriaca/R. Graffin, B167

Patrologia Syriaca/I. Ortiz de Urbina, B141

Patrologiae/J. P. Migne, B169

Patrologie et histoire de la théologie/ F. Cayre, B138

PATROLOGY, B135-B181

Patrology/B. Altaner, B135

Patrology/O. Bardenhewer, B137

Patrology/J. Quasten, B143

Paul VI/Insegnamenti, E119

Pegis, A. C./Wisdom of Catholicism, C83

Pegis, J. C./Practical Catholic Dictionary, A110

Pelliccia, G./Dizionario degli istituti di perfezione, E181

Pelloquin, G./Index et concordance, Vatican II, E162

Pelzer, A./Abréviations latines médiévales, C145

Penguin Dictionary of Saints/D. Attwater, A219

Penitente Bibliography/M. Weigle, E83

Pensiero medievale/C. Vasoli, C11

Pérennès, F. M./Dictionnaire de bibliographie catholique, A4

Perini, D. A./Bibliographia Augustiniana, E210

PERIODICALS, A142-A161

Periodicals for Religious Education Resource Centers/J. T. Corrigan, A146

Pernicone, J. M./Ecclesiastical Prohibition of Books, A46

Peterson, G. C./Books for Catholic Colleges, A41

Petit glossaire de l'argot écclésiastique/ J. Follain, A121

Peultier, E./Concordantiarum universae sacrae Scripturae thesaurus, B89

Pfaff, R. W./Medieval Latin Liturgy, B344

Pfeiffer, H. A./Catholic Picture Dictionary, A111

Pflieger, A./Liturgicae orationis concordantia verbalia, B353

Pflugt-Harttung, J. von/Acta pontificium, E101

Philosophical Dictionary/W. Brugger, C16

Philosophie des Mittelälters/F. van Steenberghen, C10

PHILOSOPHY, C1-C73

Philosophy: A Select, Classified Bibliography/S. A. Matczak, C5

Photo Directory of the U.S. Catholic Hierarchy, A193

Piccola enciclopedia ecclesiastica/
A. Ceccaroni, A129
Piepkorn, A. C./Profiles in Belief,
B206
Piercy, W. C./Dictionary of Christian
Biography and Literature to
the end of the Sixth Century,
A178
Pierre Teilhard de Chardin: A
Comprehensive Bibliography/
J. M. McCarthy, C50
Pilley, C. M./Guide to Catholic
Literature, A56
Pinard de La Boullaye, H./L'étude
comparée des religions,
B16
Piolanti, A./Dictionary of Dogmatic
Theology, B225
Pioneer Laymen of North America/
T. J. Campbell, A182
Pioneer Priests of North America/
T. J. Campbell, A183
Pitra, J. B./Analecta sacra spicilegio
solesmensi parata, B175
––––––. Iuris ecclesiastici graecorum,
D185
––––––. Spicilegium solesmense, B174
Pius XII/Discoursi e radiomessaggi,
E117
Pocket Catholic Dictionary/J. A.
Hardon, A103
Pocknee, C. E./Liturgical Vesture,
C208
Podhradsky, G./New Dictionary of
the Liturgy, B389
Prodręczna encyklopedia biblijna/
E. Dąbrowskiego, B107
POETRY, C127-C134, C141
Pogany, A. H./Political Science and
International Relations,
D148
Polgár, L./Bibliography of the
History of the Society of Jesus,
E250
––––––. Internationale Teilhard-
Bibliographie, C51
POLITICAL SCIENCE, D146-D151
Political Science and International
Relations/A. H. Pogany, D148

Pollen, J. H./Sources for the History
of Roman Catholicism in
England, Ireland and
Scotland, E64
Polska bibliografia teologiczna/
J. R. Bar, A67
Polska bibliografia teologii/
J.R. Bar, A68
Pontifical Institute of Medieval
Studies/Dictionary Catalog,
E47
Pontificale romanum, B370
Pontificia americana/D. C. Shearer,
E112
Pope, H./English Versions of the
Bible, B72
Pope Speaks, E125
Popes/E. John, E132
Popes on Youth/R. B. Fullam, D64
Popes through History/R. Schmandt,
E140
Popes through the Ages/J. S.
Brusher, E135
Porte, J./Encyclopedie des musiques
sacrées, C161
Post, W. E./Saints, Signs and
Symbols, C184, C199
Potthast, A./Bibliotheca historica
medii aevi, E48
––––––. Regesta Pontificium, E107
Poulat, É./Semaines religieuses, A153
Poulin, D./Teilhard de Chardin, C52
Pour revaloriser Migne/P. Glorieux,
B165
Pourrat, P./Christian Spirituality,
B324
Power, E. J./Catholic Education,
D19
Powers, F. J./Papal Pronouncements
on the Political Order, D149
Practical Catholic Dictionary/J. C.
Pegis, A110
Practical Commentary on the Code
of Canon Law/S. Woywood,
D183
Praktisches Bibellexikon/A. Grabner-
Haider, B100
Prat, F./Jesus Christ, B234
PRAYERS, B412-B418

Preacher's Encyclopedia/A. Herrera
Oria, B286
PREACHING, B286-B289
Précis d'histoire de la philosophie
moderne/J. Maréchal, C28
Preliminary Survey of Roman Catholic
Hymnals/M. C. Verret, C152
Preuss, A./Dictionary of Secret and
Other Societies, A165
Primer of Medieval Latin/C. H.
Beeson, C84
Principe, W. H./Bibliographies and
Bulletins in Theology, B35
Principles, Origin and Establishment
of the Catholic School System
in the U.S./J. A. Burns, D41
Proeve eener bibliographie van de
missionarissen van Scheut/
W. A. Grootaers, E229
Profiles in Belief/A. C. Piepkorn,
B206
PROSE, C135-C136
Protestant Churches of America/
J. A. Hardon, B3
PROTESTANT DENOMINATIONS,
B1-B7
Prümm, K./Religionsgeschichtliches
Handbuch, E34
Prümmer, D. M./Handbook of Moral
Theology, B279
_____. Manuale theologiae moralis,
B279
PSYCHOLOGY, C74-C76
Pszczólkowska, M./The Catholic
Book in Poland, A69
Publishers Guide: Catholic Journals/
S. J. Gaines, A150
Puech, A./Histoire de la littérature
grecque chrétienne, B142
Puglisi, J. F./Bibliography of
Interchurch and Intercon-
fessional Theological
Dialogues, B327
Pullen, G. F./Catalogue of the Bible
Collections in the Old Library
at St. Mary's Oscott, B73
Puniet, P. de/Roman Pontifical, B372
Putz, L. J./Catholic Church, U.S.A.,
E97

Quasten, J./Monumenta eucharistica
et liturgica, B250
_____. Patrology, B143
Quatorze années de bibliographie
érasmienne/J. C. Margolin,
C44
Quatrocento scrittori spirituali/
Metodio da Nembro, C. M.,
B309
Quellen zur Geschichte des Papsttums/
K. Mirbt, E111
Quétif, J./Scriptores Ordinis
Predicatorum, E231
Quinn, B./Apostolic Regions of the
U.S., D101
_____. Churches and Church
Membership in the United
States, 1980, D77
_____. Distribution of Catholic
Priests in the U.S., D102
_____. Readings for Town and
Country Church Workers,
D45
QUOTATIONS, C115

Raab, C./Twenty Ecumenical
Councils, E169
Raccolta, B414
Raccolta di concordati/A. Mercati,
D186
Radó, P./Enchiridion liturgicum,
B396
Raes, A./Introductio in liturgiam
orientalum, B422
Raeymaeker, L. de/Introduction à la
philosophie, C21
Rahner, K./Dictionary of Theology,
B195
_____. Encyclopedia of Theology:
The concise Sacramentum
mundi, B196
_____. Handbuch der Pastoral-
theologie, B283
_____. Sacramentum mundi, B197
RARE BOOKS, BIBLIOGRAPHY,
A9-A14
Rassegna di letteratura tomistica,
B36, C6, C59

Rathberger, A. M./Wissen Sie
    Bescheid?, A126
Rauch, W./Lexikon des katholischen
    Lebens, B266
Ravasi, L. R./Fontes bibliographia
    de vocatione, E175
Readings for Town and Country
    Church Workers, An
    Annotated Bibliography/
    D. M. Byers, D45
Readings in Church History/C. J.
    Barry, E3
Réau, L./Iconographie de l'art
    chrétien, C185
Recent Homiletical Thought/B288
Recommended Spiritual Reading
    Books/S. G. Matthews, B308
Records of Christianity/D. Ayerst,
    E5
Records of the American Catholic
    Historical Society, Index,
    E95
Recueil des historiens des Gaules
    et de France, E54
Recusant Books at St. Mary's
    Oscott, A14
Recusant Books in America/L. Byrns,
    A12
Recusant History/Biographical
    Studies, A197
Recusant Poets/L. I. Guiney, C134
REDEMPTORISTS, E261
REFERENCE BOOKS, BIBLIOG-
    RAPHY, A18, A47
Reference Works in the Field of
    Religion, 1977-1985/E.
    Freudenberger, A18
Regesta pontificium/A. Brackmann,
    E108
Regesta pontificium/P. Jaffe, E106
Regesta Pontificium/A. Potthast,
    E107
Regis, M./Catholic Bookman's Guide,
    A19
Register of Middle English and
    Didactic Verse/C. F. Brown,
    C131
Register zu den Konzilsdokumenten/
    R. Spiecker, E161

Registi dell'archivo (Monte Cassino),
    E220
Reich, W. T./Encyclopedia of
    Bioethics, B264
Reinsma, L. M./Aelfric, C101
Religia a literatura, C78
Religionen der Menscheit/A.
    Anwander, B13
RELIGIONS, B1-B20
Religions: A Select, Classified Bibliog-
    raphy/J. F. Mitros, B15
RELIGIONS, HISTORY, B13-B17
Religions of the World/J. A.
    Hardon, B4
Religionsgeschichtliches Handbuch/
    K. Prümm, E34
Religionswissenschaftliches Wörter-
    buch die Grundbegriffe/F.
    König, B20
Religious Art/É. Mâle, C183
Religious Aspects of Medical Care,
    B284
Religious Bodies/U.S. Bureau of
    the Census, D104
Religious Book Review, A58
RELIGIOUS ORDERS, E170-E264
Religious Orders and Congregations
    of Great Britain and Ireland/
    P. F. Anson, E179
Religious Orders in England/D.
    Knowles, E203
Religious Orders of Women in the
    U.S./E. T. Dehey, E182
RELIGIOUS ORDERS, SYMBOLS,
    C203
Religious Reading, A59
Renewing the Earth/D. J. O'Brien,
    D6
Rennhofer, F./Bücherkunde des
    katholischen Lebens, A65
Répertoire alphabétique de 15,500
    auteurs/G. Sagehomme, C79
Répertoire bibliographique, C8
Répertoire bibliographique de la
    philosophy, C7
Répertoire bibliographique de saint
    Augustin/T. J. van Bavel, C36
Répertoire de maîtres en théologie/
    P. Glorieux, B31

Répertoire des sources historiques du moyen âge/C. U. J. Chevalier, A170, E41

Répertoire des thèses des facultés ecclésiastiques de l'Université Laval, 1935-60/A. Gagne, B29

Répertoire d'incipit de prières en ancien français/J. Sonet, B418

Répertoire d'incipit des prières françaises/P. Rézeau, B415

Répertoire général de sciences religieuses, B37

Répertoire topo-bibliographique des abbayes et prieurés/L. H. Cottineau, E172

Repertorium biblicum/M. Bechis, B81

Repertorium biblicum Medii Aevi/F. Stegmüller, B76

Repertorium commentariorum in Sententias Petri Lombardi, B39

Repertorium fontium historiae medii aevi, E49

Repertorium hymnologicum/C. U. J. Chevalier, C147

Repertorium liturgicum Augustanum/ R. Amiet, B330

Repertorium repertorii/C. Blume, C146

Repertorium universale siglorum ordinem et institutum religiosorum/H. Ooms, E195

Rerum britanicarum medii aevi scriptores, E55

Rerum gallicorum et franciscarum scriptores, E54

Rerum Italicarum scriptorum, E56

Research in Philosophy/H. J. Koren, C2

Researching the Development of Lay leadership in the Catholic Church/L. T. Snyderwine, B38

Resource Guide for Adult Religious Education, D18

Resources for Religious Instruction of Retarded People/L. J. Cronin, D16

Rettger, E. A./Manual of Episcopal Ceremonies, B373

Reuss, F. X./Biographical Cyclopedia of the Catholic Hierarchy, A194

Revell, P./Fifteenth Century English Prayers and Meditations, A8

Revised Medieval Word-List/R. E. Latham, E60

Revision of Canon Law/M. Zimmerman, D157

Revue d'histoire ecclésiastique/ Bibliographie, E2

Revue internationale des études bibliques, B78

Rézeau, P./Répertoire d'incipit des prieres françaises, B415

Rhymer, J./The Bible in Order, B55

Rice, E. E./Church, A Pictorial History, E24

Richards, H. J./ABC of the Bible, B108

Richardson, A./Westminster Dictionary of Christian Theology, B198

Richter, A. L./Corpus juris canonici, D164

Rickaby, J. J./Index to the works of John Newman, C114

Riedl, J. O./Catalogue of Renaissance Philosophers, C32

Righetti, M./Manuale di storia liturgica, B409

Rites of Eastern Christendom/A. A. King, B421

Rites of the Catholic Church, B369

Rites of Western Christendom/A. A. King, B392

RITUAL, B368-B369

Road to Rome/A. J. Menendez, C77

Robbins, R. H./Index of Middle English Verse, C132

Robert, A./Guide to the Bible, B126

———. Introduction to the New Testament, B127

———. Introduction to the Old Testament, B128

Roberti, F./Dictionary of Moral Theology, B268

Roberts, A./Ante-Nicene Fathers, B154

Rocca, F./Manual of Canon Law,
D179
Rocca, G./Dizionario degli istituti
di perfezione, E181
Roeder, H./Saints and their
Attributes, C200
Rogelio Alvarez, J./Enciclopedia
de la Iglesia Católica en
México, A138
Rogers, D./Catalogue of Catholic
Books Printed in English, A11
Rohault de Fleury, C./Archéologie
chrétienne, C201
————. L'évangile, C190
————. La messe, C191
————. La Sainte Vierge, C193
Rolla, A./Enciclopedia della Bibbia
B109
Rolls Series, E55
ROMAN BREVIARY, B357-B367
Roman Breviary in English, B358
Roman Calendar, B400
Roman Martyrology/J. B. O'Connell,
B376
ROMAN MISSAL, B346-B356
Roman Pontifical, B371
Roman Pontifical/P. de Puniet, B372
Roman Ritual in Latin and English,
B368
Romani, S./Enciclopedia del
christianismo, A133
Rombach, H./Wörterbuch der
Pädagogik, D20
Romig, W./Book of Catholic
Authors, C93
Rommerskirchen, G./Bibliografia
missionaria, B290
Ronda, J. P./Indian Missions, B291
Roschini, G. G./I Grande del
Cattolicesimo, A176
Roschini, G. M./Dizionario di
mariologia, B245
Rossi, L./Dizionario enciclopedico
di teologia morale, B269
Rouet, A./Short Dictionary of
the New Testament, B110
Rouët de Journel, M. J./Enchiridion
asceticum, B314
————. Enchiridion patristicum, B222

Rouillard, P./Dictionnaire de la foi
catholique, B191
Roulin, E. A./Vestments and Vesture,
C209
Rousselot, P./Christus: manuel
d'histoire des religions,
B17
Roussos, E./Lexilogion ekklēsiastikou
dikaiou, D174
Rowlands, L./Guide Book for
Catholic Church Choir-
masters, C167
Rufino, M./Vademecum of Stories,
B289
Rules for the Catalog of Printed
Books/Biblioteca vaticana,
A80
Ruoss, G. M./World Directory of
Theological Libraries, A73
Rupke, U. I./Liturgische Zeitschriften,
B332
Russell, J. B./Medieval Heresies, E40
Russian Revolution and Religion/
B. Szczesniak, E68
Russo-Alesi, A. I./Martyrology
Pronouncing Dictionary,
B377

Sabourin, L./Names and Titles of
Jesus, B235
Sacra musica: lexikon der katholischen
Kirchenmusik/A. Weissenbäch,
C162
Sacrae theologiae summa, B228
Sacramentary, B350
Sacramentary/I. Schuster, B354
SACRAMENTS, B250-B256
Sacramentum mundi/K. Rahner,
B197
Sacramentum verbi: An Encyclopedia
of Biblical Theology/J. B.
Bauer, B94
Sacred and Legendary Art/A. B.
Jameson, C179
Sacred Canons/J. A. Abbo, D176
Sacred Congregation for the Clergy/
General Catechetical Directory,
B207

Sacred Shrine: A Study of the Poetry and Art of the Catholic Church/Y. Hirn, C173

Sacrorum conciliorum/G. D. Mansi, E145

Sáenz de Tejada, J. M./Bibliografía de la devoción al Carazón de Jesús, B310

Sagehomme, G./Répertoire alphabétique de 15,500 auters, C79

Saggio di bibliografia/Marcellino da Civezza, E239

St. John's Gospel/E. Malatesta, B68

St. John's University/Library Index to Biblical Journals, B74

St. Mary's College/Catholic Writers' Magazine Market, A154

Sante Vierge: études archéologique et iconographiques/C. Rohault de Fleury, C193

Saints, A Concise Biographical Dictionary/J. Coulson, A233

Saints and Feast Days, A234

Saints and Their Attributes/H. Roeder, C200

Saints and Their Emblems/M. Drake, C196

Saints and Their Emblems/R. L. P. Milburn, C198

SAINTS, LIVES OF, A205-A244

Saints of Cornwall/G. H. Doble, A243

Saints of the Americas/M. A. Habig, A240

Saints of the East/D. Attwater, A239

Saints, Signs and Symbols/W. E. Post, C184, C199

SAINTS, SYMBOLS, C194, C202

Santiago Vela, G. de/Ensayo de una biblioteca, E211

Sartori, C./Enchiridion canonicum, D166

Satō Seitarō/Ecclesiastical Japanese, A137

Sawyer, M. E./Bibliographical Index of Five English Mystics, B311

Scally, M. A./Negro Catholic Writers, C93

Schäfer, O./Bibliographia de vita, operibus et doctrina Iohannis Duns Scoti, C42

Schaff, P./Select Library of Nicene and Post-Nicene Fathers of the Christian Church, B156

Scheemelcher, W./Bibliographia patristica, B144

Scherer, G./Glaubersinformation, B188

Schmandt, R./Popes through History, E140

Schmaus, M./Dogma, B229

Schmidlin, J./Catholic Mission History, B299

_____. Catholic Mission Theory, B300

Schmidt, H./Introductio in liturgiam occidentalem, B397

Shmitz, W. J./Book of Ceremonies, B402

Schneider, G./Exegetisches Wörter-buch sum Neuen Testament, B99

Schneider, V. P./Parish and Catholic Lending Library Manual, A79

Schneidermeyer, W./Iris Murdoch and Muriel Spark, C117

School Directory for the Archdiocese of Detroit, F3

School Question: A Bibliography on Church-State Relations/E. G. Drouin, D17

SCHOOLS DIRECTORIES, D24-D38

Schooyans, M./Bibliographie philosophique de Saint Albert le Grand (1931-1960), C33

Schriftsteller der noch bestehenden Augustinerchorherrenstifte/ B. O. Cěrnik, E208

Schroeder, H. J./Canons and Decrees of the Council of Trent, E146

_____. Disciplinary Decrees of the General Councils, E144

Schulte, J. F./Geschichte der Quellen und Literatur des canonischen Rechts, D155

Schuster, I./Sacramentary, B354

Schütz, L./Thomas-lexikon, C68

Schwartz, E./Acta conciliorum oecumenicorum, E142

Sciacca, M. F./Augustinus, C41

Scriptores ecclesiastici de musica sacra potissimum/M. Gerbert, C171

Scriptores Ordinis minorum/L. Wadding, E242

Scriptores Ordinis Predicatorum/ J. Quétif, E231

Scriptorum de musica Medii Aevi novam seriem/C. E. H. de Coussemaker, C170

SCRIPTURE, B44-B134

Scrittori barnabiti/G. Boffito, E213

Scrittori cattolici italiani viventi/G. Casati, C95

Seasoltz, R. K./New Liturgy, B339

Secretaria Status Rationarium General Ecclesiae/Annuarium statisticum ecclesiae, D74

Seelhammer, R./Hopkins Collected at Gonzaga, C108

Séguineau, R./Dictionary of Proper Names and Places in the Bible, B106

Selección de libros católicos españoles/Instituto Nacional del Libro Español, A28

Select Bibliography of the Catholic Church in the U.S./J. T. Ellis, E76

Select Bibliography to California Catholic Literature/F. J. Weber, E82

Select Library of Nicene and Post-Nicene Fathers of the Christian Church/P. Schaff, B156

Selected Annotated Bibliography on Ecumenical and Related Matters/E. J. Sutfin, B328

Semaines religieuses/É. Poulat, A153

Seminaria ecclesiae catholicae/ Congregatio de Seminariis et Studiorum Universitatibus, D32

Senior, D./New Testament Message, B122

Senior High School Library Catalog with Catholic Supplement, A38

Separated Brethren/W. J. Whalen, B7

Seppelt, F. X./Geschichte der Päpst, E141

Seraphi, E. W./Maps of the Land of Christ, B134

Series episcoporum Ecclesiae catholicae/P. B. Gams, A175

Seubert, A. H./Index to the New Testament, B90

Shannon, T. A./Renewing the Earth, D6

Sharp, M./Guide to the Churches of Rome, C204

_____. Traveller's Guide to Saints in Europe, D191

Shea, J. D. G./Bibliographical Account of Catholic Bibles, Testaments and Other Portions of the Scripture, B75

Shearer, D. C./Pontificia americana, E112

Sheridan, L. W./Bibliography on Canon Law, 1965-1971, D156

Shooner, H. V./Codices manuscripti operum Thomae de Aquino, C57

Short Dictionary of the New Testament//A. Rouet, B110

Shorter Atlas of the Bible/L. H. Grollenberg, B132

Shuster, G./Statistical Profile of Black Catholics, D103

Shuster, G. N./World's Great Catholic Literature, C85

Signs and Symbols in Christian Art/ G. W. Ferguson, C178

Sill, G. G./Handbook of Symbols in Christian Art, C186

Silva-Tarouca, C./Fontes historiae
ecclesiasticae, E57
Sinclair, K. V./French Devotional
Texts of the Middle Ages,
B416
SISTERS READING, A48
Sixteen Documents of Vatican II,
E158
Sloyan, G. S./Commentary on the
New Lectionary, B355
Small Liturgical Dictionary/G.
Lercaro, B386
Smet, J./Catalog of the Carmelitana
Collection, E224
Smith, E. F./Baptismal and
Confirmation Names, A249
Smith, G. D./Teaching of the Catholic
Church, B230
Smith, W./Dictionary of Christian
Antiquities, E32
_____. Dictionary of Christian
Biography, A177
Smyth, D./Focus, A40
Snyderwine, L. T./Researching the
Development of Lay Leader-
ship in the Catholic Church,
B38
Social Justice/V. P. Mainelli, D7
SOCIAL SCIENCES, GENERAL
WORKS, D1-D13
Social Teachings of the Church/A.
Freemantle, D5
Social Wellsprings/J. Husslein, E116
SOCIAL WORK, D52-D64
Société Internationale pour l'Étude
de la Philosophie Médiévale/
Bulletin, C9
SOCIETIES, A162-A168
Society of St. Gregory of America/
White List, C168
Sociologie du christianisme/H.
Carrier, D46
SOCIOLOGY, D44-D69
Some Catholic Novelists/P.
Braybrooke, C122
Some Schools of Catholic Spirituality/
J. Gautier, B323
Some Victorian and Georgian
Catholics/P. Braybrooke, C98

Sommervogel, C./Bibliothèque de
la Compagnie de Jésus, E247
_____. Dictionnaire des ouvrages
anonymes et pseudonymes
(Jesuit), E251
Sonet, J./Répertoire d'incipit de
prières en ancien français,
B418
Source Book for Ancient Church
History/J. C. Ayer, E29
Source Book for Medieval Economic
History/R. C. Cave, D145
Sources chrétienne/H. DeLubac, B176
Sources for the Early History of
Ireland/J. F. Kenney, E45
Sources for the History of Roman
Catholicism in England,
Ireland and Scotland/
J. H. Hungerford, E64
Sources of Catholic Dogma/H. J. D.
Denzinger, B219
Sources of Christian Theology/P. F.
Palmer, B42
Souter, A./Glossary of Later Latin
to 600 A.D., B181
Southern, A. C./Elizabethan Recusant
Prose, C136
Spadafora, F./Dizionario biblico,
B111
SPARK, M., C117
Spicilegium solesmense/J. B.
Pitra, B174
Spiecker, R./Register zu den
Konzilsdokumenten, E161
Spirago, F./Catechism Explained,
B208
Spirit and Origins of American
Protestantism, B5
Spiritual Books for Catholic Youth/
R. B. Fullam, A33
Spiritual Life/A. Tanquerey, B321
Sprug, J. W./Index to G. K.
Chesterton, C103
Staatslexikon/Görres Gesellschaft,
D151
Stabili, E. C./Italian Americans and
Religion, E80
Stammler, W./Die Deutsche Literatur
des Mittelalters, C140

Statistical Profile of Black Catholics/
G. Shuster, D103
Statistical Yearbook of the Church/
Secretaria Status, D74
STATISTICS, D70-D143
Staudacher, J. M./Lector's Guide to
Biblical Pronunciations,
B112
Steck, F. B./Tentative Guide to
Historical Materials on the
Spanish Borderlands, E79
Steenberghen, F. van/Histoire de la
philosophie: périod chrétienne,
C29
———. Philosophie des Mittelälters,
C10
Stegmüller, F./Repertorium Biblicum
Medii Aevi, B76
———. Repertorium commentariorum
in Sententias Petri Lombardi,
B39
Stehle, A./Manual of Episcopal
Ceremonies, B373
Steiner, U. J./Contemporary
Theology, B40
Steinmueller, J. E./Catholic Biblical
Encyclopedia, B95
———. Companion to Scripture
Studies, B77
———. Gospel Harmony, B59
Sterck, L. C./Great Books of France,
C137
Stevenson, J./Creeds, Councils and
Controversies, E30
———. New Eusebius, E31
Stickler, A. M./Historia juris
canonici, D184
Stockhammer, M./Thomas Aquinas
Dictionary, C69
Stoeckle, B./Concise Dictionary
of Christian Ethics, B263
Sträter, P./Katholische Marienkunde,
B248
Stratman, C. J./Bibliography of
Medieval Drama, C120
Strayer, J. R./Dictionary of the
Middle Ages, E58
Streit, R./Bibliotheca missionum,
B292

Student's Values in Drugs and Drug
Abuse/M. V. Sztore, A39
Study of Spirituality/C. Jones,
B320
Stuhlmueller, C./Old Testament
Message, B123
SUBJECT HEADINGS, A84
Sugranyes de Franch, R./Organisa-
tions internationales
catholiques, A166
Sullivan, J. F./Externals of the
Catholic Church, D69
Sullivan, K./Catholic Biblical
Encyclopedia, B95
———. Catholic Tourist Guide,
D192
Sullivan, M. C./Flannery O'Connor
and Caroline Gordon, C115
SULPICIANS, E262
Summa theologiae (1964)/T. Aquinas,
C73
Summa theologica (1947)/T. Aquinas,
C72
Summary of Catholic History/
N. C. Eberhardt, E17
Summary of Scholastic Principles/
B. Wuellner, C22
Survey of American Church History/
N. C. Eberhardt, E96
Survey of Cathlic Literature/
S. J. M. Brown, C99
Survey of the Vatican Archives/
L. E. Boyle, E37
Sutfin, E. J./Selected Annotated
Bibliography on Ecumenical
and Related Matters, B328
Sutro Library Catalogue/C. D.
O'Malley, A10
SYMBOLISM, C174-C203
Symbolism in Liturgical Art/L. H.
Appleton, C174
SYMBOLS, *see* SYMBOLISM
Synopsis theologiae dogmaticae/A.
Tanquerey, B231
Synopsis theologiae morilis et
pastoralis/A. Tanquerey, B280
Systematisch geordnetes Repertorium
der katholische-theologischen
Litteratur/D. Gla, B30

Szczesniak, B./Russian Revolution
and Religion, E68
Szeplaki, J./Bibliography on Cardinal
Mindszenty, E65
Szövérffy, J./Die Annalen der
lateinischen Hymnendichtung,
C169
Sztore, M. V./Student's Values
in Drugs and Drug Abuse,
A39

Table Prayer/M. D. Bouyer, B412
Tanquerey, A./Brevior synopsis
theologiae dogmaticae, B232
_____. Brevior synopsis theologiae
moralis et pastoralis,
B281
_____. Manual of Dogmatic
Theology, B233
_____. Spiritual Life, B321
_____. Synopsis theologiae
dogmaticae, B231
_____. Synopsis theologiae moralis
et pastoralis, B280
Tardiff, H./Index et concordance,
Vatican II, E162
Targum und New Testament/P.
Nickels, B70
Tavagnutti, M. S./Katholisch-
theologische bücherkunde,
A31
Taylor, S. S./Who's Who in the
Catholic World, A181
Teaching of Christ/R. D. Lawler,
B202
Teaching of the Catholic Church/
G. D. Smith, B230
Teachings of the Church Fathers/J. R.
Willis, B224
Teachings of the Second Vatican
Council, E159
TEILHARD DE CHARDIN, P./
C49-C55
Teilhard de Chardin: essai de
bibliographie/D. Poulin, C52
Teilhard de Chardin: index analytique/
P. L'Archevêque, C53
TEMPLARS, E263

Tentative Guide to Historical Materials
on the Spanish Borderlands/
F. B. Steck, E79
Textus et Documenta in usam
exercitationum et
praelectionum academarum,
B43
THEOLOGY, B21-B43, B182-B329
THEOLOGY, BIBLIOGRAPHY,
B21-B41
THEOLOGY, DICTIONARIES
AND ENCYCLOPEDIAS,
B182-B198
THEOLOGY, HANDBOOKS,
B199-B210
THEOLOGY, HISTORY, B211
Theology in Transition/E. O'Brian,
B34
Theology Library/A. M. Henry,
B209
Theotokas/M. O'Carroll, B244
Thériault, M./Les instituts de vie
consacrée au Canada, E196
Thesaurus doctrinae catholicae/
F. Cavellera, B216
Theses and Dissertations/Catholic
University of America, A55
This They Wrote/A. Frederick,
E256
THOMAS AQUINAS, C56-C73
Thomas Aquinas Dictionary/M.
Stockhammer, C69
Thomas Aquinas. Scriptum super
sententiis/C. H. Lohr, C65
Thomas Aquinas/Summa theologiae
(1964), C73
_____. Summa theologica (1947), C72
Thomas, E./Women Religious
History Sources, E176
Thomas-lexikon/L. Schütz, C68
Thomas Merton/M. Breit, C109
Thomas Merton: A Bibliography/
F. Dell'Isola, C110
Thomas van Aquin/P. Wyser, C61
Thomismus/P. Wyser, C62
Thomistic Bibliography, 1920-1940/
V. J. Bourke, C56
Thomistic Bibliography, 1940-1978/
T. L. Miethe, C60

Thompson, N. W./Complete Concordance to the Bible, B91
———. Verbal Concordance to the New Testament, B92
Thornton, F. B./Our American Princes, A195
Thurston, H./Lives of the Saints, A225-A227
Thwaites, R. G./Jesuit Relations, E88
Tiso, F./Young Person's Book of Catholic Signs and Symbols, C187
Tobin, J. E./Dictionary of Catholic Biography, A172
Toelle, G./Catalog of the Carmelitana Collection, E224
Tomasi, S./Italian Americans and Religion, E80
Tomassetti, L./Bullarum, E102
Tomb of St. Peter/A. A. DeMarco, E26
Tominaga, T. T./Iris Murdoch and Muriel Spark, C117
Torres Calvo, A./Diccionario de los textos conciliares, E166
———. Diccionario de textos sociales pontificios, D10
Total Dedication for the Laity/ T. P. McCarthy, E192
Tour of the Summa/P. J. Glenn, C71
Tracey, G./John Henry Newman, C113
TRAPPISTS, see CISTERCIANS, E227-E228
TRAVEL, D187-D192
Traveller's Guide to Saints in Europe/ M. Sharp, D191
Treasury of Catholic Reading/J. Chapin, C82
Triche, C. W./Euthanasia Controversy, B261
TRINITARIANS, E264
Trinitas/M. O'Carroll, B226
Trisco, R./Guide to American Catholic History, E73

Troeyer, B. de/Bio-bibliographia franciscana neerlandica ante saeculum XVI, E241
———. Bio-bibliographia franciscana neerlandica Saeculi XVI, E240
Trudel, P./Dictionary of Canon Law, D175
Tumpach, J./Bibliografie české katolické, A62
Turin Bullarium/L. Tomassetti, E102
Turner, C. H./Ecclesiae occidentalis monumenta iuris antiquissima, D171
Twentieth Century Atlas of the Christian World/A. Freitag, D194
Twentieth Century Catholicism, A113
Twentieth Century Encyclopedia of Catholicism/H. Daniel-Rops, A112
Twenty Centuries of Catholic Church Music/E. E. Nemmers, C172
Twenty Ecumenical Councils/C. Raab, E169
Twenty-four American Cardinals/ B. A. Finn, A189
Tylenda, J. N./Jesuit Saints and Martyrs, E255

Ulanov, B./Contemporary Catholic Thought, C86
Uniate Eastern Churches/A. Fortescue, B12
Union List of Catholic Periodicals/ C. A. Fitzgerald, A157
Union List of Serials/Chicago Area Theological Library Association, A156
United States Catholic Conference/ National Inventory of Parish Catechetical Programs, D23
U.S. Bureau of the Census/Religious Bodies, D104
U.S. Catholic Mission Council/ Handbook, B298
U.S. Documents in the Propaganda Fide Archives, E74

Universal Knowledge, A114
Utz, A./Bibliographie der Sozialethik, D44

Vacant, A./Dictionnaire de théologie catholique, B185
Vademecum of Stories/M. Rufino, B289
Valsecchi, A./Dizionario enciclopedico di teologia, morale, B269
Valverde, T. E./Biobibliographia eclesiastica mexicana, A204
Van Hove, A./Commentarium lovaniense in Codicem iuris canonici, D180
Vann, J. D./Graham Greene, C103
Varia latinitatis scripta/A. Bacci, E126
Vasoli, C./Pensiero medievale, C11
Vaterunser Bibliographie/M. Dorneich, B419
Vatican, Biblioteca vaticana/Books Published by the Vatican Library, A5
Vatican Council II, More Post Conciliar Document/A. P. Flannery, E156
VATICAN COUNCILS, E149-E167
Vatican Revolution/G. MacGregor, E149
Vatican II: A Bibliography/C. Dollen, E150
Vatikanische Archiv/K. A. Fink, E6
Vaughan, K./Divine Armory of Holy Scripture, B223
Veil is Lifted/J. B. Code, E205
Vekene, E./Bibliotheca bibliographica historiae sanctae inquisitionis, E66
Verbal Concordance to the New Testament/N. W. Thompson, B92
Vermeersch, A./Epitome iuris canonici, D181
Verret, M. C./Preliminary Survey of Roman Catholic Hymnals, C152

VESTMENTS, C205-C209
Vestments and Vesture/E. A. Roulin, C209
Veuillot, P./Catholic Priesthood According to the Teaching of the Church, B254
Vienna Corpus, B164
Vies des saints et des bienheureux, A235
Vigouroux, F. G./Dictionnaire de la Bible, B113
Viller, M./Dictionnaire de spiritualité ascétique et mystique, B316
Villiers de St. Étienne, C. de/ Bibliotheca carmelitana, E223
Vincent, A. L./Lexique biblique, B115
Virtue's Catholic Encyclopedia, A108
Vision Obscured: Perceptions of Some Twentieth Century Catholic Novelists/M. J. Friedman, C126
Vismans, T. A./Critical Bibliography of Liturgical Literature, B333
Vital Tradition: The Catholic Novel in a Period of Convergence/ J. D. Kellogg, C125
Vocabulaire latin des principaux thèmes liturgiques/A. Blaise, B380
Vocabulaire Teilhard de Chardin/ H. Cuypers, C55
Voicu, S. J./Bibliography of Inter-church and Interconfessional Theological Dialogues, B327
Vollmar, E. R./Catholic Church in America, E81
Voragine, J. de/Golden Legend, A215
Vorgrimler, H./Bilan de la théologie du XXe siècle, B210
_____. Commentary on the Documents of Vatican II, E152
_____. Dictionary of Theology, B195
Vriens, L./Critical bibliography of missiology, B293
Vulgate, B44

Wace, H./Dictionary of Christian
Biography, A177
_____. Dictionary of Christian
Biography and Literature to the
End of the Sixth Century,
A178
Wadding, L./Scriptores Ordinis
minorum, E242
Wakefield, G. S./Westminster
Dictionary of Christian
Spirituality, B319
Walsh, M./Butler's Lives of the
Saints, Concise Edition,
A224
Walsh, R. J./Modification and
Expansion of the Dewey
Decimal Classification in
the 200 Class, A83
Walsh, T./Catholic Anthology, C130
WAUGH, E., C118
Way of the Lord Jesus/G. G. Grisez,
B274
Weale, W. H. J./Bibliographia
liturgica, B356
Webber, F. R./Church Symbolism,
C188
Weber, F. J./Select Bibliography to
California Catholic Litera-
ture, E82
Weigle, M./Penitente Bibliography,
E83
Weiser, F. X./Handbook of Christian
Feasts and Customs, B406
Weissenbäch, A./Sacra musica,
C162
Weller, P. T./Roman Ritual in Latin
and English, B368
Welty, E./Handbook of Christian
Social Ethics, D12
Wernz, F.X./Ius decretalium,
D182
Werth, A./Papal Pronouncements
on Marriage and the Family,
B262
Western Mysticism/M. A. Bowman,
B304
Westminster Dictionary of Christian
Ethics/J. F. Childress, B270,
C19

Westminster Dictionary of Christian
Spirituality/G. S. Wakefield,
B319
Westminster Dictionary of Christian
Theology/A. Richardson, B198
Westminster Dictionary of Church
History/J. C. Brauer, E11
Westminster Version of the Sacred
Scriptures, B56
Wetzer, H. J./Wetzer und Welt's
Kirchenlexikon, A127
Whalen, W. J./Handbook of Secret
Organizations, A167
_____. Minority Religions in
America, B6
_____. Separated Brethren, B7
What Do You Think of the Priest?/
T. T. Mierzwinski, B252
What Is the Index?/R. A. Burke,
A44
What They Ask about Morals/J. D.
Conway, B272
White List/Society of Saint Gregory
of America, C168
Who's Who in the Catholic World/
S. S. Taylor, A181
Wikenhauser, A./New Testament
Introduction, B129
Willaert, L./Bibliotheca Janseniana
Belgica, B41
Willging, E. P./Catalog of Catholic
Paperback Books, A60
_____. Catholic Serials of the
Nineteenth Century, A155
_____. Handbook of American
Catholic Societies, A168
_____. Index to Catholic Pamphlets,
A61
Williams, M. J./Catholic Social
Thought, D13
Williams, T. D./Concordance of the
Proper Names in the Holy
Scriptures, B93
Willis, J. R./Teachings of the Church
Fathers, B224
Willmann-Institut/Wörterbuch der
Pädagogik, D20
Wimmer, O./Handbuch der Namen
und Heiligen, C202

Wisdom of Catholicism/A. C.
　　Pegis, C83
Wissen Sie Bescheid?/A. M.
　　Rathberger, A126
Women Religious History Sources/
　　E. Thomas, E176
Woods, R. L./Catholic Companion
　　to the Bible, B130
Work of the Bollandists through
　　Three Centuries/H. Delehaye,
　　A214
Works and Criticism of Gerard
　　Manley Hopkins/E. H. Cohen,
　　C105
World Directory of Theological
　　Libraries/G. M. Ruoss, A73
World's Great Catholic Literature/
　　G. N. Shuster, C85
Wörterbuch der Pädagogik/H.
　　Rombach, D20
Wörterbuch der Religion/A.
　　Anwander, B18
Wörterbuch zum Codex juris cononici/
　　R. Köstler, D173
Woywood, S./Practical Commentary
　　on the Code of Canon Law,
　　D183
Wuellner, B./Dictionary of Scholastic
　　Philosophy, C20
_____. Summary of Scholastic
　　Principles, C22
Wuest, J./Matters Liturgical, B403
Wulf, M. M./History of Medieval
　　Philosophy, C30

Wyser, P./Der Thomismus, C62
_____. Thomas von Aquin, C61
Wyszynski, S./Listy pasterskie, E69

Xiberta y Roqueta, B. M./
　　Enchiridion de Verbo
　　Incarnato, B236

Yearbook of Liturgical Studies,
　　B334
YEARBOOKS, D70-D143
Young Person's Book of Catholic
　　Signs and Symbols/F. Tiso,
　　C187
YOUTH, D64

Zamarriego, T./Enciclopedia de
　　orientación bibliografica,
　　A27
Zampetti, E./Bibliografia ragionata
　　delle reviste filosofiche
　　italiane, C14
Zimmermann, M./Revision of Canon
　　Law, D157
Zulaica Garate, R./Franciscanos y la
　　imprenta en México, E244
Zumbro Valley Medical Society/
　　Religious Aspects of Medical
　　Care, B284

GRAHAM SWIFT

ENGLAND

and Other Stories

**SIMON &
SCHUSTER**

London · New York · Sydney · Toronto · New Delhi

A CBS COMPANY

First published in Great Britain by Simon & Schuster UK Ltd, 2014
A CBS COMPANY

Copyright © Graham Swift 2014

3 5 7 9 10 8 6 4 2

Simon & Schuster UK Ltd
1st Floor
222 Gray's Inn Road
London WC1X 8HB

www.simonandschuster.co.uk
www.simonandschuster.com.au

Simon & Schuster Australia, Sydney
Simon & Schuster India, New Delhi

A CIP catalogue record for this book
is available from the British Library

ISBN HB 978-1-47113-739-6
ISBN TPB 978-1-47113-740-2
ISBN E-book 978-1-47113-742-6

Typeset by M Rules
Printed and bound by CPI (UK) Ltd, Croydon, CR0 4YY

For Candice

L—d! said my mother, what is all this story about?

Laurence Sterne, *Tristram Shandy*

CONTENTS

Going Up in the World 1

Wonders Will Never Cease 13

People Are Life 23

Haematology 31

Remember This 43

The Best Days 59

Half a Loaf 75

Saving Grace 85

Tragedy, Tragedy 95

As Much Love as Possible 103

Yorkshire 113

Holly and Polly 125

Keys 133

Lawrence of Arabia 143

Ajax 149

Was She the Only One? 165

Knife 177

Mrs Kaminski 185

Dog 191

Fusilli 205

I Live Alone 213

Articles of War 229

Saint Peter 237

First on the Scene 247

England 257

Going Up in the World

CHARLIE YATES IS a small compact man with the look such men can have of inhabiting well their own modest proportions. He'd been less at ease, once, with his name. Charles Yates, the proper version, the name he had to write on forms, was a toff's name, a joke name. What had his parents been thinking? But Charlie was a joke name too, a joker's name. A right Charlie. Still, he couldn't wriggle out of it. Charlie Yates. No one else seemed to mind.

He's fifty-seven now. He's not quite sure how it's happened. He was born in Wapping in 1951. The Wapping he can remember from back then was still pretty much the Wapping that Hitler had flattened. Look at it now.

He can look at it now because more than twenty years ago

he and Brenda moved to Blackheath. Not very far as the crow flies, but in other ways a different country. They'd made the move because they could. They'd gone up in the world. And Don Abbot and Marion had made the same move at the same time. Don and Charlie were old pals and business partners. Bren and Marion got on with each other too.

Now at fifty-seven Charlie likes to keep himself in shape. He likes on crisp bright still-early Sunday mornings to take a jog. Not such a short one either: across the heath itself and into Greenwich Park, then through the trees to the brow of the hill where you get the view. Then he likes to sit for a bit on one of the benches and take it all in. My city, my London. He's sitting there now.

Jogging isn't his friend Don's idea of how to spend the early part, or any part, of a Sunday morning, even a brilliant crisp one like this, so Charlie has never jogged with Don. He jogs alone. But every other Sunday, even after Charlie has already gone for a jog, Don and Charlie meet up and go and play nine holes. At Shooters Hill or Eltham, even sometimes, if someone asks them, at Blackheath itself—'Royal Blackheath'. There, perhaps, he should be known as Charles.

There were never many golf courses in Wapping.

When he jogs Charlie wears a pale grey tracksuit, with a blue stripe, and neat trainers, nothing sloppy or cheap. The simple thin gold chain that it seems he's worn all his life flips up and down at the base of his neck. He has trim close-cropped hair that's now more white than grey, but it's soft and fine and his wife still likes to stroke it sometimes as if she might be stroking the head of a dog.

As he sits for a while he's hardly puffed at all. At fifty-seven

Charlie's father, Frank Yates, had been pretty much past it. But then he was a docker—or he had been—just like Don's father. Look at the docks now.

Francis Yates. You could say that was a toff's name too.

One fine morning in Wapping over fifty years ago Charlie Yates and Don Abbot had met in the playground at Lea Road Infants' School and for some strange reason—a big chunky kid and a little nipper—they'd known it would be a lifelong thing. Lea Road Infants' had later got flattened too, though not by bombs.

For his size, Charlie has quite broad shoulders. When he pushes up the sleeves of his tracksuit (or of his red cashmere golf sweater) you notice the tattoos on his forearms and that, for his size, he has large wrists and hands. He also has, for the size of his face, quite a big prominent but well-shaped nose. With his deep-set eyes this can give him, especially when he grins, a slightly wolfish expression which once used to help him with a certain kind of girl.

But Charlie would say—and the jogging, which is sometimes more of a gentle floating run, would back this up—that the most important item is the feet. The balance and the feet.

Once, for three or four years, Charlie was a boxer. Big hands, but it was really the feet. A bantamweight. He won a few fights and is still proud of the fact that he never got his finely shaped nose smashed out of true. Once he worked on an oil rig, which was when, more fool him, he got the tattoos. But tattoos had come back again now—so he's in fashion. Once he was a roofer. That was his main thing. He was never going to be a docker at any rate. Just as well.

A roofer. He could climb like a monkey. He had the physique. Then it seemed that the roofs just got higher and higher and he became something more than a roofer, without really reckoning on it and without knowing if there was any limit to how high he could go.

He went up in the world. He discovered that he had no fear of heights.

Once, if he'd been born earlier, Charlie might have been a steeplejack, but that was a trade, even a word—like docker— that was becoming out of date. Where were the steeples? Where were the tall chimneys? But suddenly, instead, there were the towers, springing up as if it were a race, and Charlie could work at the very top of them on the exposed girders, without a moment's giddiness or fear. A head for heights is what they say, but Charlie would say it was all in the feet. Where you are standing is just where you are standing.

He earned good money and there was no shortage of work. Some people called it danger money. Charlie didn't like to call it danger money because that implied it was dangerous, but he accepted the basic principle: no risk, no gain. Do something special—like boxing—so you might make a bit extra and put something away, not just scrape along till Friday. Don't be a docker.

Some people—quite a lot of the people Charlie has known—like to place bets, to put their hopes in dogs and horses. Charlie has never placed a bet in his life. He became a birdman, helping to build towers.

And there they are now, glinting in the early-September sunshine, the towers that Charlie Yates helped to build. There, beyond the hidden twists of the river, is Wapping. There's Stepney, there's Limehouse. There's Docklands.

*

One night, when it was still only starting with him and Brenda, when it was still a bit touch and go, Brenda had said, 'Charlie, you have lovely feet.' It was the clincher. No one had said this to him before. It went straight, not to his feet, but to his heart, not just because it had never been said before, but because it was true. He said, 'Brenda, you have lovely everything.' And that was that.

Now Brenda and Marion go on shopping sprees together. Now, twice a year, all four of them go on holidays, to faraway places. Last March it was the Maldives. Charlie couldn't say precisely where the Maldives are, but he's been there. You get out of a plane. The others were all for going again this winter, but Charlie wasn't so sure. He'd heard somewhere that the Maldives could be one of the first places in the world to be submerged by rising sea levels. It was hardly likely to happen while they were there. But he wasn't sure.

Funny, the feelings you could get. He had no fear of heights, but he'd never got on with the sea. He'd known it, working on that oil rig. Once was enough. The same perhaps was true of the Maldives, different proposition though they were. And if he was honest, Charlie would say that he'd be just as happy knocking a ball around the local course with Don as he would be sitting in the Maldives. Or wherever. He's just as happy sitting here. It's all the same place, it's sitting in your own body.

He'd said to Brenda, 'You don't have to worry, Bren, with these feet.' As if his feet had little wings. But there he'd be anyway, safe and sound every night, cuddling up with her again. A thirty-floor tower in the Isle of Dogs wasn't, in that respect as well as others, like being stuck out in the North Sea.

He said, 'Aren't you glad, Bren?'

'Glad what?'

'Glad I'm not on an oil rig.'

But it wasn't fair to her, he knew, the prospect of his going off every day indefinitely to walk in the sky. He said that when he'd stashed enough away he'd fix something else up. He hadn't a clue what. He'd come back down to earth.

At some point he twigged that those towers weren't just built with risk, they were built for it. It was risk inside and out. They were built, most of them, to be full of people dealing in their own mysterious kind of danger money. Well, that was their business. He took his money and took the risk that one day, though he never did, he might step off into space.

But one day he took another kind of risk. He followed another lifetime hunch.

It was obvious too, once you saw it, like all the big things perhaps are. It was so obvious that his immediate second thought was: If it was so obvious, how many others might already be in on the act? But it was still early days. More and more towers. And what were those towers made of—or what did it look as though they were made of? What was it that sometimes you didn't see even when it was staring you in the face?

He went to see Don, who was then—well, what was Don Abbot in those days? He was a wheeler-dealer, he was a bit of this and that. You might say he was going places, you might say he was all talk. They had a drink in the Queen Victoria. Don listened. He looked his little friend up and down. Then he spoke as if he hadn't really been listening, but that was Don's way.

6

'So what are you suggesting, Charlie? That you and me should become a pair of window cleaners?'

'No, Don. Don't muck me about.'

Then they'd talked some more.

It became the standard story anyway, the standard line. In golf club bars. In hotel bars, by the blue pools, all around the world.

'I'm Don, this is Charlie. We're window cleaners.'

He looks at the towers. He'd helped to build them. And then for twenty years or so he and Don had helped to keep them sparkling.

Don had said, 'One thing you have to understand, Charlie, I'm never getting in one of those—contraptions, I'm never even going *up* there. I'm not the kind of guvnor who likes to show everybody he can actually do the job.'

'Well you can leave that to me. I'll be the one who won't have to bullshit. But don't get me wrong, Don. I'm planning on the same as you. And I've promised Brenda.'

Abbot and Yates. No arguing about the alphabetical order. We clean windows, not just any old windows. It took a while to get it off the ground, so to speak, but then ... All that glittering glass.

Now they live with the gentry in Blackheath. And now it isn't just him and Bren and Don and Marion, but their kids, a boy and a girl each. Who aren't even kids any more. They'd grown up in Blackheath and gone to school there, and then they'd all gone, with one exception, to university. University! It had been a good move, to cross the river.

The one exception was Don and Marion's Sebastian.

Sebastian! How did Don and Marion come up with a name like that? Thank God he was known as Seb. Seb had gone straight from being sixteen, or so it seemed, to working in one of those towers. For a New York bank. At twenty-three Seb was making serious money, or crazy money—take your pick— money that made Don and him look pretty silly. That made getting A levels and going to university look pretty silly too. Or as Don put it, and Charlie was never quite sure how Don meant it, Seb was one of the barrow boys, wasn't he? One of the barrow boys who'd moved on and moved in. Moved on and moved up.

Charlie looks at the towers. His own son Ian is studying in Southampton to be a marine biologist, which makes Charlie feel—in a different way from how Don must feel about Seb— out of his depth. Ha. There was a joke there. And when Charlie had first told Don about Ian's leanings in life Don had said, 'My Uncle Eddy was in the marines in the war. I never knew they had their own biologists.'

Charlie and Don could say, 'My old man was a docker.' What else could they say? What would their kids say? 'My old man was a window cleaner'? They wouldn't even say 'my old man'. Except maybe Seb. Seb might say it, and laugh.

Down in Southampton, Ian wouldn't be able to think: My city, my London. He wouldn't be able to point and say, 'See—over there.' When Charlie and Brenda drive down to Southampton Charlie humbles himself and listens while his son talks. Maybe that thing about the Maldives came from Ian. Of course it did. But it's not difficult to be humble. Perhaps it isn't even humility. Sometimes while Ian talks Charlie feels a little quick whoosh inside. It's like the whoosh he feels when with Don on a Sunday morning he hits a really good drive. 'That one's shifting, Charlie.' It's like the whoosh he once felt years ago, after a fight, when the ref's arm would go up, lifting his.

My son Ian. A marine biologist.

He sits on the bench in his tracksuit, feeling the circulation in his veins, feeling, as he's always done, good in his own skin. Charlie is a businessman (a word he can find strange) and a successful one, yet he would still say that the most important thing is your own body. It's what you have, what you come with, and to be glad of it and trust in it is simply life's greatest gift.

So it was funny how it was the urge and aim of most people—almost a sort of law of the world—to go up into their heads, into the topmost part of themselves and live there, live in and by their heads, when most people (he was the exception proving the rule) were afraid of heights.

He looks at the towers, a hand screening his eyes from the dazzle, and smiles. Or it looks like a smile. Only Brenda would know that it's not a smile. Only Brenda would see the two little extra pinches at the corners of Charlie's mouth and understand this contradiction in his face. He has no repertoire of frowns. When Charlie's worried or puzzled he smiles, but smiles differently.

He's worried, and has been now for some time, about his friend Don, about how he's putting on weight. Don has always been a big man, but big of frame, not flabby or cumbersome or slow. Now he's spreading, he's simply expanding. It's a sort of joke—that he's putting on pounds—a joke that even Don likes to tell against himself, but it isn't really a joke at all, and when

Charlie plays golf with Don now he knows it's not just for fun, but it's important for keeping Don moving. They should play every Sunday. They should play the other nine holes, not just spend them in the bar.

He knows there's no point, there's never been, in asking Don to come jogging with him. And how would it look now, how could it possibly work: Don lumbering and sweating beside him while he, Charlie, just hovered on his toes? It has even come to seem a little wrong to Charlie that he should go jogging by himself while Don has this weight problem—which is completely illogical, even vaguely superstitious. Like thinking you shouldn't go to the Maldives because the Maldives might one day disappear.

But Charlie worries about Don. It's as if all the money is at last turning to fat. Fifty years ago and more, Charlie had thought that he was just a little scrap of nothing and this bigger kid might take him under his wing. And so it was. Though now you could also say it was Don who should be for ever grateful to Charlie. But Charlie feels the strange worrying need, like some unpaid debt, to take his ever bulkier friend under his wing. How?

And now he has the other worry too, this new worry that could knock the first one aside. He's going to talk to Don about it soon. Don will tell him what else he knows, when they play their round in just a couple of hours. By the sound of it, there won't be much concentrating on Don's weight problem or even on the golf. Crisp bright morning though it is.

Charlie is a businessman, yes that's what he can legitimately be called, but, even though he likes to sit and look at them, he doesn't keep his ear close to what goes on inside those towers. That's their business, he just cleans the windows, so to speak. But Don keeps an ear, it's even an inside ear, because of Seb. Charlie has sometimes had the bizarre vision of Don actually cleaning a window, on the twenty-fifth floor say, something Don could never do (though Charlie could, easy-peasy), and looking in and waving at his son.

Don had called and said, 'Seb's in trouble, deep trouble.'

Trouble? Wasn't Seb making telephone numbers? Wasn't Seb making them all look silly?

Don said, 'They're going to pull the rug from under him. Him and everyone else. Something big's coming, Charlie, something big and bad. If you ask me, from what Seb's heard—it's not just Seb who's in trouble, it's the whole fucking world.'

Did Don have drink in his voice? No. Charlie didn't say anything to Brenda, only that it was Don calling about tomorrow, though Brenda would have thought: Why did Don need to call? It was a Saturday night. Charlie didn't hear anything on the late-night news. Later, cuddling up, he said, 'Aren't you glad, Bren?'

'Glad what?'

'Glad I was never a marine biologist.'

'What are you on about?'

He didn't really know, himself. There was something about Don's voice, there was something about that 'whole fucking world'.

His instinct the next morning was to get up and do the usual jog, to be on his feet, to prepare—to prepare his mind by preparing his body. And it was such a beautiful morning, early September, the tingle of autumn in the air.

Now he gets up from the bench and takes a last look at the towers. They gleam back. Then he turns and jogs again through the glistening trees, feeling at fifty-seven as light on his feet as he did when he was seventeen.

WONDERS WILL NEVER CEASE

WHEN AARON AND I were younger we used to chase women. It's a phrase. How many times do you actually see a man chasing a woman, say ten yards behind and gaining? We were both runners anyway, literally—athletes. With me it was the hurdles. We both did the same PE course at college, and girls were part of our physical education. I'll be the first to say that Aaron was better at it than me. In his case it was more that the women chased him, or crawled all over him. It was how he was made. I tended to get his rejects. But even Aaron's rejects could be something, and one day I married and settled down with one of them. Patti.

After that I didn't hang out with Aaron so much. In fact we hardly heard from each other. Maybe he thought that by marrying Patti and settling down I was also letting the side down. Well, too bad.

I wouldn't have said this ten years ago, but I think I'm the type who sees life like a book, with chapters. In one chapter you mess around, then you marry, have kids, get a place of your own, and so on. I'm not like Aaron. I wouldn't like to guess how many books Aaron's read. But that's the point perhaps with physical education, it's not really about reading.

It was an option anyway. If you did the course and got the certificate you could make a career, a life out of it. It was a chance. Meanwhile we were athletes too.

I never had any illusions about making it to the big competitions. I was just quite good at hurdling, I loved the hurdles. Aaron used to say, 'Count me out, man. When I run, I want to run. I don't want to run at something that'll trip me up.'

I didn't say, 'Doesn't that apply to women?'

They tripped him up and they crawled all over him. And they crawled all over him because he was quite a specimen. It was a vicious circle. But Aaron, I believe—just to talk about his running—could have been championship stuff. I say this as a qualified PE teacher.

Anyhow, the time came, years back, when I'd settled down with Patti, and Aaron and I had almost lost touch. Just now and then Patti and I would have our 'wondering about Aaron' conversations. I was always a bit nervous about them, Patti having been one of Aaron's rejects. I sometimes thought this was the reason why the gap had opened up between Aaron and me. It was Patti's doing, it was Aaron's, it was mine. I don't know. Once—we were having Sunday break-fast—I actually said to Patti, 'I wonder if those women aren't catching up with him.' I might have said 'the years' instead. It was just a casual, private-joke thing, but it was a bit care-less perhaps.

Patti didn't pick it up one way or the other. She said, 'Mmm, I wonder too.' She took a bite of toast. Then she said, 'If you're worried about him, give him a call, look him up.' As if she was daring me.

She was pregnant with Daryl, our first, around this time. She was crazy about marmalade! Maybe she was thinking: Well, if he's hankering for a last boys' night out, he better take his chance while he can. Now we have the two boys, Daryl and Warren, two growing boys. Lots of boys' nights in.

Anyhow, I never made the call. But one day, years later, I get a call, out of the blue, from Aaron. He sounds just like the old Aaron, but he also sounds a bit cagey. It turns out he's called to tell me he's going to get married. I wait a bit, in case I'm being wound up. Then I wait anyway, in case he has some joke to make about it. I wait for an 'Okay, man, don't laugh'. But the only joke is that he's speaking in a sort of whisper, as if it's top-secret information he can trust only with me.

Then he says he'd like me—me and Patti of course—to come to the wedding. To make things clear, he says it's going to be a 'low-key' thing, in a registry office, just the two of them. Except you need a witness. So would Patti and I like to be there, to witness?

All the time, apart from swallowing back my surprise, I'm thinking: He didn't have to tell me this—a witness could be anyone—but I get the feeling he thinks that by telling me and having me as his witness he won't have to tell anyone else. I feel honoured and I also feel arm-twisted, but how could I not say yes? Even though, apparently, it means a trip to Birmingham. That's where he is now. Guess what—teaching PE.

I say, 'Yes, of course.' Before I've even spoken to Patti. I also feel like saying, 'Don't worry, Aaron, I won't breathe a word.'

I say, 'So what's her name then?'

'It's Wanda.'

'Wanda,' I say, trying to form a picture of a Wanda. I don't say, 'So, is she pregnant?'

Fortunately, Patti more or less has the same thought as me: How can we not? Perhaps she's really thinking: Must we? But she looks all keen and interested, she even makes a joke about it, a pretty good joke too. 'Well, Wandas will never cease.'

So we go through with it, this low-key, hush-hush event. We manage to park the boys with Patti's parents. We're even ready to book a hotel. But Aaron says, 'Nah, man, stay with us, no problem.' This needs a bit of thought. I don't like to spell it out: this might be intruding on Aaron and Wanda's wedding night. We aren't at PE college any more.

But I soon get the picture that, apart from the business at the registry office and a few drinks and a meal, nothing much out of the ordinary is going to happen. There's not going to be a honeymoon. Aaron and Wanda have apparently been shacked up together for quite a while. There'd be a spare room in their flat for Patti and me. It's just that they've both decided it's time to get married.

'Okay,' I say, slightly wishing it would be easier to insist on paying for a hotel anyway. With the two boys, Patti and me have to watch the cash. But of course what I'm mostly thinking, and so's Patti, is: What's this Wanda like? And, given all the years that have passed: What's Aaron like?

Well, it may put me in a bad light, but I have to say Wanda was a disappointment. At least at first. A surprise and a disappointment. Don't get me wrong. I don't mean she wasn't perfectly—fine. But if all those years of what Aaron once got up to were supposed to be a selection process, so that in the end he'd pick out a real star—well, Wanda was nothing special.

I even felt, which doesn't put me in a good light either, I did better with Patti.

I didn't share this thought with Patti, but I could feel her tuning in to it and relaxing. It put me in a good light with her. I think Patti's fear was that we were about to meet some woman who'd have me, in spite of myself, spending the whole weekend with my tongue hanging out. That this might have been the real purpose of the exercise. Aaron just wanted to show off his trophy.

To be honest, it was my fear too.

Wanda was built along pretty pared-down lines, which wasn't, as I recall, how Aaron had liked them. She wasn't skinny, but she was, well, wiry, with a tough little pair of shoulders. And her face, though it had a cheeky way of making you feel good and want to laugh, wasn't a face that would stop you in your tracks. It could even sometimes look a bit hard and locked up.

She wasn't a beauty, but she had a way of carrying herself, of moving, an energy, an intensity. I liked her. I was glad I didn't fancy her. And pretty soon I twigged it.

I found a moment to say in private to Aaron, 'She's a runner, isn't she?' This was barely an hour after the two of them had become Mr and Mrs.

'I hope she's not running anywhere, man, after what we've just done.'

'You know what I mean.'

'I know what you mean.' In fact a glint had come into his eyes. We were at a bar, fetching drinks.

'Yep,' he said. 'Four hundred. Eight hundred maybe.' He gave me a quick stare. 'Maybe hurdles. She has to find where it really is for her.' Then he said, with a certain pride in his voice, and he even looked across the crowded room to exchange a wink with his new wife, 'Yep, a runner. She's going places. Same again, man?'

As for Aaron himself, how did he look? Well, he looked good—right then he looked very good—but I could see how the years had affected him. They'd blunted and blurred him a bit, taken off some shine. Enough to make me think: How will he look in another five years? And to make me think: He'll be having the same thoughts about me.

Except I didn't kid myself and I hadn't just got married and I was a father of two. And my viewpoint had perhaps been different all along. I keep people fit for a living, so I keep fit myself, but there are limits, and no one gets any younger. That's why these days I spend a good deal of time with a man called Jarvis who's starting up a sportswear company. It's why I enrolled not long ago on a business course. It's my plan B. For the boys' and Patti's sake. For my own sake.

I could have been a hurdler? Maybe. But, as I said once to Patti a long time ago, I saw the hurdles.

All the same, people reach their peaks, I believe this. They come into their best. There's the book with the chapters, but there's something else. We reach our peaks and we pass them. There's nothing to be done about it, but it's a sad thing if you never even knew the peak you had it in you to reach. In the world of physical fitness you see a lot of this. You see the chances and you see a lot of missed ones.

What I'm really saying is that you might have thought that for Aaron and Wanda their wedding day wasn't their moment of coming into their best. It was important, but their best was somewhere else. Maybe Aaron knew that his had already gone.

Anyhow, after a few drinks—it was a three o'clock wedding—they took us back to their place before we went out again for dinner. It was a top flat, on two floors, and our room was a tiny little spare room under the roof, but I was relieved we wouldn't be sleeping just the other side of a wall from them.

More than relieved. As we went upstairs Patti was ahead. She was wearing a nice outfit for the occasion (maybe for Aaron too, but I'll let that pass). I was carrying our overnight bag, but I couldn't keep my free hand to myself. I couldn't help giving Patti a good goosing. And no sooner were we behind the door and supposed to be, according to Aaron, 'sorting ourselves out', than we were at it, quick and breathless and more or less still standing up. A chilly attic room in Birmingham, dark outside. Patti with her skirt up, holding on to the back of a chair. The kids off our hands. Two newly-weds below. Wonders will never cease.

We had a good time—I mean we had a good time, too, with Aaron and Wanda. Because of the head start we had, of having been married for five years already and having two kids, being with Aaron and Wanda was like being with a couple of kids.

And, not having our own kids around, it was like being a couple of kids ourselves.

True, when we came back later that night—it *was* their wedding night—our top room, above theirs, might still have been a bit tricky. But we'd all been drinking and then Patti and me—well, we'd had our head start. All I remember is curling up with her, this time just for warmth, and crashing.

When I woke up I could hear a lot of scuffling below. I don't mean bedroom noises. I mean scuffling, on the stairs and then in the hallway. The sound of people on their feet and busy about something—very early on a Sunday morning, in January. On the day after their wedding.

I heard muffled voices. I think I heard, 'Okay, Wan? Keys?' Then I heard the front door being shut with an effort to keep it quiet. Then I heard more voices below in the street. I wondered if Aaron and Wanda were still drunk. And I couldn't help getting up to peep through the curtains of our little front window.

It made me think of getting up once when I'd heard strange noises at home. It was just two foxes, under the streetlamps, mucking around with an upended dustbin. I remember thinking that I wasn't young any more—I was someone who worried about noises in the night.

What I saw this time, under the streetlamps, was Aaron and Wanda. To say they were mucking around wouldn't have been quite right, but not quite wrong either. They were in tracksuits and trainers. On the morning after their wedding night—it was still dark and freezing—they were going for a run. But they were also mucking around as if they couldn't yet get down to serious business. They were laughing. They were like two foxes in their own way. They more than once kissed and ran their hands over each other. I thought: They could be doing all that snuggled up in bed.

Nonetheless I saw Aaron had a stopwatch on a loop round his neck. They actually took up positions, side by side, in the middle of the road, half crouching, as if their toes were on a line. Aaron held the stopwatch, looking at it, then Wanda tensed and Aaron spoke. I'm sure I heard, 'Set! Go!' Wanda sped off and Aaron kept looking at the watch—maybe it was a ten-second handicap—then he sped off too.

His challenge to her, or hers to him? I'll never know. Or what the distance was or the route. It was 6.30 a.m.

Wanda's an eight-hundred-metre runner now. The real deal. It's less than a year to the London Olympics. And she's Aaron's missis.

I turned from the window. Patti had woken up. She switched on a bedside light and stared at me. 'What the hell are you doing? What's going on?'

Well, the phrase came to me. I had to laugh. I said, 'I've just seen Aaron chasing a woman.'

I explained. I explained what I'd heard and what I'd seen and I expected there'd now be some chuckling head-shaking discussion between us about this weird post-wedding behaviour. Or that this might be the time for our in-depth analysis of the whole Aaron-Wanda thing.

But Patti just said, 'You mean they're not here, they're not right below us? We've got the place to ourselves?'

And she grabbed my wrist and yanked me back into bed.

People Are Life

'But you have friends,' I said.

I don't know why I said it. It was somewhere between saying and asking.

'Friends?' he said.

'Friends. You know.'

He was my last of the day. I'd already told Hassan to turn the sign on the door. I was tired, but sometimes the last of the day is different, if only because it's the last. It was a little before seven, already dark.

I snipped away.

'Friends,' he said, as if he'd never heard the word before. Then he went silent. 'I have meetings,' he said.

Now it was my turn. 'Meetings?'

'Meetings. I know people and I meet them. People I've known for a long time, but I just meet them. Know what I mean? Time goes by, then we meet, for a drink or something. Then time goes by again. Is that having friends?'

I wasn't sure now if he was saying or asking.

'Well,' I said.

Maybe what I'd meant by friends was no more than just that—what he'd just said. People you could talk to. People he could talk to.

'Well,' I said.

It's not every day that one comes in and lets you know that since you did them last their mother has died. And who puts it this way: 'That's both of them. My dad last year, my mum last week.'

Well, that was certainly saying.

I'd never known, or I couldn't remember, about his dad.

'I didn't know that,' I said. 'The two of them.'

And I'd never known till now the truth of this one's situation. He didn't have to say it, I didn't have to ask. I saw it in his face in the mirror, in the way he looked at his face in the mirror.

'Well it has to happen,' I said, 'sooner or later.' I might have said, 'When you get to our age,' but I didn't.

You see things in the way people look at their own faces. It's not a thing they often do or even want to do, but in a barber's shop there's not much else to do. In a café people pay to sit and look out at the world going by. In a barber's they pay to stare at their own faces, and you see what goes on when they do.

You don't see much in the top of a head. Though sometimes

I think: Right there beneath my fingers is their skull, their brain and every thought that's in it.

What this one was telling me, by his look in the mirror, was that he'd lived with—lived for—his mum and his dad all his life. Some men are big children. That was about the whole of it. And he must have been past sixty. One of those big, hefty but soft types. What he was telling me was that he was all alone in the world.

I carried on snipping. What I thought was: Well, what can I do about it? I cut hair.

'Still, it's tough,' I said. 'How old—your mother?'

'Eighty-three,' he said.

'Eighty-three,' I said. 'That's not bad. Eighty-three's not a bad age.'

Then after a silence I said, I don't know why, 'But you have friends.'

People to talk to, I meant, in your time of trouble. Everyone has friends. But he only had 'meetings' apparently.

'Friends,' he said, as if the word was strange. 'I had friends when I was a kid. I mean a little kid. We hung around together, all the time. We were in and out of each other's homes, each other's lives. We never thought twice about it. That's having friends.'

I snipped away. 'Well that's true enough,' I said.

And how many times do I say that to a customer? 'That's true enough.' It's what you say. Whatever they say.

'The friends we make when we're young,' I said, 'they're the ones that stick, they're the ones that matter.'

That wasn't quite what he'd said, or meant, and I knew it. It wasn't quite what I meant either. I saw what he'd meant. I snipped away and looked at his hair, but I saw my friends, in Cyprus. In Ayios Nikolaos. All my nine-year-old, ten-year-old friends. I saw myself with them.

Maybe he knew that I hadn't meant what I'd said. I'd said something everyone says, or likes to think.

He said, 'It's not the same, is it? Meeting people, seeing people, talking to them. It's not the same as having friends.'

I moved the angle of his head. 'That's too hard,' I said, 'too hard.' I felt something coming, something almost like anger. I pushed it back. I almost stopped snipping. 'You're asking too much,' I said. 'All due respect—to your mother. All due respect to your feelings. If you have people to see and talk to, then you have friends. If you have people, you have life.'

It was late, it was dark. It was the nearest I could get to a little philosophy. It's what some people expect, sometimes, from a barber. A little philosophy. Especially a barber who's turned sixty himself and who's boss of his own shop (me and three juniors) and whose hair is crinkly grey. And I'm Greek too (or Cypriot) and we invented philosophy.

'People,' I said. 'People are life.'

But what I thought was: You didn't have to come and get your hair cut, did you, after your mum had just died? His hair wasn't so long, it didn't need a cut.

I put the scissors and comb in my top pocket and switched on the clippers so we couldn't speak.

People think if you're a barber then you have people, you have talk all the time, your whole day. The things you must hear, the stories, the things you must learn from all those people.

But the truth is I like to get away from people. I like it when it's the end of the day. That's why sometimes I'm different, I say things, with the last one. I get enough of people. And people are mainly just heads of hair, some of them not such nice heads of hair.

I thought: He wants it neat and tidy for the funeral.

My mother and father died years ago, in Cyprus. I hadn't seen them anyway for quite a time. I hadn't been back. As a matter of fact, my wife died too, just three years ago—my English wife, Irene. But we'd split up, we'd been split up for years. She drank all the time. She drank and she swore all the time.

Did I tell all my customers, when she died, when we split up? Did I gabble away to my customers? Did I close the shop?

I have two grown-up boys who are both in computers and are embarrassed by their father who's just been a barber all his life.

I'm glad when I get home and can be alone.

Maybe he heard all this in my voice. Or he saw it in my face, in the mirror. There's always a moment when you stand behind them, with your fingers either side of their head, holding it straight, and you both stare at the mirror as if for a photograph. As if the head you have in your hands might be something you've just made.

'People are life,' I said.

But he could see, in the mirror, that I was thinking: Don't come to me at the end of the day for wise words or comfort, or friendship, if that's what you want. What do you expect? That when I shut the shop in just a moment I'm going to say, 'Why don't you and I go for a drink? Why don't we get to know each other better?'

I'm glad when I get home and can take a beer from the fridge.

One of those heavy but soft types who look as if they've been well fed by their mothers and will end up feeding them. A regular, it's true. How many years? Always wanting me, the boss, to do him, none of the juniors. The years flash by if you count them in haircuts. I didn't know his name. That's not so strange, of course. No appointment system. No need to know their names—unless they tell you—or what they do for a living.

It's how the English are, I learnt this.

They all know my name. It's over the window. Vangeli. And they know what I do. But how many times do any of them ask, 'So how did you get to be a barber?'

I tell them, if they ask, I give them the story. I say I was born holding a comb and scissors . . .

The truth is it was something I could do. It didn't need a brain. Then I did my army service. They made me cut the whole camp's hair. There I met some people! There I got some talk! I gave them all the same shaved-rat's face. Then I came to this country and ran around for a while with a crazy bunch who'd made the journey before me. Then I settled down to be a barber.

And now I was the same age, give or take, as this man whose head was in my hands. And yes, in however many years it was, I'd seen his hair grow thinner and greyer, more pink showing through. But of course never said.

There's a joke in the barber's trade: 'I'm sorry for your loss.'

When my wife died and I went to see her, I mean in the chapel of rest, she was covered right up to her chin in a cloth. All I saw was a head. You can't get away from some things.

I went back to snipping. Outside people were hurrying home. Lucas, one of my juniors—it's what I call them, 'juniors'—was sweeping the floor.

Your turn to speak, I thought. But he didn't. For a second or so I thought: He's just glad of the touch of my fingers, through his hair, on his scalp, the flick of my comb. The smell of shampoo and talc, like the smell of being a baby again.

Vangeli. It means 'angel of good news', but I don't like to explain this to people, because of the jokes. I don't like to explain that Irene, my wife's name, is really a Greek name too. It means 'peace'.

Peace!

There's another moment when you reach for the hand mirror and hold it up to the back of their heads. And once again you have to look, both of you, straight into the big mirror, as if you're a pair who go together. It's the moment when it's almost over. Then there's the moment when you pull away the cloth and brush them down and they stand up and you give them the paper towel, then they wipe their necks, put on their jackets and pay. You give them back any change, if they don't tell you to keep it.

Then there's the moment when they turn, and you—or at least I always do it—give them a little pat, a little pat that turns into a squeeze, just half a second, on one shoulder. It means thank you, thank you for the tip, but it also means: there, that's you done, that's you all fresh and ready. Now go and live your life.

Haematology

Roehampton, Surrey
House of Eliab Harvey

7th February, 1649

Colonel Edward Francis
The Council of Officers
Westminster

My dear cousin,

Well, Ned (if I may still so call you and if you will deign to hear from me), we have lived through extraordinary times. Were there ever such times as these? And now I must cede to you that you are of the winning party and may lord it over me who was the close attendant of kings, nay of our late—of our very late— king. Or would you have me name him, if I have it right, 'tyrant, traitor, murderer'? Would you daub me with the same charges, for having been so privy to His Majesty—but must I not call him that?—for having ministered to his agues, fevers and coughs? Would you have me place my own head upon the block for having been such a bodily accomplice to tyranny? Then it would be seen, would it not, if my argument of the blood's motion held true? Physician, prove thyself!

But was it not proven when that royal blood—may we even call it that?—spurted forth but a week ago at Whitehall? And is it not proven when any man's head or limb is severed from his body, as has been the lot of many men—nay, of women and children—in these late times? A king is but a man like any other. Has it needed seven years of war and a trial by Parliament to determine the matter, when any such as I might have attested to it? Anatomy is no respecter. I have dissected criminals and examined kings. Does it need any special statute to claim the one might be the other?

That, Ned, was my grounding and my ground, long before those of your party set out to curb the King's powers, then over-throw him. There are tyrannies and tyrannies, and treacheries and treacheries. There are some even now of my party—I mean among the party of physicians—who would not blench or lament to see my old head removed from my body, to see me cut down for having raised my standard against King Galen. There are many kinds of majesty and rebellion. We were but boys, Ned, when the Armada closed upon our shores, but would we not have rallied round our monarch? Rally, I say! We were more than half the age we have now when Ralegh's head was severed from his body. Did we not then both feel not a little of the sharpness of the axe that smote him? There were many of your party for whom that day, I dare say, marked a severance. It was their beginning, their pretext. So it was with you. It was the beginning, I dare say, of our own severance.

Yet did we not feel also, if we are truthful, that there is a motion, a fluctuation—may not I use such terms?—in the fortunes of men, an ebb and flow, a rise and fall, beyond all issue of government or justice; and that it is into these unrestrained tides—we knew it by then—we enter as we enter the world? We set our little skiffs upon them, as Ralegh set many a fine vessel upon the waters of his ambition. Should I have stepped in, Ned, to bid my former master James withhold his warrant upon so worthy a head? I was but his physician, not his counsellor, and had been hardly a year in his service. And Ralegh went to his death bravely and nobly, as did, but these seven days past, my other late master Charles.

Is that what we must call him now, only Charles? Is that the ordinance? As you and I may still call each other—or so I trust—but Ned and Will, boys who once played at knuckle-bones and did battle with the wooden swords of our rulers at Canterbury. And quaked in our shoes, no doubt, at the wrath of our masters, or spoke impudence about them, behind our hands, when their gowned backs were turned. They were only our schoolmasters, but it was all our world. Such tyranny, such subjection. Such fledgling revolt. Such nursing of our destinies. And it was the *King's* School, mark you. Though it was still the reign, long to continue, of, as we would call her, even in our prayers, Our Sovereign Lady Elizabeth.

What times, Ned, what times. 'That one might read the book of fate and see the revolution of the times'—do I have it correctly? Is it not King Henry IV, deposer himself of kings? But it was you who attended the playhouses and, if I know you as I knew you in your youth, no doubt other houses as well, while I attended my lectures at Padua. You who are now of God's militia, while I, to pass the hours, read more of the poets than I read of the Bible. Is that to speak treason?

That, surely, was our first parting, though we would write much to each other. You were for the law, I was for physic. You were for the Middle Temple, I was for Padua. Was it not indeed the seed of all our future differences and of future offices we would hold as then undiscovered to us? Yet that common seed, that common stirring of the blood—quite so!—was ambition. Should we deny it? I was for anatomy, you, with your lawyer's trenchancy, were for the bones of human contention. It was always in you, Ned, though it was your profession then to fight but with words. You had the mark of a swordsman. One day you might draw a true sword. I had only a scalpel. Even with your wooden ruler you were more often than not, as I recall, the victor. Now I must own again that you, and those of your kind, are my victor. Nay, my ruler! Truly I live now under your rule.

How does it go, Ned? 'If this were seen, the happiest youth, viewing his progress through, what perils past, what crosses to ensue.' I am an old man. I read by a winter fire. But I freely admit I was ambitious too. My cause was the advancement of learning, but it was also the advancement of myself. Did I marry my late wife because I wished her to be my wife or because I wished to be the husband of the daughter of the late Queen's physician? It opened more doors than my laurels from Padua. Yet how I miss her, my dear Liz. My late Liz. Late! It is the only word now for us, now we have passed our three score and ten. All is late. Though you may think, if God (and your physician) grant you health, that you are now but in your earliness, your newness. Do we not have a new world? Is this not the seventh day of its creation?

Ambition, Ned, it was our common spurring in our separate courses. Shall we confess it? And shall we confess that for a while, for a good long while, my ambition outrode and was better stabled than yours? Now shall we see where the ambition of your master Cromwell—but I must call him master too—will take him and how it may serve and accommodate yours.

What times, what times. It is now I who must sit aside, withdraw and retire, taking shelter as I do in my brother's house. It is I who must content myself with my books and studies, I who once accompanied kings. Yet I want no more. You will perhaps smirk to know that my studies remain upon the reproduction of our kind and of the animals at large. What food for mirth and raillery have I given my enemies and detractors—who are still many and persistent—that I, an old man both wifeless and childless, should dwell upon such stuff. How they must snigger at me as we once sniggered behind the backs of our schoolmasters.

Yet I would know, Ned, perhaps before I die, how we are born, how we are shaped for the world. Leave that, some will still cry, to the doctors of divinity, tread not upon that holy ground. So are we not alike there? Do you not discern it from your present elevation? We both came moulded with the rebellious, some might say heretical, disposition to trespass upon sacred soil. In the interests, to be sure, of truth and justice. And of ambition?

I was no prostrate worshipper in the church of kingship, no more than you, but my interests, or shall I say the interests of learning, made me seek their best protection. Is it not at least food for thought for you that our late king, tyrant, traitor and murderer, who clung so much to his own divine prerogative, was yet the patron of so much that assailed the sacrosanct? And is it not also food for thought for you that those of your party who once so boldly and blasphemously rose up against him are now entrenched in their own sanctimonies? Do I blaspheme now? Will you arraign me?

The bones of human contention! Why did I hold back for some dozen years the publication of my findings, my *De Motu Cordis*? Because I lacked courage, I confess it, because—I should say this!—I was weak of heart. Because I knew it would bring down upon me the learned heavens, if not other powers-that-be. It would bring me enemies. And lose me valued practice. And so it did, and still does. There is heresy and heresy, there is dogma and dogma.

How well I remember, Ned, when we last spoke together. It was some eight years past. It was at your table. There were the bonds of our kinship and of our friendship and of host and guest, yet I felt a broil simmering. There was the whiff of smoke. You said there was a time approaching when every man would have to make his stand. Of whose party was he? I said may not a man make a stand, and a stout one, of being of no party? You said that was no stand at all. Or rather, as I recall, you said it was not the stand of a man but of a tree. Would I be a tree and not a man?

It was late August and your windows were flung open upon the view of your orchard, a whole regiment of trees, hung with blushing apples. 'No, Ned,' I said, 'I am not a tree, but let trees still decide the matter. I too have an orchard. Let us not quarrel over whose apples are the sweeter, though over lesser things men have sometimes come to blows, but here is the true quarrel: if you or any man or any man's party were to invade my orchard, cut down my trees and trample my land, why then I would be of the opposing party. There would be my allegiance.'

You would not take this for an answer (nor in all honesty did I think it quite sufficient). You said, 'Well there you have spoken wisely, Will, since the King already cuts and tramples through the orchard that is his kingdom, claiming it as his right to do so and that it is no man's land but his own. Is not then your allegiance decided?' There was a smile upon your lips, but there was a smouldering in your eyes. You poured another cup of ale. You said, 'There will come a time, Will, there will come a time.' I should perhaps have said nothing, but I said, 'Then let us hope that time does not come tomorrow, or the day after. And let us hope that when it comes we do not fall out upon our cousinship, no matter which party we choose.' I said, 'I am a doctor, Ned, I must minister to all parties.'

But you would not take that for an answer either, or your eyes would not. I had not seen them burn so before. You plainly deemed, but did not say, that for certain causes even a doctor must throw aside his phials, as a lawyer must throw aside his books of law, and buckle on armour. How little I or you knew, Ned, that one day soldiers of your party would enter my chamber and ransack its contents, casting hither and thither my precious notes, papers and experiments. There was my orchard for you, there was my party confirmed.

But, not to skirt about the nub of the matter, how could I say that my party was already chosen for me? As you knew it was. How could I, who was physician to the King, who knew the

King's very body as no other man knew it, be of any party but the King's? It was scarcely a case of cause or principle. But how, equally, could I have said that I noted that fire in your eyes? I noted it as a physician notes symptoms. It was the fire of your cause, I grant you, but it was the fire also of envy. It was the fire of an ambition not yet rewarded, and overtaken by another's eminence. And such was the fire—I can say this, now you enjoy your own eminence—that lit the eyes of many of your ranks, cause or no cause.

Orchards! Kingdoms! How could I have said, without seeming to speak like my master the King in his worst haughtiness, that my party was of bigger things? It is a small entity, the heart, it is a small allowance, the blood of any creature, yet to every creature it is the All of life. I was born, you know this, Ned, in Folkestone, which looks across to the Continent. How could I have said that I was of the Continent's party, I was of the world's party? England is but a small country, albeit my own. Why did I journey to Padua? How could I have said that I was of Fabricius's party, nay of Galileo's, whose noble hand I have clasped? Knowledge is vaster than kingdoms and, while kingdoms come and go, is the only true arbiter of the times. How could I have said this to you, a lawyer and counsellor to members of Parliament (did you not have, even then, your modicum of eminence?), without adding fuel to that fire? I can scarcely claim the licence of old age to speak it now.

I care not for kings. I cared for the King. I knew him well. I was charged with the King's body, not with the body politick. It was a small and slight body, for all its loftiness of position and mien. It was stunted by rickets. It was a body indeed that was sniggered at. How many of your party knew so well your

enemy, knew his fleshly infirmities as well as his kingly tower-
ings, knew his private graces? When I attended his hunts he
would set aside for me so much of his quarry, his stags, hinds
and hares, as I might want as fresh matter for my dissections.
He did not trample on the advancement of learning, nor even
on the defying of Galen. When he took up his headquarters in
Oxford he ensured I should have place and time for my studies. It was his fortress of war, but still a seat of learning. True,
Ned, I was a Caius man, before Cambridge was Parliament's
school, who found sanctuary in Oxford. Did I choose my party?
I was made, by the King's wish, Warden of Merton. You were
made Colonel of Horse. We find our places, Ned, we find our
colours.

Either way now, the orchard, the kingdom—the commonwealth, the republic, what are we to call it?—lies bleeding and
cut down. A commonwealth? Look at its poverty. A republic?
A headless body.

When I was at Edge Hill, in attendance, before my days in
Oxford, I observed the pallor in my master's brow. It was but
a man's pallor, the pallor of any man on hearing the opening
shots of cannon, but it was a king's pallor. No other man could
have worn that pallor. It was the first battle. Pray God, he must
have thought, it would be the only one. It was the first occasion
of his leading an army in battle, and certainly the first against
his own people.

What times, Ned, what times. We who played at knuckle-
bones. Truly that battle, if such disorderliness could be called a
battle, was well named, since was it not a great edge of things,
a great precipice overstepped? It was not for me, dissector of
corpses and philosopher of the blood, to be affrighted at the

carnage and slaughter. In truth I spent much of the time behind a hedge endeavouring to read a book. Yet I was affrighted at the look I saw on almost every man's face, be he for King or Parliament (and you could not often well tell the difference), the look that said, as it were: It is a true thing now, and it is of this sanguinary substance, this thing that was but hours ago still a thing of speech and protestation. It is a thing now of experiment, and such is the experiment.

Had they chosen their party, those green recruits who had not known a fight before? Had they chosen their party, those who turned and ran or galloped for their lives before the charge of Prince Rupert? And had they chosen their party, those of Prince Rupert's command, who knew, it seemed, no command, but charged ever on beyond the field, as if the battle were not a battle but a great chase, a great hunting of men? It almost cost the King the day. It certainly cost his winning it.

Would that he had won it. Do I speak treachery? It would have settled the matter. There would have been a battle only and no war. I believe it was in that pallor that I noted. That he knew he could win. He had the ridge, indeed the edge, and all the advantages. He held the London road. He might prevail, as a king should all at once prevail. Yet it was that day that led to his placing his neck upon the block.

But did you see it, Ned, that look upon the *common* face? I know you were there. That is, it came to my later knowledge that you had been among Sir William Balfour's horse, who led the counter-charge, against an army naked of its own horse, and very nearly seized a victory. It was the beginning of your late-won eminence, not as man of law or even of Parliament, but of arms.

But did you know, even then, that I was there? Did you know how close your cuirassiers came to the King and to those in his attendance? Did we look upon each other, Ned? This I would know. Your face would have been hidden by a helmet, but not my own. Did you see my face? Yet did you see, in any case, or were you blinded by your purposes, that look upon the general face that said all England is a butcher's yard now, a very shambles? All England is a hunting ground and every man a quarry.

I would know it, Ned. I did not fight. I carried no weapon. I carried a book, thinking I might be idle. I attended the King and I tended the wounded, of both parties. It was an October day, bitter cold, and darkness, blessedly, came early, ending the matter in no party's favour but not stopping the flow from wounds. Did we look upon each other? It is seven years past and we were both even then men with grey hairs. I was never a man of arms, but I am haunted by the dream, Ned, that we face each other on a field of battle. I have no potion to drive away the stubborn vision. We both have swords drawn. They are not wooden rulers. It is not apples and orchards. It has come to this. Did you see my face, and should I be thankful I did not see yours?

It is bitter cold this night also. I write by firelight and candlelight. Either way, the land lies ravaged. Soon, they say, Parliament's victory will be further visited upon the people of Ireland. You are surely too old now to command there a regiment. Yet, physician as I am, I know not the mettle of your ageing body. The army is a toughening and late schooling, no doubt; and the heat of battle, so it would seem, is a heater of the soul, even a forger of zeal for the Lord. We are all of God's party now, but some more so. Is it not the case? There were all along in this affair but two parties, the army and the people, that too is now more so, and either the army would be our church or the church our army. Is it not so? We have no civility but a confusion of godliness and war. Such our new world.

Well, Ned, I am of the people's party now, I am only of the people. Though I have served kings, I am, as physician, only of the party and of the care of Every Body. I believe, and indeed can demonstrate, that every man's organs obey the same internal government. I still hold faith in the advancement of learning, if I believe less that by learning we advance.

Yet tell me, did we see each other? And tell me, might we yet, in the time remaining to us, see each other again? We are kinsmen and, whatever the divisions between us, we are now old men. I would have been your physician, Ned, most happily and truly, if you had asked me. And would be so still. Old men require physicians. Unless your Cromwell takes a crown, neither of us, I dare say, will know another king. We are as one there. We have only our allotted years. You would be welcome here at my brother's house. You may view, for your amusement, my experiments. It is not a long journey from Westminster, and but a short way from Putney where you would have held your late debates. Were they not upon 'An Agreement of the People'? There is good ale. There is an orchard, be it bare. We should sit and be at peace, Ned, and talk, as old men are given to talk. And remember. What times we have seen.

Your humble servant and cousin,
Will

William Harvey, Doctor of Physic

REMEMBER THIS

THEY WERE MARRIED now and had been told they should
make their wills, as if that was the next step in life, so one day
they went together to see a solicitor, Mr Reeves. He was not as
they'd expected. He was soft-spoken, silver-haired and kindly.
He smiled at them as if he'd never before met such a sweet
newly married young couple, so plainly in love yet so sensibly
doing the right thing. He was more like a vicar than a solicitor,
and later Nick and Lisa shared the thought that they'd wished
Mr Reeves had actually married them. Going to see him was in
fact not unlike getting married. It had the same mixture of
solemnity and giggly disbelief—are we really doing this?—the
same feeling of being a child in adult's clothing.

They'd thought it might be a rather grim process. You can't

make a will without thinking about death, even when you're twenty-four and twenty-five. They'd thought Mr Reeves might be hard going. But he was so nice. He gently steered them through the delicate business of making provision for their dying together, or with the briefest of gaps in between. 'In a car accident say,' he said, with an apologetic smile. That was like contemplating death indeed, that was like saying they might die tomorrow.

But they got through it. And, all in all, the fact of having drafted your last will and testament and having left all your worldly possessions—pending children—to your spouse was every bit as significant and as enduring a commitment as a wedding. Perhaps even more so.

And then there was something . . . Something.

Though it was a twelve-noon appointment and wouldn't take long, they'd both taken the day off and, without discussing it but simultaneously, dressed quite smartly, as if for a job interview. Nick wore a suit and tie. Lisa wore a short black jacket, a dark red blouse and a black skirt which, though formal, was also eye-catchingly clingy. They both knew that if they'd turned up at Mr Reeves' office in jeans and T-shirts it wouldn't have particularly mattered—he was only a high street solicitor. On the other hand this was hardly an everyday event, for them at least. They both felt that certain occasions required an element of ceremony, even of celebration. Though could you celebrate making a will?

In any case, if just for themselves, they'd dressed up a bit, and perhaps Mr Reeves had simply been taken by the way they'd done this. Thus he'd smiled at them as if, so it seemed to them, he was going to consecrate their marriage all over again.

It was a bright and balmy May morning, so they walked across the common. There was no point in driving (and when Mr Reeves said that thing about a car accident they were glad they hadn't). There was no one else to think about, really, except themselves and their as yet unmet solicitor. As they walked they linked arms or held hands, or Nick's hand would wander to pat Lisa's bottom in her slim black skirt. The big trees on the common were in their first vivid green and full of singing birds.

They were newly married, but it had seemed to make no essential difference. It was a 'formality', as today was a formality. Formality was a lovely word, since it implied the existence of informality and even in some strange way gave its blessing to it. Nick let his palm travel and wondered if his glad freedom to let it do so was in any way altered, even enhanced, now that Lisa was his wife and not just Lisa.

Married or not, they were still at the stage of not being able to keep their hands off each other, even in public places. As they walked across the common to see Mr Reeves, Nick found himself considering that this might only be a stage—a stage that would fade or even cease one day. They'd grow older and just get used to each other. They wouldn't just grow older, they'd age, they'd *die*. It was why they were doing what they were doing today. And it was the deal with marriage.

It seemed necessary to go down this terminal path of thought even as they walked in the sunshine. Nonetheless, he let his palm travel.

And in Mr Reeves' office, though it was reassuring that

Mr Reeves was so nice, one thing that helped Nick, while they were told about the various circumstances in which they might die, was thinking about Lisa's arse and hearing the tiny slithery noises her skirt made whenever she shifted in her seat.

It was a beautiful morning, but he'd heard a mixed forecast and he'd brought an umbrella. Having your will done seemed, generally, like remembering to bring an umbrella.

When they came out—it took less than half an hour—the clouds had thickened, though the bright patches of sky seemed all the brighter. 'Well, that's that,' Nick said to Lisa, as if the whole thing deserved only a relieved shrug, though they both felt an oddly exhilarating sense of accomplishment. Lisa said, 'Wasn't he *sweet*,' and Nick agreed immediately, and they both felt also, released back into the spring air, a great sense of animal vitality.

There was a bloom upon them and perhaps Mr Reeves couldn't be immune to it.

They retraced their steps, or rather took a longer route via the White Lion on the edge of the common. It seemed appropriate, however illogical, after what they'd done, to have a drink. Yes, to celebrate. Lunch, a bottle of wine, why not? In fact, since they both knew that, above all, they were hungry and thirsty for each other, they settled for nothing more detaining than two prawn sandwiches and two glasses of Sauvignon. The sky, at the window, meanwhile turned distinctly threatening.

By the time they'd crossed back over the common the rain had begun, but Nick had the umbrella, under which it was necessary to huddle close together. As he put it up he had the fleeting thought that its stretched black folds were not unlike women's tight black skirts. He'd never before had this thought about umbrellas, only the usual thoughts—that they were like bats' wings or that they were vaguely funereal—and this was like other thoughts and words that came into his head on this day, almost as if newly invented. It was a bit like the word kindly suddenly presenting itself as the exact word to describe Mr Reeves.

As they turned the corner of their street it began to pelt down and they broke into a run. Inside, in the hallway, they stood and panted a little. It was dark and clammy and with the rain beating outside a little like being inside a drum. They climbed the stairs to their flat, Lisa going first. Nick had an erection and the words 'stair rods' came into his mind.

It was barely two o'clock and the lower of the two flats was empty. Nick thought—though very quickly, since his thoughts were really elsewhere—of how incredibly lucky they were to be who they were and to have a flat of their own to go to on a rainy afternoon. It was supposed to be a 'starter home' and they owed it largely to Lisa's dad. It was supposed to be a first stage. He thought of stages again, if less bleakly this time. Everything in life could be viewed as a stage, leading to other stages and to having things you didn't yet have. But right now he felt they had everything, the best life could bring. What more could you want? And they'd even made their wills.

He'd hardly dropped the sopping umbrella into the kitchen sink than they were both, by inevitable progression, in the bedroom, and he'd hardly removed his jacket and pulled across the curtains than Lisa had unbuttoned her red blouse. She'd let him unzip her skirt, she knew how he liked to.

*

It rained all afternoon and kept raining, if not so hard, through the evening. They both slept a bit, then got up, picked up the clothes they'd hastily shed, and thought about going for a pizza. But it was still wet and they didn't want to break the strange spell of the day or fail to repeat, later, the manner of their return in the early afternoon. It seemed, too, that they might destroy the mood if they went out dressed in anything less special than what they'd worn earlier. But just for a pizza?

So—going to the other extreme—they took a shared bath, put on bathrobes, and settled for Welsh rarebit. They opened the only bottle of wine they had, a Rioja that someone had once brought them. They found a red twisty candle left over from Christmas. They put on a favourite CD. Outside, the rain persisted and darkness, though it was May, came early. The candle flame and their white-robed bodies loomed in the kitchen window.

Why this day had become so special, a day of celebration, of formality mixed with its flagrant opposite, neither of them could have said exactly. It happened. Having eaten and having drunk only half the bottle, it seemed natural to drift back to bed, less hurriedly this time, to make love again more lingeringly.

Then they lay awake a long time holding each other, talking and listening to the rain in the gutters and to the occasional slosh of a car outside. They talked about Mr Reeves. They wondered what it was precisely that had made him so sweet. They wondered if he was happily married and had a family, a grown-up family. Surely he would have all those things. They wondered how he'd met Mrs Reeves—they decided her name was Sylvia—and what she was like. They wondered if he'd been perhaps a little jealous of their own youth or just, in his gracious way, gladdened by it.

They wondered if he found wills merely routine or if he could be occasionally stopped short by the very idea of two absurdly young people making decisions about death. He must have made his own will. Surely—a good one. They wondered if a good aim in life might simply be to become like Mr Reeves, gentle, courteous and benign. Of course, that could only really apply to Nick, not to Lisa.

Then Lisa fell asleep and Nick lay awake still holding her and thinking. He thought: What is Mr Reeves doing now? Is he in bed with Mrs Reeves—with Sylvia? He wondered if when Mr Reeves had talked to them in his office he'd had any idea of how the two of them, his clients (and that was a strange word and a strange thing to be), would spend the rest of the day. He hoped Mr Reeves had had an inkling.

He wondered if he really might become like Mr Reeves when he was older. If he too would have (still plentiful and handsome) silver hair.

Then he forgot Mr Reeves altogether and the overwhelming thought came to him: Remember this, remember this. Remember this always. Whatever comes, remember this.

He was so smitten by the need to honour and consummate this thought that even as he held Lisa in his arms his chest felt full and he couldn't prevent his eyes suddenly welling. When Lisa slept she sometimes unknowingly nuzzled him, like some small creature pressing against its mother. She did this now, as if she might have quickly licked the skin at the base of his neck.

He was wide awake. Remember this. He couldn't sleep and

he didn't want to sleep. The grotesque thought came to him that he'd just made his last will and testament, so he could die now, it was all right to die. This might be his deathbed and this, with Lisa in his arms, might be called dying happy—surely it could be called dying happy—the very thing that no will or testament, no matter how prudent its provisions, could guarantee.

But no, of course not! He clasped Lisa, almost wanting to wake her, afraid of his thought.

Of course not! He was alive and happy, intensely alive and happy. Then he had the thought that though he'd drafted his last testament it was not in any real sense a testament, it was not even *his* testament. It was only a testament about the minor matter of his possessions and what should become of them when he was no more. But it was not the real testament of his life, its stuff, its story. It was not a testament at all to how he was feeling *now*.

How strange that people solemnly drew up and signed these crucial documents that were really about their non-existence, and didn't draw up anything—there wasn't even a word for such a thing—that testified to their existence.

Then he realised that in all his time of knowing her he'd never written a love letter to this woman, Lisa, who was sleeping in his arms. Though he loved her completely, more than words could say—which was perhaps the simple reason why he'd never written such a thing. Love letters were classically composed to woo and to win, they were a means of getting what you didn't have. What didn't he have? Perhaps they were just silly wordy exercises anyway. He hardly wrote letters at all, let alone love letters, he hardly *wrote* anything. He wouldn't be any good at it.

And yet. And yet the need to write his wife a love letter assailed him. Not just a random letter that might, in theory, be one among many, but *the* letter, the letter that would declare to her once and for all how much he loved her and why. So it would be there always for her, as enduring as a will. The testament of his love, and thus of his life. The testament of how his heart had been full one rainy night in May when he was twenty-five. He would not need to write any other.

So overpowering was this thought that eventually he disengaged his arms gently from Lisa and got out of bed. He put on his bathrobe and went into the kitchen. There was the lingering smell of toasted cheese and there was the unfinished bottle of wine. They possessed no good-quality notepaper, unless Lisa had a private stash, but there was a box of A4 by the computer in the spare room and he went in and took a couple of sheets and found a blue roller-ball pen. He'd never had a fountain pen or used real ink, but he felt quite sure that this thing had to be handwritten, it would not be the thing it should be otherwise. He'd noticed that Mr Reeves had a very handsome fountain pen. Black and gold. No doubt a gift from Sylvia.

He returned to the kitchen, poured a little wine and very quickly wrote, so it seemed like a direct release of the thickness in his chest:

My darling Lisa,

One day you walked into my life and I never thought something so wonderful could ever happen to me. You are the love of my life . . .

The words came so quickly and readily that, not being a writer of any kind, he was surprised by his sudden ability. They were so right and complete and he didn't want to alter any of them. Though they were just the beginning.

But no more words came. Or it seemed that there were a number of directions he might take, in each of which certain words might follow, but he didn't know which one to choose, and didn't want, by choosing, to exclude the others. He wanted to go in all directions, he wanted a totality. He wanted to set down every single thing he loved about his wife, every moment he'd loved sharing with her—which was almost *every* moment—including of course every moment of this day that had passed: the walk across the common, the rain, her red blouse, her black skirt, the small slithery sounds she made sitting in a solicitor's office, which of course were the sounds any woman might make shifting position in a tight skirt, but the important thing was that *she* was making them. She was making them even as she made her will, or rather as they made *their* wills, which were really only wills to each other.

But he realised that if he went into such detail the letter would need many pages. Perhaps it would be better simply to say, 'I love everything about you. I love all of you. I love every moment spent with you.' But these phrases, on the other hand, though true, seemed bland. They might be said of anyone by anyone.

Then again, if he embarked on the route of detail, the letter could hardly all be written now. It would need to be a thing of stages—stages!—reflecting their continuing life together and incorporating all the new things he found to commemorate. That would mean that it would be all right if he wrote no more now, he could pick it up later. And he'd written the most important thing, the beginning. But then if he picked it up later, it might become an immense labour—if truly a labour of love—a labour of years. There'd be the question: When would he stop, when would he bring it to its conclusion and deliver it?

A love letter was useless unless it was delivered.

He'd hardly begun and already he saw these snags and complications, these reasons why this passionate undertaking might fail. And he couldn't even think of the next thing to say. Then the words that he'd said to himself silently in his head, even as he held Lisa in his arms, rushed to him, as the very words he should write to her now and the best way of continuing:

I never thought something so wonderful could happen to me. You are the love of my life. Remember this always. Whatever comes, remember this . . .

Adding those words, in this way, made his chest tighten again and his eyes go prickly. And he wondered if that in itself was enough. It was entirely true to his feelings and to this moment. He should just put the date on it and sign it in some way and give it to Lisa the next morning. Yes, that was all he needed to do.

But though emotion was almost choking him, it suddenly seemed out of place—so big, if brief, a statement looking back at him from a kitchen table, with the smell of toasted cheese all around him. Suppose the mood tomorrow morning was quite different, suppose he faltered. Then again, that 'whatever comes' seemed ominous, it seemed like tempting fate, it seemed when you followed it through even to be about catastrophe and death. It shouldn't be there at all perhaps. And yet it seemed the essence of the thing. 'Whatever comes, remember this.' That was the essence.

Then he reflected that the essence of love letters was that they were about separation. It was why they were needed in the first place. They were about yearning and longing and distance. But he wasn't separated from Lisa—unless being the other side of a wall counted as separation. He could be with her whenever he liked, as close to her as possible, he'd made love to her twice today. Though as he'd written those additional words, 'whatever comes', he'd had the strange sensation of being a long way away from her, like a man in exile or on the eve of battle. It was what had brought the tears to his eyes.

In any case there it was. It was written. And what was he supposed to do with it? Just keep it? Keep it, but slip it in with the copy of his will—the 'executed' copy—so that after his death Lisa would read it? Read what he'd written on the night after they'd made their wills. Is that what he intended?

And how did he know he would die *first*? He'd simply had that thought so it would enable Lisa to read the letter. But how did he know she wouldn't die first? And he didn't want to think about either of them dying, he didn't want to think of dying at all. And even supposing Lisa read these words—these very words on this bit of paper!—after his death, wouldn't they in one undeniable and inescapable sense be too late? Though wouldn't that moment, after his death, be in another sense precisely the right moment?

Love letters are written out of separation.

He didn't know what to do. He'd written a love letter and it had only brought on this paralysis. But he couldn't cancel what he'd written. He folded the sheet of A4 and, returning to the spare room, found an envelope, on which he wrote Lisa's name, simply her name: Lisa. Without sealing the envelope, he put the letter in a safe and fairly secret place. There were no really secret places in the flat and he would have been glad to declare that he and Lisa had no secrets. Had the opportunity arisen, he might have done so to Mr Reeves. But now—it was almost like some misdeed—there was this secret.

But he couldn't cancel it. Some things you can't cancel, they stare back at you. There was nothing experimental or feeble or lacking about those words. His heart had spilled over in them.

He went back to bed. He fitted himself against Lisa's body. She'd turned now onto her other side, away from his side of the bed, but she was fast asleep. He kissed the nape of her neck. He wanted to cradle her and protect her. Thoughts came to him that he might add to the letter, if he added to it. But the letter was surely already complete.

His penis stiffened, contentedly and undemandingly, against his wife. She knew nothing about it, or about his midnight session with pen and paper. He thought again about Mr Reeves and about last wills and testaments. Pen. Penis. It was funny to think about the word penis and the word testament in the same breath, as it were. Words were strange things. He thought about the word testicle.

The rain was still gurgling outside and whether it stopped before he fell asleep or he fell asleep first he didn't remember.

*

The truth is he did nothing with the letter the next morning. He might have propped it conspicuously, after sealing the envelope, on the kitchen table, but he didn't want to disturb the tender atmosphere that still lingered from yesterday, even though that same tenderness gave him his licence. Wouldn't the letter only endorse it? He felt a little cowardly, though why? For what he'd put in writing?

He looked adoringly, perhaps even rather pleadingly, at Lisa, as if she might have helped him in his dilemma. She looked slightly puzzled, but she also looked happy. She was hardly going to say, 'Go on, give me the letter.'

His line of thought to himself was still that the letter wasn't finished. Yes, he'd add to it later. It would be premature, at this point, to hand it over. Though he also knew there was no better point. And the moment was passing.

It was a Saturday morning. Outside, the rain had stopped, but a misty breath hung in the air, and over them hung still the curiously palpable, anointing fact that they were people who'd made their wills.

The truth is he could neither keep nor deliver, nor destroy, nor even resume the letter. It was simply there. Though he did keep it, by default. His hesitation over delivering it, a thing at first of just minutes and hours, became a prolonged, perennial reality, a thing of years, like his excuse that he'd continue it.

And one day, one bad day, he did, nearly, destroy it. It was a long time later, but the letter was still there, still as it was on that wet night in May, still in the envelope with the single word 'Lisa' on it, but now like a piece of history.

And his will, now, would certainly need altering. But not yet.

Not yet. He thought of destroying the letter. It had suddenly and almost accusingly come into his mind—that letter! But the thought of destroying a love letter seemed almost as melodramatic and sentimental as writing one.

How did you destroy a love letter? The only way was to burn it. The smell of Welsh rarebit reinvaded his nostrils. You found some ceremonial-looking dish and set light to the letter and watched it burn. Though the *real* way to burn a love letter was to fling it into a blazing fire and for good measure thrust a poker through it. And to do this you should really be sitting at a hearthside, rain at the window, in a long finely quilted silk dressing gown . . .

Then his chest filled and his eyes melted just as they'd done when he first penned the letter.

The truth is they separated. Then they needed lawyers, in duplicate, to decide on the settlement and on how the two children would be provided for. And, in due course, to draw up new wills. He didn't destroy the letter, and he didn't send it on finally to its intended recipient, as some last-ditch attempt to resolve matters and bring back the past, or even as some desperate act of guilt-inducement, of warped revenge. This would have betrayed its original impulse, and how hopeless anyway either gesture would have been. She might have thought it was all a fabrication, that he hadn't really written the letter on the 10th of May all those years ago—if so, why the hell hadn't he delivered it?—that he'd concocted it only yesterday. It was another, rather glaring, example of his general instability.

He didn't destroy it, he kept it. But not in the way he'd waveringly and wonderingly kept it for so many years. He kept it now only for himself. Who else was going to look at it?

Occasionally, he took it out and read it. He knew the words, of course, by heart, but it was important now and then, even on every 10th of May, to see them sitting on the paper. And when he looked at them it was like looking at his own face in the mirror, but not at a face that would obligingly and comfortingly replicate whatever he might do—wrinkle his nose, bare his teeth. It was a face that had found the separate power to smirk back at him when he wasn't smirking himself, and to have an expression in its eyes, which his own eyes could never have mustered, that said, 'You fool, you poor sad fool.'

The Best Days

Sean and Andy found themselves standing to one side of the
steps up to the church, on the edge of the broad sweep of driveway. Now it seemed all right to do so, Sean took a pack of
cigarettes from his jacket, took one out, then offered the pack in
his usual abrupt way to Andy. They'd been together at Holmgate
School just six years ago, then together at Wainwright's till it
closed.

The hearse and a couple of following limousines had driven
off, leaving the lingering, spreading spillage of a surprisingly large
congregation—a 'good turnout', as their former headmaster,
Clive Davenport, had been apt to say about various other occasions. He was now in the hearse on his way to be cremated.

'She looks a right little whore,' Andy said.

Sean said nothing. Then he said, breathing out smoke, 'How many whores have you seen lately?'

They were referring to Karen Shield, who'd been at Holmgate with them, in the same year. Neither had seen her for some time, but she was recognisable and certainly noticeable.

It was a grey mild blustery afternoon in April and it had rained recently. There'd been a general standing solemnly and silently as the hearse departed, then one or two people had waved. Someone had called out, 'Bye, Daffy!' and the atmosphere had broken. The new atmosphere was almost like gaiety. Everyone was freshly aware of being alive in the world and not dead in it and that they'd been involved in something dutiful but oddly animating. There were now many more waves, of recognition, much milling, hand-shaking, smiling and embracing and a good deal of sudden laughter. No one seemed to want to leave immediately.

As if to share the mood, the sun broke through a gap in the clouds and made the surface of the driveway gleam. To one side of the church, the big cedar, stirred by the breeze and with a sudden sparkle, shrugged off its burden of drops.

The news about Clive Davenport—felled by a heart attack only three years after retiring—had circulated quickly, along with tributes to the fact that he'd been head of Holmgate almost since it had opened. This accounted for the impressive gathering, which in turn had reassured many members of it who'd been uncertain about coming in the first place. Several generations of former staff and pupils were involved. Some present had few fond memories of Holmgate and had even once wished old Daffy dead, but the passage of time and the needs of the occasion had instilled an infectious makeshift nostalgia. Perhaps Daffy hadn't been such a bad headmaster. Perhaps life itself at Holmgate hadn't been so bad. Life after Holmgate hadn't always been so great.

Many had turned up simply to see who else would be there and how they were looking now. It was a way of satisfying that curiosity without having to sign up to any grim 'reunion'. But undoubtedly another motive for attending was having nothing better to do on a Thursday afternoon. It was unemployment.

St Luke's, a big stone barn of a place, stood on a hillside, within a railed enclosure large enough to feel like a small public park. Below, a good portion of the town was visible, its rooftops wetly glinting. You could even make out, appropriately enough, the playing fields at Holmgate.

'Has she seen us?' Andy said. 'Has she recognised us?'

'Doesn't look like it,' Sean said. 'Not yet.'

Though in fact, inside the church, when he'd craned his head round, Sean had received a definite look of recognition, though it hadn't come from the woman (woman was now the word) Andy was speaking of. For a fraction of a second he'd wondered *who* it had come from.

'Well, shall we say hello?' Andy said, taking a drag. He had the stance he'd many times adopted, pint glass in hand, in bars on Friday nights. When Andy said 'right little whore' he didn't necessarily mean it as a term of abuse or of rejection.

'If you want,' Sean said, but made no move.

Andy had the bravado, Sean had the actual command, it was how it had always been. But—despite the description just given her—their record with Karen Shield at Holmgate was much the same. Neither had got very far.

Andy said, 'Christ, is *that* her mother? Talking of whores.'

Sean said softly, 'Andy!' It was almost, strangely, a rebuke, as if he might have added, 'You're in church.' Except they weren't any more. And he could see Andy's point.

They were both dressed in cheap suits—their 'interview suits'. Many around them were similarly dressed, but there were also definite outbreaks, especially among the women, of something showy, even provocative. It was as if many of the former pupils of Mr Davenport, in wishing to pay their respects, wanted also to demonstrate that they weren't at school any more, they hadn't turned into obedient little adults. Or else they wanted to prove to their peers, not seen for years, that they were still alive and kicking, they hadn't turned drab and sad.

Misery and grief had anyway driven off in the two family cars behind the hearse.

The group of four, less than thirty yards away, that Sean and Andy were eyeing consisted of Karen, her mother (it was her mother), her father and some chattering friend, of the parents' age, who'd intercepted them and was preventing them looking round, back towards the church. Sean was rather glad of this.

Karen wore nothing that wasn't in theory appropriate—it couldn't be faulted on its colour—but what she was actually got up in was a pair of black ankle boots, dark tights, with a seam up the back, a tight shiny-black waist-length jacket, a black nonsense of a hat with some black gauze attached to it, and a short flouncy charcoal skirt with which the wind was now playing mischievously.

The extraordinary thing was that the mother was wearing an outfit that was almost identical—the boots, the seamed tights, the short skirt and flimsy headpiece. Her top was a little different, but if anything more tarty.

It was hard not to conclude that they'd conspired over it, even gone shopping together. If not, who had started the competition, who had copied whom? There might have been something fetching about it, if it had worked. But the big difference between them was that while the daughter got away with it—it was fancy dress, but she had the looks anyway—the mother, the other side of forty, was a sight. The daughter's hair was dark and glossy, the wind toying pleasingly with it too. The mother's hair was a brownish frizz, the face rounded, puffy and fairly smothered in make-up.

Strangely, neither woman at this moment seemed aware of the effect. They were both laughing at something the fourth person was saying. They now and then with exactly the same action curled their knuckles cutely round the hems of their skirts. They might have been two happy perky twin sisters.

The father was something else altogether. Beside the two women, he was an unredeemed scruff. No tie, not even a white shirt. His excuse might have been a blunt, 'I don't dress up for funerals.' Or, on this occasion, 'He wasn't *my* headmaster.' But his face, never mind the clothes, was a mess. It was podgy and red, the sun struck it harshly.

But he too was now laughing, as if experiencing some rush of joy or of cocky pride in his womenfolk. It was the face—both Sean and Andy could spot this even at a distance—of a man who'd been drunk when he arrived and who did his best to be drunk as often as he could.

'She looks a right old baggage,' Andy said.

Sean didn't answer this at first. Then he chose to agree. 'You can say that again.'

'And is that her dad?'

'I suppose so.'

'He looks shit-faced.'

In any case the main attraction was Karen. Sean looked at her without voicing any opinion. Tart's clothes or not, the only right word was lovely. She'd been lovely at Holmgate too, in the last couple of years, though 'lovely' wasn't in the vocabulary then. It wasn't in the vocabulary now, not with Andy Sykes around, but it was the right word.

And he was wishing Karen had worn something plainer—to curb her mum. He was also wishing that fourth person would stay there with them, so he and Andy (though Andy was clearly getting other ideas) could just slip away. They'd decided to turn up, for whatever mad reason. For a laugh? To do their duty by Daffy? What had he done for them? They'd come anyway, and now they could just clear off.

He'd tried it on, of course, with Karen at Holmgate. He wasn't the only one. How many had succeeded? Depending, of course, on what was meant by success. But he wasn't the only one to try. It seemed an age ago now, being fifteen or sixteen. It hadn't helped that he hadn't lost it yet, or not in the true sense, the big V. He didn't know if *she* had, for all the tease. The more she teased, in fact, the more he thought she hadn't. Then he'd think what would be better, for his chances? If she had, but he hadn't? If he had (theoretically), but she hadn't? If they both had? If they both hadn't?

He remembered it now, standing outside St Luke's, all those possibilities running through his head. Had old Daffy been aware of it all—all going on like a sizzling pan under his nose?

*

One day he'd gone to Karen Shield's house in Derwent Road, carrying the school bag she'd left on the bus. It wasn't until he'd got up to get off himself, two stops later, that he'd noticed the bag lying on the seat up ahead. Otherwise, when she'd brushed past him (and she liked to brush) with Cheryl Hudson and Amina Khan he'd have grabbed her wrist and when she tugged back, said, 'You've forgotten something.'

But there it was, and he knew it was hers because it was a plastic imitation leopard-skin. How could anyone forget such a bag?

He never would.

So he'd got off at Thorpe Avenue, his stop, carrying two bags. Then everything had happened. It was all a gift. It was a gift that she'd left her bag. It was a gift that he'd been sitting on his own on the bus and not sitting with handy-Andy here. He hadn't known, yet, what kind of gift.

He could still see himself walking down Thorpe Avenue, coming to a decision, with two bags, one a somewhat embarrassing pretend leopard-skin. He could still see the October sun coming out from behind the clouds and smiling at him.

The proper thing would have been to phone Karen up and say, 'I've got your bag. I can bring it round if you like.' It would have earned him points and might have led to something. But it was just a bit too goody-goody and he didn't have her number. Though that might be in the bag. As might her *phone*!

Or: he might have taken the bag with him to school the next morning and said coolly, 'Here's your bag.' And then perhaps said, 'I had a good look inside.' He decided that this option had less going for it.

Though he did look inside, right there in Thorpe Avenue. Or rather he opened the flap and saw a label underneath saying 'Karen Shield, Holmgate School'. Then her home address. Well he'd known it was Derwent Road, on the Braithwaite Estate, and now he knew the number. But something about the label made him not delve any further. An odd primness came over him. It was like the label for some little girl much younger than and quite different from Karen Shield, and he didn't want to know about her.

His feet made the decision for him anyway. He turned and walked in the direction of the Braithwaite Estate. Two stops on the bus, but not so far on foot if you cut through the back streets.

Points from Karen, he calculated, and points from her mother, if she was there. If Karen's mother was there, then Karen couldn't be anything but nice and grateful to him, her mother would ensure it. But perhaps he was only thinking of Karen's mother being there to control his excitement about the possibility he really hoped for, of Karen being there all by herself, worrying about the bag she must have stupidly left on the bus.

He rang the bell at number fifteen and, after a pause, Karen's mother stood before him, blinking at him. Perhaps his disappointment was written on his face. But he had to go ahead.

'Mrs Shield? I've got Karen's bag.' He held it up like a piece of evidence. 'She left it on the bus.'

He noticed how she blinked and he noticed her red fingernails on the edge of the half-opened door. She stopped blinking and looked at him sternly.

'Who are you?' she said slowly, as if she might have just woken up.

'I'm a friend of Karen's. At Holmgate. Is Karen here?'

He'd peered in, towards a tiny hallway and the foot of a staircase. There was no sign or sound of anyone else.

But Karen's mother was undoubtedly Karen's mother. She was like a bigger version of Karen. She was wearing a smoky-coloured dress of a close-fitting but fluffy material. It went somehow with the red nails. The dress wasn't very long, and what he mostly noticed, as he tried to look beyond her, was her hip. As she stood holding the door one hip was hidden, but the other was pushed out. It was oddly alert. The idea of a hip, even the word hip, seemed new to him. Strangely, it had never entered his mind when he thought of Karen.

'She's not here,' Mrs Shield said, still looking at him sternly. 'Karen's not here.' She said it so deliberately it almost sounded like a lie, but he felt sure himself now that Mrs Shield was alone.

Karen had got off the bus less than half an hour ago, to go home. It was a mystery. And he was somehow now under suspicion, for his good deed.

'She goes round to Cheryl Hudson's most afternoons before she comes home,' Mrs Shield said. 'God knows what they do there.'

She looked at him as if this were something he should have known already, as if he should have gone himself to Cheryl Hudson's. (What went on there?) He felt put on the spot. It was like being called out to the front by a teacher. But Mrs Shield didn't look like a teacher. And, though she was Karen's mother, she didn't really look like a mother.

'Have you got a name?'

'Sean.'

'Sean who?'

'Sean Wheatley.'

'And that's Karen's bag?'

It seemed a strange question, and even before he could answer she said, 'I can see it's Karen's bag.'

She looked at him searchingly. Her hands were still holding or rather fingering the edge of the door.

'Tell me something, Sean Wheatley. Did you come round here now to hand over Karen's bag, or did you come round here because you were really hoping to see Karen?'

It was a big question and he knew there was no ducking it. He knew that Mrs Shield would have spotted a false answer better than any teacher.

'Both, Mrs Shield. Mainly to see Karen.'

She looked at him again for a long while.

'Well, you'd better come in and wait for her.'

This was confusing. If Karen was round at Cheryl Hudson's, then how long was he going to have to wait? Did he want to wait? But he also somehow knew that just to have handed over the bag and left would have been a big mistake.

She shut the door behind him. There was the vague smell of what he thought of as 'other people's house'. It was different in every house and you could never work out exactly what it was made of. Part of it must be Mrs Shield. Part of it must be Karen.

But, now the door was shut, Karen seemed suddenly far away, even though he was for the first time inside her home and he was holding her leopard-skin bag.

'Through here,' Mrs Shield said.

There was a small cluttered living room, like any living

room, with a glass coffee table. He knew that quite often in other people's houses (sometimes in his own) there'd be a bottle of something, opened, on the coffee table, even in the afternoon. But he couldn't see any bottle. The telly was on with the sound down. She must have turned it down when she answered the door. The picture on the telly was weak because of the sunshine now streaming through the window. Outside, the clouds had completely dispersed.

He stood by the coffee table, politeness enveloping him, along with dazzling sunshine. He knew that you weren't supposed to sit in other people's houses till they asked you to.

'So, Sean—' she said, taking a breath. Then she stopped. 'God, it's blinding in here, isn't it?'

She turned. It was the first time she'd moved suddenly and spontaneously, almost girlishly. She drew the curtains. They were a pale yellow and still let through a buttery glow. To close them, she put one knee on the sofa and reached up behind it. He saw an exposed heel and again, dominantly, her hips. Both this time.

As she turned back there was a flustered smile on her face at her own agility. It made her look younger and even less like a mother, certainly not the thirty-five or more she must have been.

She came right up close to where he still stood compliantly. The scent and breath of Mrs Shield were suddenly all over him. There was no trace of drink that he could detect.

'So, Sean, how long have you been friends with Karen? I mean, friends, not just at school with her?'

But once again she didn't wait for him to answer. With one hand she pulled down his fly zip, then slipped the other hand inside, like a pickpocket stealing a wallet.

'Have you got an erection, Sean? Do you have one all the time?'

Then he was, in all senses, in her hands.

Silent seconds passed. There was the technical considera-
tion: suppose Karen were to come home any moment now.
But that seemed somehow irrelevant, or dealt with. Mrs Shield
plainly knew what she was doing, even as she deferentially
asked him, 'So what do you think we should do now, Sean?
What do you think we should do? Perhaps you should put
those bags down.'

She kept her hand where it was while he did what she suggested.

'I think we should do the whole thing, don't you? The whole
thing. Can you hang on?'

Hang on!

She took her hand away and, as nimbly as she'd managed the
curtains, she left the room, then returned with a large white
bath towel. She spread it on the sofa.

It was all done quickly. How could it not have been? Hang on!

But afterwards she'd had the goodness—if that was the right
word—just to lie with him for a while, her arms round him, or
perhaps it was more that his were round her. He'd felt his own
slightness and her bigness—if that too was the right word. She
was a fully formed complete woman, like no schoolgirl could
ever be. He'd wanted to tell her this, but didn't know how, or
if it would be wise. He'd wanted to thank her, to praise her, to
express all his grateful amazement, but hadn't a clue how to do
it. What he should have said—he knew it now, standing outside St Luke's—was that she was lovely.

In the glow from the window he tried absurdly to work out
his bearings. Which was east, which was west? Which way did
the window face? Where was Craig Road, where he lived?

Where was Holmgate School, the Town Hall, Tesco's, Skelby Moor? Minutes ago he'd been standing on a front doorstep, holding a leopard-skin bag. Less than an hour ago he'd been sitting on a number six bus.

Finally, as if a timer had registered the appropriate interval, she moved, loosened their mutual grip, kissed him, just a peck, on the cheek and made it clear they should tidy themselves up.

Had she done this before? Was she in the habit of doing it? It was certain that she knew he'd never done anything like it before, just as it was certain that he'd never do, at least in one sense, anything like it again.

'Now,' she said before he left, her stern face back again, 'you don't breathe a word of this.' And while he gravely nodded and she looked into his depths, she added, 'More than your life's worth if you do.'

Then she said, 'Don't forget *your* bag. The name's Deborah, by the way. Since you ask.'

He realised later that she'd effectively vetoed his going any further with Karen. She'd simultaneously equipped and unequipped him. He looked at Karen now with something like pity.

The sun shone on the wet driveway. That fourth person, whoever he was, seemed to be moving on. The remaining three now turned to look around and a hand suddenly went to cover the daughter's mouth in a show of recognition and surprise. Her eyes widened. She took away the hand and, at that distance, they half heard, half lip-read her words.

'Well, well, look who's here!'

She was making such a thing of it that he didn't notice the look on the mother's face. Or he didn't want to look at the mother's face, daubed with all that slap. Or at the father's. Karen's face was the only one you wanted to look at.

The mother. He knew her name.

And now all three of them were walking directly towards them and Andy was saying, flicking at his cigarette, 'Well, I don't like yours much.'

He didn't want to look at her, but he wished there were some secret sign he might nonetheless make, without the need to catch her eye, to indicate that he'd never told anyone, not at Holmgate, not at Wainwright's. Other blokes might have done, sooner or later. 'I banged her mother.' He'd never breathed a word. Least of all to his best mate Andy Sykes here, goggling like a prat.

Some sign. So at least she wouldn't feel humiliated on that score. Only on the score of looking a mess—a dressed-up, painted-over mess, which made it worse. But maybe she really didn't know that. Maybe she thought she looked the image of her daughter.

He wasn't sure at all how he was going to manage this. It was cowardice not to look at her. Were they going to have to do all that hand-shaking stuff, the hugging and kissing, the strange grown-up but childish lovey-dovey stuff that was going on all around them?

'She looks a right dog, doesn't she?'

'Shut up, Andy, they'll hear.' Just for a moment he hated Andy.

'*Where-as!*' Andy was preening himself, wriggling his shoulders. 'And she's not *with* anyone, is she?'

He looked at the father. *He* can't ever have known, or he'd have known, himself, big-time. And Karen can't ever have known, he was sure of that. Or she wouldn't be acting so full-on now.

Just for a moment, as she drew close, he hated Karen Shield too. Intensely. For looking fantastic and making a fool of her mum.

'*Ooo-ooo!*' Andy was saying, clearly about Karen. Then he said, 'Is that really her mother?'

'Yes,' he replied with an authority he didn't like. He dropped his cigarette end and trod on it. 'So, Andy boy,' he said, 'let it be a lesson to you.'

He had to say it quickly, under his breath, with no time to explain what he meant—if he knew what he meant. Though he thought, rapidly and cruelly, of what he might have gone on to say.

Karen was upon them, in her silly irresistible hat.

'Sean Wheatley and Andy Sykes! Still together after all these years!'

He'd always been a jump or two ahead of Andy; now he felt he might be twice Andy's age. He almost felt he might be like old Daffy, up there on the stage at morning assembly, telling them all what was good for them, telling them what the future held.

'Have you got an erection, Sean?' He'd hear those words on his dying day.

Karen was opening her arms as if she meant to enfold them both like lost sons.

'You run after them, Andy boy'—this is what he might have said—'you get the hots for them and you have your wicked way with them and then you end up marrying them. And then years down the road, look what you get. So—let it be a lesson to you.'

HALF A LOAF

HALF A LOAF. Not even that.

She has gone again. She's stayed the night and she's gone again. But part of 'my time', as I think of it—I don't ever dare think of it as 'our time'—is the time it takes for her to walk from the front step to the street corner, no more than a minute, the time in which I watch her, getting smaller, from the angle of the bay window. She never looks back. Perhaps she guesses that I watch her. I've never told her. To tell her would be to give her ammunition—for my eventual destruction. It's coming one day. Of course it is.

Don't give her ammunition. But then if you make out you're calm, you're equable, you will only give her the excuse she needs.

Her name is Tanya. Even to watch her walking away is something. And it's a kind of training—but I don't dwell on that. You've drunk the glass, I tell myself, till it's filled next time, but there's still this last drop. Don't waste it.

I stand at the window. It's a quiet street. She crosses it at a long, oblique, efficient angle, between the parked cars, then at the main road she disappears, but I stand perhaps for a minute more, as if I can see through walls. Just to imagine her walking along a pavement, descending into the Tube is something. Just to imagine her being in the world is something, and may be all I'll have one day, any day now.

She disappears, but I don't move. In my head already is a picture of a woman in a red coat, sitting in a Tube train. She's the woman you notice as soon as you get in, and you can't keep your eyes off her. This is true for all the men in the carriage, but I don't think of the other men. She sits as if she's entirely unaware of this swamp of attention, as if she'd be surprised, embarrassed if you put even the possibility to her. She sits as if she's also completely, nonchalantly aware of it, as if it goes with being alive. I want to reach out and touch her, but not as a young man would. I want to put my hand on the crown of her head and say, 'Stay as you are, always. May no harm ever come to you.' How absurd, when she has the power to destroy me.

Half a loaf? But isn't this life, the whole of it? Shouldn't I be thanking, praising heaven?

My mother used to say, 'All good things come to an end.' Perhaps all mothers say it. As if the worst harm she foresaw for me was the tragedy of good stuff not being constantly on tap. Lucky little brat. But she must have seen the look of abject misery on my face whenever some seaside holiday or just some happy sunny day approached its end.

There it is, there it isn't. Now you see it, now you don't. But now I know it's not as simple as that. Thank heaven.

My father was a churchman, a man of God. In the war he was an RAF padre. It wasn't a get-out card, he flew on missions too. But when others broke down, he couldn't. He had to be their comfort. He never talked about it much, but once he said, 'Believe me, Eric, a lot of praying went on, and it had nothing to do with me.'

When I grew up, because of my father, I used to think a lot of good things were bad things—or rather I secretly thought a lot of bad things were good. At any rate I thought: One day God will punish me, he'll surely punish me. And he'll surely punish me for not believing in him.

But he never did punish me. And meanwhile my mother dispensed her regular balm: 'All good things come to an end.' I sometimes wondered if she too really believed in God.

But look at me now, looking at someone who's no longer there, and rehearsing a silent prayer: Please, God, let there be another time, another week. And what would my dead father think if—as God is supposed to do—he could see my every action and could see me, as I may do very soon, go up to the bedroom to touch the still-wrinkled, faintly warm sheets. To pick up a pillow and press it to my face.

I'm an osteopath. It's my business to lay hands on people, to manipulate them, both men and women. But never, ever. Until now. There are walks of life—university lecturers, osteopaths— that must arouse the particular fears of wives, but my wife,

Anthea, never had reason, nor, having Anthea, did I. I'm not unaware—this is only alertness, not vanity—that there are certain female patients, perhaps male ones too, who come to me not exactly for their back problems. But I'm saved by the clock, by the session. Time's up—till the next time. And of course it's in my power to say (all good things) there won't be any next time.

But my wife died. Nearly three years ago. It was neurological. My field can border on the neurological, but I'm not a neurologist and there was nothing I could do for her. Nor, as it turned out, anything that neurologists could do for her either.

I wanted to die. I won't pretend. I wanted to die even before she died—to be spared the fact of her death. I prayed. And after her death I wanted to die, and prayed that I might, even more.

My life was over, I went through the motions. One, two years. To steady myself, I thought of my parents, I thought of them getting through the war. All bad things. No one ever says that. My father died fifteen years ago, and my mother barely six months afterwards. There were medical reasons, but I think she died simply of my father's death. And I wanted something similar for myself. I waited for it, willed it to happen, but I'm of sound health.

I came close to making it happen, but I'm also a coward.

Then there was Tanya. Or put it another way: I had a mental breakdown. Certainly a professional breakdown.

Lower-back pain. There's so much of it about. I bless her lower-back pain. I bless her lower back. I bless the fact that in one so young it was something readily curable, and I could cure it. I could be her magician. *Her* magician!

'There,' I said, 'that seems to have done it.'

And then suddenly there were tears running down my face because of the sheer delight on her face at having been so simply, quickly cured—there'd even been a little click—and at having been spared, or so I'd vouched, only more pain and interminable waiting on the NHS.

And because she was the most beautiful creature I'd ever seen and in a moment, if I wasn't careful, I might say so. And because I was having a mental breakdown . . .

And because if Anthea was watching me, as God is supposed to watch, I thought she might not wish to punish me, or even reproach me. She might even be thinking: About time, Eric, about time something like this happened. I'm even glad for you that it's happening. Go on, Eric, seize what you can.

The truth is I didn't even *think* this. I'm sure that I heard Anthea actually saying in my ear, 'Now I won't have to worry, Eric, and grieve for you so much. But for God's sake stop blubbering, stop making a complete spectacle of yourself. It's life, it's happening. And you're not a complete spectacle, you're still a good-looking man. I'm frankly surprised, Eric—but I'm glad too—that nothing like this ever happened when I was alive. But you're a free man now. I'm dead, you're not. Go on, don't be a bloody coward.'

All this as if she were at my shoulder, while in fact cowardly tears were rolling down my face and a partially unclad woman of extraordinary health and beauty and less than half my age was still perched on my couch, and I was saying, 'I'm sorry, I'm terribly sorry. I was thinking of my wife—my late wife. I'm most terribly sorry. But your problem is cured. You really don't have to see me again, but—but would you, could you do me the honour' (and where did I get that phrase from?) 'of having dinner with me tonight?'

I didn't delude myself that she really thought—in spite of that click—that I was Mr Magic. With a face full of tears? Perhaps for some women charm, if I have any, is well mixed with a little vulnerability. But this was hardly vulnerability, or a little of it.

Was it naked bribery? A performance I'd somehow mustered? I don't care. Was I about to say (some men must do this sort of thing all the time), 'If you'll have dinner with me I'll forget the fee'? Or was I, before she could answer, about to cut my own legs from under me by saying, 'I'm most frightfully sorry, but please forget all this, forget it ever happened'?

The fact is she said with a simple, quick, uncomplicated smile, 'I'd be happy to.' The fact is she took the box of Kleenex that I keep ready for the occasional upset patient (I'm not unfamiliar with the psychosomatic) and held a bunch of them out to me. 'Here,' she said.

The fact is we had dinner that evening at Zeppo's, the very place where I used to go with Anthea and where I still had the thought: Anthea is willing me on, this is all under her aegis. And it was Anthea who'd surely warned me in the hours beforehand: Don't go for somewhere you think is *her* kind of place, a *young* place, don't be an idiot. Stick to what you know.

And the plain fact is that she—that is, Tanya—left my bedroom (my bedroom!) early the following morning, to return home, then to go to work. It was not yet seven. Breakfast wasn't wanted. And I thought: Of course—she's leaving, she's going, that's that. But as she made her exit, urging me not to get up, I asked the ridiculous and doomed question, 'Will I see you again?' And she said, with that same uncloudy voice, 'Why not?'

I never thought to see it. A pale young body slipping through the dimness of my bedroom, like some creature glimpsed in a forest.

And of course I got up. Of course I went down, in my dressing gown, and stood, as I'm standing now, at the window. If only to tell myself that this was my home and this had really happened.

Half a loaf? So it has continued now for nearly two months. I'm not blind. I'm not, actually, foolish. It can't last. Two months is already beyond any due allowance—whatever that might be. Is it pity? Charity? Amusement? Curiosity? I don't mind. I don't ask. So long as she comes. She has the power to destroy me at any moment, and maybe that in itself is the reason why she comes: the thrill of having another human soul dangling from her fingertips—a thrill that in one so young (she's twenty-six) isn't hampered by conscience, but a thrill that can only be consummated once, then it's gone. One day she will open her fingers. There! Like the click of a bone in her back.

I don't dare believe that she comes because of something I give her. What could that possibly be? Something that she takes from me and can't find elsewhere, and is worth at least one stray, but now almost routine, night out of seven? I know she has a boyfriend—a regular boyfriend. His name is Nathan. I don't ask, I don't picture. But she talks about him freely and unprompted, which makes me think she must talk in the same way to him about me. There have been no repercussions, no phone calls, no dramas. I don't know how it works with

Nathan, this piece of her life with me, a man over twice her age. Maybe he thinks: If that's the deal . . . don't rock the boat. I'd think the same perhaps, if I were him. Maybe he thinks: Half a loaf. Or, in his case, just the one slice that's missing.

Tanya.

Only she knows. Or perhaps she doesn't. She looks at me sometimes with a clear, clean gaze as if she wouldn't know how to question, to examine anything. She looks at objects in my house, pictures on the wall, as if she wouldn't know how such things, such collections are assembled. I long ago began to accept, though I was young once, that the young are a mystery, a different species. But people are a mystery, period. You can understand, even correct their bone structure—everyone comes with a skeleton—but where does that begin to get you?

It can't be because she's still grateful for her back. Her back! It will be the last thing, standing like this one day, I'll see of her.

I don't talk to her about Anthea. I don't tell her the stories behind those objects she so vacantly inspects. I'm like my father not talking about the war. You don't want to know. She doesn't ask.

And so I don't tell her this very strangest thing, that's been true now for nearly two months (and how would it help me to tell it?): that when she's present, so too is my wife. That it's only been since all this began that I've felt my wife come back to me, after three years, as if (it sometimes really seems like this) she'd never gone.

It's all right, Eric, it's all right that this is happening. I feel her at my shoulder right now, by the window. I hear her even saying, 'I hope she comes back.'

*

Half a loaf? But surely it's the whole thing, it's everything. And I wouldn't mind if it were only a crust. I'd be as joyous, as terrified, as grateful. Some men in my bereft situation might eventually resort to prostitutes, doing so perhaps with much agony and shame, and wanting less to perform or have performed upon them certain acts than to have the simple proximity of warm female flesh. They come perhaps to some sad weekly addictive arrangement.

It's not like that with me, though I can see it has a semblance. I don't pay her, I don't offer her anything, except dinner. Nonetheless, if it were needed—a crust!—I'd empty my wallet every time.

From where I stand right now I can see the brass plate on the white stucco by the front porch (Anthea used to say it made us look like an embassy) that tells me who I am and what I do. I sometimes make bad things come to an end. It's sometimes been my professional pleasure and privilege to watch people leave me, who I'll never see again, who suddenly feel alive again 'in their very bones'.

She sits in a Tube train, no longer having to sit with care because of the pain in her back. But that's a thing of the past now, she can't even remember perhaps what it was like. Twenty-six is less than half my age, but not so young that she can afford to follow any strange, diverting path indefinitely. Not so young that, wanting to end it, she might lack the courage or heartlessness to do so.

I know it will end, of course it will end. The day will come. And when it comes I know one other terrible thing for certain. This sense that Anthea is with me and is glad for me, even egging me on, this sense that I'm wrapped in her generosity and that she no longer has to mourn for me, locked out here in the cold zone of life—that too will be gone. I won't feel her presence, won't hear her voice in my ear. I'll be just another lost, dutiful man going once a week to mutter words to a stone and getting no words back.

Saving Grace

Dr Shah had never ceased to tell the story. 'I'm as British as you are,' he might begin. 'I was born in Battersea.' Or, more challengingly: 'My mother is as white as you. You don't believe me?'

In his early days in medicine, even though by then the National Health had become awash (it was his own word) with black and brown faces, it was not uncommon for patients to cut up rough at being treated by an Asian, or an Asian-looking, doctor. Such a thing could still happen, but now his seniority, his reputation as a top consultant and his winning smile usually banished any trouble. But the story was still there, the chapter and verse of it, or just his satisfaction at relating it once again.

He tended to tell it these days, since it really required time and leisure, during follow-up sessions when the patient might be well on the mend, and in the half-hour slot there'd be little else to discuss. He'd even come to regard it as simply his way of bidding patients farewell. A final prescription. Though it had nothing to do in any clinical sense with cardiology.

'No, I've never been to India. Perhaps I never shall. But my father was born in India . . .'

It had lost none of its force, especially now his father was dead and he and his mother were sharing their mourning. Less than a year ago he'd embraced his father, so far as that was possible given his pitiful condition, for the last time. He'd held him close and had the fleeting bizarre thought that he was also holding India. He'd said to his mother, 'They're making him comfortable, making him ready, he won't feel any pain.'

His father wasn't his patient, but of course Dr Shah knew about such things. For a moment he'd quite forgotten that his mother (it was very much part of the story) had once long ago been a nurse.

As a medical man he should have been protected against grief, but he wasn't surprised by how much now it overtook him, by how much he still felt, even after several months, the non-medical mystery of his father's absence.

'My father was born in India,' he'd say, 'in Poona, in 1925. All this will seem like ancient history, I'm sure. In those days of course the British ruled. *We* ruled.' Dr Shah would smile his smile. 'He was born into one of those families who revered the British. He had an education that was better than that of many boys born at the same time in Birmingham or Bradford. Or Battersea. And spoke better English too.'

The smile would only widen.

'Yes, I know, there were many Indians who didn't revere the

British. Quite the opposite. But when the war broke out in 1939 there was no question that my father, when he came of age, would sign up with the Indian Army to fight for the British in their war. There were many Indians who felt differently. There were many Indians who wanted to fight against the British. But of course I had no say in these things, I wasn't even around. My father's name was Ranjit. As you know, that's my name too.

'So one day he found himself on a troopship bound for Italy, which was where most of the Indian soldiers who came to Europe went. The fact is I might have been Italian, I might be telling you this in Naples or Rome. Think of that.

'But because of some mishap of war—they had to switch ships—my father's unit ended up in England, in the spring of 1944, and it was decided that instead of shipping them all the way back to Italy they should be trained up for the invasion of France.'

Dr Shah would seem to wait a moment, as if to let his story catch up with him.

'England. A camp in Dorset to be precise, not far from Sturminster Newton. The truth is my father couldn't believe his luck. He'd grown up worshipping everything English. He spoke English, good English, not Italian. And there he was in the English countryside, in spring—thatched cottages, primroses, bluebells, everything he'd only read about in books. He even got himself a bicycle and whizzed round the lanes.'

Dr Shah would give a sympathetic shrug.

'No, I don't quite fully believe it either. I don't believe it can have been all fun for a bunch of Indian soldiers in Dorset in 1944. Just think about it. But I'm only telling you what my father told me. He called it luck.

'It wasn't the only piece of luck either, though you might think this next piece of luck wasn't any kind of luck at all. He took part in D-Day. He was one of very few Indian soldiers who did so. He served the British in their war. To the utmost, you might say. He was on that big fleet of ships. But he was very soon on a ship coming back, and very soon after that he was in a ward in a hospital here in London, commandeered by the Army, where all the patients had serious wounds to the leg, or legs.

'I don't know the details. It was somewhere in Normandy, not far from the beaches. I'm not sure he knew himself. All he'd say was, "I was blown up." Once he said, "I was blown up and I thought I was dead." And he went a little further still. "I thought I'd been blown to pieces," he said, "and had come back together again as somebody else." That's not physiologically possible, of course. I can't comment on that as a medical man. But then—we transplant hearts.'

Dr Shah would smile.

'He was in the leg unit, or more plainly the amputation unit, though no one, I suppose, would have called it that. The only saving grace was that it might have been better to have a leg removed there than back in the thick of things in France. Though sometimes, I believe, it's important to amputate a leg fast. But the crucial fact is that he was the only Indian man, the only brown man, occupying any of the beds. Not a saving grace you might think, but wait.

'I've never amputated a leg. It's not my field, as you know. But anyone knows it's an extreme procedure, if sometimes the only way of saving life. And I'm talking about over sixty years ago and about patients who might have had other complicated injuries too. In short, not every amputee would have survived and every man on that ward would have known the risks.

'My father once showed me a photograph when I was a boy. It was of three men in pyjamas, in wheelchairs, all of them missing a leg. But all of them smiling, as if they were pleased with their stumps. It was a rather scary photograph to show a small boy, but my father wanted me to see it. He told me the men were some of his "old pals". Then he told me that if ever I should feel disadvantaged in life I should remember his old pals. "Disadvantaged". That was his actual word. It was a big word for a small boy, but I remember it clearly.'

Dr Shah's smile would broaden again and his listener might think—as he or she was perhaps meant to think—that 'disadvantaged' sat strangely on the lips of a senior consultant in an expensive pinstriped suit.

'I used to think that the smiles on the faces of those amputees were a bit like my father saying he'd had the time of his life in Dorset. Anyway there was another photograph of him and his bicycle, and he's smiling in that. You need two legs to ride a bicycle.

'Working on the leg unit there were of course doctors, surgeons, nurses. One of the nurses was called Nurse Watts, but my father would get to know her as Rosie. And I would get to know her as my mother. One day, apparently, my father asked her if her family had kept a newspaper announcing the news of D-Day. Many families kept such a thing. Could she bring it in to show him? He wanted proof that he'd been part of history. But it was the start of something else.

'Working on the leg unit too was a doctor, a doctor and assistant surgeon—only a junior, not the top man at all—who discreetly let it be known to a few of the men that if they let him "do" them he could save their leg. Also of course, by implication, their life.

'Quite an offer, you might think. But so far not a single patient had signed up to it. It wasn't that he was only a junior. The simple reason was that the man's name was Chaudhry and he was a brown-skinned doctor. From Bombay. From Mumbai. He too had come from India to serve the British, in a medical capacity. And they—the other patients, I mean—didn't want his brown fingers meddling with them. In fact there was even a sort of soldiers' pact among them that the brown doctor's offer should be refused.

'Silly fools.'

Dr Shah would leave a well-rehearsed pause at this point.

'But you can imagine that the position and response of my father was rather different.'

There'd be another pause, almost as if he had come to the end.

'I hardly need to tell you, do I? The others underwent their amputations, successfully or not, but my father's leg was saved. After a while he was even able to walk again, almost as easily as he'd always done. He had a very slight limp and—or so he liked to say—perhaps a few tiny grains of metal still inside him, courtesy of Krupp's. But that's not all. His relations with Nurse Watts—with Rosie, my mother—had meanwhile reached a point where they both clearly wanted to take things further. Against all the odds. To take them further, in fact, for the rest of their lives.

'You can imagine it, can't you? All those men with their stumps. It wasn't just their legs they'd lost, was it? They'd lost out on something else. And there were Ranjit and Rosie, like two turtle doves. As my father put it, he got his leg and he got the girl too. Now do you see why he talked about his luck?'

Dr Shah would sometimes leave things there. It was the simple version and it was enough. He'd only add, 'And that's how I came to be born in Battersea, in 1948.' He'd leave a pause and look closely but disclaimingly at his patient. 'No, my field isn't genetics either, and I can't explain it, but it's how I came out.'

But if he wished to tell the longer and fuller version, he'd go on.

'Imagine it. London, Battersea. At the end of a war. Against all the odds. But my mother always said there were no two ways about it. Ranjit was the one. And if she could fall in love with a man with his body all smashed up and the possibility that he'd lose a leg, then wasn't that a pretty good test of love? Setting aside the other matter that had nothing to do with the war.

'Let me tell you something else. For nearly ten years my father was a hospital porter. You won't catch me talking down to a hospital porter. Then he rose to the dizzy heights of hospital administration. I mean he was a clerk, lowest grade. With his education. Having fought at D-Day. And all of that because it was all he could get. And that only because of some string-pulling from his nurse wife—and no doubt from Dr Chaudhry too.

'But he accepted it and stuck with it. Because, I have no doubt, he thought it was worth it, because he thought it was a small price. And for the same reason he began gradually to realise that he'd never go back to India. It was how it was. His home was in England now. His family, his mother and father in Poona—he'd probably never see them again.

'He once told me that he looked at it like this: he might never have gone back anyway. He might have been killed in France. Or in Italy. And hadn't he done a fine thing anyway, even in the eyes of his family? Married a British lady. Perhaps he was right. He'd been blown up and he'd become somebody else.

'And this of course was the time—just before I was born—that India got home rule. Home rule and partition. We cleared out—the British cleared out. India was divided and terrible things happened, and all this while there was this other division my father had made between India and himself. It can't have been easy. He got his leg and he got the girl, but he lost something else. They say that amputees never stop feeling the "ghosts" of their limbs.

'But of all of this, too, you could say it was a pretty good test.

'And do I have to tell you the rest? Do I have to tell you that the man who saved my father's leg, Dr Chaudhry, became a sort of second father to my father? And like an uncle to me. He became a friend of the family. And do I have to tell you that it was because of Dr Chaudhry—his name was Sunil—and with his encouragement that I set my sights on taking up medicine too? I was born in 1948. I was born along with the National Health. I was fated to spend my days in hospitals.'

Dr Shah's smile, now more like a triumphant beam, would indicate that his story was over. He'd look distinctly young, even though he was over sixty and was even mourning his father.

'But you are free to go,' he'd announce—if he were speaking to one of his recovered patients. He'd hold out his hand, his brown hand with its fine dexterous fingers.

'At this point I always like to say I hope I never see you again.

Please don't take it the wrong way. Take it the right way. Remember my father and his leg.'

There were things he might have added, but didn't, things only to be inferred. He didn't say that, though he'd been born into the Welfare State, he'd certainly known, once upon a time in Battersea, the 'disadvantages' of which his father spoke. He didn't enlarge on the fact that, though he'd been encouraged by Dr Chaudhry, he hadn't gone into orthopaedics, but cardiology. And he didn't say that in becoming a doctor himself, not to say eventually a senior consultant, he'd become, too, like a sort of second father to his own father and—there was really no other phrase for it—had gladdened his father's heart.

Cardiology, back in his days at medical school, had certainly become the glamour field. Everyone wanted to be a heart surgeon, in spite of the fact that the heart is only an organ like any other. No one gets worked up about a liver or a lung or a lower intestine. Or even perhaps a leg.

He'd held his father very gently, but wanting to hold him as tightly and inseparably as possible. His father had become as puny and as nearly weightless as a boy. He'd seen for a moment that photo, the men with their stumps. And for a moment he'd seen too the map of India as it had once appeared in old school atlases, in the 1950s, blush-red and plumply dangling, not unlike some other familiar shape.

Tragedy, Tragedy

'Tragedy, tragedy,' Mick says. 'Ever feel there's too much tragedy about?'

We're in the canteen. Morning break. Mick has the paper spread, as usual, over the table. He peers at it through his half-rims. Two damp rings where our mugs have been.

I thought: Now what?

'Tragedy,' he says. 'When bad stuff happens, when people die. It's always a tragedy, it's tragic. That's what the papers say. Tragic.'

'Well, isn't it?' I say.

He looks up at me, over the half-rims, and takes his usual pause.

'When Ronnie Meadows had his heart attack on the fork-lift, was that tragic?'

I have to take a little pause too.

'Well—no,' I say, wondering whether it's the right answer. Whether it's fair to Ronnie to say it wasn't tragic.

'Exactly,' Mick says. 'It was just Ronnie Meadows having a heart attack. But if Ronnie had died in, I don't know, a train crash and it had been in the papers, they'd have called it tragic. See what I mean?'

True. But it's not as if they'd have mentioned Ronnie at all. I could see the word printed in the paper. I could see the headline: 'Rail Crash Tragedy'. Not just 'Rail Crash'. I couldn't see the headline: 'Ronnie Meadows Dies in Rail Crash Tragedy'.

I was drumming on the edge of the table with my fingers.

'So?' I say.

'Or if Ronnie hadn't been a fork-lift driver, if he'd been, I don't know, a Member of Parliament or someone on TV, and he'd died doing something just as boring—pushing a lawn-mower—they'd have called that tragic.'

'So?' I say again.

I thought: Drink your tea, Micky, I'm gasping.

'So. So it's just a word. It's just a word they use in the papers about things that get into the papers. It's just a word they use because they can't think of what else to say. It has to be tragic.'

Mick likes to do this. He likes to read the paper—I mean not just look at it, but read it—and he likes to mouth off about whatever he's reading to anyone he's with. Which is me, Bob Lewis. But he likes to do it now specially, to make me suffer, now he's trying to quit. I wanted him to finish his tea and fold up his paper so we could go outside for a smoke.

'So it has no meaning?' I say.

I thought: Idiot, why encourage him?

But I also thought it's not true that no one called Ronnie's death tragic. Mick wasn't as close as I was, when the ambulance came. Ronnie's wife had come too. She had to come. I've forgotten her name. Sandra? Sarah? And Mercer was there, in his white shirt, he had to be. He said, 'It's tragic, Mrs Meadows. Tragic ... tragic.' He said it several times. He looked like he didn't know what else to say, and Ronnie's wife looked like she wasn't listening.

Ronnie was still lying under a pallet cover, because it was technically an industrial accident and he couldn't be moved yet. There was a pointy bit of the pallet cover that was Ronnie Meadows' nose.

Did Mick hear what Mercer said? As I remember it, he was hanging back a bit. It was over three months ago. Ronnie had to go and drop dead right in the middle of the yard where everyone crosses to get to the gate. Even for a smoke at break time. I saw people skirting round for days, weeks afterwards. I skirted round myself. Then one day I realised, same as everyone else: I've just walked over the spot where Ronnie Meadows died and never thought about it.

But now I remembered Mercer saying 'tragic' to Ronnie's wife.

'Yes it has a meaning,' Mick says. He takes a breath. I thought: Here we go. He could see me drumming my fingers.

He started wearing the half-rims a couple of months ago. Because of them everyone began calling him 'Prof'. But I think the glasses only brought out something already there. It was like his face had been waiting for the glasses to complete it. Mick himself had been waiting. Mick Hammond, the man who likes to let you know he thinks.

'It has a meaning . . .'

He was all shy at first about wearing them, but now he fancies himself in them, he likes the business of looking over the top of them. And I quite like Mick in his reading glasses. Because they make him look serious, and that makes me want to laugh.

'It has a meaning . . .'

I could see he really was doing some thinking now, but he was also in a bit of a fix. I thought: You started this, Micky mate.

But mainly I thought: I'm gasping. And I thought: He's only dawdling over his tea because he's trying to quit the fags. He doesn't want to cross the yard with me and slip out the gate to what we used to call Death Row. Till Ronnie Meadows died.

Mick's a mate, but this whole giving-up thing's a bastard. It doesn't seem right for Mick to stop me nipping off for a drag. But it doesn't seem right for me to nip off anyway without Mick. Even if he's not going to smoke himself, he should come outside with me and stand beside me while I do. But that's daft too.

'If . . .' he says, 'if . . . a famous mountaineer dies while trying to climb a new way up the north face of the Eiger, the papers would call that tragic, but it wouldn't be.'

That seems a long way from Macintyre's warehouse, but I let it go. I can see Mick is getting all important with himself. I thought: Stay calm.

'What would it be?'

'It would be. . . well, heroic maybe.'

'Or mad,' I say.

'No, no, it would be the right sort of death for a mountaineer, wouldn't it? It would be how a mountaineer might even *want* to die.'

I don't say, 'Who *wants* to die?' And I don't say, 'Why are we talking about mountaineering?'

'So?' I say.

He shifts the half-rims on his nose a little, lifts them up with one finger, lets them drop again. Any moment now he'll take them off and wipe them. He didn't just get new glasses, he got a whole new act, a whole new bloody Mick Hammond, or the one that had only been waiting.

Maybe because of Mick and his glasses, I thought: Tragedy's about acting too. It's about stuff that happens on stage. Shakespeare and stuff. That's the thing about it. It's not real life. And Mercer can't have been thinking that Ronnie Meadows dropping off his fork-lift was—well, like *Hamlet*.

Micky Hamlet, I thought. Mickey Mouse.

'If, on the other hand . . .' he says.

I thought: Here we go.

'. . . if a famous mountaineer dies not on the north face of the Eiger, but climbing up some easy-peasy little mountain in, I don't know, the Lake District, then that's tragic.'

I didn't know what to say to this. Mick must have done some thinking, I'll give him that, to come up with this. I sort of got what he was getting at, but then again I didn't, I didn't at all.

I thought: I never knew Mick had a secret hankering to be a mountaineer. And I thought: We're nowhere near the Lake District, Micky, we're in Stevenage.

So I said, 'Why?'

Which is always the killer question. When I said it I couldn't help thinking of when Gavin, our first, started up with his 'Why? Why? Why?'. It often sounded more like 'Wha! Wha! Wha!' but, God, he knew it was the killer question.

Gavin's nearly eighteen now.

'Well, don't you see?' Mick says. 'It's got something about it. It's not how a mountaineer would want to die, or should die. It's—'

'Just stupid,' I say.

'Tragic,' he says.

Mick Hammond's totally different from me. But, yes, he's my mate, has been for years. Search me.

'If you say so, Mick.'

And those glasses sometimes make Mick look like a grand-dad, twice my age, though there's only a year in it.

I didn't say, 'If you say so, Prof.' I thought: How did we get to this? The newspaper. Ronnie Meadows. The Lake District. But it was the newspaper first. I thought: I'm gasping.

And then I thought: If I get up and leave Mick here and go out across the yard to the gate to have a smoke and if I keel over while I'm doing it, would that be tragic? Smoking kills. It says so on the packet. Or would it be more tragic if Mick comes with me, is standing right beside me when it happens, and if he's smoking too? Or if he isn't, because he's trying to give up and he's just keeping me company?

Or would it be more tragic still if I go and have a smoke all by myself and feel all the better for it and meanwhile Mick here slumps forward and croaks. Slumps forward, with his tea unfinished, onto his newspaper with the word tragic dotted all over it.

'If you say so,' I say.

Mick thinks quitting smoking is wise. It goes with the glasses, maybe. But I know he only started trying to quit because of Ronnie. It wasn't because he's wise. It was because he was scared.

When Ronnie dropped off the fork-lift onto the yard floor he was still in a sitting-down position. It must have been a zonker of a heart attack.

I thought: Mick's wrong. He's talking cobblers. None of those deaths would be tragic.

I'm not a newspaper reader, I'm not any kind of reader, but when I was at primary school and it rained and we couldn't go out to the playground, there'd be this big box of old *Beanos* and *Dandys* brought out for us to read. I used to love reading them—because it wasn't reading at all. How they used to make me laugh. Biff! Bam! Kerrchow! I never thought then I'd end up being a warehouseman at Macintyre's, dying for a smoke in my break.

Mick did his nose-shift thing again. He looked very pleased with having won his argument, if that's what it was, or with me not understanding and just giving up. Or with him getting away—we'd run out of time now—with not having a smoke. If that's what this was really all about. His little score on that.

Not exactly mountain climbing, Micky.

I thought: Okay, Mick, you're my mate, if you're really giving up, then that's up to you, but next time I'm going out by myself, I'm leaving you here, matey. And don't you ever start preaching to me, with your new glasses, about how I should give up myself. Don't you ever start that.

Then I saw, in my head, Mick slumped forward over his spread newspaper, dead as a sack of cement.

And of course I understood. Of course I understood that tragic was a word people used when they didn't know what else to say—about people dropping dead. But I thought: It's not because they don't know what to say. It's not that at all. It's because they can't say the other thing, they can't ever say it. The thing that goes with tragedy and happens on the stage too, and doesn't have much to do with Macintyre's warehouse either.

Biff! Bam! Kerrzang! How I laughed. How I'd love to get out a copy of the *Beano* in the canteen. Though I'd look a bloody idiot, wouldn't I? The word you ought to use about that mountaineer in the Lake District, or about Ronnie dropping off the fork-lift still sitting down, or even about Mick here, slumped over his newspaper with his neat little new half-rims all scrunched up against his face, is comic.

Comic. That's what you ought to say. But you can't.

As Much Love as Possible

He'd been early and Sue had still been upstairs, getting ready, as Alec ushered him in. Her voice had floated down, through a half-opened door, from above. 'Hello, Bill.' Then a hurried and apologetic, 'I'm not decent.'

'You're always decent,' he'd called back.

What did that mean? And the word stuck with him: decent.

Alec had phoned days before and said that Sue was having a night out with the girls, so he'd be all on his own. Why didn't Bill come over?

'I've got a bottle of Macallan. Fifteen-year-old. It fell off the back of a lorry.'

Alec didn't say that he knew Bill would be on his own too— Sophie and the boys being away for half-term at Sophie's parents while he soldiered on at the office. Bill reckoned that it was Sue who knew this, not Alec, so this was really Sue's idea, Sue's invitation. But Alec was Bill's oldest friend.

'Come over. I haven't seen you for ages. Don't bring anything, just yersel.' Alec could get all Scots when he wanted.

So there he'd been, a little early, and Alec was giving him a cardiganed hug and there was the smell of the shepherd's pie in the oven that Sue had cooked for them. He'd driven, which was easiest, but also stupid—given the bottle of Macallan. But he'd told himself that if he drove then he'd have to go carefully on the whisky, and if he had his car outside then he'd avoid any pressure as things got late to stay the night, which was all false upside-down logic. It wasn't that he didn't like being with Alec and Sue, quite the opposite.

Alec had flicked his eyes upward and said, 'Making herself beautiful.' Then said, 'How dastardly of me, there's no making about it.' And Bill had smiled and thought nonetheless how women made themselves beautiful for nights out with other women. For a boys' night out, or in, men hardly bothered. Witness the pair of them, like two adverts for woollens.

They'd hardly settled when Sue had come down and appeared in the doorway. Many years ago Bill had thought that Sue was just the sort of dumb and ditzy blonde Alec would end up marrying, then find the novelty wearing off. It had been his own reason for not marrying her, or rather for not making any move at all, though he might have done. He'd given precedence to his friend and felt he'd been shrewd.

He'd been best man, naturally, at Alec and Sue's wedding, but by then he'd met Sophie and she and he had been the first pair to get hitched. And to have kids, pretty quickly, one after the other. Alec and Sue had waited several years. Perhaps there was a difficulty, but they hadn't seemed unhappy at the time. So much for shrewdness. Maybe they'd waited simply because of that: because they were happy and wanted to have time just with each other. Then they'd gone and had twins. A boy and girl.

They'd be upstairs right now, still only four years old. Or was it five? He ought to know, he was their godfather.

Bill had said to Sue as she appeared in the doorway, 'Sue, you look fantastic.' He should have allowed Alec to say something first, perhaps. Anyway it was true. She was wearing a dress that wasn't quite a party dress, but it had a shimmer. Or it was more that *she* had a shimmer, a kind of ready, default-mode excitement.

It was only a girls' night out, he'd thought, it wasn't a ball.

She said, 'You look pretty good yourself, Bill.' He said, 'Rubbish,' and had got up to meet her embrace which was always full-on and generous, as if she had arms for everyone. She'd been holding a black coat and a cream scarf but had slung them momentarily over the banister at the foot of the stairs, on top of his own undistinguished Puffa thing.

She picked up the coat again and looked at her watch.

'Alec, you did ring for the taxi, didn't you?'

Alec was already fetching two whisky tumblers. He thumped his forehead with his free hand.

'Oh shit! Shit! I'm sorry, sweetheart. Let me drive you.'

Sue had said, 'No, you have to look after Bill.' There wasn't any hint of anger or dramatics, just the small practical quandary. So, while Alec had done more breast-beating, he'd said, 'I'll drive you, Sue.' It seemed a neat and diplomatic solution. His car was still warm. Alec would have to get his out of the garage. And he didn't want Sue to be late.

'Where are you going?'

'Hathaway's. Park Street.'

'I know it. Good choice. No problem.'

Sue had protested, then finally said, 'You're an angel, Bill.' And Alec had said, 'The man puts me to eternal shame.'

Alec had put the tumblers down and helped Sue on with her coat. There was no reproachfulness. She said, 'Don't forget about the shepherd's pie. And the twins are sparko. I looked in.'

Alec had draped the scarf round his wife's neck then kissed her tenderly by the ear. 'Sorry, precious,' he said. 'You better give this man here a decent tip.' That word once more. Then, to him, he'd said, 'I'll see you later, buster. I'll try not to open the bottle.'

So now here he was—it was only a ten-minute drive—sitting beside Sue in the car opposite Hathaway's, and Sue, though she was several minutes late, didn't seem in a rush. All through the short journey he'd felt inevitably that they were like some couple going out on a date themselves—particularly at the start as they got into the car, he holding the door open for her, chauffeur-fashion, she swinging her legs in and gathering up her coat, and Alec watching contritely from the front porch, like some stoical father.

Sue had spent the few minutes saying how sweet it was of him and he'd spent it establishing that the 'girls' were Christine and Anita and that all three of them had been at the hair academy together and now they each had salons of their own.

He wondered what a hair academy was and had his bizarre mental pictures, but didn't ask. He'd long since stopped thinking it obvious that a fluffy blonde whose principal feature was her hair would go into hairdressing. Nothing was obvious any more.

He knew Sue's salon was called Locks and that it had been set up—funded—by Alec. For all Bill knew, Alec might have among his many business interests a small chain of hair salons which involved funding Christine and Anita as well.

Bill had often passed Locks but never entered. He'd sometimes wondered how it would be if he were to walk in and ask to have his hair cut—by Sue herself of course. It seemed the most innocent yet intimate of requests.

Salon. Hair academy. These were easily scoffed at, bogus expressions. But he no longer thought like that.

Sue said, as if she hadn't thanked him enough, 'Why don't you come in for a moment? I could introduce you to the girls.' It was a strange impetuous suggestion and was perhaps only meant jokingly.

'It's a bit late in the day for that sort of thing, isn't it?' He smiled. He hadn't meant to sound rueful.

She said, 'All okay, with you and Sophie?'

'Yes. Fine.'

'And the kids?'

He snorted. 'I hardly think of them as kids any more. They're eleven and twelve.'

There was a little weighty pause. She could just get out. It didn't need a speech.

'You know, Bill, all I've ever wanted, all that's ever made me happy, is to do something for other people that makes them feel nicer. That's all, nothing special, nothing more than that.

They come into my salon, they walk out again a little later—feeling nicer.'

His hands still held the steering wheel. He hadn't had a drink yet. He thought of Alec, waiting for him, staring at a (still virgin?) bottle of Macallan. He thought how many months since he last saw Sue? When would he see her again? And when would he again, if ever at all, sit beside her like this, just the two of them, in the convenient bubble of a car?

Across the road, Hathaway's was lit up, but curtained. If Christine and Anita were inside waiting, they couldn't be seen.

He said, 'I love you, Sue. I love you. I could say something like "I'm very fond of you", but I love you. I don't mean I don't love Sophie. I don't mean I don't love lots of people. But I love you. Don't you think there should be as much love as possible?'

There. He held the steering wheel. He held it, looking straight ahead as if he were still driving.

He heard, eventually, the slow punctilious creep of a woman's clothing as she moves deliberately to kiss a man. It was barely a touch against the side of his face, by his ear, as if she wished to say something that could only be whispered, but he felt just the brush of her lips and a small expulsion of warm breath.

'Well,' she said, drawing away, 'I better not ask you in then. You better not meet the girls.'

She could never have been so suave years ago.

She opened her door and got out, but then lingered on the pavement, despite the cold, one hand on the open door, her coat unbuttoned, leaning in while he leant across, constrained by his seat belt.

What was there to say? It was as if it was late and he was dropping her off.

'Enjoy your evening,' he said like some polite stranger. Like a cab driver.

'And you. Don't get sloshed.'

'Nor you. I'll see you later.'

'Yes. But—'

'But what?'

'Don't wait up.'

What did that mean?

'Go on,' he said. 'It's cold. The girls are waiting.' To puncture the mood and effect a disengagement he added, 'I can see down your top when you lean like that.'

It was a fifteen-year-old bottle, to be treated with respect, so they sipped slowly, both acknowledging how they couldn't cane it like they'd used to. And there was the shepherd's pie to mop it up. It was a very good shepherd's pie. Perhaps he praised it too much, but Alec had simply said, waxing Caledonian, that short of a decent haggis there was no finer accompaniment to a good whisky. Decent haggis. That word again.

All the same, after a certain point—he could recognise the symptoms—he knew he should start to put his hand over his glass or ask for a coffee. And he really didn't want, now, to have that moment when Alec would say, 'There's a spare bed upstairs, mon. No problem.' He didn't even want, now, to be around when Sue returned. Don't wait up.

The point should come, before Alec launched off on some other topic, when he should say, 'Look, if you don't mind, I'll head back now.' And make whatever feeble excuses. He'd already told Alec that, strictly speaking, he was under doctor's orders. It wasn't true, though he'd had a fairly schoolmasterly doctor's warning.

On the coffee table were two abandoned plates and the dish, with an encrusted serving spoon, that had contained the shepherd's pie. They'd eaten like slobs, on their laps. He wondered how the table was looking at Hathaway's with Christine and Anita.

He should make a move before he lost his power of decision—he was near that—and, yes, definitely before Sue returned. He needed a pee, so he went upstairs, resolving that when he came down and while still on his feet he'd mouth his garbled adieus. It had gone eleven. No, he was okay to drive. He had work to do tomorrow.

But he made the mistake, when he came out of the bathroom, of peeping into the room with the just-open door along the landing. Why did all kids want to sleep with the door just open? Had he once? He peered in, even crept in a little, and stood inside the doorway. There was that barely-lit atmosphere of utter peace, utter immersion in sleep—sleep like no grown-ups have. There were the two little concentrated forms beneath blankets, each in their own small bed. A guarding clutter of inert toys.

He knew about this from his own experience. It was a primal parental joy. But here there was an extra magic, an extra harmony and rapture: twins. He stood and looked, as if these were his own children. His heart turned over.

He stood there long enough, if it was only seconds, to hear the noise of a car creeping up the quiet cul-de-sac outside. He felt sure it was a taxi bringing Sue home. So she, at least, had kept her power of decision and made her departure before things got late and disorderly. Or—they all had their salons to think about—there'd been a general sensible dispersal.

He hurried downstairs, if only to get to the living room before Sue could reach the front door and to avoid the awkwardness—was it an awkwardness?—of coming face to face with her as she let herself in. And of course as he re-entered the living room Alec poured him another slug, even as they both heard a car door close outside, and Alec said, 'That must be Sue. Rather early. The good wee lassies.'

Half past eleven wasn't exactly early and there was a tiny touch of tension in his voice. Was he still smarting from his earlier blunder? He went through to be at the front door.

'Hello, precious,' Bill heard, holding his topped-up glass and feeling the edge of the waft of February air that Sue brought in with her. He knew now he had no control over how things would proceed. He saw himself in the spare room—further along the landing—in solitary inebriated confinement in a house of couples.

She appeared in the doorway, just as before, Alec behind her now, removing her coat. Yes, the shimmer was all hers. There was a light inside her. It was only a girls' night out, he thought again, it wasn't a ball. Life wasn't a ball.

'All well here?' she said, quickly stooping to release her high-heeled shoes. One hand on the door frame, leaning in.

'Yes,' Alec said over her shoulder. 'Look how much whisky we haven't drunk.'

Alec slipped back into the living room, touching Sue's bottom with his palm as he did so.

Bill said, 'And how was your evening?' It sounded, again, absurdly polite.

She smiled. She drew herself up, smoothed her skirt, shook her hair a little, then took a deep and, so it seemed, utterly thrilled and pure breath, like someone on a mountain top.

'Oh, I've had the most wonderful evening.'

YORKSHIRE

NOBODY SPOKE, nobody said anything. They spoke about the dead who couldn't speak back, they stood around with poppies, but the ones still alive, they shut up and got on with it. Wasn't that the best way, anyway, of being grateful to the dead? It's what you did, it's what everyone did.

And what did she know or care, a schoolgirl, a teenager on a bicycle whizzing down Denmark Hill, flashing her underwear? It had all been over before she was born, it had all been over for nearly twenty years. Her mother called her 'flighty', as if it was her new name, though her real name was Daisy. Daisy Leigh. She said, 'You'll end up in trouble, Daisy, one of these days.' But her father said nothing, he shut up and got on with it. He coughed.

She quite liked 'Daisy', she liked being a daisy, but she liked 'flighty' too. She told Larry it was her middle name, it was what her mum called her. He said, 'Flighty? Well, that settles it then, doesn't it?'

And now Larry was sleeping in the spare room. What did it mean? They'd been married for over fifty years. Her name wasn't Leigh, it was Baker. What was flighty about that? But Larry was sleeping in the spare room.

Her hair flying and her skirt too. Well if they saw it wouldn't be for long, would it? Sometimes she'd let go of the handlebars, just because she knew she could do it, and hold out her arms like wings. Wheeee! She must have been saved up for Flight Sergeant Baker.

Trouble?

All over for nearly twenty years, but it hadn't been so long since they'd told her, or rather since her mum had told her, as if it was something to be whispered between women about the man in the next room. But it must have been agreed between them. You tell her, Gracie.

'Your daddy was gassed at Wipers.'

And what was that supposed to mean? She said the word gassed as if it was a bad word that shouldn't be repeated. She said it in the way she'd hear people later say the word cancer. And she said Wipers as if it was a real name you might find on a map.

And how, at nine or ten or whenever it was, should she, Daisy Leigh, have known otherwise? All she knew was that her daddy had a 'chest', a 'funny chest', it went with him just as surely as he wore trousers. And he was still, so far as she was concerned, her same daddy with his same funny chest.

But the fact that she'd been told this thing like a secret not to be passed on had something to do, though she couldn't have said what, with her becoming the sort of girl who didn't mind too much if her skirt blew up and who got to be called flighty, not Daisy. It was a bit like the word Wipers.

Then along came another war anyway to take your mind off the old one, to wipe it away. Just come home, Larry. Just come home to your Flighty. She might be in or out of her nightie.

And now Larry was sleeping—or not sleeping—in the next room, but it was just like one of those black nights when he might never have come home. What did it mean? Tomorrow there was going to be a police investigation. He was going, voluntarily, to the police station, to 'clear all this up'. He was going *voluntarily*. No one was being arrested. So there was still this night, it could wait till the morning. And what was he going to do anyway, run off somewhere? At seventy-two?

He was going to the police station, voluntarily, to help with inquiries. He was cooperating. But then? All hell let loose, she was sure of that. All hell, either way, whatever the outcome, whatever the decision. Never mind the voluntarily. All hell, she was sure, if this wasn't hell already.

Which was what they'd all said when they didn't want to say—or couldn't think of how to say—anything. All hell. You don't want to know.

But there was still this night, this black interval, and she wished it could be truly lastingly black. She wished when she opened her eyes—what was the point of shutting them if it didn't make things go away?—there'd not be that glow, from the streetlights, round the edge of the curtains. My God, she wished

she had blackout curtains. She saw them again as if it were yesterday, the dusty black brutal things they'd had to get used to,
instead of the swirls of flowers or the Regency stripes. The curtains in her old bedroom in Camberwell had daisies. Of course.

What did it mean? Voluntarily. 'Clear all this up.'

And what did this mean, right now, him being in the other
room? That he didn't want to be near her, touching her, let
alone talking to her? Or that he thought that *she* wouldn't want
him there, not now, next to her? That she wouldn't want to be
touching him or, my God, for him to be touching her?

She told herself it was his confession, his way of saying it.
She told herself it was just the disgrace, the sheer disgrace at the
very idea of it, the very suggestion. Imagine. Either way, he was
contaminated, not to be touched. Either way it was all hell.

And how could you ever tell anyway when things themselves
went right back into blackness? It was what Addy herself had
said, it was her trump card.

'We're talking here, Mum, about earliest memories. No, not
even that. We're talking about when you shouldn't have any
memories at all. But you have them, don't you, if they're strong
enough, if they're bad enough? You just suppress them, don't
you, submerge them? You pretend to forget.'

Suppress? Submerge? It had gone through her head to say,
'You're not in one of your classes now, my girl, you're not in
front of a blackboard.' And she'd seen for a moment (something she'd never ever actually seen) her daughter facing rows
of young faces. Why had Addy chosen to be a teacher? The
thought of her becoming one had once vaguely scared her.
She'd seen herself back at school, a target for her own teachers.

Pretend to forget?

What *could* you say about that time where memory vanishes into darkness? You could say nothing. Or you could say anything, you could say what the hell you liked, it was anyone's guess, and no one could prove you wrong.

My girl. Addy—little Addy—was forty-eight.

'You tell me what your earliest memories are, Mum. Go on, try it on me.'

She actually said that, to her own mother, as if she was accusing *her*, or as if she was saying, 'Come on, join me.'

And now here she was *doing* it, at three in the morning, trying to go back in her memory as far as possible, to where memory slips down a black hole. And she couldn't tell if it was because she was searching for something—and why the hell should she be?—or because she just wanted to slip, herself, down that black hole and never come out again . . .

She could remember being held against her father's chest, when she was small enough for most of her to fit against it. She had a blue cotton dress, it was her first dress. She could remember him hugging her to his chest and her hugging him back. What was wrong with that? She could remember having her ear against her father's chest and hearing the strange sounds it made, like rocks or pebbles shifting inside a cave—a cave by the sea with waves washing into it. She could remember it being as though he was letting her listen to the sounds, just her specially. What was wrong with that?

She could remember being in the paddling pool in the children's playground in Ruskin Park, though she couldn't say how old she'd have been, and a man had popped out from behind a big tree with his trousers undone and all his stuff showing. He'd done it very quickly and cleverly, just as she'd looked up and when no one else was looking, because she'd turned round and everyone was looking the other way. And when she'd looked back the man had gone as if he'd never been there. But she could remember his stuff showing, his red bobbing thing. She couldn't have invented that. She could remember thinking what was wrong with him, what sort of—disfigurement—was that? Though she didn't know then the word disfigurement.

Anyway she'd got over it and never said a word. And it wasn't her daddy.

Her face was wet. Addy was making her do this. The bitch.

And if it had been all right to hug her father still, her father who'd been gassed, and for him to hug her since he was still her same daddy, then it was all right to hug Larry now, no matter what, to hold him and hug him against her own sad chest, against her own flat breasts, and say, 'It's all right, Larry, I'm here. You're still the same Larry.'

Except he wouldn't let her. He'd gone to the spare room. What did it mean? It could mean that he thought that *she* must think that he'd really—

The bitch, the evil bitch. She was making them lie like this in separate rooms, both in their own separate blackness.

And he was lying, for God's sake, in Addy's old room. It wasn't, at least, in her old single bed. That had gone ages ago, it had been the spare room for ages with a new double bed from Debenham's. But it was the bed where Addy and Brian had slept enough times when they'd visited, and they'd visited enough times in nearly twenty years. Brian had said once it had 'tickled' him to sleep in Addy's old room. He'd said that. And then they'd brought their kids, Mark and Judy, first one then the other, in their carry-cots, to sleep with them in that same room.

And if all this, now, was true, then how could they have done that, come here, kept visiting, with their kids too? Though it had been a while, it was true, since any of them had visited, and the kids weren't kids any more. She should have said, perhaps, like some interfering mother, 'Is everything okay?'

Which was just the point Addy was making. Years went by and people never talked, did they? She, Adele Hughes, born Baker, hadn't talked for over forty years, but she was talking now. She'd kept it to herself, she'd 'struggled', but now she had to 'speak out'. And she was talking face to face, notice, she wasn't flinching. She was looking at her own mother, hard in the eye, as if her own mother might have known all along what all this was about and covered it up. And she wouldn't be the only one to speak out, would she, not by a long way? The world knew that by now. It was others speaking out that had given her the courage.

Courage?

She said she'd been 'traumatised'. All her life she'd struggled. But it had to stop now. She had to have her 'release'. At forty-eight? And had she talked to Brian first about it all? 'Tickled'. Had she had *him* sleeping in another bed?

Or was he doing that anyway?

She said that when she was very small, almost too far back for memory—there she went again—Larry, her own father, had done things to her, had interfered with her. He'd molested her. He'd traumatised her.

'He what? He did *what*? Where? When? *What*?'

She'd exploded into questions—which seemed to be all she had now. She was lying in this bed, under a rubble of questions.

'You better have some facts, my girl! You better know what the hell you're talking about!'

It had surprised her, the fierceness and quickness of her answer. She hadn't been lost for words exactly, or for a way to say them. She'd spoken in a certain voice and with a certain look. She knew she had a certain look, because Addy had actually stepped back. She'd flinched—for all her being unflinching. And whatever else that look was saying, it was saying, 'I'm not your mother any more, my girl. I've just become your deadly enemy.'

And whatever Addy had thought that talking to her mum would achieve—she'd wanted comforting? To be told she had guts?—she knew now she'd been seriously mistaken. And anyway she'd crossed a line for ever and there was no going back. But she must have thought of that—she should have thought of that—long before she opened her mouth.

Then her own mouth had opened again and she'd said to her own daughter, her own child of forty-eight years, 'You lying evil bitch.'

He was stationed in Yorkshire. Flight Sergeant Baker, wireless-op Baker. As it turned out they were from barely a mile apart, he was from Streatham, but he was stationed in Yorkshire. It might as well have been another country. He said on the phone, 'I'm safer here than where you are, I have it cushy here.' But she knew it was a lie, or a daytime truth and a night-time lie, since any night he could be killed. That was the truth, that was the deal now. It wasn't hanky-panky any more in the back of the stalls, though there was some of that, it began with that, but it went beyond.

Night-time, bedtime. How everything was turned round. How could she sleep when he might be over Hamburg or Berlin? But she never knew where, or even if, he'd be flying that night—so she might be scaring herself stiff for nothing. She'd actually preferred it when she had to be in the shelter. At least she could think: Well he's dropping bombs on them. She didn't care about Germans at all. That was their hell.

But the nights when she just lay in bed were terrible. They were like this night now. She didn't even know where in Yorkshire, just Yorkshire. 'Believe me, Flighty, you wouldn't know where, even if I told you.' But because she didn't know anything, which nights or where, Yorkshire itself became like the place, the word for all things terrible. Yorkshire terriers. Like the word for terror itself.

That's where he was now. Or she was.

And that's where you came from, my girl.

He never talked either. He shut up and got on with it too. The fact is he came back, he always came back, but she never knew, nor did he, that that was how it would be, till it was all over. He came back and he never talked. 'I'd rather talk about this, Flighty.' His hand you know where. In the Air Force they called it Lack of Moral Fibre if you didn't shut up and get on with it. Larry never had Lack of Moral Fibre.

He had nightmares, of course, for a long time afterwards— so yes he talked, even screamed a bit, in his sleep. But that was something she could deal with simply, easily, gladly. 'You were dreaming, Larry, only dreaming. Look, you're here beside me, you're alive, these are my breasts. Put your head in my breasts.'

If only she could say that now. 'You're here, Larry, you're not in Yorkshire.'

And then, in 1947, Adele was born. Little sweet Adele. And wasn't that the universal cure? Everyone was doing it. Little babies galore. And didn't that help to wipe things away?

*

And if Addy had been waiting all this time to talk—if there were any reason to—then she might have waited till the two of them were dead. If she'd waited anyway till she was *forty-eight*. Or she might have waited till they'd lost their marbles, gone doolally, so they wouldn't know a thing anyway. Same difference.

But to say it now when they were seventy-two and seventy-one, though still going strong, in their 'sunset years' and trying to make the most of them. Having passed their Golden and hoping to make it to their Diamond (what was flighty about that?). Not to mention to the year 2000, to a new millennium. Think of that, Larry, we've lived through a millennium.

But Addy had actually given *that* as her reason. If she'd waited till they were dead, till *he* was dead, then there wouldn't have been any justice, would there?

Justice?

She actually said it was the thought of them reaching the end of their lives that had 'forced her' to it, the thought of them being dead and the thing just disappearing into the past, then her having no 'redress' and just having to carry on living with it till she was dead herself.

She actually said that. All her life she'd protected them, but enough was enough.

Protected them?

Well, she'd made the sun set now sure enough. There was only this night, which she wished would go on for ever.

No matter how tightly she closed her eyes, she couldn't make it black enough. To *want* night, to want blackness! Yet to be made to feel at the same time that you had to shine some nasty poking torch into it, like a policeman at a murky window. And there could be no stopping it, could there, no end to it, once you got into that area where memory itself stopped and no one could say what was true or false? Beneath everything a great web of—disfigurement. It must be there because no one talked about it.

How she'd dreaded it, once, sunset—the thought of the sun setting over Yorkshire. Now she wanted only darkness. She couldn't say what Larry wanted.

She saw herself on a bicycle, arms outspread. She saw again her little room in Camberwell, bands of light from the street. Her daisy curtains. Her father's cough across the landing.

Though she'd never felt it before and never imagined she might feel it, she felt it now like some black swelling creature inside her. The wish not to have been born. Or was it the wish not to have given birth? She felt it, decades on, but as if it were happening all over again, the exact, insistent, living feeling of carrying Adele inside her. Though was this Adele? At four months, at six months, at eight, at—

Then she woke up and felt sure she'd been screaming, screaming out loud. She felt sure she'd screamed—so loud that Larry, in the next room, must have heard, even if he'd been sleeping. Yes, he was in the next room, but it was only the next room, so he must have heard, a scream like that. And she wanted this to end it, she wanted it to be the thing that would make him snap out of it and leap up and come back to her and hold her and soothe her and crush her against his chest and say, 'It's all right, Flighty, you were only dreaming.'

Holly and Polly

Holly likes to say—and Holly likes to say everything—that we're in the introduction business. We can't make anything happen, but we can bring the parties together. She'll say this to men in bars when they home in on us. It's a wonderful thing to watch a pair of them edge our way and to see the light in their eyes before they get the full picture.

'So, don't tell us,' one of them says, 'the two of you work in a dating agency?'

'No, but you're close,' Holly says. 'Sure, getting the date right can be an important part of it.'

'You wouldn't be Irish by any chance?'

'By every chance. But that's not what you're guessing.'

Isn't it a wonderful thing—isn't it *the* most wonderful

thing—how things come together in this world, how they can even be meant for each other? But you can't tell, you can't guess it in advance.

'So—you've got one more guess. Yes, we work together. It's not an office. And it's not a dating agency. You two wouldn't be after a date now, would you? Without the agency?'

'We're thinking,' the other one says. 'Don't talk, we're thinking.'

Then the first one says, 'No, you'll have to tell us. We give up, you'll have to say. I'm Matt, this is Jamie.'

'I'm Holly and this is Polly. Yes, we know. But look now, we're doing what Polly and me do all day, we're making introductions. We're clinical embryologists. Have you heard of those people? We spend all day looking at sperms. We're experts on the little fellers. We pick out the good ones, the best from the rest, and then we introduce them to eggs. We say to them, "There now, say hello, youse two, and on you get with it."'

And then the lights go off, or they go brighter. A turn-off or a turn-on. They might want to get mucky. And Holly can do mucky.

And they haven't even seen the full picture.

You can't make it happen. You can bring the parties together. But tell me, please, how does *that* happen? How does it happen that there was Holly Nolan, raised in a convent (though you might not think it) somewhere in Ireland and there was me, Polly Miller, meek and mild, but raised in a comprehensive in Bolton, both of us fired by the same thing ('Sure, isn't it the only subject now, the science of life?'), both of us getting, in different places, our B.Sc.'s and our certificates, so that she should cross the sea (it not being a field that Ireland's big in) and we should meet in a brand-new clinic, in a clean white room with clean white counters and white expensive instruments, like two specimens ourselves in some sort of clinical trial, both of us in the pea-green scrubs we were provided with.

So that we would be introduced to each other.

'I'm Holly.'

'I'm Polly.'

'Would you believe it? Hello, Polly. We're to work together.'

'Yes.'

'In these things! Have I come all the way from County Kildare just to wear green?'

Both of us only twenty-three (*junior* clinical embryologists), but both of us qualified and trained for a job that some people say is the job of playing God.

'Well I like that now! Are we not a pair of goddesses?'

So that we would come together, so that it would happen. So that my life would at last begin.

When I'm out with Holly in a bar, teasing men, I sometimes see the touch of red in her black hair—what she calls her 'burn'. I see her tarty brashness, what they think is her being up for it. I hear her unstoppable voice. I think: Not my type, not my type at all.

How wrong can you be?

'Well now, Polly dear, there's such a thing as the attraction of opposites.'

When she first arrived here she used to say things about her Catholic upbringing that could make me blush. Or blush inside. That could make me think: Hold on, that's wrong, that's blasphemous. She said that she and her convent-school friends used to sing a plainsong rendering of the sexual act, in Latin.

And she sang it for me—intoned it for me—in her purest priestly voice:

Penem in vaginam intro-duxit.

To which the response was, as from a choir of monks:

Et semen e-mi-sit.

With a long sustaining of the *'mi'*.

It was hardly filth, and it was Latin. And it had me in stitches. The stitches maybe hid the blushes. But it was the very idea of it, I suppose, the idea of singing such a thing as if it were a prayer. It was the feeling of a wickedness unavailable to such as me. Me with my godless (but chaste) upbringing. My only shred of religion was that I'd worshipped once my biology teacher, Sandra Rhys.

Which is only to say I felt jealous. Why should that be? Jealous of Holly and of her convent schooling and of her chorus of profaning schoolfriends.

'I haven't shocked you now, have I, Polly? In our line of business.'

And how many jobs are there—tell me one other—in which just along a corridor men go into little rooms and, well, as Holly would say, they engage in private devotion and offer themselves up into little jars, and the jars are passed discreetly our way for us to examine closely.

For a while we couldn't mark the arrival of such a tribute without actually singing, softly, in unison, or wanting to sing:

Et semen e-mi-sit . . .

I was even jealous of her familiarity with Latin. If you're a biologist you need to know a little, but for her it had really once been a sort of second secret language.

'Introduxit'—from *introducere,* to lead into or towards. The introduction business.

*

And it's a serious one. We're not God. We're not playing either. Though sometimes you have to laugh. We're the girls in the lab, the girls in the back room. It's Dr Mortimer and his nurses who do the meeting and greeting and perform the intimate procedures, but we sometimes get to see the clients, to say hello to—Mr and Mrs Desperate. And Dr Mortimer, as *he* makes the introductions, will inevitably call us his behind-the-scenes angels, the ones who perform the real miracles. The smoothie. Or the buck passer, as Holly would say.

You have to laugh.

And we'll sometimes see in the faces of Mr and Mrs Desperate the surprise, or sheer alarm, at knowing that their chances depend on such a pair of youngsters. Two girls in green. Or else see them thinking: Well it's all right for them, it must be a lark for them, hardly out of school and with all their bits inside just as they should be, but not even thinking about it yet, not even caring about it. Though getting in plenty of practice, no doubt, on the preliminary activity.

If only they knew, if only they knew the real cause of our clinical detachment.

We don't often think about it, but sometimes we do. We know that one day in a living room somewhere, because of something we've done in our clean white lab, and because the moment has come, Mr and Mrs Desperate will squeeze each other's hand, and she will go to the bathroom where there's the testing kit our clinic has provided. And he will wait, perhaps saying a small prayer. And a little while later they'll squeeze hands again while they cry tears of joy. Or just cry.

What is it that makes things happen?

*

I thought, with all her mouth—a cherry-lipsticked gash of a mouth—and all the language spilling from it, she can't be a virgin. But why should I have had that thought at all? She was twenty-three, and had crossed the sea. They grow up, don't they, Catholics, with the Holy Virgin, they worship their Holy Virgin? Though hardly this one. But there wasn't the mention or even the hint about her of any man. Despite all the mouth. Despite the way she could twist Dr Mortimer round her little finger. And that despite the fact that Dr Mortimer, good and caring gyno though he is, likes everyone to know that *he* does the charming round here.

Is she a virgin? Why should I even have thought it? In our line of business.

For the simplest plainest reason.

She said, 'Are you doing anything tonight?' Not of itself a remarkable question. But she said it in a certain way, with a certain tilt. She said it even, I like to think now, with a little toss of her hair. Except she couldn't have done that in her scrub cap. And of course she was a virgin. For the same reason and in the same sense that I was. It takes one to know another perhaps, but there's still the attraction of opposites.

The plain truth of it was that we ourselves were two Miss Desperates. There had never been, in all our years, for me or her, a '*penem in vaginam*' situation. Oh the handiness of Latin. Though there had been some false introductions.

It takes some less time, it takes some perhaps, poor souls, much longer, but it had taken each of us all our lives to discover and acknowledge, then to nurse and hide, in our different ways, our secret. Both wondering all along, like good little girls intent on being pure even till their wedding nights, if there might be someone, the right one, one day, with whom we could share it.

Was there ever such a strange way, among our sperms and eggs—and, goodness knows, they have their difficulties—for the likes of us to come together?

'Was there ever, Polly angel darling, such a sweet and charming thing?'

That couple in the living room, with the tears running down their faces, they can't have anything to do with the likes of us, can they? And yet they have everything to do with us. And we might as well have been, that night, that couple in the living room, tears of joy—this was how the test had gone—running down our faces. How magical, how all-confessing, how all-absolving, are the little words 'Me too'. How all-embracing.

We went for a drink in the Radcliffe Arms. Then we went for a Chinese in the Blue Pagoda. And then. And then. Like the beginnings of all things everywhere. She said the province of Northern Ireland with its bloody Union Jack had been shoved up against the Republic of Ireland for nearly a century. But it hadn't taken us very long, had it?

Not my type at all. Oh how I love her. And oh how happy I am to be with her, to wear green with her, two peas in a pod, to work with her among our sperms and eggs, to have found among them the one I am and the one I should be with, so far as I'm concerned, for ever.

And if we should ever want to be what the likes of us can't be, to have the thing the likes of us can't have, then we're in the right place, aren't we? We know how it can be arranged, don't we?

*

We walked into the clinic that next morning as a couple. That's to say, we made sure we didn't walk in together, but a good half-minute apart. The nicety of lovers. It was Holly who went ahead. Naturally. And so bumped straight into Dr Mortimer, fresh from his silver BMW and his drive in from Wilmslow. How much did he see straight away? How much had he guessed already?

But it's common knowledge now anyway. I mean it's common knowledge in this place. And truly this place is a place where there's precious little to be coy and canny about, with pots of sperm being passed around all day.

But Dr Mortimer looked at Holly and said, 'You're looking particularly glowing this morning, Holly. Is there something I don't know?'

And Holly said—because I was near enough by then to hear, near enough to see and to know how much I love her—'Sure, if you're not God around here, Dr Mortimer, if you're not Our Lord Father Almighty. Don't you know everything?'

KEYS

HE DROVE CLARE to the station. The traffic was unexpectedly heavy and they just made it in time. Their goodbyes were rushed and clumsy, but this spared him. He had no idea what to say. 'Call me,' he said. Then, 'Quick!' Then he said, 'I love you.' He hadn't planned on saying it. It just happened. He watched her blink and scan his face even as she hurried.

'Quick!' he said again, and she turned, wheeling her small case into the station entrance. He loitered in the forecourt as her train arrived. He should be going with her, of course, but she'd brushed aside the need for this. They both knew he'd never got on with her brother, couldn't stand him in fact. And now her brother was suddenly, perhaps dangerously, ill.

It spared him. It would have been false. But as he watched

her train pull out he felt a pang. He thought of her sitting there like some newly made orphan or refugee. She had to cross London then take another train from Euston, some four or five hours in all. Plenty of time to be alone with her thoughts, plenty of time before she'd have any reason to call. But he somehow knew she'd only call him if things looked not too bad. If they looked really bad she'd be immersed in it all and in her family and she'd forget him. He'd be peripheral. He was just a husband.

Being an only child himself, who'd lost his parents years ago, he hated the stifling stuff of families, and sometimes couldn't hide it. It didn't sound good at all for Adam, and Adam was only forty-two.

He asked himself why he'd never been able to bear him. There was nothing rational about it. Simply because he was Clare's older brother? No, it was because he was weak. That was the truth. He hated weak men. He could spot them. And the truth about weak men was that they got ill, and even died.

He remained parked for some time after the train disappeared, as if he were now waiting for someone to arrive. It was a leaden August afternoon and thick sparse spots of rain began to fall. He thought about his affair with Vicki. It hadn't lasted long and it was the only time. He thought of how he'd hidden it from Clare—whether she'd had her inklings or not—and of how his hiding it from her had come to seem like a kindness, even a virtue.

Then he drove back home, only to discover that, in the unusual circumstances, he'd forgotten his keys.

He knew at once where they were, in the pocket of his zip-up jacket, slung over the back of his chair by his desk. He'd decided hastily not to wear it after all. Then, while he'd carried out Clare's case and put it in the boot, Clare had locked the front door. And now of course he didn't have the remedy that Clare, with her keys, could come to his rescue.

Rain started to fall in earnest as he sat outside his own home, staring at it like some riddle.

The normal thing in such a situation was to seek the help of a neighbour. He'd done it before. The houses were terraced. At the back of theirs was a window on the first floor with a broken catch. It had been possible that previous time to raise the lower sash from outside, then crawl in. Thanks to his negligence in getting the catch repaired, it might be possible to do the same again. But first he'd have to be let in by his next-door neighbour, explain himself, make embarrassed apologies, borrow a ladder and climb over the garden fence, somehow manhandling the ladder over too.

And now it was August and both the Wheelers on one side and the Mitchells on the other were on holiday. Last time, it had been the Mitchells. He knew they had a ladder. But the Mitchells would be in their place in France.

And the irony was that the window—the window that was by no means guaranteed to save him—was the window to his study and only a few feet from his abandoned jacket, with his keys in it, over the chair. Last time, he'd squirmed through the window, then found himself swimming on his desk.

He could of course call a locksmith. He'd forgotten his keys, but he had his phone. How long would it take for a locksmith to arrive?

At least he was sheltered from this rain in the car.

For a moment he did nothing, immobilised by the fact of

being excluded from his own home, his own life. There it was, but he simply couldn't get to it. There was his desk, with his zip-up jacket over the chair, his drawing board where he'd resolved just to get on with the work he'd brought home from the office—having taken today, Friday, off—right through the weekend if need be while Clare was away.

He had to revise all the drawings on the Neale Road project. It was the stupid developer's fault, but it was a significant job and they had to swallow it. There was a bit of a panic and he'd said he'd see to it by Monday. He vaguely knew it wasn't so tricky. The future residents of Neale Road would have a little less space than they might have done, that's all. But they'd never know about it.

He said he'd tackle it anyway over the weekend, and felt this piece of noble volunteering already scoring him points. Clare would have to put up with it, but he'd say he couldn't wriggle out, and she was used to work coming home with him. Then the situation had changed dramatically. His weekend commitment became another, secondary reason why he couldn't accompany her. It also became his own self-sacrificing task to counterbalance, at least a little, her more demanding mission.

Except now he had this other problem.

He realised that in confronting this minor catastrophe of being locked out, he'd for some minutes suspended all thought of his wife's much more grievous situation—or her brother's. He saw her again sitting on the train, the window streaked with rain, not thinking of him. Her keys in her handbag.

The truth was he didn't think Neale Road should take more than half a day, though he could make out it had taken longer. He saw himself handing in the results to Vicki on Monday and in doing so scoring personal points with her that he couldn't precisely analyse. 'There we are,' he'd say, as if really saying in a certain victorious way (victorious—ha!), 'No hard feelings.'

He looked at the unremitting frontage of his own home, briefly seeing the immured but none-the-wiser residents of Neale Road.

It was so strange: his life there, himself here, but the sensation was not entirely foreign, or unwelcome.

The rain grew suddenly heavier, a real downpour. Then he saw a light go on, on the first floor, in number twenty, the Mitchells' place—at 4.30 in the afternoon.

He was surprised how rapidly he solved the mystery. It would be their cleaner. He was sure of it. She came once a week, on Fridays. The Mitchells were away, till Sunday, but they'd no doubt asked her to look in and do a few chores, water the plants and so on, before their return. He remembered now—but he'd hardly forgotten—coming home once from the office early and just as he was reaching for his keys (his keys!) seeing her emerge from the adjacent front door.

She'd been visibly startled to see him standing there so close.

'I'm John. I live here,' he said reassuringly, then held up his keys by way of proof. She held up her own keys—or the set of keys the Mitchells had given her. For a moment they'd done a flustered mutual jingling with their two sets of keys, a hand dance, as if this was more effective than speech.

'Olga,' she eventually said. 'I clean.' She was blonde, indeterminately foreign, no more than twenty-five.

She'd lowered her eyes automatically, at first, from his gaze. Now she suddenly gave him a quick direct stare, half smiling, half something else. He felt the feral punch of it, even as he knew his own stare was stripping away the thinnish dress she was wearing. This mutual jolt was something he hadn't really felt (except with Vicki) since before he married Clare, though he'd felt it often enough back in those days, and he felt its submerged familiarity now.

Olga. He'd always thought it was an ugly name, implying ugly women. Olga, Friday afternoons. Perhaps he'd noted it even then. So: that light going on next door—it was in the Mitchells' bedroom—must be her. And Olga could be his legitimate means of getting into his house.

She was perhaps stranded herself, he thought. This sudden torrential rain. No umbrella. We forget things. And if it was that same thinnish dress. And this same bucketing rain, he also thought, might make rather tricky, or at least postponable, the business with the ladder and the fence-hopping and the unsecured window.

He got out and scrambled to the porch of number twenty. Even these few paces left him wet. He rang, then for good measure rattled on the letter box and rang again. It might be her policy not to answer the bell when doing the Mitchells' cleaning. But, after a moment, more lights came on and she half opened the front door.

'Remember me?' he said. 'John? And my keys? Well now I haven't got any.'

It was the same dress. A mix of washed-out pinks and greys. Maybe it was the only dress she did the cleaning in.

'I'm locked out,' he said, wondering if this was an expression a foreign woman with limited English would understand. He couldn't hold up a missing key. Was she Russian, Polish, Romanian? It turned out she was Moldovan. He wasn't quite sure where Moldova was.

But she understood the situation and what he needed to do. She even met his apologetic laugh at the comedy of it all with a cautious laugh of her own. If this was all some ruse on his part, then it was peculiarly inventive.

But it was she who made the first move. That is, the move to say that he—they—shouldn't attempt his breaking-and-entering plan, or at least not straight away. With this rain he'd get soaked. And suppose the ladder slipped. It could be dangerous.

And suppose, he might have said, the rain continued for hours still. Suppose it continued all night.

Which it did. In fact the rain, gushing down incessantly, was like some conspiring screen (had anyone seen him enter not his own house but number twenty?). More than that, there was something insistent about it, the very noise of it like a rush of blood.

He'd been here before. And she knew it. She'd been here before. Though he'd never been before, like this, inside the Mitchells' house. But he'd been in this place, or in a place like it, many times before, before Clare. He recognised it as his element.

Many years ago he'd discovered his power—a simple power that was also so like a mere proneness, a gravitation, that he wondered why other men didn't simply, naturally have it too. Why for other men it could sometimes seem so damn difficult. It was just weakness perhaps, other men were just plain weak. Or they just didn't know how to pick up a scent.

Years ago he could have said to another man, though of course it was unthinkable actually to say it, that in a little while, just a little while, he'd have that one there. That one over there. And in a little while after that, probably, he'd make her cry.

So sure was he of this repeated cycle, so familiar, even faintly fatigued by it, that he'd wanted relief and sanctuary. He'd wanted marriage, a wife, a house and all the other things that go with them. And he was an architect by choice and qualification—he fashioned domestic spaces. But he knew there was still this stray animal inside him. And now he was locked out of it all anyway.

There it was, just the other side of a wall: his life. It even seemed for a moment that he and Clare might actually *be* there. He had turned into someone else. There they were. He felt tenderly, protectively towards them. And of course if they were there, then Clare couldn't be travelling somewhere northwards on a train to where her brother was gravely ill, perhaps even dying. And he couldn't be here.

It was a weird thing to be occupying the Mitchells' house, even—as it proved—their bed. Weird and undeniably wrong, but undeniably thrilling and enveloping, like the rain, which didn't let up. It wasn't his house, it wasn't hers. They had that in common. They were both displaced people, though in his case all it took was a wall. Weird and undeniably violating. It made the Mitchells seem the imposters.

At some stage of the evening, or night, he managed to ask her where she was from and why and how she'd come to England. He couldn't get from her much more than the hint of some gaping separation, or loss, that even in his comforting arms (or he thought they might be comforting) she didn't want, or know how, to explain. Where was Moldova? She seemed to retreat behind her poor English. He didn't press or insist. No more than she did about his mysteriously absent wife.

So he just held her, as she seemed to want him to do, as if just being held was his side of a bargain that she'd secured from him.

He thought, as he held her, of how Clare hadn't called. It was really dark now, it might be the middle of the night. She could have arrived and had news, but she hadn't called. And how would he have spoken to her if she had? He hadn't switched off his mobile—as if that might have been an admission of something. But of course she would call on their home phone, the land line. He strained his ears as if to hear it ringing through the wall: an unanswered phone in an empty house. But heard nothing.

She hadn't called, so no problem. Or that is, according to his earlier logic, things must be bad for her brother.

He thought of when, if at all now, but it somehow didn't seem to matter, he'd perform that farcical act with the ladder, his legs poking from the window. He thought of himself breast-stroking on his desk. He thought of himself, earlier, driving Clare diligently to the station and saying unexpectedly 'I love you' and returning, truly meaning to knuckle down to work and not knowing at all then how this sudden chain of events would overtake him. He thought of his jacket, with the keys in the pocket, hanging over the chair.

Of course Clare had her inklings.

As he held her, she began to shudder uncontrollably, then to sob and to cry out loud. He'd somehow known this would happen, without knowing why, and knew he must hold her, it was all he could do. He held her and she cried. Then after a while, a long while it seemed, the crying and sobbing ceased and she fell asleep, but he continued to hold her, alert and alone in the dark with just the hiss of the rain.

LAWRENCE OF ARABIA

I NEVER THOUGHT this would happen to me, Hettie, though I always knew it could. But I never thought I'd be lying here like this in your spare room, looking at your picture of the 'Old Harry Rocks at Studland' on the wall. Death's a funny thing, Het. Can you say that?

Have I told you about Lawrence of Arabia?

There's supposed to be a family that rallies round. But it was just me and Roy, like it was just you and Dennis. We were the two Mrs Underwoods, but there was something tricky with the Underwood genes. Never mind. Carry on. Now it's just you and me, and it feels like we're a couple of real sisters, not sisters-in-law, and you're the older one, though you're not, because you went through all this ahead of me with Dennis. Not the right order, but what bloody order is there?

And when Dennis went you had Roy and me. Or rather we both had Roy. We both had Roy being an older brother like he'd never been before, taking charge like he'd never taken charge before. Well, he stopped taking charge just over a week ago, and it was all I could do, in the time before he went, to make him understand he didn't have to take charge any more.

I know, Het, of course I do. Studland. It was where you and Dennis went for your honeymoon. It was a joke once, wasn't it? In a different world. Honeymoon. Studland. And Roy and I went to the Scilly Isles. There was a joke there too.

A couple of sisters, a couple of widows. It makes me think of a couple of crows. Or do I mean crones? Who'd have thought it, years ago, when it was Roy the Boy and Dennis the Menace, that one day we'd become like those pairs of crumple-faced women you used to see in pubs, nursing their glasses of black Guinness.

No, all right, that's not exactly us. Nursing our glasses of white wine.

I'm so grateful to you for taking me in. You had other plans. You were going somewhere warm. I've forgotten where already. Not Studland anyhow. You said, 'I've cancelled everything, Peg. You're staying with me.' You said, 'It's Christmas, but it can be whatever you want, it can be not Christmas if you like. I don't have a bit of tinsel in the house. Don't argue, Peg, you're staying with me.'

Did I say 'taking charge'?

And why should Roy have hung on for Christmas? So he could spend it in a hospital bed? So I could come in with a cracker for us to pull, if he had the strength? So he could wear a funny hat?

They say however much you prepare, nothing prepares you. They say it doesn't hit you till after the funeral. Well, that was yesterday, the day before Christmas Eve. You can't choose your date, can you? Or the weather. A howling gale, umbrellas blowing inside-out. And you'd been going somewhere warm.

They say—who are these they with their big mouths?—that you're in a state of shock. I don't know about that. Do you know what I thought, Het, when I left that hospital, after he'd gone? I thought: This can't be happening, I can't just be sitting here on a number nine bus. I thought: He's with me still, of course he is, it's up to me now to make him be with me. I felt in a state of importance, that's what I felt. Never mind shock. Nothing so important had ever happened to me before. Except of course the importance of meeting Roy in the first place.

The Scilly Isles, 1965. Us and Harold Wilson.

A state of importance. Does that sound silly? I'm not an important person. Nor was Roy. All he did, before he retired, was get to the top of the Parks Department and run five public parks and nine other sites of horticultural amenity. And how he took charge of them.

There I was on that bus, wanting only to be with him, wanting only to make him be with me. But do you know who else was on that bus too?

Peter O'Toole.

Maybe I'd already heard it at the hospital. Maybe I'd heard one nurse say to another, 'Have you heard—Peter O'Toole has died?' And if I did hear it maybe I'd thought: No, I didn't hear that. I don't want to hear it anyway. Not now.

But the bus was full of people going to work, holding newspapers with Peter O'Toole on the front. I couldn't not know about it. And only days before it had been Nelson Mandela. Deaths don't come much bigger, do they? And I hadn't wanted to know about that either. But even Roy, lying there with his tubes and drips, had to be aware that Nelson Mandela had died. Nelson Mandela who took charge of South Africa. And you know what he said? 'Well perhaps it's all right for me then.' And perhaps in some way it was. And you know what else he said? 'All these black nurses, Peg. It matters for them, doesn't it?'

There I was on that bus, at seven in the morning, with the Christmas lights floating by outside, just two hours after Roy had died, looking at the face of Peter O'Toole. Except it wasn't even Peter O'Toole. It was Lawrence of Arabia. On every newspaper. It was as if Lawrence of Arabia had died all over again. As if Lawrence of Arabia had got on the bus.

How unfair to Peter O'Toole. How unfair to Roy.

But the truth is I couldn't help thinking, just like everyone else: Those blue eyes, that golden hair, that man in the white robes, striding along the roof of a train. How old were we when Peter O'Toole suddenly came along? And what girl wouldn't? In her dreams.

Two hours after Roy had gone and I was thinking about Peter O'Toole. Or thinking about Lawrence of Arabia. Or not thinking about either of them, since I was thinking about that man in the fluttering white robes, who only ever existed in a film, didn't he? I've seen pictures of the real Lawrence of Arabia and he looks like a little squinty man you wouldn't want to spend any time with.

But he was important, wasn't he? He'd done something

146

important. So had Peter O'Toole, if only to turn into Lawrence of Arabia. And so of course had Nelson Mandela. A state of importance, don't we all want just a bit of it?

It must be Christmas morning already, Het, no longer Christmas Eve. I'm so grateful to you. A couple of sisters, in our separate rooms, waiting for Father Christmas, in his red robes, who never existed either.

All those crazy Englishmen—and Peter O'Toole wasn't even English, was he?—who went off to foreign parts, to do crazy things, wear Arab costume or whatever, to make their mark on the world, take charge. All those crazy Englishmen in the midday sun.

There I was on that bus, riding along Fairfax Street with Lawrence of Arabia. Now here I am in your spare bedroom, with the light on because I don't want to lie in the dark, wondering who the hell was Old Harry.

Well, I'm a lucky girl. Most widows get a few flowers, I get five parks.

Roy never had blue eyes or golden hair or wore white robes, like some bloody angel. He died in one of those hospital nightie things, all peek-a-boo up the back. He had brown eyes and black hair, most of which had gone anyway. His little brother went before him. So did Nelson Mandela. And now he's gone too, Hettie, he's gone too, like his hair.

AJAX

WHEN I WAS a small boy we had a neighbour called Mr Wilkinson, who was a weirdo. He must be long gone now, but I've often wondered what became of him. I was his undoing.

Let me stress that I never thought he was a weirdo, it wasn't my word. It was an opinion I was made to have of him. I was too young to have opinions of my own, or so it was thought. I was just a small boy going to primary school. But I didn't think Mr Wilkinson was weird. I thought he was interesting, I even admired him. I was driven into taking an opposite view.

When I was with my mother and we met him in the street he'd always be well mannered. He'd doff his hat. He'd always wear a hat and be well dressed, often in a suit, even if the suit had seen better days. He'd ask courteously after my father—

'Mr Simmonds'—and he used words with a feeling for them, as if they were things you should treat appreciatively, not just mechanically, employing standard phrases. Maybe it was his enthusiastic use of language that first made my parents think he was weird.

He looked entirely respectable. The dearest wish of all the grown-ups in our street was to be respectable and, by being respectable, to better themselves. So you'd think they might have regarded Mr Wilkinson as a model. It was obvious even to me that he was in some ways a cut above our street, he'd come down in the world to it. It was also obvious that he was what people called 'educated'.

I'd had it drummed into me by my parents from the earliest age that education was the most important thing in life and the key to everything, and I believed them. 'Education' was one of the first long words I learnt, and learning it was—rather magically—an example of the thing it proclaimed. At school I had no problem with teachers. I revered them. They were the purveyors of this most important thing. It struck me that Mr Wilkinson had the qualities of a teacher and perhaps had been one once. He seemed, in fact, even more educated than any of the teachers at my primary school, and for this reason too I couldn't see why the whole street didn't look up to him, instead of thinking he was weird.

But Mr Wilkinson lived alone. That was one mark against him. And though he'd always be respectably dressed when you met him in the street, he was in the habit of engaging in physical exercises in his back garden in just his underpants. In all weathers, even in mid-January. Just his underpants.

It wasn't only exercising. There seemed to be a whole ritual medley of things that sometimes involved simply breathing—a vigorous expanding and deflating of his lungs—and sometimes involved not doing anything in particular except chanting. Chanting was the best word for it. You might sometimes have called it humming or even singing, but chanting was the word that got used. In his underpants.

Anyone can do what they like in the privacy of their own home. This was something my parents would have firmly and fairly asserted. But they also said, about many things, that there were limits.

Our street was like thousands of others built in the outer suburbs on vacant land just after the war, but for some reason it had been decided to erect a pair of semis, then a bungalow, then another pair of semis and so on. If you had a bungalow you only had the one floor, but you had the privilege of being detached. There wasn't a great deal of space, but you could walk all the way round your own home. Even in your underpants.

On the other side of us, in the adjoining semi, were the Hislops. They'd been there, as had my parents, since the houses were built, but were a slightly older generation. Their two boys—I never thought of them as 'boys'—were old enough for one of them to have done National Service. I remember him in a beret, with an unexpected moustache and a kit bag. Their father ran a small printer's. The boys had girlfriends, tinkered around with cars and got married. There was nothing particularly educated about the Hislops, they were even slightly rough-edged, but they were a family and normal.

On the other side was Mr Wilkinson.

There was a high wooden fence, with a bit of trellis on top, between ourselves and Mr Wilkinson, so the only way you could see him in his underpants was from our spare bedroom or my parents' bedroom, both at the back upstairs. This put us in the position of spies, while all Mr Wilkinson was doing was—minding his own business. Nonetheless, my parents and particularly my mother didn't want to live next door to someone who was even known to stand around in his underpants and chant. And you could hear the chanting sometimes without needing to look.

Mr Wilkinson, I should say, was quite old. By that I mean that he seemed old to me. He must have been in his fifties. He had thinning, whitish hair, but had none of the stoopingness or vulnerability of old people. He was well built, even quite muscular (as could be seen) and, plainly, he kept himself fit. He was a good advert for physical education too.

I only remember him as 'Mr Wilkinson'. I can't recall ever knowing his first name, perhaps it was considered wrong to know it. Mr Hislop was also Tony. My parents christened me James, and gradually gave up the battle against 'Jimmy'. When I was first introduced to Mr Wilkinson (before we knew anything of his habits) it was as James, but he immediately and perhaps only in a spirit of friendship called me Jimmy. I saw that this set my mother against him.

Not only was there the fence and the trellis, but because the street was on a hill and Mr Wilkinson was above us, it was virtually impossible at ground level to see the back of his bungalow or into his garden. In the months when the trellis wasn't overgrown you might just glimpse his white-haired but imposing head moving past, or even a pale pink shoulder.

Which could make you wonder if he was wearing underpants this time or nothing at all.

On warm days I used to like playing by the flower bed at the foot of the fence, near the back of the house. Playing really meant re-landscaping the flower bed according to my infant purposes, which naturally displeased my parents. But I remained so set upon this activity that they eventually allowed a (strictly limited) part of the bed to be used for it. Perhaps they thought it was good for my development and that I might one day become a civil engineer. In fact, though they didn't know it, I was rearranging, in miniature, our street. I was in charge of every household in it.

Imagine a region of pebble-dashing and occasional bursts of mock-Tudor, of rowans, laburnums, trim hedges, trim lawns and clumps of purple aubrietia. You have the picture. I think of it now with an odd fondness, but with an abiding, far-off sense of its own weirdness.

One day, engaged in my flower-bed projects, I caught Mr Wilkinson watching me intently through the trellis and the tendrils of clematis. He must have been doing it for some time before I looked up, but, if I was surprised, I wasn't frightened. He wasn't spying on me (as we spied on him) so much as waiting to speak to me.

He asked me if I was interested in agriculture and if I was a vegetarian.

These were two long words I didn't know—I found them even difficult to remember—and I must have disappointed Mr Wilkinson with my answer. But he seemed eager that I should *be* a vegetarian. I told my parents (I was at heart a truthful, conscientious boy) and I must have repeated the words accurately enough. They said agriculture was farming and vegetarians were people who didn't eat meat.

Then my mother said, and my father backed her up, that I should never speak to Mr Wilkinson through the fence, or anywhere else, if I was by myself, even if he spoke to me. This had probably been the first conversation—or one-to-one encounter—I'd had with him anyway.

He stood around in his back garden in his underpants and he was a vegetarian. This settled the question of his being a weirdo. Every Sunday, without fail, the whole street smelt of roasting meat.

If the underpants and the vegetarianism didn't clinch it, there was the matter of the visitors. Mr Wilkinson didn't go out at regular times as people did who had jobs, but he had visitors. They came just now and then, not in a steady flow, and didn't stay for very long. They were all sorts, but it's true that among them were a number of what my mother called 'young girls'.

There was nothing intrinsically improper about this and, again, you had to keep watch on Mr Wilkinson's bungalow even to notice it. The simple explanation—that went with his teacherly demeanour—was that Mr Wilkinson gave some kind of lessons. He taught music perhaps. Given the chanting, perhaps he taught singing. But no one arrived, it's true, with a musical instrument and we never heard, though we heard the chanting, the muffled sounds from within the bungalow of a piano or a poorly sung scale.

He taught something anyway, for which people were prepared to come for an hour or so and pay him. I actually had the misplaced fantasy that I might go round to Mr Wilkinson's myself and be taught whatever it was he taught. Since the key to life was education. But I was glad I kept this thought from my parents.

The teaching theory never held much water, even if it was plausible and I wanted to subscribe to it. My mother—in overheard conversations with my father—kept coming back to the young girls, as if that in itself disproved it. But I could easily imagine Mr Wilkinson teaching young girls something. Elocution, deportment. I'd discovered that even very small girls at my primary school could be subjected by their parents to bouts of extra-curricular improvement. And if Mr Wilkinson had some dubious interest in young girls that was simply to do with their being young girls (and which I knew nothing of), why didn't he restrict his visitors to young girls only? But I never voiced this argument either.

The teaching theory was scotched anyway by what, it became known, Mr Wilkinson had himself disclosed about his occupation and livelihood. Some other neighbour, bolder or more prying than my parents, had pinned him down on the matter and been obligingly told that he practised his own form of 'alternative medicine'. It was something he'd evolved over the years through study and application. He advertised professionally and had many satisfied patients. He had even asked the inquisitive neighbour (I think it was Mrs Fox at number seven) if there was anything he might do for her.

My mother said, 'Alternative medicine?' Then said, 'What's that when it's at home?'—a favourite phrase of hers which I much later thought was particularly apt in this case. Then she added, 'In his underpants?'

These were remarks put to my father that, again, weren't for my ears, though I overheard them. My father said (and, thinking about it much later too, I thought it pretty near the mark), 'Alternative medicine? If you ask me, I think he might once have practised ordinary medicine. But now—if you see what I mean—he has no alternative.'

I retained those words because, though I didn't understand them, I could tell my father thought he'd said something clever. The cleverness had even taken him by surprise. And though I didn't know what the cleverness consisted of, I felt pleased for him because for a moment at least he seemed to possess the artful and inventive way with language that was characteristic of Mr Wilkinson.

I couldn't, myself, picture Mr Wilkinson as a doctor. My childhood experience of doctors was that they were gruff, chilly people who could do nasty things to you. I continued to see him as a teacher, an educator, and perhaps alternative medicine (if it wasn't just something bad-tasting in a bottle) was really a form of teaching. Perhaps Mr Wilkinson had some special wisdom to impart. He wasn't a weirdo at all. The visitors who turned up now and then to ring his doorbell were his followers.

One day I had another 'conversation' with Mr Wilkinson which proved to be rather more than a conversation. I did the thing I wasn't supposed to do, and I exceeded even that. It was in the school holidays. My father was at work, my mother was going to see her mother for the afternoon. I was to be dispatched, while she was gone, to play with my friend Roger West at number ten, and thus be under the watchful eye of Mrs West. But some minor crisis in the West household prevented this, and my mother, for whatever reason, couldn't suddenly disappoint my grandmother.

For perhaps the first time in my life I was told that I'd have to be alone in the house for a whole afternoon, though it wouldn't be so long really and I was old enough for it. But I was, strictly, to stay in the house or in the back garden and not to answer the door to anyone.

It was a warm summer's day, so I was happy to keep to the back garden, doing more reconstruction of 'my' section of the flower bed. I don't think Mr Wilkinson can have been aware of my exact situation, because of the question he asked me. But there he was again suddenly, peering through the clematis, and there was no one to witness that I was breaking my solemn oath not to speak to him.

He said, 'Excuse me, Jimmy. Does your mother—does Mrs Simmonds—have anything for clearing drains? I'm awfully sorry to trouble her, but I've a spot of bother with my one at the back here. Nothing drastic, but in this hot weather, you know . . .'

I could see that Mr Wilkinson was sporting a shirt collar. He wasn't just in his underpants.

I had the child's instinct not to say that my mother was out, the child's alertness to the possibility of adventure—at least to the possibility of getting to know Mr Wilkinson better. Not to mention the child's excitement at the forbidden. I didn't know about clearing drains, but I knew there was a cupboard in the kitchen where the sort of thing that might clear them would be.

I said to Mr Wilkinson, 'I'll go and ask her.'

Did I say truthful and conscientious?

In the cupboard there were various jars and bottles, but there was a big tall tin labelled 'Ajax'. I vaguely knew it had a variety of uses (my father sometimes used it for something in the garden) and that it was my mother's answer to anything unpleasant. There was another tin of the stuff in the lavatory upstairs. Drains? Why not?

I picked it up and decided that, instead of trying to pass it over the fence—impossible for a small boy anyway—I should take it round to Mr Wilkinson directly. It was only a matter of opening the side door, which fastened with just a latch, then walking up his front path. The truth was that I was impelled by a sly curiosity: I would be just like one of those mysterious visitors, of whom there might already have been one or two that morning.

Mr Wilkinson opened his door. He looked at me and smiled. He was wearing clothes. His strong arms projected from rolled-up sleeves. 'Oh that's good of you, Jimmy. And so kind of your mother.' He studied the Ajax tin, perhaps frowning a little even as he continued to smile. He could hardly reject my offering. 'Well, perhaps it might do the trick.'

He looked at me again, the frown deepening, and seemed to hesitate. I can see now that he was coming to a significant decision: whether to take the tin, say he'd return it later, and send me away, or whether, since I was there and it was our tin, to make me a party to his drain-clearing operation. Perhaps he thought I was just a small boy and there was no danger—that is, to him. Or perhaps he was just infected with the same impetuous rush towards the hazardous that had overcome me.

'Well,' he said, 'we may as well go straight round the side.'

This disappointed me. I wasn't going to be allowed to pass through the house. On the other hand, I could see (or could see later with hindsight) that he'd decided, wrongly, to trust me. If trust even came into it.

He liked me, I think. He thought he'd found a friend.

We walked along by the flank wall of the bungalow. There I was on the other side of the fence over which he'd peered at me and over which he could sometimes be seen standing near-naked and ululating.

He'd taken the tin from me and, raising it now like an exhibit or something in a lesson, he said, 'Isn't it a sad thing, Jimmy, that one of the great heroes of the Greek myths, one of the most glorious of those who fought in the Trojan War, should be reduced to being a tin of scouring powder?'

I hadn't the faintest idea what he was talking about, but these words made a great impression on me and have stayed with me ever since. I still hear them being spoken in the eloquent, playful yet lamenting way Mr Wilkinson uttered them.

The fact is that it is to this unintelligible but memorable remark I owe all my later discovery and enthralled exploration of the Greek myths. I owe a whole world of narrative and magic and meaning. I owe a whole education.

When my parents asked me later that year what I wanted for Christmas I said at once (having done some precocious research at my primary school) that I wanted a book that would tell me all the stories of the Greek myths, the Trojan War included. This request rather surprised my parents, but they found me such a book. It was a little beyond me at first, but I grew into it. I have it still.

But more than this. Much more. I owe to Mr Wilkinson's remark all my lasting fascination not just with how a great Greek hero gets turned into a tin of scouring powder, but with all the strange turns and twists and evolutions this world can take, all the bizarre changes of fortune, for good and bad, it can offer. And I should know about them.

I owe to it an education. And an education.

'When we say scouring powder, Jimmy, we really mean lavatory cleaner, don't we? No doubt at your age you have your lavatorial interests. Did you know, Jimmy, that in Elizabethan times a lavatory was called a jakes? A jakes. Ajax. Do you see the connection?'

Again, I hadn't the foggiest what he was on about, but I found it all beguiling, tantalising.

He took me round to the back of the bungalow where an outflow pipe from his kitchen led into a little gully with a drain hole and a grille. We had something similar beneath our own kitchen. I could see he was now hesitating again, that he wasn't sure he should be doing this in my company, but I could also sense his mood of wilful risk-taking, that he wanted to let me, even, into his secret. I could see that he'd removed the grille and had been poking about with a stick.

'Ajax,' he said. 'Will it—will he—do the trick?'

Whatever it was that was clogging his drain it was deep down, or else there was some uncooperative bend in the pipe. The hole was abnormally full, almost to overflowing, of dirty water. But it wasn't just water, it was water with a distinctly reddish colour. It made me think at once of the slop bucket that would be sometimes visible in our local butcher's, where I'd go with my mother and where there'd be sawdust on the floor and halves of pigs hanging on huge hooks and dripping.

A little bobbing shred of something, a mere gobbet of scum, floated in the water.

Let me say that everything was so much more primitive in those days, even if gentlemen doffed hats. It was so much nearer the Middle Ages. There'd been a war and there'd been rationing. My mother was perfectly capable of skinning and cooking a rabbit, but there came a point when she wouldn't have liked to admit to this, or even to eat rabbit. When my parents developed their desire for respectability and advancement they really wanted to move into the clean modern age and leave behind them all traces of the ancient gutter. They weren't squeamish and they weren't innocent, but they wanted to live tidy lives, and they didn't like weirdness.

I could see that in theory our street didn't mind Mr Wilkinson's being weird, but they minded his being weird in our street. They hoped that somehow something would be done about it. But, short of some superior agent's stepping in, they believed that by the sheer force of their adverse opinion Mr Wilkinson might be compelled to leave and take his weirdness elsewhere. They wanted him flushed out. In this situation was the whole history of the world.

I could see that the mucky water in Mr Wilkinson's drain was composed partly of blood and I could see that for some inscrutable and perilous reason Mr Wilkinson wanted me to see it, and not to say anything.

But, yes, I was at heart a conscientious, a truthful boy. I honoured my father and mother. I had a sense of moral responsibility. I'd told my parents about the vegetarianism when I might have said nothing. Now I'd have to tell them about breaking the edict that had followed from that first honesty and—worse—about taking the Ajax tin and going round to Mr Wilkinson's when I should have stayed within clearly prescribed bounds.

But all this was capped by the greater and more glaring obligation to truth I had: to let it be known that Mr Wilkinson clearly wasn't a vegetarian—a slander of my own unwitting instigation—and was even, though I hadn't been able to see into his kitchen, a fairly zealous eater of meat. And, by implication, he was at least in that respect so much less of the weirdo than he'd been unfairly made out to be.

I can never be sure whether it was this action on my part, with all its complexity and for which I was punished by not being allowed out, even into the garden, for most of the next day, which led directly to Mr Wilkinson's leaving us, which led to his being, as I was to discover later, taken into custody while a search warrant was issued and (discreetly) acted upon for his bungalow.

Having been so roundly punished, I was soon being, confusingly, asked questions by a kindly and patient policeman while my mother tenderly held my hand.

There were things you couldn't do in those days, the law didn't allow it, which you can do now. It was all very primitive, and perhaps the changes which have occurred since then are further evidence of the importance of education. For example, Mr Wilkinson lived alone, he might have been a homosexual, but he wouldn't have been allowed by law to be one in any practical sense.

I say this because I'm a homosexual myself, though I didn't know it then, I discovered it later. You might say I had to be educated into it. There's a whole other story I might tell, involving me and my parents, which is even more painful in some ways than the story of Mr Wilkinson. But this is not the time, and perhaps you can imagine it. There are plenty of stories, but this is not the time.

But I think about Mr Wilkinson and about what I did to him.

He disappeared anyway. It was what the whole street wanted, but I missed him, I even felt a little bereft. I wish I'd known his first name. A nice couple, the Fletchers, who soon had their first baby, a little girl called Jilly—I remember *her* name—whom my mother unashamedly adored, moved in. And that was what the whole street wanted too.

There are some people who might say or think of me, now, that I'm a little weird, or at least odd. But then if you're a professor of Greek you're allowed to be that, the world even rather expects it of you, especially if your hair has become a snowy fleece and you wear tweed suits and affect white-spotted red bow ties.

I have never, so far, walked across the court here to the senior common room—across the grass on which only a few are permitted to walk—in just my underpants. Or, for extra brio, with my Fellow's gown on too. But I'm sure if I did this (and frankly I'm tempted) it would be forgiven me, at least once, since I'm the Morley-Edwards Professor of Greek. And I'm sure that far more scandalous acts have occurred in Oxford colleges and yet been permitted, or at least smoothed over—acts that would never be countenanced in suburban streets.

All my life I've taken seriously—pursued and furthered—my parents' creed that education is the most important thing, education that leads us on an ameliorating journey through life. I am their exemplar, their vindication. What could better have answered and glorified their tenet than that I should have become a professor at an Oxford college?

If you want weirdness, real weirdness, the weirdness we're all made of, if you want the primitive that never goes away, then go to the Greek myths and to what the Greeks made out of them. Though don't forget your Ajax tin.

Ajax, son of Telamon and mighty warrior, second only to Achilles, but ousted by the brain of Odysseus, went mad in the end, mistaking sheep for people. I know this now.

Was She the Only One?

Was she the only one? Was it all her fault?

Was she the only one not to wash her husband's shirt? It hung in the wardrobe with all its creases and wrinkles, his best white shirt, his Sunday shirt, the last shirt he'd worn before putting on a uniform. She took it down and pressed it to her nose. When the letters arrived she crushed it to her face and, as she read, breathed deeply. It was the best that could be done. Was she the only one?

In those days a man's white shirt was quite an item, with its long tails, double cuffs, its round neck with the stud holes. It was more like a sort of starchy nightdress, and it served her as such often enough. So the wrinkles multiplied, so there was her smell mingling with his. But that was only right. They were husband and wife. It became a superstition. If she didn't wash it, so long as she didn't wash it. Not until. Was she the only one?

Months went by. The letters came less frequently. She had to be sparing in her use of the shirt, or her smell would take away his. It was getting rather ripe, it's true. His first leave was cancelled. He couldn't say why. It was a blow that made her weep, but it wasn't like a message to say he was dead. And she hadn't washed the shirt.

This was her short marriage to Albert. Most of it was separation, most of it wasn't a marriage at all, most of it was marriage to a shirt. He was a railway clerk from Slough, but he had his notions. One day he'd be a station master. He was fussy about his shirts. He only liked to be called Albert, never Bert.

She was Lily Hobbs from Staines. She was eighteen and didn't mind: either Lily or Lil.

I'm Bert, Bert, I haven't a shirt . . .

Months went by. Then he came home. Because his previous leave had been cancelled he now had two weeks. Was it true, two whole weeks? And he was untouched—not a scratch, or so he wrote. Was it true? Was he being brave? Still she didn't wash the shirt. Seeing was believing. She'd heard stories of telegrams arriving before men due home on leave. She had two choices anyway: to wash it, specially, for his arrival, or not to wash it—until. She chose the latter. Her big mistake.

If she'd washed the shirt, would everything have been all right?

I'm Bert . . .

*

166

But there he was on the doorstep. So, it had been just as well. There he was. Or there he wasn't. Albert Tanner. He said, 'Hello, Lily. Can I come in?' Which was just like him, but not. She rather wished he'd said 'Lil'. She rather wished he'd clapped a hand quickly to her behind, but he hadn't.

He'd never mentioned the shell shock. That was news to her. Did it explain everything, and what was it anyway? Shell shock. Had he invented it? He said that he had it, like something catching, like measles. Was that why he hardly touched her? He said it was why he had the two weeks. He said he'd have to report every other day to a doctor, an MO, in London, who'd assess him to see if he was fit to return. Which was like saying—was he saying this?—that his two weeks, depending, might go on indefinitely.

In which case, God bless shell shock. In which case, Albert, be as shell-shocked as you can.

Was it all lies? Was he preparing for his desertion? Did he really have two weeks? There was something about him, standing there in his uniform. He didn't look like a soldier, or even a railway clerk. He looked like a crafty door-to-door salesman. He looked like the sort of man women left at home had to watch out for. He looked up to no good. He looked—was this really the word?—like a criminal. Albert? A criminal?

Then he saw the shirt.

He wanted to know, he *demanded* to know why it was hanging there like that, his best white shirt, 'in that filthy condition'. And before she could explain to him the several reasons (but couldn't he guess?) he was explaining to her, he was shouting in her face that the reason why it was hanging there in that filthy condition was that she'd lent it to another man, she'd been letting another man wear it. And to prove the point he thrust his nostrils into the fabric, pushing it to his face, then let out a disgusted 'Pah!'

None of this had she imagined. None of this in her wildest anticipations had she allowed for. He wouldn't be untouched, he'd have a bit missing. An ear or something.

I'm Bert, Bert, I haven't a . . .

Now that this was happening the sheer absurdity of it couldn't smother her terror. Was he going to hit her? Albert? Hit her? For a moment she actually looked at the shirt and saw it, perhaps as he was seeing it, like some other man skulking there in the wardrobe, just as they were supposed to do in naughty stage plays.

She knew she had to stand her ground, keep steady, be reasonable. Yes, of course, of course: over there (but she'd never thought of this before) it would be the constant talk, what their women got up to back home. They'd tease and torture each other with it, they'd tease and torture themselves.

It was June, 1918. No one knew the war had only five months to run. If he hadn't been a railway clerk but a railwayman—a signalman say—he might have been permanently excused, but he'd joined up anyway.

Yes, of course. She was eighteen. She walked down streets on her own, her skirt swung. But.

'It's your smell, Albert, no one but yours.'

Which was a lie, a half-lie, because the smell by then was mostly hers. But she could explain that, and wouldn't the explanation, surely, please him? Wouldn't it even be the clearest sign—it seemed ridiculous to have to grope for a word—of her loyalty?

But she never did explain. She saw his rage boil over. Was he really going to hit her?

'Wash it!' he said. 'Wash it, right now!'

He'd barely got home. It was like an order, a bellowed military order. 'Wash it!' He was a corporal now, with a stripe on his shoulder. He'd gone away a private and come back a corporal. What had he done to become a corporal so quickly? She didn't like the word corporal, she liked the word private. He'd gone away Albert too.

'Wash it!'

She couldn't disobey. He would have struck her. She washed it while he stood over her and watched her wash it. She put it through the mangle. Then later she ironed it while he stood over her too and watched her. She hadn't imagined this. But she foolishly supposed that when this task was finished all might be restored. This was her punishment—her penalty, her humiliation—all thoroughly undeserved, but so be it, she would undergo it, if it would bring Albert back again. Perhaps, when the shirt was fully laundered, he'd break down, see the obvious truth, beg her forgiveness.

But it was she who had to face the less obvious truth that, yes, she really was washing away another man's smell, and that other man was Albert.

'There's your shirt, Albert. All clean. Now, wear it. Please. Wear it for me.'

She foolishly imagined, only extending her delusions, that once he wore it, that would do the trick. It would mean, of course, having to remove his uniform. He didn't seem to want to remove it, it was like his skin. It would mean having to have a good scrub in the tub. And among her many anticipations had been seeing herself assist him in doing just that.

What she really meant by 'wear your shirt' was make love. She didn't have the way to say it directly, but might he not see that it was what she meant? Might he not see that 'wear your shirt for me, Albert' actually meant don't wear it—yet. She would have gladly washed it for him anyway, having explained to him first those reasons—as if they were needed—and having, first of all . . .

If she could only get round now to saying that she'd gone to bed with it, she'd worn it in bed—wasn't it obvious?—then wouldn't the other thing follow? And she didn't really mind, now, how it was done—gently, roughly, fumblingly, slowly, all too rushed and quickly. So long as.

But he stared at the clean shirt she held out to him and all that happened (though it was something) was that his anger seemed to leave him, even turn for a while into something like its opposite, into complete bewilderment, even panic, as if she were offering him something terrible. A white shirt, he was staring at a white shirt.

'Please, Albert.' What could she do that wasn't wrong?

If he were to wear it, if they were to be to each other like man and wife. It was all ifs. It took nearly a week before he wore the shirt. As for the other thing, as for her own desires, she understood that what Duncan, her second husband, would one day call her 'appetites' had not only been thwarted, but neutralised, chilled.

How could she do it with Albert if Albert wasn't Albert?

'You have appetites, Lily.' So Duncan had said, barely a fortnight before the Armistice. She couldn't tell if he was confused or impressed. For all his fine words, he was just a boy, like Albert.

It took nearly a week before he wore the shirt, including the days when he had to report to the MO. If that's what he did. Need it have taken so much time? Had he invented the MO just so, when he'd hardly got home, he could disappear every other day? How absurd, how humiliating—and somehow just as agonising—having waited for him all those months, to have to wait for him now to come home on a train from Paddington. Or wherever. Would he come home at all?

'Hello, Albert.'

'Hello, Lily. Can I come in?'

What was happening? He'd be in his uniform again, for the MO presumably. She had the first flicker of the thought that she wanted him back where he'd come from. Not Paddington, or wherever. Where he'd come from. Did he see it in her face?

'I want you to wear your shirt, Albert.'

She didn't give up. She had a plan. If he'd made her do what she'd done, then she'd make him do this, if it was the last thing she'd ask of him.

'Listen, Albert, listen. I want you to wear your shirt. I want you to wear your shirt and to go with me this Sunday to Marlow. The weather will be fine. I want you to take me out on a boat on the river. Remember?'

To her surprise (she was ready for more coaxing) he said, 'All right, Lil.'

'Lil'. Was it something the MO had said?

He wore the shirt. He submitted. He became so woodenly docile that this, too, alarmed her. It was tit for tat, it was his punishment? But it was hardly that, an outing on the river. He was preparing to say he was sorry? I'm sorry, Lil, I'm so sorry for everything—his eyes, Albert's pale brown eyes, trying to express the measure of what he was sorry for.

Or it was nothing of the sort, and he knew better? Yes, if she wanted, yes, if it meant so much to her. Yes, he'd fit into this foolish picture of hers. At least he didn't explode and say: So this is what she'd done all this while, gone to Marlow, on the river, with other men.

They went to Marlow. They took the train. They changed at Maidenhead. She didn't know if he still kept in his head the timetables he'd once so diligently kept there. Cookham, Bourne End . . . She didn't know any more what he had in his head. He was wearing the shirt. She was wearing her long narrow skirt and carrying the little parasol that had once been her grandmother's.

When one day she was a grandmother herself she'd find it impossible to explain to her teenage granddaughters, who wore next to nothing, that she'd once thought it the height of *sexiness* (though the word hadn't existed) to loll back in a creaking boat, water lapping at its undersides, in a long white skirt, twirling a parasol, while a man—but the man was Albert—removed his jacket, rolled up his white sleeves and rowed you rhythmically upriver.

As impossible as to explain to them about Albert anyway, though that was her firm decision. Just the name and that he'd died in the war—the first one that is. She'd had this other husband once, before Grandpa Duncan. But what should they care? He hadn't been their grandfather. Even her own daughters, Joyce and Margaret: he hadn't been their father. No logic in saying that he might have been.

'Albert,' she would say, with a fragile smile. 'He never liked to be called Bert.'

They took a boat. The water sparkled. Willows and swans. But she saw at once (if she didn't know already), from the put-upon way he shoved off from the little jetty, that this journey by river was going nowhere, certainly not back into the past. He took it out on the oars, whatever it was he had in his head. He worked it out on the oars. She could loll and twiddle her parasol as much as she liked.

When they returned to the jetty she suddenly pictured Channel steamers, packed with reeking men. She hadn't thought of it: a train, a boat. What could she do that wasn't wrong? It was as if this brief Sunday excursion was like the whole brief non-event of his leave. An hour, two weeks, what was the difference? He wanted to go back. She saw this. Did he see her tears? He wanted to go back and be really dead.

His leave was actually truncated. Was it all his invention again, the invention of an invention? The doctor had said now, apparently, that his shell shock was all an act, he should snap out of it and return. But which was the act? He said, in a flat voice more appalling than rage, that there was nothing he could do about it. He'd been 'found out'. Found out?

I'm Bert, Bert . . .

And—this was the worst part—she was actually glad. Had it shown in her face, like that other flicker? Would it have mattered? They were both glad.

And there was another level to her gladness. His too? She was glad—no chance of it in those last few days—that they'd never conceived a child.

'Goodbye then, Lily. I'll be seeing you.'

'Goodbye, Albert.'

There was only the shirt again, hanging in the wardrobe, smelling now of a sweat worked up on the River Thames. But it wasn't Albert's sweat. It had no magic. It was a general dreadful now commonly manufactured sweat and, yes, it was like an infectious disease, it was like the measles, she seemed to feel it spreading from the wardrobe all through the house. She couldn't stand the thing hanging there like that. On the other hand, she wasn't going to wash it. Not now.

It took a week, a week of contending with the shirt. It was like a miniature war. Then she could bear it no longer. She lit a fire—in June—and flung it on. She knew what she was doing. She didn't thrust it into the kitchen stove. She wanted to watch it burn.

It was the 25th of June. Two days later she got the telegram. '25th June. Of wounds.' But it came as no surprise.

So she was a widow now. Was she the only one?

Three months later she met Duncan. Duncan Ross. Of all places, it was on Slough station. The train was late. They exchanged shy words. Then he actually paid for her to travel first class, as if it was his sudden flustered duty. He had to, you see, in his uniform. They sat together to Reading, where he had to change for Aldershot, and where she was going for an interview, as a maid.

He was in intelligence, which meant he couldn't talk about it. So, how did she know? She didn't say that, of course. She looked at him, at his brown moustache, perfectly demurely. She didn't say, 'So, it was a bit like shell shock then.'

And her own private joke to herself—something else she'd never say—was that he was in intelligence, but the intelligence was all hers. In intelligence, and based at home. Neither of them knew the war had just two months left. An officer, a newly made lieutenant, an educated child. And clearly—but never mind that, she'd cope with that—above her station.

But my people are well off, you know . . .

Dear Duncan. In thirty years' time they'd have lived through another war and he'd have been safely in intelligence again—rising to major. And they'd have had Joyce and Margaret, their darling girls, who not only lived through that war too, but cut a fine swathe through it, having a high old time. Girls! You could have said this was part of her intelligence too. Though she could hardly have insisted on it from Duncan. Only girls, please. But perhaps because she wanted it so much, it was what she got. Duncan obliged. And girls for grandchildren too.

It was agreed, on the platform at Reading, that they'd meet again. Going for the interview, she'd thought, was a little like Albert going to see the MO. Duncan and Lily . . . It had a ring, like the name of a superior grocer's. They managed in due course to scrape a whole day together, in Maidenhead, by the river. It was meeting halfway.

Maidenhead! Well, it was where her new life began, her second one, her real one.

'You have appetites, Lily.'

But she'd never tell even Duncan, who had the good sense—the intelligence—not to probe for details. Not even the date. Often there wasn't any date. Often there wasn't anything.

The 25th of June: she'd have to live through it every year.

Just the bare facts: she'd been married before, then widowed. She wasn't the only one. It had all taken less than a year. His name was Albert. Just the little extra morsel, the gently smiling decoy: 'Always Albert. He never liked to be called Bert.'

KNIFE

HE STOOD BY the opened kitchen drawer. It was a warm April afternoon. He'd come home from school meaning to take the knife at some point before the following morning and hadn't thought that his best chance might be straight away. The clock on the microwave said 4.25. His mother was in her bedroom with her boyfriend Wes. He could hear them, they were loud enough. Boyfriend wasn't really the right word, but it was a word that would do. Either they hadn't heard him and didn't know he was there, or they'd heard him and didn't care. By the sink were the scattered cartons they'd been eating from. They'd been eating KFCs and fries with ketchup, just like kids who'd come home from school themselves.

They could do it without making a noise, possibly. But he

understood that the noises went with doing it. He'd been in this situation before, of having to be around and just listen, but not in the situation of taking the knife.

The brothers had told him that he should get a knife. He knew what they were saying. If you want to move on to the next stage, if you want to stay with us. So he'd thought at once of the kitchen drawer. It was the easiest way, the simplest way. 'Here is a knife.' He wasn't going to say that it was really his mum's knife. It didn't matter, it was a knife.

But perhaps it did matter. Perhaps it mattered very much that it was his mum's knife.

The noises from the other room only made it easier to take it. They were almost like a permission. So why should he hesitate? Why shouldn't he just go ahead? He understood that at this moment, though he was only twelve, he had about as much power in the world as he would ever have. He understood it almost painfully now. At twelve you could not be held responsible, even if you were. To everything you could say: So? So what are you going to do about it? And at twelve you were still small enough not to be picked on. People would think twice.

The brothers knew this. That's why it was worth their while to take on twelve-year-olds, to string them along and train them up, like dogs. But then there'd come the moment when they'd say, 'Do you really want to be one of us?'

He knew—he knew it especially now—that this place wasn't his home. If he belonged anywhere now it was with the brothers. Only with them could he have any respect. If you had nothing else, then you had to have respect.

His mother might have said to Wes, 'No, not now. Danny

will be back from school any second.' But then just caved in and not cared.

He'd meant to take the knife—it wasn't even stealing, to take a knife from your own kitchen drawer—but he hadn't thought he'd be pushed into doing it as soon as he got home. And he hadn't thought of all the other thoughts that would rush into his head—almost, so it seemed, into his hand—just before he did so. What it means to hold a knife, in a certain way, in your hand.

At twelve years old he knew he was fearless, or just about. He knew he could look anyone, or almost anyone, in the eyes and they'd give in first. So? So what are you going to do? The brothers perhaps recognised this quality in him.

So: a knife in your hand ought to make you even more fearless. But if you could be fearless without it, why have it? This was the real point. At twelve years old he understood that his fearlessness, rapidly acquired, might soon be over. He would not have the untouchability of being twelve.

He'd been in this same situation before—without the issue of the knife. In a little while Wes would emerge, perhaps buckling his belt. Wes had a belt with a big shiny buckle, part of which was shaped like a skull. But he wasn't afraid of Wes. Wes wasn't his enemy, he wasn't his friend, and he'd just want to clear off anyway, but first they'd have to look at each other. Each time they'd done this before Wes had lost. At twelve years old he was good at looking, even looking at people like Wes who were more than twice his size and twice his age. There'd be a point when Wes's eyes would flicker, as if to say, 'So what are you looking at?' Once Wes had actually said that. Now he didn't say anything. There'd be just the flicker, then he'd clear off.

Wes was afraid of him. He was twelve, but Wes was afraid of him. Wes had a skull on the buckle of his belt and shoulders that bulged through his T-shirt, but Wes was afraid of him.

And now when Wes emerged he could go a step further. What was a knife for? He might not only look at Wes, but as he did so he might be holding a knife, pointing a knife. He'd never thought about this till moments ago. He'd never thought about it as he was coming home from school. Then there'd be an even bigger flicker in Wes's eyes, not just a flicker, and he'd clear off even more quickly. And not come back.

Or he could go a step further still. This thought made his hand sweat. He could take the knife and just go into the other room and stick it in Wes's back. Wes's back might very probably be turned and bare. This is what a knife enabled you to do. The thought made him freeze.

Wes wasn't his enemy. In some deep-down way he didn't even mind his mum having Wes. He was something she needed. Maybe she got money from Wes. In any case she got something she needed. He didn't even mind them being at it right now like animals and making their noises, even as he was standing here in the kitchen. It was just how it was. He understood very clearly now that it might also have been just how it was with his father, twelve years and more ago. So if he stabbed Wes it would be like stabbing his father. Which might have been the best and the right thing to do. Except he wasn't around then to do it. If he'd stabbed his father then he'd never have been around at all. Which didn't make any sense.

His father's name was Winston. That was all he knew. Winston. Wes. Maybe his mother had invented the name Winston. She had to have a name, at least, to give him. His father had cleared off twelve years ago. Just like Wes would. And had never come back.

Outside, there were noises too, the noises of kids playing. Just kids playing, kids younger than him, cackling and screeching. Both the noises inside and the noises outside were like the sounds of animals.

Wes would emerge and look, and flicker, and clear off. Then there'd be quite a long gap, and then his mother would emerge. Then they'd look at each other too. It would be like him and Wes, but his mother would always win. When she emerged she'd have a deliberately lazy way about her, which he hated, as if she wasn't going to hurry for anyone, and once when they'd looked at each other she'd thrown up her chin and said, 'So what are you looking at?' The very same words Wes had used once and failed. But his mother would always win. She was the only one who could.

And she was the only one he was really afraid of. In all the world. He was afraid of her even now. Once, his mother had needed to come and collect him from the police station. At twelve years old, or less, you could laugh at the police. He wasn't afraid of the police. But when his mother had come to the police station she'd spoken to them all very obediently and softly, as if she were a child herself.

Then on the way home she'd changed, she'd kept trying to say things, but she couldn't, her mouth had seemed not to know how to work. Then when they'd got home her mouth had tried again, but not worked either, and then she'd beaten him—hard, with the full swing of her arm and the full whack of her hand. It was an attack. It hurt. But he'd known she was only hitting him because she was incapable of finding the right words, she might as well have been hitting herself. She was hitting him because in some way *she* was afraid. He understood this. And yet he was afraid of her. His own mum.

Even now he was afraid of her.

Fear was a strange thing. Even right now, with these noises that were like a permission, he was afraid of the simplest thing. To take a knife from a drawer.

His mother might not even notice it was missing. Since when had she taken stock of what there was in the kitchen drawer? And even if his mother were to say later, 'Where's my knife? Where's that knife?' he might simply say he didn't know, and shrug. It wasn't his knife. Or he'd say it must have got chucked in the waste bin by mistake. Plenty of things did, including once one of her big orange bangles. Or he could say that it was another of the things Wes must have walked off with.

He could simply say that. 'Wes took it.'

And if it really came to it, if his mother looked at him, not saying anything, but with a look that said, 'You took it, didn't you, Daniel?' then he could look back at her with a look that said, 'Well? So? So? What did you ever do to prevent me? What did you ever do to stop me going down this road? What did you ever do that was so right and good that you could tell me that taking a knife from a drawer was wrong?'

But he wondered if he could actually do that—and win.

It was the easiest thing. What was the simplest way of getting a knife? But he knew it wasn't simple, since he knew there was the question: Why did it have to be her knife? Why did he *want* it to be her knife? He knew this wasn't so much a question now as a question that would come later. A question that might even be his excuse. And even now it seemed he could hear people, people in the future, asking him the question.

Because . . . But couldn't they see? Wasn't it obvious? Because if it was her knife then anything he did with it—if he did anything—would have to have been done too by her. And if they didn't see it (who were these people?) *she* would.

Because . . . Because she could talk about *her* father. She could talk about him and she could even talk about *his* father, her father's father. And when you got back to him, to his mother's grandfather—he even knew that *his* name was Daniel—then you were talking about someone who'd stepped off the boat. You were talking about fucking Bridgetown, Barbados. She had all that, she belonged to all that, and if she didn't know what to do with it then that was her problem.

He belonged with the brothers.

It was a line, she had a sort of line. But he didn't have it or want it, no fucking thanks. And everyone knows what you can do with a line. Everyone knows that when you're born there's this cord, but it doesn't stay there for long.

Where is the knife, Daniel? What did you do with the knife? (Who was saying this to him?) What did you do with the knife?

Where is my knife, Daniel?

It was only something she'd have bought in a shop once. In Hanif's Handy Store. A cheap kitchen knife. He couldn't remember when he'd last seen her use it for what it was meant for. Slicing a piece of chicken.

He heard the kids outside and the thought came to him that one day he'd remember this moment, he'd remember it very clearly and precisely as if he were twelve years old all over again. Standing here like this, hand over the drawer, not yet holding the knife. The smeared cartons. The kids outside. In his white school shirt with his tie insolently knotted so that just a few striped inches of it dangled from his neck.

He heard the noise his mother would start to make when things were getting near their finish. It was a rough gasping repetition of a single word, so rough and gasping you could hardly make out it was a word. It was like when she couldn't find the words before she beat him. But it was a word, and it wasn't a word that said don't.

He put in his hand and took out the knife. It was the simplest, easiest, most ordinary thing, to take a knife from a drawer.

MRS KAMINSKI

'MRS KAMINSKI?'

'That's me, dear.'

'I'm Dr Somerfield. I need to take some blood.'

'Take as much as you like. It's no good to me.'

'We need to do some tests. Are you feeling more comfortable?'

'You should work in an English hospital, dear, a nice girl like you. The National Health Service, it's the best in the world.'

'This is an English hospital. It's St George's, Tooting.'

'It's the way to Poland.'

'Are you Polish, Mrs Kaminski?'

'No, but I'm on my way to Poland.'

'I need to ask you a few questions. Do you know how old you are?'

'Ninety-one.'

'Date of birth?'

'March the 4th, 1923.'

'And your first name?'

'Nora.'

'Can I call you Nora?'

'Please yourself. How old are you, dear?'

'Twenty-five. Do you know where you were born, Nora?'

'Carshalton, Surrey.'

'Do you know what month it is?'

'Why?'

'You had an accident. A funny turn. A fall, in the street. You were brought here. We're trying to find out what caused it all. Do you know where you live?'

'Flat four, Romsey Court, Neville Gardens, Mitcham.'

'You just said you were on the way to Poland.'

'That's right. Haven't you noticed all the Polish people? They do the plumbing, the cleaning, the central heating. They mow the lawns. They do it all for us.'

'Do you live alone there, at the address you just gave me?'

'I don't live there any more, do I?'

'Do you have a husband, Nora?'

'Yes.'

'Where is he?'

'He went to Poland.'

'When did he go there?'

'1944.'

'1944?'

'June the 18th, 1944.'

'That's a long time ago. You said you were going there too.'

'That's right. I'll soon be seeing him, won't I? I just have to find him. Or he'll have to find me. Perhaps you can help us, dear.'

'Do you have any sons or daughters, Nora? Brothers, sisters?'

'Relatives, you mean?'

'Yes, relatives.'

'I have a son. Ted.'

'Where does he live?'

'He went to Poland. He'll be with his father. He'll be there too.'

'We should let your son know that you're here.'

'Of course you should. And his father. They'll both want to know I'm here. You should go and find them for me, dear.'

'I mean we should let your son know that you're here, in hospital, that you've had a funny turn. If he's your next of kin.'

'Kinski. People sometimes just called us the Kinskis. He went to Poland. 1964.'

'You mean he's really living in Poland?'

'He got a job as a boilerman. In a hospital. He had to keep the boilers going that kept the hospital warm. They gave him a boiler suit.'

'This is a hospital, Mrs Kinski. Sorry, Kaminski.'

'It's the way to Poland.'

'You're confused. You've had a nasty turn.'

'He hung himself in the boiler room. He hung himself by the legs of his boiler suit. He went to Poland. He went to join his father.'

'I'm getting confused, Mrs Kaminski.'

'You said I was confused, dear.'

'What did your husband do?'

'He was a pilot. He went to Poland. 1944.'

'He flew there?'

'He flew into the English Channel. Haven't you heard of all the Polish pilots? There were lots of them. They came over here. They shot down Germans for us.'

'So your husband was from Poland.'

'Lodz.'

'Lots?'

'The white cliffs.'

'The white cliffs?'

'The white cliffs of Dover. The English Channel. They never found him. Little Teddy was born after. He never knew his dad. But he'll know him now, he'll have known him for a long time. They'll be getting ready to see me. You must tell them where I am. It's been such a long time. It will be so lovely.'

'I'll take that blood now. It won't hurt. I'll just dab your arm.'

'Pour it down the sink, dear, when you've finished. Down the sinkski.'

'What was your husband's name?'

'Ted. He was Teddy too. I had to call little Teddy by his dad's name, didn't I? But his real name was Tadeusz. It's a Polish name.'

'Tadeusz.'

'Tadeusz. Ted's easier. Ted Kaminski. My two Teds, they'll be here somewhere. Do you speak Polish?'

'So you have no relatives, Nora? No living relatives we can inform?'

'We'll all be together. If you just run along and find them for me, when you've finished with that blood.'

'We have to do some tests.'

'He flew into the drinkski.'

'Mrs Kaminski—'

'It was a flying bomb, dear. It wasn't the Battle of Britain. He got through all that. Do you remember the Battle of Britain?'

'I'm twenty-five. I wasn't born.'

'Nor was little Teddy. You'd like little Teddy. I can see it, you and him. But I was the lucky one, I had his father. Not for long. Tadeusz Kaminski. He flew into the Channel. I married a Pole. I didn't mind at all. The Germans invaded Poland. And we'll all be in Poland soon, we'll all be together.'

'This is England, Mrs Kaminski. It's Tooting.'

'A flying bomb. He shot it down. He blew it up, then he flew into the sea. That's what they told me. But it doesn't matter now. We'll all be together.'

'Nora—'

'They were coming over by the hundreds, nasty buzzy buzz bombs. It was worse than the Blitz. Nothing you could do, except not be under one. Fifty, a hundred people gone in a flash. If they landed on a school. Or a hospital.'

'Mrs Kaminski—'

'Just think about it, dear, just thinkski. If one of them dropped right now on this hospital. I know it's a hospital. You must have a boiler room somewhere. But I'm not here for long, I'm on my way to Poland. Just imagine. If one of them drops we'll all be gone. You, me, doctors, nurses, all gone in a flash.'

Dog

His father had once said to him, 'Money doesn't buy you happiness, Adrian, but it helps you to be miserable in comfort.'

He'd wondered ever since at this equivocal utterance. Was his father saying that his own life had been miserable? Or that life itself, as a working premise, was miserable? These possibilities were suddenly dreadful.

All he'd done—though it had taken courage—was ask for more pocket money. He wished he'd never opened his mouth. Perhaps his father, who was rich and not given to utterances, had felt the same.

His father had died long ago anyway, and he'd heeded the recommendation—if recommendation it had been. He'd made money himself, lots of it. He'd made it when it was possible to make lots of it and he was one of those clever or lucky ones who'd got out before losing it, and put it where it could keep working.

Now here he was featherbedded with the stuff. Which was just as well, with an ugly divorce and an estranged family to pay for. Though all that, too, was now some time ago and all the bills had been settled. So, had his father's words been only wise? And what counsel—the same?—had he given his own children? Hugh, Simon, Rebecca. He couldn't remember giving them any counsel at all. He couldn't remember them ever seeking it. They were all grown-up now.

He pushed the buggy which contained his daughter Lucy, though he was old enough, easily, to be her grandfather, listening to her wordless burblings and knowing that he loved her wholly, that right now he loved her more than anything in the world. She shouldn't really be there, she shouldn't be there at all. He already had, he'd already raised, a family. He shouldn't be pushing a helpless infant still years from articulate speech on a journey to the park. Yet he was, and he loved her completely and loved her burblings as if there were a string running directly from his heart to hers. He loved her as he couldn't, in all honesty, remember quite loving his other, now adult children.

Whenever his new young wife Julia urged him to take Lucy for a buggy ride to the park so that she, Julia, could have some respite, he tended to feign reluctance or even resentment, for the simple reason that he didn't want Julia to know that he really loved doing it. Nor did he want her to know that, though Lucy could sometimes be impossible at home, she instantly became utterly sweet-tempered once she felt him pushing her along.

He loved being alone with Lucy perhaps more than he loved being alone with Julia, though Julia, even after a difficult first pregnancy, was a beautiful slender woman with light brown hair, some twenty years his junior. Why, after all, had he fallen for her, then married her? But he knew (he wasn't stupid) that the question was rather: Why had she inveigled him, seduced him into marrying her? Because she'd wanted a Lucy of course. A Lucy plus security.

And now look.

There was something particularly entrancing, he couldn't say why, about this physical act of steering Lucy in her buggy, about having his hands on the handles and feeling through them the bumps and swerves that she felt through her whole body. These rides seemed to induce in her such a simple infallible delight, she became a kind of living cargo of happiness, and he could sometimes find himself, quite unselfconsciously, echoing out loud her burblings, as if infected (at last, at fifty-six!) with mindless *joie de vivre*.

His father had spoken those disenchanted words. But these babblings! And of course he didn't tell Julia that, while she put her feet up, he was only too keen to push Lucy to the park yet again.

Lucy, of course, had no control. She had no power of decision, and she had no control literally. She relied on him entirely to steer her. The fact that she did so with such delirious trust made his own steps light, and right now he loved her absolutely because her helpless burblings matched, though entirely benignly, the fact that he'd lost all control of his life and that she was the product of that loss of control.

*

It was a mild day in late February. Spring was in the air. A few innocuous white clouds hung in the sky. Crocuses were poking through by the entrance to the park.

When had he lost control? He hadn't lost control of the business of making money, he'd been a dab hand at that. He hadn't even lost control of the money itself, though he'd handed over large chunks of it. But when had he lost control of himself, of his life, of who he was?

When he was twenty-eight, say, he'd felt pretty much in control. At least he'd felt a good notch surer of himself than when he'd been eighteen or twenty-one—when all doors are supposed to open. He'd even say now—now he was exactly twice twenty-eight—that twenty-eight was actually the age he was inside. He was a twenty-eight-year-old in heavy disguise.

But by the time he was thirty-eight, or certainly forty-five, the sense he'd once had long ago as a little kid—long before that bleak interview with his father—that life and growing up could only ever be about gaining more and more control, a steady upward graph, had deserted him. It wasn't that he was losing control in some ways but gaining it in others, he was seriously and centrally losing control, and he knew it. And he knew that very probably this loss of control would only increase and accelerate for the rest of his life, he'd crossed some sort of dire threshold, till one day he'd be approaching his death in a state of utter and terrifying loss of control, never having—to put it mildly—put his affairs in order.

When he understood this he did what most people do. He ignored it. He had another drink. Was putting your affairs in order the purpose of life anyway? Affairs! A poor joke of a word. It was his affairs, having them, that had got him into this mess.

Once, when he was twenty-eight—or was it thirty-five?—he'd thought that having affairs and their rather thrilling disorder was actually the stuff of life, if not maybe its purpose. He was, he'd have to confess, quite good at it.

Did anyone put their affairs (other sense) in order? People said, didn't they—people not like his father—that you should seize life, grasp it while it was there? Which sounded like taking control, big-time. But it also sounded exactly like what he did when he toppled—dived—into another affair. It was taking control, but it was also like going full-tilt for the complete opposite.

By his forties he'd started to do something he'd never done before. He looked at people. That is, he studied them and wondered about them, as if he might be the other side of a glass wall. Did they look out of control, did they look as if they all secretly felt like him? No. The amazing thing was that they didn't. They looked as if they were pretty much holding it together, as if they were moving along paths they felt they should be moving along. How did they manage it?

He'd never had this feeling of a glass wall before, he'd never felt he was an observer, not a doer. Though what he'd been doing, perhaps for some time now, had been losing control.

And now here he was pushing a buggy along a park path—an act of control and calm purpose if ever there was—with a child in the buggy astonishingly remote from him in years yet to whom he felt closer than anything else in the world.

It was a Sunday morning. The sun, with a real warmth to it, seemed to be seeing off the clouds and the park was doing good business. There were other people pushing buggies, like him, either towards or back from the little mecca of the play area, with its brightly coloured attractions, that had opened recently and been an instant success. On Sunday mornings it could heave. It was hard to tell if adults or small children dominated. There were buggy-parking issues. There were multiple-child buggies. You understood at once one of the principal local activities: it was to breed and to do so with a certain public self-congratulation.

But there were also joggers, in Lycra, with headsets. There were people with dogs. There were also people—they were professionals—with lots of dogs, whole packs of them, because their owners were too busy, even on a Sunday, or too lazy to walk them, so they paid someone. Money, the things it could do. Even some of the buggy-pushers would be hired live-in nannies, speaking foreign languages. Nannies! He'd had a thing once—he'd lost control—with a nanny, called Consuelo. It hadn't lasted long, not long enough even to call it an affair. Now, spotting the nannies, and even though Julia wasn't around to catch him looking, he wasn't even tempted.

There were about as many dogs as buggies. And—setting aside the nannies—not a few of the buggy-pushers and dog-walkers had a similar appearance. They were men, otherwise unaccompanied. They weren't young. They were often rather chubby, jowly or flushed of face and their hair was receding, if they weren't in fact bald. If they'd had looks once, they'd lost them. Yet for all this, they didn't appear out of control. Far from it. They were in charge of a buggy or a dog after all. Some of them even had a pretty lordly air and issued, to the dogs, bellowing commands.

In other words (though he refused to acknowledge this

196

outright) they looked like him. And sometimes, in the case of the buggy-pushers, the age of the child or even children they were pushing told the whole story. It was a bit like his story.

But he was pushing Lucy. No one else was pushing Lucy. In a little while he'd unstrap her from the buggy and place her with a father's tender care—a quite experienced father's care—on one of the contraptions in the play area. She wasn't old enough to be more than placed briefly in this way, but the mere contact with the colourful apparatus seemed enough for her. It gave the buggy ride its goal, but he felt that for her as well as for him it was the ride itself that was really the thing.

All the time she was out of the buggy and just perched on one of the bits of equipment his hands would hover close to her, his whole body would want to shield her, as much from the roughness of other children and the intrusions of other parents as from any other form of harm. He'd keep guard of her and would think while he did so, as he would at other times of such close vigilance, of what would become of her in later life, of how her life would be when he was gone, of the possibility, which was not at all unreal, of his being gone before she was a woman with whom he might have a grown-up conversation. He'd feel a punishing stab. But he had her burblings.

They approached the play area. But the whole park, with its tree-lined paths and expanses of grass, its peeping bulbs and its joggers, dog-walkers and buggies, was like a play area, and on this smiling Sunday morning was the very image of communal well-being. It was the serener broader version of the kids' place, without the latter's tendency (he could see that this morning it was thickly patronised) to teeter into stressful frenzy. In truth, he didn't greatly like the play area, but Lucy wasn't able to say to him, understandingly and exoneratingly, 'It's okay, we don't really have to go there.'

The dog came from nowhere. If it was one of the many dogs he'd been loosely holding in his view, it still seemed that it hurled itself from a different place, as if through some unperceived screen, and there it suddenly and loudly was. And it was one of those breeds of dog that weren't supposed to be let off leads, or even to be owned by people, or even, possibly, to exist at all. But there it was, and it was mauling—no, it was attacking—a child strapped in another buggy on the edge of the play area. Another little girl of less than two, with pale blonde curls, only yards away. With a father and mother who appeared to be momentarily paralysed.

It seemed that he too was suddenly on the scene, like the dog—that to others looking on it would seem that he too had sprung without warning from nowhere. It seemed so even to himself. Who was this man? He was suddenly grasping, grappling with a vicious snarling dog (whatever its behaviour had been just seconds ago), a dog that, but for his action and the sturdiness of modern buggy accoutrements, might have had in its mouth, in its claws, a helpless defenceless child.

The little girl was screaming and the dog must have been making a terrible row. People all around must have been yelling, but he didn't hear them or care, and he didn't even care, for some reason, if this dog was about to savage his own flesh or claw out an eye. He was *going to stop it.*

For a moment it writhed in his weird embrace, he felt the

uncontainable spasm of its muscles—yes, it was going to bite his face off—but he wrenched it somehow from the buggy, then, as it shot from his clutches, it lost its balance and he was able to kick it, kick it *hard*, in the ribs, in the head, in its skidding legs, he didn't care. He'd won the battle, he knew, it had been a matter of seconds. Were people cheering? But he kicked it, and kicked it again.

He knew too, even as he did this, that the outcome of this episode would be that the dog would be put down. A dog that attacks a child. No arguments. It was what would happen. He could already picture the child's father—galvanised now into action—speaking righteously into a mobile phone, gathering a circle of witnesses round him. This is what would happen. And he would be a principal witness, and in some people's eyes a hero. And the dog would be put down. Professionally.

But he kicked it as if to save them the trouble. He kicked it even when it was beaten. He didn't care about its owner, who must be somewhere. The owner of a dog like this wouldn't, or couldn't, entrust it to a dog-walker, and the owner of a dog like this would only own it in order to feel a vicarious power. Yes, that was why people had dogs (he'd never had one), in order to have the illusion of mastery and control.

It was all split-second stuff, but he kicked it more than once, enough for him to imagine that when people later discussed his daring action they might add, 'But did you see the way he kicked it?' Enough for him to think (and this was perhaps what made him stop): What would Lucy think, of her father furiously kicking a dog? Would she grow up with this whole scene indelibly imprinted on her? Her first and enduringly scarring memory of her daddy.

But of course it was for *her* that he'd done it, it was because the child in the buggy might so easily have been—

Lucy in fact, he realised, was bawling, screaming. Some well-meaning bystander was seeking to comfort her. Other buggy-bound infants were also in a state of howling terror, or else of white-faced shock, at what had happened to another of their kind, and thus at what could happen—it was plainly possible—to them. Lucy wasn't concerned with the gallant actions of her father, she was concerned with her own appalling vulnerability, and she was particularly concerned with the fact that her father had taken his hands off the buggy, thus abandoning her to such horror.

He quickly went to her, to place his hands back on the handles, and almost at once, as if some electric current of safety and assurance, or of something deeper, had passed between them, she was calm again, she was almost her untroubled self again.

'It's okay, Lucy, everything's okay. I'm here.'

In a matter of moments she even began a subdued, speculative version of her customary burbling, as if this encounter with a dog, from which her father had come off visibly discomposed (he realised he was shaking a bit), was already moving out of her mental compass. She seemed, in mere seconds, almost to have forgotten it—never mind bearing the image of it for the rest of her life. Her father, wrestling with a dog! This rapid shift both relieved him and disappointed him.

'It's okay. Everything's okay.'

They had to hang around for some time while the matter was dealt with—while a parks policeman (so parks policemen had a purpose) arrived and notes were taken and calls made, and while he tried not to listen to comments being uttered about him. 'He was amazing ... Just think what might have happened, if he hadn't ... Just think what might have happened—you know—to that little kid ...'

He could have done without it all. He had never in all his fifty-six years heard himself being called amazing, but he could have done without it. All the while he kept his hands very tightly on the buggy handles, except when he stooped to pat and stroke Lucy's head. His place was with Lucy. He wasn't even interested, now, in the poor child he'd rescued—had he been told its name?—whose life he'd quite possibly saved. That wasn't so far-fetched. It wasn't every day that you, possibly, saved a child's life.

He wasn't interested in the sudden paean he was getting—distress turning to relief and almost hysterical gratitude—from the child's mother. 'How can we ever thank you enough? How can we ever repay you?' That sort of thing. He actually wanted to say, 'Control yourself, woman.' He said, 'It was nothing.' He wasn't interested in his own patent prowess. He'd moved like lightning. Younger men around him—twenty-eight-year-olds!—had stood rooted to the spot. He didn't have any of these feelings.

And he wasn't interested in the dog, least of all. He knew it was done for.

He wanted to get away. He wanted just to be pushing Lucy again. There was no question now of spending any time with her in the play area, where all activity seemed suspended anyway. He knew that she wouldn't feel let down by this. It was the buggy ride that mattered.

Eventually, with anxious looks at his watch, he excused himself and edged away. He had his own child to look after—

clearly. Her mother would be wondering. No one seemed surprised that he said 'child' not 'grandchild'. It wasn't a rare phenomenon. And anyway he'd just behaved with the speed and agility, not to say sheer ferocity, of someone half his age.

He pushed Lucy back the way they'd come, alone with her again and totally in love with her, listening to her burblings resume their joyful commentary. It was as if nothing had happened. He very much wanted it to be as if nothing had happened. He envied his daughter's eclipsing amnesia. He didn't want to tell Julia about any of this. He looked at his watch again. Allowing for the time they might otherwise have spent at the play area, they wouldn't be unduly late back, so he need say nothing.

But of course word about the incident, in which he'd played such a central and dramatic role, was bound to get around to Julia, and pretty quickly, through the local grapevine. And there was the simple obvious fact that he himself bore the immediate evidence of something. Though his hands were firmly guiding the buggy he knew he was still shaking, he was shaking in fact quite a lot. He needed to grip the handles to stop it. There was a big streak of mud down one of his trouser legs, there was a tear at one knee, and if his face and hands seemed, remarkably, to have come away unscathed, his jacket was in several places snagged if not actually torn. That was all right. You could replace clothes, with some money. He hadn't wanted any money from that child's mother, though she'd offered it, she'd offered to replace his entire wardrobe. She was blonde and totally at his service. It seemed that she might offer him anything.

You could replace a jacket. But the claw marks themselves—yes they were actually claw marks—and his general appearance of having been in some fight, of being a bit of a walking catastrophe, he hadn't the slightest idea how he was going to explain away these things to Julia.

FUSILLI

HE PUSHED THE trolley round the end of the aisle, ignoring the stacks of boxed mince pies.

It would be Christmas Day in just over two weeks' time, but he and Jenny had already agreed, without really talking about it, to abolish Christmas. They couldn't go through with it. The calendar would be different this year. Remembrance Day had come and gone, but it would be Remembrance Day on Christmas Day. Even that was going to be terrible.

On Remembrance Day itself they'd adopted, without ever talking about it either, a sort of double position, both to mark it and to ignore it, they couldn't work out which way their superstition should go. But he remembered now—how could he forget?—coming here about a month ago. It was just days before Remembrance Day. The clocks had gone back, it was dark outside. He remembered pushing the trolley then.

How he wished it was still then.

There'd been little boxes of poppies, with plastic jars for coins, by the entrance. He'd wondered whether to buy one. Yet another one. Whether to tip in all his change. But the bigger thing, already, was Christmas. Christmas stuff, Christmas offers. It was Christmas before it was even Remembrance Day. A sudden wave of anger had hit him. It had been Halloween less than a fortnight before. The shops had been full of pumpkins and skeletons.

No one saw his anger, it stayed inside. He wasn't even sure if it was anger exactly. He'd pushed the trolley in the normal way, his list stuck in one hand, his mobile in his top pocket in case of problems.

'Shop patrol to base. No fresh ginger, Jen. What do you reckon?'

That sort of problem.

He did the weekly supermarket run—his duty, or his regular volunteering—and for several months now not a time had passed when he didn't think: And what are Doug's little problems right now? His tricky two-for-one choices?

He'd never forget how his mobile had rung—right here in the rice and pasta aisle—and it had been Doug. In Afghanistan, in Helmand. That sort of thing was possible now.

He was talking to Doug. And Doug had phoned *him*. So he couldn't say, 'I'll get your mum.' (Why did he always say that anyway?) Doug had phoned *his* number.

Shit—was it something bad? Was it something he should know first?

'I'm in Waitrose, Doug. By the pasta. Doug! Doug! How's it going?'

What a stupid way of putting it: 'How's it going?'

But Doug had wanted to know all about his shopping list. He'd seemed tickled by the picture of his father pushing a trolley, holding his list, dithering by the shelves. And while Doug was so keen on the situation in Waitrose, he hadn't wanted to ask his son about the situation in Afghanistan. His anger, if that's what it was, had dropped away.

'You should stick with dried, Dad. Fresh is a scam.' Doug had said this in Helmand. 'Try the fusilli for a change. The little curly ones.'

A November evening, days before Remembrance Day. But Christmas was coming apparently. Doug had called from Helmand.

He couldn't think about it now. He couldn't not think about it. He could hardly enter Waitrose again. It was almost impossible to go now—though he had to—to the spot, in the aisle, where it had happened. Where he'd spoken to Doug and looked around at all the others with their trolleys and baskets and thought: They don't know, they don't know I'm talking to my boy in Afghanistan.

He and Jenny would never eat fusilli again, that was for sure, they'd never eat those things again.

And had it been anger, just before Doug called? Anger was sometimes supposed to be a substitute for fear, so they said. Or grief. Had that surge of anger, or whatever it was, been some sort of advance warning? If he hadn't had it, if he hadn't got angry, then would nothing have happened? But then if he hadn't had it, would Doug have called, just then?

Everything, now, was a matter of mocking superstition.

But Christmas before Remembrance Day! And now it was almost really Christmas. The aisles were crammed and glistening with it. He couldn't bear it. The only good thing was not to think. The only good thing was to ignore, ignore. But he couldn't.

He pushed the trolley. He couldn't even bear to think of Jenny. Maybe she took the opportunity while he did these supermarket trips just to sit with her head in her hands, tears trickling between her fingers.

He couldn't bear to think of calling her to ask, like he used to, about the rice. 'What sort, Jen? Regular? Basmati?' Such things. It couldn't be done, it just couldn't be done any more. Their little foodie fads, their fancy cooking. Their being nice to themselves and splashing out—Waitrose not Tesco's—now the lad had left home.

Puy lentils, Thai green sauce. That sort of shit.

He couldn't bear to think about how thinking about Jenny only half a mile away was the same as thinking about Doug three thousand miles away. He wasn't here, he was there, but you could talk, just the same, on the phone. Now the simple words 'here' and 'there' confused him utterly. Doug wasn't here, but he wasn't there. He wasn't *there* at all.

Or—and this is where it got really terrible—Doug *was* there. Doug was in a mortuary in Swindon, pending a coroner's decision. They couldn't have Doug yet. It was pretty clear now that they couldn't have Doug before Christmas, maybe even for some time after Christmas. All they wanted for Christmas was Doug. But Doug would be spending Christmas in a mortuary in Swindon. And anyway Christmas wouldn't happen this year.

'Christmas is coming.' He remembered when he was a kid how the words had excited him almost more than the word Christmas itself, the idea that it was on its way. At Christmas, or when it was coming, you made lists, you dropped hints. He wanted to remember now—but at the same time didn't want to remember—every present they'd ever bought Doug for Christmas, every one.

Had they ever bought him any kind of toy gun? If they had, then it could have been another of those signals, those things that become real. So they must have done. If only they hadn't. Or if only Doug had been a girl. If so he'd have been called Natalie and the list of presents would have been different.

He tried to think, while trying not to think, of all the presents. But it wasn't so hard to remember being the man, in years gone by, in the days when Christmas was coming, looking for a gift to give his son. Not to remember being that man was the harder thing.

Fifteen, twenty years ago. Wars on TV. But there were soldiers to do all that stuff, and he'd never thought it was wrong or unmanly of him to be traipsing round Mothercare with Jenny and Doug—'Dougie in his buggy'—while there were wars going on. He felt it was the right thing to be doing. And it had never occurred to either of them that one day Doug would get it into his head . . .

'Stick with dried, Dad.'

Why had he been so interested in pasta? Was that what they got out there? Dried stuff. Not stuff in tins. Pasta, all the varieties. Had it been a soldier's advice?

Before him suddenly was one of those floundering young mums with a loaded trolley, two small kids swinging from the sides, using it as a jumping-off point for marauding charges up and down the aisle.

Nothing, once, on these shopping trips used to get his goat more than these bawling little bastards, these kids their mums or dads seemed unable to restrain, Doug never having been a noisy, out-of-control child. He'd been proud of that. He'd been proud of his soldier-son too. But now these screaming brats in front of him simply made him stand stock-still. They were kids. There was their mother. They were, all of them, both there and here. The kids were only doing what kids do. He looked at the mother's strained, about-to-burst face. He thought: She doesn't know how lucky she is. He wanted to look hard at her, to catch her eye, so she would see something in his.

But beyond her was the pasta section. He couldn't go there. He had to go there. They were out of pasta, he'd checked. They weren't interested in food any more, but they had to eat. They were out of even basics now: pasta, rice. Fuck mince pies.

He'd told Jenny, of course, about the phone call, of course he had. Should he have kept it a secret? It was why they'd eaten the things, that same evening—with a tomato, garlic and basil sauce. A bottle of Sicilian red. They'd been Doug's 'choice'. They'd never eat the fucking things again.

He had to go there, yet he couldn't. And now anyway this losing-her-grip mother was blocking his path. She was stand-ing exactly where—

Everything was like this now: a reason for, a reason against. He was suddenly furious with this useless hopeless mum. Was it anger? What was it exactly? He understood how violence gets done. He pushed his trolley forward, in a no-swerving, no-yielding way, as if to smash into her trolley. Did she catch his eye? Did she see something in it? She was probably thinking: Bastard of a man. She moved in any case, she got out of his damn way, so did the screaming brats. And he was suddenly there, on the spot where he'd spoken to Doug.

His mobile had rung. He'd thought: What now? What had Jenny forgotten to ask him to get? It was the last time he'd heard Doug's voice. It would have been the middle of the night in Helmand.

He saw them, in their little clear-plastic bags, alongside the lasagne and the tagliatelle. He even knew what the word meant now. Had Doug known? He picked up a packet. He knew that it wasn't for them to eat. It wasn't even for Jenny to see, to know. He had to do it. He held the scrunchy packet. He'd put it separately somewhere, he'd hide it. He grabbed a big pack of spaghetti and tossed it into his trolley anyway.

'Fresh is a scam, Dad. The dried lasts for ever.'

He clasped the fusilli close to his chest. They'd never get eaten. He'd put them somewhere, God knows where. Under the seat in the car.

Christmas wouldn't happen this year. No presents, no lists. But this was his gift for Doug, or it was Doug's gift to him. He didn't know. Everything was this and that. The woman had gone. He'd somehow even cleared the aisle. He felt the pieces of pasta beneath the shiny plastic like the knobbly, guessed-at things inside a Christmas stocking long ago. The little curly things.

I Live Alone

THERE WAS A moment, as Dr Grant spoke, when he didn't see Grant's face at all. He saw Anne's face, streaming with salt water. He saw her wet arm held out to him, as if she herself had delivered this news. It made it strangely bearable.

It didn't otherwise help to know that he was the victim of a rare disease, with some foreigner's name—as if the rarity, so Grant seemed to be suggesting, was some kind of compensation. He didn't feel privileged to have been introduced, in this intimate way, to this Dubrowski or Bronowski or whoever he was—as if he too might have held out a hand across Grant's desk. He saw his wife's hand. Anne's hand, Anne's face.

He saw, but in a different way and more vividly than ever, what he'd never failed to see every day for ten years.

He stopped listening to what Grant was saying. There was only so much you could take in after the announcement of such a basic fact. He was trying to take that in—along with his vision of Anne. He was trying to take in the fact that his life was no longer the indefinite thing of which he'd always been the subject, it was a closed thing, a finite thing, an object.

And he suddenly remembered himself, distinctly, at primary school, aged perhaps ten, holding a cricket ball. It had been a matter of some debate—he remembered this—whether small boys should be allowed to use proper hard cricket balls. But this was the school team, it was serious grown-up stuff, and they were playing St Michael's. Astonishingly, he remembered even that. He saw himself in the outfield on the off side, picking up a cricket ball struck in his direction. He saw the dry summer grass beneath him, the flattened dandelions. He saw the ball he'd grabbed, its scuffed red surface, felt its solidity.

His life was now like a cricket ball.

But he saw himself, too, fling back his arm and hurl this same ball, with inspired force, not just towards the wicket keeper, but directly towards the stumps. Saw it shatter the stumps long before the running batsman—or batsboy—even with bat outstretched, could gain the crease. Saw the wicket keeper lift his gloved hands in jubilation. Saw everyone lift their hands.

It was a spectacular throw, perhaps thirty yards, and perhaps his only moment of sporting glory. And the strange thing was that he'd *known* it wouldn't miss. He hadn't thought about it in decades, but he saw it now, in Grant's consulting room, as clearly, as triumphantly as yesterday. He saw the ball, with its dense red weight, briefly clutched in his hand.

*

After leaving his office he'd taken the bus across the city and by the time he'd entered the now familiar private hospital and sat in the waiting room he'd set out in his mind three possible outcomes for this visit and given them each a percentage. One was that Grant would say the latest tests had revealed nothing of further importance and, though they should keep it under review and meet again in, say, a couple of months, there was really nothing to worry about. Thirty per cent. Second, Grant might say there was now a clear diagnosis, but the problem, though significant, could be treated. Sixty per cent. Third, Grant would say that unfortunately the diagnosis was that he had a rare incurable fatal disease. Ten per cent.

He'd considered these options to be fairly weighted, if anything rather tilted against him, and he'd believed in them like a superstition. Of course he'd hoped for option one, if not exactly for an 'all clear'. Though he was technically prepared for it, he hadn't believed in option three, but to have left it out would have been tempting fate.

Yet he'd known from Grant's face, even before Grant began properly to speak, that option three was actually the one.

There'd come to him the absurdly calming notion that since Grant was a doctor and he was a lawyer a certain professional comportment should be maintained. The roles might be reversed. As a lawyer he'd often had to give clients grave disquieting news or maintain a quasi-clinical detachment while they exhibited signs of distress. He couldn't complain if it was now the other way round. He should handle himself properly. He should look Grant in the face. He did.

But he saw Anne, he saw her arm. And seeing Anne was really the thing that saved him, not his professional decorum.

This was what kept (these very words came to him) his head above water and made it look to Grant perhaps that he was taking it rather well, he was taking it like a man.

He told himself: I deserve this, I'd even wanted it. This too was the other way round. Ten per cent.

So then.

Then the notion of his life as some small separate finite object, like a cricket ball, had rushed towards him.

He told himself (he actually had the sense of standing outside himself to do so): And anyway it's hardly unfair. I'm fifty-nine. Many will live to a much riper age. But many, many—though, above all, Anne—have died long before.

And with that supremely balanced thought there'd entered his head—no, it seemed that they *themselves* had entered Grant's room—the actual roster of all those he'd known but who'd died before him. They appeared with remarkable clarity and in remarkably organised reverse order, taking him all the way back to the very first of their kind he'd known.

Yes, he remembered now. It popped up from some submerged place as if it had only been waiting for this moment. The very first had been little Howard Clarke. Now he remembered even the name—and remembered the other thing too. Howard Clarke had been the wicket keeper, his small hands encased in monstrous gloves, the wicket keeper whose skill had not been needed when he'd made that legendary throw. The wicket keeper who'd raised his exultant arms.

The point being that Howard Clarke, aged ten yet already marked out as a wicket keeper, had gone off as they all had for the summer holiday, but had never returned. It had been somehow conveyed to them, early in September, that he was never going to return. A brain tumour, someone said, whatever that was. A brain tumour, perhaps as dense and undeniable as a cricket ball, inside his head.

Grant continued to speak, but he didn't listen or couldn't focus. It was enough—surely enough since it was everything—to have to take in the main thing. He'd already asked the question that he'd never thought he'd hear himself ask, the question people only asked in films. And Grant had answered, though through a sort of fog. Had he said six months or eighteen, or that it could be anywhere between the two? Grant was now speaking of what might be done to 'maximise his quality of life' (had he heard that phrase?). But he wasn't really listening. Oddly, given the crucial nature of it all, he wasn't concentrating.

Again, he knew this sort of thing from the other side. How many times, after telling clients some urgent sobering fact, had he watched their faces glaze over as he went on to explain the repercussions? They were still digesting the main thing. But what could you do except carry on? It was your professional obligation.

But mainly he couldn't concentrate on Grant because of the way Grant was crowded out, in his small room, by these others, by these ranks of dead ones, or of living memories, going back as far as Howard Clarke. They were far more important than Grant. Grant was being replaced by them—he'd even for a moment turned into Anne—so that his voice seemed to become increasingly feeble. It even seemed—but was this another confusion with Anne?—that Grant was the floundering and struggling one, the one in difficulties, and he felt a great gush of pity, mixed with something like wise seniority, for this man placed in the awful position of having to make the announcement he'd just made.

Grant, he supposed, when he wasn't being a physician, was a family man with a wife, and children perhaps now in their teens. He would go back to all that this evening. Which meant that he belonged, unquestionably, to the freely living, to those whose lives were not closed and finite. Whereas he, now, was of the other sort, the minority. He was not now of the same kind as Grant, though he had been moments ago, before entering his consulting room.

Yet he'd always been—or had been for the last ten years and those ten years had become a sort of 'always'—a man of a different kind of minority. Of a kind who'd sometimes say, by way of giving a general, guarded account of himself, 'I live alone.'

Had he said it at some point to Grant?

It had become his watchword. He said it to clients, particularly clients he was guiding through the troublesome process of divorce, and he could say it with a judicious ironical tone, even a crinkly smile. So they could never tell what he really meant. An expression of sad fact? Or of proud resolution? An explanation, or a recommendation?

Grant, he thought, was speaking, in his flailing voice, with the strange loquacity of the living, with the gabble with which one might speak about all the detailed necessary arrangements for a wedding while somehow forgetting the main thing, that two people were about to commit themselves to each other for life.

Except this wasn't a wedding.

Yet he saw himself clearly for a moment (no longer a small boy on a cricket field) at his own wedding, nearly thirty years ago, and all the other people at it, several of whom were now dead and thus among this muster here in Grant's room. It had been a thronged lavish wedding because Anne came from a large and wealthy family, while he was just a suburban boy who'd landed on his feet. West Ealing to Winchester. The Sixties song had lodged in his brain. *Win-chester Cathedral . . .* Would they have to get married, he'd joked, in Winchester Cathedral?

How strange to have had such a packed wedding when he was now a man who said, 'I live alone.'

And he remembered how before the wedding he'd gone with Anne down to the jetty at Lymington with two bottles of champagne clanking in a bag. And they'd rowed out to where the *Marinella* was anchored. It was theirs now. It had been in Anne's family for years, but it was officially theirs now, a wedding present, though the sort that can't be wrapped or hidden. And before they climbed aboard—to drink the second bottle and make ceremonial waterborne love in the cabin—Anne had smashed the first bottle, with a fine flourish of her arm, against the bows, saying, 'I name this yacht the *Marinella*, the yacht of our marriage. May God bless all those who navigate and copulate in her.'

He'd never thought he could become (with Anne's instruction) a sailor. That, with Anne, he could sail the *Marinella* to Jersey, Guernsey, Brittany, Portugal. He was a provincial lawyer, a decent fish in a smallish pond, whose only act of physical prowess had been that amazing throw at primary school, Howard Clarke's leathered hands raised high.

'I live alone.' Fewer and fewer people now knew, or remembered, why he said this. One of them was Janice, the receptionist, the veteran uncomplaining Janice, right now guarding his office.

Why had Janice, who was not dead, sprung suddenly into his mind?

Because, he realised, she'd almost certainly be the first person, not counting Grant himself (who was still wittering on), he'd have to confront after having received this news.

And then ... and then he'd have to confront Mrs Roberts, whom he'd never met. Mrs Roberts: 5.15. Mrs Roberts who was on the brink of that troublesome process, or precipice, known as divorce.

Why was he thinking of his office—in Grant's 'office'? 'Eliot and Holloway'. He pictured it for a moment like some distant light seen in a dark forest. Why was he thinking of Mrs Roberts whom he'd never met? But he knew now. He knew now why he'd kept his 5.15 appointment, despite Janice's puzzled and concerned gaze. 'Why don't you get me to move it?' she'd almost said. He'd read her thought: Why, if your appointment's at four, don't you just take the afternoon off? A fair question. But he'd insisted. 'I'll keep my 5.15.'

'I live alone.' Would he say it to Mrs Roberts? And in the same cryptically smiling way as ever?

I live alone. Did that fact, too, save him, come to his rescue now?

Grant was gabbling on, so it seemed, like a man put on the spot. And he was listening to him, hearing him out, like some silent patient judge. It came to him that what Grant was saying might be a fabrication, a ruse. He knew it wasn't. Little Howard Clarke had proved it. Nonetheless, the idea was somehow to be seized. There also came to him, in this meeting of two professional men bound by rules of confidentiality, the phrase he sometimes used, with a certain solemnity, in his own profession: 'Nothing need go beyond this room.'

He saw the cubicle of a room he was in like some locked vault in a bank. It was a very important room—it was the room in which he'd learnt the most important fact of his life—but nothing need go beyond it.

Except himself. He saw that it was vital that in a moment he should get up and leave and in passing through the door, crossing the waiting room, signing out at the desk, then exiting through the glass doors be absolutely no different (though he absolutely was) from the man who'd walked in.

And he *was* no different. How could he be different, even to himself? He was the same creature, with the same legs beneath him, the same mobile, thinking, breathing vessel that contained all he was.

He did get up. It wasn't difficult. He didn't totter. It was 4.25. He may have shaken Grant's hand. He may have shaken Grant's hand in a way he'd never shaken anyone's hand before. He may have looked him in the eye and nodded obligingly in response to some further reassurance on his part about 'what should happen next'.

But what should happen next was that he should put one foot in front of the other. That was the most important thing. One foot in front of the other. He walked, feeling the extraordinary exactness of his steps, to the desk in the waiting room. The nurse smiled at him. She couldn't possibly know. It was an ordinary smile. But the fact that she'd smiled so simply must mean that his own face looked ordinary. So—Janice was not, quite, the first and he'd proved that the thing could be done.

There was a name tag over the nurse's left breast: 'Gina'. He noted this fact and the smooth skin of her throat.

When the glass doors slid open and he emerged into the cold and darkening air of a November afternoon it was a sort of shock, but also a kind of cancelling continuity, to know the world was still there.

He began at once to walk, buttoning his coat: across the forecourt, through the main entrance, turning left onto the pavement. One foot in front of the other. He knew this was the walk of his life. He knew he could have picked up one of the taxis that dropped incoming patients by the glass doors, or just got the bus. He'd got the bus on the way and now he knew why. The company of other, living people. But now he knew he must walk.

Across the city, beyond the cathedral, to his office. There was time. He knew he must walk, to prove he was healthy and alive and able to place one foot in front of the other. And to give himself time, while his legs worked beneath him, to cement and seal up inside him the great secret he'd just learnt. If the secret could be successfully hidden from all but himself (and Grant) then it would be as though the secret—even perhaps to himself—might not be real.

Win-chester Cathedral . . .

He walked. It would take half an hour, perhaps a little more. He wouldn't disappoint Mrs Roberts.

Dry leaves scurried along the pavement like small alarmed animals. The lights of passing traffic glared. He couldn't drive any more, of course, because of his mysterious blackouts, and he'd supposed it was a temporary prohibition. Now he knew it wasn't. So he should sell the car perhaps. But what did it matter now to sell it or not? Six months? Eighteen months? Scores of practical considerations and decisions, as if he were being a good solicitor to himself, suddenly rose before him, then scattered meaninglessly away like the leaves at his feet.

He'd sold the *Marinella* quickly enough. That hadn't been a protracted decision. It had come with the force of a gale behind it, if not like the gale—but it had been more than a gale, it was a mad murderous whirlwind brewed up by a gale—that had smashed through the sea around them that afternoon, ten miles off the Needles, and picked up the *Marinella* like a toy boat and tossed it over. And tossed them out of it.

Hours later, close to freezing and like a drowned rat, he was winched up on the end of a wire, clutching a man in a helmet who'd said, 'Hold me, hold me,' like a lover.

This was something also that he'd never seen himself doing, or having done to him, in his life.

But Anne was never winched up. The last he'd seen of Anne alive, as a huge wave lifted her then took her sweeping away, was her face and outstretched arm—as he'd seen it in Grant's office, as he'd seen it countless times. Hold me, hold me. But she'd been too far away for holding, even reaching. Then she was gone.

He'd sold the boat, after the salvage team had brought it in and the damage was repaired and paid for. He'd never stepped in it again, would never sail again. He'd been a sailor once, to his surprise, a lawyer and weekend sailor, a solicitor and occasional marine adventurer, but he'd never be those things again, except the solicitor, and he'd never know again the joy of being married to Anne and of riding with her, in the boat of their marriage, the high, astonishing seas.

'I live alone.' Some who heard him say it understood. After all, the thing had been in the papers.

And now he'd never even drive a car again. Though, in any case, now he must walk. Now he must feel beneath him his own motor efficiently propelling him forward.

And so he did. He crossed the city, here and there taking short cuts he knew through back streets, away from traffic, so that he could even hear the rasp of his breath and steady scuff of his footsteps. Even now, there was the feeling like a patent disproof: look, there's nothing wrong with you.

Win-chester Cathedral . . .

He seemed to be walking back into all the previous bodies—which were only this same body—that had once been his. His younger stronger imperishable bodies. So that at one point the legs beneath him even seemed to be—he could feel them there again—the little stick-like but superbly alive legs he'd had when he'd once hurled a cricket ball and had, soon afterwards, resolved that Howard Clarke, who had similar stick-like, immortal legs and who'd so spontaneously applauded his spectacular throw, should become—perhaps when they all returned after the summer—his friend.

And as he walked he couldn't help noticing, within this body, this fifty-nine-year-old motor that was himself, the central pulsing component that kept now thumping out its rhythm as never before. He could feel it, hear it. Surely others must hear it. How was it possible that he'd carried this same beating thing inside him all this time, since he was a boy with stick legs? How was it possible that it had kept up its persistent and so often unappreciated beat all this time, as if it would never stop?

He reached his office. It was now completely dark and the lit-up windows and railed frontage—a fine Georgian centre-terrace converted, like others in the row, into offices—struck him, as it sometimes did but now more than ever, like a stage set, like a doll's house. 'Eliot and Holloway'. He seemed to see, through the windows, the swallow-tailed and crinolined folk who'd once inhabited it.

Janice knew, of course. Janice knew what 'I live alone' meant. Janice had been there when . . . Janice had watched and known ever since. And Janice had been there some nine months ago when he'd had that first extraordinary, and extraordinarily embarrassing, blackout in his office. She was there beside him—he'd never seen her knees so closely—with a glass of water, looking down at him on the office carpet as he came to. She'd called an ambulance. Janice was there, and he'd recognised her face, among the others (Alan Holloway looking a bit white) pressing round and looking down, before he'd even recognised who he was himself.

That's Janice. What on earth is she doing? And then he'd seen rapidly disappearing from Janice's face, but not so rapidly that he couldn't notice it, her horrified conviction that he was dead.

Janice looked up at him now as he walked in. He knew that how he looked back at her and how he spoke to her was of the utmost importance. Even so, he wondered if she could see— surely Janice must see—through his gaze and his words.

'Nothing new, Janice, don't even ask.'

Did he sound sufficiently disgruntled?

'Same as last time. More tests. Honestly, I sometimes wonder if they know what they're doing.'

When Janice kept looking he said, 'I walked. I walked all the way back. Did me more good than going there.'

He eyed his watch. Ten past five. He took off his coat. Alan had closed shop for the day, so it seemed. Good. Well, Alan would be ruling the roost before long. He peered into the open door of his own office as if into a room that some other person had left.

'So, Janice, we have . . . er . . . Mrs Roberts.'

As if Mrs Roberts hadn't become his unexpected lifeline.

Even as he spoke a figure in a black coat and red scarf entered where he'd just entered, a woman of forty or so, not unattractive, but etched by an anxiety she was clearly trying to hide.

Was it so difficult then, to wear a disguise?

'Mrs Roberts?' he said and, when she said yes, held out a hand and smiled. 'David Eliot.' How strange his own name sounded. 'And this is our receptionist, Janice. You've caught me on the hop. I've just returned from an appointment of my own.' She only blinked at this. 'So then—'

And now he extended an ushering arm, in exactly the same way, he realised, as Grant had done at his consulting-room door, just as all professional people habitually do.

He'd quickly made his assessment: Well, she's not one of the hard-bitten ones, out to grab all she can. She's one of the ones (he seemed to see this more clearly than he'd ever done) who thought this sort of thing could never happen to her, not to her—that her marriage, her life was all soundly, safely in its place. She's putting up a good front of businesslike poise, but really she's lost, she's all at sea. She's looking out over a gulf which was never meant for her and which she has no idea how to cross.

They sat down. He made some lawyer's small talk. He looked at her, at the notes he had. Then he leant back patiently and attentively in his chair.

'Now, in your own words, in your own time, tell me all about it.'

Articles of War

He had the wretchedest of coach journeys, a grey relentless drizzle shrouding everything, clogging the roads when they should have been at their firmest and denying him any farewell visions of apple-hung orchards or golden stooks. Harvest time and every field sodden. And all the while the familiar desolation claiming him, like some awful return to school.

They changed horses late in Totnes, and night had fallen when they arrived. It had been falling all day. So, he would have to wait now till dawn. It was always some small relief when you first saw the ships. He saw a distant twinkle of lanterns, through the gloom, out on the Sound.

So, he must wait. And then no doubt—he must wait. It was his experience that you sped upon their lordships' bidding only to languish indefinitely pending further orders. His chest was taken into the Bell. He had intended making some better arrangement for his shore quarters only to fall back on the known devil. It was convenient. It was convenient to say, 'I am at the Bell.' He had no money for grandeur.

He was shown to his chamber. He knew it—or one like it. He had been confined here before, as had God knows how many others like him. It was strange that it felt so immediately incarcerating when it was bigger by far than any pitching cabin.

He took off his hat and cloak and at once felt chilly. He inspected the supply of candles. There was a meagre fire that appeared to have been unwillingly lit. It was only just September after all. September, 1805. In August, three weeks ago, he had passed his twenty-fifth birthday. So—he would not have to note it solely to himself at sea. Was it noteworthy?

He removed his gloves. He resisted an attack of the ancient urge to chew his fingertips. He pissed into the chamber pot. It was too early to sup, and if he supped—then what? He would sit by this skulking fire with this cheerless companion who was himself. He would commence the melancholy business of writing letters—letters as if written on the eve of sailing, though the eve of sailing might be three weeks hence.

If he made himself visible and if he were lucky (or unlucky) some other soul in blue and gold might hail him and invite him to dine. This might allay or aggravate his dejection. 'Wives and sweethearts—may they never meet.' But he had neither. He was the Navy's wholly. So (he always told himself) he was spared the much-sung pangs. He had only these other pangs that came from some deep and solitary place within him.

Or, not to mince the matter: he had his mother and his two

older sisters, Emily and Jane. His two older brothers, Arthur and George, moved in spheres beyond him and were both of an age, it sometimes seemed, to have been his father. And then there was his father . . .

He was, in short—and he would only dwell on it in these dire intervals before embarkation—the youngest: the late and unexpected addition, the afterthought (though no thought could have gone into it), a plaything for his sisters, a thing of no account to his brothers and a conundrum to his parents.

Yet to the womenfolk at least he would write his fond, unmanning, still shore-bound letters—disguising his real misery—as if he were still the weeping schoolboy who had forgotten to pack his handkerchief. My Dearest Emily . . . My Dearest Jane . . .

How little they knew how their pet rag-doll could rasp out an order. He had sea legs (if he were allowed to find them) and sea lungs to go with them. And of what should he write to them now, long as it was since he had last beheld them? Of a perilous expedition by coach from Bridgwater?

One day his father had summoned him to the library and had spoken to him as if from an immense and patient height. It was so that he would be told the modest nature of his allowance, but it was also so that he would be given words of general advice. He had trembled before this seldom-seen figure as he would one day tremble before admirals. He would remember—as he remembered now—how his father's face briefly softened as if in recognition of his discomfort.

His father had said, 'My dear Richard, you are a member of the Longridge family. You are neither a king nor a commoner. You will understand all you need to know for your conduct in

this world if you understand these words: know your place.'
His father's features had hardened again and his eyes had
seemed to probe him, as though behind the words, clear and
implacable enough, were some other message.

The library clock had chimed, painfully, the morning hour. So
distant had he felt from his father at this point that his father
might as well have been a king and he himself the lowest of com-
moners. Or his father's bastard child. It had dawned on him
afterwards—gradually but with a nagging lucidity—that, though
the matter was apparently being charitably concealed, this might
indeed be the truth of it. It was not in his interest to question
anything. It was in his interest to conspire in the deception and
be grateful—to write milksop letters to his mother and sisters.

He was perhaps, though it was not in his interest ever to
verify it, what his schoolfellows had called a 'fitz'.

He prodded the disobliging fire with the poker. He recalled
his mother's once constant refrain to the maid, like some further, if unwitting, piece of parental advice: 'A feeble fire, Betty,
is worse than an empty grate.'

He saw again his schoolfellows, remembered their plaintive
names. Ashmole, Palgrave, Wilkes . . .

Since he had not, even with the advantages of education,
overcome by his own ingenuity the problem of his essential
superfluity, it came down to the Army, the Navy or the Church.
He preferred blue to red, and preferred either to the black-and-
white absurdity of being a parson in a pulpit.

He hadn't thought much, strangely, about a thing called the
sea. He was acquainted with it now. And he hadn't known that
service in the King's Navy, even when he was commissioned
and sea-seasoned (even more so then) would involve these vile

periods of limbo and of dismal self-exposure—a creature neither of land nor sea, caught between a dubious homesickness and three or four days, depending on the course and the weather, of actual vomiting.

There was no evil in the world but uselessness and no good but its opposite. This he understood, if he would never, precisely, understand his father's words. He knew that his present disease could only be cured by a series of remedies. It would be eased, a little, by the first sight of his ship, then, more so, by first stepping upon it, but it would only be fully purged (and only then with much retching and wishing to be dead) once that ship had drawn up its chain. Now he was denied even the weakest of those medicines. He did not even know if his ship was at anchor.

He might have enquired at once of the innkeeper, he might enquire of anyone, but he did not want to suffer the naval indignity of having to ask the whereabouts of his vessel. He went to the window and, craning his neck, saw the lights across the water. He imagined himself foolishly asking, 'Is any one of those the *Temeraire*?'

He would surely know at dawn anyway by the evidence of his own eyes. A Second Rate would be unmistakable. And the sight of it, the pride of it, even under veiling drizzle, would surely chase away this malady. He had never served before in anything so mighty. Even his sisters had understood. And the fact that their lordships had assigned him to a ship of the line must mean that he had not gone entirely unnoticed and was deemed to have some worth. It might even be the preliminary to a captaincy and a frigate.

But he had heard of the *Temeraire*. The name itself was an

audacity. Quite so. A French name when they were fighting the French. Napoleon himself might be styled '*téméraire*'. More to the point, and as everyone knew (even his sisters knew and forbore to mention it), mutiny had been committed on this ship. Men had dangled from its yardarms. And for all its guns and its belligerent name, the *Temeraire* had never seen action. Its timbers had been damaged by storm and dishonoured by sedition, but never been struck by shot.

Well, it was like him then. He had not seen action either. Action: it was the very word of validated existence. He had received such promotion as he had neither by grace and favour (perhaps the whole fleet knew who, or what, he really was) nor by exploit. Their lordships must have dispatched him to the *Temeraire* because of his competence at gun practice. What else was there to do on the blockade? Gun practice, and more gun practice.

Now he would command a bigger battery of guns on a bigger gun deck. But as a proportion of the ship's sum of guns his command would be less than what it had been on a Fourth Rate. And on the same gun deck, commanding the other battery, might be another lieutenant—call him Lieutenant Lanyard—and Lieutenant Lanyard might be a squeak of eighteen, and have seen action.

But the *Temeraire* had seen no action save mutiny.

Why, every time, must he suffer these forebodings, like Jonah going down to Joppa—and now be posted to a ship accordingly?

He turned from the window back to the fire. He might go out into the dripping lamp-lit darkness, to stretch his coach-cramped legs, to breathe at least the salt-flavoured air, to soothe his spleen. But he did not want, for some reason, to walk, as he would have to, among seamen, though he would walk among them continually soon—let it be soon—on a heaving deck. He had noticed, even as the coach rolled in, that there were many of them. He had not before seen Plymouth so crowded, nor felt—but this was some sixth sense and not a matter of the eyes—the place so pregnant with preparation. So, it would not be so long perhaps.

His reluctance was not from any cocked-hatted nicety. They would of course make way for him and touch their temples, and should he wish (but he would not) to snap at them they would jump. As sailors ashore they were not technically under the full articles of war, but it was not in their interest not to look lively. Everyone minded their interest.

It was more that such contact, or non-contact, might only make him think of his hidden respect for them, or even—and this was mutinous thinking indeed—his kinship. Aboard ship it was different. You acted within timber bounds and iron laws. A sea creature? More a sea mechanism. You did not think. This was precisely his affliction now. He was thinking.

But it was one thing the Navy had taught him, or confirmed in him. He was not, essentially, different from them. Mutinous meditation indeed. Perhaps his competence in the matter of gunnery, his quality of leadership in this regard, his ability at least to achieve what others achieved, but without threats of the lash or other fulminations—with only firmness of voice and no other tyranny than that of his pocket watch—owed itself to this inadmissible fact. Again, boys, and again! And yet again, till you are but part of your guns. As if, as he commanded them, he were really proclaiming: Know your place, know your place.

Neither God nor man will find any other place or use for you than this. It is what you are for.

But he had not known action. He knew about noise and smoke and hissing steam that became as great as the smoke. He knew about powder in the mouth and nostrils. But he did not know about splinters. He trusted that, should the occasion arise and they were flying about, he would not lose his power of command. He would not lose his voice. He would not flinch or duck or wish to cover his face, not just because this would be unexemplary, but because he had been led to understand that whatever you did it made no difference.

He had not seen action, but some other sixth sense—a seventh sense—told him that this time might be the occasion. He trusted, simply, that he would do his duty. As he had done his careful, grateful, unmutinying duty to his father and (if such she was) his mother.

My dearest Mama . . . My dearest . . .

He stabbed the fire. All boldness and lustre had fled from his heart. He chewed his fingers savagely. He was himself like one of his mother's empty grates.

Temeraire. It was a mocking name, it was an inglorious, ill-fated ship.

Saint Peter

It embarrassed him now, so many years later, to say he was a vicar's son, that he'd been raised in a vicarage. It was like saying he'd been raised in some cosy cottage in the country—even if the vicarage had been in one of the less appealing suburbs of Birmingham. It was an ordinary house with a bay window. If you stood by the window you could see the church a little way along the road on the other side. 'A stone's throw' was what his father always said, they were a stone's throw. It was a common enough expression, but when he was small he always used to picture someone actually lifting their arm and tensing their back to throw a stone. He'd wonder whether the throwing was from or to the church. He was troubled by the idea of anyone throwing a stone at a church, or even from one.

He could still summon up now, though it was long ago, his father's keen but gaunt face. His father had died when he was still small, so it was always the same unageing face that he saw, while his own face in more than fifty years had changed immensely. There was something about that time, when he was only eight and when his father, though no one knew it yet, was dying, that was imprinted on him. He couldn't picture nearly so clearly, though he'd actually known him for longer, the face of Peter Wilson, his stepfather. And he'd never known, though the question remained, if when his father had been dying Peter Wilson had been just his mother's friend and a friend of the family or something more, even at that time. And if his father had known it.

It was like picking up a stone and trying to guess its weight. And not knowing, even now, which way to throw it. His mother knew, but had never said. Why should she? And now that she was old and frail and losing her memory he had even less reason to press her. He could only wonder if it all still pressed upon her anyway.

His mother hadn't met him in any case, that afternoon, at the school gates. He was eight years old and he didn't need his mother to meet him. The school wasn't much further away than the church. But she was one of those mothers who'd still turn up, perhaps because she was the Vicar's wife. And he was one of those kids who, though he might have preferred his mother not to turn up, was secretly glad that she did.

But this time it was his father. It was a cold grey day in March. A mean buffeting wind was blowing. It was also the last day of term before the Easter holiday, and he wondered, though there was no logic to it, whether it was because of this that his father and not his mother had come to meet him.

He certainly hadn't known then that his father would be dead by Christmas. Nor could his mother have known, nor even his father himself. He wasn't well and he looked tired, standing by the school gates, but not especially ill. He'd been clearly able to manage the walk to the school, something that would prove impossible soon. He'd been told by his doctor that he shouldn't overdo things, at just the time, around Easter, when his duties were particularly demanding, but he'd made a joke about this. There was a deputy vicar lined up to take at least some of the services, and since 'vicar' meant deputy anyway that meant there was a deputy-deputy.

It had disappointed him to be told that a vicar was only a deputy. It seemed like a mark of unimportance. And he'd been troubled by the idea that a doctor could tell a vicar what to do.

They'd walked back together. He felt that his father had come to the school gates in order to tell him something, to have his exclusive attention as they returned home. But something—perhaps the evil wind, constantly sending up clouds of dust and grit as they walked—had forestalled this.

It was anyway only when they got back that he realised his mother wasn't at home. He'd assumed she'd simply indulged his father's whim, but now his father said, 'Mum's sorry she couldn't meet you, but she'll be home any moment.' It was said in a way that made him understand he shouldn't ask why. In any case, almost in the same breath, his father said, rather strangely, 'Easter is coming.' It was hardly necessary to say it, everyone knew Easter was coming, but since he'd said it so quickly after what he'd said about his mother it made him think that Easter was like a person too who'd turn up at any moment—from wherever it was that Easter went.

His father put the kettle on and cut a thick slice of bread which he plastered with butter, then with strawberry jam. This was his regular reward for coming home from school. His father was doing exactly what his mother would normally do, though he was doing it, sleeves rolled up, with his sinewy arms, which for the first time he'd thought were not like a vicar's arms, but just like any man's arms.

They took their tea, and the bread and jam, into the front room. They used their front room regularly. A lot of people seemed not to do this—they reserved their front rooms for special occasions. Perhaps their own case was different because the house was a vicarage and because from the front room you could see the church. From where his father now chose to sit he couldn't have seen the church—you had to be close to the window—but he sat so that he was nonetheless looking out, at their gate and the privet hedge juddering in the wind. It was clear that he wanted to say something.

It was St Peter's Church and it was only a coincidence that it was Peter Wilson. There were lots of Peters. His own name was Paul. There was a St Paul too. Since his father was the Vicar of St Peter's, he'd absorbed a few facts, even when he was very small, about St Peter. That his symbol was the crossed keys. That these keys represented the keys to heaven, since St Peter was the keeper of the gates to heaven. That Jesus had once said to St Peter that he was the rock on which he'd build his church, since the name Peter was also just an ordinary word meaning 'rock'. It had seemed to him that, with all these attributes, Peter

240

must be the best and most important of all the saints. So he'd been proud and glad that his father was the Vicar of St Peter's.

But his father now said, with the tiredness in his face showing in the light from the window, that St Peter had once been no kind of saint at all. It was like his remark about Easter. It came from nowhere and seemed to be heading nowhere, but he said it with some emphasis. He said it was important to understand this. St Peter had once been no saint at all. Then he said, and this was a rather shocking remark, that it was important to understand too that there had once been no such thing as Easter.

It became rather difficult to eat his bread and jam. It felt wrong while his father was pronouncing such things. It had been wrong perhaps of his father to prepare it for him. But his father had only been doing, decently, what was expected, what his mother would have done. And, until moments ago, he'd been a hungry boy, home from school.

He'd remember always that slice of bread—it was rather thicker than his mother would have cut—that he wasn't able, even with an effort, to finish. His father must have seen his struggle, but, caught in a quandary of his own, been unable to say anything. He was talking about St Peter.

He'd remember always his challenging bread and jam, the blue-orange glow of the gas fire, which his father had turned on, and the noise behind him, through the window, of their gate knock-knocking in the wind.

'Can you imagine that?' his father had said. 'Can you imagine when there wasn't any such thing as Easter?'

He couldn't. Easter was something that came round every year, like birthdays and holidays, like Christmas. Then his father had told him the story that, even at eight, he probably mostly knew, and even knew mostly from his father. But his father had never told it like this, as if it were a story that had never been told before.

It was important to remember that there'd once been no such thing as Easter. It was important to remember that when Jesus spoke to Peter on the night before Good Friday it wasn't the night before Good Friday, because Good Friday didn't exist then. There was no such thing. And Peter wasn't a saint either. He was just Peter. But this was nonetheless the night, the real and actual night before Jesus was put on the cross, if no one but Jesus understood it. Peter didn't understand it, and didn't believe it when Jesus said to him that before the cock crowed in the morning he, Peter, would deny him three times. Peter didn't know what was happening. He was only Peter.

Jesus had gone to a place to pray, and though he knew what was to come he'd begged God to spare him. He'd said, 'Let this cup pass from me.' All through the night Jesus had stayed awake and prayed, but the three disciples who were with him had just slept in a huddle close by. Despite what their master was going through, they'd just slept. One of them was Peter.

More than once Jesus had woken them, but they'd just slept again, even at such a time. Because their eyes were heavy, his father had said, and they were only human. They didn't really know what was happening. Jesus had already that night named the disciple, Judas, who would betray him, but he'd said to Peter too those words about the cock crowing. Even knowing this, Peter had just slept.

His father had said all these things not like a vicar speaking in church, but as if they were being said for the first time. Some of his father's words were just words from the Bible and perhaps, even at eight, he knew this, but he felt them, saw them, like real things. He felt the weight of the disciples' eyes. Saw that cup, though it was only a cup in Jesus's mind. Felt the passing of that long night and the stern exactness of those three times.

He couldn't finish his bread and jam. It was what his mother had said, almost immediately, when she came in: 'You haven't finished your bread and jam.' She'd noticed very quickly the little remnant of bread with the small half-moon shape in it of his mouth. But she must have noticed too that there was an atmosphere inside the house. An atmosphere. She must have noticed it more than the piece of bread.

Let this bread and jam pass from me.

It was only a story. But he lay awake that night, listening to the wind and feeling somehow that he should stay awake the whole night, he should do this, for his father's sake. But he'd slept too, despite the story. He'd simply fallen asleep. He was eight years old and he slept deeply and sweetly and when he woke up it was bright daylight and he knew that he didn't have to get up to go to school. He could shut his eyes and go back to sleep if he wished. It was a delicious feeling. For a moment he hadn't remembered his father speaking to him or anything about the previous day. Then there was a sort of shadow in his head. Then he remembered.

Outside, the sky was clear. The wind had stopped. It was Birmingham, and no cocks crowed. In a while his mother would come in to see if he was awake. She would stoop to kiss him. Sometimes, so as to enjoy her kiss, he'd pretend he was still asleep and that it was her kiss that had woken him. He wondered if she guessed this. It was a little like wishing she wouldn't come to the school gates, but being glad, inside, that she did.

He'd surely have remembered if his mother had kissed him that morning.

Peter Wilson was a teacher at the primary school. Peter Wilson had once taught him. He'd become a friend of the family, as teachers can become, perhaps a particular friend of his mother. He'd been Mr Wilson, then he became Peter. Then he became his stepfather.

If his father had known that Peter Wilson was something more than just his mother's friend, then he'd have known, when he became more seriously ill, that if he died it would give her her freedom. And if he'd died knowing—or even wishing— this, then that would, surely, have been not unsaintly. In any case, being a Christian, a vicar, his father would have known that he'd have to die without anguish or bitterness, accepting that it was God's will.

When his father died—it was early December and now it was Christmas that was coming—his mother hadn't cried, or not much, or not in front of him. But then she too had to behave with composure, like the wife of a vicar. But she cried a lot, and in front of him, when Peter Wilson, many years later, left her, just suddenly left her. It's more uncomfortable, perhaps, for a mother to cry in front of her twenty-year-old son than in front of her eight-year-old son—setting aside which is more uncomfortable for the son. But she cried anyway, uncontrollably, as if she were crying two times over on the one occasion. He'd hesitated to embrace her.

What's in a word? Words aren't things. Cup, stone, rock. He didn't really believe, even at eight, though his father must have believed it, that St Peter had a pair of keys that opened the gate to heaven. How could heaven have a gate? How could heaven have the same arrangement as his school, or even their front garden? People say of themselves, it's the commonest excuse, and he must have said it of himself more than once in his life, 'I'm no saint.'

He's no saint. Or: She's no angel.

Could he have thought it, of his own mother, as she stooped like that to kiss him in the morning? She's no angel.

His father had said that it had all happened just as Jesus had said. Those who came to accuse and arrest him accused Peter too—of being a follower of Jesus. Three times, in fact, Peter was accused and three times he said that he had nothing to do with Jesus. Even though he'd been told by Jesus that this was just what he'd do—which should have been the severest and most unbreakable command not to do it—Peter had gone ahead three times with his denials.

His father didn't say about this that it was because Peter was only human and he was afraid. He just said it was what happened. Peter had slept because his eyes were heavy. Now he made his denials, three times. Immediately after the third time the cock suddenly crowed. Then Peter had wept.

FIRST ON THE SCENE

NEARLY EVERY WEEK now—more often if he could and if the weather was good—Terry would catch a train to the country and take a walk in one of the places where, not so long ago, he and his late wife Lynne used to walk together. They'd discovered these places and the appropriate train timetables when he'd had to give up driving because of his Parkinson's, and because Lynne had never learnt to drive. In just an hour or so from town they'd be stepping out into quiet countryside with good walks, fine views and maybe a handy pub. It was all a lot better, in fact, more free and easy, than driving somewhere. They'd never have discovered these places in a car. It made him less miffed about not being able to drive, even about his altered state of health.

He'd always thought that, with his Parkinson's, he would go first, but it was Lynne.

Now Terry went on these same walks, caught exactly the same trains on his own, because it was the nearest he could get to being with Lynne and enjoying it. At home, in the house they'd shared for years, the same theoretically applied, but it wasn't enjoyable, it was the opposite. He needed the country-side, the trees, the open air, the familiar paths.

On these walks he'd sometimes say to himself: This is as good as it gets. It was something he'd never have thought of saying to himself when he was young, it would have seemed foolish, but there'd come a point in his life when he began to say it quite often, like a reminder. He used to say it to himself nearly every time he walked with Lynne. But he said it also now. It was important. It wasn't true now, because when he'd said it to himself while walking with Lynne everything had been so much better. But it was also true now. It was true and it wasn't.

When Terry took the trains for these walks he would look at other passengers as if he were a complete outsider, as if he might be invisible. He'd listen to their chatter. All of this wasn't an uncomfortable feeling, in fact he sometimes felt a strange tug of warmth, of soothing fascination for these creatures he was no longer one of. He couldn't have had these feelings driv-ing in a car.

It might have been that on these walks he would have just felt lonely, but it was the opposite. It was only on these walks that he felt totally free to imagine that his wife was walking beside him, that he could be uninhibited about talking to her out loud, not even in his head. He couldn't do this at home, it would seem like the first sign of madness, but on these walks he'd initiate and conduct whole conversations with his wife, and, yes, as he spoke or even as he just walked he'd sometimes really believe, turning his head quickly to check, that she was there.

It might have been, too, that, wrapped up in this process, Terry wouldn't have been so attentive to the countryside around him, to the pleasing views, to the observation of nature. Yet it was all the more important to notice these things, to point them out to his wife, to see the butterfly, or the woodpecker, like a speck of paint, against the tree, or the kestrel quivering in mid-air. These things were alive.

So, in fact, he was all the more observant. He'd sometimes be drawn, with a surprisingly tender concentration, to just a cluster of primroses or a clump of moss. He'd notice things even at a distance.

So he noticed very quickly now, through the ferns, the patch of bright colour—bright red—up ahead.

There was a place where if you left the main path and struck out through the undergrowth you emerged onto the brow of a hill. There were bramble bushes, a thick bank of ferns, then a small clearing of grass and more ferns. Then the woods encroached again. It was a semi-secret place and, with the grass and the view and the enclosing bushes and ferns, a perfect spot in fine weather just to sit for a while and rest before walking on, or walking back. Or (with Lynne) to have had a small picnic—to have got out the thermos and the plastic box of stuff he'd carry in his backpack. He'd sat here with Lynne many times and, surprisingly, they'd never found it occupied by anyone else.

He thought that this might be the case now and that he

should stop, back-track into the woods and circle round. Too bad, that the place was taken. But the red patch, though it seemed like a patch of clothing, didn't move and there were no sounds. He concluded that it was something left by somebody, and this at first annoyed him. How could anyone leave behind anything so glaring?

After a few more steps and without yet emerging from the narrow gap through the ferns he saw that the red patch was indeed an item of clothing. It was a woman's red T-shirt and it was being worn by a woman in her mid-twenties, and the woman was alone and very still and dead.

He knew this at once and for certain, without ever drawing close: the woman was dead. She was lying on her side in a curled-up position, in what is known as the foetal position, but she wasn't asleep, she didn't stir. She was dead. If he were questioned—and he soon realised that he would be—as to how he knew the woman was dead, it wouldn't be easy to explain. He'd never come across a dead person in a clearing before, but some ability in him that perhaps all humans come equipped with, to recognise another human who is dead, instantly asserted itself. Perhaps he possessed this ability more keenly now that Lynne was dead.

There was nothing else in the clearing and the woman appeared unmarked, but she was dead. There was the unavoidable impression that she'd lain there for some time. There was a total immobility about her and a sense that the passage of hours, the weather and other, more mysterious processes had worked on her to claim her as just an inanimate part of the surroundings.

Apart from the red top, she wore blue jeans and lightweight, stylish trainers—clothes for a summer's day, but not for sleeping outside through a summer's night. This thought was merely technical. The thought that she would have been cold was irrelevant. The clothes seemed attached to her in a way that was not the usual way of clothes. Her hair was strangely tangled about her face as if the hair and the face were only incidental to each other. There were tiny bits of vegetation, things that might fall from trees or be blown about the air, dotted all over her. A small leaf was lodged in her exposed upturned ear.

He was no expert, but he didn't need to go any further to verify that she was not alive and had lain there like that, without stirring, since at least the preceding evening. He was sure of this, if he was sure of nothing else.

It was now not long after ten on a warm Sunday morning. He'd taken a fairly early train.

He stood still. He didn't want to emerge from the screen of the ferns. He peered carefully around. There was only the innocent sunny aspect the scene would have had if he were the only one there—which he was in a sense. Or if nobody was there. Indeed the absurd phrase came to him: 'first on the scene'.

In all his life—and he was sixty-nine—he'd never been first on the scene. Was this remarkable, a sort of achievement, or just the norm? In all his life with Lynne, in all their walks, they'd never been first on the scene either. It had never even occurred to them that it might happen. But he was now, for the first time, first on the scene. He was the one who 'while out walking' ... It was another phrase that came to him.

He stood and looked. He also shook. But this was his Parkinson's, his occasional and really not so violent tremor. It was another virtue of his solitary walks that this sometimes embarrassing symptom no longer mattered. It was anyway the lesser of his plights. He was so constituted now as to have from time to time a condition usually associated with strong emotion—and now he was under the sway of strong emotion his body had no separate way of signalling it. But he wasn't sure what the emotion was. Was it fear? Or rather anger?

Whatever else this sight before him signified, it was something that had brutally interrupted—swept away, cancelled—his much-needed conversation with his wife, his being still with her though she wasn't there. It had desecrated the memory of being here, in this same grassy clearing, with her in the past. It had made it impossible ever to walk this way with her (though without her) again.

It was hardly the appropriate emotion: anger. Yet he felt it. He would never tell anyone about it, though he understood that he'd have to tell people about other things. It was an inescapable consequence of his being here right now that he'd have to explain things and carefully answer questions. He'd have to justify his actions.

What were you doing walking in the woods? Why were you there?

She was in her twenties. If she were alive (and since he was sixty-nine) he might have called her a girl. The trainers were pale blue and white and had red laces to match her top. There was something impossible about the small swell of her ankle bone.

'Stumbled upon': that was another phrase. In all his life he'd never stumbled upon. He understood that his role in all this—though it was not as if he'd been assigned a role—was minor, incidental, the result of the merest chance, yet at the same time it was critical and would involve him a great deal. He might have walked another way, he might have caught a later train, he might not have come for a walk at all. This encounter might have been entirely someone else's, but it was his.

If he gave an honest answer to why he was walking in the wood he might at once be thought to be a little peculiar. Why are you trembling? It's Parkinson's disease. I have Parkinson's disease. Anyway, why shouldn't he tremble? Who wouldn't tremble at such a thing?

As the first on the scene, he might automatically—this possibility suddenly hit him—come under suspicion himself. Automatically and provisionally, yet almost definitely. A young woman, a girl. A retired man, a widower, with a tremble, walking alone in a wood . . .

What would Lynne think of this predicament he'd walked into? Suppose it had happened while he'd been walking with her. But he couldn't now turn to his wife and say, 'Lynne, what should I do? What should we do?' Lynne, who just moments ago had seemed so assuringly to be with him, had now totally disappeared.

And that was really the worst of it all.

A great temptation came over him: to make the hypothesis, the other, not realised possibility be true. He might simply retrace his steps, go back into the woods, rejoin the main path. He might never, after all, have forked off through the undergrowth to this spot that only he, he and Lynne, and perhaps just a few other walking folk knew. He might just carry on with his walk. He might contemplate nature. There would be a story, a news story, which he might not even hear about, which would have nothing to do with him.

But he knew he couldn't do this. It was true that he hadn't gone near the body, let alone touched it, he'd only stood here and looked. Yet he felt that his presence, the path he'd taken, brushing aside twigs and stems, his tread on the ground beneath him were as indelibly imprinted as any scent an animal might pick up. There was something irrevocable about his being here. It was so much the case that the emotion afflicting him was perhaps neither anger nor fear but a sort of contaminating, trapping, but unjustifiable guilt. And he wanted to cry out suddenly to Lynne, who wasn't there, to be his witness, his alibi.

The woman was not in any way like Lynne. She was not even like Lynne had been when she was, say, twenty-four. Except, of course, she was like Lynne in one fundamental way.

The trees, the ferns all around him were trembling, shaking in their way too. It was just the summer breeze. It was only for entirely extraneous reasons, an unlucky gene, that he was trembling himself. And yet he made a determined and futile effort—as if it were something both vital and within his power—to stop doing so.

Then he saw the whole truth of what must ensue, of what he and no one else must inescapably instigate, the truth of what was embodied before him—setting aside the immense riddle of why it was there at all. This was someone's daughter, someone's . . .

He reached for his mobile phone. It wasn't easy. Mobile phones aren't designed for people with Parkinson's, but he still carried one, even on solitary walks, and would have said that it was in case he got into difficulties, in case of emergencies. And this was certainly an emergency. Even before his symptoms had appeared he hadn't been a great user of his mobile and had called it his 'walkie-talkie' because he used it almost solely for communicating with his wife. Walkie-talkie: he should never have used those mocking words. When Lynne died he wished he hadn't recently deleted all her inconsequential voice messages. But how should he have known?

It took time and was a struggle, with the shaking of his hand. But then others in his circumstances, without his condition, might have found this to be the case. He had no choice but to remain here, to be fixed to this spot. He even resolved not to budge from his position among the ferns, to stay as still as possible (setting aside his tremor), as still as that woman over there. Look at the ferns, the green ferns. Look at the butterfly, the woodpecker. Look—

He looked at the woman in her red top and saw, almost with a longing, the absolute absence the dead have even as they are there.

A voice crackled in his ear. He hadn't a clue how to begin. He hadn't a clue how to describe his situation or to pinpoint exactly where he was. What a terrible thing it can be just to be on this earth.

ENGLAND

HE CAME OVER the familiar brow and saw at once the red lights of the solitary vehicle, perhaps half a mile ahead on the otherwise empty stretch of road. It wasn't moving, it had pulled up. Then, as he drew closer, he saw the odd angle. Its nearside wheels had lodged in one of the treacherous roadside gullies where the tarmac stopped.

It was not yet five. His watch began at 5.30. Only minutes ago, while Ruth still slept, he'd eased the car, in the dim light, from the garage. At this hour the straight stretch of road, the only straight stretch in his short journey, was normally all his own. He seldom rushed it. It was so starkly beautiful: the mass of the moor to his left and up ahead, in the scoops between the hills, the first glimpses of the sea. He told himself, routinely, not to take it for granted.

It was dawn, but overcast, there was even a faint mist—a general breathy greyness. The sort of greyness that would burn off, to give full sunshine, by mid-morning. The weather was in his professional blood. Fair weather, calm seas, late July. But it was the busy season.

He looked at the dashboard. He could spare perhaps ten minutes. He slowed and pulled over—not too far over, taking his warning from the car ahead. In it he could see a solitary figure in the driver's seat, who must be amply aware by now that help was at hand. It was a blue BMW, but of a certain vintage, not a rich man's car. Exmoor, these days, was full of rich men's cars. Every species of plush four-by-four. Well, it was four-by-four territory. The joke was that since they drove the things around Chelsea, then here, surely, they should use their dinky little town cars. He didn't quite get the joke, never having been to Chelsea.

He stopped. He could, in theory, have driven on. He was under no obligation. But how could you? In any case rescue was in his professional veins too. He understood at once what the situation might look like—he was even wearing a dark uniform. It must be why the driver didn't open his door and, back turned, seemed almost to be cowering.

He walked forward, inhaling the cool air. A thin dreamy envelope of sleep still clung to him. There was the tiny cluck of water in the gully. A stream, barely more than a trickle through the grass, came down off the hillside and, in the slight dip, cut away at the edge of the road. It was a dodgy spot.

The driver's window was down. He was met by a sudden blast of the foreign.

'Fookin' 'ell. Fookin' 'ell!'

The driver's face was black. He had, in silently noting the fact, no other word for it. You might say it wasn't deep black, as black faces go, but it was black. This was not a place, an area, for black faces. It was remarkable to see them. There was, on top, a thick bizarre bonnet of frizzy hair. It looked cartoonish in its frizziness.

'Fookin' 'ell.'

'It's okay,' he quickly and pacifyingly said, 'I'm not a policeman. I'm a coastguard. It's not a crime to be stuck in a ditch. Can I help?'

'Co-ahst-guaard!'

The man's voice had changed in an instant. The first voice (the normal one?) had a strong accent which, nonetheless, he couldn't place, because all northern accents eluded him. The second voice was a foreign voice in the sense that the accent wasn't English at all. He couldn't place it exactly either, just that it was broadly—very broadly—Caribbean. But the man had slipped into it as if it were not in fact his natural voice. It was turned on and exaggerated, a joke voice.

On the other hand, since both voices were alien to him, both voices were like joke voices. That wasn't a fair-minded thought, but he knew that people not from the West Country made a joke of the West Country accent all the time. It was one of the standard joke accents.

'Where de co-ahst, man? Where de co-ahst? I is lookin' for de co-ahst. You guard it, you tell me where it is.'

He felt at once compelled to comply.

'It's over there.' He actually lifted an arm. 'You're looking at it.'

The man wrinkled his face as if he couldn't see anything.

'I is lookin' for Ilfracombe, man.' Then he pronounced the word at full-pitch and with declamatory slowness, as if it were a place in Africa.

'Il-frah-coombe!'

Then the voice broke up into little screechy, hissy laughs. He couldn't tell if it was nervous laughter, panicky laughter or a sort of calculated laughter. Or just laughter. It was like a parrot. He couldn't help the thought. It was like a parrot laughing.

'Ilfracombe is over there.' Again he felt the ridiculous need to raise an arm. 'You're in the right direction. You'll need the thirty-nine, then the three-nine-nine. An hour, at this time of day.'

The man peered, putting a visoring hand to his eyes. 'I no see it, man. I no see no three-nine-nine. Ilfracombe, Deh-von. We in Deh-von, man?'

'We're in Somerset.' (He almost said, 'We in Somerset.') It surely didn't need saying, but he announced it, 'This is Exmoor.'

'*Ex*moor! Fookin' 'ell. *Ilkley* Moor, that's me. Ilkley Moor bar tat. Ilkley Moor bar fookin' tat.'

The voice had completely changed again. What was going on here? He was used—occupationally used—to the effects of shock and exposure. He was used to the phenomenon of dis-orientation. To gabble, hysteria, even, sometimes, to the effects of drug taking.

He wanted to say a simple 'Calm down'. He wanted to exert a restorative authority. But he felt that this man, stranded in what seemed to be, for him, the middle of nowhere and talk-ing weirdly, somehow had the authority. He peered into the car's interior. He saw that on the not unroomy back seat there was a grubby blanket and a pillow. It was five in the morning. He got the strong impression that this man, going about whatever could possibly be his business, used his car as at least an emergency place of overnight accommodation. Having just affirmed that he wasn't one, he felt like a policeman. He felt out of his territory, though he couldn't be more in it. He knew this road like the back of his hand. But he was a coastguard, not a policeman.

The voice changed again. 'I is in de right direction, man. But I is goin' nowhere.'

'No. I can see that. What happened?'

'Fookin' deer.' It was the other man—the other other-man—again.

'What?'

'Fookin' deer. Int' middle of road. Joost standin' there.'

'You saw a deer?'

'Int' middle of road. Five fookin' minutes ago.'

He looked around, over the roof of the car. It was Exmoor. There were deer. You saw them sometimes from the road, especially in the early morning. But there was little cover for them here and he'd never, in over twenty years, come upon a deer just standing in the middle of the road. If they stepped on the road at all, they'd surely dart off again at even the distant sight of a vehicle. This man had come from—wherever he'd come from—to see something he'd never seen in decades.

He had the feeling that the deer might be another symptom of disorientation. A hallucination, an invention. Yet the man (the other one again) spoke about it with beguiling precision.

'A lee-tal baby deer, man. I couldn't get by he. I couldn't kill he. A lee-tal baby Bambee.'

He looked over the roof of the car. Nothing moved in the greenish greyness. It was just plausible: a young stray deer, separated and inexperienced, in the dip, in a pocket of mist, near a source of drinking water. It was just plausible. He was a coastguard, not a deer warden. He asked himself: Would he have had any sceptical thoughts if this were just some unlucky farmer?

'I see his lee-tal eyes in me headlights. I couldn't kill he.'

The man was behaving, it was true, as if he were being doubted, were under suspicion, as if this were a familiar situation.

He saw, in his mind's eye, a deer's eyes in the headlights, the white dapples on its flank. A small trembling deer. It was a startling but magical vision. That alone, on this routine journey to work, would have been something special to talk about.

He tried to give his best, friendly passer-by's smile. 'Of course you couldn't kill it. You didn't hit it?'

'No. He hop it. I the one who end up in de shit, man.'

It might shake you up a bit, nearly hitting a deer.

The man changed voices yet again. 'Fookin' deer.' Then he said, in the other voice, 'I is a long way from Leeds.'

So it was Yorkshire. He was from Leeds, but he was on the edge of Exmoor, at five in the morning. Which was even more bewildering perhaps than a deer in your headlights. He felt a moment's protectiveness. He wasn't sure if it was for the lost man, or the lost deer, the little Bambi. He'd helped to return many a lost child, over the years, to its distraught parents. It was one of the happier duties. Now was the peak time for it.

'So. Let's get you out of here. You've tried reversing?'

'I've tried reversing.' It was the northern voice, but with no manic exaggeration.

He stepped round to the back of the car. Either he'd reversed clumsily and the back wheel had slipped into the gully or it had gone into the gully in the first place when he'd braked and swerved—for the phantom deer. He'd got stuck anyway. And what were the chances—they were remote, extraordinary and barely believable too—that in such circumstances help would come along, uniformed help, in a matter of minutes?

The man got out to inspect the damage for himself. He didn't look like a man who'd have regular roadside-assistance cover. He was shorter and slighter than he'd supposed. It was the hair, the two-inch hedge of it, that made him tall. But he had a strutting way of carrying himself. The gait of a cocky, belligerent Yorkshireman? No, not exactly.

In the dampish dawn air—his own sidelights lighting up the gully—they assessed the situation. No harm done, just the misplaced wheels.

'If we do it together,' he said, 'we could just lift her so the back wheel's on the road again. Then you can reverse. I can push from the front if you spin. But you should be okay.'

'You tell me, skipper.'

This was no doubt a reference to the looped stripe on his sleeve. It was a perk of his job occasionally to be mistaken for a ship's captain. But he'd said, and noticed it even as he said it, the nautical 'lift her'.

'We lift her arse, skipper, nice and easy.' The man even crouched, ready to take the bumper, like a small sumo wrestler.

'Wait.'

He went round to the left-open driver's door. He checked the position of the gear stick. Then he took off his jacket and, folding it, placed it on the passenger seat. He felt chilly without it, but he didn't want to arrive on duty looking as if he'd been in an accident himself.

The man watched him and said, 'That's righ', man. We don't wahnt you messin' de natty tailorin'.'

The man's own clothes might have been natty once, long ago, in their own way. There was a faded sweater—purple and black horizontal stripes—over which there was a very old, perhaps once stylish full-length leather jacket. It hung about him like a droopy black second skin, which was an unfortunate way of thinking of it. The clothes looked anciently lived-in.

He rolled up his own crisp white sleeves. He walked round to the gully. There were some convenient small stream-washed rocks and he jammed a few against the stricken front wheel. He surreptitiously checked, as if trained for it, the front of the car—for dents, for possible bits of deer. There were none. That is, there were many dents, but they were old.

He walked back. He now felt, if it was only fleetingly, in charge, as if the man had become his appointed junior.

'Okay.' They crouched. 'You have a hold? On "three" then.'

'You give the word, skip.'

The man seemed calmer, less disoriented—if that was the proper diagnosis—even appreciative and submissive. The mere fact of doing together what couldn't have been done by one man alone seemed to have put everything into a complete and, if just for a moment, composed perspective. Around them was Exmoor being slowly unveiled by the dawn. Except for a few sparse, travelling lights in the distance on the main road up ahead, they were alone in the landscape. There was a tiny, seemingly stationary light in the further distance. It was the light of a ship in the Bristol Channel. It would be in the station's log.

'One—two—*three!*'

It was simply achieved. A heave, an instinctive sideways thrust to the right. The back wheel was returned safely to the tarmac. The boot can't have contained anything heavy. No dead deer, for example.

'Fookin' champion!'

What was it about these voices—both of them? But the man seemed genuinely elated, as if wizardry had just occurred.

'You have to reverse her out yet.'

Again he'd said 'her'. They both went to the front. While the man got in and turned the ignition, he continued to the near-side front wing. In another situation he might have said, '*Reverse*, and gently.' Fortunately, his own car—engine off and lights on—was parked at a comfortable distance.

There was no difficulty. There was a slight skittering, but the gully wasn't deep and the back wheels hauled the car entirely onto the road again. His own bit of effort on the front bumper was almost superfluous. He looked at his watch. Five minutes had passed. The man cut his engine, yanking on the handbrake, and the sudden returning silence made the brief grinding of reverse gear seem almost like some effrontery.

The man got out.

'Fookin' champion!'

He came forward, hand extended. Like everything else about him, the extended hand was like an act, it was like something not quite as it should be. But he took it and shook it.

'I've got a thermos inside, man. Black coffee. Want some?' The voice was normal now—normal with its Yorkshire tones.

He'd had coffee at home, minutes ago, and there'd be more at the station. But it seemed wrong not to accept the man's gesture of gratitude. There had to be a gesture, a little ritual. Besides, he was curious.

'Okay.' He looked at his watch.

'I know. You have to—clock on.'

'Be on watch,' he said, a little stiffly.

'Aye aye.'

He vaguely allowed for the fact that in Yorkshire, so he believed, they said 'aye' for 'yes'. All the same.

'A cup of coffee,' the man said. ''Tain't every day, is it?'

He had to agree, even give a yielding chuckle. 'No, it's not every day,' he said, not really knowing exactly what the man meant. But, true, it wasn't every day.

The man groped inside the car, first graciously producing the folded jacket from the passenger seat, then a thermos. He shook it, judging the contents, close to his ear. He unscrewed a pair of cups, one inside the other.

'Black coffee. While I'm driving, to keep me awake. Same as you, I suppose, when you're—on watch.'

Like the rest of the world, the man had a picture of a coastguard as a solitary figure, eyes glued to the horizon, telescope to hand, maintaining a sentry-like vigil. It wasn't quite like that. It was a big station. A huddle of white buildings, with masts and dishes, beneath the tower of a decommissioned lighthouse. There was a rotating watch of staff. At any one time there'd be at least two on duty. There was an array of monitoring and communications equipment.

Never mind. It was a coastguard station. It was an outstandingly beautiful, dramatic section of coast. People came at weekends and for holidays. He was there all the time. He was exceptionally lucky, in his work, in his life. Ruth, the job, the two kids who'd made him, twice over, a grandfather—though they were still kids in his mind. The only cloud, it seemed, was retirement. Having to stop it all one day. He was fifty-three. The man was—what? He sometimes seemed young, then not young at all.

'Yes,' he said. 'Coffee helps.'

'Black coffee,' the man said. 'I never know whether to make a joke. And I never know whether to make a joke out of the black or the coffee. See my face, man? Black or coffee?'

He tried to look obtuse and passive. But there was something he genuinely didn't understand.

There was a pause while Exmoor reasserted its presence. Then the man cackled. It was the shoulder-shaking, oddly engaging parrot-laugh.

'I'm a joker, man. My business. I'm a comedian.'

That in itself seemed a possible joke, a possible trick. I met a strange man today, he was quite a comedian.

'A co-me-di-ahn!'

And now the man—or one of his personas—was back at full frantic tilt again, even while pouring not very warm-looking coffee. He had no choice, nor did Exmoor, but to listen.

'Ah coom all the way from Yorkshire, from fookin' West Ridin', just to get rescued by a coastguard, a fookin' *coastguard*, on Exmoor. Serious. *Exmoor.* What's a *coast*guard doing on fookin' Exmoor? Ilkley Moor, me. Ah never knew you 'ad moors down 'ere an' all. Ilkley Moor bar tat. Ilkley Moor bar mitzvah! Ee but ah do luv Ilfracombe. Il-frah-*combe*. Ave ah said? Ah *combe* from Yorkshire. Ee bah goom! But ah tell yer what they *do* 'ave on Exmoor. Apart from coastguards. Fookin' deer. Did yer know? 'Erds of fookin' deer, and 'erds of fookin' coastguards. Ave ah told yer me deer joke? It's the one where ah tell it and yer all go, "Dear oh dear oh dear."'

It was astonishing. It was a performance, an unabashed performance—in the middle of nowhere. It was utterly disconcerting, but now, at least, he understood. And, actually, he was laughing, he couldn't help it. A comedian.

The man saw that he understood. He slowed down, became near-normal again. He grinned. He held out his hand once more, as if he had to introduce himself twice.

'Johnny Dewhurst,' he said. Then, grasping his coffee in one hand, he slipped the other inside his jacket and pulled out a card. It said 'Johnny Dewhurst, Comedian and Wayfarer'. Underneath, in smaller print, were the words 'All Engagements Gratefully Appreciated'. And to one side there was a picture of a clown, a standard circus clown—big feet, big nose, made-up face. The picture bore no resemblance to Johnny Dewhurst (if that was his actual name). On the other hand, you could see that, with the topiary of hair and mobility of face, not to say voice, he could play the clown if needed—if he wasn't doing it already. And who knows what comic paraphernalia might be stored in the boot of his car?

He laughed his parrot-laugh again. It seemed like a laugh of conspiracy, of complicity now, because his audience had laughed too.

'Il-frah-coombe!' The personas switched again. 'Tonight I play Ilfracombe. Then I play Barnstaple. Baahrn-stable! I sleep in de barn or I sleep in de stable? Barnstable not very far, I tink. Then I play Plymouth. That far enough for Johnny. That like

Land's End. I next play Verona. No, that different gig. That *Kiss Me Quick* or someting. By Cole Porter. Wid name like that, he must be *black man*! Night before last I play Yeovil. Yo-Ville! I say, "Yo brother, this my kind of town, this where Johnny belong." But they don't understan' me, they don't clap very much. Then they send me on to Taunton. They send me to *Tawny Town*! I say, "This some kind of a *joke*? This some kind of a *rayssiahl* ting?"'

He couldn't help but laugh, whether or not he was meant to. But at the same time he felt that it didn't matter whether he laughed or not, since he understood it now—it was rather like the worn-smooth wrinkled leather coat—the man was inured to the reactions of audiences, be they friendly, hostile, hard-to-please or indifferent. Or perhaps absent.

But the man laughed too.

'How you going to be my straight-man, man, you keep laughing like that? You have a name? You save my life, you haven't told me your name.'

'Ken,' he said. Now he too held out his hand a second time, but with concealed caution. He desperately wanted to avoid giving his second name. It was Black. He was Kenneth Black. Lots of people are called Black, but he shuddered to think of the comic repercussions.

'Johnny Dewhurst and Kenny—Coastguard. I see it, man. I see it!'

He hid his relief. 'Is it your real name, "Johnny Dewhurst"?'

'Hey, you tink I's a liar, man? You tink I gives you joke name? I have a card made up with some joker's name?'

The shoulders shook, he hee-hawed and he was off again. It bubbled out of him. It was hard to see where the one thing stopped and the other thing began. He'd always supposed that comedians (was there truly a section of humanity called comedians?) were really hard-nosed crafty individuals. There was a gap between the act and the person. But with this man you couldn't tell. There even seemed to be something wished-for in the confusion.

'Johnny Dewhurst, it no joker's name, it a butcher's name. I say, "First Johnny tell de joke, then—he get butchered for it!"'

He reached inside his jacket again, pulled out a folded slip of paper and handed it over. It was a flyer, a flyer for a tour—'The Johnny Dewhurst Tour'. It was a list, a remarkably long one, of places and dates. The places criss-crossed and circumscribed England. The tour began—or had begun—in Scarborough, then had taken in several northern locations, then worked circuitously south. It had networked the Midlands, then struck southwest. It had touched Lincoln, Nottingham, Derby, Shrewsbury, Rugby . . . as well as towns he couldn't exactly place. The first date was in late June and there was still over a month to go. It had still to track the length of the south coast and to reach such venues as Lowestoft and Skegness. It was a list of theatres, corn exchanges, seaside palaces and pavilions, and indeterminate halls. And it must be a very ambitious list, because he'd never heard of Johnny Dewhurst, though he'd met him now, and at many of these places, some of them even having a faint hint of glamour, Johnny Dewhurst must be very far from star billing—'on tour' as he was—he must be a very short spot a long way down the programme.

And now he was stranded, or he was rescued, on Exmoor.

'Johnny Dewhurst wish he were back in Leeds, man. Johnny Dewhurst wish he were back in Dewsbury.'

He seemed to speak from the depths of his soul. But you really couldn't tell.

A moment had come. They both upended their thermos cups, both making the same, mutually accepted, grimace. They shook out the dregs, roadside fashion. It was a piece of perfect mime. There was no one to see it.

'You come to my show in Ilfracombe, if you like. Il-frah-coombe! Bring your Missis Coastguard. I don't have a bag of money to give you, I don't have any free tickets. But you come if you want. Johnny Dewhurst entertain you.'

A challenge? A genuine invitation? A forlorn hope?

'Then I know I have an audience?' He screeched and hissed and pistoned his shoulders again.

Then, by more mutual, resigned understanding, they turned to their cars.

'You go first, Mister Coastguardman. Johnny Dewhurst have to water Exmoor. Three-nine-nine. I remember. I see it, man! I see it up in lights!'

He couldn't think of anything witty or memorable to say, but then he was the straight-man, apparently. He said, 'Take care now.' It was what coastguards said when they put some foolish member of the public right. Take care now.

He started his car and drove slowly by with a final wave, then continued along the straight, gradually rising road. He didn't speed. He would make it. He also needed to think. Now he was back in his car, with his lights on, it seemed that dawn had retreated, it was semi-dark again. He looked in the rear-view mirror. The other car remained stationary.

How did someone decide to be a comedian? He'd wanted to be a coastguard since he was small. It was no more than a boy's yen, perhaps, for the seaside, for things maritime, though he hadn't wanted, clearly, the perils of the open sea. He'd wanted perhaps the taste of adventure, but with a good measure of its opposite. He'd never wanted to be a sailor, a soldier—or even a policeman. He'd seen himself, yes, with a vigilant stare and a mug of cocoa. It was a commendable, if not necessarily a courageous thing, to guard the nation's coastline. He'd wanted, if he were honest, to be a preserver of safety, while having—and perhaps the one thing conferred the other—a large slice of safety himself.

Was being a coastguard courageous? No. It was ninety-five per cent not courageous. There were incidents, some of them nasty, there were rescues. You were in the business of rescue. Was rescue courageous?

But it was certainly courageous, it was unfathomably courageous to do what Johnny Dewhurst did. Could he, a man from Somerset, possibly go to Leeds (he'd never been to Leeds, he'd only twice been to London) and, with his West Country voice, his joke of a voice, get up in front of a local audience? And make them *laugh*. His knees buckled at the thought of it.

He looked in the rear-view mirror. The car hadn't moved. It was just a distant twinkle. The poor man had hundreds of miles yet to drive. Did he really sleep in it? What the hell would he do in Ilfracombe at six in the morning? But what the hell was he doing anyway, there, at five?

He hadn't done enough, surely, not nearly enough, just to lift him back onto the road.

But, as he mounted another ridge and the car behind disappeared, it seemed somehow that its existence and everything that had happened, from the ghostly deer onwards, became obscure and doubtful too. Had it really all happened?

He should now be eagerly working out how he'd tell the story, to his colleagues, his fellow coastguards, and then, later, Ruth. You'll never guess, you'll never guess. On the Culworthy road, at five in the morning. I met a comedian.

But the more he reflected, the more it seemed impossible. How to begin, how to be believed? How to convey every important detail? It was a story he didn't have the power of telling. So, better not to tell it. It was one of those stories you didn't tell. He wondered, already, if he believed it himself.

He reached the main road, which he would briefly follow before turning off again. There was the conspicuous sign: 'Barnstaple, Ilfracombe'. The man could hardly get lost. To his right now were bigger, broader pockets of sea, touched, as the land wasn't yet, by rays of pink-gold light from the east. It was the Bristol Channel. It was also the Atlantic Ocean. It was, at this point, a satisfying expanse of water. Swansea lay beyond the horizon, further away than Calais from Dover. Ships, he knew, had once sailed up the Bristol Channel with cargoes of sugar. On the way out they'd made for Africa. Then sailed west.

He took the familiar right turn, the narrow twisting road. In a while he'd see the white buildings with the lighthouse. On some mornings it could still take his breath away. And if you arrived at sunset . . .

It wasn't a head-in-the-sands job—if that wasn't a joke in bad taste. There was bad stuff. There were suicides, washed-up bodies. But he could never go to Leeds. And it was a job, by very definition, perched on the edge and looking out. It was also, by definition too, mainly stationary. A coastguard station. He thought of Johnny Dewhurst's amazing itinerary.

Was it true? Was it really a story to be told? He patted suddenly his breast pocket, containing the flyer and the card, as if even that hard evidence might have been mysteriously whisked away from him.

Should he take Ruth to Ilfracombe? Tonight. Should he explain, and should he take her, even under protest? I think we should go. But would that risk having his roadside encounter hurled outrageously back at him—and at Ruth? Have you heard the one about the lost coastguard? On Exmoor. That's right, missis, a *coastguard* on Exmoor. Would he risk discovering that he'd now become 'material'—in Ilfracombe and all points to Skegness?

He thought of that double-act that was never going to happen. Kenny Coastguard—or Kenny Black?

No, he'd tell no one. Not even Ruth. In time even Johnny Dewhurst, like that questionable deer, might start to seem like a hallucination.

The familiar tower of the lighthouse appeared before him, its topmost, no longer functioning section nonetheless touched with pink glinting light. He sat on the edge of England, supposedly guarding it, looking outwards. He knew a bit about the Bristol Channel, its present-day shipping and its history. He knew a bit about Exmoor. But Exmoor wasn't England—much as you might want it to be. Brand-new shiny SUVs nosed around it like exploring spacecraft. He knew what he knew about this land to which his back was largely turned, this strange expanse beyond Exmoor, but it was precious little really. He really knew, he thought, as he brought his car to a halt again, nothing about it at all.